PERSONNEL MANAGEMENT AND HUMAN RESOURCES

McGRAW-HILL SERIES IN MANAGEMENT

Fred Luthans and Keith Davis, Consulting Editors

PERSONNEL MANAGEMENT AND HUMAN RESOURCES

SECOND EDITION

WILLIAM B. WERTHER, Jr., Ph.D.

KEITH DAVIS, Ph.D.
Arizona State University

McGRAW-HILL BOOK COMPANY

New York | St. Louis | San Francisco | Auckland | Bogotá | Hamburg | Johannesburg
London | Madrid | Mexico | Montreal | New Delhi | Panama | Paris
São Paulo | Singapore | Sydney | Tokyo | Toronto

**PERSONNEL MANAGEMENT
AND
HUMAN RESOURCES**

1234567890HALHAL898765

ISBN 0-07-069433-8

This book was set in Cheltenham Light by Black Dot, Inc. (ECU).
The editors were John R. Meyer and Laura D. Warner;
the designer was Nicholas Krenitsky;
the production supervisor was Marietta Breitwieser.
The drawings were done by J & R Services, Inc.
Halliday Lithograph Corporation was printer and binder.

Library of Congress Cataloging in Publication Data

Werther, William B.
Personnel management and human resources.

(McGraw-Hill series in management)
Includes bibliographies and indexes.
1. Personnel management.   I. Davis, Keith, date
II. Title.   III. Series.
HF5549.W439   1985   658.3   84-19449
ISBN 0-07-069433-8

ABOUT THE AUTHORS

WILLIAM B. WERTHER, Jr., received his Ph.D. (Phi Beta Kappa) from the University of Florida, where he taught for two years before joining the faculty of Arizona State University in 1971. His teaching and research interests included personnel management, employee relations, productivity management, corporate strategy, and computer conferencing approaches to communications and productivity improvement.

He has written four books and more than fifty articles on a variety of employee relations topics and is the award-winning author of *Labor Relations in the Health Profession.* His writings have appeared in *Personnel Administrator*, *Personnel Journal*, *Compensation Review*, *Labor Law Journal*, *California Management Review*, *National Productivity Review*, and other major business publications. He serves as a North American editor for the *Journal of Management Development* and is on the editorial advisory board of the *National Productivity Review.*

Dr. Werther has served as a consultant to a number of leading firms in the aerospace, aluminum, banking, beverage, communications, electronics, hospitality, and steel industries—including American Productivity Center, Anheuser-Busch Companies, Citicorp, State Farm Insurance Companies, and TRW, Inc.—and has worked with local, state, and federal government agencies. He is currently a productivity and human resource consultant to several companies where he assists in the design and implementation of employee involvement approaches to productivity improvement. He also has worked with organizations in the evaluation and operation of computer conferencing networks. His consulting work has involved both diagnostic assistance and over 400 executive development seminars.

Werther also is a labor arbitrator, listed with the National Panel of Arbitrators for the American Arbitration Association and the Federal Mediation and Conciliation Service. From 1980 to 1982 he served as chairman of the Public Employment Relations Board for the City of Phoenix.

He has been active in a variety of professional associations and has served on the program committee of the Western Division of the Academy of Management, on the executive board of the Arizona Industrial Relations Association, and as president of the East Valley Personnel Management Association, a chapter of the American Society for Personnel Administration. He is a member of the Academy of Management, the Industrial Relations Research Association, and the American Institute for Decision Sciences.

His awards include an NDEA Title IV Fellowship and membership in such honorary societies as Phi Beta Kappa, Beta Gamma Sigma, Phi Kappa Phi, and Sigma Iota Epsilon. His expertise on employee relations matters has been recognized in *The Wall Street Journal* and *U.S. News and World Report*, and in testimony for the Arizona State Senate and the U.S. House of Representatives.

KEITH DAVIS is professor emeritus of management at Arizona State University, College of Business. He is the author of prominent books on management and the consulting editor for approximately eighty books in the McGraw-Hill Series in Management. He is a fellow in both the Academy of Management and the International Academy of Management. Prior to entering the teaching field Davis was a personnel specialist in industry and a personnel manager in government.

He received his Ph.D. from Ohio State University and has taught at the University of Texas and at Indiana University. His fields of work are organizational behavior, personnel management, and social issues in management. Davis has been visiting professor at a number of universities, including the University of Western Australia and the University of Central Florida. He also has served as a consultant to a number of business and government organizations—including Mobil Oil Company, Texaco, the U.S. Internal Revenue Service, and the state of Hawaii.

Davis is a former president of the Academy of Management, and he received the National Human Relations Award from the Society for Advancement of Management. He has been a national Beta Gamma Sigma distinguished scholar and is an accredited Senior Professional in Human Resources.

Two of Davis's most popular books are (with John W. Newstrom) *Human Behavior at Work: Organizational Behavior* (7th ed., 1985) and (with William C. Frederick) *Business and Society* (5th ed., 1984), both published by McGraw-Hill Book Company. He also has contributed chapters to over 100 other books and is the author of over 150 articles in journals such as *Harvard Business Review*, *Academy of Management Journal*, *Management International*, and *California Management Review*. Four of his books have been translated into other languages.

This book is dedicated to
RICHARD E. WERTHER and SUE DAVIS

CONTENTS

PART IV COMPENSATION AND PROTECTION

PART V EMPLOYEE RELATIONS

We believe that personnel departments will play a key role in determining the success of our organizations and society during the remaining years of the twentieth century.

The Authors

The first edition of *Personnel Management and Human Resources* took nearly six years to research and write. It exacted a high price in time, effort, and emotion. So when the book was published, we were most gratified by its wide acceptance. More than 100 colleges and universities in the United States adopted it as the cornerstone of their personnel management course. The Canadian edition (adapted by Professors Hermann F. Schwind, T. P. Hari Das, and Frederick C. Miner, Jr., of St. Mary's University) quickly became the leading personnel textbook in Canada. Interest in the book even led to Spanish, Portuguese, and French translations—in addition to an international student edition, published in Japan.

We attribute the book's widespread acceptance to its practical orientation. Professors and students report to us that it is understandable and pragmatic. As we wrote in the preface to the first edition:

> Although balanced and thorough coverage is the most important feature of the book, we believe that readers and instructors want more than that. Comments from colleagues and students convinced us that an introductory personnel management text also must be readable and teachable. It should:
>
> - Capture the interest of readers
> - Reflect the flavor and challenges of this exciting field
> - Provide instructors with a flexible teaching tool

We retained this same approach and purpose in the second edition—while updating the content, coverage, features, and supplementary material.

Purpose

This book builds on the premise that modern organizations are the most important innovations of our era. Organizations succeed by effectively and efficiently combining resources to achieve stated objectives. Although all resources are necessary for success, readers will sense our belief that people are the pivotal resource for any employer. How well an organization attains, maintains, and retains its human resources determines its success or failure. And the success or failure of our organizations shapes the well-being of every person on the planet.

The purpose of this book is to explain the personnel department's role in dealing with human resources. It introduces the foundations and challenges of modern personnel management, presenting the key concepts, issues, and practices of this dynamic field without being encyclopedic. Our focus is practical. We emphasize the applications of this knowledge so that readers will gain a useful understanding of the subject, whether they seek careers in personnel management or in other disciplines.

Balanced Coverage

Throughout the book, we aim for a balanced coverage of traditional topics and emerging concerns. We explore the well-established concepts and practices that form the core of modern personnel management and then go beyond these proven techniques to discuss the challenges and innovations that confront today's personnel professionals.

In the second edition we have undertaken a major revision of the content to reflect the dynamic changes occurring in personnel management and human resources. Greater emphasis has been put on the theme of productivity improvement and on how personnel departments can contribute to this important organizational goal. More than 100 examples from named companies have been added to illustrate the applicability of key concepts.

New chapters have been included—such as Chapter 5, "Job Analysis and Design," and Chapter 8, "Orientation and Placement." Chapter 17, "Personnel Communications Systems," and Chapter 19, "Quality of Work Life," have been revised to reflect new approaches in these areas. In other cases—such as in Part VI, on union-management relations—we have carefully consolidated the material into fewer chapters with very little loss of content. The continued importance of equal employment opportunity is reflected in a much more rigorous treatment of this topic in Chapter 3. Readers are introduced to key court decisions and such persistent issues as comparable worth. Subsequent chapters integrate issues of equal employment opportunity into the discussion of specific personnel activities. For example, Chapter 7, "Employee Selection," examines the EEOC's uniform selection guidelines, the four-fifths rule, bottom-line results, and other EEO issues. Besides the integration of key concepts from one chapter to the next, a variety of new topics have been introduced within each of the chapters. A few of the new or expanded subjects include quality circles, burnout, attitude survey feedback, obsolescence, productivity, ergonomics, and relevant court cases.

The updating and upgrading of content take place within a traditional format that addresses the major functions of personnel management. The book is organized into seven parts, each with a brief overview about its importance to the reader. Part I, "Foundations and Challenges," discusses the internal, external, and equal employment challenges that are shaping the field of personnel management. Part II, "Preparation and Selection," examines human resource planning and the analysis and design of jobs and then concludes with a discussion of recruitment and employee selection. Part III, "Development and Evaluation," picks up where the selection process ends. The need for careful attention to orientation and placement is discussed in one chapter; the importance of training and development is emphasized in the next. The popular career planning chapter that follows describes corporate and individual approaches to career advancement. The performance appraisal chapter explains how performance is evaluated.

Once human resources are obtained, developed, and evaluated, they must be maintained. Part IV, "Compensation and Protection," discusses how organizations compensate employees with wages, benefits, and services. Since the personnel department plays a key role in the security, safety, and health of the workers, these topics and their legal ramifications also are explored. Part V, "Employee Relations," treats many of the day-to-day issues confronting modern personnel departments. Here the topics of motivation and satisfaction are discussed, as well as stress, counseling, and discipline. Personnel communications systems, change, and organizational development are areas of growing concern to many personnel departments, and so they also are explained. Part V ends with a look at efforts in quality of work life, which are becoming major personnel tools as organizations battle for higher productivity.

The topics in Part VI, "Union-Management Relations," remain an ongoing concern for many personnel departments. Readers will find a concise explanation of the union-management framework used in unionized and nonunionized organizations. An examination of bargaining techniques and contract administration also is included. Part VII, "Personnel Management in Perspective," ends the book with a look at personnel research and audits.

Key Features

The first edition incorporated a variety of features that added relevance and interest to the material. As we revised the book, we were able to modify many features to further their contribution to the learning process.

1. *Real-life examples.* The second edition contains over 200 examples drawn from business and government organizations. Many of these are new. They demonstrate the relevancy of personnel topics, create interest for the reader, and reinforce key concepts. Since users told us that they prefer examples from named organizations, virtually all the new vignettes are from readily recognizable North American corporations. To provide greater continuity and integration, the book uses the same organizations in different examples throughout a chapter.

2. *Two-color figures.* Over 130 two-color figures appear throughout the text. These figures illustrate concepts and their relationships while adding visual variety to the book. Where appropriate, new figures have been added or old ones have been updated.

3. *Chapter objectives.* Each chapter begins with an expanded list of learning objectives that prepare the reader for the major ideas ahead and help identify key concepts. (These objectives are useful review tools, especially when comprehensive final examinations are used.)

4. *Chapter quote.* Each chapter opens with a brief quotation or two by a leading authority in the field. These quotes are designed to stimulate interest, provide a perspective on the chapter, and offer an interesting counterpoint to today's conventional wisdom.

5. *Opening example.* To focus attention on a key concept, the text of each chapter usually starts with an example drawn from a major North American corporation.

6. *Chapter summary.* Each chapter concludes with a brief summary that captures its main thoughts.

7. *Terms for review.* Following the summary is a list of the key terms introduced in the chapter. These terms are italicized and explained in the text, and their number has been expanded in the second edition. Definitions of key terms are listed in the glossary at the end of the book.

8. *Review and discussion questions.* Each end-of-chapter section includes several review and discussion questions. Some request a summarization of the ideas found in the chapter, and others seek an application of the chapter's concepts to specific problems.

9. *Chapter incidents.* Each chapter presents classroom-tested incidents that are suitable for discussion or independent study. These incidents emphasize the application of the material in the chapter to realistic situations that the readers may encounter.

10. *References.* Each chapter provides a mixture of classic and current references that enable the reader to pursue topics in greater depth. The second edition has greatly expanded the number of references to provide readers with more detailed documentation.

11. *Glossary.* Since this book is intended as an introduction to personnel management and human resources, a thorough glossary is included in the Appendix. The glossary has been significantly expanded in this edition to include many new concepts.

12. *Personnel publications.* Another Appendix section provides a brief list of major journals, magazines, and other periodicals relating to the fields of personnel management and human resources.

Supplementary Materials

To augment the balanced coverage and interest-building features of the book, a comprehensive instructor's manual and a test bank are available to adopters. Users of the first edition reported that the instructor's manual and test bank were two of the most thorough teaching resources available in the personnel management field. For the second edition, we have expanded these useful teaching tools.

Instructor's manual The instructor's manual is a resource book. Section 1 contains the sample course syllabus, alternate course designs, suggested term projects, a film and videotape bibliography, and other instructional resources. Section 2 provides chapter-by-chapter materials such as lecture notes keyed to chapter outlines, experiential in-class exercises, answers to review and discussion questions, and comments on chapter incidents. Section 3 holds a complete set of transparency masters selected from figures in the text. Even experienced professors who seldom use an instructor's manual have commented on its comprehensive steps and useful suggestions.

Test bank   The test bank contains approximately 1000 questions drawn from the text material. The questions include true-false, multiple-choice, essay, and other formats. The test bank has been expanded for coverage of new materials in the second edition.

Acknowledgments

We owe a great debt to many scholars and practitioners who pioneered the innovations this book discusses. In particular, our greatest appreciation goes to those who gave so freely of their time and advice; their good counsel enriched the book in many ways. Where we failed to heed their advice, we remain responsible.

In particular, we are most grateful to John W. Newstrom of the University of Minnesota—Duluth and to William E. Reif, Associate Dean of the College of Business at Arizona State University. Along with Professor Fred Luthans of the University of Nebraska, these scholars played an important role in the formulation of the first edition. The authors also wish to thank Professors Harold E. Fearon and William A. Ruch, respectively chairman and acting chairman of the Management Department at Arizona State University during the writing of the second edition.

At McGraw-Hill we would like to thank a long line of editors beginning with Bill Kane and John F. Carleo, and continuing with Kathi A. Benson and John Meyer, who helped bring the second edition to life. The fine assistance of Laura Warner allowed many of the production issues to be smoothly handled. We would also like to express our thanks for the many useful comments and suggestions provided by colleagues who reviewed this text during the course of its development, especially George Biles, American University; George Bohlander, Arizona State University; Tom Chacko, Iowa State University; Joseph DiAngelo, Widener University; Robert Gatewood, University of Georgia; Joyce Giglioni, Mississippi State University; Stephen Hartman, New York Institute of Technology; Wallace Johnson, Virginia Commonwealth University; Thomas Johnston, Nassau County Community College; Robert McGinty, Eastern Washington University; George E. Stevens, University of Central Florida; and Arthur Whatley, New Mexico State University.

Finally, we owe thanks to the thousands of students at Arizona State University who helped in the classroom testing of these materials.

William B. Werther, Jr.
Keith Davis

PERSONNEL MANAGEMENT AND HUMAN RESOURCES

PART

I

FOUNDATIONS AND CHALLENGES

A personnel department helps people in organizations reach their goals. But it faces many challenges along the way. These challenges arise from the demands of people, organizations, and their environment. Other challenges result from the need for equal employment opportunity.

The first three chapters of this book explore these challenges. Your success as a manager or as a personnel specialist depends on how these challenges are met. You are affected because organizations touch your life every day. How well our organizations succeed also determines our well-being and the well-being of our society.

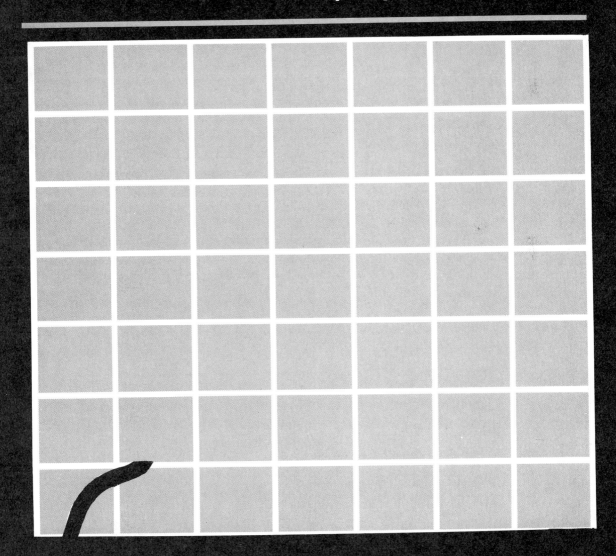

CHAPTER

1

Human resources are the key to economic development!

Eli Ginzberg[1]

THE CHALLENGES OF PERSONNEL MANAGEMENT

CHAPTER OBJECTIVES

After studying this chapter, you should be able to:

1 <u>Discuss</u> the central challenge facing our society.

2 <u>Explain</u> the purpose and objectives of personnel management.

3 <u>Summarize</u> the major activities associated with personnel management.

4 <u>Describe</u> the personnel responsibilities of all managers.

5 <u>Identify</u> the key jobs in a personnel department.

6 <u>Diagram</u> the relationships among basic personnel management functions.

What is the greatest accomplishment of the twentieth century? Landing on the moon? Computers? Biogenetic engineering? The most significant achievement may not even have happened yet. But every major advance of this century shares a common feature: organizations.

The Apollo missions to the moon were made possible by an organization called the National Aeronautics and Space Administration, or NASA. Likewise, computers were first developed by Sperry Rand and other organizations. Even on a day-to-day basis, organizations play a central role in our lives. The water we drink, the food we eat, the clothes we wear, and the vehicles we drive are products of organizations. When future historians view our era, they may see twentieth-century organizations as our greatest accomplishment. Certainly, they will agree with the essayist who said:

> Organizations are the most inventive social arrangements of our age and of civilization. It is a marvel to know that tens of thousands of people with highly individualized backgrounds, skills, and interests are coordinated in various enterprises to pursue common institutionalized goals.[2]

People are the common element in every organization. They create the innovations and accomplishments for which organizations are noted. When looked at from the perspective of an organization, people are resources. They are not inanimate resources, such as land or capital; instead they are *human resources*. When properly managed and combined with other resources, these human resources produce a nation's valued products and services. And it is these valued outputs that determine a society's well-being and its standard of living.

Among the resources available to an organization, none are more important than its people. As a slogan at one Union Carbide plant puts it, "Assets make things possible, people make things happen." With this philosophy, Union Carbide's Y-12 facility in Oak Ridge, Tennessee, has become a more productive and more satisfying place to work. And this plant is not an isolated example. More and more top managers recognize that success depends upon careful attention to human resources. Despite severe financial difficulties caused by deregulation in the early 1980s, Delta Air Lines provides a long-standing example of effective personnel management.

Success depends on human resources.

C. E. Woolman was a major force in the creation of Delta Air Lines. As its longtime president, he stamped his image on the company through his employee relations philosophy. He treated employees as though they were part of a large family. Personnel policies and management actions were designed to take care of Delta's human resources.

The company went beyond merely promoting from within and offering superior wages and benefits. For example, when other airlines furloughed employees during fuel crises and the air traffic controllers' strike, Delta put surplus pilots and flight attendants to work selling tickets, loading bags, and even washing airplanes. Through these turbulent times, not one full-time Delta employee was laid off. As Delta's senior vice president for administration and personnel observed, "The whole company saw what we did for the pilots and flight attendants . . . to keep paychecks coming and benefits intact. . . . And I think the company is better off for what we did. Everyone knows we went the extra mile for them, and so today our folks seem to be willing to go the extra mile for us."[3]

A year after these comments were made, Delta gave its employees an 8 percent raise while many other employers were actually cutting wages. The majority of Delta's employees responded by chipping in to buy their employer a $30 million Boeing 767 jet.

Although Delta's balance sheet does not list its human "assets," those assets are the backbone of the airline that *Business Week* labeled "the world's most profitable."[4] Its billion-dollar fleet of jets and its valuable airport leases would be of little use without its human resources: The fundamental point of this example is that people and organizations depend on each other. Individual employees rely on Delta for jobs. This airline exists only through the cooperative efforts of its people. And those of us outside the "Delta family" depend on organizations like it to provide goods and services, such as air transportation. In fact, without our modern organizations, society as we know it could not even exist.

People and organizations depend on each other.

THE CENTRAL CHALLENGE

This mutual dependence among individuals, organizations, and society is almost certain to grow during the remainder of this century and into the next.[5] As the challenges shown in Figure 1-1 become more complex, our society will face further demands to feed the hungry, find new energy sources, cure diseases, curb inflation, lower unemployment, and meet other challenges that we cannot imagine. Individually and collectively we will respond to these challenges through our most creative invention: our organizations. The better our organizations work, the easier our society can meet these challenges and opportunities. *Therefore, the central challenge facing our society is the continued improvement of our organizations, both private and public.*

Progress depends on better organizations.

Only if our public and private organizations continue to improve will our society prosper and meet the challenges shown in Figure 1-1. But how do they improve? Organizations improve through the more effective and efficient use of their resources. *Effective* means producing the right goods or services in a way that society deems appropriate. In Delta's case, effective means providing safe and reliable air transportation of people and freight. But Delta must do more than just the right things; it must also perform its activities in the right ways. Since Delta competes with Eastern, American, and other carriers, it must be efficient to survive. *Efficient* means that an organization must use the minimum amount of resources needed to produce its goods and services. If Delta, for example, can do a better job of scheduling its planes, it can serve more customers with fewer planes, pilots, and fuel. Eastern, American, and other airlines must then serve more customers with fewer planes in order to re-

Effectiveness versus efficiency

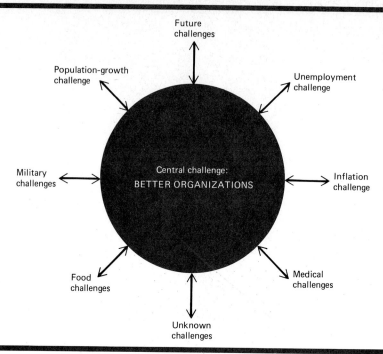

Figure 1-1
The Central Challenge to Organizations

main competitive. The result for society is an improvement in this industry's productivity.

As shown in Figure 1-2, *productivity* is the ratio of an organization's outputs (goods and services) to its inputs (people, capital, materials, and energy).[6] Productivity increases as an organization finds new ways to use fewer resources to produce its output. In a business environment, productivity improvement is essential for long-run success. Through gains in productivity, managers can reduce costs, save scarce resources, and enhance profits. In turn, improved profits allow an organization to provide better pay, benefits, and working conditions. The result can be a higher quality of work life for employees, who are more likely to be motivated toward further improvements in productivity. Personnel departments contribute to improved productivity *directly* by finding better and more efficient ways to meet their objectives and *indirectly* by improving the quality of work life for employees.[7]

Figure 1-2
Productivity Defined as a Ratio

$$\text{PRODUCTIVITY} = \frac{\text{OUTPUTS}}{\text{INPUTS}} \quad \text{or} \quad \frac{\text{GOODS AND SERVICES}}{\text{PEOPLE, CAPITAL, MATERIALS, ENERGY}}$$

This chapter begins the explanation of how organizations become more productive through the effective and efficient use of one resource: people. It shows the purpose of personnel departments and how they respond with clear objectives and specific activities to improve the productive contribution of human resources. The chapter ends with an overall framework in the form of a model. Subsequent chapters expand the model and provide details.

THE RESPONSE OF PERSONNEL MANAGEMENT

As challenges become more complex, organizations have responded with increased sophistication. One area of rapid advancement is in the management of human resources, also called *personnel management.*[8] *The purpose of personnel management is to improve the productive contribution of human resources to the organization.* This purpose guides the study and practice of personnel management. The study of personnel management describes what human resource managers do and what they should do. In practice, this definition demands that personnel departments take actions that enhance the contribution of human resources to the organization's productivity.[9]

Purpose of personnel management

Improving the contribution of human resources is both ambitious and important. It is ambitious because personnel departments do not control many of the factors that shape the employee's contribution, such as the capital, materials, and procedures.[10] A personnel department decides neither strategy nor the supervisors' treatment of employees, although it strongly influences both. Nevertheless, the purpose of personnel management is important. Without gains in employee productivity, organizations eventually stagnate and fail. To guide its many activities, a personnel department must have objectives.

The Objectives of Personnel Management

In practice, personnel management achieves its purpose by meeting objectives. *Objectives* are benchmarks against which personnel management actions are evaluated. Sometimes these objectives are carefully thought out and expressed in writing. (This approach to management by objectives will be explained more fully in subsequent chapters.) More often, objectives are never formally stated. Either way, objectives guide the personnel management function in practice. To do this, personnel objectives must recognize challenges from society, the organization, the personnel function, and the people who are affected. Failure to do so can harm the firm's performance, its profits, and even its survival. These challenges spotlight four objectives that are common to personnel management.

- *Societal objective.* To be socially responsible to the needs and challenges of society while minimizing the negative impact of such demands upon the organization. The failure of organizations to use their resources for society's benefit may result in restrictions.[11] For example, society may pass laws that limit personnel decisions.

- *Organizational objective.* To recognize that personnel management exists to contribute to organizational effectiveness. Personnel management is not an end in itself; it is only a means to assist the organization with its primary objectives. Simply stated, the personnel department exists to serve the rest of the organization.

- *Functional objective.* To maintain the personnel management contribution at a level appropriate with organization's needs. Resources are wasted when personnel management is more or less sophisticated than the organization demands. A personnel department's level of service must be appropriate for the organization it serves.

- *Personal objective.* To assist employees in achieving their personal goals, at least insofar as these goals enhance the individual's contribution to the organization. Personal objectives of employees must be met if workers are to be maintained, retained, and motivated (see Chapter 15). Otherwise, employee performance and satisfaction may decline, and employees may leave the organization.

Consider how one personnel manager contributed to organizational productivity by solving a long-standing employee turnover problem. Notice how this solution helped meet each of the four personnel management objectives:

"Best" versus "appropriate" recruits

At a Frigidaire plant, the personnel department always sought the best workers it could find. "Best" meant, among other things, the brightest and most intelligent applicants. On one job, this strategy created high turnover. The job required an employee to drill holes in sheets of metal. The employee would pick up the sheet metal, center it on the upright drill press, and drill a hole in it. (The hole was for the intake and discharge tubes of a washing machine.) The typical employee quit within three months.

The use of bright employees for this simple job led to boredom and then resignations. The problem was solved by filling the job with a mentally handicapped worker who became a productive, long-service employee. The personnel manager contributed to society's objective of finding suitable employment for the handicapped and at the same time was able to serve the organization's objective of effectiveness. The functional objective of assuring an appropriate contribution from the personnel department was met because the organization benefited from a revision in the department's selection procedures. And the new employee's personal objective of a decent job also was satisfied.

Not every personnel decision meets these four objectives every time. Trade-offs do occur. But these objectives serve as a check on decisions. The more these objectives are met by the personnel department's actions, the better will be the department's contribution to the organization. Moreover, by keeping these objectives in mind, personnel specialists are able to see the reason behind the many activities personnel departments perform.

Personnel Management Activities

11

To achieve its purpose and objectives, personnel departments obtain, develop, utilize, evaluate, maintain, and retain the right numbers and types of workers to provide the organization with an appropriate work force. As Figure 1-3 shows, these activities meet personnel objectives. When these objectives are met, the purpose of personnel management is achieved through human resources that contribute to the overall organizational goals of effectiveness and efficiency.[12] And it is only through such organizations that societal needs and challenges are satisfied.

Key personnel activities *Personnel activities* are those actions taken to provide and maintain an appropriate work force for the organization. Not every personnel department undertakes every activity discussed in this book. Small personnel departments often do not have sufficiently large budgets or enough staff members. They simply focus upon the activities that are most important for their organization. Large personnel departments usually are "full-service" departments; they do all the activities described in the following paragraphs to contribute to the overall organizational objectives found in Figure 1-3.

"Full-service" departments

Once an organization grows beyond a few employees, attempts are made to estimate the organization's future human resource needs through an activity called *human resource planning.* With an idea of future needs, *recruitment* seeks to secure job applicants to fill those needs. The result is a pool of applicants who are screened through a *selection process.* This process chooses those people who meet the needs uncovered through human resource planning.

Since new workers seldom fit the organization's needs exactly, they must be *oriented* and *trained* to perform effectively. Subsequent human resource plans reveal new demands upon the organization. These demands are met by recruitment of additional workers and by *development* of present employees. Development teaches employees new skills to ensure their continued usefulness to the organization and to meet their personal desires for advancement. Then as demands change, *placement* activities transfer, promote, demote, lay off, or even terminate workers.

Figure 1-3
The Response of Personnel Management to
Societal Needs and Challenges

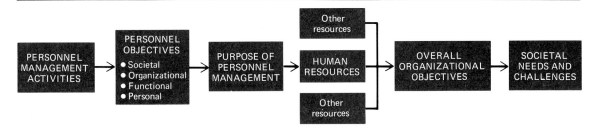

To check on these various personnel activities, individual performance is *appraised.* Not only does this activity evaluate how well people perform, but it also indicates how well personnel activities have been done. Poor performance might mean that selection, training, or developmental activities should be reconsidered. Or there may be a problem with employee motivation and satisfaction.

When employees perform, they receive *compensation* in the form of wages and salaries, along with a wide variety of employee benefits such as insurance and vacations. Some rewards are *required services* dictated by *legal compliance* —such as social security contributions, safe working conditions, and overtime pay. *Communications* and *counseling* efforts are other techniques used to maintain employee performance and satisfaction.

When employees are dissatisfied, they may band together and take collective action. Then personnel management is confronted with a new situation: *union-management relations.* To respond to collective demands by employees, personnel specialists may have to negotiate a *labor agreement* and administer it.

Even when personnel activities appear to be going smoothly, modern personnel departments apply *controls* to evaluate their effectiveness and assure continued success. Traditional budgetary limitations are one form of control. Another means of control might be to conduct an evaluation of each activity's effectiveness in meeting the personnel management objectives.

Activities contribute to objectives.

Figure 1-4 matches these different activities against the four personnel management objectives previously discussed. The figure shows that each activity contributes to one or more personnel objectives. For example, appraisal contributes to organizational, functional, and personal objectives. If an activity does not contribute to one or more of the personnel department objectives, the resources devoted to that activity should be redirected.

Responsibility for personnel activities The responsibility for personnel management activities rests with *each manager.* If managers throughout the organization do not accept their responsibility, then personnel activities may be done only partially or not at all. Even when a personnel department is created within the organization, a dual responsibility exists among operating managers and personnel experts. Individual managers remain involved with human resource planning, selection, orientation, training, development, evaluation, compensation, and other personnel activities, even though these activities may be done primarily by personnel experts.

Each manager is responsible.

Delegation

When operating managers find that personnel work seriously disrupts their other duties, the work may be reassigned. The assignment might be to another worker or to a specialized department that handles personnel matters. This process of getting others to share the work is called *delegation.*[13] Delegation requires the manager to assign duties, grant authority, and create a sense of accountability in those to whom the delegation was given. Duties, authority, and accountability must be explained clearly or the delegation will fail. And even though others may have been asked to handle personnel activities, the manager still remains responsible. The action of delegation does not reduce a manager's

PERSONNEL MANAGEMENT OBJECTIVES	SUPPORTING ACTIVITIES	**13**
SOCIETAL OBJECTIVE	1. Legal compliance 2. Required services 3. Union-management relations	
ORGANIZATIONAL OBJECTIVE	1. Human resource planning 2. Required services 3. Selection 4. Training and development 5. Appraisal 6. Placement 7. Control activities	
FUNCTIONAL OBJECTIVE	1. Appraisal 2. Placement 3. Control activities	
PERSONAL OBJECTIVE	1. Training and development 2. Appraisal 3. Placement 4. Compensation 5. Control activities	

Figure 1-4
The Relation of Personnel Management Activities to
Personnel Management Objectives

responsibility; it only shares that responsibility with others who become accountable. For example, a manager may ask a senior worker to train a new employee. If the experienced worker errs and the new employee makes a costly mistake, the manager will be held responsible for the problems that result. As personnel activities become more complex and time-consuming, the need for a separate department of personnel management may arise.

THE ORGANIZATION OF PERSONNEL MANAGEMENT

A separate personnel department usually emerges when personnel activities become a burden to other departments in the organization. At that point, the expected benefits of a personnel department usually exceed its costs. Until then, managers must handle personnel activities themselves or delegate to subordinates.

When the personnel department first emerges, it is typically small and is the responsibility of some middle-level manager. Figure 1-5 illustrates a common placement of a personnel department at the time it is first formed. Such departments are usually limited to maintaining employee records and helping managers find new recruits. Whether the department performs other activities depends upon the needs of other managers in the firm.

As the demands grow, the personnel department increases in importance and complexity.[14] Figure 1-6 demonstrates the increased importance by showing

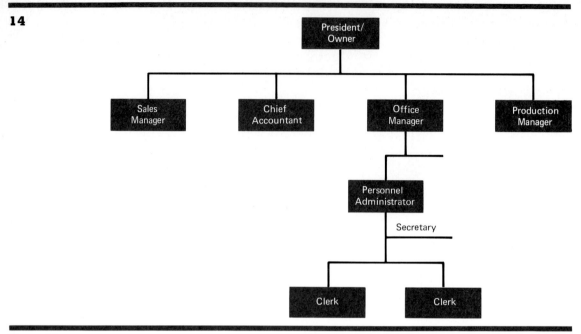

Figure 1-5
The Personnel Department in a Small Organization

Figure 1-6
The Hierarchy of Jobs within
a Large Personnel Management Department

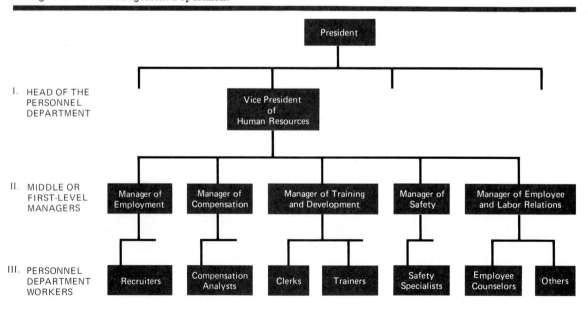

the head of personnel reporting directly to the chief operating officer, who in this figure is the company president. Increased importance may be signified by a change in title to vice president. In practice, increased complexity also results as the organization grows and new demands are placed on the personnel department. To deal with growth and new demands, jobs in the personnel department become more specialized. As the personnel department expands and specializes, it may be organized into highly specialized subdepartments and provide a wide range of services as shown in levels II and III of Figure 1-6.

New demands may mean more specialization.

Departmental Components

The subdepartments of a large full-service personnel department approximately correspond with the personnel activities shown in Figure 1-6. For each major activity, a subdepartment may be established to provide the specialized service. The employment department, for example, involves recruitment and selection. Other divisions in the figure perform the activities their names imply. This specialization allows members of the personnel department to become extremely knowledgeable in a limited number of personnel activities.

Activities not shown in Figure 1-6 are shared among the different sections. For example, employment, training, and development may share in human resource planning and placement. Performance appraisals are used to determine pay, and so the compensation division may assist managers with appraising performance. Required services come under the benefits and safety sections. Control activities, communications, and counseling are divided among all subdepartments, with employee and labor relations doing most of these tasks. Employee and labor relations sections also provide the official union-management coordination, when unions exist. Figure 1-7 shows the organization chart for Delta's personnel division.

Key Roles in Personnel

The personnel department contains a hierarchy of jobs, as shown in Figure 1-6. The top job varies in importance and title in different organizations.[15] When the department first is formed, the head of it is often called a personnel manager, director, or administrator. The title of vice president of personnel or vice president of human resources becomes more likely as the department's contribution, sophistication, and responsibility grow. If unions make a major demand on the personnel function, the title typically becomes director or even vice president of industrial relations.

Departmental hierarchy

Personnel departments in large organizations have a variety of positions. The manager of employment assists other managers with recruiting and selection. The compensation manager establishes fair pay systems. The training and development manager provides guidance and programs for those managers who want to improve their human resources. Other activity managers contribute their expertise and usually report directly to the head of personnel.[16] Activity managers may be supported by an assortment of specialists, secretaries, and clerks. These are the people who carry out the department's activities. It is the specialists in large organizations who actually do the recruiting, training, or

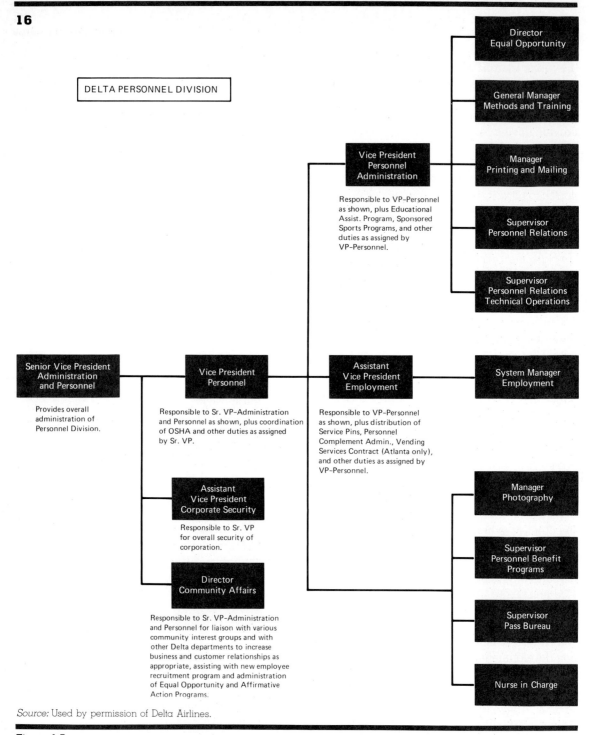

DELTA PERSONNEL DIVISION

Director
Equal Opportunity

General Manager
Methods and Training

Manager
Printing and Mailing

Supervisor
Personnel Relations

Supervisor
Personnel Relations
Technical Operations

Vice President
Personnel
Administration

Responsible to VP-Personnel
as shown, plus Educational
Assist. Program, Sponsored
Sports Programs, and other
duties as assigned by
VP-Personnel.

Senior Vice President
Administration
and Personnel

Provides overall
administration of
Personnel Division.

Vice President
Personnel

Responsible to Sr. VP-Administration
and Personnel as shown, plus coordination
of OSHA and other duties as assigned
by Sr. VP.

Assistant
Vice President
Employment

Responsible to VP-Personnel
as shown, plus distribution of
Service Pins, Personnel
Complement Admin., Vending
Services Contract (Atlanta only),
and other duties as assigned by
VP-Personnel.

System Manager
Employment

Assistant
Vice President
Corporate Security

Responsible to Sr. VP
for overall security of
corporation.

Director
Community Affairs

Responsible to Sr. VP-Administration
and Personnel for liaison with various
community interest groups and with
other Delta departments to increase
business and customer relationships as
appropriate, assisting with new employee
recruitment program and administration
of Equal Opportunity and Affirmative
Action Programs.

Manager
Photography

Supervisor
Personnel Benefit
Programs

Supervisor
Pass Bureau

Nurse in Charge

Source: Used by permission of Delta Airlines.

Figure 1-7
Organizational Chart of the Delta Airlines Personnel Division

other necessary tasks. These specialist positions are the jobs that college graduates often use to start careers in personnel work.[17]

The Service Role of Personnel

Personnel departments are service departments. They exist to assist employees, managers, and the organization. Personnel managers do not have the authority to manage other departments. Instead, they have *staff authority,* which is the authority to advise, not direct, other managers. *Line authority* is the right to direct the operations of those departments that make or distribute the organization's products or service. Those who have line authority are sometimes called line managers. Line managers make the decisions about production, performance, and people. They decide promotions, job assignments, and other people-related decisions. Personnel specialists advise these line managers, who are ultimately responsible for employee performance.

Types of authority

Even though it is advisory, staff authority is powerful. When the personnel manager advises a line manager about a human resource issue, the line manager may reject the advice. In doing so, however, the line manager bears the full responsibility for the outcome. If the results cause employee relations problems, the consequences fall on the line manager. To avoid disruptive consequences, line managers usually consider personnel's advice and follow it. The result is that the personnel department has considerable influence in shaping the actions of line managers.

In some situations, the cost of not following the personnel department's counsel is so high that top management grants the department functional authority over specific issues. *Functional authority* is the right given to specialists to make the final decision in specified circumstances. In highly technical or routine decisions, functional authority allows the personnel department to make decisions that would otherwise be made by line managers. For example, some employee benefits are technically complex. If each department manager made separate decisions about employee benefits, the result would be excessive costs and inequities. So the right of line managers to determine their employees' benefit package is given to the personnel department by top management. If line managers disagree with the department's actions, they can ask top management to review and even veto the personnel department's plans. Otherwise, the personnel department makes the decisions about employee benefits to ensure control, uniformity, and the use of their expertise. When a personnel department is given functional authority, it no longer advises. It decides. However, like all organizational decisions, the use of functional authority is subject to review by top management.

The use of line, staff, and functional authority can result in a *dual responsibility for personnel management.* Both line and personnel managers are responsible for employee productivity and quality of work life. Personnel departments are responsible for creating a productive climate by finding ways to enhance the organization's quality of work life through its many activities and advice to line managers. At the same time, line managers are responsible for their employees' day-to-day treatment and for the quality of work life in their

18

departments. Conflicts between line and staff managers occur when their objectives clash. A production manager, for example, may want to reduce costs through layoffs at the first sign of declining sales. The personnel manager, however, may see a temporary layoff of short duration as damaging to the organization's quality of work life. Or a line manager might want to hire someone at a salary above the level recommended by a compensation analyst in the personnel department. Although potentially disruptive to smooth line and staff relations, such conflict has the benefit of causing both groups to review their objectives and methods.

Line versus staff
conflict

Departmental size

The size of the personnel department also affects the type of service provided to employees, managers, and the organization. In small departments, the personnel manager handles many of the day-to-day activities related to the organization's human resource needs. Other managers bring their problems directly to the head of personnel, and these meetings constantly remind the personnel manager of the contribution that is expected.

When the personnel function grows larger, problems are handled by subordinates. Not only do personnel managers have less contact with lower-level managers, but others in the personnel department grow increasingly specialized. At this point, personnel managers and their subordinates may lose sight of the overall contributions that are expected of them or of the limits on their authority. Instead, experts sometimes become more interested in perfecting their specialty than in asking how they may serve others. While improving their expertise, they may fail to uncover new ways of serving the organization and its people. Or specialists may assume authority they do not have.[18] For example, consider what happened at a fast-growing maker of minicomputers.

For the past five years, Harris Mini-Computers, Inc., had grown at an average rate of 25 percent a year. To keep up with this growth, the personnel department manager, Earl Bates, used budget increases to hire new recruiters. His strategy meant that the personnel department was well prepared to find new employees. But recruiting specialists paid little attention to other human resource problems. In one month, three of the company's best computer design engineers quit to go to work for a competitor. Before they left, they were interviewed. They complained that they saw desirable job openings being filled by people recruited from outside the organization. No design engineer had been promoted to supervisor in the past three years, so each of these engineers found jobs where the promotion possibilities looked better.

When Earl reminded these engineers that they lacked experience or training as supervisors, one of them commented that the company should have provided such training. With the next personnel department budget increase, Earl hired a specialist in employee training and development, who designed a supervisory development program.

The personnel manager and the recruiting specialists at Harris Mini-Computers overlooked the variety of activities that the personnel department is supposed to perform. And they failed to identify the services that the organization needs from the personnel department. They also did not recognize the connection between different personnel management activities.

THE PERSONNEL MANAGEMENT MODEL

Personnel management is a system of many interdependent activities. These activities do not occur in isolation. Virtually every one affects some other personnel activity.

> In preparing a bid for a construction contract, an estimator miscalculated the human resource requirements. Too many unskilled workers and too few skilled employees were hired. As the expansion of the football stadium fell behind schedule, supervisors tried to get work done more quickly. This speedup led to complaints from the union. Finally, the project manager realized the problem. The manager fired one-third of the unskilled workers and replaced them with skilled cement masons and carpenters. This decision led to legal problems over unemployment compensation claims, and the higher-paid skilled workers caused the original payroll estimates to be wrong. The personnel manager had to intervene. The stadium seats were in place by the first home game. But the contractor lost $385,000 on the job.

As this illustration shows, personnel management activities are connected. A poor decision about human resource requirements can lead to problems in employment, placement, legal compliance, union-management relations, and compensation. When personnel activities are involved as a whole, they form an organization's personnel management system.

A Systems Model

When activities are related, a system exists. A *system* consists of two or more parts (or subsystems) working together as an organized whole with identifiable boundaries.[19] Examples are numerous. A car is a system composed of subsystems (engine, transmission, radio, and the like). A human body is a system with respiratory, digestive, circulatory, and other subsystems. Cars, people, and personnel departments have identifiable boundaries.

Personnel management activities form an interconnected system with boundaries, as shown in Figure 1-8. The figure indicates that each activity (or subsystem) relates directly to every other activity. For example, the challenges faced by personnel departments affect their selection of employees. The selection subsystem influences the department's development and evaluation of human resources. In addition, each subsystem is affected by the personnel department's objectives and policies and by the external environment in which personnel management takes place, as shown in Figure 1-8.

Thinking in terms of systems is useful because it enables one to recognize the interrelationships among parts. If one adopts a systems view of personnel,

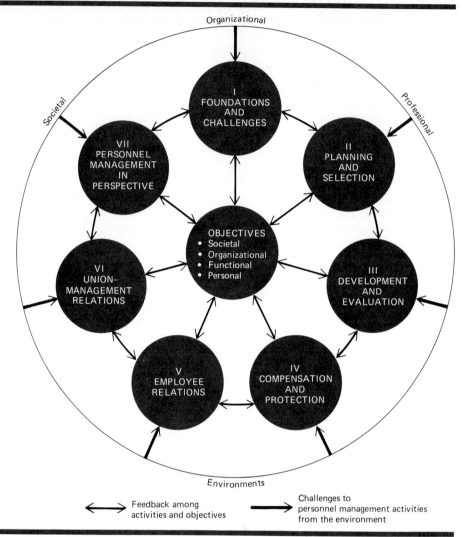

Figure 1-8
Personnel Management Model and Subsystems

the relationships between personnel activities are less likely to be overlooked. In the example of the football stadium, the manager failed to recognize the interdependence between the subparts of the personnel system.

Systems thinking also requires the recognition of the system's boundaries, which mark the beginning of its external environment. The environment is an important consideration because most systems are open systems. An *open* **Open systems** *system* is one that is affected by the environment. Organizations and people are an open system because they are affected by their environments. Personnel management is also an open system, influenced by the external environment. For example, the stadium contractor's organization is an open system because the society, organization, and professional personnel practices impact how the personnel department responds.

A brief discussion of this model appears below. It explains the role of major personnel subsystems. It also serves as a preview of the seven parts of this book and their major topics. Each part of the book is identified in the model by a Roman numeral.

I. Foundations and challenges Personnel management faces many challenges in dealing with human resources. The central challenge is to assist organizations in improving their effectiveness and efficiency. To do so requires personnel departments to be organized in a way that allows them to meet their objectives while serving their organization. Other challenges arise from the environment in which organizations operate; economics, markets, pressure groups, professional ethics, and government are just a few. Challenges also spring from within the organization. For example, other departments compete with the personnel department for larger budgets, for a larger share of their organization's resources. Perhaps the most pervasive force is the government requirement for equal employment opportunity.[20] To respond to this societal demand, personnel departments become more actively involved in line management decisions that affect employees. And their success in advising other managers depends upon a continued awareness of the objectives and challenges facing personnel management.

Challenges to personnel

II. Planning and selection At the heart of personnel management is the need for a sound information base. Without accurate and timely information, personnel departments are seriously limited in their ability to meet the challenges before them. To build this information base, data are gathered about each job and about the organization's future human resource needs.[21] From this information, personnel specialists can advise managers about the design of jobs they supervise and even find ways to make those jobs more productive and satisfying. Estimates of future human resource needs allow the personnel department to become proactive in the recruitment and selection of new workers.

Information base

III. Development and evaluation Once hired, new employees are oriented to the company's policies and procedures. They are then placed in jobs and given needed training to be productive. With a sound human resource information base, personnel specialists can help determine the orientation, training, development, and career counseling needs of present employees. Through these activities, many job openings can be filled from within, rather than by recruiting new employees from outside the firm. Training develops employees for future jobs. The results of the personnel department's efforts should lead to a more effective work force. To evaluate employees, formal performance appraisals are conducted periodically. Appraisals give workers feedback on their performance and can help the personnel department spot its own weaknesses.

Employee development

22

Retaining and maintaining employees

IV. Compensation and protection One element of retaining and maintaining an effective work force is compensation. Employees must be paid a fair wage or salary relative to their productive contribution. When compensation is too low, turnover and other employee relations problems are likely. If pay is too high, the company can lose its competitive position in the marketplace. But modern compensation management goes beyond just pay. Benefits are an increasingly important part of any compensation package and must be at a level appropriate to employee productivity if the company is to retain its work- ers and remain competitive. At the same time, the organization needs to protect its workers from occupational hazards. Through safety and health programs, personnel departments not only assure a safe work environment but also keep the employer in compliance with the many health and safety laws.

Motivation, satisfaction, and productivity

V. Employee relations To maintain an effective work force requires more than just pay, benefits, and safe working conditions. Employees need to be motivated, and the personnel department is partially responsible for ensuring employee satisfaction with the job. Personal and job-related problems may lead to employee stress and the need for counseling or discipline. Here again, the personnel specialists can provide effective programs or specific advice to line managers. To further employee satisfaction and organizational productivity, communications are used to keep people informed. More and more companies today are seeing personnel communications systems as an effective way to improve employee motivation, satisfaction, and productivity. When the organi- zation is confronted with the need to change, personnel specialists become involved by assisting line managers or even conducting companywide efforts aimed at improving the performance of the company through organizational development activities. In fact, personnel departments are becoming increasing- ly involved in planned efforts to improve the quality of work life for employees, and these efforts lead to improved productivity.

Unions and personnel management

VI. Union-management relations For a variety of reasons, employees may join together and form self-help groups, called unions. When this occurs, personnel departments are usually responsible for dealing with the union's attempt to organize the workers. If a union is formed, the personnel department assumes the responsibility for negotiating a labor agreement with the union and administering its terms.

Audits

VII. Personnel management in perspective As with any ongoing system, personnel departments need to uncover their successes and failures through self-evaluation. Full-service personnel departments regularly conduct audits of their performance and do research to uncover more effective ways to serve their organization. Often this research is helpful in uncovering future challenges in order to anticipate their impact on the organization and its human resources.

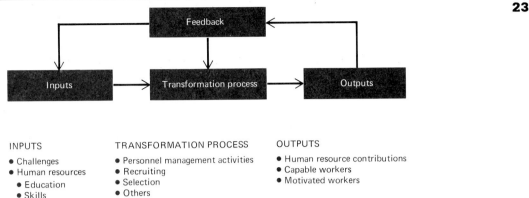

INPUTS
- Challenges
- Human resources
  - Education
  - Skills

TRANSFORMATION PROCESS
- Personnel management activities
- Recruiting
- Selection
- Others

OUTPUTS
- Human resource contributions
- Capable workers
- Motivated workers

Figure 1-9
Input-Output Simplification of
the Personnel Management System

An Applied Systems View

Personnel subsystems affect each other, and personnel specialists must remain aware of this interdependency. Perhaps the most effective way to recognize possible complications is through systems thinking. Figure 1-9 provides a simplified visual model for applying systems thinking.

An applied systems view describes personnel activities as taking *inputs* and *transforming* them into *outputs*. Then the personnel specialist checks on the results to see if they are correct. This checking process produces *feedback,* which is information that helps evaluate success or failure. Consider the situation faced by Carol Torres, the personnel manager at a Veterans Administration hospital:

> A predicated shortage of medical technologists caused Carol to start an in-house development program to prepare six lab assistants to become licensed medical technologists. After fifteen months, they finished the program and passed the state certification test. Since the program was a success and the shortage had grown worse, eight more lab assistants were recruited for the second program.

Transforming inputs into outputs

The knowledge of a shortage was one *input.* Another *input* was the lab assistants who signed up for training. The program itself was the *transformation process* that created the desired *output,* a new supply of technologists. When all six technologists passed the state certification test, those results gave Carol *feedback* that the program was a success. In summary, the personnel management system transforms inputs into desired outputs. The inputs are challenges (usually in the form of information) and human resources. Through personnel activities, these inputs are transformed into the desired outputs, which become feedback to the personnel management system.

In practice, systems thinking helps personnel specialists identify the key variables with which they are dealing. After viewing new information as an input, specialists decide what the desired output is. With inputs and outputs known, decision makers draw on their knowledge of personnel activities to transform the inputs into outputs in the most effective way. To verify their success, they acquire feedback about the outcome. Negative feedback means that other inputs (information or people) are needed or that the transformation process (a specific personnel activity) is malfunctioning. Negative feedback demands corrective action.

Proactive versus Reactive Personnel Management

Personnel departments cannot always wait for feedback and then respond. To wait may expose the organization to needless damage from changes in its environment. For example, reconsider the situation of Carol Torres when she learned of the impending shortage of technologists and discussed it with her manager:

> Carol Torres: My department budget must be increased by $12,000 so we can train more lab technologists. With the impending shortage of technologists, we will have serious staffing, performance, and employee relations problems if we don't take action now.

> Anna Newman: Hold on! Washington has put a freeze on the budget for six months, and as director of administrative services my hands are tied. Why not wait until we can show Congress complaints from doctors? Then the shortage will be real, and we can get Congress to expand our budget.

> Carol Torres: But then we will probably have to spend $15,000 for training. We will probably have to pay another $30,000 for overtime to the technologists we now have while we train new ones. Besides, with all that overtime, error rates are sure to jump and so will lawsuits for faulty lab work. All I need is $12,000, but I need it now.

Anna was suggesting that Carol's department wait until an actual problem occurred and then react. Carol wanted to take action in anticipation of the problem without waiting for the feedback of doctors' complaints or lawsuits. Anna's approach was reactive, while Carol's was proactive. *Reactive* personnel management occurs when decision makers respond to human resource problems. *Proactive* personnel management occurs when human resource problems are anticipated and corrective action begins before the problem exists.[22]

Proactive versus reactive

Effective and efficient personnel departments seek proactive solutions. By applying systems thinking to personnel management, managers like Carol Torres can take action before serious problems arise. This proactive approach improves productivity by minimizing the resources needed to produce the organization's goods or services. In short, a proactive approach to the management of human resources is a major step in enhancing organizational productivity.[23]

PERSONNEL MANAGEMENT VIEWPOINTS

━━━━━━━━━━━ Throughout this chapter several viewpoints of personnel management stand out. These approaches provide complementary themes that we will pursue throughout the book to keep personnel management and human resources in perspective. They include:

Complementary themes

- *Human resource approach.* Personnel management is the management of human resources. The importance and dignity of human beings should not be ignored for the sake of expediency.[24] Only through careful attention to the needs of employees do successful organizations grow and prosper.

- *Management approach.* Personnel management is the responsibility of every manager. The personnel department exists to serve managers and employees through its expertise. So in the final analysis, the performance and well-being of each worker is the dual responsibility of that worker's immediate supervisor and the personnel department.

- *Systems approach.* Personnel management takes place within a larger system: the organization. Therefore, personnel management must be evaluated with respect to the contribution it makes to the organization's productivity. In practice, experts must recognize that the personnel management model is an open system of interrelated parts. Each part affects the others and is influenced by the external environment.[25]

- *Proactive approach.* Personnel management can increase its contribution to employees, managers, and the organization by anticipating challenges before they arise. If efforts are reactive only, problems may be compounded and opportunities may be missed.

Since the practice of personnel management is an open system, it is affected by the environment in which it is practiced. The historical evolution of personnel management and standards of professionalism in the field help shape that environment. Other challenges arise from society and even from the organization that the department serves. These historical, environmental, and professional challenges set the context in which personnel management is practiced. Recognition and understanding of these challenges are fundamental to the proper practice of personnel management. Each of these challenges is explored more fully in the next chapter.

Next chapter

SUMMARY

━━━━━━━━━━━ The central challenge facing society is the continued improvement of our organizations, both private and public. Personnel management exists to improve the contribution made by human resources to organizations.

To carry out its role, personnel management departments need to satisfy multiple, and sometimes conflicting, objectives. Societal, organizational, and personal needs must be met. But they must be met in a way that is appropriate to the organization being served. These objectives are achieved through a variety of personnel activities that are designed to obtain, maintain, utilize, evaluate, and retain an effective work force. These activities are the responsibility of all managers in the organization, even though many of them may be delegated to the personnel department.

The activities of a personnel department can be viewed as a system of interrelated actions. Each activity affects other personnel activities directly or indirectly. Personnel specialists view information and human resources as the primary inputs. They transform these inputs through various activities to produce results that help the organization meet its goals and further its productivity. Ideally, personnel experts undertake this role proactively.

TERMS FOR REVIEW

Human resources	Functional authority
Personnel management	Dual responsibility for personnel
Purpose of personnel management	System
Productivity	Open system
Delegation	Feedback
Staff authority	Reactive
Line authority	Proactive

REVIEW AND DISCUSSION QUESTIONS

1. What is productivity and why is it important to organizations?

2. What are the objectives of personnel management?

3. Explain the relationship between societal needs and the activities of a personnel department.

4. Why is a systems approach to personnel management useful?

5. Explain the difference between proactive and reactive approaches to personnel management.

6. Suppose you worked for a maker of automobile parts and the company decided to open a chain of parts stores. Briefly describe what areas of personnel management would be affected if you become the personnel manager for the chain of stores.

7. If a bank opened a branch in a distant city, what activities would the personnel department need to undertake before a fully operational and staffed branch was ready for business?

INCIDENT 1-1

People, Productivity, and Profits at Delta Air Lines

Delta Air Lines was used as an example several times throughout the chapter because it represents an organization that is successful in a variety of ways. Its treatment of employees, its profitability, and its productivity help set the standards for its industry. As *Business Week* stated:

> Delta's secret is simple. It combines good planning—15 years ahead for flight equipment and support facilities—with a massive effort to motivate employees. The result: the highest productivity in the trunk airline industry.[26]

To continue its success, Delta's personnel policies try to assure good treatment of its human resources. So pervasive is the commitment to its people that the organization generates a strong commitment, even zeal, from its employees. Some of Delta's policies include:

● Reassignment of employees to avoid layoffs, even at the expense of short-term profits and productivity

● Payment of wages that are 5 to 10 cents per hour above the rates paid to unionized workers in other airlines

● Fringe benefits for employees that are considered to be some of the most generous in the industry and that provide employees with sound economic security in the event of disability or retirement

● Rewards for employees who do an exceptional job of helping passengers in need of assistance

● Communications from top management with all employees in groups of twenty-five to thirty every year and a half

Although good planning, modern planes, lean staff, and effective equipment scheduling contribute to Delta's favorable record, the core of its success is its people who do the planning, scheduling, and serving of customers. By creating and maintaining an effective work force, Delta has been able to grow and prosper at times when other airlines, such as Braniff, declared bankruptcy.

1. Since Delta must pay approximately the same as other airlines for its planes, equipment, fuel, and facilities, how can it pay higher wages and fringe benefits while remaining one of the industry's most profitable carriers?

2. From this incident, give examples of how Delta's management uses the human resource, management, systems, and proactive approaches discussed in the chapter.

INCIDENT 1-2

Personnel Decision Making at Benlux, Inc.

Benlux, Inc., is a very large importer of linens, china, and crystal. It has operations in nine countries and has long been plagued by problems in its personnel practices. These problems led to the following discussion between the vice president of personnel and the vice president of distribution:

Rob Whittier: You may not agree with me, but if we are going to have consistency in our personnel policies, then key personnel decisions must be centralized in the personnel department. Otherwise, branch managers continue to make their own decisions differently. Besides, the personnel department has the experts. If you needed financial advice, you would not ask your doctor; you would go to a banker or other financial expert. When it comes to deciding compensation packages or hiring new employees, those decisions should be left to experts in salary administration or selection. To ask a branch manager or supervisor to make these decisions deprives our firm of all of the expertise we have in the personnel department.

Henri DeLahn: I have never questioned your department's expertise. Sure, the people in personnel are more knowledgeable than the line managers. But if we want those managers to be responsible for the performance of their branches, then we must not deprive those managers of their authority to make personnel decisions. Those operating managers must be able to decide whom to hire and whom to reward with raises. If they cannot make those decisions, then their effectiveness as managers will suffer.

1.   If you were the president of Benlux, Inc., and were asked to resolve this dispute, which argument would you select? Why?

2.   Can you suggest a compromise that would allow line managers to make these decisions consistently?

REFERENCES

1.   Eli Ginzberg, "Man and His Work," *California Management Review,* Winter 1962, p. 21.

2.   Robert Granford Wright, "Managing Management Resources through Corporate Constitutionalism," *Human Resource Management,* Summer 1973, p. 15.

3.   "Delta: The World's Most Profitable Airline," *Business Week,* Aug. 31, 1981, p. 71.

4.   Ibid., pp. 68–72.

5.   Karen E. Debats, "The Continuing Personnel Challenge," *Personnel Journal,* May 1982, pp. 332–336, 338, 340, 342, 344.

6. William A. Ruch and James C. Hershauer, *Factors Affecting Worker Productivity,* Tempe, Arizona: Bureau of Business and Economic Research, Arizona State University, 1974, pp. 9–14.

7. Harold C. White, "Personnel Administration and Organizational Productivity: An Employee View," *Personnel Administrator,* August 1981, pp. 37–42, 44, 46, 48.

8. Dennis R. Briscoe, "Human Resources Management Has Come of Age," *Personnel Administrator,* November 1982, pp. 75–77, 80–83.

9. Joyce D. Ross, "A Definition of Human Resources Management," *Personnel Journal,* October 1982, pp. 781–783.

10. Ruch, op. cit. Also see Arnold S. Judso, "The Awkward Truth about Productivity," *Harvard Business Review,* September–October 1982, pp. 93–97.

11. Keith Davis and William C. Frederick, *Business and Society,* New York: McGraw-Hill, 1984, pp. 33–35. Also see Sandra L. Holmes, "Corporate Social Performance: Past and Present Areas of Commitment," *Academy of Management Journal,* September 1977, pp. 443–448.

12. Briscoe, op. cit., p. 77.

13. Patrick J. Montana and Deborah F. Nash, "Delegation: The Art of Managing," *Personnel Journal,* October 1981, pp. 784–787.

14. Lena B. Prewitt, "The Emerging Field of Human Resources Management," *Personnel Administrator,* May 1982, pp. 81–83, 84–85. See also Russell J. Johnson, "The Personnel Administrator of the 1970s," *Personnel Journal,* April 1971, p. 298; and Robert H. Meehan, "The Future Personnel Executive," *Personnel Administrator,* January 1981, pp. 25–28.

15. Meehan, ibid. See also Roger Kenny, "The Future Top Personnel Executive," *Personnel Administrator,* February 1980, pp. 77–82.

16. Herbert E. Meyer, "Personnel Directors Are the New Corporate Heros," *Fortune,* February 1976, pp. 84–88, 140. Also see Wendell French and Dale Henning, "The Authority-Influence Role of the Functional Specialist in Management," *Academy of Management Journal,* September 1966, pp. 187–203.

17. Duff A. Greenwell, "Not for Students Only," *Personnel Administrator,* September 1981, pp. 16, 19–20.

18. Joseph A. Litterer, "Pitfalls for 'Professionals,'" *Personnel Journal,* May 1982, pp. 383–385.

19. James Grier Miller and Jessie Louise Miller, "Systems Science: An Emerging Interdisciplinary Field," *The Center Magazine,* September–October 1981, pp. 44–45. For a more detailed discussion of systems theory also see Daniel L. Katz and Robert L. Kahn, *The Social Psychology of Organizations,* New York: Wiley, 1966, pp. 14–29; and Fremont E. Kast and James E. Rosenzweig, *Organization and Management,* 2d ed., New York: McGraw-Hill, 1974, pp. 100–125.

20. Briscoe, op. cit., p. 76.

21. Richard P. Shenetulskis, "Implementing a Personnel Data System," *The Personnel Administrator,* October 1978, pp. 24–27.

22. Alfred W. Hill, "How Organizational Philosophy Influences Management Development," *Personnel Journal,* February 1980, pp. 118–120, 148. See also Paul R. Westbrook, "A Practical Approach to Personnel," *Personnel Journal,* September 1977, p. 459.

23. William B. Werther, Jr., "Productivity through People," *Arizona Business,* February 1981, pp. 14–19.

24. Walter R. Nord and Douglas E. Durand, "What's Wrong with the Human Resources Approach to Management?" *Organizational Dynamics,* Winter 1978, pp. 13–25.

25. David R. Leigh, "Business Planning Is People Planning," *Personnel Journal,* May 1984, pp. 44, 47–48.

26. "Delta: The World's Most Profitable Airline," op. cit., p. 68. See also "Delta: Top Brass Listens to Staff," *Dallas Times Herald,* Monday, Dec. 27, 1982, pp. B-1, B-3.

CHAPTER 2

The innovative organization, the organization that resists stagnation rather than change, is a major challenge to management, private and public.

Peter F. Drucker[1]

ENVIRONMENTAL CHALLENGES

CHAPTER OBJECTIVES

After studying this chapter, you should be able to:

1 Explain the historical challenges that have led to the need for personnel departments.

2 Identify the external forces that affect today's personnel practitioners.

3 Isolate the challenges to personnel management that come from within the organization served.

4 Describe the challenge of professionalism facing the personnel field.

5 Discuss how human resource policies can further organizational strategy.

6 Put personnel management concepts into an understandable framework.

Origins of personnel practices

As discussed in Chapter 1, organizations and their personnel departments are open systems. Both are affected by the changing environment in which they operate. Changes that impact an organization almost always affect and challenge its people and its personnel department. Although some challenges are unique to a firm or an industry, many of them affect personnel professionals in all organizations. For example, most personnel practices have historical origins earlier in this century that have led most personnel departments to use similar methods and procedures. However, today's practitioners must adapt these practices or create new ones to meet the challenges that result from the external, organizational, and professional environments in which they work. Their proactive responses assume an awareness of their organization's environment and how it may impact their efforts. An example of how the human resources department of one company is responding to its environmental challenges comes from Motorola.

Motorola's semiconductor operation is one of the world's leading producers of solid-state electronics, from transistors to state-of-the-art "computer-on-a-chip" technology. Its environment is highly competitive on a worldwide basis. Not only must it compete with domestic rivals—such as Texas Instruments, Intel, and National Semiconductor—but it must also face increasing competition from Japanese manufacturers.

As envisioned by the Japanese Ministry of International Trade and Industry, "Japan's goal for the 1980s is to dominate the computer business, but to do that it must first dominate the semiconductor business."[2] Toward that end, Japanese manufacturers became a major force in the worldwide semiconductor market by the early 1980s. "As the battle for semiconductor supremacy unfolds, the Japanese have a clear advantage because they have an aggressive consumer electronics industry, while U.S. companies have virtually given up on designing and manufacturing such equipment."[3] This large base of consumer-oriented uses for semiconductors gives the Japanese significant economies of scale that allow for high-volume, low-cost production.

Motorola's "participative management program"

To compete in this environment, Motorola has implemented a variety of business strategies. One of those strategies is called the "participative management program." PMP, as it is called at Motorola, began in the mid-1970s, before the Japanese became a significant force in the semiconductor market. This proactive response to the management of human resources involves employees at Motorola in the decisions that affect their productivity and quality of work life. Through training and subsequent group meetings, employees learn to solve problems and find better ways to make the company's products. The result is not only higher productivity and product quality but also increased employee satisfaction and quality of work life. Through its PMP and other strategies, Motorola does not try to copy the Japanese. Instead, as one senior executive commented, "We plan to be the leaders in technology and people management. We want the Japanese to chase us for worldwide leadership. And we are going to win."[4]

Whether Motorola will maintain its dominant position in these important markets during the 1990s is too early to tell. What is clear, however, is that the personnel professionals and line managers at Motorola have responded proactively to their environment. They were aware that changes in the external environment meant that the company had to adapt its business and human resource strategies to the new reality of increased foreign competition.

This adaptation process affects nearly every part of the personnel management system shown in Figure 2-1. With an already strong foundation in human resource management, Motorola's personnel experts had to modify the type of supervisors they sought to hire and develop. More emphasis is placed upon the *development* of employees through the PMP *training;* and *performance evaluation* of managers is influenced by how successful their PMP efforts are working. These evaluations, in turn, are reflected in *compensation* decisions that determine incentives and more traditional pay raises. And the ideas of employees often lead to improvements in productivity, quality, and *safety,* which furthers their protection. As the PMP effort enhances the workers' *quality of work life,* employee relations are improved, too. Finally, the already high stature of the personnel function at Motorola will increase if the PMP effort continues to improve the company's productivity. In short, the PMP effort enables the personnel department to meet the societal, organizational, functional, and personal objectives discussed in Chapter 1.

PMP's impact

Personnel professionals at Motorola, or at any other company, cannot meet the objectives in Figure 2-1 without an understanding and awareness of environmental challenges. One of the most pervasive environmental challenges faced by personnel professionals is government. Through laws and regulations, it has such a major impact that the next chapter is devoted to just one aspect: equal employment opportunity. Other government challenges affect compensation, safety and health, and labor relations. These challenges are discussed in subsequent chapters. This chapter focuses on the nongovernmental challenges that arise from the external, organizational, and professional environments. These challenges are added to the personnel management model in Figure 2-1, which was first presented in Chapter 1. The rest of this chapter explains these challenges. Throughout the book, we will return to these challenges to see how they affect specific personnel activities.

Additions to model

HISTORICAL FOUNDATIONS
The field of personnel management did not suddenly appear. It evolved into its present form. A review of this evolution shows how the efforts of early pioneers led to today's more proactive methods. By tracing this evolution, we can also sense the newness and growing importance of personnel management.

Early Causes and Origins
The origins of personnel management are unknown. Probably the first cave dwellers struggled with problems of utilizing human resources. Even the Bible records selection and training problems faced by Moses.[5]

Biblical mention

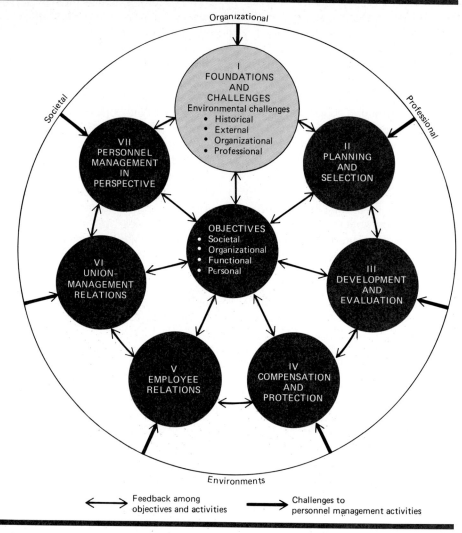

Figure 2-1
A Model of the Personnel Management System
and Its Major Environmental Challenges

During the thousands of years between Moses and the industrial revolution, there were few large organizations. Except for religious orders (the Roman Catholic Church, for example) or governments (particularly the military), most work was done in small groups. Whether on the farm, in small shops, or in the home, the primary work unit was the family. There was little need for a formal study of personnel management. However, the industrial revolution changed the nature of work. Big textile mills, foundries, and mines sprang up in England and then in North America. Expensive facilities, steam engines, and other innovations required large numbers of people to work together to attain economies of scale. Collectively, people were still an important resource, but the industrial revolution meant greater mechanization and unpleasant working conditions for many workers.

By the late 1800s, a few employers reacted to the human problems caused by industrialization and created the post of *welfare secretary*. Welfare secretaries existed to meet worker needs and to prevent workers from forming unions. Social secretaries, as they were sometimes called, helped employees with personal problems such as education, housing, and medical needs. These early forerunners of personnel specialists also sought to improve working conditions for workers. The emergence of welfare secretaries prior to 1900 demonstrates that the personnel activities in large organizations had already become more than some top operating managers wanted to handle. Thus, social secretaries marked the birth of specialized human resource management, as distinct from the day-to-day supervision of personnel by operating managers.

Welfare secretary

Scientific Management and Human Needs

The next noteworthy development was scientific management, as advocated by Frederick Taylor, for example. The scientific management movement showed the world that systematic, scientific study of work could lead to improved efficiency. Their arguments for specialization and improved training furthered the need for personnel departments.

Stimulated by the developments of scientific management and early unions, the first decades of this century saw primitive personnel departments replace welfare secretaries. These new departments contributed to organizational effectiveness by maintaining wages at proper levels, screening job applicants, and handling grievances. They also assumed the welfare secretary's role of improving working conditions, dealing with unions, and meeting other employee needs.

By World War I, personnel departments were becoming common among very large industrial employers. But these early departments were not important parts of the organizations they served. They were record depositories with advisory authority only. At that time, production, finance, and marketing problems overshadowed the role of personnel management. The importance of personnel departments grew slowly as their contribution and responsibilities increased. During World War I, selection tests were developed to match recruits with their roles in the Army. This advancement led to the industrial use of tests that continues today and is usually a responsibility of the personnel department.

From the end of World War I until the Great Depression in the 1930s, personnel departments assumed growing roles in handling compensation, testing, unions, and employee needs. More and more attention was paid to employee needs. The importance of individual needs became even more pronounced as a result of the research studies at Western Electric's Hawthorne plant during this period.[6] These studies showed that the efficiency goals of

Hawthorne studies

scientific management had to be balanced by considerations of human needs. These elementary observations eventually had a profound impact on personnel management. But the Depression and World War II diverted attention to more urgent matters of organizational and national survival.

Modern Influences

The Depression of the 1930s led citizens to lose faith in the ability of business to meet society's needs. They turned to government. Government intervened to give workers unemployment compensation, social security, minimum wages, and even the federally protected right to join unions. The government's emphasis was on improving employee security and working conditions. This outpouring of legislation during the 1930s helped to shape the present role of personnel departments by adding legal obligations. Organizations now had to consider societal objectives and the need for legal compliance, which elevated the importance of personnel departments. In practice, personnel departments were made responsible for discouraging unionization among employees. But with new-found legal protection, unions grew dramatically. These organizing successes startled many organizations into rethinking their use of *paternalism,* their "management-knows-best" approach to employee welfare. Personnel departments began replacing paternalism with more proactive approaches that considered employee desires. When workers did organize, responsibility for dealing with unions also fell to the personnel department, sometimes renamed the industrial relations department to reflect these new duties.

Personnel departments continued to increase in importance during the 1940s and 1950s. The recruiting and training demands of World War II added to the credibility of personnel departments that successfully met these challenges. After the war, personnel departments grew in importance as they contended with powerful unions and an expanding need for knowledge workers, such as engineers and accountants. The explosive growth of employee benefits also contributed to the personnel department's importance. At the same time, the widespread understanding of the Hawthorne studies and newer behavioral findings led to concern for improved human relations. These findings helped underscore the importance of sound personnel management practices.

Personnel legislation   In the 1960s and 1970s, the central influence on personnel was again legislation. Laws were passed to eliminate discrimination in pay between men and women. Laws to end discrimination in employment because of sex, race, religion, national origin, and age were also enacted. Safety and health legislation and pension laws followed in the 1970s. These acts gave personnel departments a still larger voice—a voice that began to equal those of production, finance, and marketing executives in major corporations.

Figure 2-2 summarizes the key historical developments in the personnel field. As is evident from the figure, many of the historical factors that affected personnel management resulted from external changes. And although these historical events have shaped the role of personnel departments, current challenges from the external, organizational, and professional environments mean more changes are likely.

Paternalism fades appears in the left margin alongside the first body paragraph.

YEAR	DEVELOPMENTS AND EVENTS
1806	Members of the Philadelphia Cordwainers (shoemakers) are convicted of a criminal conspiracy for striking their employers.
1842	Merely joining unions is no longer considered illegal, according to the Massachusetts Supreme Court ruling in *Commonwealth v. Hunt.*
1848	Pennsylvania passes child labor laws setting 12 as the minimum working age.
1875	American Express starts a pension plan.
1886	The American Federation of Labor is formed.
1911	F. W. Taylor's book, *The Principles of Scientific Management,* is printed.
1917	World War I selection tests are applied to Army recruits.
1923	American Telephone and Telegraph establishes the position of vice president of personnel relations.
1926	The *Railway Labor Act* sets union-management relations rules in the railroad industry.
1935	Congress passes the *National Labor Relations Act* and the *Social Security Act.*
1938	The *Fair Labor Standards Act* is passed, establishing minimum wages and overtime for hours over forty. President Roosevelt orders government agencies to establish personnel departments.
1939	*Management and the Worker,* describing the Hawthorne experiments, is published.
1941	World War II starts, with attendant shortages of human resources and a sudden need to train large numbers of workers.
1947	The *Labor-Management Relations Act* is passed to protect workers and management from union activities.
1955	The American Federation of Labor merges with the Congress of Industrial Organizations to create the AFL-CIO.
1959	The *Labor-Management Reporting and Disclosure Act* provides union members with a "Bill of Rights" in dealing with their union in addition to other labor law change.
1963	The *Equal Pay Act* is passed by Congress, requiring that women be paid the same as men for similar jobs.
1964	The *Civil Rights Act* is passed by Congress, prohibiting discrimination in employment based on race, color, religion, sex, or national origin.
1967	The *Age Discrimination in Employment Act* is passed by Congress.
1970	The *Occupational Safety and Health Act* is passed by Congress.
1972	The *Equal Employment Opportunity Act* is passed by Congress to amend and strengthen the 1964 Civil Rights Act.
1973	The *Rehabilitation Act* is passed by Congress to aid handicapped workers.
1974	Congress passes *Employee Retirement Income Security Act* to regulate pension plans. Congress passes the *Vietnam Era Veterans Readjustment Act*, requiring federal contractors to undertake affirmative action for Vietnam era veterans.
1976	The American Society of Personnel Administrators begins an accreditation program for personnel experts.
1978	The *Pregnancy Discrimination Act* prohibits discrimination against pregnant women. The *Comprehensive Education and Training Act* is passed to provide federally funded training programs.
1983	The *Job Training Partnership Act* replaces the Comprehensive Education and Training Act, providing for increased consultation with industry about its training needs.

Figure 2-2

Key Developments in the Evolution of
Personnel Management

38   **EXTERNAL CHALLENGES**

Organizations are surrounded by an external environment filled with challenges that can be viewed as variables—variables over which the organization and its personnel department have little influence. Many of these variables affect the way the organization is operated and, in turn, affect personnel policies and practices indirectly. For example, after scientists at Western Electric developed the transistor, the management at Motorola opened a research facility in Phoenix, Arizona, to study the applications of this new technology. Their early successes led Motorola's management to formulate a corporate strategy centered around high technology. From this strategy and its modest research facility, Motorola's operations in Arizona have grown to more than 20,000 employees who had to be recruited, selected, oriented, trained, compensated, and maintained. As this example illustrates, changes in the external environment, such as a new technology, may impact corporate strategy and planning. Personnel departments then are affected as they respond to these changes and help the organization meet its strategy and objectives.

Corporate strategy and personnel

Some of the external challenges facing organizations evolve gradually, while others occur quickly. Changes in the composition of the work force take place over many years, for example, while new laws or court rulings seemingly can occur overnight. Personnel professionals deal with these changes by following the steps in Figure 2-3. As the figure explains, they constantly search the environment for changes and evaluate their impact on the organization and on the personnel function. When noteworthy changes are uncovered through reading, continuing education, or studying company strategy, proactive plans are developed and implemented. The personnel department's success is measured through feedback about the plans it has implemented. Although challenges may arise from many areas, the most common sources are technology, economics, work force composition, cultural values, and government. Each of these challenges is discussed in the following sections.

Sources of challenges

Technological Challenges

Technology impacts personnel management by changing jobs and the skills required to do them. This happens when technology alters entire industries.

Figure 2-3
Steps in Dealing with Environmental Challenges

1. *Monitor the environment.* Personnel specialists must stay informed about likely changes in the environment by belonging to professional associations, attending seminars, furthering their formal education, and reading widely.

2. *Evaluate the impact.* As new information is acquired, personnel experts ask: "What impact will this information have on the organization today? Tomorrow?" Specialists must diagnose the future meaning of today's events.

3. *Take proactive measures.* Once changes and their impact are evaluated, personnel specialists implement approaches that help the organization reach its goals.

4. *Obtain and analyze feedback.* The results of proactive personnel activities are then evaluated to see if the desired outcomes are reached.

The technology of cars and airplanes modified the transportation industry. Automobile and aviation companies grew. Growth created demand for more employees and training. For those already employed within these firms, growth provided promotional opportunities. Railroad companies were also affected by the same technology, except the personnel management challenges differed. Revenue lost to cars, trucks, and airplanes limited growth. Advancement opportunities—even employment opportunities—shrank. Personnel departments in these companies had to reduce the work force and create early retirement systems.

Automation is another way that technology affects the field of personnel management.

The introduction of computers into banks changed employment needs. Before computers, personnel specialists recruited large numbers of unskilled and semiskilled clerks. Computers, however, required highly skilled programmers and systems analysts. Also needed were semiskilled employees to process information into computer-usable form. Bank systems that could be observed by outsiders changed very little. But personnel departments of banks had dramatically changed their recruiting and training programs.

One specific form of automation that is likely to have a significant impact on organizations is robotics. As robots become more common and sophisticated, they will affect organizational productivity and the quality of work life for employees. Their increased use seems a certainty since their cost relative to human resources is declining.[7] The good news is that hazardous and boring jobs will be taken over by robots. Dangerous jobs—such as working with toxic chemicals and paints—will be changed by substituting robots for people. Likewise, highly repetitive assembly tasks increasingly will be taken over by robots during the late 1980s and early 1990s. General Motors, for example, plans to use more than 1500 robot painters by 1990, when it will have more than 13,000 robots doing welding, assembly, and other work.[8] New jobs will appear, from robotics engineers to robotics technicians and assemblers. The result will be more challenges for personnel departments to recruit and train these specialists. The jobs that remain are likely to be upgraded in importance and pay because those who control and maintain the robots will possess a higher level of skills than the workers who will be replaced.

Robotics

The bad news is that personnel professionals may have to contend with increased worker alienation since job opportunities may shrink along with opportunities for socialization on the job. To effectively utilize expensive robots, more and more factories may find it necessary to work two or three shifts a day. If these changes do occur on a wide scale, personnel departments will face even more challenges in recruiting and retaining qualified workers. And it is likely that these departments will become more involved with helping line managers introduce robots into the workplace in ways that minimize employee fears of displacement and unemployment.[9]

Personnel implications

40

Economic Challenges

Business cycles

As the economy changes from expansion to contraction during the course of a business cycle, organizations must modify their plans. These changes in the business cycle make demands on personnel specialists, who must assist their organization in meeting its new plans. When the economy expands, new employees and training programs are needed. Voluntary departures by employees increase. Pressures for higher wages, better benefits, and improved working conditions also grow. Personnel departments must act cautiously, however. Overstaffing, bloated benefit programs, and higher wages become serious burdens when the business cycle turns down. A recession creates a need to maintain a competent work force and reduce labor costs. Decisions to reduce hours, lay off workers, or accept lower profit margins involve the advice of personnel experts. The more effectively personnel departments monitor the economy, the better they can anticipate the organization's changing needs. Sometimes personnel departments can even develop proactive policies that anticipate changes in the business cycle. Motorola provides another example.

Contract labor at Motorola

Motorola uses contract labor to staff its human resource needs during periods of peak business activity. *Contract labor* consists of people who are hired (and often trained) by an independent agency that supplies companies such as Motorola with needed human resources for a fee. When Motorola finds that it needs assemblers of electronic components to finish a project, for example, it recruits, hires, and trains most of these people through its own personnel department. But some of the workers it uses will be contracted from a temporary help agency. Not only can the agency provide extra staff more quickly, but these agency workers do not become Motorola employees; instead, they work for their agency and are assigned to Motorola to meet the temporary need for more workers. When the project is completed or when the business cycle declines, Motorola informs the agency that it needs fewer of these temporary contract workers. The result is that the personnel department is able to meet the staffing needs of its divisions while providing high levels of employment security to Motorola's employees. Of course, Motorola has less control over the quality of these contract workers, whose loyalty and dedication to Motorola objectives may be less than that of career Motorolans.

This policy of using contract labor is another example of how proactive personnel departments seek ways to meet the needs of an organization and its people while remaining sensitive to the firm's economic environment. In Motorola's case, the personnel department did not wait for the economy to go up or down before it reacted. Rather, these practitioners developed policies that allow the organization to adjust smoothly to changes caused by technological, economic, and other challenges.

Demographic Challenges

The *demographics* of the work force describe its composition: the education level, age, race, sex, the percentage of the population participating in the work force, and other descriptive characteristics. Changes in work-force demographics are usually known in advance, occur slowly, and are well measured. For example, increases in the educational levels of the population are a slow-moving trend. Some companies, such as General Motors, find demographics to be so important that they have hired their own demographers.[10] Although slow-moving, these trends can have a significant impact on a personnel department's activities.

The Depression of the 1930s and World War II led to a decline in the birthrate. This meant fewer people in the 35 to 44 age range during the late 1960s and throughout the 1970s. Most middle-level managers come from this age group. Reactive personnel departments did little until the shortage became acute. Proactive ones implemented training programs in the early 1960s to groom lower-level managers to fill the foreseeable shortages. Likewise, the post-World War II "baby boom" peaked in the late 1950s, and the birthrate declined through the 1960s and most of the 1970s. As a result, the growth rate of the work force will slow down in the late 1980s and through the 1990s unless a large number of immigrants move to the United States and Canada.[11] Personnel departments in businesses that rely heavily on young workers—such as McDonalds, retail stores, and newspapers—will find a less plentiful supply of new employees.[12] Other organizations will be affected in the late 1990s and beyond as they search for technical and managerial talent in a work force that begins to grow more slowly.[13]

Many projections of demographic changes in the work force are provided by the U.S. Department of Labor.[14] Figure 2-4 shows, for example, the past and projected participation rates in the work force. *Participation rates* are the percentage of working-age men and women who are in the work force. During the past couple of decades, the percentage of men in the work force has been declining gradually while the rate for women has grown steadily. The labor department's middle-of-the road assumptions indicate that both trends will continue. Another projection in Figure 2-5 reveals that the percentage of

Work-force projections

Figure 2-4
Actual and Projected Work Force Participation Rates of
Men and Women in the United States

	ACTUAL PARTICIPATION RATE, %			PROJECTED PARTICIPATION RATE, %	
	1965	1975	1979	1985	1990
Total	58.9	61.2	63.7	66.5	67.9
Men	80.7	77.9	77.9	77.7	77.2
Women	39.3	46.3	51.0	56.5	59.6

Source: Based on Department of Labor figures and adapted from Ronald E. Kutscher, "New Economic Projections through 1990—An Overview," *Monthly Labor Review,* August 1981, pp. 9–16.

OCCUPATIONAL GROUP	1978		1990		PERCENTAGE CHANGE BETWEEN 1978 AND 1990
	NUMBER	PERCENT	NUMBER	PERCENT	
Total	97,610	100.0	121,447	100.0	24.4
WHITE-COLLAR WORKERS	48,608	49.8	61,570	50.7	26.7
• Professional and technical	15,568	15.9	20,295	16.7	30.4
• Managerial and administrators	8,802	9.0	10,677	8.8	21.3
• Salesworkers	6,420	6.6	8,079	6.7	25.3
• Clerical workers	17,818	18.3	22,519	18.5	26.4
BLUE-COLLAR WORKERS	31,812	32.6	38,330	31.6	20.5
• Craft and kindred	11,705	12.0	14,668	12.1	25.3
• Operatives	14,205	14.6	16,584	13.7	16.8
• Nonfarm labor	5,902	6.0	7,078	5.8	19.9
SERVICE WORKERS	14,414	14.8	19,220	15.8	33.3
• Private household workers	1,160	1.2	988	0.8	− 14.9
• Other service workers	13,254	13.6	18,232	15.0	37.6
FARMWORKERS	2,775	2.8	2,327	1.9	− 16.3

Source: Based on Department of Labor statistics and adapted from Max L. Cavey, "Occupational Employment Growth through 1990," *Monthly Labor Review,* August 1981, p. 45.

Figure 2-5

Employment by Major Occupational Groups for 1978 and Projections for 1990

white-collar and service workers will grow as the percentage of blue-collar and farm workers declines.[15] While the changes in the blue-collar and farm-worker groups largely reflect technological developments and an evolution of the economic structure of the United States, participation rates of men and women mirror cultural changes.

Cultural Challenges

Attitudes toward work and leisure can cause changes in the demographics of the work force and result in new challenges for personnel management. The increased participation of women in the labor force is an example of a cultural change that has demographic implications.

Women in the work force

During the 1970s, for example, more than half of the growth in the United States work force came from women seeking employment.[16] Except during World War II, the majority of the growth in the labor force historically came from men. Changing values and laws have caused greater participation rates by women in the employment market. The old cultural value that "men work and women stay home" underwent radical modification. The implications for personnel departments have been many. For example, child-care facilities provided by employers are becoming a more common demand on personnel departments and benefit administrators. Motorola, for example, responded to this pressure by selling a piece of land near one of its facilities to a child-care company in order to have day care near its plant. In many companies, sick days—paid days off for illness—are becoming "personal leave days" so that working parents can be absent to meet the needs of their children. And with the increasing frequency of "dual career families," more and more personnel departments find themselves helping the spouses of newly hired employees to find jobs in their local communities.

Other changes in attitudes toward work and leisure have confronted personnel departments with requests for longer vacations, more holidays, and nontraditional work schedules.[17] Changes in cultural attitudes about work have also caused personnel departments to find new ways to motivate employees. Motorola's participative management program mentioned earlier in this chapter is an example. Even attitudes toward honesty are reflected in the growing rates of employee theft with which many personnel departments must contend. Perhaps the most dramatic change in cultural values is reflected in attitudes about the work ethic. Figure 2-6 shows the results of a nationwide survey conducted by Louis Harris & Associates for Sentry Insurance. Of the almost 1200 people surveyed, the vast majority reported that pride, loyalty, motivation, workmanship, and hard work declined during the last ten years.[18] During the same time period, the growth rate of productivity improvement in the United States also declined. Against this backdrop of changing values, personnel departments must still recruit, motivate, and retain qualified employees.

Sentry Insurance survey

It is impossible to identify every changing value in society. However, organizations represent a small sample of society. As cultural values change, personnel departments must try to anticipate the impact of these changes on their employer and *act* accordingly. Failure to anticipate changing values can lead to lower effectiveness or even government involvement.

Government Challenges

Few challenges encountered by personnel departments are as overwhelming as those presented by government. Government—through the enforcement of laws—has a direct and immediate impact on the personnel function. The federal

Figure 2-6

Changing Cultural Values toward Work in the United States

	PERCENTAGE AGREEING
The American public believes:	
● Most people do not work as hard as they did ten years ago.	63
● Workmanship today is not as good as it was ten years ago.	71
● Most people have less pride in their work than they did ten years ago.	76
● Employees today are less loyal to their employers than they were ten years ago.	76
● People are not as motivated to work today as they were ten years ago.	73

Source: Adapted from *Perspectives on Productivity: A Global View*, Stevens Point, Wisconsin: Sentry Insurance Company, 1981, pp. 9–10.

laws that regulate the employee-employer relationship challenge the methods personnel departments use. Some laws, such as the Occupational Safety and Health Act or the Civil Rights Act, make major demands on personnel departments. The impact of these laws has helped elevate the importance of personnel decisions.

Government involvement in the employment relationship seeks to achieve societal objectives—usually the elimination of practices that are considered contrary to public policy. To personnel specialists, government involvement requires compliance and proactive efforts to minimize the organizational consequences. Throughout this book, employee-related laws are explained to illustrate the challenges and actions modern personnel departments encounter.

ORGANIZATIONAL CHALLENGES

Besides external demands, personnel departments find current challenges within the organizations they serve. Internal challenges arise because employers pursue multiple objectives. These objectives required trade-offs between financial, sales, service, production, employee, and other goals. Since personnel objectives are just one set among many in the eyes of top management, personnel managers must confront internal challenges with a balanced concern for other needs. The employer does not exist solely, or even largely, to meet personnel objectives. Instead, personnel departments exist to assist the organization in meeting its other objectives successfully. Personnel departments find several internal challenges in helping the organization achieve its objectives. Included are challenges from unions, informational needs, and organizational character.

Unions

Unions are an actual or potential challenge.

Unions represent an *actual* challenge in unionized companies and a *potential* challenge to those that are not. In companies with unions, the employer and union sign a labor agreement that specifies compensation (wages and benefits), hours, and working conditions. The agreement limits the personnel activities of supervisors and personnel departments. For both, the challenge is to achieve objectives without violating the agreement.

> Karl McPheters wanted to promote Jill Wang to chief switchboard operator because Jill was an excellent employee. The labor contract called for promotions to go to the most experienced worker, which meant Pam Hale. To promote Jill, Karl found Pam a production job at more money. She took it. This now made Jill the most senior switchboard operator and next in line for the promotion. The contract was honored, and management achieved its objective of promoting the best person, Jill.

Employers *without* unions are affected too. To retain the flexibility of nonunion status, personnel departments implement compensation policies, hours of work, and working conditions similar to those found in unionized operations. Here the personnel challenge is usually determined by top management; try to operate so that unionization is discouraged. For example, major firms in the electronics industry, such as Motorola and Texas Instruments, are mostly nonunion.

Information Systems

Personnel departments require large amounts of detailed information. Increasingly, the quality of the personnel department's contribution depends on the quality of its information. Many personnel activities and much effort by personnel professionals are devoted to obtaining and refining the department's information base. The information requirements of a full-service department are only hinted at by such questions as:

- What are the duties and responsibilities of *every* job in the organization?   Some key questions

- What are the skills possessed by *every* employee?

- What are the organization's future human resource needs?

- How are external constraints affecting the organization?

- What are the current trends in compensation of employees?

And this list could be continued for pages!

Clearly, the acquisition, storage, and retrieval of information present a significant challenge.[19] One key part of the challenge is gaining cooperation from others in the organization who provide the department with much of its information. Employee responses to personnel department questionnaires, supervisors' absentee control reports, and most other sources of human resource information come from others. Line managers may see personnel's request for information as far less important than producing or selling the firm's goods and services. To ensure a timely flow of accurate information, personnel specialists must not only communicate the importance of their requests, but they must maintain good working relationships with other managers to earn their cooperation. To store and retrieve information, personnel departments increasingly rely on computer-based information systems—systems that store detailed information about employees, jobs, laws, unions, economic trends, and other internal and external factors. But massive information systems challenge the personnel department's ability to safeguard the privacy of employee records. As a manager at a consulting firm specializing in computer security observed:

> Computer security is more important in the human resource management   Computer security
> field than in any other area where computers might be used.   and privacy
>
> There is an ethical responsibility to protect the individual. But more importantly and certainly more of a problem is the legal aspect of privacy.
>
> I don't know of any state that doesn't have some sort of privacy legislation on the books regarding the confidentiality of . . . personnel records in general. HRM administrators can be held criminally liable if they do not take adequate measures to protect that data. . . .[20]

46

Organization Character

Each organization is unique.

Every employer is unique. Similarities between organizations can be found among their parts, but each whole organization has a unique character.[21] *Organization character* is the product of all the organization's features: its people, its successes, and its failures. Organization character reflects the past and shapes the future.

The challenge for personnel specialists is to adjust proactively to the character of the organization. For example, it is sometimes overlooked that objectives can be achieved in several acceptable ways. This idea, called *equifinality,* means there are usually multiple paths to objectives. The key to success is picking the path that best fits the organization's character.

> As personnel manager, Aaron Chu feared that his request to hire a training assistant would be turned down. Instead of asking for funds to hire someone, Aaron expressed concern that poor supervisory skills were contributing to employee complaints and some resignations. He observed at the weekly management meeting that unskilled replacements could lead to rising labor costs.
>
> Knowing that top management was concerned about remaining a low-cost producer, Aaron was not surprised when the plant manager suggested hiring "someone to do training around here." Aaron got a budget increase for training by adjusting to the organization's character.

Core values and excellent organizations

In nearly every organization, a few core values or beliefs shape its culture. Sometimes service is highly valued, as at IBM. Other times, product innovation is seen as the key to the firm's success, as at the 3M Company. At Aaron's firm, it is labor costs. Top management evidently holds the belief that success depends on low labor costs, and it is willing to support actions that promise to keep labor cost low. Effective practitioners identify the values or beliefs in their organization and strive to further those values.[22]

PROFESSIONAL CHALLENGES

The newest challenge for personnel experts is professionalism. Personnel management skills are too important to organizations and society to be ignored. External and internal challenges require practitioners who are at least minimally qualified. Since the actual capabilities of practicing personnel experts vary widely, it became increasing evident during the 1970s that professionalism of the personnel management field was needed. The *American Society for Personnel Administration* (usually referred to as ASPA) took an important step toward building the profession of personnel management: *accreditation.*

Accreditation

ASPA

ASPA studied the question of accreditation for a decade.[23] By late 1975, ASPA established standards and credentials for accreditation. Experienced practitioners and academicians were admitted under a "grandfather" clause, which

ASPA ACCREDITATION   **47**

SENIOR LEVEL	BASIC LEVEL
Senior Professional in Human Resources	Professional in Human Resources
(SPHR)	(PHR)

Figure 2-7
Professional Designations Granted by the American
Society for Personnel Administration

granted them accreditation based on letters of recommendation and their experience. This clause ended after the first year, and credentials are now earned by testing, which ensures a minimum level of competence among those who receive a professional designation from ASPA.

ASPA created two professional designations to distinguish between different levels, as shown in Figure 2-7. The senior level requires experience with policy-developing responsibilities. If these responsibilities are limited to a segment of the field, the designation is Senior Professional in Human Resources (Specialist). One is an SPHR (Generalist) if responsibilities span the field. A Professional in Human Resources (PHR) designation is for those in the field who are not at the policy level. The designations require varying years of experience and successful completion of ASPA examinations. For the PHR designation, examinations require a basic understanding of personnel management. At the senior level, specialized tests from the following areas are given:

1. Employment, placement, and personnel planning

2. Training and development

3. Compensation and benefits

4. Health, safety, and security

5. Employee and labor relations

6. Personnel research

Other Professional Requirements

Accreditation does not make personnel management a profession. Some argue that the field will never become a profession because there is no common body of knowledge. Personnel management is not a clearly separate discipline like law, medicine, or economics. It draws on a variety of disciplines.

Individual personnel practitioners have little control over their activities, and this limits their professionalism. Unlike self-employed physicians or attorneys who are independent decision makers, or teachers who have some traditionally guaranteed rights under tenure rules, personnel experts are dependent upon the direction of top management and have few rights. And unlike most professions, there are no legal certification or licensing requirements. Most professions have

American Society for Personnel Administration

Code of Ethics

Each member of the American Society for Personnel Administration shall acknowledge his or her personal responsibility to strive for growth in the field of human resources management, and will pledge to carry out the following Society objectives, to the best of his or her ability:

♦ Support the goals and objectives of the Society in order to reflect the highest standards of the human resource management profession.

♦ Support the personal and professional development programs of the Society in Personnel Administration and Industrial Relations to help create an environment of recognition and support of human values in the workplace.

♦ Support the self-enforcement provisions in the codes of other associations to achieve the overall goal of development of each person to his/her full human potential.

♦ Display a unity of spirit and cohesiveness of purpose in bringing fair and equitable treatment of all people to the forefront of employers' thought; transmit that cohesive-

ness to academia by actively cooperating to instill the PAIR ethic into the curricula of accredited institutions.

♦ Practice respect and regard for each other as a paramount personal commitment to a lifestyle exemplary in its motivation toward making business profitable in both human and monetary values.

♦ Express in the workplace through corporate codes the basic rules governing moral conduct of the members of the organization in order to provide employees and the public with a sense of confidence about the conduct and intentions of management.

♦ Personally refrain from using their official positions (regular or volunteer) to secure special privilege, gain or benefit for themselves, their employers or the Society.

Source: Reprinted by permission of the American Society for Personnel Administration, 30 Park Drive, Berea, Ohio 44017.

Figure 2-8
Code of Ethics of the American Society for Personnel Administration

legally sanctioned procedures to establish minimum competency. There are no such requirements in the personnel field. Even ASPA's accreditation program is voluntary. As a result, there are no standard codes of conduct or ethics that are widely recognized. Although Figure 2-8 reproduces ASPA's code, neither practitioners nor the public uniformly supports it. So there is little reason for the public to recognize the personnel field as a profession.

While debate will continue over whether the field of personnel is or will become a profession, the field is *becoming* more professional through the leadership of ASPA, more highly educated practitioners, and more advanced university education in personnel management. The result is a challenge to every practitioner that goes beyond organizational boundaries: Can the personnel management field become a profession?[24]

> **Becoming professional**

PERSONNEL MANAGEMENT IN PERSPECTIVE

Amid historical, external, internal, and professional challenges, it is important to keep personnel management in perspective. Its purpose is to assist in the attainment of organizational objectives with maximum effectiveness. Personnel management aids other departments. It does not direct operations or decide organizational objectives. Its authority is limited. Although research shows that personnel managers perceive themselves as having more authority than they really do,[25] their authority is usually viewed as *advisory* (or staff) *authority*. That is, personnel managers primarily advise and assist, not decide and direct. In recent years, however, the complexity of the employment environment has meant that personnel managers get more *decision-making* (or line) *authority*.

> **Limited authority**

> Carlos Ortega has been personnel manager for A & M Lumberyards for seven years. Carlos usually recommended to department managers the best three applicants he could find for each opening. The department managers then made the final hiring decision. Because some of these managers made statements to applicants that could be interpreted as racially or sexually discriminatory, lawsuits resulted. The owners of A & M eventually decided to grant Carlos the final hiring authority.

Carlos and many of his peers in other companies now have more decision-making authority as the result of legal changes. Authority to manage other departments still remains with the managers in those departments, however. In using their authority, personnel experts must recognize different groups within the organization. Research shows that executives and lower-level managers have different expectations about personnel activities.[26] Figure 2-9 illustrates the dozen most important personnel activities as viewed by executives. Note how these perceptions differ from the perceptions of lower-level managers. For example, executives and managers rank selection testing differently. Likewise, according to this survey, health and safety concerns are more important to lower-level managers than they are to executives. To be effective, personnel

	RANKINGS BY EXECUTIVES	RANKINGS BY MANAGERS
Fringe benefits	1	1
Selection testing	2	16
Orientation of new employees	3	3
Recruiting	4	11
Job descriptions	5	21
Training	6	8
Selection	7	13
Personnel surveys	8	12
Complaints and grievances	9	5
Health and safety	10	2
Employee communications	11	14
Civil rights	12	6

Source: Harold C. White and Robert E. Boynton, "The Role of Personnel Administration: A Management View," *Arizona Business,* October 1974, p. 19.

Figure 2-9

The Importance of Different Personnel Functions as Perceived by Executives and Lower-Level Managers

specialists must determine the areas of concern to different levels of management. Otherwise their advisory authority will be less effective and more likely ignored.

Limited resources and unlimited challenges

The use of authority by personnel specialists is important because the resources of personnel departments are extremely limited. One study found that the average budget of the personnel department amounts to barely 1 percent of the organization's total budget. This same study showed that the average personnel department contains less than 1 percent of the organization's total employees.[27]

With limited authority and resources, the personnel department is expected to meet the challenges discussed in this chapter and in the following ones. These challenges affect the department's ability to meet its purpose of contributing to the organization's effectiveness. If these challenges are not met, then personnel management does not achieve its purpose. Moreover, its challenges are likely to grow in the future, unless personnel specialists can take proactive measures now.[28]

Next chapter

Perhaps the most extensive challenge comes from the need to provide equal employment opportunity. A detailed examination of this challenge in the next chapter reveals how critical the personnel function can be to organizations. Other challenges are reviewed in more depth throughout the book.

SUMMARY

The practice of personnel management is shaped by a variety of environmental challenges. These challenges arise from the historical, external, organizational, and professional demands confronting personnel specialists.

The historical challenges began with the industrial revolution, which led to the scientific study of work and workers. As the tools available to managers became more sophisticated, the need for specialists in personnel management and human resources grew. Early in this century, personnel departments emerged to deal with these demands. Today, personnel departments are responsible for meeting the external, organizational, and professional issues that affect employees.

The external challenges to personnel management come from several different sources. The major external concerns are created by changing technologies, economic cycles, demographic developments, cultural changes, and government involvement. Each of these factors influences the ways in which personnel departments meet their objectives.

Organizational challenges include those elements within the organization that personnel departments cannot ignore if they are to be successful. Unions are one obvious example. They demand that management meet and satisfy its economic objectives within the constraints imposed by labor organizations. Even employers who do not have a union must be aware of actions that can cause workers to unionize. A professionally managed personnel department must develop and maintain a sophisticated data base in order to be effective. The need for information and the best way to implement personnel activities are also dependent on unique aspects of the organization's character.

The newest challenge to personnel management is professionalism. The important role that personnel departments and their members play in modern organizations requires a professional approach and professionally trained people. The growing importance of this function requires practitioners to strive for the high standards expected of professionals. The accreditation program of the American Society for Personnel Administration is a major step in that direction.

If personnel departments can successfully meet the environmental challenges discussed in this chapter, they are more likely to contribute effectively to the goals of the organization and its people.

TERMS FOR REVIEW

Welfare secretary

Paternalism

Demographics

Organization character

Equifinality

American Society for Personnel
  Administration

Accreditation

Advisory (staff) authority

Decision-making (line) authority

Contract labor

Participation rate

REVIEW AND DISCUSSION QUESTIONS

1. Explain how increased competition—particularly from the Japanese—has made personnel management more important at Motorola's semiconductor group.
2. In what ways did the industrial revolution influence the practice of personnel management?
3. Describe how a proactive personnel department would be affected by the introduction of robotics and other forms of automation into a production department.
4. What are the characteristics of demographic changes? Why should personnel specialists monitor demographic trends?
5. How would the increased professionalization of the personnel field benefit personnel practitioners and their employers?
6. What is the purpose of a code of ethics, such as the one developed by ASPA? Can you suggest any additions to ASPA's code?
7. Defend or refute the following statement: Since personnel department budgets usually amount to only 1 percent of the organization's total budget, top management should not devote more than 1 percent of its time to personnel management issues.
8. How do economic cycles affect the personnel function? Give an example of a personnel policy that considers variations in the economy.

INCIDENT 2-1

A Possible Technological Scenario

Sometime within the near future electronic technology will advance to the point where the average home will have:

•   A computer console and access to several on-line computer systems via satellite communications

•   A television set (with more than a hundred working channels fed by a cable system) that serves as a visual display for computer outputs and inputs

•   A photocopy machine connected to the television that permits photocopies of screen information

•   A two-way video phone

About the time this all becomes a reality, serious people will ask, "Why do we still follow the primitive ritual of going to work? Why don't we do our jobs at home, since most workers are now white-collar information handlers?" Shortly after, the practice of going to work, which began with the industrial revolution, will end for some workers. People will still work. Some will even have to "go to work." But most people will stay at home, plugged into a worldwide information grid.

Assuming this scenario comes true during your career:

1. What implications does it hold for our culture and our society?

2. What are the implications of these probable changes for personnel management?

INCIDENT 2-2

Government Intervention

Since the 1930s, the federal government has increased its regulation of how employers treat employees. Laws have been passed that permit workers to join unions, require employers to pay minimum wages, ensure safe and healthy work environments, prohibit discrimination, and restrict the freedom of employers to make personnel decisions in other areas.

Some futurists believe the trend of increasing government intervention will continue. To support their argument, these thinkers point to Japan and Europe, where government involvement is far more extensive than in the United States and Canada. These people believe that the federal government will require employers to provide even greater job security against layoffs, develop more extensive training programs for the disadvantaged and handicapped, and follow other regulations that will further limit personnel decisions.

Other experts think that the trend of growing government involvement is beginning to end. Complaints about taxes, deregulation of the airlines and other industries, and the demographic trend toward an older population are the evidence these people cite in support of their position. These people also argue that regulation cannot continue if United States and Canadian firms are to remain competitive in international markets.

1. Which trend do you think will occur and why?

2. If government regulation continues to increase, how will personnel departments be affected?

REFERENCES

1. Peter F. Drucker, *Management: Tasks, Responsibilities, Practices,* New York: Harper & Row, 1973, 1974, p. 803.

2. *Vision of Industry in the Eighties,* Tokyo: Ministry of International Trade and Industry, 1980.

3.   "Japan Inc. Goes International with High Technology," *Business Week*, Dec. 14, 1981, p. 44. See also Bro Uttal, "Here Comes Computer Inc.," *Fortune*, Oct. 4, 1982, pp. 82–90.

4.   Ibid., p. 48. See also "Motorola's New Strategy: Adding Computers to Its Base in Electronics," *Business Week*, Mar. 29, 1982, pp. 128–132.

5.   Moses was confronted by one of the earliest recorded personnel challenges when Jethro, his father-in-law, advised: "And thou shalt teach them ordinances and laws, and shalt shew them the way wherein they must walk, and the work they must do. Moreover, thou shalt provide out of all the people able men . . . to be rulers." (*The Holy Bible, Exodus*, 18 Verses 20 and 21.)

6.   Elton Mayo, *The Human Problems of an Industrial Civilization*, Cambridge, Mass.: Harvard University Press, 1933. See also F. J. Roethlisberger and W. J. Dickson, *Management and the Worker*, Cambridge, Mass.: Harvard University Press, 1939.

7.   George L. Whaley, "The Impact of Robotics Technology upon Human Resource Management," *Personnel Administrator*, September 1982, p. 70.

8.   "GM's Ambitious Plans to Employ Robots," *Business Week*, Mar. 16, 1981, p. 31.

9.   Whaley, op. cit., pp. 61–63. See also John Dodd, "Robots: The New 'Steel Collar' Workers," *Personnel Journal*, September 1981, pp. 688–695.

10.   James C. Hyatt, "People Watchers: Demographers Finally Come into Their Own in Firms, Government," *The Wall Street Journal*, Western ed., July 19, 1978, pp. 1, 31.

11.   Joan Lindroth, "How to Beat the Coming Labor Shortage," *Personnel Journal*, April 1982, pp. 268–272.

12.   Melinda Beck et al., "The Baby Boomers Come of Age," *Newsweek*, Mar. 30, 1981, pp. 34–37.

13.   Valerie A. Personick, "The Outlook for Industry Output and Employment Through 1990," *Monthly Labor Review*, August 1981, pp. 28–41.

14.   Ronald E. Kutscher, "New Economic Projections through 1990—An Overview," *Monthly Labor Review*, August 1981, pp. 9–16.

15.   Max L. Carey, "Occupational Employment Growth through 1990," *Monthly Labor Review*, August 1981, pp. 42–55.

16.   Ibid. See also "Single Men and Married Women Show Unusually Large Labor Gains," *United States Department of Labor News Release*," Sept. 14, 1977.

17.   John D. Owne, "Workweeks and Leisure: An Analysis of Trends, 1948–1975," *Monthly Labor Review*, August 1976, pp. 3–8.

18.   *Perspectives on Productivity: A Global View*, Stevens Point, Wis: Sentry Insurance Company, 1981, pp. 9–10.

19.   Alfred J. Walker, "The Newest Job in Personnel: Human Resources Data Administrator," *Personnel Journal*, December 1982, pp. 924–928.

20.   "Securing Computerized Personnel Records," *Resource*, November 1982, p. 2. See also John Rahiya, "Privacy Protection and Personnel Administration: Are New Laws Needed?" *The Personnel Administrator*, April 1979, pp. 19–21, 28.

21. William B. Wolf, "Organizational Constructs: An Approach to Understanding Organizations," *Journal of the Academy of Management,* April 1968, pp. 7–15. Also see Robert Granford Wright, *Mosaics of Organizational Character,* New York: Dunellen, 1975, p. 39.

22. "Putting Excellence into Management," *Business Week,* July 21, 1980, pp. 196–197, 200, 205.

23. Wiley Beavers, "Accreditation: What Do We Need That For?" *The Personnel Administrator,* November 1975, p. 39.

24. George Ritzer, "The Professionals: Will Personnel Occupations Ever Become Professions?" *The Personnel Administrator,* May–June 1971, pp. 34–36.

25. Wendell French and Dale Henning, "The Authority-Influence Role of the Functional Specialist in Management," *Academy of Management Journal,* September 1966, p. 203.

26. Harold C. White and Robert E. Boynton, "Role of Personnel: A Management View," *Arizona Business,* October 1974, pp. 17–21. See also Harold C. White and Michael N. Wolfe, "The Role Desired for Personnel Administration," *Personnel Administrator,* June 1980, pp. 87–97.

27. Oscar A. Ornati, Edward J. Giblin, and Richard R. Floersch, *The Personnel Department: Its Staffing and Budgeting* (An AMA Research Study), New York: AMA Research and Information Service, 1982. See also "ASPA-BNA Survey No. 43, Status of Human Resources Programs—Mid-Year 1982," The Bureau of National Affairs, Inc., 1982.

28. Robert A. Holmes, "What's Ahead for Personnel Professionals in the 80's?" *Personnel Administrator,* June 1980, pp. 33–37, 82.

CHAPTER

3

The impact of Title VII of the Civil Rights Act, which prohibits discrimination in employment based on race, color, religion, national origin, or sex, has been far greater than even opponents of some of its provisions envisaged.

Mary Green Miner and John B. Miner[1]

EQUAL EMPLOYMENT OPPORTUNITY

CHAPTER OBJECTIVES

After studying this chapter, you should be able to:

1 <u>Identify</u> the major sources of equal employment law.

2 <u>List</u> the major equal employment laws and their main provisions.

3 <u>Discuss</u> the leading court cases that interpret equal employment laws.

4 <u>Match</u> major equal employment laws with the remedies for violations.

5 <u>Explain</u> the effect of equal employment laws on the role of human resource specialists.

6 <u>Outline</u> the key elements of an affirmative action program.

Few of the challenges discussed in Chapter 2 affect organizations as much as government. It acts with the force of law. Organizations must comply or face potential lawsuits and penalties. Personnel departments become involved when laws deal with the employment relationship.

Governmental attention to personnel issues reflects changes in our society undreamed of a century ago, when laws covering the employment relationship were virtually nonexistent. Then most jobs were found on the farm, in skilled trades, or with small proprietorships. Most people worked for themselves or for the owner-manager of small business. However, a society of mostly farmers, ranchers, skilled craft workers, and proprietors in the 1800s became a nation of mostly wage earners in the 1900s. As the well-being of society increasingly came to depend on employment relationships, Congress and state legislatures passed laws and established agencies to administer them. Personnel specialists became involved because these laws and regulations impact the use of human resources.

Equal employment opportunity laws create an extensive legal challenge for personnel departments to provide equal employment opportunity without regard to race, religion, sex, pregnancy, national origin, or age. Unlike other employment laws, equal employment is not limited to one or two personnel activities. It affects nearly every personnel function including: human resource planning, recruiting, selection, training, placement, compensation, and labor relations. Perhaps no other single development rivals the impact of these laws on the management of human resources. To illustrate the scope of these laws, consider how equal employment laws affected the American Telephone and Telegraph Company (AT&T).

AT&T's landmark case
In the early 1970s, the American Telephone and Telegraph Company asked the Federal Communication Commission for approval to increase long-distance telephone rates. The Equal Employment Opportunity Commission (the federal agency that is largely responsible for policing equal employment laws) filed a petition to stop the rate increases. The EEOC argued that "approval of the rate increase would be both unconstitutional and contrary to the public interest because AT&T had engaged . . . in extensive violations of Federal, State and constitutional prohibitions against job discrimination."[2] This case "was the first government effort to attack all significant patterns and practices of discrimination of a major national employer."[3]

After more than two years of hearings and negotiations—and hundreds of thousands of pages of exhibits, testimony, and statistical data—AT&T negotiated a settlement. It outlined a series of actions that AT&T would take to remedy the alleged patterns and practices of discrimination. As the federal district court judge who signed the consent decree commented, it was "the largest and most impressive civil rights settlement in the history of the nation."[4]

The consent decree required AT&T to pay some $45 million to affected employees during the first year.[5] Officially, the EEOC estimates that AT&T has spent $100 million in back pay and incentive awards.[6] Not only was money paid to nearly 50,000 AT&T employees who had been financially affected by past practices, but AT&T was required to become more aggressive in recruiting, hiring, developing, and promoting women and minorities. Labor relations problems also resulted since suits by AT&T's unions were filed to protect the seniority rights of those employees who did not benefit from the back pay and accelerated training opportunities.

These personnel issues were not resolved quickly. AT&T remained under the consent decree for six years before the EEOC agreed that the company had met most of its equal employment objectives.

As the AT&T example illustrates, virtually every aspect of personnel management in Figure 3-1 is affected by equal employment opportunity law.

EEO and personnel activities

Figure 3-1
A Model of the Personnel Management System and Its Major Environmental Challenges

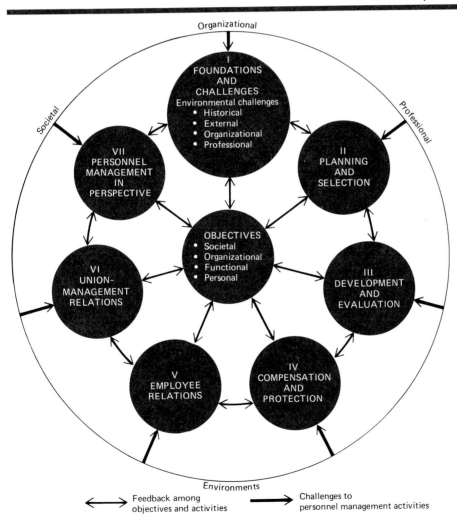

Feedback among objectives and activities

Challenges to personnel management activities

60

Preparation, selection, development, evaluation, and compensation must all be done without discriminating because of a person's race, religion, color, sex, age, or national origin. If past actions have had a discriminatory result, the government can require that corrective action be taken, including affirmative actions by the employer to remedy past discrimination. Although equal employment is only one of the challenges listed in Figure 3-1, its impact on personnel management may be the most pervasive.

Practitioners have responsibilities.

Since regulation of the employment relationship concerns personnel practitioners, they have three responsibilities. First, they must stay abreast of new laws, agency decisions, and court rulings. Otherwise, these experts soon find their knowledge outdated and useless to the organization. Second, they must develop and administer programs that ensure their organization's compliance with the laws. Failure to do so may lead to discrimination, loss of government contracts, poor public relations, and suits by government agencies or affected individuals. Third, they must pursue their traditional roles of obtaining, maintaining, and retaining an optimal work force. No organization benefits from compliance with government constraints at the expense of a poorly qualified work force.

Since equal employment opportunity laws are a major challenge to personnel management, they are examined in this chapter. The implications of these laws will then be discussed throughout the book.

EQUAL EMPLOYMENT LAWS:
AN OVERVIEW

EEO objectives

Equal employment opportunity laws have the common objective of providing equal employment opportunity for members of *protected groups.* These acts outlaw discrimination in employment based on race, color, religion, national origin, sex, pregnancy, or age (between 40 and 70). Vietnam era veterans and qualified disabled workers are also covered under specific conditions discussed later in the chapter.

Overlapping jurisdiction

Equal employment constraints emerged during the 1960s and 1970s. They had three origins: federal acts, state and local legislation, and executive orders of the president. Each source sought similar—and sometimes overlapping—objectives and jurisdictions.[7] Figure 3-2 summarizes 'he three sources of employment law. As the figure implies, coverage overlaps because federal jurisdiction includes only those employers whose operations affect interstate commerce, some government agencies, and federal government contractors. Employers who do not fall into these categories might discriminate if state and local legislative bodies did not pass fair employment practice laws to fill this void. Executive orders are presidential decrees that affect federal agencies and contractors. To comply with equal employment laws or to remedy past discrimination, human resource specialists develop affirmative action plans. These programs set forth the employer's plan and timetable for ensuring compliance with the equal opportunity laws.

But before affirmative action programs are reviewed, the three layers of equal employment law will be discussed. We will look at the purpose,

TYPES	SOURCE	OBJECTIVES AND JURISDICTION
FEDERAL ACTS	Passed by Congress and enforced by the executive branch.	To ensure equal employment opportunities with employers involved in interstate commerce, with government agencies, and with most government contractors.
STATE AND LOCAL LAWS (Sometimes called fair employment practices)	Enacted by state legislatures or local lawmakers and enforced by state or local executive branches.	To ensure equal employment opportunities within the state or local community.
EXECUTIVE ORDERS	Decreed by the president and enforced by the executive branch.	To ensure equal employment opportunities with federal agencies and with certain government contractors.

Figure 3-2

Types, Sources, Objectives, and Jurisdiction
of Equal Employment Laws

prohibitions, enforcement, implications, and major court decisions of these laws.

FEDERAL EQUAL EMPLOYMENT LAWS

To the personnel specialist, the federal equal employment acts are an important group of laws. They form the basis for nearly all attempts to provide equal employment opportunity. Most state and local fair employment practices are modeled after the acts in Figure 3-3. When conflicts arise among federal and other laws, the most demanding—usually a federal law—dominates. And among federal laws, none is as encompassing as Title VII of the 1964 *Civil Rights Act.*

The key law

Figure 3-3

Major Federal Equal Employment Opportunity Laws

EQUAL EMPLOYMENT ACTS	MAJOR PROHIBITIONS	JURISDICTION
TITLE VII OF THE CIVIL RIGHTS ACT OF 1964 As amended in 1972, and as amended again in 1978 by the Pregnancy Discrimination Act	Outlaws discrimination in employment based on race, color, religion, sex, pregnancy, or national origin.	Employers with fifteen or more employees; unions with fifteen or more members; employment agencies; union hiring halls; institutions of higher education; federal, state, and local governments.
AGE DISCRIMINATION IN EMPLOYMENT ACT OF 1967	Outlaws discrimination in employment against those who are between the ages of 40 and 65 (since raised to 70).	Employers with twenty or more employees; unions with twenty-five or more members; employment agencies; federal, state, and local governments.
EQUAL PAY ACT OF 1963	Outlaws discrimination in pay based on the sex of the worker.	Employers engaged in interstate commerce and most employees of federal, state, and local governments.

62

All aspects of employment affected

Title VII

Title VII of the *Civil Rights Act* of 1964 attempts to ensure equal employment opportunity by prohibiting discrimination in hiring, promoting, and compensating, and in any other conditions of employment. As a result, discrimination in employment based upon race, color, religion, sex, pregnancy, or national origin is illegal. Sections 703(a) and (d) are presented in Figure 3-4 and discussed below.

As sections 703(a) and (d) indicate, the intent of Title VII was to cover all aspects of the employment relationship. Included are all actions by an employer that adversely affect an individual's status or opportunities because of that person's membership in a protected group. The range of affected classes is specified in Title VII, as it has been amended since 1964. Discrimination on the basis of a person's sex, race, or color is the most common violation. However, discrimination because of one's national origin or the national origin of one's parents is also a violation.[8] Likewise, an employer cannot discriminate because of a person's religion. In fact, an employer must accommodate an employee's religious observances or practices, as long as they do not impose an undue hardship on the employer.[9]

TWA and religious discrimination

A Trans World Airlines employee, Hardison, wanted Saturdays off for religious reasons. The company refused on the grounds of undue hardship since making the changes would have meant additional costs. Hardison sued on the basis of religious discrimination. He argued that TWA is obligated to accommodate his religious practices.[10] TWA won. Hardison had to work Saturdays because TWA showed undue hardship in the form of higher costs.

Discrimination among workers because of their effort, performance, or other work-related criteria remains both *permissible* and *advisable*. Equal

Figure 3-4

Excerpts of Title VII of the Civil Rights Act of 1964, as Amended

TITLE VII OF THE CIVIL RIGHTS ACT OF 1964 AS AMENDED

Section 703. (*a*) It shall be an unlawful employment practice for an employer—

(1) to fail or refuse to hire or to discharge any individual or otherwise to discriminate against any individual with respect to his compensation, terms, conditions, or privileges of employment, because of such individual's race, color, religion, sex, or national origin; or

(2) to limit, segregate, or classify his employees or applicants for employment in any way which would deprive or tend to deprive any individual of employment opportunities or otherwise adversely affect his status as an employee, because of such individual's race, color, religion, sex, or national origin.

(*d*) It shall be an unlawful employment practice of any employer . . . controlling . . . training programs to discriminate against any individual because of his race, color, religion, sex, or national origin in admission to, or employment in, any program established to provide apprenticeship or other training.

employment laws *do* permit employers to reward outstanding performers and penalize unacceptable productivity. These laws only require that the basis for rewards and punishment be work-related—not unrelated issues such as a person's sex, race, religion, or other prohibited measures. Not only do these laws prohibit intentional discrimination, but they also prohibit disparate treatment and disparate impact even when such discrimination is unintentional.

Disparate treatment   *Disparate treatment* occurs when members of a protected class receive unequal treatment. If AT&T regularly hired female applicants as telephone operators without letting them apply for the higher-paid and more skilled craft jobs, the result would be unequal or disparate treatment. Unequal treatment also occurs when different standards are applied to different groups. For example, an employer who refuses to hire women with small children because those children may cause her to miss work, but hires men with young children, is applying a different standard.

Disparate impact   *Disparate impact* occurs when the results of an employer's actions have a different impact on one or more protected classes. Even when an employer develops a uniform standard and applies it equally to all classes, the results may be discriminatory. Consider the comments of Gerald H. Trautman, former chairman of the board for the Greyhound Corporation, when he observed that the federal government:

> . . . went after us in San Francisco to eliminate our safety rule which required any applicant, male or female, for the driver's position to be five foot seven. They took us to court and wanted us to give up the rule. But we finally decided it just wasn't worth the fight. . . . The first four people who were under five foot seven . . . flunked the test. They weren't able to handle the bus. But we don't have that rule any more.[11]

When standards discriminate against one or more protected groups, the burden is on the employer to prove the standard is necessary. In the Greyhound example, management thought the standard was reasonable. However, the impact of a height standard was to discriminate against women and males of Asian descent, since these groups tend to be shorter than males of European or African heritage. Treatment was equal, but the impact was discriminatory. In *Griggs v. Duke Power Company*,[12] a similar outcome was ruled upon by the U.S. Supreme Court.

> The Duke Power Company had a long-standing policy of requiring a high school degree for all jobs except those in the labor pool. As a result, the labor pool consisted mostly of black men who were denied an opportunity for better jobs at the utility because they did not have a high school degree. The requirements of a high school diploma and general intelligence test were challenged in court. Duke Power Company could not show that a high school diploma was necessary to perform many jobs or that the test bore any relationship to on-the-job performance.

Disparate treatment versus disparate impact

Greyhound and employment rules

Griggs v. Duke Power Company: landmark case

64

Intents versus results

Regardless of the company's intent, the result of its actions was discriminatory because the degree requirement and tests tended to have an unequal impact on one protected class: blacks. The test and degree requirements were disallowed even though they were applied equally to black and white workers.

From the *Griggs* case and other examples, it is clear that equal employment opportunity laws place a burden on employers to demonstrate that their personnel actions are based on sound business reasons. However, even if business reasons are used and a disparate impact results, the personnel department should find other methods that do not have a disparate impact. In *Albemarle Paper Company v. Moody*,[13] the company used business reasons for its actions. However, the U.S. Supreme Court found discrimination resulted because other methods could have been used that were not discriminatory. The implication for personnel specialists is that all personnel actions must be related to a business purpose and not be discriminatory in intent or result. If job-related actions discriminate against a protected class, those actions should be discontinued in favor of nondiscriminatory approaches.

Albemarle Paper Company v. Moody

Even though pregnancy affects one protected group, the U.S. Supreme Court ruled in *General Electric v. Gilbert*[14] that the denial of pregnancy-related benefits *did not* violate Title VII. Congress subsequently amended Title VII with the *Pregnancy Disability Amendment of 1978*, and employers could no longer require women to take leaves of absence or resign because of pregnancy. As long as the woman was still capable of doing her job, the employer could not discriminate in benefits or other conditions of employment.[15]

Pregnancy and discrimination

Harassment Perhaps the most difficult form of discrimination to deal with is harassment. Whether it occurs because of someone's race or sex, it is prohibited. Although racial harassment may exist as open racism or subtle comments, it creates a discriminatory environment that violates Title VII. Open or subtle sexual harassment also violates the law. Although one experienced mediator made the following statement about sexual harassment, these comments and the ones that follow could well apply to any form of prohibited harassment.

Racial and sexual harassment

The most serious aspect of almost all reported cases is the power relationship between the alleged offender and the offended person. (I believe that most sexual aggressiveness that occurs *outside* a power relationship is simply ignored or adequately dealt with by the offended party.) In any case, reports of harassment usually involve fear of retribution because of the supposed power of a . . . supervisor. In fact, most reported cases do involve a supervisor-subordinate relationship; hence, productivity is threatened.[16]

The difficulty with allegations of racial or sexual harassment is proof. These allegations often become one person's word against another's. As a result, it is believed that most offenses go unreported to company officials or government agencies.[17]

Human resource departments usually develop and communicate a strongly worded policy about harassment. The policy clearly states that racial or sexual harassment violates company rules. Those who use their position in the company to harass other employees can expect harsh discipline, often termination of their employment. Finally, the policy directive usually indicates what actions an offended party should take.[18]

Exceptions   Although sexual or racial harassment is never permitted, Title VII and the courts do permit some exceptions to equal employment opportunity. These exceptions include bona fide occupational qualifications, seniority systems, and preferential quota systems.

A *bona fide occupational qualification* (BFOQ) exists when discrimination against a protected group is reasonably necessary to the normal operation of the organization. A preference by the employer, personnel specialists, or long standing tradition is insufficient. There must be a "justified business reason." For example, a hotel seeking a rest room attendant can specify the sex of the applicant because a specific sex is reasonably necessary to do the job. Whenever a personnel department alleges a BFOQ, the burden of proof obviously falls to the employer to show that a compelling business reason exists. In the Greyhound example, company officials believed that people who were less than five feet seven inches tall probably could not change bus tires and make other minor road repairs. Changing large bus tires was a requirement of the job. But since the company could not demonstrate that being five foot seven or taller was a BFOQ, Greyhound had to drop this rule because it had a disparate impact on women and those of Asian descent.

BFOQ as a defense

In labor agreements negotiated between employers and their unions, *seniority clauses* are common. These provisions usually require that promotions, pay, and other conditions of employment are preferentially affected by how long the worker has been employed. When the senior workers are predominantly of one race or sex, the application of seniority may lead to a disparate impact on those in protected classes. However, Title VII anticipates this issue with the following section:

Seniority system as a defense

> *Section 703(h).* Notwithstanding any other provision of this title, it shall not be an unlawful employment practice for an employer to apply different standards of compensation, or different terms, conditions, or privileges of employment pursuant to a bona fide seniority or merit system. . . .

In *International Brotherhood of Teamsters v. United States*,[19] the U.S. Supreme Court has upheld this section of Title VII, provided that the seniority system was not created to discriminate against some protected class. Furthermore, the seniority system must apply equally to all people covered by it.

A third exception is *preferential quota systems*. These approaches reserve a proportion of job openings, promotions, or other employment opportunities for

Quotas as a defense

members of protected classes who may have been discriminated against previously. When an employer recognizes that members of a protected class have unequal representation in a particular job classification, an employer may develop a plan to correct this imbalance. Kaiser Aluminum & Chemical Corporation's Gramercy, Louisiana, plant provides a landmark example.

Kaiser's work force at the plant was 14.8 percent black, and the labor force in the area was 39 percent black. But in the skilled (and better paying) craft jobs, less than 2 percent of the craft workers were black. Kaiser's management entered into a nationwide collective bargaining agreement with the United Steelworkers. An on-the-job training program for craft jobs was established. It was decided that the entry ratio into the program would be one white and one black until minority representation equaled the same percentage as the area's civilian labor force.

Weber v. Kaiser

Eventually this preferential quota system was challenged in the courts by Brian F. Weber, an employee of the plant, who believed the one-to-one ratio discriminated against him. In the case, the U.S. Supreme Court ruled that preferential systems would help undo the effects of past discrimination. Although not every preferential quota approach is sure to be legal, they may offer a defense against allegations of discrimination when their purpose is to remedy past discrimination.[20]

Key summary

Intentional discrimination and practices that lead to disparate treatment or impact are prohibited. When they occur, personnel professionals further their functional, organizational, and societal objectives by ending these forms of discrimination. The only exceptions are bona fide occupational qualifications, valid seniority systems, and appropriate preferential quota systems.

Employer retaliation   As with most employment laws, it is a separate violation to retaliate *in any way* against those who exercise their Title VII rights. Those who file charges, testify, or otherwise participate in any Title VII action are protected by the law. If a supervisor tries to "get even" with an employee who filed charges, the act is violated.[21]

Enforcement   The five-member Equal Employment Opportunity Commission enforces Title VII through offices in major cities. The EEOC was created to enforce Title VII, but its powers were limited. Congress expanded the authority of the commission by passing the *Equal Employment Opportunity Act* of 1972. Under the 1972 act, the EEOC was empowered to initiate court action against noncomplying businesses.[22]

EEOC and enforcement

Figure 3-5 summarizes the EEOC's enforcement procedures. Enforcement begins when a charge is filed. It may be filed by the aggrieved person, someone acting on behalf of the aggrieved person, or one of the EEOC commissioners. In states with fair employment laws, charges can be filed with the state agency. If charges are filed with EEOC, it defers jurisdiction to qualified state or local agencies for sixty days. These jurisdictions are known as *deferral jurisdictions.*

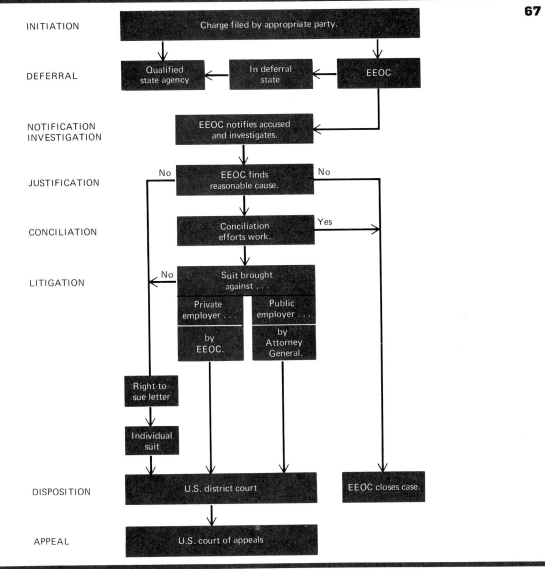

INITIATION — Charge filed by appropriate party.

DEFERRAL — Qualified state agency ← In deferral state ← EEOC

NOTIFICATION INVESTIGATION — EEOC notifies accused and investigates.

JUSTIFICATION — No / EEOC finds reasonable cause. / No

CONCILIATION — Conciliation efforts work. / Yes

LITIGATION — No / Suit brought against . . . / Private employer . . . by EEOC. / Public employer . . . by Attorney General.

Right-to-sue letter

Individual suit

DISPOSITION — U.S. district court / EEOC closes case.

APPEAL — U.S. court of appeals

Figure 3-5
EEOC Enforcement Procedure

Charges are filed directly with the EEOC in *nondeferral states*—states without qualified agencies. The accused parties are notified within ten days by the EEOC once charges are filed. It then conducts an investigation and decides whether the charges are a violation. If there is reason to believe a violation has occurred, the EEOC seeks a *conciliation agreement*. This agreement is a negotiated settlement acceptable to the EEOC and all parties involved. Its acceptance closes the case.

If conciliation fails, court action may result. A suit can be brought by the EEOC when the wrongdoer is a private employer or by the U.S. attorney general when the charges are against a public employer. Even individuals may file suit within ninety days once a *right-to-sue letter* has been issued by the EEOC. A right-to-sue letter is granted when:

- The EEOC dismisses the charges.

- No suit is brought after the EEOC fails to obtain a conciliation agreement.

Remedies   Title VII clearly acknowledges that remedies can include a wide range of penalties.

Penalties

Section 203(g). If the court finds that the respondent has intentionally engaged in or is intentionally engaging in an unlawful employment practice charged in the complaint, the court may enjoin the respondent from engaging in such unlawful employment practice, and order such affirmative action as may be appropriate, which may include, but is not limited to, reinstatement or hiring of employees, with or without back pay (payable by the employer, employment agency, or labor organization, as the case may be, responsible for the unlawful employment practice), or any other equitable relief as the court deems appropriate.

AT&T reconsidered

Whether compliance results from a conciliation agreement or a court order, remedies have similar characteristics. Reconsider the AT&T example described earlier in this chapter. AT&T agreed to:

- Cease and desist from practices that caused disparate treatment or impact

- Preferential hiring, training, and promoting of those in protected classes that are allegedly discriminated against

- Financial payments to compensate for past discrimination in order to "make whole" those affected

As the AT&T example points out, remedies typically include an agreement by the company to cease and desist from discriminatory practices. Past patterns and practices of discrimination against entire groups (for example, women and minorities at AT&T) may have to be corrected with affirmative action plans that may include special hiring, training, and promoting quotas and programs. If there has been any financially measurable harm done to those in protected classes, the employer often must pay financial restitution to "make whole" those who were affected. This requirement means making up losses suffered because of the discriminatory actions. Reinstatement with no loss of seniority and full

"Make-whole" remedies

payment of back wages are common *make-whole* remedies in illegal discharge cases, for example. Even when no discharges are involved, monetary adjustments may be required to compensate those who were discriminated against. When funds are paid to those affected, the company receives little benefit.

Therefore, most human resource professionals try to have financial penalties put in the form of dollars to be spent on training those who were discriminated against. This way the company captures some value for its often huge outlays.

Age Discrimination in Employment

Equal opportunity is sometimes denied because of age. To prevent this form of discrimination, Congress passed the *Age Discrimination in Employment Act* of 1967, as amended. It prohibits discrimination against those between ages 40 and 70, when the person's age is a factor in employment-related decisions. Violations can be time-consuming, costly, and difficult to separate from legitimate business decisions.[23]

> Shortly before Christmas . . . Philip W. Houghton was fired by his employer of 25 years, the McDonnell Douglas Corporation. The stated reason: unsatisfactory performance in a new assignment. But Houghton was certain the real reason was his age—52. He had been chief production test pilot, flight checking the supersonic F-4 Phantom jet fighter. Because of declining orders, the company had been reducing its corps of test pilots by grounding the oldest members.
>
> Houghton resolved to fight. Then he hired a lawyer and sued McDonnell Douglas, under the Age Discrimination in Employment Act. . . .
>
> [A] three-judge appeals court panel ruled unanimously that McDonnell Douglas had violated the Federal law. It ordered the company to reinstate Houghton as a test pilot if he still meets the physical qualifications, and to pay him lost wages, plus damages. The amount could exceed $400,000, says Houghton's attorney. . . .[24]

Employee suits are possible.

Although an employer has the right to reduce its work force, age cannot be the deciding reason.

Exceptions and retaliation   As with Title VII, bona fide occupational qualifications are permitted, but they are extremely limited. For example, a casting director can discriminate against older actors when hiring for children's roles. Discrimination against someone who has filed a complaint, given testimony, or otherwise exercised their rights under the act is also forbidden.

Enforcement and remedies   When someone believes a violation has occurred, that person may file charges with the EEOC or their state agency, if one exists. In states with a qualified agency, the federal government defers the charge to the state agency for sixty days. Otherwise, the EEOC investigates the charge.

Federal law requires that an attempt to achieve voluntary compliance must be made by government before legal action is taken. If voluntary compliance efforts fail, a suit can be filed in federal court, as was done in the McDonnell Douglas case above. Such suits may be brought by an individual employee, groups of employees, or the government. Since courts have wide latitude in deciding remedies, personnel managers often find voluntary compliance to be

Voluntary compliance comes first.

less costly. Compliance may be reactive and not take place until after the government investigates some specific charge. Or even better, personnel experts may take proactive steps to gain compliance before charges are brought against the employer. When guilty employers wait for court-imposed solutions, personnel departments are ordered to cease and desist from past actions and provide make-whole remedies—such as reinstatement, back pay, legal fees, and court costs. If the past discrimination involved *patterns and practices* of discrimination against an entire class of workers, the personnel department usually must draft plans to correct past patterns of discrimination.[25]

Equal Pay Act

Historically, employers have viewed men as heads of households and women as supplemental wage earners. Therefore, men have often received higher wages than women who do the same job.[26] The growing number of households headed by women and the obvious discrimination behind this tradition led Congress to pass the *Equal Pay Act* in 1963.

The Equal Pay Act requires employers to pay equal wages for equal work.[27] Jobs are considered equal when both sexes work at the same place and the job demands substantially the same skill, effort, responsibility, and working conditions. When one of these factors differs, the employer is justified in paying different wages. As Figure 3-6 lightheartedly illustrates, the greater effort of Santas justifies a higher wage rate. Had male Santas been paid more than female Santas, a violation would have existed. The figure also shows that equal work is determined by an examination of the job duties, not simply job titles.

Santa Claus versus the Easter Bunny

Exceptions and retaliation   The Equal Pay Act does permit employers to reward workers for individual merit or performance. Even seniority can be rewarded with higher pay. As long as seniority and merit pay differentials are not based on the sex of the worker, they are legal. Likewise, companies can pay employees according to their productivity, paying for each unit produced. As with other employment laws, those who exercise their rights under the Equal Pay Act are protected against employer retaliation.

Figure 3-6
Sad News for the Easter Bunny

The Easter Bunny lost its sex discrimination dispute with Santa Claus yesterday.

Because Santa works harder, keeps longer hours and sees more children each year, he's worth 90 cents more an hour than department store bunnies, a California deputy labor commission ruled.

. . . After a two hour hearing in San Jose conducted by Commissioner Andrew Evans of the state's Division of Labor Standards, . . . he found no evidence of discrimination.

"There are some basic differences in the job," Evans noted. "Santa works harder."

He found that Santa sees more children and is twice as successful as the Easter Bunny in the business of selling parents snapshots of their children on his lap.

However, Evans said, he found that a man or a woman who suits up as Santa earns the same wage; and a male and female Easter Bunny earn equal pay, even though it's less than Santa's.

Source: San Francisco Chronicle, Feb. 25, 1976, p. 5. Used by permission.

Comparable worth   The Equal Pay Act has been law since 1963. However, women still earn only about 60 percent of the income that men do. This disparity has many origins. Women tend to concentrate in low-paying jobs like elementary school teacher, nurse, and clerical worker. Many women—even those in managerial and professional positions—will leave their careers to have and raise children. When they return to their careers, some find they must begin all over again, while their male counterparts have made steady progress in their careers and compensation.[28] And some of the difference in income probably results from discrimination.

Some advocates of income equality between the sexes doubt equality will occur through the Equal Pay Act, which only seeks to assure equal pay for people doing equal work. Instead, some suggest that equality depends on the comparable worth doctrine becoming law. The concept of *comparable worth* requires that jobs equal in value to the organization be equal in pay.[29] For example, if an electrician and a nurse are of equal value to a hospital, they would be paid the same under the comparable worth doctrine. The compensation methods used by virtually all organizations differ from the comparable worth approach. Compensation specialists compute a job's pay based on the job's content, responsibilities, and going wage rate in the labor market. If electricians are better compensated than nurses in the labor market, the hospital must pay more to obtain and retain electricians. Should Congress modify the law or the courts interpret present laws to include comparable worth, new methods of determining pay levels would have to be devised. How much value a nurse brings to a hospital compared with how much value an electrician brings to the hospital, for example, is difficult to judge. Present approaches rely heavily on the rates being paid in the labor markets for electricians and nurses. However, distortions in the marketplace—such as union wage scales or supply-and-demand relationships—lead to different wage rates that often favor "male dominated" jobs, such as electrician. Without a comparable worth law, women as a group are likely to earn substantially less than men until the patterns of traditional male and female occupations disappear. Enactment of comparable worth probably would mean increases in labor costs and inflation in addition to the need for new compensation procedures.

Equal pay versus comparable worth

Enforcement and remedies   The Equal Pay Act of 1963 may be enforced by either the federal government or state agencies. In the absence of state laws and agencies, the EEOC handles equal pay violations. Its enforcement procedures are the same as those applied to age discrimination cases, except the Equal Pay Act does not require voluntary conciliation before a suit is brought against the employer.[30] Since courts have wide discretion under this act, they have granted back-pay awards in some cases to thousands of workers.

Jurisdiction

> A federal court found Wheaton Glass Company had violated the Equal Pay Act. The court ordered Wheaton to pay $900,000 in back pay and interest to 2000 female employees.[31]

Timely attention to the requirements of the Equal Pay Act by personnel specialists can eliminate such costly back-pay settlements, the adverse publicity involved, and the hardship of female workers.

Other Federal Laws

The remaining federal acts are the Rehabilitation Act of 1973 and the Vietnam Era Veterans Readjustment Act of 1974. These laws are more limited in scope than other federal laws. Their major provisions are summarized in Figure 3-7 and discussed below.

Rehabilitation Act   Probably the group most widely discriminated against in the United States is the handicapped. Numbering 12 million, these people are often denied equal opportunity. Congress passed the *Rehabilitation Act* of 1973 to partially remedy this social problem. The act outlaws discrimination against mentally or physically handicapped individuals who, with reasonable accommodation, can perform successfully. These people are the *qualified handicapped.*[32]

Qualified
handicapped

> Lisa Hope had been an assembly-line worker for almost two years when she was paralyzed from the waist down in a hang glider accident. Her employer had a platform and ramp built so that Lisa could resume her job as an assembler while seated in her wheelchair. Although Lisa's employer was not a government contractor, the personnel department recognized that she was qualified to do her job if some reasonable accommodations were made.

Not all employers
are covered.

One section of the act provides equal employment for federal employees and applicants who are among the qualified handicapped. Another section of the law applies to federal government contractors with contracts of $2500 or more. In both situations, handicapped applicants and employees may not be discriminated against because of their handicap as long as these workers can perform their job duties. For the personnel departments of government contractors, compliance is crucial; failure to comply can lead to the loss of government contracts. Compliance is likely when personnel departments attempt to accommodate handicapped employees and seek applicants through college and community groups that work with the disabled.

Figure 3-7

Equal Employment Opportunity Laws Applicable to
Government Contractors and Government Agencies

EQUAL OPPORTUNITY LAWS	PRIMARY PROHIBITIONS	JURISDICTION
REHABILITATION ACT OF 1973	Outlaws discrimination in employment based on handicaps of workers who, with reasonable employer accommodation, could do the job.	Section 501 covers employment with the federal government. Section 503 covers federal government contractors with contracts of $2500 or more.
VIETNAM ERA VETERANS READJUSTMENT ACT OF 1974	Outlaws discrimination in employment against Vietnam era veterans.	Covers federal government contractors with contracts of $10,000 or more.

Vietnam Era Veterans Readjustment Act   As Vietnam era veterans

were discharged from military service, many found it difficult to obtain employment. To assist their integration into the private economy, Congress passed the *Vietnam Era Veterans Readjustment Act* of 1974. The act requires government contractors with contracts of $10,000 or more to provide equal employment opportunity to Vietnam era veterans. Violations can lead to the loss of government contracts. Personnel departments help ensure compliance by actively seeking applications from veterans through contacts at local military bases and through work with veteran's affairs offices at most large universities.

Honeywell, Inc.'s efforts go even further than the law requires. As a proactive move, the company appointed a "Vietnam veterans program coordinator" to help workers who are veterans deal with psychological problems and advance their careers. The coordinator works to get vets hired, organizes family counseling sessions, and publishes a company newsletter for them.[33]

Honeywell's proactive effort

STATE AND LOCAL FAIR EMPLOYMENT PRACTICES

State and local laws, which are often called *fair employment practices,* are the second major source of equal employment laws. These laws are limited to employers within the jurisdiction of state or local governments. Although important to personnel experts whose companies are covered, fair employment practices are too numerous and too varied to be discussed here in detail. In general, however, they seek objectives similar to federal acts: providing equal opportunity. They provide equal opportunity in two ways. One is to extend state or local protection to groups exempted from federal laws. The other way is by sharing jurisdiction with the federal government in deferral states. Except in circumstances where fair employment standards cover omissions in federal laws or federal agencies have agreed to defer to state agencies, federal law is supreme when conflicts exist.

Overlapping jurisdictions in some states

Besides similar objectives, enforcement and remedies under state and local laws parallel federal procedures. Administration of these practices is typically the responsibility of state or local fair employment practices commissions. These commissions can normally be found in the executive branch of state or local government. In nearly all situations, compliance with the federal laws results in compliance with state and local fair employment practices. Nevertheless, experienced personnel practitioners also stay informed of state and local laws.

EXECUTIVE ORDERS

The executive branch of the federal government is the single largest employer and consumer in the United States. By applying equal employment opportunity standards to itself, it sets an example for other employers; by requiring its contractors to follow equal employment rules, government can influence many employment relationships. Toward these ends,

74

EXECUTIVE ORDERS	MAJOR PROHIBITIONS	JURISDICTION
E.O. 11246	Outlaws discrimination in employment based on race, color, religion, or national origin.	Government contractors
E.O. 11375	Revises E.O. 11246 to prohibit sex discrimination.	Government contractors
E.O. 11478	Outlaws discrimination in employment based on race, color, religion, national origin, sex, political affiliation, marital status, or physical handicap.	Government agencies and the Postal Service
E.O. 11141	Outlaws discrimination in employment based on age.	Government agencies Government contractors

Figure 3-8
Executive Orders Designed to Ensure
Equal Employment Opportunity

Presidential decrees

different presidents have issued *executive orders,* described in Figure 3-8. The purpose and content of these executive orders parallel the federal equal employment laws already discussed. But, like the Rehabilitation and Vietnam Era Veterans Readjustment Acts, executive orders have a narrow jurisdiction. These presidential orders are aimed at federal government agencies and contractors.

Government Agencies

Federal agencies are required to provide equal employment opportunity on the basis of race, color, religion, national origin, sex, political affiliation, marital status, and physical handicap under Executive Order 11478. Likewise, these agencies are prohibited from discrimination on the basis of age under Executive Order 11141. Under both orders, those who think they have been mistreated may file complaints and have the discrimination ended by the offending agency.

Government Contractors

Personnel specialists are affected by executive orders when their employer is a government contractor. Government contractors must abide by all equal employment laws: *Title VII of the Civil Rights Act, the Age Discrimination in Employment Act, the Equal Pay Act, the Rehabilitation Act,* and *The Vietnam Era Veterans Readjustment Act.* In addition, they must comply with Executive Order 11246, as revised, which duplicates Title VII. It outlaws discrimination based on race, color, religion, national origin, and sex. Age discrimination by these employers also is illegal according to Executive Order 11141.

Government contractors are significantly affected by Executive Order 11246. This presidential decree applies to an entire company even though only one plant or division sells to the federal government. The order requires that government contractors take affirmative action—systematic steps to ensure that past discrimination is remedied and that further discrimination does not occur. To enforce this affirmative requirement, government contractors must file affirmative action plans with the Office of Federal Contract Compliance Programs (OFCCP), which is located in the U.S. Department of Labor. The OFCCP devotes most of its efforts to reviewing contractors' affirmative action plans and visiting sites to interview managerial and nonmanagerial employees. Violation of OFCCP rules and regulations can lead to the loss of government contracts, although this penalty is seldom used.

Office of Federal Contract Compliance Programs

Executive Orders and Equal Employment Laws

Executive orders overlap federal and state acts. This duplication exists for two reasons. First, some federal equal employment acts specifically exempt agencies of the federal government, and state laws do not apply to federal employees. To assure federal employees of equal employment opportunities, executive orders were passed to fill the void. Second, since government agencies and contractors spend public funds, they are subject to close examination.

The enforcement procedures under federal and state laws are largely reactive. Investigations normally do not start until a complaint is made against the employer. But under the executive orders, the federal government can demand compliance whether a charge is filed or not. Compliance before charges are filed often takes the form of requiring government contractors to submit affirmative action programs.

AFFIRMATIVE ACTION

Employers develop affirmative action programs to qualify as government contractors, to remedy past discrimination, or to prevent discrimination in the future. Personnel departments in most large employers develop these plans whether their organization is a government contractor or not. *Affirmative action programs* are written, systematic plans that outline goals in hiring, training, promoting, and compensating those groups protected by federal equal employment laws, fair employment practices, and executive orders.[34] They exist for several reasons. From a practical standpoint, employers seldom benefit by excluding people who belong to some particular group. Excluding an entire class of workers, such as women or minorities, limits the labor pool from which the personnel department can draw. Open discrimination can also lead to negative public relations, boycotts by consumers, and government intervention. To ensure that such discrimination does not occur, employers often develop affirmative action programs voluntarily.

Voluntary compliance is also a practical way to correct past discrimination because compliance can avoid costly and time-consuming legal battles. As the Kaiser and steelworker's efforts to train more black craft workers illustrated, voluntary affirmative action programs are a legal way to remedy past discrimination. Sometimes compliance is the best course even when the company thinks its past actions were legal, as was the case with Greyhound dropping its height rule. At other times compliance results from a *consent decree,* which is a legally binding agreement to undertake specific actions. AT&T's massive affirmative action plan began with the consent decree it signed with the EEOC, Department of Justice, and the Department of Labor.

76

AT&T was a target.

Title VII coverage

Qualifiable workers

AT&T was in a delicate position.[35] As the largest private employer in the United States at the time of the suit, it made an attractive target for the government. The EEOC's victory put large and small employers on notice that the government was serious about enforcement. AT&T recognized that its ability to get rate increases on long-distance business calls might have been delayed for years if it had fought the EEOC all the way through court appeals.

Since every employer with fifteen or more employees is covered under Title VII of the 1964 Civil Rights Act, as amended, virtually all companies have some form of affirmative action. These activities are usually the responsibility of the personnel department, which develops a plan to achieve the organization's affirmative action goals in the least disruptive manner.

Affirmative Action Issues

The design and implementation of an affirmative action plan may lead the personnel department to take action that employees and line managers do not like. For example, an aggressive plan may cause the personnel department to hire and promote *qualifiable* workers, rather than qualified ones. A *qualifiable worker* is one who does not currently possess all the required knowledge, skills, or abilities to do a job but through additional training and experience will become qualified. Other employees—such as Brian Weber in *United Steelworkers v. Weber*—may well resent being passed over by a qualifiable worker, especially if those employees believe themselves to be qualified already. Likewise, line managers may resent the loss of their authority to make final hiring, firing, or other employment decisions. The issues of reverse discrimination and the impact on line management merit further discussion.

Reverse discrimination   The use of affirmative action plans has led to charges of reverse discrimination against employers. These charges usually arise when an employer seeks to hire or promote a member of a protected class over an equally (or better) qualified candidate who is not a member of the protected class. For example, if an employer has an affirmative action program that gives preference to women over men when promotions occur, a qualified male may sue the employer and claim he was discriminated against because of his sex. Since equal employment laws prohibit discrimination on the basis of sex, courts have entertained such suits in the past.

Charges of reverse discrimination have placed personnel departments in a difficult position. On one hand, the personnel department is responsible for eliminating discrimination. On the other hand, to give preference to members of a protected class (such as women) raises questions about whether the personnel department is being fair.[36]

For example, it is easy to imagine how special treatment toward women would evoke strong negative feelings. These negative feelings could easily lead to frustration, tensions, employee turnover, and lower employee satisfaction.[37]

Although preferential treatment will always raise questions of fairness, the U.S. Supreme Court has ruled in *United Steelworkers v. Weber* that such treatment is not discriminatory when done to meet the objectives of a bona fide affirmative action program. Even when such programs are voluntary and not required by law or courts, preferential treatment to meet the goals of these programs is considered permissible and not in violation of Title VII of the 1964 Civil Rights Act.

Line management   The implementation of an affirmative action program may cause line managers to feel a loss of authority.[38] Operating managers may lose the right to make final hiring and promotion decisions. To achieve the objectives of the plan, the personnel department may even have to overrule line managers. In time, supervisors may believe that members of protected classes are getting different treatment. If workers also sense an element of reverse discrimination, conflicts may arise and lessen the effectiveness of the work group.

To overcome potentially damaging side effects of affirmative action plans, personnel specialists must educate line managers—particularly first-line supervisors. Training programs, seminars, and explanations of personnel decisions affecting protected classes must be given to managers. Otherwise, their support and understanding of affirmative action are likely to be low; and, in turn, the perceived quality of the work environment may decline.

Line management support is crucial.

Developing Affirmative Action Plans

Affirmative action plans are situational. Their design depends on the specific discriminatory practices that are involved. For example, when an employer has a high number of protected class members doing a particular job, concentration exists. *Concentration* occurs when the proportion of protected class members holding a particular job is greater than their availability in the labor market. When AT&T signed its consent decree, for example, women represented less than half of the labor market but held more than 98 percent of all telephone operator jobs. *Underutilization* is just the opposite. It occurs when protected class members are underrepresented in particular jobs compared to their availability in the work force. The scarcity of women in middle-level management positions at AT&T at the time of the consent decree is an example of underutilization. Thus the affirmative action strategy used by an organization must consider the extent of concentration or underutilization.

The nature of the program also depends on the organization's growth rate. A slow-growing employer uses affirmative action strategies that are different from those of a growth company with greater opportunities for promotions. Likewise, the reasons for the affirmative action plan influence its final form. For example, a large government contractor's program must meet every agency regulation, whereas a totally voluntary program need only meet the employer's objectives.

Regardless of these situational variables, resistance to the plan is likely by those who fear reverse discrimination and by managers who believe their authority may be diminished. To gain acceptance, some authorities recommend using an educational strategy before the plan is developed.[39] Preplan development may begin with the creation of an Affirmative Action Advisory Committee that includes line managers, workers, and staff members from the human resource department. If well chosen, the committee can be used to reflect the concerns of others in the organization. It may even conduct a survey to learn

Resistance to affirmative action

1. *Exhibit* strong employer commitment.

2. *Appoint* a high-ranking director.

3. *Publicize* commitment internally and externally.

4. *Survey* the work force for underutilization and concentration.

5. *Develop* goals and timetables.

6. *Design* remedial and preventive programs.

7. *Establish* control systems and reporting procedures.

Figure 3-9
Major Action Steps in Affirmative Action Programs

about the perceptions held by others. As they help design the plan, committee members not only increase their understanding of affirmative action but also are likely to educate their peers as to the scope, goals, and need for it. Goals they set participatively are more likely to be accepted by them and their peers. Certainly, resistance from those on the committee is apt to be lower and support higher than if they had not served in an advisory role.

Beyond the internal strategies used to educate and win support for affirmative action, personnel departments usually follow common steps in developing these plans. The major action steps are summarized in Figure 3-9.

A key aspect of affirmative action planning is overcoming past perceptions. For example, a major problem faced by AT&T was overcoming perceptions that telephone operator jobs were for "women" and outside repair jobs were for "men." To break down these perceptions AT&T had to exhibit strong employer commitment to affirmative action. Managers were evaluated on how well they met their affirmative action plans, and the company appointed a high-ranking director to manage affirmative action. The company also publicized its commitment by declaring in its internal and external communications that it was an "equal opportunity employer."

The company also followed the other action steps in Figure 3-9. It surveyed its work force to find areas of concentration and underutilization. Then it developed goals and timetables to systematically correct these situations. AT&T also designed remedial and preventive programs. For example, some equipment used in training and in the field was redesigned to accommodate members of protected classes so that more would successfully complete training and be promoted.

Beyond the required reports for the Equal Employment Opportunity Commission, AT&T developed its own internal reporting and control systems to ensure that affirmative action would become an ongoing way of life and would receive proper visibility within the company.

EQUAL OPPORTUNITY
IN PERSPECTIVE

Equal employment laws have a broad impact on the practice of personnel management. Professionally, the challenge of equal employment has given personnel professionals more visibility and power within

**Personnel and
its relationships**

their organizations. Threats of suits and government investigations, and even the remote possibility of losing a government contract, have caused top management to lend more support to activities that further equal employment opportunity. At the same time, some personnel departments have found that their relationships with other managers in the organization can suffer. When line managers believe that the personnel department's rules prevent them from hiring the best candidates or require them to spend valuable hours completing reports, these managers question whether the department is truly furthering organizational objectives. At the extreme, the personnel department can be viewed as a hindrance. When this happens, many of the other services provided by the department are too often overlooked. The result can be that operating managers may not seek the assistance they need to improve their operation's productivity and their workers' quality of work life.

As mentioned in Chapter 1, personnel is a service department. The department may be required to carry out societal and even organizational objectives that line managers do not appreciate and may even dislike. Nevertheless, activities such as assuring equal employment are critical to personnel management. What personnel professionals must do, however, is meet their organizational, societal, functional, and personal objectives simultaneously. As illustrated in the model shown in Figure 3-1, these objectives are at the center of all human resource activities. They must be pursued. But care must be taken so that personnel's pursuit of these objectives causes the least disruption to the organization's performance. One way to minimize the disruption caused by equal employment opportunity is to consider its impact on the other personnel activities:

EEO is critical to personnel management.

- *Human resource plans* must reflect the organization's affirmative action goals.

- *Job descriptions* must not contain unneeded requirements that exclude members of protected classes.

- *Recruiting* must ensure that all types of applicants are sought without discriminating.

- *Selection* of applicants must use screening devices that are valid and nondiscriminatory.

- *Training and development* opportunities must be available to workers without regard to factors that discriminate.

- *Performance appraisals* must be free of biases that discriminate.

- *Compensation programs* must be based on skills, performance, and/or seniority and cannot discriminate against jobholders because of their membership in some protected class.

Virtually every personnel activity is affected by equal employment and affirmative action plans. If the equal employment implications are weighed when other personnel activities are undertaken, the need for remedial programs

Next chapter

will decline as organizations move closer to complete equal employment opportunity.

Human resource planning is one way personnel departments help meet their affirmative action goals. But human resource planning is more than just a tool to achieve equal employment opportunity. It is a vehicle that allows personnel departments to overcome the challenges mentioned in Chapters 2 and 3. At the same time, human resource planning contributes to personnel's societal, organizational, functional, and personal objectives discussed in Chapter 1. The next chapter explores the pivotal role human resource planning can play in modern personnel departments.

SUMMARY

Since government acts with the force of law, it presents a major challenge to the practice of personnel management. Its influence is through laws aimed at the employment relationship. Although most laws are limited in scope, equal employment opportunity laws affect virtually every personnel activity.

The three main sources of equal employment laws are federal acts, state and local fair employment practices, and executive orders. The most significant law is Title VII of the 1964 Civil Rights Act. Along with the Age Discrimination in Employment Act, it defines the major protected classes. Other federal equal employment laws include the Equal Pay Act, the Rehabilitation Act, and the Vietnam Era Veterans Readjustment Act.

Title VII seeks to eliminate intentional discrimination in employment in addition to employment practices that cause disparate treatment or impact. Racial and sexual harassment also are prohibited.

To eliminate past discrimination and ensure future compliance, most organizations have developed affirmative action programs. These programs are designed to identify areas of past and present discrimination, develop affirmative goals, and implement corrective programs. Many government contractors develop affirmative action plans in order to comply with the OFCCP in the Department of Labor.

TERMS FOR REVIEW

Protected groups

Affirmative action programs

Disparate treatment and impact

Civil Rights Act

Equal Employment Opportunity Commission

Bona fide occupational qualification

Conciliation agreement

Deferral and nondeferral jurisdictions

Concentration

Harassment

Age Discrimination in Employment
   Act

"Make-whole" remedy

Qualified handicapped

Executive orders

Underutilization

REVIEW AND DISCUSSION QUESTIONS

1.   Suppose during your first job interview after graduation you are asked, "Why should a company have an affirmative action plan?" How would you respond?

2.   If you are a supervisor in the production department of a textile mill and an employee demands to be allowed to miss work on Fridays for religious reasons, what would you do? Under what circumstances would you be required to let the employee have time off? Under what circumstances could you require attendance?

3.   List the major equal employment laws and their primary prohibitions.

4.   Since the personnel department is not the legal department, what role does personnel play in the area of equal employment law?

5.   Suppose you are told that your first duty as a personnel specialist is to construct an affirmative action plan. What would you do? What types of information would you seek?

6.   What conditions would have to be met before you could bring suit against an employer who discriminated against you because of your sex?

7.   Under what circumstances would a disabled veteran have special legal protections?

8.   During the 1990s, do you think other groups will receive special legislation to protect them from discrimination? Which groups might get additional protection?

9.   Explain disparate impact.

INCIDENT 3-1

Metropolitan Hospital's Affirmative Action Needs

A large metropolitan hospital in a northern city recently developed an affirmative action program. The program was required by the then Department of Health and Human Services because the hospital was a major government contractor;

the hospital received $14 million a year in government research contracts and medicare payments.

Under the affirmative action program the hospital agreed to promote two women into supervisory ranks for each man promoted. This practice was to continue until 40 to 45 percent of all supervisory jobs in the hospital were held by women.

The need for the first supervisory promotion occurred in the medical records department. The manager of medical records was one of the few female managers in the hospital. Nevertheless, she argued that Roy Biggs should become a medical records supervisor since he was best qualified. Roy had spent two years in medical school and was a graduate of a medical records program at the local community college. The assistant director of hospital operations agreed that Roy should get the promotion. The equal employment compliance specialist in the personnel department argued that Kate Van Dam should get the promotion because of the affirmative action program and because she had more seniority and experience in the department than Roy. The records manager, the assistant administrator, and the compliance specialist decided that the personnel manager should make the final decision.

1. What weight would you give to (a) Kate's seniority and experience, (b) Roy's superior training, (c) the recommendation of the records manager, (d) the new affirmative action program?

2. What are the implications for the affirmative action program if Roy gets the job? What are the implications for the employees presently taking job-related courses if Kate gets the promotion?

3. What decision would you make if you were the personnel manager?

EXERCISE 3-1

CARVER JEWELRY COMPANY

The Carver Jewelry Company, Inc., has the following work-force composition:

JOB CLASSES	MALE	FEMALE	WHITE	BLACK	HISPANIC	OTHER
Executive	9	1	10			
Management	71	9	68	8	3	1
Salaried with commission	43	31	70	3	1	
Hourly	24	164	96	67	22	3

An analysis of the local labor force from which Carver draws its employees is as follows:

MALE	FEMALE	WHITE	BLACK	HISPANIC	OTHER
51%	49%	62%	30%	5%	3%

On the basis of this information:

1. Identify which job classes at Carver exhibit underutilization.

2. Identify which job classes at Carver exhibit concentration.

REFERENCES

1. Mary Green Miner and John B. Miner, *Employee Selection within the Law,* Washington, D.C.: The Bureau of National Affairs, 1978, p. 3.

2. *Equal Employment Opportunity Commission Eighth Annual Report* (Fiscal Year, 1973), Washington, D.C.: 1975, p. 25.

3. Ibid.

4. "U.S. Government Finds AT&T in Compliance," *U.S. Equal Employment Opportunity Commission News Release,* p. 3.

5. Eighth Annual Report, op. cit.

6. *Equal Employment Opportunity Commission, Tenth Annual Report* (Fiscal Year, 1975), Washington, D.C.: 1977, p. 5.

7. Roger B. Jacobs, "Employment Discrimination and Continuing Violations: An Update of *Ricks* and Recent Decisions," *Labor Law Journal,* October 1982, pp. 684–689. See also Richard Peres, *Dealing with Employment Discrimination,* New York: McGraw-Hill, 1978, p. 4; James M. Higgins, "A Manager's Guide to the Equal Employment Opportunity Laws," *Personnel Journal,* August 1976, pp. 406–411, 418; Charles F. Schanie and William L. Holley, "An Interpretive Review of the Federal Uniform Guidelines on Employee Selection Procedures," *Personnel Administrator,* June 1980, pp. 44–48; also the enforcement agencies provide many free or low-cost pamphlets on nearly every aspect of equal employment.

8. Paul S. Greenlaw and John P. Kohl, "National Origin Discrimination and the New EEOC Guidelines," *Personnel Journal,* August 1981, pp. 634–636.

9. Charles J. Hollon and Thomas L. Bright, "Avoiding Religious Discrimination in the Workplace," *Personnel Journal,* August 1982, pp. 590–594.

10. *Trans World Airlines v. Hardison,* 432 U.S. 63 (1970).

11. Gerald H. Trautman, "Greyhound Ain't No Dog," *Arizona,* June 12, 1977, p. 10. According to Charlotte M. Cloninger, director of women's affairs for the Greyhound Corporation, the height rule required applicants to be "more than five-feet, six inches tall."

12. *Griggs v. Duke Power Company,* 401 U.S. 424 (1971).

13. *Albemarle Paper Company v. Moody,* 422 U.S. 405 (1975).

14. *General Electric v. Gilbert,* 429 U.S. 125 (1976).

15. Richard Trotter, Susan Rawson Zacur, and Wallace Gatewood, "The Pregnancy Disability Amendment: What the Law Provides," *Personnel Administrator,* February 1982, pp. 47–48, 50–54.

16. Mary P. Rowe, "Dealing with Sexual Harassment," *Harvard Business Review,* May–June 1981, p. 42; see also Gary D. Brown, "How Type of Employment Affects Earnings Differences by Sex," *Monthly Labor Review,* July 1976, pp. 25–30.

17. Eliza G. C. Collins and Timothy B. Blodgett, "Sexual Harassment . . . Some See It . . . Some Won't," *Harvard Business Review,* March–April 1981, pp. 77–95.

18. Donald J. Petersen and Douglass Massengill, "Sexual Harassment—A Growing Problem in the Workplace," *Personnel Administrator,* October 1982, pp. 79–89. See also Patricia Linenberger and Timothy J. Keaveny, "Sexual Harassment in Employment," *Human Resource Management,* Spring 1981, pp. 11–17; and George E. Biles, "A Program Guide for Preventing Sexual Harassment in the Workplace," *Personnel Administrator,* June 1981, pp. 49–54, 56.

19. *International Brotherhood of Teamsters v. United States,* 431 U.S. 324 (1977).

20. *Weber v. Kaiser Aluminum and Chemical Corp.,* 443 U.S. 193.

21. Bette Bardeen Durling, "Retaliation: A Misunderstood Form of Employment Discrimination," *Personnel Journal,* July 1981, pp. 555–558.

22. Robert H. Sheahan, "Responding to Employment Discrimination Charges," *Personnel Journal,* March 1981, pp. 216–220.

23. Susan R. Rhodes, Michael Schuster, and Mildred Doering, "The Implications of an Aging Workforce," *Personnel Administrator,* October 1981, pp. 19–22.

24. Morton C. Paulson, "How to Protect Your Job If the Boss Says You're Too Old," *National Observer,* July 4, 1977, p. 1.

25. Paul S. Greenlaw and John P. Kohl, "Age Discrimination in Employment Guidelines," *Personnel Journal,* March 1982, pp. 224–228.

26. D. Brown, op. cit.

27. Paul S. Greenlaw and John P. Kohl, "The EEOC's New Equal Pay Act Guidelines," *Personnel Journal,* July 1982, pp. 517–521.

28. Brown, op. cit.

29. Thomas A. Mahoney, "Approaches to the Definition of Comparable Worth," *Academy of Management Review,* January 1983, pp. 14–22; see also John R. Schnebly, "Comparable Worth: A Legal Overview," *Personnel Administrator,* April 1982, pp. 43–48; George L. Whaley, "Controversy Swirls over Comparable Worth Issue," *Personnel Administrator,* April 1982, pp. 51–56, 58–61.

30. Richard J. Schonberger and Harry W. Hennessey, Jr., "Is Equal Pay for Comparable Work Fair?" *Personnel Journal,* December 1981, pp. 964–968. See also Michael F. Carter, "Comparable Worth: An Idea Whose Time Has Come?" *Personnel Journal,* October 1981, pp. 792–744.

31. *Schultz v. Wheaton Glass Company,* 421 F. 2d, 259.

32. Gopal C. Pati and John I. Adkins, Jr., "Hire the Handicapped—Compliance Is Good Business," *Harvard Business Review,* January–February 1980, pp. 14–22; Cheryl Grazulis, "Understanding Section 503: What Does It Really Say?" *The Personnel Administrator,* January 1978, pp. 22–23; Bob Gatty, "Business Finds Profit in Hiring the Disabled," *Nation's Business,* August 1981, pp. 30–35.

33. "Veterans' Advocate: A Firm Makes Special Efforts to Solve Vets' Problems," *The Wall Street Journal,* Western ed., Dec. 28, 1982, p. 1.

34. The U.S. Equal Employment Opportunity Commission has published a useful pair of booklets related to affirmative action: *Affirmative Action and Equal Employment: A Guidebook for Employees,* vol. 1 and 2, January 1974. See also Daniel Seligman, "Affirmative Action Is Here to Stay," *Fortune,* Apr. 19, 1982, pp. 143–144, 148, 152, 156, 160, 162.

35. *News Release,* op. cit.

36. Eleanor Holmes Norton, "Comment on the Bakke Decision," *The Personnel Administrator,* August 1978, pp. 26–28.

37. Benson Rosen and Thomas H. Jerdee, "Coping with Affirmative Action Backlash," *Business Horizons,* August 1979, pp. 18–19.

38. Tove Helland Hanner, "Affirmative Action Programs: Have We Forgotten The First Line Supervisor," *Personnel Journal,* June 1979, pp. 384–389.

39. David A. Brookmire, "Designing and Implementing Your Company's Affirmative Action Program," *Personnel Journal,* April 1979, pp. 232, 235–237; see also Benson Rosen, Thomas H. Jerdee, and John Huonker, "Are Older Workers Hurt by Affirmative Action?" *Business Horizons,* September–October, 1982, pp. 67–70.

PART

II

PREPARATION AND SELECTION

An employer hires people to do jobs that support organizational objectives. To staff effectively, a company plans its human resource needs and studies the requirements of its jobs. Then the personnel department recruits and selects people to fill the jobs, from internal and external sources.

The next four chapters discuss the activities used to select employees. You are affected as either a personnel specialist or as a manager. The quality of workers you select helps to shape the company's success and yours. You also are involved in the selection process each time you look for a job.

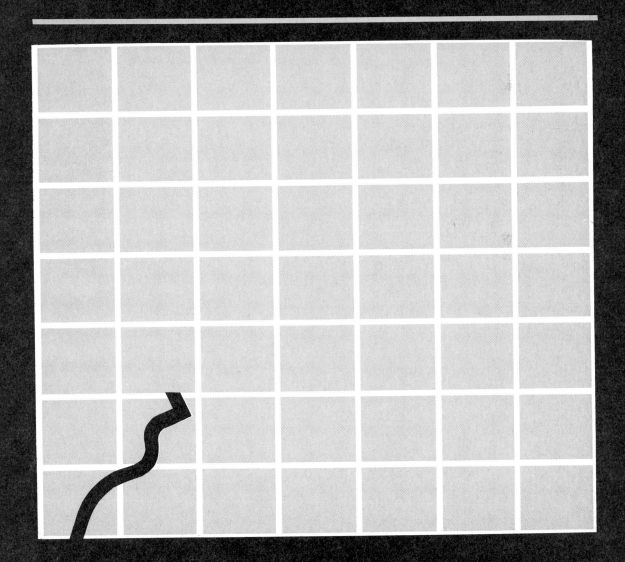

CHAPTER 4

Through human resource planning, management prepares to have the right people at the right places at the right times to fulfill both organizational and individual objectives.

James W. Walker[1]

HUMAN RESOURCE PLANNING

CHAPTER OBJECTIVES

After studying this chapter, you should be able to:

1 <u>Explain</u> why large organizations use human resource planning more than small ones do.

2 <u>Discuss</u> the relationship between human resource planning and strategic planning.

3 <u>Identify</u> the factors that shape an organization's demand for human resources.

4 <u>Describe</u> the shortcomings of human resource forecasting methods.

5 <u>Develop</u> a skills inventory as part of a human resource audit.

6 <u>Recommend</u> solutions to shortages or surpluses of human resources.

Many of the challenges faced by organizations are beyond the direct responsibility of personnel managers and their employees. From the examples used in the first three chapters, we saw that human resource specialists at Delta Air Lines could do little about rising fuel prices. Likewise, Motorola's personnel experts could not change the market strategies of Japanese competitors. Even their counterparts at AT&T could not dismantle traditional hiring practices without the strong top management commitment that followed the court order. As these and other examples illustrate, organizations are affected by their environment, and virtually every action they take to deal with it involves their people. When the personnel department can anticipate the organization's human resource needs, it can better help the organization meet its challenges, as illustrated at Delta Air Lines and Motorola. Personnel specialists in these companies did not do anything to reduce fuel prices or foreign competition. Instead, they sought ways to enlist even greater commitment from employees.

Approaches to personnel management

As described in Chapter 1, however, personnel professionals need more than just a proactive viewpoint to be successful. They must also apply a human resource approach, which recognizes the importance and dignity of employees as human beings. Likewise, they must remember the management approach described in Chapter 1, which makes "personnel management . . . the responsibility of every manager." With the human resource and management approaches in mind, personnel professionals can take a systems viewpoint by identifying how their proactive efforts contribute to the organization and what other parts of the organization will be affected. When these viewpoints—human resources, management, systems, and proactive approaches—are considered, personnel professionals are better able to develop plans that meet the objectives shown in Figure 4-1, the personnel management model. Reconsider the Delta Air Lines and Motorola examples from earlier chapters.

Delta's people make it successful.

At Delta Air Lines, the rapid rise in oil prices and the severe recession that followed reduced the need for flight personnel. Instead of ordering layoffs, Delta's personnel department found other jobs for pilots and cabin attendants, as discussed in Chapter 1. These actions obviously furthered the personal objectives of the flight personnel who otherwise would have been unemployed. The societal objective of stable employment for employees and the organizational objectives of high morale and a nonunion status also were aided. And none of these actions materially changed the appropriate size and scope of the personnel department, so the functional objective was met, too.

At Motorola, concern for human resources and competition led human resource specialists to develop the participative management program, or PMP. The PMP effort helped meet the personal needs of Motorolans because it gave them greater involvement in the decisions that affected them and their jobs. PMP also meets societal and organizational objectives of higher productivity and employee satisfaction. As a result, the contribution of personnel management has improved, which furthers the department's functional objective. In short, Motorola's PMP met the human

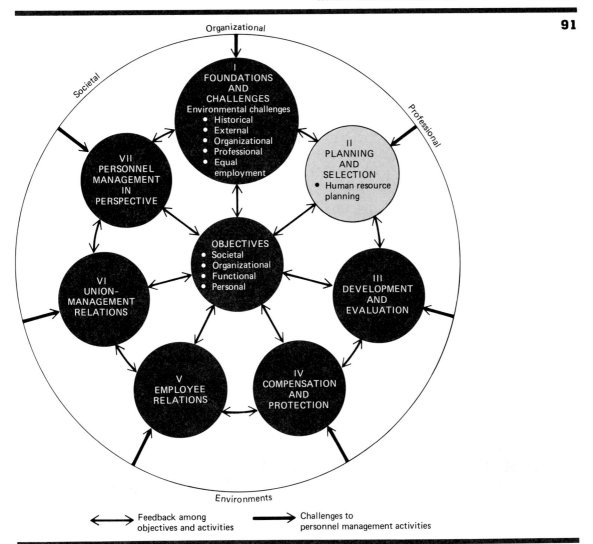

Figure 4-1
A Model of the Personnel Management System

resource objectives of the personnel management model. And the PMP did it while furthering the human resource, management, systems, and proactive viewpoints at Motorola.

These two examples underscore the importance of a personnel department meeting the objectives listed in Figure 4-1. When the department's activities meet those objectives, it is making a positive contribution to the challenges facing the organization. Actions undertaken by the personnel department are more likely to meet the objectives in Figure 4-1 if the department's plans consider the human resource, management, systems, and proactive approaches. One way Delta Air Lines, Motorola, AT&T, and other organizations achieve their objectives in a proactive and systematic fashion is through human resource planning.

OVERVIEW OF
HUMAN RESOURCE PLANNING

Definition

Human resource planning (HRP) systematically forecasts an organization's future supply of, and demand for, employees.[2] By estimating the number and types of employees that will be needed, the personnel department can better plan its recruitment, selection, training, career planning, and other activities. Human resource planning—or employment planning, as it is also called—allows the department to staff the organization at the right time with the right people. Not only can it help companies like AT&T meet their affirmative action goals, but human resource planning can help firms such as Motorola and Delta Air Lines implement their short- and long-range strategic business plans.

People constraints

Short- and long-range business plans are carried out by people. If the organization is not properly staffed with the right number and types of people, corporate plans may fail. Of course, production, financial, and marketing plans are important cornerstones of a company's strategic plans. More and more executives realize, however, that well-conceived human resource plans are another cornerstone of company plans.[3] For example, the decision of high-technology firms like Motorola and IBM to develop new products and enter new markets often depends on the availability of qualified technical and support people. Without sufficient engineering talent, market opportunities can be lost to more appropriately staffed competitors.

Ideally, all organizations should identify their short-run and long-run employee needs through planning. Short-range plans point out job openings that must be filled during the coming year. Long-range plans estimate the human resource situation for two, five, or, occasionally, ten years into the future. Examples of employment planning are more common in large organizations because it allows them to:

Benefits of HRP

- Improve the utilization of human resources

- Match personnel activities and future organization objectives efficiently

- Achieve economies in hiring new workers

- Expand the personnel management information base to assist other personnel activities and other organizational units

- Make major demands on local labor markets successfully

- Coordinate different personnel management programs such as affirmative action plans and hiring needs

A small organization can expect similar advantages, but the gains in effectiveness are often considerably less because its situation is less complex. In fact, the benefits of human resource planning for small firms may not justify the time and costs. Consider the different situations faced by a small-and large-city government.

> Rural City employs 20 workers and is growing 10 percent a year. Metropolis has 8000 employees, and it is growing by 5 percent. That means 400 new employees plus replacements for those who leave. If it costs $400 to find and hire a typical employee, Rural City will spend $800 to hire 2 more workers. Metropolis will spend $160,000 just to add new employees. If employment planning saves 25 percent, Rural City's manager cannot justify detailed planning efforts for $200. But for $40,000, Metropolis can afford a specialist and still save thousands of dollars after planning expenses are deducted.

Nevertheless, knowledge of human resource planning is useful to personnel specialists in *both* small and large organizations. It shows small employers the human resource considerations they face if they should expand rapidly. (For example, if Rural City attracted several large factories to its area, expansion of city services would depend partly on the city's human resource planning.) Large organizations can benefit from knowledge of employment planning because it reveals ways to make the personnel function more effective.

This chapter examines the two dimensions of human resource planning. The chapter begins with an explanation of how the personnel department estimates future job openings. It ends by showing the methods used by personnel experts to isolate potential sources of employees to meet those vacancies.

THE DEMAND FOR HUMAN RESOURCES

An organization's future demand for people is central to employment planning. Most firms predict their future employment needs (at least informally) even if they do not estimate their sources of supply. For example, one study found that employers are two times more likely to estimate human resource demand than supply.[4] The challenges that determine this demand and the methods of forecasting it merit brief review.

Causes of Demand

Although many challenges influence the demand for human resources, changes in the environment, organization, and work force usually are involved.[5] These factors are common to short-range and long-range employment plans. The causes of these changes are summarized in Figure 4-2. Some of these causes are within the organization's control and others are not.

What influences the demand for people?

External challenges   Developments in the organization's environment are difficult for personnel specialists to predict in the short run and sometimes impossible to estimate in the long run. Reconsider the example of the small-city government. City planners seldom know of major factory relocations until shortly before construction begins. Other *economic* developments have a

EXTERNAL	ORGANIZATIONAL	WORK FORCE
• Economics	• Strategic plans	• Retirement
• Social-political-legal	• Budgets	• Resignations
• Technology	• Sales and production forecasts	• Terminations
• Competitors	• New ventures	• Deaths
	• Organization and job designs	• Leaves of absence

Figure 4-2

Causes of Demand for Human Resources in the Future

noticeable effect but are difficult to estimate. Examples include inflation, unemployment, and interest rates that curtail construction and the need for construction workers.

Social, political, and *legal* challenges are easier to predict, but their implications are seldom clear. The impact on human resource planning of civil rights laws passed in the 1960s was unclear until the 1970s. Now most large firms have affirmative action programs and compliance officers, as discussed in Chapter 3. Likewise, the implications of raising the mandatory retirement age in 1978 may be unknown until a generation has lived without the "65 and out" tradition.[6]

Technological changes are difficult to predict and difficult to assess. Many thought the computer would cause mass unemployment, for example. Today the computer field is one of the fastest growing industries, employing hundreds of thousands directly and indirectly. Very often human resource planning is complicated by technology because it tends to reduce employment in one department (for example, bookkeeping) while increasing employment in anoth-

Robots and HRP   er (such as computer operations). The use of robots, as discussed in Chapter 2, will undoubtedly complicate future employment planning even more.

Competitors are another external challenge that affects an organization's demand for human resources. Employment in the automobile and steel industries barely grows, partially because of foreign competition. But in the electronics industry, competition results in lower prices, larger markets, and additional employment.

Organizational decisions   Major organizational decisions affect the

Strategic plans   demand for human resources. The organization's *strategic plan* is the most influential decision.[7] It commits the firm to long-range objectives—such as growth rates and new products, markets, or services. These objectives dictate the number and types of employees needed in the future. If long-term objectives are to be met, personnel specialists must develop long-range human resource plans that accommodate the strategic plan. In the short run, planners find that strategic plans become operational in the form of *budgets.* Budget increases or cuts are the most significant short-run influence on human resource needs.

Sales and production forecasts are less exact than budgets but may provide even quicker notice of short-run changes in human resource demand.

> The personnel manager for a nationwide chain of furniture outlets observed a sharp decline in sales brought on by a recession. The personnel manager quickly discarded the short-run human resource plan and imposed an employment freeze on all outlets' hiring plans.

New ventures mean changing human resource demands. When a new venture is begun internally from scratch, the lead time may allow planners to develop short-run and long-run employment plans. But new ventures begun by acquisitions and mergers cause an immediate revision of human resource demands and can lead to new organization and job designs. A reorganization, especially after a merger or an acquisition, can radically alter human resource needs. Likewise, the redesign of jobs changes the required skill levels of future workers.[8]

Work-force factors   The demand for human resources is modified by such employee actions as retirements, resignations, terminations, deaths, and leaves of absence. When large numbers of employees are involved, past experience usually serves as a reasonably accurate guide. However, reliance on past experiences means that personnel specialists must be sensitive to changes that upset past trends.

Turnover

> Jim Santino used to keep close track of employees nearing retirement so that his human resource plan remained accurate. But in 1978 Congress prohibited employers from requiring mandatory retirement at age 65. This meant that all employees of Universal Book Publishers could continue to work until age 70. As a result, Jim can no longer use past experience as a guide to when older workers will retire. This change has caused Jim to seek other ways to forecast his short-run human resource needs.

Forecasting Techniques

Human resource forecasts are attempts to predict an organization's future demand for employees.[9] As Figure 4-3 shows, forecasting techniques range from the informal to the sophisticated. Even the most sophisticated methods are not perfectly accurate; instead, they are best viewed as approximations. Most firms make only casual estimates about the immediate future. As they gain experience with forecasting human resource needs, they may use more sophisticated techniques (especially if they can afford the specialized staff). Each of the forecasting methods in Figure 4-3 is explained below.

Predicting human resource needs

Expert forecasts   *Expert forecasts* are based on the judgments of those who are knowledgeable of future human resource needs. Since most employment decisions are made by line managers, human resource planners must devise methods to learn about these managers' staffing needs. In small organizations, the director of operations or the personnel manager may have all the needed knowledge. In larger organizations, the simplest method is to *survey*

EXPERT	TREND	OTHER
• Informal and instant decisions	• Extrapolation	• Budget and planning analysis
• Formal expert survey	• Indexation	• New-venture analysis
• Delphi technique	• Statistical analysis	• Computer models

Figure 4-3
Forecasting Techniques for Estimating
Future Human Resource Needs

these managers, who are the ultimate experts about the future staffing needs of their departments.

Delphi survey   Additional sophistication can be added to the survey approach with the Delphi technique.[10] The *Delphi survey* also solicits estimates from a group of experts, usually managers. Then personnel department planners act as an intermediary, summarize the various responses, and report the findings back to the experts. The experts are surveyed again after they get this feedback. Summaries and surveys are repeated until the experts' opinions begin to agree on future developments. (Usually four or five surveys are enough.) For example, the personnel department may survey all production supervisors and managers until an agreement is reached on the number of replacements needed during the next year.

Trend projection forecasts   Perhaps the quickest forecasting technique is to project past trends. The two simplest methods are extrapolation and *Extrapolation*   indexation. *Extrapolation* involves extending past rates of change into the future. For example, if an average of 20 production workers were hired each month for the past two years, extrapolating that trend into the future means 240 production workers will be added during the upcoming year.

Indexation is a method of estimating future employment needs by matching employment growth with some index. A common example is the ratio of production employees to sales. For example, planners may discover that for each million dollar increase in sales, the production department requires ten new assemblers.

Extrapolation and indexation are crude approximations in the short run because they assume that the causes of demand—external, organizational, and work-force factors—remain constant, which is seldom the case. These methods are very inaccurate for long-range human resource projections. More sophisticated *statistical analyses* make allowances for changes in the underlying causes of demand.[11]

Other forecasting methods   There are several other ways planners can estimate the future demand for human resources. One approach is through *budget and planning analysis*. Organizations that need human resource planning generally have detailed budgets and long-range plans. A study of department budgets reveals the financial authorizations for more employees. These data plus extrapolations of work-force changes (resignation, terminations, and the like) can provide short-run estimates of human resource needs. Long-term estimates can be made from each department or division's long-range plans.

When new ventures complicate employment planning, planners can use new-venture analysis. *New-venture analysis* requires planners to estimate human resource needs by comparison with firms that already perform similar operations. For example, a petroleum company that plans to open a coal mine can estimate its future employment needs by determining them from employment levels of other coal mines.

The most sophisticated forecasting approaches involve computers. *Computer models* are a series of mathematical formulas that simultaneously use extrapolation, indexation, survey results, and estimates of work-force changes to compute future human resource needs. Through time, actual changes in human resource demand are used to refine the computer's formulas.

Computer modeling

One expert suggests that there are four levels of complexity in human resource forecasting.[12] These stages of forecasting sophistication are summarized in Figure 4-4. As can be seen, they range from informal discussions to highly complex computerized forecasting systems. The more sophisticated techniques are found among large organizations that have had years of experience in human resource planning. Small firms or those just beginning to forecast human resource needs are more likely to start with stage 1 and progress to other stages as planners seek greater accuracy.

Figure 4-4

Stages of Complexity and Sophistication
in Human Resource Forecasting

STAGE 1	STAGE 2	STAGE 3	STAGE 4
• Managers discuss goals, plans, and thus types and numbers of people needed in the short term.	• Annual planning budgeting process includes human resource needs.	• Using computer-generated analyses, examine causes of problems and future trends regarding the flow of talent.	• On-line modeling and computer simulation of talent needs, flows, and costs to aid in a continuing process of updating and projecting needs, staffing plans, career opportunities, and thus program plans.
• Highly informal and subjective.	• Specify quantity and quality of talent needs as far as possible.	• Use computer to relieve managers of routine forecasting tasks (such as vacancies or turnover).	• Provide best possible current information for managerial decisions.
	• Identify problems requiring action: individual or general.		• Exchange data with other companies and with government (such as economic, employment, and social data).

Source: James W. Walker, "Evaluating the Practical Effectiveness of Human Resource Planning Applications," *Human Resource Management,* Spring 1974, p. 21.

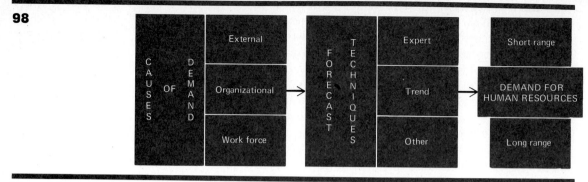

Figure 4-5
Components of the Future Demand for
Human Resources

Human Resource Requirements

Figure 4-5 depicts an overview of the key considerations involved in estimating demand for human resources. It shows that forecasts translate the causes of demand into short-range and long-range statements of needs. The resulting long-range plans are, of necessity, general statements of *probable* needs. Specific numbers are either estimated or omitted entirely because initially they have a low level of accuracy. But as planners become more familiar with the causes of demand and the forecasting techniques, their estimates of human resource demand become more accurate.

Short-term plans are more specific and may be reported as a staffing table (Figure 4-6). A *staffing table* lists the future employment needs for each type of job. The listing may be a specific number or an approximate range of needs, depending on the accuracy of the underlying forecast. Staffing tables (also called manning tables) are neither complete nor wholly accurate. They are only approximations. But these estimates allow personnel specialists to match short-run demand and supply. They help operating departments run more smoothly and can enhance the image of the personnel department.

With specific estimates of future human resource needs, personnel specialists can become more proactive and systematic. For example, a review of Figure 4-6 shows that the city's personnel department must hire thirty-two police academy recruits every three months. This knowledge allows recruiters in the personnel department to plan their recruiting campaign so that it peaks about six weeks before the beginning of the next police academy class. The advanced planning allows the department to screen applicants and notify them at least three weeks before the class begins. For those still in school or for other applicants who cannot be ready that quickly, recruiters can inform them of when the next class will begin. If the personnel department waited for the police department to notify them, notification might come too late to allow a systematic recruiting and screening process. Staffing tables enable recruiters to be proactive and to plan their activities better.

METROPOLIS
CITY GOVERNMENT
STAFFING TABLE

Date Compiled: _____

Budget Code Number	Job Title	Using Department(s)	Anticipated Openings by Months of the Year												
			Total	1	2	3	4	5	6	7	8	9	10	11	12
100–32	Police Academy Recruit	Police	128	32			32			32			32		
100–33	Police Dispatcher	Police	3	2					1						
100–84	Meter Reader	Police	24	2	2	2	2	2	2	2	2	2	2	2	2
100–85	Traffic Supervisor	Police	5	2			1			1			1		
100–86	Team Supervisor –Police (Sergeant)	Police	5	2			1			1			1		
100–97	Duty Supervisor –Police (Lieutenant)	Police	2	1						1					
100–99	Shift Officer– Police (Captain)	Police	1	1											
200–01	Car Washer	Motor Pool	4	1			1			1			1		
200–12	Mechanic's Assistant	Motor Pool	3				1			1			1		
200–13	Mechanic III	Motor Pool	2	1									1		
200–14	Mechanic II	Motor Pool	1						1						
200–15	Mechanic I (Working Supervisor)	Motor Pool	1	1											
300–01	Clerk IV	Administration	27	10			5			6			6		

Figure 4-6
A Partial Staffing Table for a City Government

THE SUPPLY OF HUMAN RESOURCES

Once the personnel department projects future demand for human resources, its next major concern is filling projected openings.[13] There are two sources of supply: internal and external. The internal supply consists of present employees who can be promoted, transferred, or demoted to fill expected openings. For example, some of the previously mentioned openings at the police academy might be filled by other city employees who want to transfer from their present jobs into police work. Those people represent the internal supply. The external supply consists of people who do not work for the city, such as employees of other organizations and the unemployed.

Two sources of supply

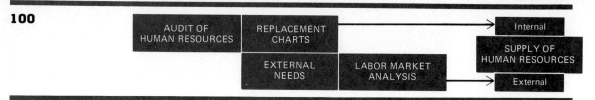

Figure 4-7
Factors that Determine the Future Supply of
Human Resources

Estimates of Internal Supply

Estimates of the internal supply involve more than merely counting the number of employees. As Figure 4-7 implies, planners audit the present work force to learn about the capabilities of workers. This information allows planners to estimate tentatively which openings can be filled by present employees. These tentative assignments usually are recorded on a replacement chart. Considering present employees for future job openings is important if workers are to have lifelong careers with their employer rather than dead-end jobs.

Identify internal candidates.

Audits and replacement charts also are important additions to the personnel department's information base. With greater knowledge of employees, the department can plan recruiting, training, and career planning activities more effectively. The knowledge can even help personnel meet its affirmative action plan by identifying internal minority candidates for job openings. Since audits and replacement charts are important to proactive personnel work, they are explained more fully below.[14]

Human resource audits   *Human resource audits* summarize each employee's skills and abilities. The audits of nonmanagers are called *skills inventories;* the audits of managers are called *management inventories.* Whatever name is used, an inventory catalogs each employee's skills and abilities. This summary gives planners a comprehensive understanding of the capabilities found in the organization's work force.

Inventories of human talent

An example of a skills inventory form is shown in Figure 4-8. It is divided into four parts. Part I can be completed by the personnel department from employee records. It identifies the employee's job title, experience, age, and previous jobs. Part II seeks information about the skills, duties, responsibilities, and education of the worker. From these questions, planners learn about the mix of employee abilities. The personnel department may collect these data through telephone or face-to-face interviews. Or the questions may be sent periodically to the employee through the company mail. In addition, most firms encourage employees to update their information when significant changes occur. The employee's future potential is briefly summarized by the immediate superior in Part III. Performance, readiness for promotion, and any deficiencies are noted here. The supervisor's signature helps ensure that the form's accuracy is reviewed by someone who knows the employee better than the personnel specialists do. Part IV is added as a final check for completeness and for the

METROPOLIS
CITY GOVERNMENT
SKILLS INVENTORY   Date: _____

PART I (To be completed by personnel department)
1. Name _____   2. Employee Number _____
3. Job Title _____   4. Experience _____ Years
5. Age _____   6. Years with City _____
7. Other Jobs Held:
    With City: Title _____   From _____ to _____
                    Title _____   From _____ to _____
    Elsewhere: Title _____   From _____ to _____
                    Title _____   From _____ to _____

PART II (To be completed by employee)
8. Special Skills. List below any skills you possess even if they are not used on your present job.
Include types and names of machines or tools with which you are experienced.
        Skills: _____
                _____
    Machines: _____
        Tools: _____
9. Duties. Briefly describe your present duties.
    _____
10. Responsibilities. Briefly describe your responsibilities for:
        City Equipment: _____
            City Funds: _____
        Employee Safety: _____
    Employee Supervision: _____
11. Education. Briefly describe your education and training background:
        Academic: (Circle highest grade)   6   7   8   9   10   11   12   Fr   So   Jr   Sr   Gr
        Job Training: _____
                      _____
        Special Courses: _____
        Military Training: _____

PART III (To be completed by personnel department with supervisory inputs)
12. Overall Evaluation of Performance _____
    _____
13. Overall Readiness for Promotion _____
        To What Job(s): _____
        Comments: _____
14. Current Deficiencies _____
    _____
15. Supervisor's Signature _____ Date: _____

PART IV (To be completed by personnel department representative)
16. Are the two most recent performance evaluations attached?   ____ Yes ____ No
17. Prepared by _____ Date: _____

Figure 4-8
A Skills Inventory Form

addition of recent employee evaluations, which give more insight into past performance.

Inventories of human resources are often computerized to match talent with openings and are updated periodically. Large organizations, such as General Electric and the U.S. Air Force, use computer-based systems to quickly match jobs with skilled personnel. Computerized records also facilitate updating, which should be done at least every two years if employees are encouraged to report major changes to the personnel department when they occur. Major changes include new skills, degree completions, changed job duties, and the like. Failure to update skills inventories can lead to present employees being overlooked for job openings within the organization.

> After working hours, Rafael Corda "moonlighted" by helping his brother do maintenance work at a large paint factory. Rafael became interested in maintenance work and completed several courses in air conditioning and plumbing. Since his full-time employer seldom updated its skills inventory on employees, the personnel manager at the First National Bank was unaware of Rafael's diverse skills. After several weeks of searching, the personnel manager hired a maintenance worker from outside the bank's present work force. The bank spent $1000 to find this new maintenance worker. When Rafael found out, he was understandably upset.

Management inventories should be updated periodically since they are also used for key personnel decisions. In fact, some employers use the same form for managers and nonmanagers. When the forms differ, the management inventory requests information about management activities. Common topics include:

- Number of employees supervised

- Total budget managed

- Duties of subordinates

- Types of employees supervised

- Management training received

- Previous management duties

Replacement charts   *Replacement charts* are a visual representation of

Replacement charts

who will replace whom in the event of a job opening. The information for constructing the chart comes from the human resource audit. Figure 4-9 illustrates a typical replacement chart. It shows the replacement status of only a few jobs in the administration of a large city.

Although different firms may seek to summarize different information in their replacement charts, the figure indicates the minimum information usually included. The chart, much like an organization chart, depicts the various jobs in the organization and shows the status of likely candidates. Replacement status consists of two variables: present performance and promotability. Present

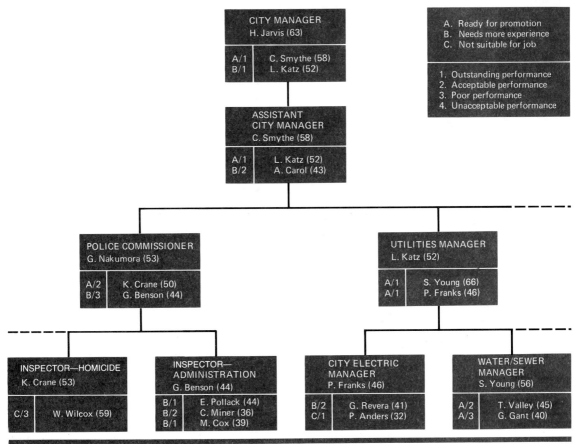

Figure 4-9
A Partial Replacement Chart for a City Government

performance is determined largely from supervisory evaluations. Opinions of other managers, peers, and subordinates may contribute to the appraisal of present performance. Future promotability is based primarily on present performance and on the estimates by immediate superiors of future success in a new job. The personnel department may contribute to these estimates through the use of psychological tests, interviews, and other methods of assessment. Replacement charts used to show the candidates' ages, which could have led to allegations of age discrimination. As a result this information is now deleted on many replacement charts.

Personnel and management decision makers find these charts provide a quick reference. Their shortcoming is that they contain very limited information.[15] To supplement the chart, and increasingly, to supplant it, personnel specialists develop replacement summaries. *Replacement summaries* list likely replacements for each job and indicate their relative strengths and weaknesses. As Figure 4-10 shows, the summaries provide considerably more data than the

Replacement summaries give more detail

Replacement Summary for the Position of <u>City Manager</u>

Present Office Holder <u>Harold Jarvis</u>   Age <u>63</u>

Probable Opening <u>In two years</u>   Reason <u>Retirement</u>

Salary Grade <u>99 ($58,500 yearly)</u>   Experience <u>8 years</u>

Candidate 1 <u>Clyde Smythe</u>   Age <u>58</u>

Current Position <u>Assistant City Manager</u>   Experience <u>4 years</u>

Current Performance <u>Outstanding</u>   Explanation <u>Clyde's performance evaluations by</u>
<u>the City Manager are always the highest possible.</u>

Promotability <u>Ready now for promotion.</u>   Explanation <u>During an extended illness of the</u>
<u>City Manager, Clyde assumed all duties successfully including major policy decisions</u>
<u>and negotiations with city unions.</u>

Training Needs <u>None</u>

Candidate 2 <u>Larry Katz</u>   Age <u>52</u>

Current Position <u>Utilities Manager</u>   Experience <u>5 years</u>

Current Performance <u>Outstanding</u>   Explanation <u>Larry's performance has kept costs of</u>
<u>utilities to citizens 10 to 15 percent below that of comparable city utilities through</u>
<u>careful planning.</u>

Promotability <u>Needs more experience.</u>   Explanation <u>Larry's experience is limited to</u>
<u>utilities management. Although successful, he needs more broad administrative experience in</u>
<u>other areas. (He is ready for promotion to Assistant City Manager at this time.)</u>

Training Needs <u>Training in budget preparation and public relations would be desirable before</u>
<u>promotion to City Manager.</u>

Figure 4-10
A Replacement Summary for
the Position of City Manager

replacement chart. This additional information allows decision makers to make
more informed decisions.

Most companies that are sophisticated enough to engage in detailed human
resource planning typically computerize their personnel records, including
human resource inventories. Then through a simple computer program, plan-

ners can compile replacement summaries each time a job opening occurs. These summaries also indicate which positions lack human resource backups. In the long run, the personnel department can encourage employees to upgrade their capabilities and prepare for future vacancies. In the short run, an opening without a suitable replacement requires someone to be hired from the external labor market. Whether replacement charts or summaries are used, this information is normally kept confidential. Confidentiality not only guards the privacy of employees, but it prevents dissatisfaction among those who are not immediately promotable.[16]

Estimates of External Supply

Not every future opening can be met with present employees. Some jobs lack replacements to fill an opening when it occurs. Other jobs are entry-level positions. That is, they are beginning jobs that are filled with people who do not presently work for the organization. When there are no replacements or when the opening is for an entry-level job, there is a need for external supplies of human resources.

Entry-level jobs

External needs   Employer growth and the effectiveness of the personnel department largely determine the need for external supplies of human resources. Growth is primarily responsible for the number of entry-level job openings, especially if the company promotes from within to fill job vacancies. The number of non-entry-level openings also depends on how well the personnel department assists employees to develop their capabilities. If workers are not encouraged to expand their capabilities, they may not be ready to fill future vacancies. The lack of promotable replacements creates job openings that need to be filled externally.

Labor market analysis   Success in finding new employees depends on the labor market and on the skills of the employment specialists in the personnel department. Even when unemployment rates are high, many needed skills are difficult to find.[17]

> In 1982, the unemployment rate in the United States reached 10.8 percent, the highest level since the closing years of the Great Depression four decades earlier. But personnel departments that sought managers and administrators had to compete in a labor market with less than 4 percent of these people unemployed.

In the short run, the national unemployment rate serves as an approximate measure of how difficult it is to acquire new employees. Personnel specialists realize that this rate varies among different groups as well as from region to region and from city to city.

> During 1983, there were wide variations in the unemployment rate. In Houston, Texas, the rate was less than 5 percent. But in Flint, Michigan, the rate exceeded 22 percent.

Regardless of the unemployment rate, external needs may be met by attracting employees who work for others. In the long run, local developments and demographic trends have the most significant impact on labor markets.[18] Local developments include community growth rates and attitudes. For example, many midwestern farm towns find their population in decline. When they attempt to attract new business, employers fear declining population may mean future shortages in the local labor market. So the new businesses often locate elsewhere. The lack of jobs results in still more people leaving the local labor market. Conversely, sun-belt cities are attractive to employers because these growing cities promise even larger labor markets in the future.

Community attitudes   Community attitudes also affect the nature of the labor market. Antibusiness or no-growth attitudes may cause employers to locate elsewhere. Fewer jobs mean a loss of middle-class workers. The shrinking work force discourages new businesses, and the cycle is complete.

"No-growth" attitudes

> The people of Santa Barbara, California, limited growth in their community by restricting the number of permits available for connecting to the city water system. Construction slowed. In time, housing prices increased dramatically. Young families that could not afford housing left the Santa Barbara labor market. New employers found the situation discouraging. Established employers found it difficult to attract new workers, especially the low-paid workers required for one of the town's major industries, tourism. Regardless of the unemployment rate, personnel departments in Santa Barbara faced a difficult task when they had to rely on external supplies of workers.

Demographics   Demographic trends are another long-term development that affects the availability of external supply. Fortunately for planners, these trends are known years in advance of their impact.

Population trends

> The low birthrates of the 1930s and early 1940s were followed by a baby boom during the late 1940s and 1950s. When the post-World War II babies started to go to college in the 1960s, the low birthrates of the 1930s led to a shortage of college teachers. These demographic trends were already in motion by 1950. Long-range human resource planning, which was sensitive to demographic developments, could have predicted the shortage soon enough for proactive colleges to take corrective action.

As for the specific shortages that affect a particular industry or occupation in the long run, ample information is readily available. The National Commission for Manpower Policy issues reports on major developments in the labor force.[19] The U.S. Department of Labor publishes the *Occupational Outlook Handbook* and quarterly reports in the *Occupational Outlook Quarterly*. These publications discuss the expected developments in various occupational groupings. Similarly, the department publishes the population estimates of the Census Bureau;

	PROJECTED NUMBERS (THOUSANDS)		
AGE, BOTH SEXES	1980	1985	1990
16 years and over:	103,759	110,688	115,925
16 to 24	25,453	24,254	22,139
25 to 54	63,396	71,515	79,466
25 to 34	27,342	30,810	32,201
35 to 44	19,516	24,198	28,532
45 to 54	16,538	16,507	18,733
55 years and over:	14,910	14,919	14,320
55 to 64	11,903	11,902	11,218
65 and over	3,007	3,017	3,102

Source: Employment and Training Report of the President, Washington: U.S. Government Printing Office, 1977, p. 254.

Figure 4-11
Changes in the Total Labor Force

projections of the total labor force; the percentage of the population that will be in the work force; and the changes in the work force by sex, age, race, marital status, and other criteria.[20] For example, Figure 4-11 shows the composition of the work force by age from 1980 to 1990. Hidden in that table are implications for many businesses.[21]

Fast-food restaurants depend on 16- to 24-year-olds for many jobs. But by 1990 this group will have declined by over 3 million. At the same time, population growth and the trend toward eating more meals away from home will cause an increased demand for fast-food employees.

IMPLEMENTATION OF
HUMAN RESOURCE PLANS

Figure 4-12 summarizes the key concepts discussed throughout the chapter. The left side of the figure identifies the major causes of human resource demand—which are external, organizational, and work-force factors. These causes of demand are forecast by experts, trend data, and other methods to determine the short- and long-range demand for human resources. This demand is fulfilled either internally by present employees or externally by newcomers. The internal supply is shown in replacement charts, which are based on audits of the organization's human resources. External sources are identified by analysis of the labor market. The results include short- and long-range human resource plans that are fulfilled by internal and external staffing processes.

Once the supply and demand of human resources are estimated, adjustments may be needed. When the internal supply of workers exceeds the firm's demand, a *human resource surplus* exists. Most employers respond to a surplus   **Surplus**

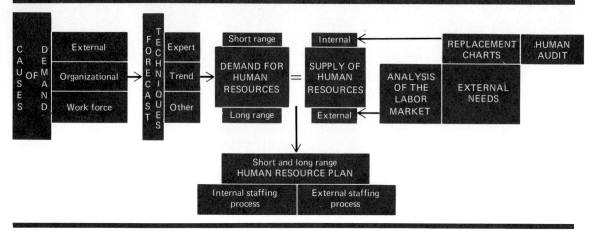

Figure 4-12
Supply and Demand Considerations
in Human Resource Planning

Attrition

with a hiring freeze. This freeze stops the personnel department from filling openings with external supplies. Instead, present employees are reassigned. Voluntary departures, called *attrition,* slowly reduce the surplus.[22] If it persists, leaves of absence are encouraged.

> After the summer tourist peak, TWA and other airlines often grant leaves of absence to employees who request them. These leaves help reduce the total work force during the slack fall and winter months.

Layoffs, which are a temporary loss of employment to workers, are also used in cases of short-run surplus. If the surplus is expected to persist into the foreseeable future, employers often encourage early retirement on a *voluntary* basis. (Forced early retirement could violate the *Age Discrimination in Employment Act.*) Should the surplus still persist, employees are discharged. The blow of discharge may be softened through formal *outplacement* procedures, which help present employees find new jobs with other firms. These efforts may include office space, secretarial services, use of photocopying machines, long-distance phone calls, counseling, instructions in how to look for work, and even invitations to competitors to meet with employees.[23]

Outplacement

If the internal supply cannot fulfill the organization's needs, a human resource *shortage* exists. Planners have little flexibility in the short run. They must rely on the external staffing process and find new employees. In the long run, responses can be more flexible. Planners can use the internal staffing process; that is, they can redouble efforts to have employees develop the necessary knowledge, skills, and attitudes to fill these jobs.

Shortage

Whether staffing needs are met internally or externally, planners must consider their employer's affirmative action plan. That plan, as discussed in Chapter 3, contains the company's strategy for undoing past discrimination and

Affirmative action

ensuring that future discrimination does not occur. As internal and external candidates are selected to fill job openings, these decisions must match the goals and timetables found in the affirmative action plan. The human resource plan also indicates whether or not the employer's affirmative action goals will be met. For example, even modest goals of increasing minority representation in a company are unlikely if the human resource plan indicates that no new hires are planned and the company intends to reduce overall employment through attrition.

The human resource plan does more than serve as a check on the likelihood of the affirmative action plan's success. It is an important part of the organization's *human resource information system.* The information contained in the plan serves as a guide to recruiters, trainers, career planners, and other human resource specialists. With the knowledge of the firm's internal and external employment needs, personnel specialists, operating managers, and individual employees can direct their efforts toward the organization's future staffing needs. Managers can groom their employees through specific training and development efforts. Even individual employees can prepare themselves for future openings through education and other self-help efforts. From the perspective of the personnel department, however, the human resource plan is only one part of the department's information system. Another important part is information about the specific jobs in the organization. The next chapter, "Job Analysis and Design," shows how personnel professionals learn about the content of the jobs in their organization. Once armed with the knowledge of job openings (through human resource planning) and the content of jobs (through job analysis), personnel professionals can then begin the staffing process in an efficient, effective, and proactive manner.

Human resource information system

Next chapter

SUMMARY

Human resource planning requires considerable time, staff, and financial resources. The return for this investment may not justify the expenditure for small firms. Increasingly, however, large organizations use human resource planning as a means of achieving greater effectiveness. Human resource planning is an attempt by personnel departments to estimate their future needs and supplies of human resources. Through an understanding of the factors that influence the demand for workers, planners can forecast specific short-term and long-term needs.

Given some anticipated level of demand, planners try to estimate the availability of present workers to meet that demand. Such estimates begin with an audit of present employees. Then possible replacements are identified. Internal shortages are resolved by seeking new employees in the external labor markets. Surpluses are reduced by normal attrition, leaves of absence, layoffs, or terminations.

As Figure 4-12 illustrates, both the external and internal staffing processes are used to fulfill human resource plans. The result is short- and long-range human resource plans that outline the organization's future human resource demands and the likely sources of supply. This information becomes an important addition to the personnel department's data base.

TERMS FOR REVIEW

Strategic plan	Skills inventories
Forecasts	Replacement charts
Delphi technique	Replacement summaries
Extrapolation	Labor market analysis
Indexation	Attrition
Staffing table	Outplacement

REVIEW AND DISCUSSION QUESTIONS

1. Why is human resource planning more common among large organizations than among small ones? What are the advantages of human resource planning for large organizations?

2. List and briefly describe the factors that change an organization's demand for human resources.

3. What is a staffing table? Of what use is it to human resource planners?

4. What is the purpose of a human resource audit? Specifically, what information acquired from a human resource audit is needed to construct a replacement chart?

5. Suppose human resource planners estimated that because of several technological innovations your firm will need 25 percent fewer employees in three years. What actions would you take today?

6. Suppose you manage a restaurant in a winter resort area. During the summer it is profitable to keep the business open, but you need only one-half the cooks, table servers, and bartenders. What actions would you take in April when the peak tourist season ended?

7. Review the demographic trends in Figure 4-11. What industries might have problems finding enough employees externally in 1990?

8. If your company locates its research and development offices in downtown Flint, Michigan, the city is willing to forgo city property taxes on the building for ten years. The city is willing to make this concession to help reduce its high unemployment rate. Houston, Texas, your company's other choice, has a low

unemployment rate and is not offering any tax breaks. Based on just these considerations, which city would you recommend and why?

INCIDENT 4-1

Metropolis City College's Human Resource Needs

For years Metropolis City College had operated at a deficit. This loss was made up from the city budget since Metropolis was city-supported. Because of the inflation and recession, the drain on the city's budget had tripled to $21 million by 1984.

Several members of the city council had heard that college enrollments were going to decline during the late 1980s. A decline in enrollment would lead to overstaffing and even larger deficits. The president of the college hired Bill Barker to develop a long-range human resource plan for the college. An excerpt of his report stated:

> The declining birthrates of the 1960s and 1970s mean that there will be a decline in college-age students at least to the year 2000. If the college is to avoid soaring deficits, it must institute an employment freeze now. Furthermore, a committee should be formed to develop new curriculums that appeal to those segments of the work force that are going to experience rapid growth between now and the year 2000.

The president of Metropolis City College argued, "An employment freeze would cut the college off from hiring new faculty members who have the latest training in new areas. Besides, our enrollments have grown by 2 to 4 percent every year since 1970. I see no reason to doubt that trend will continue."

1. Assuming you are a member of the city council, would you recommend that the college implement an employment freeze or not?

2. If Bill Barker used national birthrate information, what other population information could the president use to support his argument that the college will probably keep growing?

3. Are there any strategies that you could recommend that would allow the college to hire newly trained faculty and avoid serious budget deficits in the 1990s if enrollments do drop?

INCIDENT 4-2

Human Resource Planning in the Bell System

For many years, the American Telephone and Telegraph Company was the largest private employer in the United States. At a conference on human resource planning, Mr. W. S. Cashel, Jr., vice chairman and chief financial officer of AT&T, made the following observations about employment in the Bell System of AT&T:

- In 1977, the Bell System had to process and interview thirty applicants in order to hire one new employee.

- In 1966, telephone operators represented about 24 percent of the phone company's work force. Ten years later, operators counted for only 17 percent of the work force.

- Between 1978 and 1980, employment in the central office will fall from 2733 to 850 because of automation and technological advances.

- Between 1978 and 1983, about half (180) of the officers of the Bell System will have to be replaced.

- Nearly three-fourths of the company's operating expenses go to people-related costs.

- During the next twenty-five years, the Bell system will be serving about 28 million more households—a 50 percent increase.

1. Assume that the Bell System is able to meet its increasing demand for services primarily through automation of clerical, operator, and technical positions without changing its total employment. What implications exist for meeting future staffing needs?

2. How might detailed staffing tables help the Bell System reduce the number of applicants that must be processed for each new employee hired?

3. Since Mr. Cashel's observations were made, AT&T divested itself of the operating Bell subsidiaries. What are the implications for AT&T's long-range human resource plan?

REFERENCES

1.   James W. Walker, "Linking Human Resources Planning and Strategic Planning," *Human Resource Planning*, Spring 1978, p. 2.

2.   George T. Milkovich and Thomas A. Mahoney, "Human Resource Planning Models: A Perspective," in James W. Walker (ed.), *The Challenge of Human Resource Planning: Selected Readings*, New York: Human Resource Planning Society, 1979, pp. 73–84.

3.   Eddie C. Smith, "Strategic Business Planning and Human Resources: Part I," *Personnel Journal*, August 1982, pp. 606–610. (Part II appears in *Personnel Journal*, September 1982, pp. 680–682.)

4.   Herbert Heneman and G. Seltzer, *Employer Manpower Planning and Forecasting* (Manpower Research Monograph No. 19), Washington, D.C.: U.S. Department of Labor, 1970, p. 42.

5.   Elmer H. Burack, *Strategies for Manpower Planning and Programming,* Morristown, N.J.: General Learning, 1972, pp. 1–6.

6.   Morgan Lyons, "The Older Employee as Resource: Issues for Personnel," *Personnel Journal,* March 1981, pp. 178, 180, 184. See also James W. Walker and Harriet L. Lazer, *The End of Mandatory Retirement,* New York: Wiley, 1978.

7.   Smith, op. cit. See also Walker, op. cit.; and David R. Leigh, "Business Planning Is People Planning," *Personnel Journal,* May 1984, pp. 44, 47–48, 50, 52, 54.

8.   Gregory Moorhead, "Qualitative Factors of Corporare Fit in Mergers and Acquisitions," *The Merger/Acquisition Consultant,* Dallas: Pritchard and Associates, 1982.

9.   Richard B. Frantzreb, "Human Resource Planning: Forecasting Manpower Needs," *Personnel Journal,* November 1981, pp. 850–857; see also Norman Scarborough and Thomas W. Zimmerer, "Human Resources Forecasting: Why and Where to Begin," *Personnel Administrator,* May 1982, pp. 55–61.

10.   James W. Walker, *Human Resource Planning,* New York: McGraw-Hill, 1980, pp. 105, 124–125.

11.   Don Bryant, "Manpower Planning Models and Techniques," *Business Horizons,* April 1973, pp. 69–73; also see David J. Bartholomew, "Statistics in Human Resource Planning," *Human Resource Planning,* November 1978, pp. 67–77.

12.   James W. Walker, "Evaluating the Practical Effectiveness of Human Resource Planning Applications," *Human Resource Management,* Spring 1974, p. 21; Paul Pakchan, "Effective Manpower Planning," *Personnel Journal,* October 1983, pp. 826–830.

13.   Douglas B. Gehrman, "Objective Based Human Resources Planning," *Personnel Journal,* December 1981, pp. 942–946.

14.   David L. Chicci, "Four Steps to an Organizational/Human Resource Plan," *Personnel Journal,* June 1979, p. 392.

15.   James W. Walker, "Human Resource Planning: Managerial Concerns and Practices," *Business Horizons,* June 1976, pp. 56–57.

16.   "Respecting Employee Privacy," *Business Week,* Jan. 11, 1982, p. 131.

17.   Joan Lindroth, "How to Beat the Coming Labor Shortage," *Personnel Journal,* April 1982, pp. 268–272.

18.   William Bamberger, "Understanding and Applying Demographic Information and Techniques," *Personnel Journal,* January 1983, pp. 65–70; also see Eli Ginzberg, *The Manpower Connection,* Cambridge, Mass.: Harvard University Press, 1975.

19.   "Washington Tightens Its Grasp on CETA," *Business Week,* Oct. 3, 1977, pp. 120, 124.

20.   *Employment and Training Report of the President,* Washington, D.C.: U.S. Government Printing Office, 1980.

21.   Donald E. Pursell, "Planning for Tomorrow's Personnel Problems," *Personnel Journal,* July 1981, pp. 559–561. See also Malcolm H. Morrison, "Retirement and Human Resource Planning for the Aging Work Force," *Personnel Administrator,* June 1984, pp. 151–152, 154–159.

114

22. Kendrith M. Rowland and Scott L. Summers, "Human Resource Planning: A Second Look," *Personnel Administration,* December 1981, pp. 73–80; see also William H. Hoffman and L. L. Wyatt, "Human Resource Planning," *The Personnel Administrator,* January 1977, pp. 19–23.

23. Dane Henriksen, "Outplacement: Guidelines That Ensure Success," *Personnel Journal,* August 1982, pp. 583–589; also see Joel A. Bearak, "Termination Made Easier: Is Outplacement Really the Answer?" *Personnel Administrator,* April 1982, pp. 63–71, 99; Jack Mendleson, "Does Your Company Really Need Outplacement?" *SAM Advanced Management Journal,* Winter 1975, pp. 4–12; Jack Mendleson, "What's Fair Treatment for Terminated Employees?" *Supervisory Management,* November 1974, pp. 25–34; and Donald H. Sweet, *Decruitment: A Guide for Managers,* Menlo Park, Calif.: Addison-Wesley, 1975.

The attempt to account for, understand, and use human resource information is one of the more significant challenges faced today.

William P. Anthony[1]

To be concerned about the design of work is to be concerned about tapping the tremendous wellspring of productivity tied up in the motivation of people to perform.

Richard W. Woodman and John J. Sherwood[2]

JOB ANALYSIS AND DESIGN

CHAPTER OBJECTIVES

After studying this chapter, you should be able to:

1 <u>Explain</u> why personnel departments must have job analysis information.

2 <u>List</u> the major methods of collecting job analysis information.

3 <u>Describe</u> the content of a job description.

4 <u>Identify</u> the efficiency and behavioral considerations in job design.

5 <u>Discuss</u> the different job-redesign techniques used to improve jobs and improve the quality of work life.

6 <u>Explain</u> how a human resource information system affects most other personnel activities.

J obs are at the core of every organization's productivity. If they are designed well and done right, the organization makes progress toward its objectives. Otherwise, productivity suffers, profits fall, and the organization is less able to meet the demands of society, customers, employees, and others with a stake in its success. The importance and implications of well-designed jobs are, perhaps, best illustrated by an example.

Jobs are at the core
of productivity.

> Monsanto Company's central accounts payable department in St. Louis, Missouri, began a pilot project in job redesign. Called work effectiveness, their innovative approach to restructuring office jobs led to increased productivity, lower costs, improved quality of services, and greater job satisfaction among workers.[3]
>
> The job-redesign effort resulted from an increase in the number of invoices and a decrease in the quality and timeliness of the department's performance. Consultants conducted workshops and taught members of a task force to apply job diagnostic tools to the department's work. Interviews and surveys of incumbents provided additional inputs. As a result, the work effectiveness program redesigned jobs and "helped the department achieve (1) an increase of 12.3% in invoices processed, (2) cost savings (in salaries and overtime) of $15,200, (3) job restructuring to meet the growth needs of workers by permitting them to fully utilize their capabilities, and (4) the creation of better understanding among workers of . . . the role they play in helping the department reach its objectives."[4]

Monsanto benefits by
changing job design.

Not all attempts to restructure jobs succeed as well as this example from Monsanto. However, improvements in productivity, quality, and cost often begin with the job employees do. For a personnel department to be effective, its members must have a clear understanding of the jobs found throughout organizations. But with hundreds or even thousands of jobs, it is nearly impossible for the personnel professionals at Monsanto to know the details of every job. The solution is an effective human resource information system that contains detailed information about every job in the organization. With this written or electronically stored information, personnel specialists can quickly learn the details of any job. This knowledge is crucial to the success of a personnel department, especially in a large corporation like Monsanto, because it enables personnel specialists to be more proactive in their efforts to assist the organization. Without this information base, they would be less able to redesign jobs, recruit new employees, train present employees, determine appropriate compensation, and perform many other human resource functions.

Adding to the
human resource
information base

This chapter describes how personnel professionals expand their department's information base through job analysis. The chapter concludes by showing how personnel specialists use job analysis information to help design and redesign jobs. Subsequent chapters will detail other applications of job analysis information.

JOB ANALYSIS INFORMATION: AN OVERVIEW

Before a personnel department is created in the organization, line managers handle all personnel matters. Since operating managers are familiar with all the jobs they supervise, they seldom need recorded job information. They already know the characteristics, standards, and human abilities required of the jobs they supervise. As the personnel activities grow in scope and complexity, many of these duties—such as recruiting and compensating—are delegated to the personnel or human resource department. But the people in the personnel department seldom have much knowledge about the jobs in other departments. Knowledge about jobs and their requirements must be collected through job analysis. *Job analysis* systematically collects, evaluates, and organizes information about jobs. These actions are usually done by specialists, called *job analysts*, who gather data about each position but not about every person.

Job analysis defined

For example, suppose Monsanto had fifty accounts payable clerks in its central accounts payable department. Each job is the same since each clerk does the same work—process incoming invoices so they can be paid. Job analysts do not need to study all fifty clerks. Instead, the analyst only needs to review a random sample of these positions. Data collection on a few of these clerical jobs generates an accurate information base for all fifty positions. Simply stated, a job analyst can understand the accounts payable clerk's job without studying the job of each clerk.

Recorded job information plays a crucial role in personnel departments because it affects so many personnel activities. Some of the affected areas are listed in Figure 5-1. For example, without job analysis information, personnel specialists would find it difficult to evaluate how environmental challenges or specific job requirements affect workers' quality of work life. To match job

Job analysis has a broad impact.

Figure 5-1
Major Personnel Management Actions
that Rely on Job Analysis Information

1. *Evaluate* how environmental challenges affect individual jobs.
2. *Eliminate* unneeded job requirements that can cause discrimination in employment.
3. *Discover* job elements that help or hinder the quality of work life.
4. *Plan* for future human resource requirements.
5. *Match* job applicants and job openings.
6. *Determine* training needs for new and experienced employees.
7. *Create* plans to develop employee potential.
8. *Set* realistic performance standards.
9. *Place* employees in jobs that use their skills effectively.
10. *Compensate* jobholders fairly.

applicants to openings, personnel specialists must have an understanding of what each job requires. Similarly, compensation analysts could not be expected to determine a fair salary without detailed knowledge of what a job requires. Although line managers may know the details of every job they supervise, for example, the personnel department must formalize the collection, evaluation, and organization of job analysis information. In fact, research shows that this information is so important that 75 percent of all organizations collect it.[5]

COLLECTION OF JOB ANALYSIS INFORMATION

Job analysts gather information about jobs and jobholder characteristics. Before studying jobs, analysts study the organization—its purpose, design, inputs (people, materials, and procedures), and outputs (products or services).[6] They also review company, industry, and government reports about the work to be analyzed.[7] Armed with a general understanding of the organization and its work, they:

- Identify the jobs to be analyzed
- Develop a job analysis questionnaire
- Collect job analysis information

Job Identification

Analysts identify the different jobs in the organization before they collect job information. This process of job identification is simple in small organizations because there are few jobs. In large companies, analysts may have to construct lists of jobs from payroll records, organization charts, or discussions with workers and supervisors. If job analysis has been done before, analysts may be able to use previous records to identify many of the jobs in the firm.[8]

Questionnaire Development

To study jobs, analysts develop checklists or questionnaires that are sometimes called *job analysis schedules.* Regardless of what they are called, these forms seek to collect job information uniformly. The questionnaire uncovers the duties, responsibilities, human abilities, and performance standards of the jobs investigated. It is important to use the same questionnaire on similar jobs. Analysts want differences in job information to reflect differences in the jobs, not differences in the questions asked. Uniformity is especially hard to maintain in large organizations. When analysts study similar jobs in different departments, only a uniform questionnaire is likely to result in usable data.

Job analysis schedules

After two appliance producers merged, each initially retained its separate personnel department and separate job analysis schedule. As a result, all the production supervisors evaluated by one form had their jobs and pay substantially upgraded. The supervisors in the other plant had identical jobs, but they received only modest pay raises.

Uniformity is essential.

As this example points out, similar jobs should be studied with identical checklists. This does *not* mean that the personnel department is limited to one questionnaire. Job analysts often find that technical, clerical, and managerial jobs require different checklists. Different checklists, however, should never be applied to similar jobs.

What are the questions asked in a job analysis questionnaire? Figure 5-2 shows an abbreviated sample form. The major parts are discussed in the following paragraphs.

Status and identification   The first two headings in the figure show how current the information is and identify the job being described. Without these entries, users of job analysis data may rely on out-of-date information or apply it to the wrong job. Since most jobs change over time, outdated information may misdirect other personnel activities.

> Job analysis information about the position of billing clerk at Brevard General Hospital had not been collected for two years. This outdated information indicated that bookkeeping experience was the major skill needed. But since the hospital's entire billing system recently had been computerized, bookkeeping skills actually were unimportant. Instead, new billing clerks needed typing skills to process billing information into the computer.

Duties and responsibilities   Many forms briefly explain the purpose of the job, what it does, and how it is performed. This summary provides a quick overview of the job. The specific duties and responsibilities are listed to give a more detailed insight into the position. Questions on responsibility are expanded significantly when the checklist is applied to management jobs. Additional questions map areas of responsibility for decision making, controlling, organizing, planning, and other management functions.

Matching people to jobs

Human characteristics and working conditions   Besides information about the job, analysts need data about the people who do the work. This section of the checklist uncovers the particular knowledge, skills, abilities, training, education, experience, and other characteristics that jobholders should possess. These facts are invaluable when filling job openings or advising workers about new job assignments or career planning. Information about the job environment also improves the understanding of the job. Working conditions may explain the need for particular skills, training, knowledge, or even a particular job design. Knowledge of hazards allows the personnel department to redesign the job or protect workers through training and safety equipment. Unique working conditions influence hiring, placement, and compensation decisions.

> During World War II, one airplane manufacturer had problems installing fuel tanks inside the wings of the bombers it was building. The crawl space was extremely narrow and cramped. These tight conditions caused consid-

BREVARD GENERAL HOSPITAL
Job Analysis Questionnaire

(Form 110-JAQ)

A. Job Analysis Status
   1. Job analysis form revised on _____
   2. Previous revisions on _____
   3. Date of job analysis for specified job _____
   4. Previous analysis on _____
   5. Job analysis is conducted by _____
   6. Verified by _____

B. Job Identification
   1. Job title _____   2. Other titles _____
   3. Division(s) _____   4. Department(s) _____
   5. Supervisor(s) title _____

C. Job Summary
Briefly describe purpose of job, what is done, and how. _____
_____

D. Duties
   1. The primary duties of this job are best classified as:

      _____ Medical   _____ Technical   _____ Managerial
      _____ Clerical   _____ Professional

   2. List *major* duties and the proportion of time each involves:

      a. _____, _____ %
      b. _____, _____ %
      c. _____, _____ %

   3. List other duties and the proportion of time each involves:

      a. _____, _____ %
      b. _____, _____ %
      c. _____, _____ %

   4. What constitutes successful performance of these duties? _____
_____

   5. To perform these duties, how much training is needed for normal performance?
_____
_____

Figure 5-2
A Job Analysis Questionnaire

erable production delays. When the personnel department learned about this situation, it recruited welders who were less than 5 feet tall and weighed under 100 pounds.

Performance standards The job analysis questionnaire also seeks information about job standards that are used to evaluate performance. This information is collected on jobs with obvious and objective standards of

E. Responsibility

1. What are the responsibilities found in this job and how significant are these responsibilities?

Significance of Responsibility

Responsibility for:	Minor	Major
a. Equipment operation		
b. Use of tools		
c. Materials usage		
d. Protection of equipment		
e. Protection of tools		
f. Protection of materials		
g. Personal safety		
h. Safety of others		
i. Other's work performance		
j. Other (Specify _____)		

F. Human Characteristics/Job Specifications

1. What physical attributes are necessary to perform the job? _____
_____
_____

2. Of the following characteristics, which ones are needed and how important are they?

Characteristic	Unneeded	Helpful	Essential
1. Vision			
2. Hearing			
3. Talking			
4. Sense of smell			
5. Sense of touch			
6. Sense of taste			
7. Hand-eye coordination			
8. Overall coordination			
9. Strength			
10. Height			
11. Health			
12. Initiative			
13. Ingenuity			
14. Judgment			
15. Attention			
16. Reading			
17. Arithmetic			
18. Writing			
19. Education (Level ____)			
20. Other (Specify _____)			

Figure 5-2
(Continued)

3. Experience for this job:

——————— a. Unimportant

——————— b. Includes ——————— (months) as (job title) ———————————

4. Can training be substituted for experience?

——————— Yes   How: ———————————————————————————————

——————— No   Why: ———————————————————————————————

G. Working Conditions

1. Describe the physical conditions under which this job is performed.———————

——

2. Are there unusual psychological demands connected with this job?———————

——

3. Describe any conditions under which the job is performed that make it unique.

——

——

H. Health or Safety Features

1. Describe fully any health or safety hazards associated with this job. ———————

——

——

2. Is any safety training or equipment required? ———————————————————

——

I. Performance Standards

1. How is the performance of this job measured? ————————————————

——

2. What identifiable factors contribute most to the successful performance of this job?

——

J. Miscellaneous Comments

Are there any aspects of this job that should be noted? ——————————————

——

——

————————————————————   ————————————————
Job Analyst's Signature   Date Completed

Figure 5-2
(Continued)

performance. When standards are not readily apparent, job analysts may ask supervisors or industrial engineers to develop reasonable standards of performance.

Data Collection

There is no best way to collect all the information found on the job analysis questionnaire. Analysts must evaluate the trade-offs between time, cost, and accuracy associated with the use of interviews, juries of experts, questionnaires, employee logbooks, observations, or some combination of these techniques.[9]

Interviews Face-to-face interviews are an effective way to collect job information. The analyst has the job checklist as a guide but can add other questions where needed. Although the process is slow and expensive, it allows the interviewer to explain unclear questions and probe into uncertain answers. Both jobholders and supervisors are usually interviewed. The analyst often talks with a limited number of workers first. Then interviews with supervisors verify the information. This pattern ensures a high level of accuracy.

Jury of experts Another expensive and time-consuming method is to use a jury of experts. The jury consists of senior job incumbents and immediate supervisors. Together the group represents considerable knowledge and experience about the job. To get the job analysis information, the analyst conducts an interview with the group. The interaction of the members during the interview can add insight and detail that the analyst might not get from individual interviews. A side benefit of this process can be a clarification of expected job duties among workers and supervisors who are on the jury.[10]

Mail questionnaires A fast and less costly option is a mail questionnaire developed from the job analysis checklist. This approach allows many jobs to be studied at once and at little cost. However, there is less accuracy because of misunderstood questions, incomplete responses, and unreturned questionnaires. Supervisors can also be given mail questionnaires to verify employee responses.

Employee log An employee log or diary is another option. Workers periodically summarize their tasks and activities in the log. If entries are made over the entire job cycle, the diary can prove quite accurate. It may even be the only feasible way to collect job information.

> A New York public relations firm has three dozen account executives. Each handles a bewildering array of activities for clients. Since interviews and questionnaires often overlooked major parts of the job, the personnel department suggested a logbook. Most account executives initially resisted, but eventually they agreed to a one-month trial. The personnel department obtained the information it wanted, and account executives learned how they *actually* spent their days.

Logs are not a popular technique. They are time-consuming for jobholders and personnel specialists. This makes them costly. Managers and workers often see them as a nuisance and resist their introduction. And after the novelty wears off, accuracy may decline as entries become infrequent.

Observation Another approach is direct observation. It is slow, costly, and potentially less accurate than other methods. Accuracy may be low because the analysts may miss irregularly occurring activities. But observation is the preferred method in some situations. When analysts question data from other techniques, observation may confirm or remove doubts. Language barriers may cause observation to be used, especially with foreign-language workers.

Combinations Since each method has faults, analysts often rely on combinations. That is, two or more techniques are used concurrently.

The typical method

A lumber company has six facilities scattered throughout the United States and Canada. To interview a few workers and supervisors at each facility was considered prohibitively expensive; to rely only on questionnaire data was thought to be too inaccurate. So the personnel department interviewed selected employees at the home office and sent questionnaires to other facilities.

Combinations can ensure high accuracy at minimum costs, as the lumber company example implies. Personnel departments may even use multiple methods to improve accuracy when all employees are at the same location. Regardless of the technique used, the job analysis information is of little value until analysts convert it into more usable forms.

APPLICATIONS OF JOB ANALYSIS INFORMATION

Through preparation and collection phases of job analysis (Figure 5-3) personnel departments obtain information about jobs. This information is put into such usable forms as job descriptions, job specifications, and job standards. Together, these applications of job analysis information provide a minimum human resource information system.

Job Descriptions

A *job description* is a written statement that explains the duties, working conditions, and other aspects of a specified job. Within a firm, all the job descriptions should follow the same format, although between companies form and content may vary. One approach is to write a narrative description in a few paragraphs. Another way is to break down the description into several subparts, illustrated in Figure 5-4.[11] This figure shows a job description that parallels the job analysis checklist, which originally generated the data.

Figure 5-3
The Three Phases of Job Analysis Information

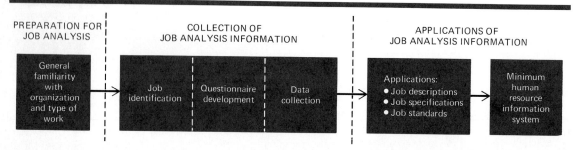

PREPARATION FOR JOB ANALYSIS	COLLECTION OF JOB ANALYSIS INFORMATION			APPLICATIONS OF JOB ANALYSIS INFORMATION	
General familiarity with organization and type of work	Job identification	Questionnaire development	Data collection	Applications: • Job descriptions • Job specifications • Job standards	Minimum human resource information system

BREVARD GENERAL HOSPITAL
Job Description

Job Title: Job Analyst   Job Code: 166.088

Date: January 3, 1985   Author: John Doakes

Job Location: Personnel Department   Job Grade:

Supervisor: Harold Grantinni   Status: Exempt

Job Summary: Collects and develops job analysis information through
              interviews, questionnaires, observation, or other
              means. Provides other personnel specialists with needed
              information.

Job Duties: Designs job analysis schedules and questionnaires.
              Collects job information.
              Interacts with workers, supervisors, and peers.
              Writes job descriptions and job specifications.
              Reports safety hazards to area manager and safety
              department.
              Verifies all information through two sources.
              Performs other duties as assigned by supervisors.

Working Conditions: Works most of the time in well—ventilated mod-
              ern office. Data collection often requires on—site work
              under every working condition found in company. Works
              standard 8 a.m. to 5 p.m., except to collect second—shift
              data and when traveling (one to three days per month).

The above information is correct as approved by:

(Signed) _____   (Signed) _____
           Job Analyst   Department Manager

Figure 5-4
A Job Description

In a job description, the section on job identity may include a *job code.* Job **Job codes** codes use numbers, letters, or both to provide a quick summary of the job. These codes are useful for comparing jobs. Figure 5-5 explains the code used in the *Dictionary of Occupational Titles* (DOT). It is an all-numeric code that helps arrange jobs into occupational groups. Once grouped, codes can be compared to see what relationships exist between different jobs. The code also identifies relationships between data, people, and things.[12]

The job identity section contains other useful information:

Date. The date is essential. It tells subsequent users how old the description is. The older the description, the less likely it is to reflect the current job.

Author. The writer of the description is identified so that questions or errors can be brought to the attention of the author.

Each job in the *Dictionary of Occupational Titles* has a six-digit code. The first digit divides all jobs into nine occupational categories.

0.
1. } Professional, technical, or managerial occupations

2. Clerical and sales occupations
3. Service occupations
4. Farming, fishery, forestry, and related occupations
5. Processing occupations
6. Machine trades occupations
7. Bench work occupations
8. Structural work occupations
9. Miscellaneous occupations

The second and third digits narrow the occupation to one of 603 occupational groups. For example, a job analyst's code is 166.088. The 1 indicates a job analyst is a "professional, technical, or managerial occupation." The first two digits (16) indicate "occupations in administrative specializations." The addition of the third digit (166) classifies the job as being in "personnel and training administration occupations." Thus, from the DOT code, the 166 means a professional, technical, or managerial administrative specialization in personnel or training administration.

The last three digits explain the job's relationship to data (fourth digit), people (fifth digit), and things (sixth digit). The job analyst code of 166.088 means that the analyst synthesizes data but has no significant relationship with people or things.

DATA (FOURTH DIGIT)	PEOPLE (FIFTH DIGIT)	THINGS (SIXTH DIGIT)
0. Synthesizing	0. Mentoring	0. Setting up
1. Coordinating	1. Negotiating	1. Precision working
2. Analyzing	2. Instructing	2. Operating-Controlling
3. Compiling	3. Supervising	3. Driving-Operating
4. Computing	4. Diverting	4. Manipulating
5. Copying	5. Persuading	5. Tending
6. Comparing	6. Speaking-Signaling	6. Feeding-Offbearing
7. No significant	7. Serving	7. Handling
8. relationship	8. No significant relationship	8. No significant relationship

For those familiar with the DOT code, just the six digits of the job analyst's code indicates "a professional, technical, or managerial administrative specialization in personnel or training administration that synthesizes data but bears no significant relationship to people or things." (Compare this explanation with the more verbal explanation in Figure 5-4.)

Source: Dictionary of Occupational Titles (vol. 1), U.S. Department of Labor, 1978, p. xvi.

Figure 5-5
Explanation of Job Codes in
the *Dictionary of Occupational Titles*

• *Location.* The department (or departments) where the job is located helps identify the job for future reference. Location references may include division, plant, or other organization breakdowns.

• *Job grade.* Job descriptions may have a blank for adding the job grade or level. This information helps rank the job's importance for pay purposes.

- *Supervisor.* The supervisor's title may be listed to help identify the job and its relative importance.

- *Status.* Analysts may identify the job as exempt or nonexempt from overtime laws.

Job summary and duties   After the job identification section, the next part of the description is the job summary. It is a written narrative that concisely summarizes the job in a few sentences. It tells what the job is, how it is done, and why. Most authorities recommend that job summaries specify the primary actions involved. Then in a simple, action-oriented style, the job description lists the job duties. Figure 5-4 provides an example of this style.

This section is important to personnel specialists. It explains what the job requires. Since the effectiveness of other personnel actions depends upon an understanding of the job, each major duty is described in terms of the actions expected. Tasks and activities are identified. Performance is emphasized. Even responsibilities are implied or stated within the job duties. If employees are in a union, the union may want to narrow the duties associated with specific jobs.

Emphasize performance.

> Before the union organized, the employee job descriptions contained the phrase "or other work as assigned." The union believed supervisors abused this clause by assigning idle workers to do unrelated jobs. With the threat of a strike, management removed the phrase, and supervisors lost much of their flexibility in assigning work.

Working conditions   A job description also explains working conditions. It may go beyond descriptions of the physical environment. Hours of work, safety and health hazards, travel requirements, and other features of the job expand the meaning of this section.

Approvals   Since job descriptions affect most personnel decisions, their accuracy should be reviewed by selected jobholders and their supervisors. Once acceptable, supervisors are asked to approve the description. This approval serves as a further test of the job description and a further check on the collection of job analysis information. Neither personnel specialists nor managers should consider approval lightly. If the description is in error, the personnel department will become a source of problems, not assistance.

Verification aids accuracy.

> In explaining the job of foundry attendant to new employees, personnel specialists relied on an inaccurate job description. Many new employees quit the job during the first two weeks. When asked why, most said the duties were less challenging than they were led to believe. When analysts checked, they found that the job description had never been verified by the supervisors.

Job Specifications

The difference between a job description and a job specification is one of perspective. A job description defines what the job is; it is a profile of the job. A

The "people
characteristics"

job specification describes what the job demands of employees who do it and the human skills that are required.[13] It is a profile of the human characteristics needed by the person performing the job. These requirements include experience, training, education, and physical and mental demands. Since the job description and specifications both focus on the job, they are often combined into a document. The combination is simply called a job description. Whether part of a job description or a separate document, job specifications include the information illustrated in Figure 5-6. The data to compile specifications also come from the job analysis information collected with the aid of a functional questionnaire or checklist.

Job specifications, if they are a separate document, contain a job identification section. The form lists the skills and effort required by each job—which may include specific tools, actions, experience, education, and training require-

Figure 5-6
A Job Specification Sheet

BREVARD GENERAL HOSPITAL
Job Description

Job Title:	Job Analyst	Job Code:	166.088
Date:	January 3, 1985	Author:	John Doakes
Job Location:	Personnel Department	Job Grade:	
Supervisor:	Harold Grantinni	Status:	Exempt

Skill Factors
Education: College degree required.
Experience: At least one year as job analyst trainee, recruiter,
                    or other professional assignment in personnel area.
Communication: Oral and written skills should evidence ability
                    to capsulize job data succinctly.

Effort Factors
Physical demands: Limited to those normally associated with clerical
                    jobs: sitting, standing, and walking.
Mental demands: Extended visual attention is needed to observe jobs.
                    Initiative and ingenuity are mandatory since job
                    receives only general supervision. Judgment must be
                    exercised on job features to be emphasized, jobs to
                    be studied, and methods used to collect job
                    data. Decision-making discretion is frequent.
                    Analyzes and synthesizes large amounts of abstract
                    information into job descriptions, job specifica-
                    tions, and job standards.

Working Conditions
Travels to hospital clinics in county from one to three days per
month.
Travels around each work site collecting job information.
Works mostly in an office setting.

HOSPITAL ORDERLY

JOB DESCRIPTION STATEMENT ON WORKING CONDITIONS	JOB SPECIFICATIONS INTERPRETATION OF WORKING CONDITIONS
1. Works in physically comfortable surroundings.	1. Must be willing to work inside.
2. Deals with physically ill and diseased patients.	2. Exposed to unpleasant situations and communicable diseases.
3. Deals with mentally ill patients.	3. Exposed to verbal and physical abuse.

Figure 5-7

Translation of Working Conditions
for Job Description to Job Specifications

ments that help clarify individual requirements for successful job performance. Job specifications also describe the physical effort in terms of the actions demanded by the job. Again, specifics are preferred to generalizations. For example, "lifts 100-pound bags" is better than "lifts heavy weights."[14] Specifications of mental effort required of jobholders help personnel experts determine the intellectual abilities that are needed. Figure 5-6 contains several examples of the physical and mental efforts required by jobs in a hospital.

Do the working conditions make any unusual demands on jobholders? The working conditions found in job descriptions may be translated by job specifications into demands faced by workers. Figure 5-7 provides examples for the job of hospital orderly. It shows that a simple statement of working conditions found in the job description can hold significant implications for jobholders. For example, compare points 2 and 3 under the job description column with points 2 and 3 under job specifications.

Job Performance Standards

Job analysis has a third application, *job performance standards*. These standards serve two functions. First, they become objectives or targets for employee efforts. The challenge or pride of meeting objectives may serve to motivate employees. Once standards are met, workers may feel accomplishment and achievement. This outcome contributes to employee satisfaction. Without standards, employee performance may suffer.

Second, standards are criteria against which job success is measured. They are indispensable to managers or personnel specialists who attempt to control work performance. Without standards, no control system can evaluate job performance.[15]

Success criteria aid feedback.

All control systems have four features: standards, measures, correction, and feedback. The relationship between these four factors is illustrated in Figure 5-8. Job performance standards are developed from job analysis information, and then actual employee performance is measured. When measured performance strays from the job standard, corrective action is taken. That is, personnel experts or line managers intervene. The corrective action serves as feedback to

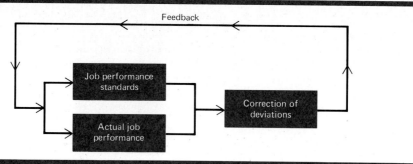

Figure 5-8
Diagram of a Job Control System

the standards and actual performance. This feedback leads to changes in either the standards (if they were inappropriate) or actual job performance.

At a regional Veterans Administration (VA) office, each loan supervisor was expected to review a standard of sixteen VA mortgage applications per day. Actual output averaged twelve. After new job analysis information was collected, analysts discovered that Congress, the VA, and area banks had added new duties since the standard was first set. Corrective action involved new job designs, revised job descriptions, and lower standards.

Job standards are a key part of any control system. When the standards are wrong, as in the VA example, they alert managers and personnel specialists to problems that need correction. The VA example also underscores the need for keeping job analysis information current.

THE HUMAN RESOURCE INFORMATION SYSTEM

Job descriptions, job specifications, and performance standards are the minimum data base needed by personnel departments. Together, these outputs of job analysis information explain each job. Supported with this information, personnel specialists can make intelligent decisions concerning jobs and human resources.[16] But there are two concerns with the minimum human resource information system as it has been explained so far: organization and legal considerations.

Organization of the Data Base

Whether job information is on written forms or in computer memories, it is organized around individual jobs.[17] Although useful, personnel departments also

Job families

need job analysis information that is organized around job families. *Job families* are groups of jobs that are closely related by similar duties, responsibilities, skills, or job elements. The jobs of clerk, typist, clerk-typist, and secretary constitute a job family, for example. These groups allow personnel departments to facilitate permanent job transfers and other personnel decisions.

Job families can be constructed in several ways. One way is to carefully study existing job analysis information. Matching of the data in job descriptions can identify jobs with similar requirements. A second method is to use the codes in the *Dictionary of Occupational Titles*. Similarities in the job codes indicate similarities in jobs. A third approach uses the *position analysis questionnaire.* The position analysis questionnaire (also called the PAQ) is a standardized, preprinted form used to collect specific information about job tasks and worker traits. Through statistical analysis of the PAQ responses, related jobs are grouped into job families.

Legal Considerations

For the most part, job analysis information is an internal matter that is little affected by external challenges. But as personnel specialists rely on job analysis information to pursue other activities, legal considerations arise in the area of equal employment opportunity.[18] As discussed more fully in Chapter 3, *Griggs v. Duke Power Company* provides a classic example of how unneeded job requirements can lead to a violation of equal employment laws.

> In *Griggs v. Duke Power Company,* the employer required a high school degree for nearly all jobs within the company, except those in the labor pool. When the need for a high school diploma was challenged in court, the employer could not show that this job specification was absolutely necessary to perform many of the jobs for which it was required. Although this requirement was applied equally to all applicants, it had an *unequal impact* on minority job applicants. As a result, many blacks were offered jobs only in the labor pool.

As the Duke Power Company case illustrates, it is important for personnel specialists to include in job descriptions and specifications only those items that are job-related.[19] Otherwise, charges of discrimination may result from the unequal impact of some needless job requirement. Even if legal considerations are ignored, needless job requirements exclude potentially qualified individuals from consideration, which can reduce the effectiveness of other personnel activities, such as human resource planning or recruiting.

Unneeded demands may discriminate.

OVERVIEW OF JOB DESIGN

Perhaps the most important reason for understanding how job design affects quality of work life is that *jobs are the link between people and the organization.* Job openings are why organizations need human resources. If personnel departments are going to help the organization obtain and maintain a desired work force, people specialists must have a thorough understanding of job designs.

Jobs link people to organizations.

Figure 5-9 illustrates a systems view of job design. The design of a job reflects the organizational, environmental, and behavioral demands placed on it.[20] Job designers attempt to consider these elements and create jobs that are both productive and satisfying. However, trade-offs among these elements of job design mean that some jobs are more or less satisfying than others. Employee

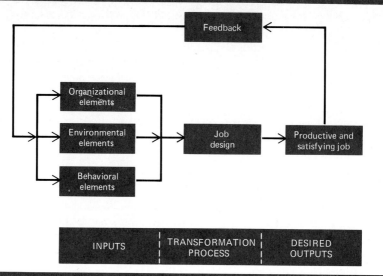

Figure 5-9
The Job Design Input-Output Framework

productivity and satisfaction provide feedback on how well designed a job is. Poorly designed jobs not only lead to low productivity, but they can also cause employee turnover, absenteeism, complaints, sabotage, unionization, resignations, and other problems. Returning to the Monsanto example introduced earlier in the chapter, consider the impact job redesign had in one department.

> In the central accounts payable department at Monsanto, the jobs were perceived as important by the people who did them, but these incumbents did not feel their personal growth needs were being met. Part of the problem stemmed from employees not knowing where their jobs fit into the overall flow of work. In addition, employees felt that they had little autonomy and received little performance feedback.
>
> At the time the job analysis interviews were conducted, the accounts payable jobs were broken down into three phases: processing invoices, handling correspondence over payment discrepancies, and providing general information to vendors and other Monsanto employees about the status of invoices. No one clerk handled all three phases. Each person had important tasks to perform, but no one had entire responsibility for all phases of accounts payable.
>
> The redesign of the jobs gave individual employees full responsibility for groups of accounts. This meant an accounts payable clerk would process invoices, resolve discrepancies, and handle inquiries from vendors and Monsanto employees about "his" or "her" group of accounts. As suggested by Figure 5-9, the environmental and organizational demands by

Monsanto's employees benefit from job design changes.

ORGANIZATIONAL ELEMENTS	ENVIRONMENTAL ELEMENTS	BEHAVIORAL ELEMENTS
• Mechanistic approach • Work flow • Work practices	• Employee abilities and availability • Social expectations	• Autonomy • Variety • Task identity • Task significance • Feedback

Figure 5-10
Elements of Job Design

those outside vendors and Monsanto employees were better met through the redesigned jobs. Feedback was especially affected because now one clerk dealt with a vendor and its in-house counterpart. Perhaps the biggest improvements occurred in the behavioral elements listed in Figure 5-10. With their broader responsibilities, the employees had a greater sense of autonomy in resolving issues. They also felt that their jobs had more variety, significance, and, of course, more feedback. Since they could identify with a set of accounts, they also received a greater sense of task identity because they could point to a completed set of accounts as "theirs."[21]

Job redesign does have some trade-offs. Under the new structure in Monsanto's accounts payable department, each clerk must now have knowledge of both bookkeeping *and* vendor relations. More training for these clerks is likely. And as they become more qualified, Monsanto will have to pay them a higher salary. To explain these trade-offs more fully, a review of the organizational, environmental, and behavioral elements of job design follows. Then the chapter will conclude with a discussion of job-redesign techniques.

Organizational Elements of Job Design

Organizational elements of job design are concerned with efficiency. Efficiently designed jobs allow a highly motivated and capable worker to achieve maximum output. This concern for efficiency was formalized by the management scientists around the turn of the century. They devoted much of their research to finding the best ways to design efficient jobs. Their success with stopwatches and motion pictures even gave rise to a new discipline, industrial engineering. They also contributed to the formal study of management as a separate discipline. From their efforts, we have learned that specialization is a key element in the design of jobs. When workers are limited to a few repetitive tasks, output is usually higher. The findings of these early researchers are still applicable today. They can be summarized under the heading of the mechanistic approach.

Efficiency in job design

Mechanistic approach   The mechanistic approach seeks to identify *every* task in a job so that tasks can be arranged to minimize the time and effort of workers. Once task identification is complete, a limited number of tasks are grouped into a job. The result is *specialization.* Specialized jobs lead to short *job cycles,* the time to complete every task in the job. For example:

Job cycles

An assembly-line worker in Detroit might pick up a headlight, plug it in, twist the adjustment screws, and pick up the next headlight within thirty seconds. Completing these tasks in thirty seconds means this worker's job cycle takes one-half a minute. The job cycle begins when the next headlight is picked up.

Headlight installation is a specialized job. It is so specialized that training takes only a few minutes. And the short job cycle means that the assembler gains much experience in a short time. Said another way, short job cycles require small investments in training and allow the worker to learn the job quickly. Training costs remain low because the worker only needs to master one job.

This mechanistic approach stresses efficiency in effort, time, labor costs, training, and employee learning time. Today, this technique is still widely used in assembly operations. It is especially effective when dealing with poorly educated workers or workers who have little industrial experience. But the efficient design of jobs also considers such organizational elements as work flow and work practices.

Work flow   The flow of work in an organization is strongly influenced by the nature of the product or service. The product or service usually suggests the sequence of and balance between jobs if the work is to be done efficiently. For example, the frame of a car must be built before the fenders and doors can be added. Once the sequence of jobs is determined, then the balance between jobs is established.

Suppose it takes one person thirty seconds to install each headlight. In two minutes, an assembler can put on four headlights. If, however, it takes four minutes to install the necessary headlight receptacles, then the job designer must balance these two interrelated jobs by assigning two people to install the receptacles. Otherwise, a production bottleneck results. Since the work flow demands two receptacle installers for each headlight installer, one worker specializes on the right-side receptacles and another specializes on the left side.

Work practices   Work practices are set ways of performing work. These methods may arise from tradition or the collective wishes of employees. Either way, the personnel department's flexibility to design jobs is limited, especially when such practices are part of a union-management relationship. Failure to consider work practices can have undesired outcomes.

Poor job design contributes to strike at G.M.

General Motors decided to increase productivity at its Lordstown, Ohio, plant by eliminating some jobs and adding new tasks to others. These design changes caused workers to stage a strike for several weeks because traditional practices at the plant had required a slower rate of production and less work by the employees. The additional demands on their jobs by management were seen as an attempt by the company to disregard past work practices.[22]

Environmental Elements of Job Design

A second aspect of job design concerns environmental elements. As with most personnel activities, job designers cannot ignore the influence of the external environment. In designing jobs, personnel specialists and managers should consider the ability and availability of potential employees. At the same time, social expectations also have to be weighed.

Employee abilities and availability Efficiency considerations must be balanced against the abilities and availability of the people who are to do the work. When Henry Ford made use of the assembly line, for example, he was aware that most potential workers lacked any automobile-making experience. So jobs were designed to be simple and require little training. Thought must be given to who will actually do the work. An extreme example underlines this point.

> Governments of less developed countries often think they can "buy" progress. To be "up to date," they seek the most advanced equipment they can find. Leaders of one country ordered a computerized oil refinery. This decision dictated a level of technology that exceeded the abilities of the country's available work force. As a result, these government leaders have hired Europeans to operate the refinery.

In less developed nations, the major risk is jobs that are too complex. Jobs that are too simple can produce equally disturbing problems in industrial nations with highly educated workers. For example, even when unemployment rates are high, many simple and overly specialized jobs are sometimes hard to fill, as long-standing newspaper want ads for dishwashers and janitors attest.

Social expectations The acceptability of a job's design is also influenced by the expectations of society. For example, many uneducated immigrants to this country during the early days of the railroad and automobile industries readily accepted highly specialized jobs that demanded long hours and hard physical labor. Often they had fled countries where jobs were unavailable; this made a job—any job—acceptable to them. Today, industrial workers are much better educated and have higher expectations about the quality of work life. Although work flow or work practices may suggest a particular job design, the job must meet the expectations of workers. Failure to consider these social expectations can create dissatisfaction, low motivation, hard-to-fill job openings, and a low quality of work life.

Today's expectations differ.

Behavioral Elements of Job Design

Jobs cannot be designed by using only those elements that aid efficiency. To do so overlooks the human needs of the people who are to perform the work.

Instead, job designers draw heavily on behavioral research to provide a work environment that helps satisfy individual needs. Higher-level needs are of particular importance. (See Chapter 15 for a more detailed discussion of human needs.) One pair of researchers provided a useful framework when they suggested:

People with a strong desire to satisfy higher order needs perform their best when placed on jobs that were high on certain dimensions. These were:

- Autonomy—responsibility for work

- Variety—use of different skills and abilities

- Task identity—doing the whole piece of work

- Feedback—information on performance[23]

Task significance should be added to the list because people like to feel that their work has meaning to others inside and outside the organization.

Autonomy   *Autonomy* is having responsibility for what one does. It is the freedom to control one's response to the environment. Jobs that give workers the authority to make decisions provide added responsibilities that tend to increase the employee's sense of recognition and self-esteem. The absence of autonomy, on the other hand, can cause employee apathy or poor performance.[24]

"Freedom on the job"

A common problem in many production operations is that employees develop an "I don't care attitude" because they believe they have no control over their jobs. On the bottling line of a small brewery, teams of workers were allowed to speed up or slow down the rate of the bottling line as long as they met daily production goals. Although total output per shift did not change, there were fewer cases of capping machines jamming or breaking down for other reasons. When asked about this unexpected development, the supervisor concluded, "Employees pride themselves on meeting the shift quota. So they are more careful to check for defective bottle caps before they load the machine."

Variety   A lack of variety may cause boredom. Boredom in turn leads to fatigue, and fatigue causes errors. By injecting variety into jobs, personnel specialists can reduce fatigue-caused errors. Being able to control the speed of the bottling line in the brewery example added variety to the pace of work and probably reduced both boredom and fatigue.

One research study found that diversity of work was partially responsible for effective performance.[25] And another study found that autonomy and variety were major contributors to employee satisfaction.[26]

Task identity   One problem with some jobs is that they lack any *task identity*. Workers cannot point to some complete piece of work. They have little sense of responsibility and may lack pride in the results. After completing their job, they may have little sense of accomplishment. When tasks are grouped so that employees feel they are making an identifiable contribution, job satisfaction may be increased significantly.[27] Again, returning to the Monsanto example, we saw that productivity and satisfaction increased when employees had a set of accounts for which they were expected to process invoices, resolve discrepancies, and handle inquiries. They became responsible for an identifiable and sensible group of tasks.

Task significance   Closely related to task identity is task significance. Doing an identifiable piece of work makes the job more satisfying. Task significance, knowing that the work is important to others in the organization or outside it, makes the job even more meaningful for incumbents. Their personal sense of self-importance is enhanced because they know that others are depending on what they do. Pride, commitment, motivation, satisfaction, and better performance are likely to result.

Does anyone care?

Feedback   When jobs do not give the workers any feedback on how well they are doing, there is little guidance or motivation to perform better. For example, by letting employees know how they are doing relative to the daily production quota, the brewery gives workers feedback that allows them to adjust their efforts. In the Monsanto example, each bookkeeper receives feedback on client errors and is able to implement changes in billing or posting procedures to avoid future problems. In both instances, feedback leads to improved motivation.[28]

BEHAVIORAL AND EFFICIENCY TRADE-OFFS

Behavioral elements of job design tell personnel specialists to add more autonomy, variety, task identity, task significance, and feedback. But efficiency elements point to greater specialization, less variety, and minimum autonomy. Thus, to make jobs more efficient may cause them to be less satisfying. Conversely, satisfying jobs may prove to be inefficient. What should personnel specialists do? There is no simple solution. Instead, personnel experts often make trade-offs between efficiency and behavioral elements. Figure 5-11 depicts the most significant trade-offs faced by job designers in the personnel department.

Graph A: Productivity versus Specialization

The assumption that additional specialization means increased output is true only up to some point. As jobs are made more specialized, productivity climbs until behavioral elements such as boredom offset the advantages of further specialization. In Figure 5-11A, additional specialization beyond point *b* causes productivity to drop. In fact, jobs that are between *b* and *c* can have their productivity *increased* by reducing the degree of specialization.

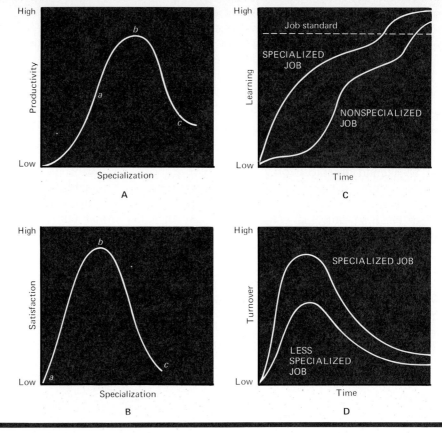

Figure 5-11
Efficiency versus Behavioral Trade-offs in Job Design

Graph B: Satisfaction versus Specialization

Another interesting relationship exists between satisfaction and specialization. Here satisfaction first goes up with specialization, and then additional specialization causes satisfaction to drop quickly. Jobs without any specialization take too long to learn; frustration is decreased and feedback is increased by adding some specialization. However, when specialization is carried past point *b* in Figure 5-11B, satisfaction drops because of a lack of autonomy, variety, and task identification. Notice that even while satisfaction is falling in graph B, productivity may still increase in graph A, from *a* to *b*. Productivity continues to go up only if the advantages of specialization outweigh the disadvantages of dissatisfaction.

Graph C: Learning versus Specialization

When a job is highly specialized, there is less to learn. Therefore, it take less time to learn a specialized job than a nonspecialized one. Graphically, this means that the rate of learning reaches an acceptable standard more quickly (shown as a dashed line).

Graph D: Turnover versus Specialization

Although overspecialized jobs are quicker to learn, the lower levels of satisfaction generally associated with them can lead to higher turnover rates. When turnover rates are high, redesigning the job with more attention to behavioral elements may reduce this quit rate.

TECHNIQUES OF JOB REDESIGN

The central question often facing job designers is whether a particular job should have more or less specialization. As can be seen in graph A in Figure 5-11, the answer depends on whether the job is near point *a, b,* or *c.* Jobs near point *a* may need more specialization to become more effective. Analysis and experimentation are the only sure ways to determine where a particular job is located on the graph.

Underspecialization

When personnel specialists believe jobs are not specialized enough, they engage in *work simplification*. That is, the job is simplified. The tasks of one job may be assigned two jobs. Unneeded tasks are identified and eliminated. What is left are jobs that contain fewer tasks.

More specialization may be a solution.

> When the *Allyndale Weekly Newspaper* operated with its old press, Guy Parsons could catch the newspapers as they came off the press, stack them, and wrap them. But when a new high-speed press was added, he could not keep up with the output. So the circulation manager simplified Guy's job by making him responsible for stacking the newspapers. Two part-time high school students took turns catching and wrapping.

The risk with work simplification is that jobs may be so specialized that boredom causes errors or resignations. This potential problem is more common in advanced industrial countries that have a highly educated work force. In less developed countries, highly specialized factory jobs may be acceptable and even appealing because they provide jobs for workers with limited skills.

Overspecialization

As the labor force in advanced industrial societies becomes more educated and affluent, routine jobs that are very specialized, such as assembly-line positions, hold less and less appeal for many people. These jobs seldom offer opportunities for accomplishment, recognition, psychological growth, or other sources of satisfaction. To increase the quality of work life for those who hold such jobs, personnel departments can use a variety of methods to improve jobs through redesign. The most widely practiced techniques include job rotation, job enlargement, and job enrichment.

Less specialization may be a solution.

Job rotation   *Job rotation* moves employees from job to job. Jobs themselves are not actually changed; only the workers are rotated. Rotation breaks the monotony of highly specialized work by calling on different skills and abilities. The organization benefits because workers become competent in several jobs rather than only one. Knowing a variety of jobs helps the worker's self-image, provides personal growth, and makes the worker more valuable to the organization.

Personnel experts should caution those who desire to use job rotation. It does not improve the jobs themselves; the relationships between tasks, activities, and objectives remain unchanged. It may even postpone the use of more effective techniques while adding to training costs. Implementation should occur only after other techniques are considered.

Job enlargement   *Job enlargement* expands the number of related tasks in the job. It adds similar duties to provide greater variety. Enlargement reduces monotony by expanding the job cycle and drawing on a wider range of employee skills. According to one summary of job design research:

IBM and Maytag enlarge jobs.

IBM reported job enlargement led to higher wages and more inspection equipment, but improved quality and worker satisfaction offset these costs.

Maytag Company claimed that production quality was improved, labor costs declined, worker satisfaction and overall efficiency were increased, and management production schedules became more flexible.[29]

Job enrichment   *Job enrichment* adds new sources of need satisfaction to jobs. It increases responsibility, autonomy, and control. Adding these elements to jobs is sometimes called *vertical loading. Horizontal loading* occurs when the job is expanded by simply adding related tasks, as with job enlargement. Job enrichment sees jobs as consisting of three elements: plan, do, and control.[30] Job enlargement (or horizontal loading) adds more things to *do*. Enrichment (or vertical loading) attempts to add more *planning* and *control* responsibilities. These additions to the job coupled with rethinking the job itself often lead to increased motivation and other improvements, as was seen in the Monsanto example. A similar example comes from one of the former members of AT&T's Bell System.

Ohio Bell enriches jobs.

The Ohio Bell Telephone Company reported that the work force needed to compile directories in one office declined from 120 to 74 as the result of job enrichment and other changes.[31]

Directory compilation improvements resulted from allowing individual clerks to have broad responsibility for entire rural (small) directories or identifiable sections of large metropolitan directories. Prior to the change, each clerk's activities were narrowly defined with close controls, little task identity, and limited autonomy. Vertical and horizontal loading lengthened job cycles, added task identity and autonomy, reduced turnover, increased productivity, and lowered labor costs.

Job enrichment, however, is not a cure-all. If it were, this book could end here. Instead, job enrichment techniques are merely tools. They are not applied universally. When the diagnosis indicates that jobs are unrewarding and unchallenging and that they limit the motivation and satisfaction of employees, personnel departments *may* find job enrichment to be the most appropriate strategy. Even then, job enrichment faces problems. One author listed twenty-two reasons against job enrichment.[32] The most compelling points are union resistance, cost of design and implementation, and limited research on the long-term effects of enrichment. Another criticism of job enrichment is that it does not go far enough. To enrich the job and ignore other variables that contribute to the quality of work life may simply increase dissatisfaction with the unimproved aspects of the job environment.[33]

SUMMARY

Job analysis information provides the foundations of an organization's human resource information system. Analysts seek to gain a general understanding of the organization and the work it performs. Then they design job analysis questionnaires to collect specific data about jobs, jobholder characteristics, and job performance standards. The job analysis information can be collected through interviews, juries of experts, mail questionnaires, employee logs, direct observation, or some combination of these techniques. Once collected, the data are converted into such useful applications as job descriptions, job specifications, and job standards.

Job analysis information is important because it tells personnel specialists what duties and responsibilities are associated with each job. This information is then used when personnel specialists undertake other personnel management activities such as job design, recruiting, and selection. Jobs are the link between organizations and their human resources. The combined accomplishment of every job allows the organization to meet its objectives. Similarly, jobs represent not only a source of income to workers but also a means for fulfilling their needs. However, for the organization and its employees to receive these mutual benefits, jobs must provide a high quality of work life.

To achieve a high quality of work life requires jobs that are well designed. Effective job design seeks a trade-off between efficiency and behavioral elements. Efficiency elements stress productivity. Behavioral elements focus on employee needs. The role of personnel specialists is to achieve a balance between these trade-offs. When jobs are underspecialized, job designers may simplify the job by reducing the number of tasks. If jobs are overspecialized, they must be expanded or enriched.

TERMS FOR REVIEW

Job analysis

Job analysis schedule

Job description

Job code

Dictionary of Occupational Titles (DOT)

Job specifications

Job performance standards

Job families   Task identity

Position analysis questionnaire   Task significance

Specialization   Work simplification

Job cycle   Job rotation

Autonomy   Job enrichment

REVIEW AND DISCUSSION QUESTIONS

1. What types of raw data do the questions on a job analysis checklist seek to obtain? Are there other data you should seek for management jobs?

2. What are the different methods of collecting job analysis information, and what are the advantages and disadvantages of each technique?

3. Describe three ways jobs can be grouped into job families.

4. Suppose you were assigned to write the job descriptions in a shirt factory in Tucson, Arizona, that employed mostly Mexican immigrants who spoke little English. What methods would you use to collect job analysis data?

5. If a manager in the shirt factory refused to complete a job analysis questionnaire, what reasons would you use to persuade this reluctant manager?

6. If, after your best efforts at persuasion failed, you still wanted job analysis information on the manager's job, how would you get it?

7. What are some of the problems you would expect to arise in an organization that had carefully designed its jobs for maximum efficiency without careful consideration of each employee's individual priority of needs?

8. Suppose you have been assigned to design the job of ticket clerk for an intrastate airline. How would you handle the following trade-offs?
    a. Would you recommend highly specialized job designs to minimize training or very broad jobs with all clerks cross-trained to handle multiple tasks? Why?
    b. Would you change your answer if you knew that employees tended to quit the job of ticket clerk within the first six months? Why or why not?

9. Assume you are told to evaluate a group of jobs in a boat-building business. After studying each job for a considerable amount of time, you identify the following activities associated with each job. What job-redesign techniques would you recommend for these jobs, if any?
    a. *Sailmaker.* Cuts and sews material with very little variety in the type of work from day to day. Job is highly skilled and takes years to learn.

b. *Sander.* Sands rough wood and fiberglass edges almost continuously. Little skill is required in this job.

c. *Sales representative.* Talks to customers, answers phone inquiries, suggests customized additions to special-order boats.

d. *Boat preparer.* Cleans up completed boats, waxes fittings, and generally makes the boat ready for customer delivery. Few skills are required for this job.

INCIDENT 5-1

Hedges Electronics Computerized Job Data

Hedges Electronics is a small manufacturer of remote access consoles, cathode-ray-tube display terminals, and other on-line computer equipment. The remote consoles and cathode displays are widely used within the company. Through the consoles, most managers can store and retrieve data from the company's mainframe computer. This information appears on cathode-ray displays, which are similar to small television screens.

Since most line and staff managers were familiar with on-line equipment, it was decided to store the human resource information system on the main computer. Then when managers or personnel specialists needed a job description, they could simply secure one from the computer.

After computerizing all human resource information, job analysts began to notice that job descriptions, job specifications, and job standards were being changed by jobholders. Whenever a manager or worker reviewed a job description or job specification that seemed outdated, they would "write in" a correction on the computer's memory.

In the beginning, personnel specialists were glad that workers were taking an interest in updating the computerized job analysis information. But workers with the same job title had different views of their job. Since changes could come from almost anyone, there was no consistency in style of content.

A subroutine was programmed into the computer that prevented unauthorized changes. Job analysts then reviewed the job descriptions and job specifications to ensure uniformity of style. Line and staff managers could still obtain copies of job analysis information.

1. Assuming you are the personnel manager at Hedges, what steps would you want followed to ensure that the restudied job analysis information was correct?

2. Given the ability of most managers to "communicate" directly with the computer, does Hedges Electronics have a new way to collect job analysis information? Explain.

EXERCISE 5-1

Preparation of a Job Description

As discussed in the chapter, there are several ways to collect job analysis information. One way is through observation. Using the form in Figure 5-2, complete parts C through J for the job of professor. After you have completed those sections of the job analysis questionnaire, use the format in Figure 5-4 and write a job description for the job of professor. When finished, look up the definition of professor provided in the *Dictionary of Occupational Titles.*

1.   How does the description in the *Dictionary of Occupational Titles* vary in format and content from the one you wrote?

2.   What parts of the professor's job are the most important in your opinion?

EXERCISE 5-2

A Good Work Environment

Think of some work-related situation that you found enjoyable. In thinking about that job, identify the features of the job that made it more enjoyable than the other jobs you have held. The job you think of need not be a formal full-time job. It simply may have been some temporary job or even some chore you had to perform. What were the characteristics of the job that made it so enjoyable? Make a list of those characteristics.

1.   In reviewing your answers with others, do you find any similarities between your list and theirs.

2.   Do these characteristics indicate what job features provide a good work situation?

REFERENCES

1.   William P. Anthony, "Get to Know Your Employees—The Human Resource Information System," *Personnel Journal,* April 1977, p. 179.

2.   Richard W. Woodman and John J. Sherwood, "A Comprehensive Look at Job Design," *Personnel Journal,* August 1977, pp. 384–385.

3.   "Job-Restructuring Plan Adds to Satisfaction of Monsanto Employees," *The Office,* March 1981, pp. 63–64, 68, 74.

4.   Ibid., p. 63.

5.   Jean Jones, Jr., and Thomas A. DeCottis, "Job Analysis: National Survey Findings," *Personnel Journal,* October 1969, p. 805.

6.   For a different approach to developing job analysis information, see Richard I. Henderson, *Compensation Management,* Reston, Va.: Reston Publishing, 1976, pp. 87–107.

7.   Herbert G. Zollitsch and Adolph Langsner, *Wage and Salary Administration,* 2d ed., Dallas: South-Western, 1970, pp. 275–276, 279.

8.   J. D. Dunn and Frank M. Rachel, *Wage and Salary Administration: Total Compensation Systems,* New York: McGraw-Hill, 1971, pp. 139–141.

9.   Ibid., p. 143.

10.   Jerrold Markowitz, "Four Methods of Job Analysis," *Training and Development Journal,* September 1981, pp. 115–117.

11.   Zollitsch and Langsner, op. cit., pp. 290–301. See also Mark A. Jones "Job Descriptions Made Easy," *Personnel Journal,* May 1984, pp. 31–34.

12.   U.S. Department of Labor, *Dictionary of Occupational Titles,* Washington, D.C.: U.S. Superintendent of Publications, 1965, vol. I, p. xvi. For a criticism of this approach, see Edwin T. Cornelius II and William Sanders, "A Scalogram Analysis of the Worker Function Hierarchies," unpublished paper presented at the Academy of Management Meetings, (New York, New York), August 1982.

13.   Zollitsch and Langsner, op. cit., pp. 301–311. See also Allan N. Nash and Stephen J. Carroll, Jr., *The Management of Compensation,* Monterey, Calif.: Brooks/Cole, 1975, pp. 116–117.

14.   Paul Sheibar, "A Simple Selection System Called 'Job Match,'" *Personnel Journal,* January 1979, p. 26.

15.   Donald E. Klingner, "When the Traditional Job Description Is Not Enough," *Personnel Journal,* April 1979, pp. 243–248.

16.   Anthony, op. cit., pp. 179–183, 202–203.

17.   Michael N. Wolfe, "Computerization—It Can Bring Sophistication into Personnel," *Personnel Journal,* June 1978, pp. 325–325, 336.

18.   George R. Wendt, "Should Courts Write Your Job Descriptions?" *Personnel Journal,* September 1976, pp. 442–445, 450. See also Frederick S. Hills, "Job Relatedness vs. Adverse Impact in Personnel Decision Making," *Personnel Journal,* March 1980, pp. 211–215, 229.

19.   Mary Green Miner and John B. Miner, *Employee Selection within the Law,* Washington, D.C.: Bureau of National Affairs, 1978, pp. 329–331.

20.   Bruce H. Johnson, Gregory Moorhead, and Ricky W. Griffin, "Integration of Job Design Variables into a Human Resource Information System: Conceptually Supportable Yet Not Done," unpublished paper, 1981.

21.   "Job Restructuring Plan," op. cit.

22.   Barbara Garson, "Luddites in Lordstown," *Harpers,* June 1972, pp. 68–73.

23.   J. R. Hackman and E. E. Lawler III, "Employee Reactions to Job Characteristics," in W. E. Scott and L. L. Cummings (eds.), *Readings in Organizational Behavior and Human Performance,* Homewood, Ill.: Richard D. Irwin, 1973, p. 231. For a detailed summary of research on job design see C. L. Hulin and M. R. Blood, "Job Enlargement, Individual Differences, and Worker Responses," *Psychological Bulletin,* 1968, pp. 41–55. For a more

recent summarization see Jon L. Pierce and Randall B. Dunham, "Task Design: A Literature Review," *The Academy of Management Review,* October 1976, pp. 83–97; also see Ricky W. Griffin, Ann Welsh, and Gregory Moorhead, "Perceived Task Characteristics and Employee Performance: A Literature Review," *Academy of Management Review,* October 1981, pp. 644–664.

24. Frederick Herzberg, Bernard Mausner, and Barbara Snyderman, *The Motivation to Work,* New York: Wiley, 1959. See also E. F. Stone and L. W. Porter, "Job Characteristics and Job Attitudes: A Multivariate Study," *Journal of Applied Psychology,* 1975, pp. 57–64.

25. G. E. Farris, "Organizational Factors and Individual Performance: A Longitudinal Study," *Journal of Applied Psychology,* 1969, pp. 87–92.

26. Stone and Porter, op. cit.

27. Hackman and Lawler, op. cit.

28. Edward E. Lawler III, "Job Attitudes and Employee Motivation: Theory, Research, and Practice," *Personnel Psychology,* Summer 1970, p. 234.

29. Woodman and Sherwood, op. cit., p. 386.

30. M. Scott Myers, *Every Employee a Manager,* New York: McGraw-Hill, 1970.

31. Robert N. Ford, "Job Enrichment Lessons from AT&T," *Harvard Business Review,* January–February 1973, p. 105.

32. Robert H. Schappe, "Twenty-Two Arguments against Job Enrichment," *Personnel Journal,* February 1974, pp. 116–123.

33. William B. Werther, Jr., "Beyond Job Enrichment to Employment Enrichment," *Personnel Journal,* August 1975, pp. 438–442.

CHAPTER

In many instances, there was no overt discrimination in hiring because there were no applicants from the protected groups and the recruitment system tended to perpetuate the same racial composition of the workforce.

Mary Green Miner and John B. Miner[1]

RECRUITMENT OF HUMAN RESOURCES

CHAPTER OBJECTIVES

After studying this chapter, you should be able to:

1 Describe how human resource planning and job analysis information help recruiters to be more effective.

2 Explain how recruiters can further or obstruct their organization's commitment to equal employment opportunity.

3 Identify the constraints under which the recruitment process occurs.

4 Recognize the appropriate recruiting methods for finding and attracting different types of recruits.

5 Explain the role of state unemployment offices, placement firms, and other organizations that help personnel departments recruit.

6 Develop an appropriate application blank.

Recruitment is the process of finding and attracting capable applicants for employment. The process begins when new recruits are sought and ends when their applications are submitted. The result is a pool of applicants from which new employees are selected. (The process of selecting from among these applicants is the topic of Chapter 7.) Responsibility for recruitment usually belongs to the personnel department. This responsibility is important because the quality of an organization's human resources depends on the quality of its recruits. Since large organizations recruit almost continuously, their personnel departments use specialists in the recruiting process, called *recruiters.*

Recruiters work to find and attract capable applicants. Their methods depend on the situation since there is no best recruiting technique. However, the job descriptions and specifications described in Chapter 5 are essential tools, especially for recruiters in large organizations. With hundreds of jobs to recruit for, it is impossible for recruiters to know the duties and employee requirements of every job. Job descriptions and specifications provide the needed information upon which the recruitment process rests.

Recruitment process Normally, recruiters follow several steps. As Figure 6-1 illustrates, recruiters identify job openings through human resource planning or requests by managers. The human resource plan can be especially helpful because it shows the recruiter both present openings and those expected in the future. As mentioned in Chapter 4, "Human Resource Planning," advanced knowledge of all expected openings allows the recruiter to be proactive. With job openings identified, the recruiter then learns what each job requires by reviewing the job analysis information, particularly the job descriptions and job specifications. This information tells the recruiter the characteristics of both the jobs and the people who will fill them. When the job analysis information appears outdated or seems superficial, recruiters can learn more about a job's requirements from the requesting manager. The potential importance of recruitment to the organization is shown by the following illustration.

Shirley Dodd was a junior mechanical engineer for Blakely Electronics when she quit to work for a competitor. Her resignation created a serious problem in the mechanical engineering department at Blakely. The department manager's reaction was, "She was doing an important job of developing the mechanical tolerances for our new electronic scales. It was

Figure 6-1
An Overview of the Recruitment Process

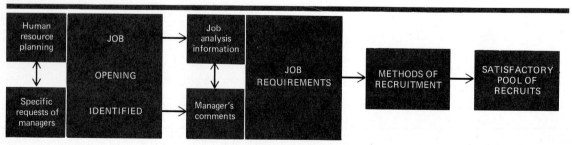

all theoretical work, but it was going to save three months' worth of product development time. We must have a bright junior engineer to complete her work. I hope someone can be recruited quickly."

A recruiter in the personnel department received the request from the head of mechnical engineering and began the recruitment process. First, the recruiter reviewed the job's requirements and discovered that applicants should have a basic understanding of mechanical engineering concepts. Then the recruiter began to seek applicants from among the graduating class of a nearby college.

This illustration implies that several assumptions were made by the recruiter. It assumes that the recruiter is aware of the organizational and environmental constraints that exist at Blakely. It also assumes that the recruiter is aware of other sources of recruits but rejected those options as inferior. Finally, the illustration assumes that the recruiter will find people at the nearby college who are willing to apply for work at Blakely Electronics.

Assumptions recruiters make

These assumptions outline the key issues covered in this chapter: the constraints on recruitment, the channels through which recruits are found and attracted, and the nature of employment applications.

Key issues in chapter

CONSTRAINTS ON RECRUITMENT

Recruiters must be sensitive to the constraints on the recruitment process. These limits arise from the organization, the recruiter, and the external environment. Although the emphasis may vary from situation to situation, the following list includes the most common constraints and challenges faced by recruiters:

- Organizational policies
- Human resource plans
- Affirmative action plans
- Recruiter habits
- Environmental conditions
- Job requirements

Organizational Policies

Organizational policies seek to achieve uniformity, economies, public relations benefits, or other objectives that are sometimes unrelated to recruiting. At times, policies can be a potent source of constraints. Those policies that may affect recruitment are highlighted below.

Promote-from-within policies Promote-from-within policies are intended to give present employees the first opportunity for job openings. These policies are widespread. In one research study, 76 percent of the organizations reported that they fill a majority of their openings internally.[2] Promote-from-within policies aid employee morale, attract recruits looking for jobs with a future, and help retain present employees. When such policies have a disparate impact, the EEOC may rule this approach to be illegal. Although these policies reduce the flow of new people and ideas into different levels of the organization,

Most jobs are filled from within.

the alternative is to pass over employees in favor of outsiders. Bypassing current employees can lead to employee dissatisfaction and turnover. In the junior engineer example, the recruiter should check with present employees—such as technicians who have been studying engineering at night school—before a new engineer is recruited.

Compensation policies   A common constraint faced by recruiters is pay policies. Organizations with personnel departments usually establish pay ranges for different jobs. If the recruiter finds a promising candidate, the pay range will influence the job seeker's desire to become a serious applicant. Recruiters seldom have the authority to exceed stated pay ranges. For example, when the market rate for junior engineers is $2200 to $2400 per month, satisfactory applicants will be few if all a recruiter can offer is $1800 to $2000 per month.

Employment status policies   Some companies have policies on hiring part-time and temporary employees. Although there is growing interest in hiring these types of workers, policies can cause recruiters to reject all but those seeking full-time work. Limitations against part-time and temporary employees exclude 18 percent of the work force in the United States.[3] Likewise, policies against hiring employees who "moonlight" by having second jobs limit recruiters by excluding over 5 percent of the work force.[4] Prohibitions against holding multiple jobs are intended to ensure a rested work force.

International hiring policies   Policies also may require foreign job openings to be staffed with local citizens. The use of foreign nationals, however, reduces relocation expenses, lessens the likelihood of nationalization, and—if top jobs are held by local citizens—minimizes charges of economic exploitation. Unlike relocated employees, foreign nationals are more apt to be involved in the local community and understand local customs and business practices.

Human Resource Plans

HRP affects recruiting.

The human resource plan is another factor that recruiters consider. Through skills inventories and promotion ladders, the human resource plan outlines which jobs should be filled by recruiting outside the firm and which are to be filled internally. A little foresight by a recruiter can lead to considerable economies for the company.

> Suppose, for example, the recruiter at Blakely reviewed the human resource plan and discovered that during the next six months the company was going to need six junior electrical engineers. The recruiter could arrange to recruit both mechanical and electrical engineers on the same recruiting trip. If advertisements were to be placed in the school newspaper, there would be no additional cost for seeking both types of engineers. Travel costs, advertising costs, and the time devoted to a second recruiting trip would be saved.
>
> Since junior engineer is the lowest-level engineering position, it is unlikely that there would be any internal candidates identified in the human resource

plan. However, if the opening had been for a more experienced worker, the human resource planning process may have identified potential candidates from within the company.

Affirmative Action Plans

Before recruiting for any position, the recruiter would want to review the firm's affirmative action plan for guidance. Affirmative action plans (discussed in Chapter 3) may alert a recruiter to the need to recruit more minority or female candidates. When affirmative action needs suggest a greater balance in the mix of employees, recruiters must adjust their plans accordingly. Reconsider Blakely Electronics. If the nearby college graduated primarily white male engineers and Blakely's affirmative action plan uncovered a lack of minority and female engineers, the recruiter at Blakely would want to use different colleges, perhaps those in large cities of the East and South. In one case, *United States v. Georgia Power Company,* the Fifth Circuit Court of Appeals ruled that recruitment only at particular scholastic institutions can exclude members of protected classes. Although recruiting at any one school is not wrong, the effect of such a limited recruitment policy can be to exclude members of protected classes. When that result occurs, the employer may be guilty of discrimination because its recruiting policies have a disparate impact on protected classes.[5]

> AAP affects recruiting.

> U.S. v. Georgia Power Company

Recruiter Habits

A recruiter's past success can lead to habits. Admittedly, habits can eliminate time-consuming decisions that reach the same answers. However, habits may also continue past mistakes or avoid more effective alternatives. Even though recruiters need positive and negative feedback, they must guard against habits, which are self-imposed constraints.

Reconsider the recruitment of the junior engineer at Blakely Electronics. Suppose the engineering department expresses satisfaction with recruits from the nearby college. Such positive feedback encourages recruiters to make a habit of this source for beginning engineers. Since these engineers share a similar curriculum, they may share similar strengths and weaknesses. As a result, the engineering department may suffer because of the educational uniformity of new recruits.

> Habits can be traps.

Environmental Conditions

External conditions strongly influence recruitment. Changes in the labor market and the challenges mentioned in Chapter 2 affect recruiting. The unemployment rate, the pace of the company, spot shortages in specific skills, projections of the labor force by the Department of Labor, labor laws, and the recruiting activities of other employers each impact the recruiter's efforts. Although these factors are considered in human resource planning, the economic environment can change quickly after the plan is finalized. To be sure that the plan's economic assumptions remain valid, recruiters can check three fast-changing measures:

> Quick measures

Leading economic indicators. Each month the U.S. Department of Commerce announces the direction of the leading indicators. These economic indexes suggest the future course of the national economy. If these indexes signal a sudden downturn in the economy, recruiting plans may have to be modified.

• *Predicted versus actual sales.* Since human resource plans are partially based upon the firm's predicted sales, variations between actual and predicted sales may indicate that these plans also are inaccurate. Thus, recruiting efforts may need to be changed accordingly.

• *Want-ads index.* The Conference Board monitors the volume of want ads in major metropolitan newspapers. An upward trend in this index indicates increased competition for engineers and managers who are recruited on a nationwide basis. For clerical and production workers, who are usually recruited on a local basis, the personnel department may want to create its own index to monitor local changes in want ads.

As the economy, sales, and want ads change, recruiters also must adjust their efforts accordingly. Tighter competition for applicants may require more vigorous recruiting efforts. When business conditions decline, an opposite approach is called for, as the following example illustrates.

As a major amusement park was opening in central Florida, the leading economic indicators dropped. Although the human resource plan called for recruiting 100 workers a week for the first month, the employment manager set a revised target of 75. Lower recruiting and employment levels helped establish a profitable operation even though first-year admissions fell below the projections used in the human resource plan.

Job Requirements

Of course, the requirements of each job are a constraint. Highly specialized workers, for example, are more difficult to find than unskilled ones. Recruiters learn how demanding a job is from job analysis information and from conversations with the requesting manager. Knowledge of a job's requirements allows the recruiter to choose the best way to find recruits, given all the other constraints under which the recruiter must operate.

The "find-the-best" pitfall

"Find the best and most experienced applicant you can" is often a constraint that is imposed on recruiters as though it were a job requirement. At first, this demand by a requesting manager seems reasonable. Everyone wants to have the best and most experienced people working for them. However, several potential problems exist with this seemingly innocent request. One problem in seeking out the best and most experienced applicants is cost. People with greater experience usually require a higher salary than less experienced people. If a high level of experience is not truly necessary, the recruit may become bored shortly after being hired. Moreover, if the personnel department cannot show that a high degree of experience is needed, then experience may be an artificial job requirement that discriminates against applicants who are members of protected classes. Another point about experience is worth remembering: For some people in some jobs, ten years of experience is another way of saying one

Ten years of experience may be one year repeated ten times.

year of experience repeated ten times. Someone with ten years of experience may not be any better than an applicant who has only one year of experience.[6]

CHANNELS OF RECRUITMENT

The ways of finding recruits are sometimes referred to as *channels*. Recruiters and applicants historically use a limited number of channels through which they pursue one another. The channels used by workers to seek jobs are summarized in Figure 6-2. As can be seen from the research report in the figure, applying directly to the employer (66 percent), asking friends about jobs where they work (51 percent), and answering local newspaper ads (46 percent) are the most commonly used methods. Managers also use job-hunting techniques that are similar to those shown in Figure 6-2.[7]

Which sources of job information give applicants the best insights about the organization's job? Information that comes from friends and relatives or that

Where are applicants found?

Figure 6-2

Methods Used to Look for Work

JOB SEARCH METHOD	PERCENTAGE WHO USED EACH METHOD
Total number (thousands): 10,437	
Applied to employer without suggestions or referrals.	66
Asked friends:	
About jobs where they work.	51
About jobs elsewhere.	42
Asked relatives:	
About jobs where they work.	28
About jobs elsewhere.	27
Answered newspaper ads:	
Local.	46
Nonlocal.	12
Checked with private employment agency.	21
Checked with state employment service.	34
Contacted school placement office.	12
Took civil service test.	15
Asked teacher or professor for job leads.	10
Checked with union hiring hall.	6
Contacted local organization.	6
Answered ads in professional or trade journals or periodicals.	5
Placed ads in newspapers:	
Local.	2
Nonlocal.	1
Went to place where employers come to pick up people.	1
Placed ads in professional or trade journals or periodicals.	1
Other.	12

Note: The approximately 3.5 million people in this survey who checked for jobs with state employment services do not represent all those who filed new or renewed job applications during 1973.

Source: Carl Rosenfeld, "Jobseeking Methods Used by American Workers," *Monthly Labor Review,* August 1975, p. 40.

NUMBER OF METHODS USED TO FIND A JOB	PERCENTAGE WHO USED EACH METHOD
One method	20
Two methods	18
Three or four methods	26
Five methods or more	36

Source: Carl Rosenfeld, "Jobseeking Methods Used by American Workers," *Monthly Labor Review,* August 1975, p. 42.

Figure 6-3
Number of Methods Used to Find a Job

Most workers use multiple channels.

results from a job seeker applying in person as a walk-in applicant often proves to be the most specific and accurate, according to one researcher.[8] Perhaps that is why Figure 6-3 reveals that a majority (64 percent) of workers use three or more channels to search for employment. The channels used by employers parallel those used by workers in order to achieve a match between job seekers and job openings. Each of these various channels is described below.

Walk-ins and Write-ins

Walk-ins are job seekers who arrive at the personnel department in search of a job. *Write-ins* are those who send a written inquiry. They normally are asked to complete an application blank to determine their interests and abilities. Usable applications are kept in an active file until a suitable opening occurs or until the application is too old to be considered valid, usually six months.

Employee Referrals

Employees may refer job seekers to the personnel department. Employee referrals have several distinctive advantages. First, employees with hard-to-find job skills may know others who do the same work. For example, a shortage of welders on the Alaskan pipeline was partially solved by having welders ask their friends in the "lower forty-eight states" to apply for the many unfilled openings. Second, new recruits already know something about the organization from those employees who referred them. Thus, referred applicants may be more strongly attracted to the organization than are casual walk-ins. Third, employees tend to refer their friends, who are likely to have similar work habits and work attitudes. Even if work values are different, these candidates may have a strong desire to work hard so that they do not let down the person who recommended them.

EEO implications of referrals

Employee referrals are an excellent and legal recruitment technique. However, recruiters must be careful that this method does not intentionally or unintentionally discriminate. The major problem with this recruiting method is that it tends to maintain the status quo of the work force in terms of race, religion, sex, and other features. Those results can be viewed as discriminatory. Returning to the Georgia Power Company case mentioned earlier in this chapter we see that the company not only limited its recruitment to a few scholastic institutions but also made extensive use of employee referrals. As one civil rights expert noted:

In *United States v. Georgia Power Company,* the Fifth Circuit Court of Appeals ruled that the respondents' form of recruitment by referrals from present workers had the effect of excluding blacks because it perpetuated the generally all-white makeup of its employees. The court stated:

> "Word-of-mouth hiring and interviewing for recruitment only at particular scholastic institutions are practices that are neutral on their face. However, under the facts of the instant case, each operates as a 'built-in-headwind' to blacks and neither is justified by business necessity."[9]

A key case

Advertising

Advertising is another effective method of seeking recruits. Since ads can reach a wider audience than employee referrals or unsolicited walk-ins, many recruiters use them as a key part of their efforts.

Want ads describe the job and the benefits, identify the employer, and tell those who are interested how to apply. They are the most familiar form of employment advertising. For highly specialized recruits, ads may be placed in professional journals or out-of-town newspapers located in areas with high concentrations of the desired skills. For example, recruiters in the aerospace industry often advertise in Los Angeles, St. Louis, Dallas–Ft. Worth, and Seattle newspapers because these cities are major aerospace centers.

Want ads have some severe limitations. They may lead to thousands of job seekers for one popular job opening. Or few may apply for less attractive jobs. For example, few people apply for door-to-door sales jobs if they know the product is encyclopedias. Likewise, the ideal recruits are probably already employed and not reading want ads. Finally, secretly advertising for a recruit to replace an incumbent cannot be done with traditional want ads. These limitations are avoided with *blind ads.* A blind ad is a want ad that does not identify the employer. Interested applicants are told to send their résumé to a mailbox number at the post office or to the newspaper. The *résumé*, which is a brief summary of the applicant's background, is then forwarded to the employer. These ads allow the opening to remain confidential, prevent countless telephone inquiries, and avoid the public relations problem of disappointed recruits.

"Blind ads" are useful.

As one writer observed, "Recruitment advertising should be written from the viewpoint of the applicant and his or her motivations rather than exclusively from the point of view of the company."[10] Since the cost of most classified advertising is determined by the size of the advertisement, short blurbs are the norm. These ads usually describe the job duties, outline minimum job qualifications, and tell interested readers how to apply. Short telegraphic phrases and sentences, sometimes written in the second person, are the usual format. Figure 6-4 provides an example. However, some experts doubt that traditional approaches will remain sufficient, particularly when recruiting people with hard-to-find skills or whenever labor markets are tight. As one researcher suggested, employment ads:

What should a want ad say?

> . . . must contain not only information about the job but also information presented in a way that effectively portrays a message about the job and the

Blakely Electronics seeks junior mechanical and electrical engineering trainees for our growing team of engineering professionals. You will work with senior engineers in designing state-of-the-art electronic equipment for home and industry. Qualified applicants will be engineers graduating by the end of this term and wanting immediate employment. Send your résumé and transcripts to: Chuck Norris, Employment Office, Blakely Electronics, P.O. Box 473, Salt Lake City, Utah 84199. Do it today for an exciting career tomorrow.

Blakely Electronics is an equal opportunity employer of minority, female, and handicapped workers.

Figure 6-4
A Sample Want Ad

company. This can't be done if the ad contains information that explains only what responsibilities the job includes, who can be qualified, where it is located, and how and when to apply.[11]

More important, in today's labor market, where increasing demands are being made for job relevance, quality of work life, and other job satisfaction factors . . . the need for more descriptive job information and information concerning working environment, supervisory style and organizational climate are necessary.[12]

Advertisements for recruits through other media—billboards, television, and radio, for example—are seldom used because the results seldom justify the expense. However, these approaches may be useful when unemployment is low and the target recruits are not likely to be reading want ads.[13]

State Employment Security Agencies

Every state government has a *state employment security agency*. Often called the unemployment office or the employment service, these state agencies match job seekers with job openings. The agencies result from a federal and state partnership that was established in 1933. At the federal level, the U.S. Employment Service sets national guidelines. Within these uniform regulations, state agencies operate more than 2400 local offices that help more than one-fifth of all unemployed workers find jobs.

State unemployment offices are changing.

To match candidates with job openings, the employment services in virtually every state use a statewide *job bank*. It works as follows: When an employer has a job opening, the personnel department voluntarily notifies the employment service of the job and its requirements. Then job openings are computerized and reduced to a printout each workday morning. This updated information helps employment service counselors identify appropriate openings. Increasingly, data about job seekers are also computerized so that the matching process can be done electronically.

Two useful spin-offs of job banks are the job information service and job-flo. Both are aimed at matching recruiters and recruits. The *job information service* provides self-service stations within local unemployment offices. Job seekers who know the jobs they want can review the job bank listing quickly without waiting to speak with a counselor.[14] Then they can contact the employer that has the desired opening. *Job-flo* is a monthly report on frequently listed openings from job banks throughout the country. Issued by the U.S. Department of Labor, job-flo is designed to give nationwide exposure to hard-to-fill job openings. It lists pay, duration of unfilled openings, location, and job qualifications.[15] These listings encourage geographic mobility by job hunters, which helps balance supply and demand in the labor market. For example, if a construction boom in the West creates a shortage of carpenters, job-flo reports alert employment offices in the East to advise unemployed carpenters of employment possibilities.

For many years state employment service offices suffered from a poor image. Recruiters often viewed these agencies as a source of unskilled or poorly qualified workers. Such self-fulfilling attitudes encouraged many skilled workers to use other channels to find employment. However, politicians increasingly see the employment service as an important weapon against unemployment. As a result, new programs have been initiated and funded, such as job-flo.[16] These changes and equal employment legislation have caused many personnel departments to list all their openings with state agencies to ensure wide exposure. Today, government-run employment services are becoming an important source of recruits and services for personnel departments, especially since they are free to both employers and applicants.

Private Placement Agencies

Private placement agencies developed in the vacuum created by the poor image of the public employment service. These for-profit companies—which exist in every major metropolitan area—arose to help employers find capable applicants. Placement firms take an employer's request for recruits and then solicit job seekers, usually through advertising or among walk-ins. Candidates are matched with employer requests and then told to report to the employer's personnel department for an interview. The matching process conducted by private agencies varies widely. Some placement services carefully prescreen applicants for the personnel department. Other firms simply provide a stream of applicants and let the personnel department do most of the screening.[17]

"People vendors"

Users of private placement agencies should realize that payment is handled in one of two ways: either the employer or the applicant pays the placement firm a fee. It commonly equals 10 percent of the first year's salary or one month's wages. *Fee-paid* positions are those openings that the employer agrees to pay. Other positions require the recruits to pay once they are offered a job or begin employment.

Professional Search Firms

Professional search firms are much more specialized than placement agencies. *Search firms* usually recruit only specific types of human resources for a fee paid by the employer. For example, some search firms specialize in executive talent, while others use their expertise to find technical and scientific personnel. Perhaps the most significant difference between search firms and placement agencies is their approach. Placement agencies hope to attract applicants through advertising, but search firms actively seek out recruits among the employees of other companies. Although they may advertise, search firms use the telephone as their primary tool to locate and attract prospective recruits.[18]

The Nelson Radar Company needed a quality control manager for its vacuum-tube assembly line. After several weeks of unsuccessful recruiting effort, the personnel manager hired a search firm. The search firm reviewed the in-house phone directories of competing firms and telephoned the assistant quality control manager at one of Nelson's competitors. The phone call was used to encourage this assistant manager to apply for the position at the Nelson Company.

This brief example illustrates several important points. First, search firms may have an in-depth experience with specific types of applicants. Second, search firms are often willing to undertake actions that an employer would not do, such as calling a competitor. Third, some personnel professionals consider search firms unethical because these firms engage in "stealing," "raiding," or "pirating" among their client's competitors. This last point shows why search firms sometimes are called "headhunters."[19]

"Headhunters" can help recruiters.

Educational Institutions

Schools are another common source of recruits. Many universities, colleges, and vocational schools offer their current students and alumni placement assistance. This assistance helps employers and graduates to meet and discuss employment opportunities and the applicant's qualifications. Distributive education programs, counselors, and vocational teachers may also provide recruiters with leads to desirable candidates in local high schools.[20]

A view of what one group of university students sought in a recruiter is found in Figure 6-5. It shows that students desire well-informed and skilled campus

Figure 6-5
A Profile of the Ideal Recruiter

On the basis of a survey of second-year students in a university MBA program, the following profile of the ideal college recruiter emerged. The ideal recruiter:

1. Was actually hiring for a specific position.
2. Was very knowledgeable about and close to the job that was open.
3. Knew the company well and could discuss both good and bad points.
4. Didn't try to oversell the company.
5. Had read the résumé before the interview.
6. Found out how much the candidate knew about the job and the company.
7. Was interested in the student as an individual.
8. Was happy with the company and felt he or she was going places.
9. Was personable, polite, on time, and sincere.
10. Asked thought-provoking questions without being too direct or personal.
11. Followed up promptly with feedback and evaluation.

Source: John E. Steele, "A Profile of the Ideal Recruiter," *Personnel Journal,* February 1977, pp. 58–59. Used by permission.

recruiters. It also indicates that candor among recruiters is an important characteristic.[21] Another study reports that the recruiter's title and age are important factors in creating a favorable impression on recruits.[22]

Professional Associations

Recruiters find that professional associations can also be a source of job seekers. Many associations conduct placement activities to help new and experienced professionals get jobs, especially at meetings and conventions. Some even have publications that accept classified advertisements. Professionals who belong to the appropriate associations are considered more likely to remain informed of the latest developments in their field, and so this channel of recruitment may lead to higher-quality applicants. Another advantage of this source of applicants is that it helps recruiters zero in on specific specialities, especially in hard-to-fill technical areas.

Labor Organizations

When recruiters want people with trade skills, local labor organizations have rosters of those people who are looking for employment. The local union of plumbers, for example, keeps a list of plumbers who are seeking jobs. In the construction industry, many contractors get their skilled workers from the local labor organizations. Since contractors often hire on a per-project basis, a union hiring hall is a convenient channel for attracting large numbers of pretrained recruits for new projects.

Unions supply construction help.

Military Operations

Trained personnel leave the military service every day. Some veterans—such as those who have been trained as mechanics, welders, or pilots—have hard-to-find skills. Personnel departments that need skills similar to those found in the military often find nearby military installations a valuable source of recruits. Many of the technicians who maintain commercial jet airliners were first trained in the military, for example.[23]

Government-Funded Training Programs

In an effort to reduce unemployment among the unskilled, the federal government has instituted a variety of programs that train unemployed individuals. Government concern stems from the belief that *some* unemployment is structural in nature. *Structural unemployment* occurs when people are ready, willing, and able to work, but their skills do not match the jobs available. For example, an unemployed coal miner in the Appalachian region of the United States is of little use to an electronics firm that seeks trained assemblers and technicians. Through government-sponsored training and retraining programs, unemployed workers are given skills to make them employable in today's labor markets.

Toward solving the "skill gap" for unemployable people

One of the problems with these programs has been that the training sometimes prepared people for jobs that were unneeded. For example, trucking deregulation and recessions combined to create a surplus of truck drivers in the early 1980s. Yet some of the government-sponsored training centers kept graduating truck drivers. Likewise, some of the centers focused on such low-paying jobs that trainees found it economically advantageous to remain on government welfare and assistance programs. For example, some entry-level jobs in banks, restaurants, hotels, and motels proved to pay less than welfare. Nevertheless, whenever unemployment is high, the federal government usually funds training and retraining for the unemployed.

Training legislation

One example of this type of legislation is the *Job Training Partnership Act* of 1983. This law, like its predecessor the *Comprehensive Education and Training Act,* provides federal funds to authorized training contractors, often city or state government agencies. These moneys are used to train people in new, employable skills. The Job Training Partnership Act differs from previous government-sponsored training laws because it mandates greater consultation between industry and the government contractors that do the training. As a result of this consultation, it is hoped that graduates will meet the needs of employers. A better match between job openings and training will mean that more of these graduates can leave the welfare and unemployment rolls in favor of meaningful and productive jobs.

Personnel departments that have an ongoing demand for skilled or semi-skilled entry-level employees should work closely with their local training centers. These centers can prove to be a low-cost source of recruits who are trained in the specific areas of interest to the company. And since many of the centers are operated by minority groups and often seek trainees from protected classes, their graduates may help the firm meet its affirmative action plans. At the same time, the personnel department can help fulfill societal goals of turning the unemployed into productive, tax paying citizens.

Temporary-Help Agencies

An outside source of short-run staffing

Most large cities have temporary-help agencies that can respond quickly to an employer's need for help. These agencies do not provide recruits. Instead, they are a source of supplemental workers. The temporary help actually work for the agency and are "on loan" to the requesting employer. For temporary jobs—during vacations, flu epidemics, or peak seasons—these agencies can be a better alternative than recruiting new workers for short periods of employment. Some companies—such as Motorola, TRW, Merrill Lynch, Control Data, and IBM—actually rely on temporary workers to fill a part of the company's staffing

"Temps" as a buffer

needs. They use "temps" as a buffer of people who can be put on layoff status quickly without having to layoff the company's full-time, career-oriented employees when sales fall short of expectations. Besides handling the recruiting and bookkeeping tasks associated with hiring new employees, these agencies often can provide clerical and secretarial talent on short notice—sometimes less than a day.[24] And when the temporary shortage is over, there is no need to lay off surplus workers because temporaries work for the agency, not the company. They can be put on layoff without creating unemployment claims against the employer. Occasionally, temporary workers are recruited to become permanent employees. However, many of the people who work for temporary-help agencies do so because they do not seek long-term, full-time careers. College students, retirees, and others who do not want a long-term job are the bulk of the temporary's work force.[25]

Departing Employees

Two often overlooked sources of recruits are retirees and other departing employees. These workers might gladly stay if they could rearrange their schedules or change the number of hours worked. Family responsibilities, health, or other circumstances may lead a worker to quit when a transfer to a part-time job may retain their valuable skills and training.[26] Even if part-time work is not a solution, a temporary leave of absence may satisfy the employee and some future recruiting need of the employer.

An overlooked source of help

Buy-backs are a channel worthy of mention, although personnel specialists and workers tend to avoid them. A *buy-back* occurs when an employee resigns to take another job, and the original employer outbids the new job offer. The following dialogue provides an example:

Employee: I quit. I am going to work as a computer programmer for International Plastics.

Manager: You are too valuable for us to just let you walk out the door. How much is International offering?

Employee: They are offering me $3000 a year more!

Manager: Stay and I'll make it $4000.

Employee: No. I'm going.

Manager: How about $5000?

Employee: Well, OK.

Even when the authority to enter into a bidding war exists, the manager may discover that other workers expect similar raises. Employees may reject a buy-back attempt because of the ethical issue raised by not reporting to a job that has already been accepted. Besides, what is to prevent the manager from using a blind ad to find a replacement? Then after International has filled its job in the example above, the employee is terminated.

Open House

A relatively new technique of recruiting involves holding an open house. People in the adjacent community are invited to see the company facilities, have refreshments, and maybe view a film about the company. This method has proved successful to recruit clerical workers when people with office skills are in tight supply.[27]

Innovative recruiting tool

G. D. Searle & Co., in Skokie, Illinois, used this method when it had problems recruiting enough clerical help. From the seventy-five people who attended the open house, the company expected to hire twenty secretaries and clerks.[28]

Figure 6-6 summarizes the recruiting process and identifies each of the commonly used channels of recruitment. As the figure indicates, the recruitment

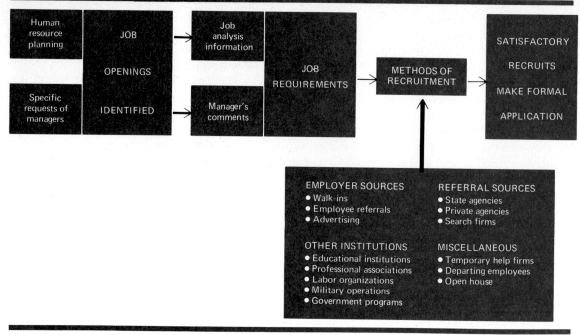

Figure 6-6
A Summary of the Recruiting Process

process ends when a recruit makes formal application, usually by completing an application blank.

JOB APPLICATION BLANKS

The *job application blank* collects information about recruits in a uniform manner. Even when recruits volunteer detailed information about themselves, applications are often required so that the information gathered is comparable. Each personnel department generally designs its own application blank. Nevertheless, common features exist. Figure 6-7 provides a typical example of an application blank and its major divisions. Although the application blank is a fairly typical one, it may contain questions that are illegal under some state jurisdictions. As one writer observed:

State jurisdictions may mean other limits.

While the majority of employers may be aware of . . . relevant federal regulations, many aren't aware that equal opportunity laws in some states are more stringent than federal requirements. For example, while federal regulations require the employer to be able to justify pre-employment inquiries as bona fide occupational qualifications (BFOQs) upon request, Ohio law says inquiries into inappropriate areas (i.e., sex, race, etc.) must be certified by the Ohio Civil Rights Commission prior to their use.

In states where local laws are more stringent than federal law, job application forms are an even more critical concern. . . .[29]

It is not enough to be in compliance with just the federal laws. State laws are important, too. When the two levels of law conflict, usually the most stringent one must be followed. And ignorance of the state laws is no defense in court. In one study of application blanks, two researchers reported that 73 percent of the forms had one or more inappropriate preemployment inquiries.[30] The remainder of this chapter discusses the various parts of the application blank in Figure 6-7.

Personal Data

Most application blanks begin with a request for personal data. Requests for name, address, and telephone number are nearly universal. But requests for some personal data such as place of birth, sex, race, religion, or national origin may lead to charges of discrimination. Since it is illegal to discriminate against applicants who are members of a protected class, an unsuccessful applicant may conclude that rejection was motivated by discrimination when discriminatory questions are asked. The personnel department must be able to show that these questions are job-related.

Applications may solicit information about health, height, weight, handicaps that relate to the job, major illnesses, and claims for injuries. Here again, there may be legal problems. Government contractors are prohibited from discriminating against handicapped individuals under the *Rehabilitation Act* of 1973. The burden of proof to show the job-relatedness of such questions falls on the employer.[31] Information about marital status and dependents and about whom to contact in a medical emergency is also commonly sought. Here again, this information cannot be used to discriminate against members of a protected class.

Handicapped are protected.

Employment Status

Some application questions concern the applicant's employment objective and availability. Included here are questions about the position sought, willingness to accept other positions, date available for work, salary or wages desired, and acceptability of part-time and full-time work schedules. This information helps a recruiter match the applicant's objective and the organization's needs. Broad or uncertain responses can prevent the application from being considered. An example follows:

> Inexperienced recruiter: Under "position sought," this applicant put "any available job." Also, under "wages desired" the applicant wrote "minimum wage or better." What should I do with this application?

> Employment manager: You are not a career counselor. You are a recruiter. Put that application in the inactive file and forget about it.

Education and Skills

The education and skills section of the application blank is designed to uncover the job seeker's abilities. Traditionally, education has been a major criterion in evaluating job seekers, but its importance has been diminished by the requirement that personnel departments show how the education is job-related. Edu-

BLAKELY ELECTRONICS, INC.
"An Equal Opportunity Employer"

Application for Employment

Personal Data

1. Name _____

2. Address _____   3. Phone number _____

   _____

Employment Status

4. Type of employment sought _____ Full-time _____ Part-time

   _____ Permanent _____ Temporary

5. Job or position sought _____

6. Date of availability, if hired _____

7. Are you willing to accept other employment if the position you seek is unavailable?

   _____ Yes _____ No

8. Approximate wages/salary desired $ _____ per month.

Education and Skills

9. Circle the highest grade completed:

   8 9 10 11 12   13 14 15 16   Graduate School

   High School   College

10. Please provide the following information about your education. (Include high school, trade or vocational schools, and colleges.)

    a. School name _____ Degree(s) or diploma _____

       School address _____

    b. School name _____ Degree(s) or diploma _____

       School address _____

11. Please describe your work skills. (Include machines, tools, equipment, and other abilities you possess.) _____

    _____

Figure 6-7

A Typical Application Blank

cational attainment does imply certain abilities and, therefore, is a common request on virtually all applications. Questions about specific skills are also used to judge prospective employees. More than any other part of the application blank, the skills section reveals the suitability of a candidate for a particular job.

Work History

Job seekers must frequently list their past jobs. From this information, a recruiter can tell whether the applicant is one who hops from job to job or is someone likely to be a long-service employee. A quick review of the stated job title, duties,

‹ Work History

Beginning with your most recent or current employer, please provide the following information about each employer. (If additional space is needed, please use an additional sheet.)

12. a. Employer _____ Dates of employment _____

      Employer's address _____

      Job title _____ Supervisor's name _____

      Job duties _____

      Starting pay _____ Ending pay _____

   b. Employer _____ Dates of employment _____

      Employer's address _____

      Job title _____ Supervisor's name _____

      Job duties _____

      Starting pay _____ Ending pay _____

Military Background

If you were ever a member of the Armed Services, please complete the following:

13. Branch of service _____ Rank at discharge _____

    Dates of service _____ to _____

    Responsibilities _____

Memberships, Awards, and Hobbies

14. What are your hobbies? _____

15. List civic/professional/social organizations to which you have belonged. _____

_____

16. List any awards you have received. _____

_____

References

In the space provided, list three references who are not members of your family:

17. a. Name _____ Address _____

   b. Name _____ Address _____

   c. Name _____ Address _____

18. Please feel free to add any other information you think should be considered in evaluating your application. _____

_____

_____

By my signature on this application, I:

    a. Authorize the verification of the above information and any other necessary inquiries that may be needed to determine my suitability for employment.

    b. Affirm that the above information is true to the best of my knowledge.

_____ Date _____

    Applicant's Signature

Figure 6-7
(Continued)

and responsibilities also shows whether the candidate is a potentially capable applicant.[32] If this information does not coincide with what an experienced recruiter expects to see, it may be that the candidate exaggerated job title, duties, or responsibilities.

Military Background

Many applications request information on military experience. Questions usually include date of discharge, branch of service, and rank at discharge. This information helps explain the applicant's background and ability to function in a structured environment.

Memberships, Awards, and Hobbies

Recruits are more than potential workers. They are also representatives of the employer in the community. For managerial and professional positions, off-the-job activities may make one candidate preferable over another. Memberships in civic, social, and professional organizations that are related to the job indicate the recruit's concern about community and career. Awards show recognition for noteworthy achievements. Hobbies may reinforce important job skills and indicate outlets for stress and frustration, or opportunities for further service to the company.

Personal interests may serve a business purpose.

When handed a pile of completed applications for manager of the car- and truck-leasing department, Frank Simmons (the personnel manager for a New Orleans Ford dealership) sorted the completed applications into two piles. When asked what criteria were being used to sort the applicants, he said, "I'm looking for golfers. Many of our largest car and truck accounts are sold on Saturday afternoons at the golf course."

References

Besides the traditional references from friends or previous employers, applications may ask for other "referencelike" information. Questions may explore the job seeker's criminal record, credit history, friends and relatives who work for the employer, or previous employment with the organization. Criminal record, credit history, and friends or relatives who work for the company may be important considerations if the job involves sensitive information, cash, or other valuables. Job-relatedness must be substantiated if these criteria disproportionately discriminate against some protected group. Previous employment with the organization means there are records of the applicant's performance.

Signature Line

Candidates usually are required to sign and date their applications. Adjacent to the signature line, a blanket authorization commonly appears. This authorization allows the employer to check with references; verify medical, criminal, or financial records; and undertake any other necessary investigations. Another common provision of the signature line is a statement that the applicant affirms the information in the application to be true and accurate as far as is known. Although many people give this clause little thought, falsification of an application blank is grounds for discharge in most organizations.

> Jim LaVera lied about his age to get into the police officers training program. As he neared retirement age, Jim was notified that he would have to retire in six months, instead of thirty months as he had planned. When Jim protested, the lie he made years before came to the surface. Jim was given the option of being terminated or taking early retirement at substantially reduced benefits.

When the application is completed and signed, the recruitment process is finished. Its unanswered questions and implications continue to affect personnel management, as the Jim LaVera example illustrates.[33] In fact, the end of the recruitment process marks the beginning of the selection process, which is discussed in the next chapter.

SUMMARY

Recruitment is the process of finding and attracting capable applicants for employment. This responsibility is normally associated with specialists in the personnel department, called recruiters. Before recruiters solicit applications, they should be aware of the constraints under which they operate. Of particular importance are such limitations as organizational policies, human resource plans, affirmative action plans, recruiter habits, environmental conditions, and the requirements of the job.

At the recruiter's disposal are a variety of methods to find and attract job seekers. Employer sources include walk-ins, write-ins, employee referrals, and direct solicitations through want ads and other forms of advertisement. Applicants can be found through the referrals of state unemployment agencies, private placement agencies, or search firms. Of course, recruits can be found through a variety of institutions too, for example, educational institutions, professional associations, labor organizations, military operations, and government training programs. Some firms have even reported success with converting temporary or departing employees into permanent ones, on a full-time or part-time basis. Even an open house may bring people into the facility and cause them to subsequently submit an application.

The end results of recruiting are completed application blanks from ready, willing, and able candidates. Application blanks seek a variety of different answers from recruits including personal, employment, educational, and work history information. Questions may even be asked about hobbies, memberships, awards, and personal interests. References are usually solicited by the application blank, too. With a pool of recruits and the information contained in completed application blanks, the personnel department is now ready to assist line managers in the process of selecting new employees, which is discussed in the next chapter.

TERMS FOR REVIEW

Recruitment	Job information service
Walk-ins	Job-flo
Write-ins	Search firms
Blind ads	Job Training Partnership Act
Résumé	Buy-back
State employment security agency	Structural unemployment
Job bank	

REVIEW AND DISCUSSION QUESTIONS

1.   What background information should a recruiter know before beginning to recruit job seekers?

2.   Give three examples of how organizational policies affect the recruitment process. Explain how these influence a recruiter's actions.

3.   Under what circumstances would a blind ad be a useful recruiting technique?

4.   After months of insufficient recognition (and two years without a raise), you accept an offer from another firm for $2500 a year more than your present salary. When you tell your boss that you are resigning, you are told how crucial you are to the business and are offered a raise of $4250 a year. What do you do? Why? What problems might exist if you accept the buy-back?

5.   Suppose you are a manager who just accepted the resignation of a crucial employee. After you send your request for a replacement to the personnel department, how could you help the recruiter do a more effective job?

6.   If your company's regular college recruiter became ill and you were assigned to recruit at six universities in two weeks, what information would you need before leaving on the trip?

7.   In small businesses, managers usually handle their own recruiting. What methods would you use for the following situations? Why?

   a. The regular janitor is going on vacation for three weeks.
   b. Your secretary has the flu.
   c. Two more sales people are needed: one for local customers and one to open a sales office in Puerto Rico.
   d. Your only chemist is retiring and must be replaced with a highly skilled individual.

8.   "If a job application omits important questions, needed information about recruits will not be available. But if a needless question is asked, the information can be ignored by the recruiter without any other complications." Do you agree or disagree? Why?

INCIDENT 6-1

Blakely Electronics Expansion

Blakely Electronics developed a revolutionary method of storing data electronically. The head of research and development, Guy Swensen, estimated that Blakely could become a supplier to every computer manufacturer in the world. The future success of the company seemed to hang on securing the broadest possible patents to cover the still-secret process.

The personnel director, Carol Kane, recommended that Swensen become a project leader in charge of developing and filing the necessary patent information. Swensen and Kane developed a list of specialists who would be needed to rush the patent applications through the final stages of development and the patent application process. Most of the needed skills were found among Blakely's present employees. However, after a preliminary review of skills inventories and staffing levels, a list of priority recruits was developed. It required the following:

• An experienced patent attorney with a strong background in electronics technology.

• A patent attorney familiar with the ins and outs of the patent process and the patent office in Washington, D.C.

• Twelve engineers. Three had to be senior engineers with experience in the latest computer technology and design. Four had to be senior engineers with experience in photographic etching reduction. Five junior engineers were also requested in the belief that they could handle the routine computations for the senior engineers.

• An office manager, ten typists, and four secretaries to transcribe the engineering notebooks and prepare the patent application.

Swensen wanted these twenty-nine people recruited as promptly as possible.

1.   Assuming you are given the responsibility of recruiting these needed employees, what channels would you use to find and attract each type of recruit sought?

2.   What other actions should the personnel department take now that there is the possibility of very rapid expansion?

170

INCIDENT 6-2

The Ethics of Headhunting

Darrow Thomas worked as a professional placement specialist for L. A. and D., Inc., an executive search firm. For the last three months Darrow had not been very successful in finding high-level executives to fill the openings of L. A. and D.'s clients. Not only did his poor record affect his commissions, but the office manager at L. A. and D. was not very pleased with Darrow's performance. Since Darrow desperately needed to make a placement, he resolved that he would do everything he could to fill the new opening he received that morning.

The opening was for a director of research and development at a major food processor. Darrow began by unsuccessfully reviewing the in-house telephone directory of General Mills, General Foods, and Quaker Oats. Finally, he stumbled across the directory of a small food processor in the South. In the directory he found a listing for Suzanne Derby, assistant director of product development. He called her, and the following conversation took place.

Suzanne: Hello. P.D. Department, Suzanne speaking.

Darrow: Hello. My name is Darrow Thomas, and I am with L. A. and D. One of my clients has an opening for a director of research and development at a well-known food processor. In discussions with people in the industry, your name was recommended as a likely candidate. I was. . . .

Suzanne: Who recommended that you call me?

Darrow: I'm awfully sorry, but we treat references and candidates with the utmost confidentiality. I cannot reveal that name. But rest assured, he thought you were ready for a more challenging job.

Suzanne: What company is it? What does the job involve?

Darrow: Again, confidentiality requires that the company name go unmentioned for now. Before we go any further, would you mind answering a few questions? Once I feel confident you are the right candidate, I can reveal my client.

Suzanne: Well, OK.

Darrow: Good. How many people do you supervise?

Suzanne: Three professionals, seven technicians, and two clerks.

Darrow: Approximately how large a budget are you responsible for?

Suzanne: Oh, it's about half a million dollars a year.

Darrow: What degree do you hold, and how many years have you been assistant director?

Suzanne: My undergraduate degree and master's are in nutrition science. After I graduated in 1975, I came to work as an applications researcher. In 1980, I was promoted to chief applications researcher. In 1984, I was appointed assistant director of product development.

Darrow: Good career progress—two degrees and managerial experience. Your background sounds great! This is a little personal, but would you tell me your salary?

Suzanne: I make $32,500 a year.

Darrow: Oh, that is disappointing. The opening I have to fill is for $46,500. That would be such a substantial jump that my client would probably assume your past experience and responsibility are too limited to be considered.

Suzanne: What do you mean?

Darrow: Well, the ideal candidate would be making about $40,000 a year. That figure would indicate a higher level of responsibility than your low salary. We could get around that problem.

Suzanne: How?

Darrow: On the data sheet I have filled out I could put down that you are making, oh, say $41,500. That sure would increase my client's interest. Besides, then they would know a salary of $46,500 was needed to attract you.

Suzanne: Wow! But when they checked on my salary history, they'd know that $41,500 was an inflated figure.

Darrow: No, they wouldn't. They wouldn't check. And even if they did, companies never reveal the salary information of past employees. Besides, my client is anxious to fill the job. I'll tell you what, let me send them the data sheet; I'm sure they'll be interested. Then we can talk more about this. OK?

Suzanne: Well, if you think it would mean a raise to $46,500, and they really need someone with my background, I guess I'd be interested.

1.   Although headhunters do not necessarily engage in the practice of inflating an applicant's wage, it does happen occasionally. What would you do in Suzanne's place? Would you allow your name to be used?

2.   Since most headhunters receive a commission that is a percentage of the successful applicant's starting salary, what safeguards would you suggest to prevent them from inflating salaries?

3.   If Suzanne goes along with Darrow's inflated salary figure and she is hired, what possible problems may she face?

REFERENCES

1.   Mary Green Miner and John B. Miner, *Employee Selection within the Law*, Washington, D.C.: Bureau of National Affairs, 1978, pp. 25–26.

2.   Herbert J. Sweeney and Kenneth S. Teel, "A New Look at Promotion from Within," *Personnel Journal,* August 1979, p. 535.

3.   U.S. Department of Labor, Bureau of Labor Statistics, "Selected Employment Indicators, Seasonally Adjusted," *Monthly Labor Review,* December 1977, p. 83.

4.   Vera C. Perrella, "Multiple Job Holders in May, 1969," *Special Labor Force Report 123,* U.S. Department of Labor, p. 63.

5.   Miner and MIner, op. cit., p. 25.

6.   Gene E. Burton and Dev S. Pathak, "101 Ways to Discriminate against Equal Employment," *The Personnel Administrator,* August 1977, pp. 42–45.

7.   Lee D. Dyer, "Managerial Jobseeking: Methods and Techniques," *Monthly Labor Review,* December 1972, pp. 29–30. For a broad view of the methods used by a variety of workers see Carl Rosenfeld, "Jobseeking Methods Used by American Workers," *Monthly Labor Review,* August 1975, pp. 39–42. See also Richard H. Coffina, "Management Recruitment Is a Two-Way Street," *Personnel Journal,* February 1979, pp. 86–89.

8.   Stephen L. Mangum, "Recruitment and Job Search: The Recruitment Tactics of Employers," *Personnel Administrator,* June 1982, pp. 96–102.

9.   Richard Peres, *Dealing with Employment Discrimination,* New York: McGraw-Hill, 1978, p. 20.

10.   Van M. Evans, "Recruitment Advertising in the '80's," *The Personnel Administrator,* March 1978, p. 23.

11.   James W. Schreier, "Deciphering Messages in Recruitment Ads," *Personnel Administrator,* March 1983, p. 35.

12.   Ibid., p. 39.

13.   Jo Bredwell, "The Use of Broadcast Advertising for Recruitment," *Personnel Administrator,* February 1981, pp. 45–49.

14.   *The Employment Service,* Washington: Manpower Administration, U.S. Department of Labor, 1975, pp. 1, 3–4.

15.   Neale Baxter, "Job-Flo: How to Learn If There's a Job in Dallas When You're Jobless in Des Moines," *Occupational Outlook Quarterly,* Summer 1976, p. 2.

16.   James M. Carter, "The Role of the Job Bank in the Placement Process," *Monthly Labor Review,* December 1972, pp. 28–29.

17.   Ronald V. Raine, "Selecting the Consultant," *Personnel Administrator,* December 1980, pp. 41–43.

18.   William Dee, "Evaluating a Search Firm," *Personnel Administrator,* March 1983, pp. 41–43, 99.

19.   John D. Erdlen, "Ethics and the Employee Relations Function," *The Personnel Administrator,* January 1979, pp. 41–43, 68.

20.   Bonnie Nunke, "The Successful Components of College Recruiting," *Personnel Journal,* November 1981, pp. 859–862.

21.   Madalyn Freund and Patricia Somers, "Ethics in College Recruiting: Views from the Front Lines," *The Personnel Administrator,* April 1979, pp. 30–33. See also Joe Thomas,

"College Recruitment: How to Use Student Perceptions of Business," *Personnel Journal,* January 1980, pp. 44–46.

22. Donald P. Rogers and Michael Z. Sincoff, "Favorable Impression Characteristics of the Recruitment Interviewer," *Personnel Psychology,* Autumn 1978, pp. 495–504.

23. Patrick L. Townsend, "A Practical Guide for Hiring A Retired Military Officer," *Personnel Administrator,* June 1984, pp. 67–68, 70, 72–73.

24. Martin J. Gannon, "A Profile of the Temporary Help Industry and Its Workers," *Monthly Labor Review,* May 1974, pp. 44–49. See also Karen E. Debats, "The Temporary Service Industry," *Personnel Journal,* February 1983, pp. 120–121; 124–125.

25. Gladys Fazio Garlitz, "Temporary Workers: A Changing Industry," *Personnel Administrator,* March 1983, pp. 47–48. See also C. Edward Kur and Philip G. Sone, "An Untapped Source of Consulting Help," *Personnel Administrator,* December 1980, pp. 29–33.

26. Barney Olmsted, "Job Sharing—A New Way to Work," *Personnel Journal,* February 1977, pp. 78–81. See also William B. Werther, Jr., "Part-timers: Overlooked and Undervalued," *Business Horizons,* February 1975, pp. 13–20.

27. Roberta M. Kenney, "The Open House Complements Recruiting Strategies," *Personnel Administrator,* March 1982, pp. 27–32.

28. "Open House: It's a New Technique for Employers to Find the Workers They Want," *The Wall Street Journal,* Western ed., May 23, 1978, p. 1.

29. Carl Camden and Bill Wallace, "Job Application Forms: A Hazardous Employment Practice," *Personnel Administrator,* March 1983, p. 31.

30. Ibid.

31. Edwin A. Fleishman, "Evaluating Physical Abilities Required by Jobs," *The Personnel Administrator,* June 1979, pp. 82–90.

32. Bernard M. Bass, "Interface between Personnel and Organizational Psychology," in W. Clay Hammer and Frank L. Schmidt (eds.), *Contemporary Problems in Personnel,* Chicago: St. Clair, 1974, pp. 44–45.

33. Robert W. Ericson, "Recruitment: Some Unanswered Questions," *Personnel Journal,* February 1974, pp. 136–140, 147. See also Stephen J. Wilhelm, "Is On-Campus Recruiting on Its Way Out?" *Personnel Journal,* April 1980, pp. 302–304, 318.

CHAPTER 7

The policy of "hire—then qualify" is replacing
the old method of "hire qualified people."

George S. Odiorne[1]

EMPLOYEE SELECTION

CHAPTER OBJECTIVES

After studying this chapter, you should be able
to:

1 Explain the dependency of personnel
   management activities on the selection
   process.

2 Describe the major test found in the EEOC's
   Uniform Guidelines on Employee Selection.

3 List and explain each step in the selection
   process.

4 Explain the importance of validity and
   reliability in employee selection.

5 Conduct an employment interview and avoid
   the major pitfalls.

6 Describe the supervisor's role in the selection
   process and in realistic job previews.

Once a pool of suitable applicants is created through recruiting, the process of selecting applicants begins. This process involves a series of steps that add time and complexity to the hiring decision. Although important, this time and complexity can lead to frustration for applicants who need jobs and for operating managers who need their job openings filled. By way of introduction, consider an overview of the hiring process at Merrill Lynch, Pierce, Fenner & Smith Inc., the largest securities firm in the United States.

Applicants for the position of account executive at Merrill Lynch complete an application, take a written test, and undergo an interview. But none of these steps prepare them for the account-executive simulation test. As described by a reporter for *The Wall Street Journal,* the test can be unnerving.

"Welcome to the Merrill Lynch account-executive simulation exercise, or, as dubbed by some, the Merrill Lynch stress test. It's a nail-biting three hours . . . that leaves many longing for the good old days of calculus finals.

The stakes are high, too. Those taking part in the simulation, except me, are applicants for the job of account executive, or stockbroker. . . . The simulation exercise is designed to gauge how they will perform under conditions similar to those that a real stockbroker faces."[2]

The test works by telling each applicant that he or she is replacing a stockbroker who has gone to another office. The stockbroker left the client book, which describes the accounts of each client. In addition, the applicants are given a variety of unanswered memos, letters, and telephone messages that they must sort through and take action on. In the background, recorded sounds of a brokerage office are played to add an air of confusing noises, shouts, telephone rings, and other unexpected distractions. During the three hours, fictitious clients call, and other messages and reports are dropped on the applicant's "desk." As one applicant commented an hour after the simulation was over, "I just can't calm down. It was a real high."[3]

The point of this illustration is simply that the simulation exercise is only one part of Merrill Lynch's selection process. Other steps precede and follow it. Although most employers do not use this elaborate a screening device, all but the smallest employers put applicants through a selection process. The *selection process* is a series of specific steps used to decide which recruits should be hired. The process begins when recruits apply for employment and ends with the hiring decision. The steps in between match the employment needs of the applicant and the organization. When these steps are not understood, selection seems like a stressful time and bureaucratic process rather than the important function it is.

In many personnel departments, recruiting and selection are combined and called the *employment function.* In large personnel departments, the employment function is the responsibility of the employment manager. In smaller departments, personnel managers handle these duties.[4] Employment is closely associated with the personnel department. It is often the primary reason for the department's existence, since the selection process is central to personnel management. Improper selection causes the personnel department to fail at the objectives set forth in Chapter 1 and the challenges discussed in Chapter 2. Even worse, improper selection can crush individual hopes and violate equal employment laws. Subsequent personnel activities (discussed later in the book) lose much of their effectiveness when they must contend with improperly selected workers. Therefore, it is not an exaggeration to say that selection is central to the success of personnel management and even to the success of the organization.

INPUTS TO SELECTION

Employment managers use the selection process to find new workers. As Figure 7-1 reveals, the selection process relies on three helpful inputs. Job analysis information provides the description of the jobs, the human specifications, and the performance standards each job requires. Human resource plans tell employment managers what job openings are likely to occur. These plans allow selection to proceed in a logical and effective manner. Finally, recruits are necessary so that the employment manager has a group of people from which to choose. These three inputs largely determine the effectiveness of the selection process. If job analysis information, human resource plans, and recruits are of high quality, the selection process should perform well. At the same time, there are other inputs into the selection process that limit its success. To succeed, employment managers must meet the challenges of limited labor supply, ethical considerations, organizational policies, and equal employment laws.

Supply Challenges

It is important to have a large, qualified pool of recruits from which to select applicants. But some jobs are so hard to fill that there are few applicants. Low-paying jobs or openings for extremely specialized work are examples of positions with small selection ratios. A *selection ratio* is the relationship between the number of applicants hired and the total number of applicants available. A large selection ratio is 1:25; a small selection ratio is 1:2. A small selection ratio means there are few applicants from which to select. In many

Selection ratio

Figure 7-1
Dependency of Personnel Management Activities
on the Selection Process

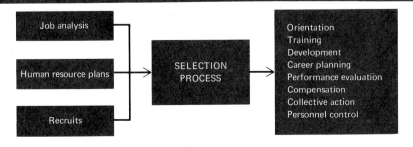

instances a small selection ratio also means a low quality of recruits. The ratio is computed as follows:

$$\frac{\text{Number of applicants hired}}{\text{Total number of applicants}} = \text{selection ratio}$$

Wes Klugh, an employment manager for a chain of motels, faced a low selection ratio for the third-shift desk clerk's job. Although it paid 25 cents an hour more than the day or evening clerk jobs, few people applied for it. Wes decided to redesign the job by enriching it. The job was expanded to include responsibility for completing the daily financial report and other bookkeeping tasks. The additional duties justified a substantial raise and new title—night auditor. The result was more applicants.

Ethical Challenges

Since employment specialists strongly influence the hiring decision, that decision is shaped by their ethics.[5] Hiring a neighbor's relative, gifts from a placement agency, and bribes (especially overseas) all challenge the employment specialists' ethical standards. If those standards are low, new employees may not be properly selected.

What would you have done?

Each summer, Athena Klemmer was told to find jobs for some of the executives' children. To disobey would affect her career. On the other hand, hiring some of them would be an admission that she selected people on criteria other than merit. Although many of her peers in the local personnel association thought employing the boss's child was merely a benefit of the executive suite, Athena felt it was improper. So each summer she found jobs in other companies for some of the executives' children.

Organizational Challenges

The selection process is not an end; it is a means through which the organization achieves its objectives. Naturally, the organization imposes limits, such as budgets and policies, that may hinder the selection process. Without budget limitations, recruiting efforts and selection techniques could be refined. But without limits, employment expenses may be so high that organizational effectiveness would suffer. Policies may expand existing challenges or simply add more constraints. Policies against discrimination reinforce external prohibitions, for example. Or internal decrees may exceed legal demands from outside. For example, policies to hire ex-convicts further societal objectives but are not legally required. Yet such internal policies add still another challenge for employment specialists.

Equal Employment Challenges

An ongoing challenge to all phases of personnel work is equal employment opportunity. However, the high visibility and importance of the selection process demand that personnel professionals give careful consideration to ensuring that all selection steps in the process are free from discriminatory bias.

Even unintentional bias—such as tests that disproportionately discriminate against members of one protected class—must be eliminated by those involved in the selection process.[6]

In an attempt to reduce discrimination in selection, the Equal Employment Opportunity Commission has created the *Uniform Guidelines on Employee Selection*. These guidelines establish certain standards that employers must meet before they can consider their selection procedures to be nondiscriminatory. A primary goal of the guidelines is to prevent adverse impact. As described in Chapter 3, adverse impact results when an employer's actions have a disproportionate effect on members of protected groups. One quick test for adverse impact suggested by the guidelines is the *four-fifths rule*. Generally, adverse impact is assumed when the selection ratio of protected-class applicants is less than 80 percent (or four-fifths) of the selection ratio for majority applicants. For example, assume an employer has 100 white male applicants for an entry-level job and hires one-half of them, or 50 percent (50/100). During the same time period, the employer has 50 minority applicants but only hires 10 of them, or 20 percent (10/50). The result is that the employer hires only 40 percent as many minority applicants as majority ones. This ratio can be calculated as follows:[7]

Uniform guidelines

$$\frac{S \text{ (PCM)}}{A \text{ (PCM)}} \div \frac{S \text{ (MAJ)}}{A \text{ (MAJ)}} = \frac{10}{50} \div \frac{50}{100} = 40\%$$

where S (PCM) = number of applicants selected from protected class members

A (PCM) = number of applicants from protected class

S (MAJ) = number of selected applicants who are members of the majority group

A (PCM) = number of applicants from the majority group

Since the ratio of protected class members hired to the ratio of the majority hired is less than four-fifths (40 percent, in this example), it would be reasonable to assume that the employer's selection procedures have an adverse impact on members of the protected class. The personnel department may have been very careful not to discriminate at any stage of the selection process. However, the overall result of its procedures has a disproportionate effect on members of a protected class. Not only will the department have to revise its selection procedures, but if it has used these procedures for long, it probably has an imbalanced work force that will require an affirmative action plan to correct. (See Chapter 3 for a more detailed explanation of adverse impact and affirmative action plans.)

When an employer's overall selection process meets the four-fifths rule, the EEOC and other government agencies will not normally apply the four-fifths rule to every step in the selection process. This "bottom-line" test, as it is called in the guidelines, allows some steps within a firm's selection process to have an adverse impact as long as the overall selection process does not. The implication for personnel professionals is obvious: When one step in the selection process has an adverse impact, it should be reviewed and improved to ensure that the overall selection process stays within the four-fifths rule.[8]

180

SELECTION: AN OVERVIEW

The selection process is a series of steps through which applicants pass. Sometimes the process can be made simple and effective, especially when selecting employees to fill internal openings.

At Citibank in New York City, the selection process has been simplified and computerized in order to match present employees with internal openings. The "Job Match" selection system rests upon matching a profile of candidates for a nonprofessional job and the task requirements of the job. The specific tasks required of the job are programmed into the computer along with the specific abilities of employees. Those employees with the highest match for a given opening are then considered for the job. One shortcoming of the Job Match system is that it does not consider nontask factors, such as whether the employee actually wants the job.[9]

To ensure that task and nontask factors are considered, personnel departments commonly use a more involved sequence of steps in selecting employees, as shown in Figure 7-2. When internal applicants are being considered, there is seldom a need to provide a preliminary reception of applicants, verify references, or do a medical evaluation. But when external applicants are being considered, the steps in Figure 7-2 are common. The remainder of the chapter explains the selection process by examining each step in this figure.

PRELIMINARY RECEPTION: STEP 1

The selection process is a two-way street. The organization selects employees, and *applicants select employers.* Selection starts with a visit to the personnel office or with a written request for an application. On the basis of how this initial reception is handled, the applicant begins to form an opinion of the employer. And two researchers suggest that a potential applicant's perceptions of an organization tend to

Figure 7-2
Steps in the Selection Process

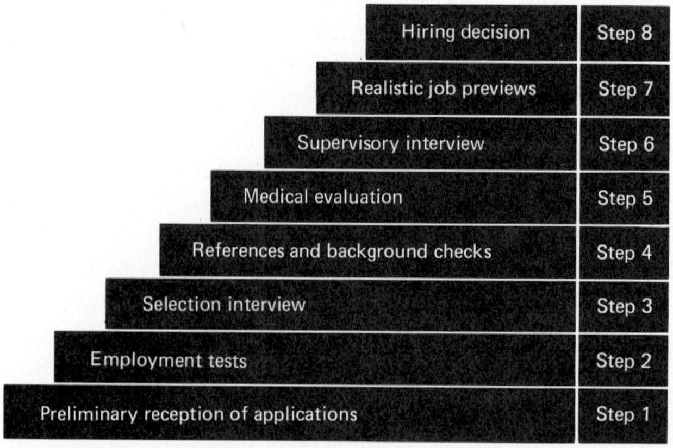

Hiring decision	Step 8
Realistic job previews	Step 7
Supervisory interview	Step 6
Medical evaluation	Step 5
References and background checks	Step 4
Selection interview	Step 3
Employment tests	Step 2
Preliminary reception of applications	Step 1

influence the applicant's intentions to sign up for interviews and request further information.[10]

When the applicant appears in person, a preliminary interview may be granted as a courtesy. This "courtesy interview," as it is often called, is simply a matter of good public relations. It also helps the personnel department screen out obvious misfits and get background information on these "drop-in" applicants who often are evaluated informally on their appearance, mannerisms, and other characteristics. A completed application usually is requested during this initial meeting. Later steps in the selection process verify this application information.

Good PR is part of the job.

EMPLOYMENT TESTS: STEP 2

Employment tests are devices that assess the probable match between applicants and job requirements. Some are paper-and-pencil tests; others are exercises that simulate work conditions. A math test for a bookkeeper is an example of paper-and-pencil test, and the account executive test at Merrill Lynch is an example of a simulation. Tests are used more frequently for hourly paid jobs than for management or staff openings because hourly jobs usually have a limited number of skills or activities that are tested easily.

Management and staff jobs are often too complex to be tested fairly and economically. When tests are used for these positions, however, they often are a simulation of real-life situations that are evaluated by several raters, as is the case at Merrill Lynch. "Estimates of the percentage of major corporations that use formal tests of some sort as guides to hiring or promotions range as high as 40%. Included are a number of not exactly flaky outfits—AT&T, IBM, Knight-Ridder Newspapers, J. C. Penney, and Sears Roebuck."[11]

Test Validation

Testing became popular on a large scale during World War I when intelligence tests were given to army recruits. During the following sixty years, tests were developed for a wide range of employment uses, but many of these tests were assumed to be valid without sufficient proof. For a test to be relied upon, it should be valid. *Validity* means that the test scores significantly relate to job performance or to some other relevant criterion. The stronger the relationship between test results and performance, the more effective the test is as a selection tool. When scores and performance are unrelated, the test is invalid and should not be used for selection.

Validity

A Miami, Florida, trucking company gave all applicants an extensive reading test. Between 1967 and 1972, one-third of its applicants were Cuban immigrants. But by 1972, there were no Cuban drivers. Since the drivers received their instructions orally and were shown on a map where to go, the reading test had no relationship to job performance. It was invalid. The test did not distinguish good drivers from bad ones. It only distinguished between those who could read English well and those who could not.

**Unintentional
discrimination
is illegal.**

Key cases

When an invalid test rejects people of a particular race, sex, religion, or national origin, it violates the 1964 Civil Rights Act. The U.S. Supreme Court has ruled that any test (or any other selection method) that has an unequal impact on a protected class and is not job-related violates the act.[12] This ruling in the *Griggs v. Duke Power* case means that personnel specialists should be especially cautious when a test disproportionately excludes some identifiable group. In *Griggs,* and later in *Albemarle Paper Co. v. Moody,* the U.S. Supreme Court gave recognition to the EEOC Uniform Guidelines on Employee Selection, which outline how tests should be evaluated to determine if they are valid.[13] To ensure that its tests are valid, personnel departments conduct validation studies. These studies compare test results with performance or traits needed to perform the job. Figure 7-3 summarizes the most common approaches to validation.

Empirical approaches rely on predictive or concurrent validity. Both methods attempt to relate test scores to some criterion, usually performance. The higher the correlation between test scores and the criterion, the more effective the test is. Courts and the EEOC guidelines generally prefer empirical approaches because they are less subjective than rational methods.

Rational approaches include content and construct validity. These techniques are used when empirical validity is not feasible because the small number of subjects does not permit a reasonable sample upon which to conduct the validation study.

Figure 7-3

An Explanation of Common Approaches to
Test Validation

EMPIRICAL APPROACHES

Empirical approaches to test validation attempt to relate test scores with a job-related criterion, usually performance. If the test actually measures a job-related criterion, the test and the criterion exhibit a positive correlation between 0 and 1.0. The higher the correlation, the better the match.

• *Predictive validity* is determined by giving a test to a group of applicants. After these applicants have been hired and mastered the job reasonably well, their performance is measured. This measurement and the test score are then correlated.

• *Concurrent validity* allows the personnel department to test present employees and correlate these scores with measures of their performance. This approach does not require the delay between hiring and mastery of the job.

RATIONAL APPROACHES

When the number of subjects is too low to have a reasonable sample of people to test, rational approaches are used. These approaches are considered inferior to empirical techniques, but are acceptable validation strategies when empirical approaches are not feasible.

• *Content validity* is assumed to exist when the test includes reasonable samples of the skills needed to successfully perform the job. A typing test for an applicant that is being hired simply to do typing is an example of a test with content validity.

• *Construct validity* seeks to establish a relationship between performance and other characteristics that are assumed to be necessary for successful job performance. Tests of intelligence and scientific terms would be considered to have construct validity if they were used to hire researchers for a chemical company.

Regardless of which approach is used, testing experts advise separate validation studies for different subgroups, such as women and minorities. The use of separate studies for different subgroups is called *differential validity.* Without differential validity, a test may be valid for a large group (white male applicants) but not for subgroups of minorities or women. Even when tests are validated, courts may examine how effective such validation attempts are. Invalid procedures, no matter how well intentioned, cannot be relied on to prove a test's validity.

Differential validity

The Albemarle Paper Company gave several black workers a battery of tests that had not been validated. The workers sued Albemarle, and so the company then implemented a validation study. But the study had several weaknesses, and the court ruled the tests invalid and discriminatory.

The problem faced by Albemarle was that:[14]

- The company used the tests that had been validated for advanced jobs, not for the entry-level positions to which the tests were being applied. Validation on advanced jobs does not prove that the tests are valid for entry-level positions. Tests must be validated on those jobs to which they are being applied.

- The company validated the test on one group (white workers) and then applied the test to another group (black workers). Tests must be validated for all the groups to whom they are applied.

Besides being valid, a test should also be reliable. *Reliability* means that the test should yield consistent results each time an individual takes it. For example, a test of manual dexterity for an assembly worker should give a similar score each time the person takes the test. If the results vary widely with each retest because good scores depend on luck, the test is not reliable. When tests are not reliable, they may also be invalid.

Reliability

Testing Tools and Cautions

There are a wide variety of employment tests. But each type of test has only limited usefulness. The exact purpose of a test, its design, its directions for administration, and its applications are recorded in the test manual, which should be reviewed before a test is used. The manual also reports the test's reliability and the results of validation efforts by the test designer. Today, many tests have been validated on large populations. But personnel specialists should conduct their own studies to make sure a particular test is valid for its planned use. Each type of test has a different purpose. Figure 7-4 lists examples and gives a brief explanation of several different types of tests.

Tests have limited usefulness.

Psychological tests are those that measure personality or temperament. They are among the least reliable. Validity suffers because the relationship between personality and performance is often vague or nonexistent.

Knowledge tests are more reliable because they determine information or knowledge. Math tests for an accountant and a weather test for a pilot are examples. But personnel specialists must be able to demonstrate that the

NAME	APPLICATION (SUBJECTS)
PSYCHOLOGICAL TESTS	
• Minnesota Multiphasic Personality Inventory	Measures personality or temperament (executives, Nuclear Power Security)
• California Psychological Inventory	Measures personality or temperament (executives, managers, supervisors)
• Guilford-Zimmerman Temperament Survey	Measures personality or temperament (sales personnel)
• Watson-Glaser Critical Thinking Appraisal	Measures logic and reasoning ability (executives, managers, supervisors)
• Owens Creativity Test	Measures creativity and judgment ability (engineers)
KNOWLEDGE TESTS	
• How Supervise?	Measures knowledge of supervisory practices (managers and supervisors)
• Leadership Opinion Questionnaire	Measures knowledge of leadership practices (managers and supervisors)
• General Aptitude Test Battery	Measures verbal, spatial, numeric, and other aptitudes and dexterity (job seekers at unemployment offices)
PERFORMANCE TESTS	
• Stromberg Dexterity Test	Measures physical coordination (shop workers)
• Revised Minnesota Paper Form Board Test	Measures spatial visualization (draftsmen and draftswomen)
• Minnesota Clerical Test	Measures ability to work with numbers and names (clerks)
• Job Simulation Tests	Measures a sample of "on-the-job" demands (managers, professionals)
GRAPHIC RESPONSE TEST	
• Lie Detector	Measures honesty and truthfulness (police, retail store workers)

Figure 7-4
Some Applications of Employment-Related Tests

knowledge is needed to perform the job. The Miami trucking company example is a case where the tested knowledge (reading at an advanced level) was unneeded.

Performance tests measure ability of applicants to do some parts of the work for which they are to be hired—for example, a typing test for typists. Validity is often assumed when the test includes a representative sample of the work the applicant is to do upon being hired. However, if the test discriminates against some protected group, personnel's assumption must be backed by detailed validation studies. Merrill Lynch's test is considered valid because the test includes a sample of the work an account representative would be expected to do.

Graphic response tests are a more recent development that seek information about applicants in ways that cannot be distorted easily. The *polygraph* (or lie detector) is the most common, with over a fifth of all firms in one study reporting its use.[15] It measures physiological changes as a person responds to questions. When a person tells a lie, the conscience usually causes involuntary physiological reactions that are detected by the polygraph. At $25 to $50 per test, it is more economical than a detailed background check on applicants. In addition to ethical and public relations considerations, however, there are serious questions about the ability of most lie detector operators to administer and interpret results in a valid manner. Since many people feel such a test is an invasion of their privacy, some states have prohibited its use.[16]

> Lie detectors in personnel

Besides heeding specific cautions associated with individual tests, personnel specialists should realize that testing is not always feasible. Even when tests can be developed or bought, their cost may not be justified for jobs that have low selection ratios or that are seldom filled. Examples include technical, professional, and managerial jobs. Even when feasible, the use of tests must be flexible. They need not always be the first or last step in the selection process. Instead, personnel experts use tests during the selection process at the point they deem appropriate. Consider the comments of an experienced personnel manager for a chain of grocery stores.

Many personnel managers in other industries use testing only after other steps in the selection process. In the grocery business you must test first. Why waste time interviewing a grocery clerk who doesn't know that three for 88 cents is 30 cents a piece? Besides, when we take applications on Tuesdays, we may have 300 of them. Interviews would take 75 hours a week, and my staff consists of a clerk and myself. But through testing, we can test the entire group in an hour. Then we interview only those who score well.

> Industry peculiarities exist.

Finally, the employment test is only one of several techniques in the selection process because its use is limited to factors that can be easily tested and validated. Other items, not measurable through testing, may be equally important, such as the enthusiasm and manners of a cashier.

SELECTION INTERVIEW: STEP 3

The *selection interview* is a formal, in-depth conversation conducted to evaluate the applicant's acceptability. The interviewer seeks to answer two broad questions: Can the applicant do the job? How does the applicant compare with others who are applying for the job?

Selection interviews, or in-depth interviews as they are also known, are the most widely used selection technique. One study reports that 90 percent of all companies surveyed had more confidence in interviews than in any other source of selection information.[17] Their popularity stems from their flexibility. They can be adapted to unskilled, skilled, managerial, and staff employees. They

> The heart of selection: interviews

also allow a two-way exchange of information: interviewers learn about the applicant, and the applicant learns about the employer.

Interviews do have shortcomings. Their most noticeable flaws are in the areas of reliability and validity. Good reliability means that the interpretation of the interview results should not vary from interviewer to interviewer. But it is common for different interviewers to form different opinions. Reliability is improved when identical questions are asked, especially if interviewers are trained to record responses systematically.[18] Validity is questionable because few personnel departments conduct validation studies on their interview results. However, proactive personnel departments are beginning to realize this problem and are comparing interview results with actual performance or other criteria, such as stability of employment.[19] More validation of interviews is needed because they may relate more to personal features of candidates than to the candidates' potential performance. For example, one study reported that two of the most important variables that influence an interview are fluency of speech and composure.[20] If these findings are applicable to most employment interviews, the results of the interviews may correlate with fluency and composure, instead of potential performance. However, whether validated or not, interviews persist because of their adaptability and believed effectiveness.

Types of Interviews

Interviews are commonly conducted between the interviewer and the applicants, on a one-to-one basis. Group interviews, however, are sometimes used. Variations of group interviews appear in Figure 7-5.

One form of group interview is to have applicants meet with two or more interviewers. This allows all interviewers to evaluate the individual on the same questions and answers. Another major variation in the figure is to have two or more applicants interviewed together, by one or more interviewers. This saves time. It also permits the answers of different applicants to be compared immediately. Whether a group interview or not, there are different interview formats. Questions can be structured, unstructured, mixed, problem-solving, or stress-producing. Figure 7-6 compares these different formats. The mixed format

Figure 7-5

Different Combinations of Interviewers and Applicants

NUMBER OF INTERVIEWERS	NUMBER OF APPLICANTS
INDIVIDUAL INTERVIEW	
1	1
GROUP INTERVIEWS	
2 or more	1
1	2 or more
2 or more	2 or more

INTERVIEW FORMAT	TYPES OF QUESTIONS	USEFUL APPLICATIONS
UNSTRUCTURED	Few if any planned questions. Questions are made up during the interview.	Useful when trying to help interviewees solve personal problems or understand why they are not right for a job.
STRUCTURED	A predetermined checklist of questions, usually asked of all applicants.	Useful for valid results, especially when dealing with large numbers of applicants.
MIXED	A combination of structured and unstructured questions, which resembles what is usually done in practice.	Realistic approach that yields comparable answers plus in-depth insights.
PROBLEM SOLVING	Questions limited to hypothetical situations. Evaluation is on the solution and the approach of the applicant.	Useful to understand applicant's reasoning and analytical abilities under modest stress.
STRESS INTERVIEW	A series of harsh, rapid-fire questions intended to upset the applicant.	Useful for stressful jobs, such as handling complaints.

Figure 7-6
Different Question Formats in Interviews

is most common in practice, although each of the others has an appropriate role to play.[21]

Unstructured interviews   As the summary in Figure 7-6 indicates, the unstructured interview allows personnel specialists to develop questions as the interview proceeds. The interviewer goes into topic areas as they arise, much like a friendly conversation. Unfortunately, this unstructured method, which also is called nondirective interviewing, lacks the reliability of a structured interview because each applicant is asked a different series of questions. Even worse, this approach may overlook key areas of the applicant's skills or background.

Structured interviews   Structured, or directive, interviews rely on a predetermined set of questions. The questions are developed before the interview begins and are asked of every applicant. This approach improves the reliability of the interview process, but it does not allow the interviewer to follow up interesting or unusual responses. Here the end result is an interview that seems quite mechanical to all concerned. The rigid format may even convey disinterest to applicants who are used to more flexible interviews.

Mixed interviews   In practice, interviewers typically use a blend of structured and unstructured questions. The structured questions provide a base of information that allows comparisons between candidates. But the unstructured questions make the interview more conversational and permit greater

Most common

insights into the unique differences between applicants. College recruiters, for example, use mixed interviews most of the time.[22]

Problem-solving interviews Problem-solving interviews focus on a problem or series of problems that the applicant is expected to solve. Often these are hypothetical interpersonal situations, and the applicant is asked what should be done. Both the answer and the approach used by the applicant are evaluated. This interview technique has a very narrow scope. It primarily reveals the applicant's ability to solve the types of problems presented. Validity is more likely if the hypothetical situations are similar to those found on the job. The actual interview might consist of ten situations similar to the following:

> Suppose you had to decide between two candidates for a promotion. Candidate A is loyal, cooperative, punctual, and hard-working. Candidate B is a complainer and is tardy and discourteous, but is the best producer in your department. Whom would you recommend for promotion to supervisor? Why?

The way the applicant reacts to the questions is noted. Since this type of interview produces modest amounts of stress, it gives an indication of how the applicant can function under moderately stressful situations.

Stress interviews When the job involves much stress, a stress interview attempts to learn how the applicant will respond to the pressure. Originally developed during World War II to see how selected recruits might react under stress behind enemy lines, these interviews have useful applications in civilian employment. For example, applicants for police work are sometimes put through a stress interview to see how they might react to problems they encounter in the streets. The interview itself consists of a series of harsh questions asked in rapid-fire succession and in an unfriendly manner. Since stressful situations are usually only part of the job, this technique should be

Bad PR is possible. used in connection with other interview formats. Even then, negative public relations are likely among those who are not hired. Reliability and validity are hard to demonstrate since the stress on the job may differ from the stress posed in the interview.

The Interview Process

The five stages of a typical employment interview are listed in Figure 7-7. These stages are interviewer preparation, creation of rapport, information exchange, termination, and evaluation. They are discussed to illustrate how the actual interview process occurs.[23]

Interviewer preparation Before beginning the interview, the interview-
What to ask? er needs to prepare. This preparation requires that specific questions be developed by the interviewer. It is the answers to these questions that the interviewer will use to decide the applicant's suitability. At the same time the interviewer must consider what questions the applicant is likely to ask. Since

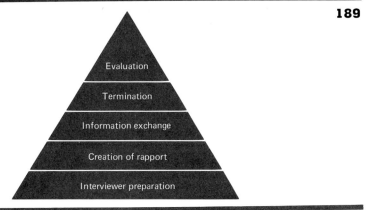

Figure 7-7
Stages in the Typical Employment Interview

they use the interview to persuade top applicants to accept subsequent job offers, interviewers need to be able to explain job duties, performance standards, pay, benefits, and other areas of interest.

A list of typical questions asked by college recruiters and other interviewers appears in Figure 7-8. As can be seen from that list, these questions are intended to give the interviewer some insight into the applicant's interests, attitudes, and background. Specific or technical questions are added to the list according to the type of job opening. A review of the job description and position specifications helps the interviewer prepare specific questions. In preparing those questions, the interviewers must be especially careful not to ask any that could be interpreted as discriminatory. As one researcher concluded, "the employment interview has increasingly come under judicial scrutiny as a result of charges that . . . questions are biased or unfair toward racial, religious and ethnic minorities, females, the handicapped, and elderly persons."[24] Questions asked of a protected group but not of members of the majority are usually the ones that cause violations. An example is asking women about child-care arrangements but not asking men the same question. Likewise, questions about sex, age, national origin, handicaps, religion, race, or color are likely to be considered discriminatorily motivated, unless there is a bona fide occupational qualification. (See Chapter 3 for a discussion of BFOQs.)[25]

Interviews and judicial scrutiny

Another action the interviewer should undertake before the interview is to review the application blank. Research shows that the quality of the interviewer's decision is significantly better when the application blank is present.[26] With or without the application blank, interviewers seem to take about the same length of time to reach a conclusion, from four to ten minutes.[27] The longer the interview is scheduled to last and the better the quality of the applicant, the longer it takes the interviewer to reach a decision.[28]

Tips for good employment interviewing

Because the average cost of hiring new employees is estimated to be as high as $4000 in the cases of managerial and professional employees, the interviewer's preparation should be aimed at making the interview process efficient and comfortable for the applicant.[29] Often the interviewer is one of the first

1. How do you spend your spare time? What are your hobbies?
2. What community or school activities have you been involved in?
3. Describe your ideal job. In what type of work are you interested?
4. Why do you want to work for our company?
5. What were your favorite classes? Why?
6. Do you have any geographic preferences?
7. Why did you select your college major?
8. What do you know about our company's products or services?
9. Describe the ideal boss.
10. How often do you expect to be promoted?
11. What is your major weakness? Strength?
12. Why do you think your friends like you?
13. Do you plan to take additional college courses? Which ones?
14. What jobs have you had that you liked the most? Least?
15. Describe your least favorite boss or teacher?
16. What are your career goals?
17. If you could go back five years, what would you do the same? Different?
18. Why should you be hired by our company?
19. Describe your last job.
20. How many hours do you think you will have to work at your job?
21. What job skills do you have?
22. What is your favorite sport?

Figure 7-8
Sample Questions Used in Employment Interviews

representatives of the employer with whom the applicant has had an opportunity to talk. A strong and lasting opinion of the company is likely to be formed.[30] If the interviewer does not show courtesy to the applicant, misperceptions may result. If the applicant is a quality candidate for the job, it is likely that the person has other job opportunities.[31]

Creation of rapport   The burden to establish rapport falls on the interviewer. As one author commented:

The heart of interviewing

> The heart of the interview process is rapport. Only in a relationship of mutual trust and comfort—a relationship largely free of anxiety—will a candidate talk freely. . . . No interview is without stress, however. The candidate is anxious about making a favorable impression. . . . In view of this mutual anxiety, every effort should be made to allay the normal fears of both parties. This can be done by . . . projecting an image of confidence, competence and concern, especially in the early stages of the interview.[32]

Rapport is aided by beginning the interview on time and starting with nonthreatening questions such as, "Did you have any parking problems?" At the same time, the interviewer may use body language to help relax the applicant. A smile, a handshake, a relaxed posture, and the moving aside of paperwork—all communicate without words. This rapport is maintained through such nonverbal communications as nodding one's head affirmatively, smiling, and relaxing one's posture during the interview session.[33]

Information exchange   The interview process is a conversation that exchanges information. To help establish rapport while learning about the candidate, some interviewers begin by asking the interviewee if he or she has any questions. This establishes two-way communication and allows the interviewer to begin to judge the recruit by the type of questions asked. Consider the responses to the interviewer's opening statement: "Let's start with any questions you may have." Which of the following responses gives you the most favorable impression?

Applicant 1:   I don't have any questions.

Applicant 2:   I have several questions. How much does the job pay? Will I get a two-week vacation at the end of the first year?

Applicant 3:   What will my responsibilities be? I am hoping to find a job that offers me challenges now and career potential down the road.

Each response creates a different impression on the interviewer. But only the third applicant appears concerned about the job. The other two applicants are either unconcerned or interested only in the benefits they will receive.

In general, an interviewer will ask questions in a way to learn as much information as possible. Questions that begin with how, what, why, compare, describe, expand, or "could you tell me more about . . ." are more likely to get an open response. Questions that can be answered with a simple "yes" or "no" do not give the interviewer much insight. For example, an interviewer is likely to get narrow, limited answers by asking questions that begin "Are you . . ." or "Did you . . ." These questions often result in very abbreviated answers.[34] Specific questions and areas of interest to an interviewer are suggested in Figure 7-8. Besides knowing the answers to those questions, the interviewer may want more specific information about the applicant's background, skills, and interests.

Types of questions

Termination   As the list of questions dwindles or available time ends, the interviewer must draw the session to a close. Once again, nonverbal communication is useful. Sitting erect, turning toward the door, glancing at a watch or clock—all clue the applicant that the end is near. Some interviewers terminate the interview by asking, "Do you have any final questions?" At this point, the interviewer notifies the applicant of the next step in the interview process, which may be to wait for a call or letter. Regardless of the interviewer's opinions, the applicant should not be given an indication of his or her prospects for getting the job. Not only may a subsequent candidate look better, but subsequent steps in the selection process may cause the final selection decision to be much different than it might appear at the end of the interview.

Use body language.

EMPIRE INC.
"An equal opportunity employer"

Postinterview Checklist

Applicant's Name _____ Date _____

Position under Consideration _____ Interviewer _____

Interviewer's Comments

A. Rate the applicant on the following (1=low; 10=high):

_____ Appearance   _____ Ability to perform job

_____ Apparent interest   _____ Education/training

_____ Experience/background   _____ Timely availability

_____ Reasonable expectations   _____ Past employment stability

B. List specific comments that reveal the candidate's strengths and weaknesses for the job being considered:

1. Attitude toward previous job _____

2. Attitude toward previous boss _____

3. Expectations about job duties _____

4. Career or occupational expectations _____

5. Other specific comments about applicant _____

_____

_____

Follow-up Actions Required

_____ None   _____ Follow-up interview with personnel

_____ Testing   _____ Applicant unacceptable (file)

_____ Supervisory interview _____ Notify applicant of rejection

_____ Applicant unacceptable for job under consideration. Reconsider for job as

_____

Figure 7-9
A Post-Interview Checklist

Evaluation Immediately after the interview ends, the interviewer should record specific answers and general impressions about the candidate. Figure 7-9 shows a typical checklist used to record the interviewer's impressions. Use of a checklist like the one in the figure can improve the reliability of the interview as a selection technique.[35] As the checklist shows, the interviewer is able to obtain a large amount of information even from a short interview.

Get reactions on paper.

Interviewer Errors

Regardless of the particular pitfall that traps the interviewer, failure to recognize the cautions in Figure 7-10 lowers the effectiveness of the interview. When the applicant is judged according to the halo effect or personal biases, the results of the interview are misinterpreted. Applicants are accepted or rejected for reasons that may bear no relationship to their potential performance. Likewise, leading questions and domination do not allow the interviewer to learn of the applicant's potential. The evaluation of the applicant is then based on guess-

Biases

HALO EFFECT

Interviewers who use limited information about an applicant to bias their evaluation of that person's other characteristics are subject to the halo effect.

Examples:

● An applicant who has a pleasant smile and firm handshake is considered a leading candidate before the interview begins.

● An applicant who wears blue jeans to the interview is rejected mentally.

LEADING QUESTIONS

Interviewers who "telegraph" the desired answer by the way they frame their questions are using leading questions.

Examples:

● "Do you think you'll like this work?"

● "Do you agree that profits are necessary?"

PERSONAL BIASES

Interviewers who harbor prejudice against specific groups are exhibiting a personal bias.

Examples:

● "I prefer sales personnel who are tall."

● "Some jobs are for men and others for women."

INTERVIEWER DOMINATION

Interviewers who use the interview to oversell the applicant, brag about their successes, or carry on a social conversation instead of an interview are guilty of interviewer domination.

Examples:

● Spending the entire interview telling the applicant about company plans or benefits.

● Using the interview to tell the applicant how important the interviewer's job is.

Figure 7-10
A Summary of Typical Interviewer Errors

work, with little or no substantiation. No matter which pitfall is involved, it reduces the reliability and validity of the interview. When biases are presented, the interview only wastes both organizational resources and the applicant's time.

REFERENCES AND BACKGROUND CHECKS: STEP 4

What type of person is the applicant? Is the applicant a good, reliable worker? To answer these questions, employment specialists use references and background checks.

Many professionals have a very skeptical attitude toward references. *Personal references*—those that attest to the applicant's sound character—are usually provided by friends or family. Their objectivity and candor are certainly

Personal references

194

Employment references

questionable. When writing a reference, the author usually emphasizes only positive points. Thus personal references are less commonly used. *Employment references* differ from personal references because they discuss the applicant's work history. Many personnel specialists doubt the usefulness of these references because former supervisors or teachers may not be completely candid, especially with negative information. As privacy legislation continues to expand,[36] many supervisors and personnel departments are growing less willing to provide employment references—they fear potential lawsuits. Even though supervisors or personnel specialists are protected under what the law calls "qualified privilege," that protection ends if there are any doubts about the truth of the recommendation, whether the recommendation is made with malice, or whether the information goes into issues not covered by privilege—such as personal information not related to employment.

Qualified privilege

A judge decides if a communication is privileged. However, a jury decides if malice existed. Even if the company wins a suit brought by a former employee, the costs to the company are often many thousands of dollars and much wasted time. If the company loses, a sympathetic jury might award an expensive settlement, even into the millions of dollars. As a result, most personnel departments develop a policy where the company will do little more than verify that the person actually worked for them. Some personnel departments will not even do that much.

This lack of candor has caused some personnel specialists to omit entirely this step from the selection process. Other specialists have substituted telephone inquiries for written references. Besides a faster response, often at lower cost, voice inflections or hesitancy to blunt questions may tip off underlying problems. In practice, less than 22 percent of all reference checks seek negative information, according to one study.[37] That same study revealed that 48 percent of reference checks are used to verify application information and 30 percent are used to gather additional data.

Detailed checks may be needed.

When an applicant is going to have access to money, valuables, or classified information—as an account executive at Merrill Lynch would have—a background search may be conducted that goes far beyond letters of reference. Bonding companies may want far more detail than appears in the application blank. The personnel department may want to check the applicant's credit rating through a commercial credit bureau or local financial institutions. If national defense security is involved, a detail background check may be needed before the employee can receive the necessary clearances to work on classified materials. For some highly secret jobs with the government or defense contractors, these clearances may take up to six months or longer and often involve checks on family members and the applicant's past all the way back to high school.[38]

MEDICAL EVALUATION: STEP 5

The selection process may include a medical evaluation of the applicant before the hiring decision is made. Normally, the evaluation is a health checklist that asks the applicant to indicate health and accident information. The questionnaire is sometimes supplemented with a physical examination by a company nurse or physician. The medical evaluation may:

- Entitle the employer to lower health or life insurance rates for company-paid insurance

- Be required by state or local health officials—particularly in food-handling operations where communicable diseases are a danger

- Be useful to evaluate whether the applicant can handle the physical or mental stress of a job

Many employers have done away with this step because of the costs involved. Government contractors are especially reluctant to use medical evaluations before the hiring decision. If an applicant is rejected, charges of discrimination under the Rehabilitation Act of 1973 may be brought. A preexisting health condition may be considered a disability, and failure to hire may be seen as discrimination against the qualified handicapped. If the employer wants a medical evaluation, it may be scheduled after the hiring decision.

Watch out for discrimination.

SUPERVISORY INTERVIEW: STEP 6

The immediate supervisor ultimately is responsible for newly hired workers. Since that responsibility is ever-present, supervisors should have input into the final hiring decision. The supervisor is often able to better evaluate the applicant's technical abilities. Likewise, the immediate supervisor can often answer the interviewee's specific job-related questions with greater precision. As a result, one study reported that in over three-fourths of the organizations surveyed the supervisor has the authority to make the final hiring decision.

When supervisors make the final decision, the role of the personnel department is to provide the supervisor with the best prescreened applicants available. From these two or three applicants, the supervisor decides whom to hire. Some organizations leave the final hiring decision to the personnel department, especially when applicants are hired into a training program instead of a specific job. If supervisors constantly reject particular groups of applicants, such as minorities or women, the personnel department may be given final hiring authority to avoid future charges of discrimination.

Regardless of who has the final hiring authority, the personal commitment of supervisors is generally higher when they participate in the selection process. Their participation is best obtained through the supervisory interview. Through a variety of structured and nonstructured questions, the supervisor attempts to assess the technical competency, potential, and overall suitability of the applicant. The supervisory interview also allows the recruit to have technical, work-related questions answered. When the supervisor recommends hiring an individual, it creates within the supervisor a psychological commitment to assist the new employee. If the candidate turns out to be unsatisfactory, the supervisor who participated is more likely to accept some of the responsibility for failure.

Get the future supervisor involved.

REALISTIC JOB PREVIEWS: STEP 7

Often the supervisory interview is supplemented with a realistic job preview. A *realistic job preview* (RJP) allows the employee to understand the job and the job setting before the hiring decision is made. Often this involves showing the candidate the type of work, equipment, and working conditions involved.

Unmet expectations about a job probably contribute to initial job dissatisfaction. The realistic job preview attempts to prevent job dissatisfaction by giving the newcomer an insight into the job.[39] Recently hired employees who have had a realistic job preview are less likely to be shocked by the job or by the job setting on the first day they report to work. Two writers concluded that:

A partial "cure" for early turnover

> The RJP functions very much like a medical vaccination. . . . The typical medical vaccination injects one with a small, weakened dose of germs, so that one's body can develop a natural resistance to that disease. The RJP functions similarly by presenting job candidates with a small dose of "organizational reality." And, like the medical vaccination, the RJP is probably much less effective after a person has already entered a new organization.[40]

Research on the effectiveness of realistic job previews has shown that employee turnover was higher when the job previews were not used. The average turnover rate in nine out of ten studies was 28.8 percent higher.[41] Clearly, realistic job previews are an effective way to reduce turnover;[42] however, as two other researchers concluded:

> Telling prospective employees about unpleasant working conditions may improve the probability that they will remain on the job in comparison to those who are not told about the conditions. However . . . those who are told about less pleasant conditions will be no more satisfied with them once they are experienced than will those who are not told. To improve satisfaction and the quality of work, ultimately some changes must be made in those aspects of the work environment with which employees are dissatisfied.[43]

HIRING DECISION: STEP 8

Whether made by the supervisor or by the personnel department, the final hiring decision marks the end of the selection process. To maintain good public relations, employers should notify applicants who were not selected. Employment specialists may want to consider rejected applicants for other openings since these recruits already have gone through various stages of the selection process. Even if no openings are available, applications of unsuccessful candidates should be kept on file for future openings. Retaining these applications can be useful if the employer is charged with employment discrimination.

The applications of those hired should also be retained. The application blank begins the employee's personnel file and contains useful information for studies that the personnel department may conduct to learn about the source of its applicants—such as age, sex, race, or other work-force characteristics. If some recruits prove unsatisfactory after they are hired, for example, personnel specialists may be able to reconstruct the selection process beginning with the application. In their reconstruction, they may uncover invalid tests, improperly conducted interviews, or other flaws in the selection process.

OUTCOMES AND FEEDBACK

The final outcome of the selection process is the people who are hired. If the preselection inputs are considered carefully and the major steps of the selection process have been followed correctly, then new employees are likely to be productive. And productive employees are the best evidence of an effective selection process.

To evaluate both new employees and the selection process requires feedback. Feedback on successful employees is sometimes hard to find since supervisors usually claim responsibility for them. Feedback on failures is ample. It can include legal suits, displeased supervisors, growing employee turnover and absenteeism, poor performance, low employee satisfaction, and even union activity.

Quality control in personnel means feedback.

More constructive feedback is obtained through specific questions. How well does the new employee adapt to the organization? To the job? To the career of which the job is a part? And finally, how well does the employee perform? Answers to each of these questions provide feedback about the employee and the selection process. The following chapters examine each of these questions in depth.

SUMMARY

The selection process depends heavily upon inputs such as job analysis, human resource plans, and recruits. These inputs are used within the challenges of ethical, supply, organizational, and equal employment guidelines established by the organization.

The key challenges that underlie the entire selection process are to secure qualified employees and to provide equal employment opportunity. In all phases of the selection process, personnel professionals must be concerned about the potential for adverse impact among the various steps of the selection process. Even when the overall selection process does not show an adverse impact upon members of protected classes, evidence of a discriminatory impact at any step in the process should be investigated and the discrimination eliminated where found.

With these inputs and challenges, the selection process takes recruits and puts them through a series of steps to evaluate their potential. These steps vary from organization to organization and from one job opening to another. In general, the selection procedure relies on testing for many hourly jobs and on interviews for virtually every opening that is to be filled. References and medical evaluations are common steps found in the selection process of most employers.

The supervisor's role should include participation in the selection process, usually through an interview with job candidates. As a result of this participation, the supervisor is more likely to be committed to the new worker's success.

The growing research evidence supports the use of realistic job previews. After considerable expense and effort to recruit and select employees, the use of realistic job previews seems well advised as a means of reducing employee turnover among new employees.

TERMS FOR REVIEW

Selection process	Selection interview
Employment function	Structured interviews
Selection ratio	Stress interviews
Four-fifths rule	Bottom-line test
Validity	Reliability
Differential validity	Realistic job previews
Halo effect	

REVIEW AND DISCUSSION QUESTIONS

1.   Suppose you are an employment specialist. Would you expect to have a large or small selection ratio for each of the following job openings?
   a. Janitors
   b. Nuclear engineers with five years of experience designing naval nuclear reactors
   c. Clerk-typists
   d. Supervisors
   e. Elementary school teachers in northern Alaska? In southern Florida?

2.   List and briefly describe each of the steps in the selection process.

3.   If the employment manager asked you to streamline the firm's selection process for hourly workers, which steps described in this chapter would you recommend cutting? Why?

4.   The interview used for selection has five definite steps. What are those steps? Briefly explain each.

5.   Why should tests be validated?

6.   As you begin interviewing a job applicant, you notice this person is very nervous. Your evaluation of the application blank indicates that this person is a highly qualified applicant. What should you do to put this person at ease in order to establish rapport?

7. Some people believe that the personnel department should have the authority to decide who is hired because personnel contains the experts on hiring. Others say that the immediate supervisor is responsible for employee performance and should have the final authority. Support one argument or the other and explain your reasoning.

8. Explain why realistic job previews help reduce turnover among recently hired employees.

INCIDENT 7-1

A Selection Decision at Empire, Inc.

At Empire, Inc., the turnover rate is very high among assembly workers. Supervisors in the production department have indicated to the personnel department that they do not have time to conduct a supervisory interview with the large number of applicants that are processed to fill assembly-line openings. As a result, the personnel department's employment specialists make the final hiring decisions.

The profiles of three typical applicants are presented below:

	APPLICANT A	APPLICANT B	APPLICANT C
Years of experience	4	7½	1
Education	1 year of college	Finished eighth grade	General equivalency degree
Age	24	43	32
Test score	76/100	73/100	85/100
Medical evaluation	OK	OK	OK
Job knowledge	Very good	Excellent	Fair/good
Work history	Limited data	Stable	Stable
Ranking by:			
Interviewer 1	1	2	3
Interviewer 2	3	2	1
Apparent eagerness	Moderate	Strong	Weak/average
Availability	4 weeks	2 weeks	Immediately

The nature of the assembly jobs is rather simple. Training seldom takes more than an hour or two. Most people master the job and achieve an acceptable level of production during the second full day on the job. The tasks involve very little physical or mental effort. The test is valid, but only has a weak relationship between scores and actual performance.

1. What information would you consider irrelevant in the selection profiles above?

2. Are there any changes you would recommend in the selection process?

3. Which of the three candidates would you select given the limited knowledge you possess? Why?

INCIDENT 7-2

National Food Brokers Selection Process

National Food Brokers buys carload orders of nonperishable food products for resale to food wholesalers. Phone-sales personnel take orders from major food wholesalers, write up the orders, and send them to the appropriate food producers. Nearly 90 of National's 130 employees work in the phone-sales department. Since the job requires long hours on the phone to different accounts, the work is not very plesant and turnover is high.

The manager of the phone-sales department, Carol Decinni, told the following observations to the personnel manager, Craig Reems:

> Most of the people that work in the department fall into two groups. There are those who have been here for two or more years. They seem reasonably content and are the top sellers we have. The other group consists of people who have been here for less than two years. Most of our turnover comes from this group. In fact, we lose one of every three new employees during the first two months. When I talk with the people who are quitting, most of them tell me that they have no idea how much time they had to spend on the phone. I am generally pleased with the quality of recruits the personnel department provides. But we cannot continue with this high turnover. My supervisors are spending most of their time training new workers. Is there anything the personnel department can do to hire more stable workers?

1. Suppose you are asked by the personnel manager to suggest some strategies for improving the selection process in order to hire more stable workers. What suggestions do you have for (a) preemployment testing and (b) reference checks?

2. Do you believe an interview with a supervisor in the department would help applicants understand the work better?

3. What do you think the supervisors should do to give the applicants a realistic understanding of the job before they are hired?

EXERCISE 7-1

Uniform Guidelines: The Four-Fifths Rule versus the Bottom-Line Test

During the last three years a company had 600 applicants, 400 whites and 200 blacks. Of this group, 100 whites and 20 blacks passed the company's standardized preemployment test. Of the 100 whites who passed the test, 80 were rated by interviewers as usable candidates; and of the 80, 60 passed the company's detailed background check. Of the 20 blacks who passed the test, 18 received acceptable evaluations from the interviewers, and 9 passed the detailed background check. The end result was that the company hired 60 white and 9 black workers during the past three years.

1. Would this company pass the bottom-line test specified by the EEOC in its uniform guidelines?

2. Which of the selection steps mentioned above, if any, fail the four-fifths rule?

3. What recommendations would you make to this company?

REFERENCES

1. George S. Odiorne, *Programmed Learning Aid for Personnel Administration: A Management by Objectives Approach,* Homewood, Ill.: Richard D. Irwin, 1973, p. 71.

2. Lawrence Rout, "Going for Broker: Our Man Takes Part in Stock-Selling Test," *The Wall Street Journal,* Eastern edition, Apr. 4, 1979, p. 1.

3. Ibid.

4. American Society of Personnel Administrators, *The Personnel Executive's Job,* Englewood Cliffs, N.J.: Prentice-Hall, 1977.

5. John D. Erdlen, "Ethics and the Employee Relations Function," *The Personnel Administrator,* January 1979, pp. 41–43, 68.

6. Richard Peres, *Dealing with Employment Discrimination,* New York: McGraw-Hill, 1978, pp. 18–37.

7. James Ledvinka, *Federal Regulation of Personnel and Human Resource Management,* Belmont, Calif.: Wadsworth, 1982, pp. 101–110.

8. Ibid.

9. Paul Sheibar, "A Simple Selection System Called 'Job Match,'" *Personnel Journal,* January 1979, pp. 26–29, 53. See also Robert P. Delamontagne and James B. Weitzul, "Performance Alignment: The Fine Art of the Perfect Fit," *Personnel Journal,* February 1980, pp. 115–117, 131.

10. Thomas A. Loenko and M. Susan Taylor, "Organizational Image: Dimensionality and Relationships to Job Search Attitudes & Behaviors," *Wisconsin Working Paper* (8-82-36), August 1982.

11. Walter Kiechel III, "The Managerial Mind Probe," *Fortune,* Feb. 7, 1983, p. 113.

12. *Willie S. Griggs et al. v. Duke Power Company,* 401 U.S. 424 (1971). For other considerations in testing see C. H. Lawrence and Michael J. Balma, *Principles of Personnel Testing,* 2d ed., New York: McGraw-Hill, 1966. Also see David E. Robertson, "Updating on Testing and Equal Employment," *Personnel Journal,* March 1977, pp. 144–147; Charles F. Schanie and William F. Holley, "An Interpretive Review of the Federal Uniform Guidelines on Employee Selection Procedures," *Personnel Administrator,* June

1980, pp. 44–48; and Bonnie Sandman and Faith Urban, "Employment Testing and the Law," *Labor Law Journal,* January 1976, pp. 38–54.

13. In *Griggs v. Duke Power Company* the U.S. Supreme Court said that the EEOC's uniform guidelines were "entitled to great deference." *Albemarle Paper Company v. Moody,* 422 U.S. 405 (1975). See also Douglas D. Baker and David E. Terpstra, "Employee Selection: Must Every Job Test Be Validated?" *Personnel Journal,* August 1982, pp. 602–604.

14. James Ledvinka and Lyle F. Schoenfeldt, "Legal Developments in Employment Testing: Albemarle and Beyond," *Personnel Psychology,* Spring 1978, pp. 1–13.

15. John A. Belt and Peter B. Holden, "Polygraph Usage among Major U.S. Corporations," *Personnel Journal,* February 1978, p. 82. See also "Business Buys the Lie Detector," *Business Week,* Feb. 6, 1978, pp. 100–191, 104; and Philip G. Benson and Paul S. Koris, "The Polygraph in Employment: Some Unresolved Issues," *Personnel Journal,* September 1979, pp. 616–621.

16. "The Intimidation of Job Tests," *The AFL-CIO American Federationist,* January 1979, pp. 1–8.

17. Bureau of National Affairs, *Personnel Policies Forum,* survey no. 114, September 1976.

18. Robert N. McMurray, "Validating the Patterned Interview," *Personnel,* January 1947, pp. 263–272. See also Eugene Mayfield, "The Selection Interview—A Reevaluation of Published Research," *Personnel Psychology,* Autumn 1964, pp. 239–260; Edward C. Andler, "Preplanned Question Areas for Efficient Interviewing," *Personnel Journal,* January 1976, pp. 8–10; and Frederick S. Hills, "Job Relatedness vs. Adverse Impact in Personnel," *Personnel Journal,* March 1980, pp. 211–215, 229.

19. McMurray, op. cit.

20. James G. Hollandsworth, Jr., and others, "Relative Contributions of Verbal, Articulative, and Nonverbal Communication to Employment Decisions in the Job Interview Setting," *Personnel Psychology,* Summer 1979, pp. 359–367.

21. R. D. Avery and J. E. Champion, "The Employment Interview: A Summary and Review of Recent Literature," *Personnel Psychology,* Summer 1982, pp. 281–322.

22. Ibid.

23. Jeffrey D. Latterell, "Planning for the Selection Interview," *Personnel Journal,* July 1979, pp. 466–467, 480.

24. Fredic M. Jablin, "Use of Discriminatory Questions in Screening Interviews," *Personnel Administrator,* March 1982, p. 44.

25. Ibid., p. 41.

26. William L. Tullar, Terry W. Mullins, and Sharon A. Caldwell, "Effects on Interview Length and Applicant Quality on Interview Decision Time," *Journal of Applied Psychology,* vol. 64, no. 6, 1979, pp. 669–674.

27. D. H. Tucker and P. M. Rowe, "Consulting the Application Form Prior to the Interview: An Essential Step in the Selection Process," *Journal of Applied Psychology,* vol. 62, no. 5, 1977, pp. 558–664.

28. Tullar, Mullins, and Caldwell, op. cit.

29. Hall A. Acuff, "Quality Control in Employee Selection," *Personnel Journal,* July 1981, p. 565.

30. Scott T. Rickard, "Effective Staff Selection," *Personnel Journal,* June 1981, pp. 475–478.

31. Nancy J. Schweitzer and John Deely, "Interviewing the Disabled Job Applicant," *Personnel Journal,* March 1982, pp. 205–209.

32. John W. Cogger, "Are You a Skilled Interviewer," *Personnel Journal,* November 1982, pp. 840–843.

33. Richard G. Nehrbass, "Psychological Barriers to Effective Employment Interviewing," *Personnel Journal,* December 1976, pp. 598–600. See also S. Trevor Michaels, "Seven Questions That Will Improve Your Managerial Hiring Decisions," *Personnel Journal,* March 1980, pp. 199–200, 224.

34. Michael H. Frisch, *Coaching and Counseling Handbook,* New York: Resource Dynamics, 1981.

35. Avery and Champion, op. cit. See also Kenneth A. Kovach, "Subconscious Stereotyping in Personnel Decisions," *Business Horizons,* September–October, 1983, pp. 60–66.

36. Virginia E. Schein, "Privacy and Personnel: A Time for Action," *Personnel Journal,* December 1976, pp. 604–607, 615. See also John Rahiya, "Privacy Protection and Personnel Administration: Are New Laws Needed?" *The Personnel Administrator,* April 1979, pp. 19–21, 28.

37. George M. Beason and John A. Belt, "Verifying Applicants' Backgrounds," *Personnel Journal,* July 1976, p. 345. See also Jeremiah Bogert, "Learning the Applicant's Background through Confidential Investigations," *Personnel Journal,* June 1976, p. 272.

38. Carole Sewell, "Pre-Employment Investigations: The Key to Security in Hiring," *Personnel Journal,* May 1981, pp. 376–377. See also Bruce D. Wonder and Kenneth S. Keleman, "Increasing the Value of Reference Information," *Personnel Administrator,* March 1984, pp. 98–103.

39. Lyman Porter and Richard Steers, "Organizational, Work, and Personal Factors in Employee Turnover and Absenteeism," *Psychological Bulletin,* vol. 80, 1973, pp. 151–176.

40. Paula Popovich and John P. Wanous, "The Realistic Job Preview as a Persuasive Communication," *Academy of Management Review,* October 1982, p. 571.

41. Ibid., p. 572.

42. John P. Wanous, "Realistic Job Previews: Can a Procedure to Reduce Turnover Also Influence the Relationship between Abilities and Performance," *Personnel Psychology,* Summer 1978, pp. 249–258.

43. Bernard L. Dugoni and Daniel R. Ilgen, "Realistic Job Preview and the Adjustment of New Employees," *Academy of Management Journal,* September 1981, p. 590; see also James A. Breaugh, "Realistic Job Previews: A Critical Appraisal and Future Research Directions," *The Academy of Management Review,* October 1983, pp. 612–619.

PART

III

DEVELOPMENT AND EVALUATION

When a new employee is hired or a present employee is reassigned, orientation should follow. Without a solid orientation program, worker productivity and quality of work life may fall short of their potential. But orientation alone is insufficient. New jobholders need to be trained to do their present jobs and developed to handle future responsibilities. Some employers even offer career planning assistance to further encourage the development of employees. The success of the individual and of the personnel department depends on receiving feedback about performance. Through performance appraisal, the employee and the personnel department learn how successful their efforts have been.

The next four chapters are about employee development and evaluation. The personnel department's role in these activities affects you whether you work in a personnel department or elsewhere in an organization. Knowledge of these activities allows you to be a better employee and a more effective manager.

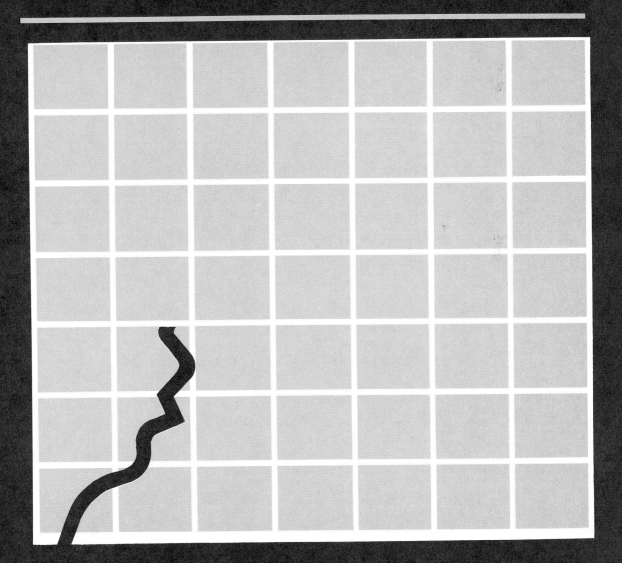

CHAPTER

8

Effective socialization means an *internal commitment* to the organization, rather than just compliance with organization practices.

John P. Wanous[1]

Two kinds of tasks confront new employees. The first kind have to do with meeting the company's expectations. . . . The second kind of tasks have to do with meeting the needs of the employee.

Joan M. Pearson[2]

ORIENTATION AND PLACEMENT

CHAPTER OBJECTIVES

After studying this chapter, you should be able to:

1 <u>Describe</u> the content and scope of a two-tier orientation program.

2 <u>Explain</u> the impact of a new employee orientation program on turnover and learning.

3 <u>Identify</u> the personnel department's and the supervisor's responsibilities in employee orientation.

4 <u>Explain</u> how placement decisions affect the personnel department.

5 <u>Discuss</u> the personnel department's role in separation decisions.

6 <u>Identify</u> several strategies that organizations use to reduce layoffs among their full-time employees.

Personnel management is much more than just hiring people. Once employee selection is completed, a proactive personnel department helps the "new hire" become a productive and satisfied employee.

The process of becoming a productive and satisfied employee is important to the organization and to the employee. As the last two chapters on recruitment and selection have shown, organizations devote considerable time and resources to hiring people. By the first day of work, the employer already has an investment in the new worker. And there is a job—or at least a potential job—that the organization needs to have done. At the same time, the newcomer has needs that may hinder the transition from recruit to worker. Anxieties leading to questions such as Will I be able to do the job? or Will I fit in around here? or Will the boss like me? are common among new employees. These "first day jitters" may be natural, but they reduce both the employee's ability to learn and the employee's satisfaction with the organization. Psychologists tell us that initial impressions are strong and lasting because newcomers have little else by which to judge the organization and its people. As a first step to helping the employee become a satisfied and productive member of the organization, the personnel department must make those initial impressions favorable.

PLACEMENT OBSTACLES
TO PRODUCTIVITY

One obstacle to a productive and satisfied work force is that employees are more likely to quit during their first few months than at any other time in their employment. This initial turnover is common. Some of it may even be beneficial if it is among those new hires who sense that the organization or the job is not right for them.[3] Realistic job previews are a partial solution to this type of turnover. As discussed at the end of Chapter 7, realistic job previews let applicants understand what their jobs entail. Then when they first report to work, the psychological gap between what they expected and what they find is easier to bridge. This difference between what one expects and what one finds is called *cognitive dissonance.*[4] If dissonance is too high, people take action. For new employees, that action may mean quitting. Realistic job previews can reduce the dissonance newcomers often encounter.

Other potential causes of dissonance exist besides the job itself. New employees may not like work-related policies, coworkers, supervision, or other aspects of their employment relationship. And until the newcomer reports to work, neither the employee nor the personnel department can tell which areas will be of concern. Nevertheless, a proactive personnel department can help employees fit into the organization. The department's efforts help integrate the newcomer into the organization and enable socialization to take place. *Socialization* is the ongoing process through which an employee begins to understand and accept the values, norms, and beliefs held by others in the organization. The socialization process helps the organization meet its needs for productive employees while enabling the new employee to meet his or her needs. As described in Chapter 1, an important objective of personnel management is to assist employees in achieving their personal goals, at least insofar as these goals enhance the individual's contribution to the organization. Personal objectives of employees must be met if workers are to be maintained and retained. Otherwise, employee performance and satisfaction may decline, and employees may leave the organization.

New Employee Turnover

When the personnel department helps employees meet their personal objectives, employee satisfaction tends to improve, which may benefit the organization through lower turnover costs.[5] Turnover is expensive. Not only the recruiting and selection expenses but also the costs associated with creating new employee records in the personnel department, establishing payroll records in accounting, giving new employees training, and providing them with necessary safety equipment are lost when employees leave. These costs never appear on the profit and loss statement as "turnover expenses," although maybe if they did top management might pay closer attention to turnover. Instead, the costs of turnover are reflected in the budgets of the personnel, accounting, training, and safety departments. The exact cost per employee probably can never be determined accurately. For entry-level, unskilled workers who quit in the first day or so, the expense is likely to be a few hundred dollars. For newly hired salaried managers and professionals—particularly if the employer had to pay a search firm fee—the cost of turnover can be many thousands of dollars.

Costs of turnover

To a large firm, a few thousand dollars may seem inconsequential. But if thousands of employees leave each year, the costs of turnover can quickly escalate into the millions of dollars. And when experienced, long-service employees quit, the loss may be incalculable because of the training, knowledge, and skills that these workers take with them.[6] In general, the personnel department can reduce turnover by meeting the personal objectives of employees. When that happens, both the employee and the organization can benefit. One widespread method for reducing turnover among newly hired employees uses an *orientation program* that familiarizes new employees with their roles, the organization, its policies, and other employees. For example, consider the situation faced some years ago by one department at Texas Instruments, a worldwide producer of microelectronics and electronic equipment.[7]

Orientation program defined

At Texas Instruments—or TI, as it is called by the employees—the orientation program was superficial at best. New employees went to a large room where they were quickly told about the company and its fringe benefits. They completed forms about benefits and other job-related matters and then were sent to their supervisor to report for work.

Texas Instrument's solution

Most supervisors took a few minutes to introduce the newcomer to the other assemblers. The supervisor often "assigned" the new employee to a work station with instructions for nearby workers to show the newcomer what to do. After being put through a superficial orientation program and quickly introduced to coworkers, the employee found himself or herself (most of the employees were female) sitting between two other employees trying to learn the job of assembling electronic components.

As many groups of workers do, the experienced assemblers had developed a little ritual for newcomers to endure. It was mild hazing. The trainees were told that Texas Instruments treated employees unfairly and that their present supervisor was one of the worst in the company. The newcomers' anxieties were greatly increased, to say the least. Their ability to learn and do the job suffered and some of the new employees would even go on a break or go to lunch and never return—not even to pick up their one-half day paycheck.

The personnel department reacted by recruiting an even larger number of new employees to offset the high initial turnover. After an internal investigation into the causes of this turnover, the department revamped its entire orientation process. New employees were given an extended orientation. The session, which lasted nearly all morning, explored the background and personnel policies of the company. Some forms were completed at the session, but the thrust of the orientation was to create a more positive attitude about TI among the recently hired recruits. Newcomers also were told that they had a high probability of success. Shortly before lunch, the new employees were taken to a roped-off section of the cafeteria where they had lunch with their future supervisors.

Following lunch, the supervisor would take the new employee back to the department and provide introductions to the other assemblers. Although the hazing went on for some time, the new employees had a more wholesome understanding of the company and were apparently better able to recognize the hazing for what it was, a ritualized introduction to the work group.

Drop in turnover

The newly revised orientation approach led to some significant changes at TI. The two major developments are illustrated in Figure 8-1. Turnover among recently hired employees dropped, as seen in Figure 8-1A. A higher percentage of employees stayed on the job. The turnover lines merge after a short time because orientation programs have little measurable impact on workers' intentions to remain after they have been with the company for a year or more. Other factors such as supervision, policies, and pay seem to have more impact on turnover among long-service employees. Both turnover curves in the figure start at the same point because an orientation program cannot have any impact on the "turnover" that occurs before the first day of work. For example, if a personnel department hires twenty people and asks them to report for orientation in two weeks, it is likely that some of the twenty will find even better jobs in the interim and not show up at all.

Acceleration in learning

The orientation program had another interesting impact, which is diagrammed in Figure 8-1B. Recipients of the new orientation program learned their jobs more quickly. That is, the more fully oriented employees mastered their jobs at the acceptable level of productivity more quickly than those employees who had the short orientation. This outcome was unexpected, since the workers in the new program were off the job for four hours while the workers in the shorter program missed only an hour or so of work. It would seem, particularly since this job was not very skilled, that a short orientation would get newcomers on the job quicker so they might learn their jobs faster. But the more fully oriented employees probably had fewer anxieties. They probably felt more at

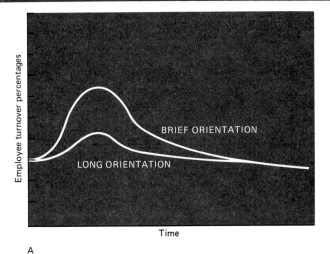

Figure 8-1
The Impact of Thorough Orientation on
Employee Turnover and Employee Learning

ease and more motivated to stay with the organization, which seems to explain why they mastered their jobs sooner than those with the shorter and more superficial orientation. Quick mastery of the job also may help lower turnover even further because research suggests that good performers are more likely to stay with an organization.[8]

Socialization

The TI orientation program succeeded because it accelerated the socialization of new employees. *Socialization* is the ongoing process through which an employee begins to understand and accept the values, norms, and beliefs held by others in the organization. Figure 8-2 depicts the socialization process as the meeting of the organization's culture and the individual's personality. Through

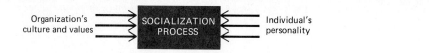

Figure 8-2
The Socialization Process

Formal and informal approaches

formal methods such as orientation programs and informal ones such as hazing in the TI example, the values of the organization are transmitted to newcomers.

Orientation programs are particularly effective socialization tools because they are used among new employees. Since most newcomers have a strong desire to be accepted, they attempt to internalize "the way things are done in the organization" and make it "their way," too. Training (discussed in Chapter 9) furthers the socialization process by having the employee actually learn and perform the desired behavior.

As a person is exposed to orientation, training, and peer group, the organizational values, beliefs, and traditions are slowly absorbed. Eventually, the newcomer becomes more fully integrated into the organization. Acceptable levels of satisfaction, productivity, and stability of employment are then more likely. The orientation process is an effective way to speed up socialization so that employees can become more productive contributors to the organization sooner.

The remainder of this book discusses what personnel departments can do to maintain and retain a productive work force. This chapter shows how a personnel department can ease an employee's transition into a new job. As Figure 8-3 suggests, a new employee's capabilities are seldom enough to meet the demands of the job. Those capabilities need to be supplemented with orientation and training. This chapter discusses how orientation facilitates the placement of employees into productive roles within the organization. The following section outlines the content, responsibilities, and benefits of orientation programs. The last section of the chapter identifies other issues in the placement of human resources within the organization.

Figure 8-3
The Balance between New Employee Capabilities
and Job Demands

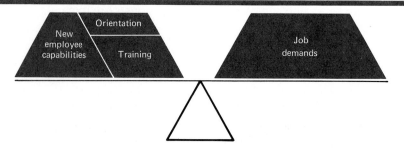

ORIENTATION PROGRAMS

Formal orientation programs usually rely on the personnel department and on the supervisor.[9] This two-tiered approach is common because the issues covered in an orientation fall into two broad categories: general topics of interest to most new employees and specific, job-related issues of concern only to specific jobholders. Figure 8-4 shows the common topics in an orientation program. Those labeled "organizational issues" and "employee benefits" are general concerns to virtually every new employee, so they are explained by representatives from the personnel department. The coverage of organizational issues and fringe benefits often is supplemented with an *employee handbook* that describes company policies, rules, regulations, benefits, and other items. Sophisticated orientation programs may include films or videotapes about the company's history as well as videotaped greetings from key executives. However, the bulk of the information comes from the personnel department representative.[10]

In addition to the department's presentation, the orientation is continued by the employee's supervisor. The supervisor handles the job-related introductions. This tier of the orientation program should include introducing new employees to the coworkers. Sometimes newcomers also need to meet others who work in different departments. Inspectors, supervisors, accountants, and even peers in

Two-tiered orientation

Employee handbook

Supervisor's role

Figure 8-4

Topics Often Covered in Employee Orientation Programs

ORGANIZATIONAL ISSUES

History of employer	Product line or services provided
Organization of employer	Overview of production process
Names and titles of key executives	Company policies and rules
Employee's title and department	Disciplinary regulations
Layout of physical facilities	Employee handbook
Probationary period	Safety procedures and enforcement

EMPLOYEE BENEFITS

Pay scales and paydays	Insurance benefits
Vacations and holidays	Retirement program
Rest breaks	Employer-provided services to employees
Training and education benefits	Rehabilitation programs
Counseling	

INTRODUCTIONS

To supervisor	To coworkers
To trainers	To employee counselor

JOB DUTIES

Job location	Overview of job
Job tasks	Job objectives
Job safety requirements	Relationship to other jobs

other departments may be part of the social network to which the employee becomes attached. Equally important are job duties and related issues. These items are normally explained by the supervisor, too. The supervisory-level orientation reviews the job and its objectives. The session covers specific information about tasks, safety requirements, job location, the relationship of the job to other jobs, and other issues in Figure 8-4. To be truly effective, employees need a two-tiered orientation using both the personnel department and the supervisor.

Opportunities and Pitfalls

The weakest part of most orientation programs is at the supervisory level. Even when the personnel department has designed an effective orientation program and trained supervisors to conduct their part of it, orientation still may not be effective. In their defense, it is only fair to say that supervisors may have more pressing problems or that everything seems so familiar to them that nothing really stands out as important for the newcomer to learn. Supervisors are often more interested in immediate production issues and may see orientation as far less important then other problems they face. To help ensure a systematic orientation, the supervisor may be given a checklist of topics to

Supervisor's checklist cover. The *supervisor's checklist* focuses on the introductions and job duties in Figure 8-4.

Buddy system One helpful supplement to the job-related orientation is the assignment of the newcomer to a buddy. Under the *buddy system* of orientation, an experienced employee is asked to show the new worker around, conduct the introductions for the supervisor, and answer the newcomer's questions. One advantage of this approach is the candid insights the newcomer is likely to gain. Moreover, the "buddy" will probably bring the new employee along to lunch and maybe to after-work activities. These social interactions give the newcomer an introduction to people in a relaxed setting and can help accelerate his or her feelings of acceptance within the work group.

The buddy system is a *supplement* to the supervisor's orientation efforts. If the buddy system is *substituted* for the supervisory orientation, the supervisor loses an excellent opportunity to establish open communications with new employees. Very soon, newcomers may find it more comfortable to ask coworkers, rather than the supervisor, about job-related issues. Supervisors who pass up the opportunity to spend some time with new employees miss a chance to create a favorable relationship before the employee becomes influenced by what other people think about the supervisor and the organization.

Other pitfalls Besides the ever-present potential for a weak supervisory orientation, other common pitfalls exist that the personnel department *and* supervisor should consider. Both the personnel department and the supervisor are responsible to see that the employee is not:

- *Overwhelmed* with too much information to absorb in a short time

- *Overloaded* with forms to complete

- *Given* only menial tasks that discourage job interest and company loyalty

- *Asked* to perform tasks where there is a high chance for failure that could discourage the employee needlessly

- *Pushed* into the job with a sketchy orientation under the mistaken belief that "trial by fire" is the best orientation

- *Forced* to fill in the gaps between a broad orientation by the personnel department and a narrow orientation at the department level

Benefits of Orientation Programs

Although research about orientation programs is limited, several benefits are commonly reported.[11] Most benefits center around reducing the employees' anxieties. With less anxiety, newcomers can better learn their duties. Hazing by peers or criticism by supervisors can be kept in perspective since properly oriented workers have more realistic job expectations. As a result, well-oriented newcomers need less attention from coworkers and supervisors, perform better, and are less likely to quit.[12] Reconsider the Texas Instruments example from earlier in this chapter.

> At Texas Instruments, one group of employees received an extended orientation program. The special program focused on the social adaptation problems usually encountered by employees at TI. They were told that they had a high probability of success, that other employees might kid or haze them, that their supervisors were helpful people, and that as new employees they should initiate communications with supervisors if there were any questions.
>
> The results of the specially oriented group showed that material waste **Results at TI** was reduced by 80 percent; training costs dropped by two-thirds; product costs were 15 percent lower; and training time, absenteeism, and tardiness were cut in half.[13]

These types of benefits occur because the orientation program helps an individual understand the social, technical, and cultural aspects of the workplace. As new employees are accepted, they become a part of the social fabric of the organization. Orientation programs help speed up that socialization process and benefit both the employee and the organization.

Orientation Follow-up

Successful orientation programs include built-in follow-up procedures. Follow-up is needed because new employees often are reluctant to admit that they do not recall everything they were told in the initial orientation sessions. Without follow-up, their questions might go unanswered. The personnel department often uses a prescheduled meeting or a simple checklist that asks the employee to critique the weaknesses of the orientation program. Weaknesses, presumably, are topics about which an employee needs more information. The checklist also serves as feedback to help the personnel department identify those parts of the program that are strong. Although the checklist can be effective, face-to-face meetings between the employee and the supervisor are the most important type of orientation follow-up.

Real versus superficial follow-up

Many supervisors believe they follow up with the new hire frequently, but many new employees often do not perceive their supervisor's actions as true follow-ups. One problem may be the supervisor's body language, for example. A supervisor may ask, "Is everything OK? Let me know if you have any questions." But if this is stated as the supervisor continues to walk past the employee, the body language received by the employee is, "My supervisor really doesn't want to stop and talk." Instead of raising questions, the employee responds with some affirmative indication that all is OK. Or the supervisor appears and disappears so quickly that even an assertive employee may not think of appropriate questions before the supervisor is gone.

Sometimes the supervisor cannot answer an employee's question and must refer it to someone else. Even though a referral may be the best answer, the employee may feel that the supervisor does not really care about the problem. An even worse situation occurs when the supervisor says "I'll find out" and never gets back to the employee with the correct answer. That *is* indifference. Consider how Exxon attacked this problem of weak follow-up by supervisors at its Research and Engineering Company in Florham Park, New Jersey.

Exxon's approach

At Exxon Research and Engineering Company, 50 to 150 engineers have been hired each year for several years. In recognition of the need for a smooth entry into the organization, Exxon had an action guide and reference manual developed for supervisors to help them do a better job with newcomers. The manual outlines actions the supervisor should take before the employee arrives, such as arranging for workspace, telephones, office supplies, and the like. It also describes the actions a supervisor should take after the new employee arrives.

The particularly innovative parts of the program are the follow-up meetings that supervisors are supposed to have with their new engineers. These sessions are called "How's It Going" meetings. They are intended to open up communications between the newcomer and the supervisor. Information is shared, concern is shown, and matters of interest are discussed. To make these sessions as effective as possible, they are held separately from meetings that give work assignments or review performance. Supervisors also are trained to conduct these meetings. The objectives of the training are to increase the supervisor's awareness of the new employee's needs, introduce the supervisors to the company's socialization procedures, and improve the supervisor's skills at communicating with new employees.

Internal company research showed that after the training, supervisors were 40 percent more likely to hold initial orientation discussions with newcomers and were 20 percent more likely to hold follow-up sessions at the end of three months.[14]

EMPLOYEE PLACEMENT

Placement is the assignment or reassignment of an employee to a new or different job. It includes the initial assignment of new employees and the promotion, transfer, or demotion of present employees. Similar to newcomers, present employees must be internally recruited, selected, and oriented before they can be placed in different positions. However, these activities are seldom as elaborate for placement decisions as they are for new hires.

Placement defined

The placement of present workers is less elaborate because the personnel department maintains employee records that contain the internal candidate's original application, skills inventory, and work history. With this information, recruitment of internal candidates is easier, particularly if employee career paths have been recorded and computerized. Likewise, selection goes more quickly because the past performance and abilities of employees are better known than those of external recruits. Time and effort also are saved in orientation. When present employees are assigned to a new job, for example, they seldom need both tiers of the orientation program. The personnel department's part usually can be skipped, although the supervisory orientation still is needed to speed up the socialization within the new work group.

Reduced need for orientation

Most placement decisions are made by line managers. Usually the employee's supervisor in consultation with higher levels of line management decides the future placement of each employee. When the placement decision involves the employee going to work in a different part of the organization, placement decisions usually are made by the employee's prospective supervisor. The personnel department's role is to advise these line managers about the company's policies and to provide counseling to the employees. The three major classes of placement decisions are promotions, transfers, and demotions. Each of these will be reviewed in the next section, followed by a discussion of separations.

Classes of placement decisions

Promotions

A *promotion* occurs when an employee is moved from one job to another that is higher in pay, responsibility, and/or organizational level. It is one of the more pleasant events that happens to people in an organization. Generally, it is given as a recognition of a person's past performance and future promise. Promotions usually are based on merit and/or seniority.[15]

Merit-based promotions   Merit-based promotions occur when an employee is promoted because of superior performance in the present job. In cases where promotion is mostly a "reward" for past efforts and successes, two problems may be encountered.

One problem is whether decision makers can objectively distinguish the strong performers from the weak ones. When merit-based promotions are being used, it is important that the decision reflect the individual's performance and not the biases of the decision maker. An example occurs when the best performer is a member of a protected class and the decision maker is

Problems with merit approaches

prejudiced. The decision maker should not allow personal prejudices to affect promotions. Decisions that are swayed by personal feelings are more common when job performance is not measured objectively. When promotion decisions result from personal biases, the organization ends up with a less competent person in a higher, more important position. The resulting resentment among those not promoted is likely to harm employees' motivation and satisfaction.

Peter Principle

A second problem with merit-based promotions is the *Peter Principle.*[16] It states that in a hierarchy people tend to rise to their level of *incompetence.* Although not universally true, the "principle" suggests that good performance in one job is no guarantee of good performance in another. For example, if one of the new engineers hired at Exxon's Research and Engineering Company consistently made major cost-saving design changes in a refinery, that would be an example of superior performance. However, suppose the engineer were promoted to supervisor. The skills needed to be an effective supervisor are very different from those needed to be a top engineer. As a result of such a promotion, Exxon might gain an ineffective supervisor and lose a superior engineer.

Seniority-based promotions   In some situations, the most senior employee gets the promotion. "Senior" in this case means the employee who has the longest length of service with the employer. The advantage of this approach is that it is objective. All one needs to do is compare the seniority records of the candidates to determine who should be promoted.

Unions prefer seniority-based promotions.

Part of the rationale for this approach is to eliminate biased promotions and to require management to develop its senior employees since they will eventually be promoted. Seniority-based promotions usually are limited to hourly employees. For example, a promotion from mechanic second class to mechanic first class may occur automatically by seniority whenever an opening for mechanic first class occurs. Labor organizations often seek this type of promotion to prevent employer's from discriminating among union members.

Most personnel experts express concern about the competency of those promoted solely because of seniority since not all workers are equally capable. Sometimes the person who is the best mechanic, for example, is not the most senior one. Under seniority-based promotions, the best person is denied the job unless the individual happens to be the most senior worker as well. This approach to promotion causes personnel departments to focus their efforts on training senior workers to ensure that they are prepared to handle future promotions. In addition, the personnel department must be concerned with maintaining an accurate seniority list. Where promotions are not based solely on seniority, both *merit* and seniority are guiding factors.

Transfers and Demotions

Definition

Transfers and demotions are the other two major placement actions available to the organization. *Transfers* occur when an employee is moved from one job to another that is relatively *equal* in pay, responsibility, and/or organizational level. *Demotions* occur when an employee is moved from one job to another that is *lower* in pay, responsibility, and/or organizational level.

Flexibility is often one key to organization success. Decision makers must be able to reallocate their human resources to meet internal and external challenges. One common tool is the employee transfer. By moving people into jobs that are neither a promotion nor a demotion, managers may be able to improve the utilization of their human resources. Transfers may even be beneficial to jobholders. The broadening experience of a transfer may provide a person with new skills and a different perspective that makes him or her a better candidate for future promotions. Transfers may even improve an individual's motivation and satisfaction, especially when a person finds little challenge in the old job. The new position, although not a promotion, may offer new technical and interpersonal challenges. In turn, these challenges may prove to be a growth opportunity for the transferee. Even when the challenges are minimal, the transfer at least offers some variety, which may enhance feelings of job satisfaction.

Transfers broaden one's experience.

Demotions generally hold few positive outcomes for the individual or the organization. Usually they are associated with discipline; the individual is demoted for poor job performance or for inappropriate behavior such as excessive absenteeism. One problem with demotions is that the demoted employee may become "demotivated" or, worse, openly antagonistic toward those responsible for the demotion decision. Besides being a negative influence on the morale of others, this person is likely to be a poor producer.

Demotions and antagonism

Sometimes demotions are intended to be a kindly alternative to firing an employee who cannot do his or her present job. Rather than sever the employment relationship, a decision is made to retain the employee but at a lower level of responsibility. If the reasons for the demotion are beyond the employee's control—such as poor health—the wage or salary may even be left unchanged, although future raises are unlikely.

When employees are members of a union, they may be "bumped" into a lower job. Bumping occurs when a worker with more seniority is told that his or her job is being eliminated. That worker can either become unemployed or take a lower-level job for which the union member is qualified. In other words, the senior employee can bump another employee out of a job. In turn, the newly bumped employee can displace a still less senior worker in a similar or lower-level job, which sets off another round of bumping and demotions. These bumping rights give senior workers greater job security.

Job-Posting Programs

Job-posting programs inform employees about unfilled job openings and qualifications. The announcement of the opening invites qualified employees to apply. The notices usually are posted on company bulletin boards or placed in the company newspaper. The posted qualifications and other facts typically are drawn from the job analysis information (discussed in Chapter 5). Then through *self-nominations* or the recommendation of a supervisor, employees who are interested in the posted opening report to the personnel department and apply.

Self-nominations

The purpose of job posting is to encourage employees to seek promotions and transfers that help the personnel department fill internal openings and meet employees' personal objectives. Not all job openings are posted. Besides entry-level positions, senior management and top staff positions may be filled by merit or by external recruiting. Job posting is most common along lower-level clerical, technical, and supervisory positions.[17] When lower-level jobs are filled without posting them, employees may believe that they should have been allowed to apply through the posting program. Therefore, it is important for the personnel department to make the rules of the job-posting program known and to consistently follow them.

A trend toward posting even higher-level management jobs may be suggested by some firms' responses to affirmative action:

> The Ralph Parsons Company, a construction firm based in California, began posting jobs to give qualified minorities knowledge of job openings. Likewise, the Consolidated Edison Company of New York posts 40 percent of its management openings, partly for reasons of affirmative action. CBS, Inc., in New York and Bendix in Michigan also post jobs, including some in management.[18]

Although most job bidders seek promotions, some self-nominations are likely from those who seek a transfer to broaden their skills or for personal reasons. Even self-nominated demotions are possible if the person is frustrated in his or her present job or if the person sees the demotion as a means to a job with more favorable promotion possibilities. For example, a typesetter at a newspaper might seek a "demotion" to a junior reporter because the long-term career options as a reporter may be more favorable.

Self-nominations may also be used by management trainees. Many organizations hire recent college graduates for management training programs. Many of these programs are little more than an extended job rotation throughout each of several departments. After this rotation is completed, the company may allow the trainees to nominate themselves to fill posted job openings.

SEPARATIONS

A *separation* is a decision for the individual and the organization to part. It may be motivated by disciplinary, economic, business, or personal reasons. Regardless of the reasons behind the decision, the personnel department's role is to find the most satisfactory method of conducting the separation in a way that minimizes the harm to the organization and to the individual. Separations can take several forms such as attrition, layoffs, and termination.

Forms of separation

Attrition

Attrition is the normal separation of people from an organization as a result of resignation, retirement, or death. It is initiated by the individual worker and not by the company. In most organizations, the key component of attrition is resignation, which is a voluntary separation.

Although attrition is a slow way to reduce the employment base in an organization, it presents the fewest problems for employees. Voluntary departures simply create a vacancy that is not filled, and the staffing level declines without anyone being forced out of a job. Human resource planning enables organizations to rely more heavily on attrition rather than on layoffs because this planning process attempts to project future employment needs, as explained in Chapter 4. When those projections indicate that a surplus of employees is likely, the personnel department can recommend an *employment freeze,* which curtails future hiring. Then the employment level begins to decline as people voluntarily leave the organization. When there is sufficient lead time, attrition can reduce or even eliminate the projected surplus.

Employment freeze

The effect of attrition can be significant even in a short time period. In a five-year span, Bank of America (B of A) added 14,500 people and reached a total of 87,500 employees. However, as an article in *Forbes* observed, "The expansion did nothing for profitability—Citicorp netted about $9,000 for each of its 58,000 employees . . . compared with B of A's $5,000 per employee. . . . However, B of A's employee count is dropping as the California division alone reduced its rolls 4.5% . . . all by attrition."[19] And this decrease in staff size took place during a one-year period.

Bank of America versus Citicorp

A special form of attrition is early retirement. It is one form of separation that the personnel department can actively control. It is used to reduce staffing levels and to create internal job openings. Early retirement plans are designed to encourage long-service workers to retire before the traditional retirement age of 65. Since people who retire before age 65 are going to draw benefits longer, their monthly retirement benefits may be reduced proportionately. Of course, an employer must take care not to discriminate against those who wish to stay until age 70, since they are protected under the Age Discrimination in Employment Act, as amended. If the employer is anxious to reduce the number of senior workers, the early retirement provisions may be supplemented so that there is no reduction in retirement benefits. The advantage of this form of separation is that it can start a chain reaction of promotions for several layers of junior workers. Moreover, senior workers tend to be the highest paid employees; when they resign, the employer's labor costs may decline.[20]

Early retirement: A special case

Layoffs

Layoffs are the separation of employees from the organization for economic or business reasons. The separation may last only a few weeks if its purpose is to adjust inventory levels or to allow the factory to retool for a new product. When caused by a business cycle, the layoffs may last many months or even years. However, if the layoff is the result of a restructuring or rescaling of an industry, the "temporary" layoffs may be permanent.

As unpleasant as layoffs are for both workers and management, they may be required when attrition is insufficient to reduce employment to acceptable levels. In some industries, such as the automobile industry, each employee may receive a supplemental unemployment benefit (SUB), which is added to state unemployment compensation. However, during severe economic downturns, the employer's SUB reserves may be depleted quickly. And if unemployment

Supplemental unemployment benefits

lasts for an extended period of time, eligibility for state unemployment benefits may be exhausted.

When the layoffs are expected to be of a short duration—as when an automobile plant temporarily closes to change its tooling for a new model— layoffs may not follow the normal pattern of forcing the most recently hired employee to accept unemployment. Rather than following seniority, some contracts have "juniority" clauses. *Juniority* provisions require that layoffs be offered first to senior workers. If the senior worker wants to accept the layoff, that person collects unemployment and SUB moneys while less senior workers keep their jobs. Senior workers are likely to accept layoffs of short duration because they receive almost the same take-home pay without working. When the layoff is of an unknown duration, the senior workers usually decline to exercise their juniority rights and fewer senior employees are put on layoff.

Juniority

Termination

Of course, employees may be separated by termination of the employment relationship. *Termination* is a broad term that encompasses the permanent separation from the organization for any reason. Usually this term implies that the person was fired as a form of discipline. When people are discharged for business or economic reasons, it is commonly, although not always, called a layoff. Sometimes, however, the employer needs to separate some employees for business reasons and has no plans to rehire them. Rather than being laid off, those people are simply terminated. In these cases, the employees may receive severance pay.

Severance pay

Severance pay is money—often equal to one or more week's salary—that is given to employees who are being permanently separated. Many organizations give severance pay only for involuntary separations and only to employees who have been performing satisfactorily. For example, if a factory is going to close and move operations to another state, employees who are terminated may be given an extra week's salary for each year they have worked for the company. It is unlikely that someone who is being fired for poor performance or for other disciplinary reasons will receive severance pay, unless the individual has been a very long service employee.

Prevention of Separations

A creative challenge

One of the more creative areas of personnel management is the prevention of separations. Obviously, anything that the personnel department can do to lessen unwanted separations benefits the organization. Restated, when personnel departments can prevent their organizations from losing valuable human resources, the moneys invested in recruitment, selection, orientation, and training are not lost. Although a minimum amount of attrition ensures a flow of new people into the organization and promotional opportunities for those already there, each departing employee is a lost investment.

To reduce the loss of valuable human resources, personnel departments can undertake a variety of actions. Through proactive programs, employee losses through voluntary resignations, death, layoffs, and terminations can be reduced.

Voluntary resignations Voluntary resignations are reduced by a satisfying work environment, a challenging job, high-quality supervision, and personal opportunities for growth. Personnel departments are involved with these issues through supervisor training, career planning, and other activities. As described in Chapter 5, for example, the personnel department can play an especially powerful role as an adviser to line managers who seek better ways to redesign the jobs they supervise. Realistic job previews and orientation programs are two other ways the department may reduce voluntary turnover.

How personnel reduces resignations

Retirement is another type of separation. Some companies offer part-time work to retiring employees as a means of helping them move from work to retirement while at the same time retaining access to the employee's valued skills and knowledge.[21]

> Equitable Life Assurance Society's part-time program for retirees is called "Retiree Talent Bank." Salaried employees who have retired are used to staff temporary openings instead of hiring workers from temporary help providers or consultants. Retirees may work up to 780 hours per year while drawing full-time retirement benefits.

Death Even death as a source of separation is a target for progressive personnel departments. Sentry Insurance Company, for example, installed a multi-million-dollar recreational complex in its western regional office in Scottsdale, Arizona. Part of the plan for this combinanion of weight rooms, jogging tracks, tennis courts, and other athletic-oriented facilities is to encourage employees to maintain better physical health in order to continue working longer.

Layoffs Layoffs are minimized in some companies by careful human resource planning. By projecting employment needs several years into the future, employers like IBM and State Farm Insurance Company have avoided layoffs even during the worst recessions. Then as the needed skill mix of their business changes, training and transfers help these organizations adjust to economic challenges while providing secure employment for their employees. Companies such as Control Data, Motorola, and IBM take another step to protect their full-time workers. As Figure 8-5 illustrates, Control Data Corporation uses a "rings of defense" approach. At the center ring are the prized full-time Control Data employees. At the next level are permanent part-time employees who would be put on layoff before the full-timers. Before permanent part-timers are laid off, temporary employees would be given their notices to leave. Suppliers and vendors become the first line of defense because Control Data (along with Motorola, IBM, and other companies) contracts out some jobs that its own people could do. Before Control Data employees would be separated, janitorial, maintenance, and other jobs that are now done by contractors would be done by Control Data employees.

"Rings of defense" at Control Data

Layoffs also can be reduced through other approaches.[22] One method that has gained popularity is the use of reduced workweeks or *"part-time layoffs,"*

"Part-time" layoffs

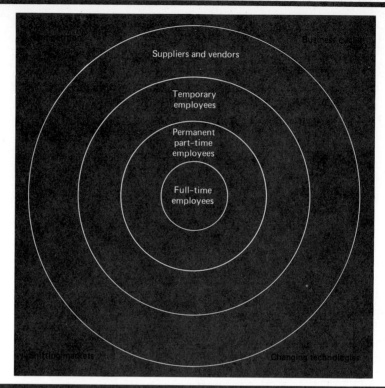

Figure 8-5
"Rings of Defense" at Control Data Corporation

which allow employers to lay off workers for part of each week. In such cases, the employees can collect a pro rata share of their weekly unemployment benefits. A person must usually be out of work for an entire week to collect unemployment compensation. However, new laws allow employees to collect unemployment insurance if they are put on a short-time or reduced workweek. For example, employees having their workweek reduced from five to four days can collect unemployment compensation for the one day they are "unemployed." This approach spreads the available work among employees while allowing the employer to retain the work force without traditional layoffs. *Job sharing* allows two or more workers to do the same job by each working part-time. Although most workers who want full-time work may find a part-time job unacceptable, job sharing may be preferable to a layoff, especially if the job sharing is of short duration or if both employees want part-time work.

Terminations Personnel departments can reduce terminations through other means besides orientation, which was discussed earlier in this chapter. For example, training and development activities help reduce terminations for poor performance. Through effective training, new and long-service employees can be taught how to do their jobs successfully. Training and development are so important to the success of most organizations that the next chapter will discuss this tool of personnel management. In Chapter 9, the distinction between training and development will be clarified, and different training approaches will be reviewed.

SUMMARY

Once the selection process is completed, new employees must be oriented in order to become productive contributors to the organization. Orientation not only improves the rate at which employees are able to perform their jobs but also helps employees satisfy their personal desires to feel a part of the organization's social fabric. The personnel department generally orients newcomers to broad organization issues and fringe benefits. Supervisors complete the orientation by introducing new employees to coworkers and others involved in the job. The supervisory orientation also explains the job's duties, safety requirements, and relationship with other jobs. The purpose of orientation is to expedite the socialization process through which the employee absorbs the values, beliefs, and traditions of the organization. Proactive personnel departments follow up after the orientation to ensure that the employees do not have any remaining questions and to check on the quality of the orientation.

When job openings are filled internally with present employees, part of this placement process also should include an orientation. This orientation, however, tends to be informal and focuses on job-related issues since the employee is already familiar with the organization and its benefits.

The process of placing present employees in different jobs or separating them from the organization is often a decision made by line managers in consultation with the personnel department. Placement decisions include promotions, transfers, and demotions. Although promotions come about in a variety of ways, they usually result because of merit, seniority, self-nomination, or some combination of these approaches. Transfers and demotions also call for the advice of the personnel department. Demotions, although rare, are a particularly sensitive issue and require careful planning and employee counseling. Separations from the organization may result from disciplinary, economic, or business reasons. The personnel department's job is to minimize the harm done to the organization and to the individual. Separations may be caused by attrition, layoffs, and terminations.

TERMS FOR REVIEW

Cognitive dissonance	Two-tiered orientation programs
Socialization	Attrition
Orientation programs	Placement
Employee handbook	Employment freeze
Buddy system	Demotions

Part-time layoffs	Merit-based promotions
Early retirement	Seniority-based promotions
Layoffs	Job posting
Juniority	Transfers
Severance pay	Peter Principle
Promotions	

REVIEW AND DISCUSSION QUESTIONS

1. If employees are properly selected, there should be no need for an orientation program. Do you agree or disagree with this statement? Why?

2. What are the benefits to the employee of a comprehensive orientation program? To the organization?

3. If you were going to design an orientation program for a retail store, describe the issues that would be covered by the personnel department and the issues that would be covered by the first-level supervisor.

4. Who is responsible for a two-tiered orientation program? Describe the issues that should be handled at each tier.

5. Why would a personnel department use seniority-based promotions and what problems might arise?

6. Why would a company have a job-posting program? How does it work?

7. How can organizations improve the stability of employment they offer and minimize the use of layoffs?

8. If you worked in the employee relations department of the Exxon Research and Engineering Company, what could you do to ensure greater use of the "How's It Going?" meetings as a follow-up to the formal orientation program?

INCIDENT 8-1

Orientation at Warehousing of North America, Inc.

Warehousing of North America, Inc., is a chain of public warehouses in the United States and Canada. The corporate personnel department requested that the local personnel managers develop their own orientation program but gave these managers few guidelines. About a year after the program was designed and installed, the personnel manager decided that follow-up interviews would be a useful way to learn how the orientation program had been received by those who went through it. Leslie Coulter was asked by the personnel manager to interview Oliver Talbot, the newest warehouse supervisor, about the orientation he had received. When asked about the program, Talbot made the following statement:

> For an international company with nearly a thousand employees, I was very disappointed with the orientation program. It began the first day when the secretary in the personnel department brought me in to see Mr. Cheever, the general manager. I was in there for about a half hour. For twenty-five minutes of that time, Mr. Cheever was on the phone. Most of the other top managers I was introduced to spent the few minutes we were together either on the phone or complaining about their problems. By lunch, I seriously thought about quitting.
>
> Luckily, my boss, the warehouse manager, spent a couple of hours with me after work the first day and explained all the forms we use. I didn't understand them all, but at least I had a general idea of the paper flow around here. It probably took two weeks to figure out all the things I was supposed to do. I really felt foolish asking some of my employees about these forms, and I was supposed to be the boss.
>
> Whenever a new person starts with me, I make sure that they understand what all these forms are for. I figure that they will ask about fringe benefits when they want to know about them. The important thing around here is to do the paperwork right. My people learn about every form the first morning. It's a lot, but knowing that paperwork is important.

A number of other interviews confirmed Talbot's observations.

1. On the basis of what Oliver Talbot said, what changes would you recommend in the part of the orientation program he does?

2. Since the top management at the warehouse appears to create an unfavorable impression, what recommendations do you have to change that part of the orientation?

EXERCISE 8-1

Reductions in Force at Chrysler Corporation

The economic difficulties faced by the Chrysler Corporation in the late 1970s and early 1980s had a variety of causes, both domestic and foreign. The reality faced by top management was that the size of the organization—in both physical and human assets—was too big. For the level of sales that could be expected, the company had too many facilities and too many people. Systematically, top management began to "shrink" the size of the corporation until the early 1980s when the company was about one half its original size. This radical transformation and the short-run survival of the corporation could not depend on attrition

228

because attrition was too slow, especially since other automobile makers and parts suppliers were, in general, not hiring. As a result, Chrysler put thousands of workers on layoff status. Most may never again work for Chrysler, or for any other car maker, because the industry is rapidly automating and foreign producers have won a larger share of the market.

For the purposes of this exercise, assume that you are asked to draw up a plan to reduce the work force from 15,000 to 10,000 employees at one very large factory.

1. What programs discussed in this chapter would you consider suggesting to the vice president of human relations before the actual layoffs begin?

2. Once people have to be given their "notice of layoff," what other actions could the company take to assist those who would be separated?

REFERENCES

1. John P. Wanous, *Organization Entry Recruitment, Selection and Socialization of Newcomers,* Reading, Mass.: Addison-Wesley, 1979, p. 171.

2. Joan M. Pearson, "The Transition into a New Job: Tasks, Problems, and Outcomes," *Personnel Journal,* April 1982, p. 287; see also James A. Breaugh, "Realistic Job Previews: A Critical Appraisal and Future Research Directions," *The Academy of Management Review,* October 1983, pp. 612–619.

3. Dan R. Dalton and William D. Todor, "Turnover: A Lucrative Hard Dollar Phenomenon," *Academy of Management Review,* April 1982, pp. 212–218.

4. L. Festinger, *A Theory of Cognitive Dissonance,* Evanston, Ill.: Row, Peterson, 1957.

5. Pearson, op. cit., p. 286.

6. William H. Mobley, "Some Unanswered Questions in Turnover and Withdrawal Research," *Academy of Management Review,* January 1982, pp. 111–116.

7. Earl G. Gomersall and M. Scott Myers, "Breakthrough in On-the-Job Training," *Harvard Business Review,* July–August 1966, pp. 66–72.

8. George F. Dreher, "The Role of Performance in the Turnover Process," *Academy of Management Journal,* March 1982, pp. 137–147.

9. "ASPA-BNA Survey No. 32," *Employee Orientation Programs,* Bulletin to Management, no. 1436, Washington, D.C.: Bureau of National Affairs, Aug. 25, 1977, p. 1.

10. Robert W. Hollmann, "Let's Not Forget about New Employee Orientations," *Personnel Journal,* May 1976, pp. 244–247, 250. See also Thomas LaMott, "Making Employee Orientation Work," *Personnel Journal,* January 1974, pp. 35–37, 44; and Walter D. St. John, "The Complete Employee Orientation Program," *Personnel Journal,* May 1980, pp. 373–378.

11. "ASPA-BNA Survey No. 32," *Employee Orientation Programs,* op. cit., p. 5. See also Richard Pascale, "Fitting New Employees into the Company Culture," *Fortune,* May 1984, pp. 28, 30, 34, 38–40.

12. Gomersal, op. cit.

13. Ibid.

14. Thomas K. Meier and Susan Hough, "Beyond Orientation: Assimilating New Employees," *Human Resource Management*, Spring 1982, pp. 27–29.

15. Alfred W. Swinyard and Floyd A. Bond, "Who Gets Promoted?" *Harvard Business Review*, September–October 1980, pp. 6–8, 12, 14, 18.

16. Laurence J. Peter and Raymond Hull, *The Peter Principle*, New York: William Morrow, 1969.

17. Gary G. Wallrapp, "Job Posting for Nonexempt Employees: A Sample Program," *Personnel Journal*, October 1981, pp. 796–798. See also J. Robert Garcia, "Job Posting for Professional Staff," *Personnel Journal*, March 1981, pp. 189–192.

18. "Job Posting Gains Favor in Private Firms as an Affirmative Action Tool," *The Wall Street Journal*, Western ed., Nov. 22, 1977, p. 1.

19. John Merwin, "The Logical Leader," *Forbes*, Nov. 2, 1983, p. 157.

20. James B. Shaw and Lisa L. Grubbs, "The Process of Retiring: Organizational Entry in Reverse." *Academy of Management Review*, January 1981, p. 41–47.

21. "Bring 'em Back to Work," *The Arizona Republic*, Jan. 17, 1983, p. A-14. See also "When Retirees Go Back on the Payroll," *Business Week*, Nov. 22, 1982, pp. 112, 116; and William B. Werther, Jr., "Part-Timers: Overlooked and Undervalued," *Business Horizons*, February 1975, pp. 13–29.

22. Alan H. Locher, "Short-Time Compensation: A Viable Alternative to Layoffs," *Personnel Journal*, March 1981, pp. 213–216.

CHAPTER

It is no longer a question of whether we want to develop our human resources or whether we should develop our human resources. . . . It is a matter of survival for our society that we develop human resources.

James L. Hayes[1]

Our refusal to spend money on investing in a skilled work force shows up in large numbers of people who are unemployable.

Herbert E. Striner[2]

TRAINING AND DEVELOPMENT

CHAPTER OBJECTIVES

After studying this chapter, you should be able to:

1 <u>Distinguish</u> between training and development of human resources.

2 <u>Identify</u> the benefits of training for employees and for the organization.

3 <u>Explain</u> different approaches to needs analysis in designing training and development programs.

4 <u>Describe</u> the major learning principles associated with each training technique.

5 <u>Identify</u> the equal employment opportunity implications that surround training and development.

6 <u>Develop</u> an evaluation process to assess the results of a training and development program.

Orientation is not enough.

Even after a comprehensive orientation, new employees seldom are able to perform satisfactorily. Often they must be trained in the duties they are expected to perform. Even experienced employees who are placed in new jobs may need training to do their jobs properly. Internal candidates may not have all the necessary capabilities or may have bad work habits that need to be overcome through training. This balance between capabilities and job demands was first illustrated in Chapter 8 and is shown again in Figure 9-1. As the figure shows, orientation and training can help bolster a worker's capabilities to do the job.

Training is for present jobs.

Development is for future jobs.

Although *training* helps employees do their present job, the benefits of training may extend throughout a person's entire career and may help *develop* that person for future responsibilities.[3] Developmental activities, on the other hand, help the individual handle future responsibilities, with little concern for present job duties. As a result, the distinction between training and development often is blurred. What starts out as training frequently develops people into better workers or managers. Since the distinction between training and development is primarily one of intent, both are discussed together throughout the chapter, with significant differences noted where important. To illustrate the developmental impact of training, consider one personnel director's observations.

> When I was first promoted to head all the job analysts many years ago, I did not know the first thing about supervising. So I was sent to a supervisory training program for new supervisors. In that seminar I learned a lot of things, but the section on delegation really impressed me the most. I have relied on that knowledge ever since. Probably the reason I head the personnel department today is because that training helped to develop me into a manager.

Training and development often blur.

When looked at from the overall perspective of a corporate training and development effort, the distinction between training for a present job and development for future ones blurs even further. Consider an outline of the training program at one company.

Figure 9-1
The Balance between New Employee Capabilities and Job Demands

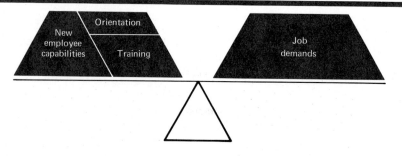

"At the Corning Glass Works plant in Harrodsburg, Kentucky, we adopted a systematic approach in the development of a plant-wide training program. Our concept of training focuses on the individual. We at the Harrodsburg plant believe all employees, regardless of salary grade, position or department assignment, can benefit from quality training."[4]

The Corning Glass Works program

The training program at Corning has four phases. The first phase is called individual training. Included here is an extensive orientation program for new employees and on-the-job training for those who have transferred to a new job. The second phase is departmental training. Hourly and management employees receive specialized courses that are intended to increase departmental productivity. These courses focus primarily on standard operation procedures used to run specific operations in the department. The third phase, plant or facilities training, contains information of general interest to those at the plant. Safety training and courses for personal or professional development are included in this category. The final phase is corporate and outside training and development. It includes training and development efforts done by the corporate offices, private consultants, and universities. These courses tend to be more general and more developmental in nature.

To support these various levels of training the plant training coordinator develops a master training schedule that is published monthly on a department-by-department basis. It shows the name, type, and appropriate audience for each training session to be held that month. This calendar is supplemented by a catalog that shows whether the training subject is an operational, safety, departmental, or plantwide session.[5]

This comprehensive array of learning opportunities includes some very specific training modules that teach people the company's standard operating procedures for doing specific jobs. At the other end of the course spectrum are seminars that grapple with broad developmental issues that upwardly mobile managers at Corning can expect to face during their careers. Many of the other seminars are training employees for their present jobs while helping others develop their skills for future jobs at Corning. Neither the training coordinator nor the students are much concerned whether a class is intended to be "training" or "development."

The more appropriate concern is whether the seminars help the employees and the organization. Corning believes that its approach to training and development benefits both employees and the company. And judging from some of the results that Corning has been able to report, the training and development have had some identifiable payoffs in productivity and in quality of work life.

As the personnel assistant and plant training coordinator at Corning asked: "So, where have over two hundred various courses for our employees taken us? First, we have increased productivity."[6] In one department, record production runs were achieved following the formalized on-the-job training of some departmental employees. Workplace practices also have become more standardized, and employees have an in-plant means of self-improvement.[7]

Other gains from training and development often result in addition to those found at Corning. Figure 9-2 summarizes some of the more common benefits. As can be seen in the figure, training helps the organization, the individual, and the human relations of the work group. Perhaps the easiest way to summarize these benefits is to consider training and development as an investment the organization makes in employees. That investment pays dividends to the employee, to the organization, and to other workers.

T & D are an "investment".

STEPS TO TRAINING AND DEVELOPMENT

To receive the benefits listed in Figure 9-2, personnel specialists and managers must assess the needs, objectives, content, and learning principles associated with training. Figure 9-3 diagrams the sequence that should be followed before training and development begin. As implied by the figure, the person who is responsible for the training or development (usually a trainer) must assess the needs of the employee and the organization in order to learn what objectives should be sought. Once objectives are set, the specific content and learning principles are considered. Whether the learning process is to be guided by trainers in the personnel department or by first-level supervisors, these preliminary steps should be undertaken to create an effective program.

Needs Assessment

The cost of training and development in the United States has been estimated at over $100 billion per year.[8] If organizations are to get maximum benefit for this staggering expenditure, then efforts must concentrate on the people and situations that can benefit the most.[9] To decide what approach to use, the trainer assesses the needs for training and development. *Needs assessment* diagnoses present problems and environmental challenges to be met through long-term development. For example, changes in the external environment may present an organization with new challenges. To respond effectively, employees may need training to deal with these changes. The comments of one training director illustrate the impact of the external environment.

Is training needed?

What kind of training is needed?

> After the Equal Employment Opportunity Act in 1972 changed the Civil Rights Act of 1964, we had to train every interviewer in the personnel department. This training was needed to ensure that our interviewers would not ask questions that might violate federal laws. When managers in other departments heard of the training, they too wanted to sign up. We decided that since they interviewed recruits, they should also be trained. What was to be a one-time seminar became a monthly session for nearly three years.

How Training Benefits the Organization

- Leads to improved profitability and/or more positive attitudes toward profit orientation.
- Improves the job knowledge and skills at all levels of the organization.
- Improves the morale of the work force.
- Helps people identify with organizational goals.
- Helps create a better corporate image.
- Fosters authenticity, openness and trust.
- Improves the relationship between boss and subordinate.
- Aids in organizational development.
- Learns from the trainee.
- Helps prepare guidelines for work.
- Aids in understanding and carrying out organizational policies.
- Provides information for future needs in all areas of the organization.
- Organization gets more effective decision making and problem solving.
- Aids in development for promotion from within.
- Aids in developing leadership skill, motivation, loyalty, better attitudes, and other aspects that successful workers and managers usually display.
- Aids in increasing productivity and/or quality of work.
- Helps keep costs down in many areas, e.g., production, personnel, administration, etc.
- Develops a sense of responsibility to the organization for being competent and knowledgeable.
- Improves labor-management relations.
- Reduces outside consulting costs by utilizing competent internal consulting.
- Stimulates preventive management as opposed to putting out fires.
- Eliminates suboptimal behavior (such as hiding tools).
- Creates an appropriate climate for growth, communication.
- Aids in improving organizational communication.
- Helps employees adjust to change.
- Aids in handling conflict, thereby helping to prevent stress and tension.

Benefits to the Individual Which in Turn Ultimately Should Benefit the Organization

- Helps the individual in making better decisions and effective problem solving.
- Through training and development, motivational variables of recognition, achievement, growth, responsibility and advancement are internalized and operationalized.
- Aids in encouraging and achieving self-development and self-confidence.
- Helps a person handle stress, tension, frustration and conflict.
- Provides information for improving leadership knowledge, communication skills and attitudes.
- Increases job satisfaction and recognition.
- Moves a person toward personal goals while improving interaction skills.
- Satisfies personal needs of the trainer (and trainee!).
- Provides trainee an avenue for growth and a say in his/her own future.
- Develops a sense of growth in learning.
- Helps a person develop speaking and listening skills; also writing skills when exercises are required.
- Helps eliminate fear in attempting new tasks.

Benefits in Personnel and Human Relations, Intra and Intergroup Relations and Policy Implementation

- Improves communication between groups and individuals.
- Aids in orientation for new employees and those taking new jobs through transfer or promotion.
- Provides information on equal opportunity and affirmative action.
- Provides information on other governmental laws and administrative policies.
- Improves interpersonal skills.
- Makes organization policies, rules and regulations viable.
- Improves morale.
- Builds cohesiveness in groups.
- Provides a good climate for learning, growth, and coordination.
- Makes the organization a better place to work and live.

Source: From M. J. Tessin, "Once Again, Why Training?" *Training,* February 1978, p. 7. Reprinted by permission.

Figure 9-2
The Benefits of Employee Training

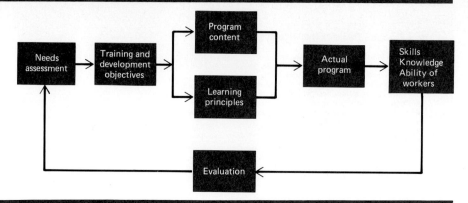

Figure 9-3
Preliminary Steps in Preparing
a Training and Development Program

Sometimes a change in the organization's strategy can create a need for training. For example, new products or services usually require employees to learn new procedures. Xerox encountered this challenge when it decided to produce computers. Sales personnel, programmers, and production workers had to be trained to produce, sell, and service this new product line. Training also can be used when high scrap or accident rates, low morale and motivation, or other problems are diagnosed. Although training is not an organizational cure-all, undesirable trends may be evidence of a poorly prepared work force.

Xerox faced a challenge.

Regardless of these challenges, needs assessment must consider each person.[10] His or her needs may be determined by the personnel department, by supervisors, or by self-nomination. The personnel department may find weaknesses among those who are hired or promoted. Supervisors see employees on a daily basis, and so they are another source of recommendations for training. However, supervisors may use training sessions as a means to banish troublemakers, "hide" surplus employees who are temporarily not needed, or to reward good workers. Since these are not valid reasons, the personnel department often reviews supervisory recommendations to verify the need for training. Likewise, the department also reviews self-nominations to learn if the training actually is needed. In one research study, more training attendees were chosen through supervisor recommendation than through self-nomination.[11] Self-nomination appears to be less common for training situations but more common for developmental activities, such as getting an M.B.A. degree under the employer's tuition reimbursement program.

Self-nominations for training

Even when employees are allowed to nominate themselves for available training programs, training directors have little assurance that the courses they offer fit the needs of the workers. To better narrow the range of courses and to define their content, more refined approaches to needs assessment are used. One approach is task identification. Trainers begin by evaluating the job description to identify the salient tasks that the job requires. Then with an understanding of these tasks, specific plans are developed to provide the necessary training so that job incumbents can perform the tasks.[12] The individual and departmental training phases of the Corning Glass Works training program are an example of a task identification approach.

Another approach is to survey potential trainees to identify specific topical areas that they want to learn more about.[13] The advantage of this method is that trainees are more likely to see the resulting programs as relevant, and thus they are more likely to be receptive to the subsequent training. Of course, this approach presumes that those surveyed know what training they need. For new employees needing specific individual or departmental training at Corning, for example, this method is not likely to be successful. However, for the more general needs that are found in Corning's plant or facilities and corporate training, group recommendations may be the best way to identify training needs. The groups' expertise may be tapped through a group discussion, questionnaire, Delphi procedure (see Chapter 4, "Human Resource Planning"), or nominal group meeting.

Surveys of potential trainees

The *nominal group technique* (NGT) is a method for drawing ideas out of a group of people on a specified topic.[14] For example, ten to fifteen trainers, managers, or potential trainees are asked to quietly list on a piece of paper all the training needs they can think of. After the group has gone through this silent generation phase, each person is asked to give one idea in round-robin fashion. This process of soliciting an idea from each person continues until each one has exhausted his or her ideas and "passes." The moderator (or a scribe) lists every idea without allowing any praise, criticism, or discussion until all the ideas are listed. Participants then vote for the five most important training needs. The votes are tabulated to determine which needs are seen by the group as the most pressing. Unlike brainstorming, where some people may not offer any ideas at all, NGT taps everyone's suggestions and allows the ideas of others during the round-robin session to stimulate additional ideas among the group members. The final "voting" ensures that the outcome reflects the group's collective wisdom.

Nominal group technique

Trainers are alert for other sources of information that may indicate a need for training. Production records, quality control reports, grievances, safety reports, absenteeism and turnover statistics, and exit interviews among departing employees may evidence problems that should be addressed through training and development efforts. Training needs may also become apparent from career planning and development discussions or from performance appraisal reviews—both of which are covered in Chapters 10 and 11.[15] Regardless of how needs assessment takes place, it is important because the success of the remaining steps in Figure 9-3 depends on an accurate assessment. If the trainer's assessment of need is not correct, it is unlikely that training objectives and program content will be appropriate.

Training and Development Objectives

An evaluation of training needs results in training and development objectives. These objectives should state the desired behavior and the conditions under which it is to occur and should serve as the standard against which individual performance and the program can be measured. For example, the objectives for an airline reservationist might be stated as follows:

Specific behavioral objectives

1.   Provide flight information to call-in customers within thirty seconds.

2.   Complete a one-city, round-trip reservation in two minutes after all information is obtained from the customer.

Objectives like these for a reservationist give the trainer and the trainee specific goals that can be used to evaluate their success. If the objectives are not met, failure gives the personnel department feedback on the program and on the participants.

Program Content

The program's content is shaped by the needs assessment and by the learning objectives. This content may seek to teach specific skills, provide needed knowledge, or simply try to influence attitudes. Whatever its content, the program must meet the needs of the organization and the participants. If company goals are not furthered, resources are wasted. And participants must view the content as relevant to their needs or else their motivation to learn may be low.

Learning Principles

Although the learning process is widely studied, little is known about it. Part of the problem is that learning cannot be observed: only its results can be measured. From studies of learning, however, researchers have sketched a broad picture of the learning process and have developed some tentative principles of learning. Perhaps the best way to understand learning is through the use of a *learning curve,* shown in Figure 9-4. As the curve illustrates, learning takes place in bursts (from points *A* to *B*) and in plateaus (from points *B* to *C*). Trainers have two goals related to the shape of each employee's learning curve. First, trainers want the learning curve to reach a satisfactory level of perform-

Figure 9-4
A Typical Learning Curve

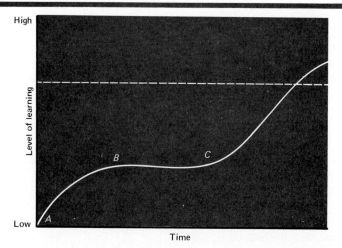

ance. This level is shown as a dashed line in the figure. Second, they want the learning curve to get to the satisfactory level as quickly as possible. Although the rate at which an individual learns depends upon the person, the use of various learning principles helps speed up the learning process.

Learning principles are the guidelines to the ways in which people learn most effectively. The more these principles are included in training, the more effective training is likely to be. These principles are participation, repetition, relevance, transference, and feedback.

Participation   Learning usually is quicker and more long-lasting when the learner can participate actively. Participation improves motivation and apparently engages more senses that help reinforce the learning process. As a result of participation, we learn more quickly and retain that learning longer. For example, most people never forget how to ride a bicycle because they actively participated in the learning process.

Repetition   Although seldom fun, repetition apparently etches a pattern into our memory. Studying for an examination, for example, involves repetition of key ideas so that they can be recalled during the test. Likewise, most people learned the alphabet and the multiplication tables by repetition.

Relevance   Learning is helped when the material to be learned is meaningful. For example, trainers usually explain the overall purpose of a job to trainees before explaining specific tasks. This explanation allows the worker to see the relevance of each task and the relevance of following the correct procedures.

Transference   The closer the demands of the training program match the demands of the job, the faster a person learns to master the job.[16] For example, pilots usually are trained in flight simulators because the simulators very closely resemble the actual cockpit and flight characteristics of the plane. The close match between the simulator and the plane allows the trained to transfer quickly the learning in the simulator to actual flight conditions.

Feedback   Feedback gives learners information on their progress. With feedback, motivated learners can adjust their behavior to achieve the quickest possible learning curve. Without feedback, the learners cannot gauge their progress and may become discouraged. Test grades are feedback on the study habits of test takers, for example.

TRAINING AND DEVELOPMENT APPROACHES

Before reviewing the various training and development approaches, it is important to remember that any method may be applied to both training and development. For example, a class on management techniques may be attended by supervisors and by workers who are likely to be promoted to these positions.[17] For supervisors, the class is training in how to do their present job better. For workers who have no management responsibilities, the classes are intended to develop these employees into supervisors. The classroom instruction is identical for both groups, but it has two different intents: training for supervisors and development for workers.

Trade-offs   In selecting a particular technique to use in training or development, there are several trade-offs. That is, no one technique is always best; the best method depends upon:

- Cost-effectiveness

- Desired program content

- Appropriateness of the facilities

- Trainee preferences and capabilities

- Trainer preferences and capabilities

- Learning principles

The importance of these six trade-offs depends upon the situation. For example, cost-effectiveness may be a minor factor when training an airline pilot in emergency maneuvers. But whatever method is selected, it has certain learning principles associated with it. Figure 9-5 lists the most common training and development techniques and the learning principles each includes. As the figure reveals, some techniques make more effective use of learning principles than others. Even those approaches that use few learning principles, such as the lecture, are valuable tools because they may satisfy one of the other six

Figure 9-5

Learning Principles in Different Training and
Development Techniques

	PARTICIPATION	REPETITION	RELEVANCE	TRANSFERENCE	FEEDBACK
ON-THE-JOB TECHNIQUES					
Job instruction training	Yes	Yes	Yes	Yes	Sometimes
Job rotation	Yes	Sometimes	Yes	Sometimes	No
Apprenticeships	Yes	Sometimes	Yes	Sometimes	Sometimes
Coaching	Yes	Sometimes	Yes	Sometimes	Yes
OFF-THE-JOB TECHNIQUES					
Lecture	No	No	No	Sometimes	No
Video presentation	No	No	No	Yes	No
Vestibule training	Yes	Yes	Sometimes	Yes	Sometimes
Role playing	Yes	Sometimes	Sometimes	No	Sometimes
Case study	Yes	Sometimes	Sometimes	Sometimes	Sometimes
Simulation	Yes	Sometimes	Sometimes	Sometimes	Sometimes
Self-study	Yes	Yes	Sometimes	Sometimes	No
Programmed learning	Yes	Yes	No	Yes	Yes
Laboratory training	Yes	Yes	Sometimes	No	Yes

Source: From *Training in Industry: The Management of Learning,* by B. M. Bass and J. A. Vaughn. Copyright © 1966 by Wadsworth Publishing Company, Inc. Reprinted by permission of the publisher, Brooks/Cole Publishing Company, Monterey, Calif.

trade-offs listed above. For example, a lecture may be the best way to communicate some academic content in the most cost-effective manner, especially if the classroom is large and the room does not lend itself to other approaches. Although these trade-offs affect the methods used, personnel specialists must be familiar with all the techniques and learning principles found in Figure 9-5.

Job Instruction Training

Job instruction training is received directly on the job, so it is often simply called "on-the-job" training. It is used primarily to teach workers how to do their present job. A trainer, supervisor, or coworker serves as the instructor. When it is properly planned and executed, this method includes each of the learning principles shown in Figure 9-5. In most cases, however, the trainer's focus is on making a product, not on good training technique.

On-the-job training (or OJT) has several steps. First, the trainee receives an overview of the job, its purpose, and its desired outcomes, with emphasis on the relevance of the training. Then the trainer demonstrates the job to provide the employee with a model to copy. Since the employee is shown the actual actions that the job requires, the training is transferable to the job. Next the employee is allowed to mimic the trainer's example. Demonstrations by the trainer and practice by the trainee are repeated until the job is mastered by the trainee. Repeated demonstrations and practice provide the advantage of repetition and feedback. Finally, the employee performs the job without supervision, although the trainer may visit the employee to see if there are any lingering questions.

Job Rotation

To cross-train employees in a variety of jobs, some trainers will move the trainee from job to job. Each move normally is preceded by job instruction training. Besides giving workers variety in their jobs, cross-training helps the organization when vacations, absences, and resignations occur. Learner participation and high job transferability are the learning advantages to job rotation.

Creating backups

Apprenticeships and Coaching

Apprenticeships involve learning from a more experienced employee or employees. This approach to training may be supplemented with off-the-job classroom training. Most craft workers, such as plumbers and carpenters, are trained through formal apprenticeship programs. Assistantships and internships are similar to apprenticeships. These approaches use high levels of participation by the trainee and have high transferability to the job.

Coaching is similar to apprenticeships because the coach attempts to provide a model for the trainee to copy. Most companies use some coaching. It tends to be less formal than an apprenticeship program because there are few formal classroom sessions, and the coaching is provided when needed rather than being part of a carefully planned program. Coaching is almost always handled by the supervisor or manager and not by the personnel department. Participation, feedback, and job transference are likely to be high in this form of learning.[18]

Someone who accepts the "coaching" of one person to learn that person's specific job is called an understudy. The star of a theater production often will have an understudy, for example. Likewise, a senior executive may designate his or her replacement well before retirement so that person can serve as an understudy.

Assignments to task forces or committees also may help develop people in much the same way that apprenticeships and coaching do. Through periodic staff meetings or work with task forces and committees, a manager develops interpersonal skills, learns to evaluate information, and gains experience in observing other potential models.

Lecture and Video Presentations

Lecture and other off-the-job techniques tend to rely more heavily on communications rather than on modeling, which is used in on-the-job programs. These approaches are applied in both training and development. Lecture is a popular approach because it offers relative economy and a meaningful organization of materials. However, participation, feedback, transference, and repetition are often low. Feedback and participation can be improved when discussion is permitted along with the lecture process.

Television, films, slides, and filmstrip presentations are similar to lectures. A meaningful organization of materials is a potential strength, along with initial audience interest. Interestingly, one survey of training directors revealed that they thought films were superior to lectures with questions.[19]

Vestibule Training

So that instruction does not disrupt normal operations, some organizations use *vestibule training*. Separate areas or vestibules are set up with equipment similar to that which will be used on the job. This arrangement allows transference, repetition, and participation. The meaningful organization of materials and feedback are also possible.

At the corporate training facilities of Best Western motels and hotels, vestibules exist that duplicate a typical motel room, a typical front counter, and a typical restaurant kitchen. This allows trainees to practice housekeeping, front counter, and kitchen skills without disrupting the operations of any one property.

Role Playing and Behavior Modeling

Role playing is a device that forces trainees to assume different identities. For example, a male worker may assume the role of a female supervisor, and the supervisor may assume the role of a male worker. Then both may be given a typical work situation and told to respond as they would expect the other to do. The result? Usually participants exaggerate each other's behavior. Ideally, they both get to see themselves as others see them. The experience may create greater empathy and tolerance of individual differences. This technique is used to change attitudes (for example, to improve racial understanding). It also helps develop interpersonal skills.[20] Although participation and feedback are present, the inclusion of other learning principles depends on the situation.

The U.S. Navy has used role playing to reduce racial tensions. Friction among sailors of different races—within the limited confines of ships on extended patrol duty—not only harmed morale and crew efficiency but also caused low rates of reenlistment among highly trained personnel. High turnover impaired the Navy's ability to function.

U.S. Navy uses role playing.

The role-playing exercises required small groups of black and white sailors to assume the role of the opposite race. The role-playing leader gave the members of each group an assignment and then directed them to carry it out as they thought members of the other race would. With the other group watching, each group in turn acted out the behavior of the others. Through these exercises and the subsequent discussions, members of the different races were able to learn how their behavior and attitudes affected one another.

Closely related to this form of role playing is behavior modeling. *Behavior modeling* was described by two writers as follows:

Modeling is one of the fundamental psychological processes by which new patterns of behavior can be acquired, and existing patterns can be altered. The fundamental characteristic of modeling is that learning takes place, *not* through actual experience, but through observation or imagination of another individual's experience. Modeling is a "vicarious process," which implies sharing in the experience of another person through imagination or sympathetic participation.[21]

Copying the ideal may help.

Whether behavior modeling is referred to as "matching" or "copying," "observational learning" or "imitation," "all of these terms imply that a behavior is learned or modified through the observation of some other individual. . . ."[22] Employees may learn a new behavior through modeling by observing a new or novel behavior and then imitating it. The re-creation of the behavior may be videotaped so that the trainer and the trainee can review and critique it. Often when watching the ideal behavior, the trainee also gets to see the negative consequences that befall someone who does not use it as recommended. By observing the positive and negative consequences, the employee receives vicarious reinforcement that encourages the correct behavior. One area where this approach has been used successfully is in teaching supervisors how to discipline employees.

In the supervisory training program of a large unionized steel company, supervisors were put through a half-day disciplinary training session that used videotape-based behavior modeling. After a short lecture on the principles of discipline, trainees were shown a brief tape of a supervisor conducting a disciplinary interview incorrectly and another where the

Modeling trains specific patterns of response.

discipline was handled properly. Then the supervisors were paired into groups of two. Each supervisor was told to "discipline" his or her partner using the correct method they had just observed. These mock discipline sessions were filmed and played back—often to the horror of the partici-pants. Each saw how others saw him or her when they conducted a disciplinary interview. After a brief and largely positive critique from the trainer, each supervisor conducted a second and a third discipline session that was followed by a critique. By the end of the morning, each supervisor was capable of conducting a disciplinary interview in the correct manner. Whether this training was actually transferred to their day-to-day behavior on the job was not evaluated by the training department nor by the shop manager.

Case Study

By studying a case situation, trainees learn about real or hypothetical circum-stances and the actions others take under those circumstances. Besides learning from the content of the case, a person can develop decision-making skills. When cases are meaningful and similar to work-related situations, there is some transference. There also is the advantage of participation through discussion of the case. Feedback and repetition, though, are usually lacking. Research indicates that this technique is most effective for developing problem-solving skills.[23]

Simulation

Simulation exercises are in two forms. One form involves a mechanical simulator that replicates the major features of the work situation. Driving simulators used in driver's education programs are an example. This training method is similar to vestibule training, except that the simulator more often provides instantaneous feedback on performance.

Computer games   Computer simulations are another technique. For training and development purposes, this method is often in the form of games. Players make a decision, and the computer determines the outcome, given the conditions under which it was programmed. This technique is used most commonly to train managers, who otherwise might have to use trial and error to learn decision making.

Self-Study and Programmed Learning

Carefully planned instructional materials can be used to train and develop employees. These are particularly useful when employees are dispersed geo-graphically or when learning requires little interaction. Self-study techniques range from manuals to prerecorded cassettes or videotapes. Unfortunately, few learning principles are included in this type of training.

Pepsi Cola uses videotaped training.   The Pepsi Cola Management Institute is responsible for training bottlers all over the world. To contend with this dispersion, it created a network of videotape recorders and supplied bottlers with videotaped materials. The institute also uses other techniques.

Programmed learning materials are another form of self-study. Usually these are printed booklets that contain a series of questions and answers. After reading and answering a question, the reader can immediately uncover the correct response. If it matches the reader's answer, the reader proceeds. If not, the reader is directed to review accompanying materials. Of course, computer programs with visual displays may be used instead of printed booklets.[24] The Control Data Corporation, for example, has spent hundreds of millions of dollars on an interactive computer-based system called PLATO. It allows a large number of users to interact with the system to learn at their own pace. Similarly, with the growth in personal computers, programmed learning materials on floppy disks are growing in popularity. Programmed materials do provide learner participation, repetition, relevance, and feedback. Transference, however, tends to be low.

Laboratory Training

Laboratory training is a form of group training primarily used to enhance interpersonal skills. It, too, can be used to develop desired behaviors for future job responsibilities. Participants seek to improve their human relations skills by better understanding themselves and others. Laboratory training involves sharing experiences and examining the feelings, behaviors, perceptions, and reactions that result. Usually a trained professional serves as a facilitator. The process relies on participation, feedback, and repetition. One popular form of laboratory training is sensitivity training, which seeks to improve a person's sensitivity to the feelings of others.

DEVELOPMENT OF HUMAN RESOURCES

The long-term development of human resources—as distinct from training for a specific job—is of growing concern to personnel departments. Through the development of present employees, the personnel department reduces the company's dependence on hiring new workers. If employees are developed properly, the job openings found through human resource planning are more likely to be filled internally. Promotions and transfers also show employees that they have a career, not just a job. The employer benefits from increased continuity in operations and from employees who feel a greater commitment to the firm.

Human resource development is also an effective way to meet several challenges faced by most large organizations. These challenges include employee obsolescence, sociotechnical changes, affirmative action, and employee turnover.[25] By meeting these challenges, the personnel department can help maintain an effective work force.

Employee Obsolescence

Obsolescence results when an employee no longer possesses the knowledge or abilities to perform successfully. In fast-changing and highly technical fields, such as engineering and medicine, obsolescence can occur quickly. Among

Obsolescence in a changing world

managers, the change may take place more slowly and be more difficult to determine. Other people in the organization may not notice obsolescence until it is advanced. Too often, favorable opinions about a manager, which are formed over years of association, prevent others from seeing telltale signs of obsolescence such as inappropriate attitudes, poor performance, or incorrect or outdated procedures.

Although obsolescence may develop from some change in the individual, it is more likely to result from that person's failure to adapt to new technology, new procedures, or other changes. The more rapidly the environment changes, the more likely employees will become obsolete.[26]

Some employers are reluctant to take strong action and fire obsolete employees, particularly those who have been with the company for a long time. Instead, such workers may be given jobs where their obsolescence does not matter so much or where their skills are not as obsolete. For example, when top executives fail to perform satisfactorily, they sometimes are "promoted" to vice chairperson of the board, where their primary role is to attend ceremonial functions such as banquets for retiring employees. For lower-level workers, the solution is often additional development programs.

To avoid the problem of obsolescence before it occurs is a major challenge for the personnel department. By periodically assessing the needs of employees and by giving them programs to develop new skills, the department is using development programs proactively. If programs are designed reactively, after obsolescence occurs, they are likely to be less effective and more costly. For example, consider the situation faced by a personnel department of a regional airline.

> Sam Oliver had been a ground crew chief in the Air Force for many of his twenty years in the service. After retirement, he joined a regional airline as a mechanic. Since he had extensive supervisory experience, he was promoted to ground crew chief. Sam had been successful in the Air Force by giving direct orders with little explanation, and he followed the same leadership style in his civilian job.
>
> The personnel department realized something was wrong when an unusually large number of grievances were filed with the union by Sam's ground crew. To correct the problems, Sam was enrolled in an intensive sixteen-week supervisory training program at the local community college. Although he changed his approach after the program, Sam now showed resentment toward those subordinates who filed the grievances.

Had the personnel department undertaken proactive supervisory development before Sam was promoted, rather than reacting to his obsolescence after problems arose, his resentment might have been avoided.

Career plateau   When an employee reaches a career plateau, obsolescence may even be more likely. A *career plateau* occurs when an employee is in a position that he or she does well enough not to be demoted or fired, but not so well that the person is likely to be promoted.[27] When the employee realizes that he or she is at this plateau, the motivation to stay current as a manager, professional, or technician may be reduced.[28]

Continuing education: a lifelong process

Many companies use continuing education for middle- and upper-level management to combat obsolescence. Western Electric conducts "Corporate Symposiums on Emerging Issues" at its corporate education center in Hopewell, New Jersey. General Electric operates the GE Management Institute on the General Electric Campus outside of New York City. IBM runs the IBM Country Club and Management Institute on Long Island, and the federal government operates the Federal Executive Institute on its own campus in Virginia.[29] These developmental opportunities are supplemented by educational leaves at companies like IBM and Xerox and by university-based advanced management education programs that typically last from four to fourteen weeks. An example of how one company deals with continuing education for selected managers comes from the Phillips Petroleum Company.

Phillips Petroleum approach

On the basis of performance and future promotability, Phillips Petroleum selects thirty middle managers with high potential to go to its internal management training program. About one-fourth of the time is devoted to issues in the external environment—macroeconomics, international economics, public policy formulation, congressional dynamics, and ethics. The remainder of the four weeks deals with business management subjects such as planning, financial management, marketing, individual and organizational behavior, and the like.

The purpose of the four-week program is not to replace university-based education, which is still used. Instead, the intent of the training is to give these high-potential managers a broader perspective on Phillips and the business environment in which they must operate. One of the hoped-for outcomes of this training is to help these managers identify areas where they need further training and development rather than try to make them experts in the topic areas that are discussed. The $3000 cost per participant is not cheap; however, the broadened perspective and the intellectual stimulation of these key middle managers can help Phillips deal with the issue of obsolescence in part. And if the attendees are motivated by the experience to further their education formally or informally, obsolescence may be avoided entirely.[30]

Sociotechnical Changes

Social and technological changes also challenge the personnel department. For example, cultural attitudes about women in the work force caused many companies, such as American Telephone and Telegraph, to redesign their development programs in order to meet societal pressures for equal employment. AT&T redesigned an existing program for outside craft workers to enable more women to qualify for outside jobs, such as installer and line worker, that previously had been dominated by men. The social changes brought about by equal employment opportunity and the company's affirmative action program even led to a redesign of the equipment used by outside craft people in order to better accommodate more female workers.

Likewise, rapid changes in technology require technology-based firms to engage in nearly continuous development. Consider the technological changes that occurred during Frank T. Carey's career with IBM, for example:

> Mr. Carey joined IBM in 1948 "because he liked its bright prospects in the office-equipment business."[31] Although IBM is still a major producer of office equipment today, most people associate it with giant computers. While Mr. Carey advanced to the position of chairman of the board at IBM, technology radically transformed IBM into the largest computer manufacturer in the world. Undoubtedly, his career, like that of many others at IBM, was marked by nearly continuous development activities in order to keep up with rapid technological change.

AT&T versus IBM: Is training a key weapon?

The social and technical changes that have taken place during the 1980s have made AT&T and IBM major competitors. The improvements in information handling and transmission technology have opened up new markets for these two ultralarge organizations. At the same time, society decreed a greater move toward deregulation of businesses. This deregulation caused AT&T to spin off most of its assets that were tied up in basic phone service in order to become deregulated and compete with IBM in the emerging information industry. These sociological and technological changes are having a profound impact on the training and development functions in these corporations. There is an increased need to assess the developmental requirements of current and future managers, professionals, and technical people. Not only are the social and technological forces changing quickly, but in the case of AT&T, this once largely regulated monopoly is now trying to adjust its corporate culture to that of a market-oriented competitor. These marketing changes are further compounding the complexities faced by AT&T training and development specialists.

Development and Affirmative Action

Companies like AT&T and IBM also face the challenge of providing equal opportunity. Many large and small corporations alike have developed affirmative action plans as remedial or preventative moves to deal with the issue of discrimination. However, the Civil Rights Act prohibits discrimination with respect to terms, conditions, or privileges of employment. As a result, training and development activities must be conducted in such a way that they do not discriminate against protected classes.[32]

Affirmative action and training

When successfully passing a training program or course is a condition of employment or promotion, for example, the personnel department must be able to show that the training requirements are related to job success. If the training or development activities are not validated, the employer may be faced with violations of the act. Even admission into a training or development program can be discriminatory if the admission criteria have an adverse impact on members of protected classes. Likewise, the training or development program itself may have a discriminatory impact if barriers to training are not related to subsequent job success. (For example, women had significant difficulty passing the training for outside craft positions at AT&T subsidiaries. Part of the problem was that some of the training equipment had been designed for the larger feet of men, thus causing a disproportionate number of women and smaller men to fail the course.) Still another problem may occur when the scores obtained from various parts of the training program are used for future placement decisions. Under these circumstances, the burden falls on the personnel department to show that these scores are in fact valid.[33]

In *Weber v. Kaiser Aluminum and Chemical Corporation,* the U.S. Supreme Court recognized that affirmative action may require a disproportionately high number of minorities to be admitted to training programs. If this form of "reverse discrimination" occurs to achieve the goals of an affirmative action plan, the courts consider it legal.

Employee Turnover

Turnover—the willingness of employees to leave one organization for another— creates a special challenge for human resource development. Because these departures are largely unpredictable, development activities must prepare present employees to succeed those who leave. Although research shows that leaders of very large industrial companies spend nearly all of their careers with one firm, the same research found that mobility is widespread among other managers.[34] Therefore, development programs must prepare other employees to replace these mobile managers. Sometimes an employer with excellent development programs finds that these programs actually *contribute* to employee turnover.

> Ironically, the widely recognized development programs of such companies as General Electric, Procter & Gamble, General Motors and IBM partially cause some employee mobility. Their programs produce such high-quality results that recruiters from other companies are attracted to these employees.

Training may create turnover opportunities.

EVALUATION OF TRAINING AND DEVELOPMENT

The implementation of training and development serves as a transformation process. Untrained employees are transformed into capable workers, and present workers may be developed to assume new responsibilities. To verify a program's success, personnel managers increasingly demand that training and development activities be evaluated systematically.

The lack of evaluation may be the most serious flaw in most training and development efforts. Simply stated, personnel professionals too seldom ask, "Did the program achieve the objectives established for it?" They often assume it had value because the content seemed important. Or trainers may rely on the evaluations of the trainees, who reported how enjoyable the experience was for them, rather than evaluate the content themselves.

Did training work?

Evaluation of training and development should follow the steps in Figure 9-6. First, evaluation criteria should be established before training begins. These

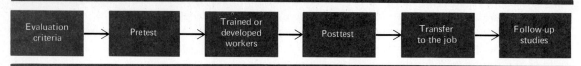

Figure 9-6
Steps in the Evaluation of Training and Development

criteria may be the same as the training and development objectives set in Figure 9-3. Then participants should be given a pretest. That is, they should be tested to establish their level of knowledge before the program begins. Sometimes selection tests can serve this purpose. After training or development is completed, a posttest should reveal any improvement that may have resulted from the program. If the improvement is significant, that is, it probably did not result from chance, it can be assumed that the program actually made a difference. The program is a success if the improvement met the evaluation criteria and is transferred to the job. Transference is best measured by improved job performance. Follow-up studies may be conducted months or even years later to see how well learning was retained.[35]

Does learning impact the job?

Plagued by a disturbing number of accidents, a local home builder contracted with a management consulting firm to receive a safety training program. The training included a variety of techniques, but the builder wanted "proof" that it was effective without waiting to see if accidents declined. A safety quiz was given to the builder's field employees. The average score was 39. After training, a posttest revealed that the average score was 67, a result that was not likely due to chance.

The management consultant claimed that the posttest proved that the training was successful. The builder's personnel manager correctly argued:

"The training is a qualified success. The posttest reveals that the training did increase the field personnel's knowledge of safety. But the only measure of success is whether that new knowledge results in behavioral changes—namely the lowering of the frequency and severity of accidents. We won't know if the training was successful until we get the quarterly accident reports in three months. In fact, I would like to run a follow-up study in a year to see how well the knowledge was retained."

As this example illustrates, posttests do not prove the success of the training. Success is best illustrated by behavioral changes. Therefore, the evaluation criteria should be stated in behavioral terms whenever possible. For the home builder's example, the learning objectives and the evaluation criteria might have read as follows:

A reduction of the frequency and severity of work-related accidents per 10,000 work hours during the subsequent calendar quarter

The posttest is still useful to determine if the information was communicated. It may also be useful to evaluate which applicants failed to understand the materials. However, the success of a program eventually is measured against specific behavioral changes that occur on the job.[36]

SUMMARY

After workers are selected and oriented, they may still lack the necessary skills, knowledge, and attitudes to perform successfully. Most workers require some training to do their present job properly. If the organization wishes to use these employees in more responsible positions in the future, then developmental activities also will have to take place. For most workers and trainers, individual learning sessions are a blend of training and development.

Most large organizations make available a broad array of educational opportunities. However, trainers should conduct a needs analysis for each course, to determine if the training is truly needed and, if it is needed, what the training should cover. Training and development, or learning, objectives result from the needs analysis. Trainers can then plan the content of the course from these objectives and incorporate as many learning principles as is feasible.

Human resource development prepares individuals for future job responsibilities. At the same time, it attempts to contend with employee obsolescence, sociotechnical change, affirmative action, and employee turnover.

To merely conduct training—even when a careful needs assessment has been undertaken—is insufficient. Experienced trainers seek to evaluate the impact of training and development activities. Often this involves a pretest and posttest and even follow-up studies to see if the learning was transferred to the job.

TERMS FOR REVIEW

Needs assessment	Job instruction training
Learning curve	Vestibule training
Learning principles	Laboratory training
Repetition	Role playing
Transference	Behavior modeling
Feedback	Obsolescence
Nominal group technique	Career plateau

REVIEW AND DISCUSSION QUESTIONS

1. Why is needs assessment an important first step in any training program? Explain three ways that a trainer might learn about the training needs faced by employees.

2.   What purpose do learning objectives serve?

3.   Explain what is meant by obsolescence and career plateaus.

4.   If you had an employee who had been working for six or seven years in the same job, what signs would you look for to tell if this person was becoming obsolete?

5.   Which training techniques do you recommend for each of the following occupations. Why?
   a. A cashier in a grocery store
   b. A welder
   c. An assembly-line worker
   d. An inexperienced supervisor

6.   If you were directed to design a managerial development program that made use of all five learning principles, which two training techniques would you combine? Why?

7.   Suppose you were a supervisor in an accounting department and the training manager wanted to implement a new training program to teach bookkeepers how to complete some new accounting forms. What steps would you recommend to evaluate the effectiveness of the training program?

8.   Assume you were hired to manage a research and development department. After a few weeks you noticed that some researchers were more effective than others and that the less effective ones received little recognition from their more productive counterparts. What forms of development would you consider for both groups?

INCIDENT 9-1

Developing a Training Program at Johnson Wax Company

How can we develop a training program which will have a significant impact on new first-line supervisors, experienced supervisors (first and second level) and on staff personnel, both new and experienced?

This was the question we faced at the Johnson Wax Company, Racine, Wisconsin . . . at an initial task force meeting of seven middle managers (section managers). The challenge had been issued to the task force by the two vice presidents of major divisions (manufacturing and distribution) to build a practical, participative, results-oriented training program for newly appointed unit managers, our title for first-line supervisors.[37]

1.   Describe the steps you would go through before actually designing the content of the training.

2.   How would you evaluate the final training modules to determine how effective each was?

3. Do you think these line managers were the right people to design the training program? Who else would you add, if anyone, to this group?

INCIDENT 9-2

Development of Human Resources at CT-General Hospital

Clayton Dahl was appointed director of human resource development at CT-General. The hospital director, Andrea Hess, suggested that Clayton could best familiarize himself with the hospital's development needs by compiling a report about past development efforts.

In gathering the information for the report, Clayton made several interesting observations:

- Development activities had been limited to preparing nonprofessionals to assume supervisory positions.

- Most department managers and staff directors took the attitude that it was easier to hire talent as it was needed rather than develop present employees.

- Those managers who supervised professional hospital employees took the attitude that development is the responsibility of each professional.

- Most other managers viewed voluntary attendance at management development programs as an admission of inability.

- During each of the last three years, the development budget had been cut by about 10 percent.

1. What would you recommend if you were in Clayton's position?

2. What type of support should Clayton seek from the hospital administrator?

3. If a new development program is offered, what type of attendance policy should Clayton set? Why? What types of problems will your answer cause?

REFERENCES

1. James L. Hayes, "Human Resources—The Last Resource of a Frontier Society," *Training and Development Journal,* June 1976, p. 9.

2. "Retraining Displaced Workers: Too Little, Too Late?" *Business Week,* July 19, 1982, p. 178.

3. Gale E. Newell, "How to Plan a Training Program," *Personnel Journal,* May 1976, pp. 220–224. See also Bonnye L. Matthes and Virginia Sweet Lincoln, "Try S.T.A.R.T.: The Systematic Training Aid Resource Tool," *Training,* January 1978, pp. 32–33; and S. D.

Inderlied and D. L. Bates, "A Practical Approach to Determining Training Solvable Problems," *Personnel Journal,* January 1980, pp. 121–125. Also see Donald B. MIller, "Training Managers to Stimulate Employee Development," *Training and Development Journal,* February 1981, pp. 47–53; and Anthony P. Carnevale and Harold Goldstein, *Employee Training: Its Changing Role and An Analysis of New Data,* Washington, D. C.: ASTD Press, 1983.

4. John D. Dickey, "Training with a Focus on the Individual," *Personnel Administrator,* June 1982, p. 35.

5. Ibid., pp. 35, 37.

6. Ibid., p. 38.

7. Ibid., p. 7.

8. Thomas F. Gilbert, "The High Cost of Knowledge," *Personnel,* March 1976, p. 23.

9. William C. Byham and James Robinson, "Building Supervisory Confidence—A Key to Transfer of Training," *Personnel Journal,* May 1977, pp. 248–250, 253. See also Richard Beckhard, "The Changing Shape of Management Development," *The Journal of Management Development,* vol. 1, no. 1, 1982, pp. 51–62.

10. John W. Lawrie, "A Guide to Customized Leadership Training and Development," *Personnel Journal,* September 1979, pp. 593–596.

11. "Employee Training," *Personnel Management: Policies and Practices,* Englewood Cliffs, N.J.: Prentice-Hall, 1979, p. 9.

12. Kenneth N. Wexley and Gary P. Latham, *Developing and Training Human Resources in Organizations,* Glenview, Ill.: Scott, Foresman, and Company, 1981, p. 35.

13. Mariless S. Niehoff and M. Jay Romans, "Needs Assessment as Step One toward Enhancing Productivity," *Personnel Administrator,* May 1982, pp. 35–39.

14. Andre Delbecq and A. Van de Ven, "A Group Process Model for Problem Identification and Program Planning," *Journal of Applied Behavioral Science,* August 1971, pp. 78–83. See also Mark Martinko and Jim Gepson, "Nominal Grouping and Needs Analysis," in Francis L. Ulschak (ed.), *Human Resource Development: The Theory and Practice of Needs Assessment,* Reston, Va.: Reston Publishing, 1983, pp. 101–110.

15. Martinko and Gepson, op. cit.

16. Byham and Robinson, op. cit.

17. Ernest D. Jobe, W. Randy Boxx, and D. L. Howell, "A Customized Approach to Management Development," *Personnel Journal,* March 1979, pp. 150–153.

18. Joseph Yeager, "Coaching the Executive: Can You Teach an Old Dog New Tricks?" *Personnel Administrator,* November 1982, pp. 37–42.

19. Stephen J. Carroll, Frank T. Paine, and John J. Ivancevich, "The Relative Effectiveness of Training Methods—Expert Opinion and Research," *Personnel Psychology,* Autumn 1972, p. 499.

20. Ibid.

21. Henry P. Sims, Jr., and Charles C. Manz, "Modeling Influences on Employee Behavior," *Personnel Journal,* January 1982, p. 58.

22. Ibid.

23. John W. Newstrom, "Evaluating the Effectiveness of Training Methods," *Personnel Administrator,* January 1980, pp. 55–60.

24. John R. Hinrichs, "Personnel Training," in Marvin D. Dunnette (ed.), *Handbook of Industrial and Organizational Psychology,* Chicago: Rand McNally, 1976, pp. 850–851.

25. Edward J. Mandt, "A Basic Model of Manager Development," *Personnel Journal,* June 1979, pp. 395–400. See also Alfred W. Hill, "How Organizational Philosophy Influences Management Development," *Personnel Journal,* February 1980, pp. 118–120, 148.

26. Elmer Burack and Gopal Pati, "Technology and Managerial Obsolescence," *MSU Business Topics,* Spring 1970, pp. 49–56. See also Herbert Kaufman, *Obsolescence and Professional Career Development,* New York: AMACOM, 1974.

27. Christopher M. Dawson, "Will Career Plateauing Become a Bigger Problem?" *Personnel Journal,* January 1983, pp. 78–81. See also Richard A. Payne, "Mid-Career Block," *Personnel Journal,* April 1984, pp. 38–40, 42, 44, 46–48.

28. Morley D. Glicken, "A Counseling Approach to Employee Burnout," *Personnel Journal,* March 1983, pp. 222–228; see also Jack Brewer and Carol Dubnicki,"Relighting the Fire with an Employee Revitalization Program," *Personnel Journal,* October 1983, pp. 812–818.

29. Matt M. Starcevich, Ph.D., and J. Arnold Sykes, "Internal Advancement Programs for Executive Development," *Personnel Administrator,* June 1982, pp. 27–33.

30. Ibid. See also Stanley Truski, "Guidelines for Conducting In-House Management Development," *Personnel Administrator,* July 1981, pp. 25–27.

31. "In the News," *Fortune,* Feb. 27, 1979, pp. 15–16.

32. Donald W. Myers, "The Impact of a Selected Provision in the Federal Guidelines on Job Analysis and Training," *Personnel Administrator,* July 1981, pp. 41–46.

33. Wexley and Latham, op. cit., pp. 22–27.

34. William B. Werther, Jr., "Management Turnover Implications of Career Mobility," *The Personnel Administrator,* February 1977, pp. 63–66. See also Simeon J. Touretzky, "Changing Attitudes: A Question of Loyalty," *The Personnel Administrator,* April 1979, pp. 35–36.

35. Wexley and Latham, op. cit., pp. 78–100. See also Frank Hoy, W. Wray Buchanan, and Bobby C. Vaught, "Are Your Management Development Programs Working?" *Personnel Journal,* December 1981, pp. 953–957. See also Charles Margerison, "How to Avoid Failure and Gain Success in Management Development," *Journal of Management Development,* vol. 1, no. 1, 1982, pp. 3–17.

36. Jonathan S. Monat, "A Perspective on the Evaluation of Training and Development Programs," *Personnel Administrator,* July 1981, pp. 47–54.

37. Thomas J. Newman, "How to Develop a Practical, Participative, Manager Development Program," *Training and Development Journal,* August 1975, pp. 36–40.

An organization needs to move individuals along career paths, to develop the . . . capabilities necessary to staff various levels and types of jobs.

James W. Walker[1]

In the long run companies will not be successful if they do not learn how to develop management talent internally. We could all learn from those elite firms . . . who year after year have had record profits and earnings and concurrently breed their own.

Eugene E. Jennings[2]

CHAPTER

10

CAREER PLANNING

CHAPTER OBJECTIVES

After studying this chapter, you should be able to:

1 <u>Advise</u> someone about the major points in career planning.

2 <u>Describe</u> how personnel departments encourage and assist career planning.

3 <u>Discuss</u> what employees seek from career planning and development.

4 <u>Identify</u> the major advantages of career planning.

5 <u>Explain</u> the relationship between career planning and career development.

6 <u>List</u> the major actions that aid career development.

s a consultant to several companies, one of the authors of this book is frequently asked the following questions:

- "How do I get ahead in this company?"

- "Are promotions around here based on seniority or on performance?"

- "Why hasn't my boss given me career counseling?"

- "Don't you think that most promotions are based on luck and knowing the right people?"

- "Do I need a degree for that job?"

- "Do company training programs help my chances for a promotion?"

Nearly everyone asks these important questions at some point during their working life. The answers to these questions help guide the personnel department, the supervisor, and the employee to the appropriate training and development activities discussed in Chapter 9. But to understand what it takes to "get ahead" requires a basic understanding of career planning and development. Armed with that understanding, training and development activities become more relevant because the employee sees how those actions benefit his or her career.

What is a career?   A *career* is all the jobs that are held during one's working life. For some people, these jobs are part of a careful plan. For others, their career is simply a matter of luck. Merely planning a career does not guarantee career success. Superior performance, experience, education, and some occasional luck play an important role. When people rely largely on luck, however, they seldom are prepared for career opportunities that arise. Successful people identify their career goals, plan, and then take action. Restated, successful careers are managed through careful career planning. People who fail to plan their careers may do so because they think that their company or their boss will assume that responsibility. Or perhaps they are unaware of the basic career planning concepts described in Figure 10-1. Without an understanding of career goals and career paths, planning is unlikely. The absence of career planning means that career development is likely to be haphazard at best. Some people argue, Who can look ten, twenty, or thirty years into the future and predict where my career

Figure 10-1
Selected Career Planning Terms

- *Career.* A career is all the jobs that are held during one's working life.
- *Career path.* A career path is the sequential pattern of jobs that forms one's career.
- *Career goals.* Career goals are the future positions one strives to reach as part of a career. These goals serve as benchmarks along one's career path.
- *Career planning.* Career planning is the process by which one selects career goals and the path to those goals.
- *Career development.* Career development is those personal improvements one undertakes to achieve a personal career plan.

will lead? I never thought it would lead to where I am now!" True, an accurate prediction that far into the future is almost impossible. However, by asking: What are my career goals? and What is my first step? a career plan can be started. But it is important for the employee to take responsibility for asking these questions. All that the personnel department can do is facilitate the process.

"The longest journey begins with the first step.

Although each person's career is unique, consider the insights contained in one executive's career path. This executive's name and the name of his employers have been changed to protect his privacy, so we will call him "Joe." Joe was in banking for forty-one years. His career progress is summarized in Figure 10-2 and explained below:

> After graduation from college and three years in the Marine Corps, Joe joined the First National Bank as a teller trainee. At that point in his career, his *goal* was to become a banking executive. He had no idea of the *career path* he would follow. But Joe realized that his first step was to become a supervisor. This *career planning* caused him to enroll in the bank's supervisory management training program. After being promoted to teller, he enrolled in other training programs and also took some noncredit courses from the American Banking Institute. These programs were the first of many *career development* actions that Joe undertook. He received two more promotions and at age 30 was made head teller.
>
> After four years, Joe felt his career plan was stalled, and so he accepted

Figure 10-2
The Career Path for a Retired Executive Vice President
in the Banking Industry

JOB NUMBER	JOB LEVEL	JOB TITLE	TYPE OF JOB CHANGE	YEARS IN JOB	ENDING AGE
1	Worker	Teller Trainee	———	½	24
2	Worker	Teller	Promotion	3½	28
3	Worker	Asst. Head Teller	Promotion	2	30
4	Supervisory	Head Teller	Promotion	4	34
5	Supervisory	New Account Supervisor	Transfer	3	37
6	Management	Asst. Branch Manager for Loans	Promotion	3	40
7			Educational leave (finish M.B.A.)	1	41
8	Management	Asst. Branch Manager	Transfer	1	42
9	Management	Branch Manager	Promotion	3	45
10	Management	Branch Manager	Transfer	4	49
11	Management	Loan Officer	Transfer	5	54
12	Management	Chief Loan Officer	Promotion	3	57
13	Executive	Vice President Operations Center	Resignation/Promotion (joins another bank)	3	60
14	Executive	Senior Vice President for Operations	Promotion	1	61
15	Executive	Executive Vice-President	Promotion	4	65
16			Retired		

a transfer into the bank's new account department. Although the transfer was not a promotion and did not even include a raise, Joe knew that some diversification in his background would increase his chances of becoming an assistant branch manager.

After three years as an assistant branch manager, Joe again felt that his career progress was too slow, and so he took an educational leave and finished his master of business administration degree (M.B.A.). With the M.B.A., he returned to the bank as an assistant manager in a new branch. A year later he was promoted to a branch manager's job. To gain a wider breadth of skills, Joe transferred to another branch as manager and then to the home office as a loan officer. After five years he became chief loan officer, and then three years later he achieved his goal by accepting a job as vice president in a competing bank. His success as an executive led to two more promotions before he retired as an executive vice president at age 65.

As a review of Figure 10-2 indicates, Joe's career plan involved well-timed transfers and an educational leave. Figure 10-3 superimposes Joe's career changes on the organization charts of the two banks for which he worked. As the organization charts show, career progress is seldom straight up in an organization. Lateral transfers, leaves, and even resignations are used. When Joe started as a teller trainee at age 24, there was no way he could have predicted the career path he would follow. But through periodic career planning, he reassessed his career progress and then undertook development activities to achieve intermediate career goals, such as becoming a supervisor. As a result of career planning and development, Joe's career consisted of a path that led him to his goal of becoming an executive in the banking industry.

Careers move sideways too.

CAREER PLANNING AND EMPLOYEE NEEDS

During the forty years of Joe's career, personnel departments in banks and in other large organizations gave little support to career planning. When promotable talent was scarce, personnel departments usually reacted with crash training programs or additional recruitment. Human resource planning and career planning seldom occurred. Instead of seeking proactive solutions, organizations and employees reacted to new developments.[3] Historically, this limited role for personnel departments was understandable because career plans were seen as largely an individual matter.[4] Even when personnel managers wanted their departments to provide assistance in career planning, they often lacked the resources to become involved. As a result, only a few (mostly large) organizations encouraged career planning by employees.

Career planning helps internal staffing needs.

Today, an increasing number of personnel departments see career planning as a viable way to meet their internal staffing needs.[5] Although this service may be limited to managerial, professional, and technical employees because of available funds, ideally all workers should be able to receive career planning. When employers encourage career planning, employees are more likely to set career goals and work toward them. In turn, these goals may motivate employees to pursue further education, training, or other career development

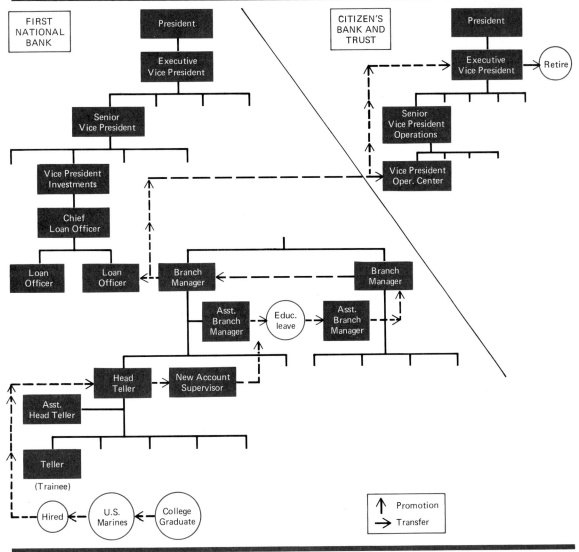

Figure 10-3

A Career Path Diagram for an Executive Vice President
in the Banking Industry

activities. These learning activities then improve the value of employees to the organization and give the personnel department a larger pool of qualified applicants from which to fill internal job openings.

But what do employees want? A study of one group of employees revealed five factors of concern.[6] These include:

• *Career equity.* Employees want to perceive equity in the organization's performance and promotion system with respect to career advancement opportunities.

262

- *Supervisory concern.* Employees want their supervisors to play an active role in career development and to provide timely performance feedback.

- *Awareness of opportunities.* Employees want knowledge of the career advancement opportunities that exist in their organization.

- *Employee interest.* Employees need different amounts of information and have different degrees of interest in career advancement depending on a variety of factors.

- *Career satisfaction.* Employees, depending on their age and occupation, have different levels of career satisfaction.

Factors that affect career planning

Effective career planning and development programs must consider these different perceptions and desires of employees. What workers expect from the career programs developed by the personnel department will vary according to age, sex, occupation, education, and other variables. In short, whatever approach the personnel department takes toward career planning and development, it must be flexible and proactive. As a personnel manager with the Hanes Group in Winston-Salem, North Carolina, concluded:

> Flexibility in career development programs is paramount if the goals of improved productivity, increased personal satisfaction, growth and ultimately increased organizational effectiveness are to be achieved. In many cases, this will require the modification of basic existing programs to address the specific needs of a particular group of employees.[7]

PERSONNEL DEPARTMENTS AND CAREER PLANNING

Personnel departments should, and increasingly do, take an active interest in employee career planning. For example, in one survey of 210 employers with career planning programs, the personnel department is responsible for this activity in over 60 percent of the cases.[8] Personnel departments often handle career planning because their human resource plans indicate the organization's future employment needs and related career opportunities. In addition, personnel experts are more likely to be aware of training and other developmental opportunities. Of course, individual managers also should encourage career planning. However, if personnel specialists leave career planning to managers, it may not get done. Not all managers take a strong interest in their employees' careers.

The involvement of personnel managers in career planning has grown during recent years because of its benefits. Here is a partial list of those benefits:

Benefits of career planning

- *Develops promotable employees.* Career planning helps to develop internal supplies of promotable talent.

- *Lowers turnover.* The increased attention and concern for individual careers generate more organizational loyalty and, therefore, lower employee turnover.

- *Taps employee potential.* Career planning encourages employees to tap more of their potential abilities because they have specific career goals.

- *Furthers growth.* Career plans and goals motivate employees to grow and develop.

- *Reduces hoarding.* Without career planning, it is easier for managers to hoard key subordinates. Career planning causes employees, managers, and the personnel department to become aware of employee qualifications.

- *Satisfies employee needs.* With less hoarding and improved growth opportunities for employees, an individual's esteem needs, such as recognition and accomplishment, are more readily satisfied.

- *Assists affirmative action plans.* Career planning can help members of protected groups prepare for more important jobs. This preparation can contribute to meeting affirmative action timetables.

To realize these benefits, more personnel departments are following the lead of a few pioneers and supporting career planning. In practice, personnel departments encourage career planning through career education, information, and counseling.

Career Education
Surprisingly, many employees know very little about career planning. Often they are unaware of the need for and advantages of career planning. And once made aware, they often lack the necessary information to plan their careers successfully. Personnel departments are suited to solve both of these shortcomings, and they can increase employee awareness through a variety of educational techniques. For example, speeches, memoranda, and position papers from top executives stimulate employee interest at low cost to the employer. If executives communicate their belief in career planning, other managers are likely to do the same.

Workshops and seminars on career planning increase employee interest by pointing out the key concepts associated with career planning.[9] Workshops help the employee set career goals, identify career paths, and uncover specific career development activities. These educational activities may be supplemented by printed or taped information.

The John Deere Harvester Works has been in East Moline, Illinois, since the company moved into the "new" technology of combine harvesting around the turn of this century. Although many of its employees have thirty or more years of service, the company has hired newcomers to fill the increasing number of jobs. These new employees have not developed the loyalty of their long-service coworkers and are more prone to ask, "What is the company doing for my career?"

At this operation, members of the personnel department have taken the view that career planning and development are the responsibility of the

John Deere's approach

employee. With that philosophy in mind, a four-hour career planning workshop was developed. Attendance is voluntary. Employees go to the workshop on their own time and do not receive any pay for attending. This "on-your-own-time" approach is intended to reinforce the point that career development rests with the individual. Instructors from the personnel department are not paid either; the fact that they volunteer to do the sessions helps to convey the idea that members of the department are interested in the participants as people, not only as employees.

Figure 10-4 lists the goals of these career information seminars. As the seminars begin, participants are assigned to teams. Introductions and a discussion about the confidentiality of the sessions follow. Then the groups discuss career planning and list enjoyable and not-so-enjoyable activities as a step to creating a personal inventory and identifying alternatives. Discussions also center around an internal staffing decision where the teams are asked to fill a hypothetical opening immediately. As two members of the personnel department observed: "The arguments which are created in this exercise are highly beneficial for promoting acceptance of the management perspective on internal selection and promotion, a perspective which many have not previously considered. Many participants realize for the first time that being passed over only means someone else was slightly better qualified—not that they're in disfavor with the company."[10]

When the personnel department lacks the necessary staff to design and conduct educational programs, public programs conducted by local colleges or consultants may help.

One consulting firm's approach   One worldwide consulting firm—Towers, Perrin, Forster & Crosby—provides its clients with a four-step package. The packaged program develops (1) a strategy for the organization to solve its unique needs, (2)

Figure 10-4
Goals of the Career Information Seminar at the John Deere Harvester Works

JOHN DEERE HARVESTER WORKS

Career Information Seminar

Goals

1. To help employees better understand how their jobs and careers at John Deere can contribute to their goals.

2. To provide employees with an approach to individualized career planning.

3. To define the roles of employees, their supervisors, and the personnel department in career planning and personal development.

4. To provide realistic job and career information upon which to build career plans.

Source: Reprinted, with permission, from Karl A. Hickerson and Richard C. Anderson, "Career Development: Whose Responsibility?" *Personnel Administrator,* June 1982, p. 45. Copyright © 1982, the American Society for Personnel Administration, 30 Park Drive, Berea, Ohio 44017.

support systems based upon the present personnel management information system to give employees the data they need to plan their careers, (3) workbooks that allow employees to perform career planning, and (4) a career resource center that offers employees assistance with their career planning.

Information on Career Planning

Regardless of the educational strategy the personnel department selects, it should provide employees with other information they need to plan their careers. For example, one research study showed that after being exposed to a career planning program, employees had a significantly increased knowledge of how to initiate a career change.[11] Much of this information is already a part of the personnel department's information system. For example, job descriptions and specifications can be quite valuable to someone who is trying to estimate reasonable career goals. Likewise, personnel departments can identify future job openings through the human resource plan. Personnel specialists can also share their knowledge of potential career paths. For example, they are often keenly aware of the similarities between seemingly unrelated jobs.

> Consider the possible career paths faced by a clerk-typist who works in a newspaper. In this type of work, the jobs of typist, Linotype operator, and Teletype operator have a similar characteristic: finger dexterity. But a clerk-typist in the advertising department may not realize that similar skills applied to a Linotype machine may earn three times as much as the other jobs.

When different jobs require similar skills, they form job families. Career paths within a job family demand little additional training since the skills of each job are closely related.[12] If personnel departments make information about job families available, employees can find feasible career paths. They then can assess the career paths by talking to those who already hold these jobs. One problem with job families is that employees may want to skip over less pleasant jobs. To prevent employees from rejecting some jobs in a job family the personnel department may establish a sequential progression of jobs. A *job progression ladder* is a partial career path where some jobs have prerequisites, as shown in Figure 10-5. The job progression ladder shown in the figure requires a clerk-typist to become a Teletype operator before moving to the better-paying job of Linotype operator. This requirement assures the personnel department of an ample internal supply of Teletype operators because this job is a prerequisite to the well-paid position of Linotype operator.

Job progression ladder

The personnel department also can encourage career planning by providing information about alternative career paths. Figure 10-6 shows that clerk-typists face multiple career paths. If a particular clerk-typist does not want to become a Teletype operator, personnel specialists can provide information about alternatives. In the newspaper example a clerk-typist might prefer a career in editorial, secretarial, or advertising occupations because these careers offer more long-term potential.

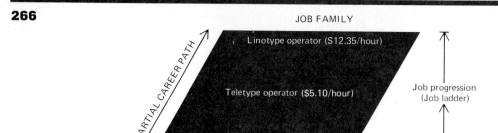

Figure 10-5

Three Jobs with Similar Requirements
Grouped into a Job Family

Figure 10-6

Alternative Career Paths Available to
a Clerk-Typist in a Newspaper Company

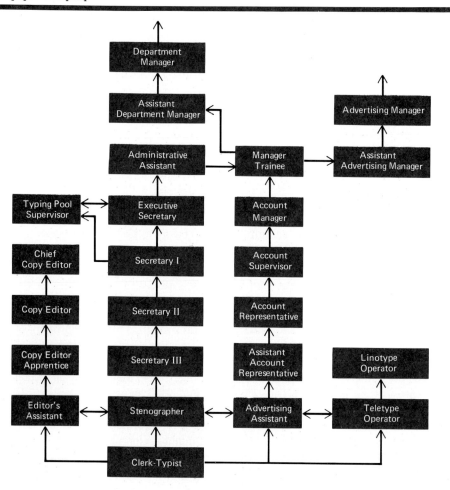

At the John Deere Harvester Works, the personnel department provides an extensive brochure that describes every department and all factory jobs below the level of management. However, the brochure is only available through the career information seminar.[13]

Career Counseling

To help employees establish career goals and find appropriate career paths, some personnel departments offer career counseling. The career counselor may simply be someone who listens to the employee's interests and provides the specific job-related information.[14] Or the counselor may help employees uncover their interests by administering and interpreting aptitude and skills tests.[15] Two tests in particular—the *Kuder Preference Record* and the *Strong Vocational Interest Blank*—are useful for guiding people into occupations that are likely to be of interest. Other tests also are available to measure individual abilities and interests in specific types of work. But to be truly successful, career counselors must get employees to assess themselves and their environment.

Job interests can be tested.

Employee self-assessment   Career counselors realize that a career is only a part of one's life. It may be a large part or even a central part. But it is only a part of one's life plan. A *life plan* is that often ill-defined series of hopes, dreams, and personal goals that each person carries through life. For example, broad objectives to be happy, healthy, and successful combine with specific goals to be a good spouse, parent, student, citizen, neighbor, and manager. Together these roles form one's life plan. Ideally, a career plan is an integral part of one's life plan. Otherwise, career goals become ends (sometimes dead ends!) rather than means toward fulfilling a life plan. An example can be drawn from an overworked motion picture plot:

Life plans

> The husband struggles for decades to achieve a degree of career success. When that success is within reach, he realizes his personal life—friendships, marriage, and paternal relationships—is in shambles. It is in shambles because career plans were pursued to the exclusion of an integrated life plan.

Trite plots result when no life plan exists.

Besides a life plan, self-assessment includes a self-inventory. Components of a self-inventory are listed in Figure 10-7. If a career counselor can get employees to complete a detailed and honest self-evaluation, it helps to focus their thinking about themselves. Then employees can match their interests and abilities on the self-inventory with the career information available to them from the personnel department. Likewise, they can match their aptitudes and career paths with their personal life plan.

Environmental assessment   A career plan that matches employee interests with likely career paths actually may do a disservice to the employee if environmental factors are overlooked. A return to the choices faced by clerk-typists at the newspaper provides an example.

WORK INTERESTS AND APTITUDES	LOW 1	2	3	4	HIGH 5
Physical work (fixing, building, using hands)	—	—	—	—	—
Written work (writing, reading, using words)	—	—	—	—	—
Oral work (talking, giving speeches, using words)	—	—	—	—	—
Quantitative work (calculating, doing accounting, using numbers)	—	—	—	—	—
Visual work (watching, inspecting, using eyes)	—	—	—	—	—
Interpersonal work (counseling, interviewing)	—	—	—	—	—
Creative work (inventing, designing, ideas)	—	—	—	—	—
Analytical work (doing research, solving problems)	—	—	—	—	—
Managerial work (initiating, directing, coordinating)	—	—	—	—	—
Clerical (keeping records)	—	—	—	—	—
Outdoor work (farming, traveling, doing athletics)	—	—	—	—	—
Mechanical (repairing, fixing, tinkering)	—	—	—	—	—

WORK SKILLS AND ABILITIES

List below specialized skills, unique personal assets, enjoyable experiences, and major accomplishments. Then evaluate.

	PHYSICAL	WRITTEN	ORAL	QUANTITATIVE	VISUAL	INTERPERSONAL	CREATIVE	ANALYTICAL	MANAGERIAL	CLERICAL	OUTDOOR	MECHANICAL
_____	—	—	—	—	—	—	—	—	—	—	—	—
_____	—	—	—	—	—	—	—	—	—	—	—	—
_____	—	—	—	—	—	—	—	—	—	—	—	—
_____	—	—	—	—	—	—	—	—	—	—	—	—
_____	—	—	—	—	—	—	—	—	—	—	—	—
_____	—	—	—	—	—	—	—	—	—	—	—	—
_____	—	—	—	—	—	—	—	—	—	—	—	—
_____	—	—	—	—	—	—	—	—	—	—	—	—
_____	—	—	—	—	—	—	—	—	—	—	—	—

Figure 10-7
A Self-Inventory for Career Planning

The job family of clerk-typist, Teletype operator, and Linotype operator may appear to be a reasonable career path since clerk-typists possess the basic typing skills needed for all three jobs. But technological changes in the newspaper industry may reduce the need for Linotype operators in the future. Photographic and computer developments are quickly replacing the use of Linotype machines in newspaper printing. If career counselors in the personnel department do not point out this development, clerk-typists may find their careers stalled in the job of Teletype operator.

Regardless of the match between one's skills and the organization's career paths, counselors need to inform employees of likely changes that will affect their occupational choices. Occupational information is readily available from the U.S. Department of Labor's Bureau of Labor Statistics.[16]

Career counseling process One of the problems often encountered by career counselors is employee reaction to the counseling process. Counseling about careers is a very sensitive, potentially explosive issue. Employees may see only parts of some jobs that pay much better and think that they are qualified. When the counselor tries to explain the need for additional skills that are not apparent, employees may feel that they are not being treated fairly. "If old Mary can do that job, certainly I can do it," is a typical reaction. Even if that reaction is true, others who are even more qualified may be better choices. Or when the counselor points out necessary steps to become qualified for a job, the employee may resist additional training or schooling. Finally, the mere presence of career counselors may be a trap. Employees might think that some-one else is taking responsibility for their career planning and development. Returning to the observations of two personnel specialists at John Deere Harvester Works:

269

"If he can, I can, too!"

> "We find, for example, there is a great unspoken lesson about the nature of competition for 'career' advancement at the moment people gather on their own time at the workplace on a Saturday morning. All they have to do is look around."[17]
>
> "Looking around" emphasizes that there are other people who are interested in advancing, too. Although a counselor can point this out, seeing thirty or forty people at the plant on a Saturday morning probably makes a deeper impression. The group training sessions also can illustrate some issues that counseling may not be able to do as well. When the personnel specialists state during the seminar that people who are flexible, energetic, and willing to improve their skills have an advantage, there is less defensive behavior than when those comments are made in a private counseling session.[18]

Counseling versus training

CAREER DEVELOPMENT

The implementation of career plans requires career development. Career development comprises those personal improve-ments one undertakes to achieve a career plan. These actions may be sponsored by the personnel department, or they may be activities that employees undertake independent of the department. This section reviews the tactics employees may use to achieve their career plans and then discusses the department's role in career development.

Individual Career Development

Career development begins with the individual. Each person must accept his or her responsibility for career development, or career progress is likely to suffer. Once this personal commitment is made, several career development actions may prove useful. These actions involve:

- Job performance
- Exposure
- Resignations
- Organizational loyalty
- Mentors and sponsors
- Key subordinates
- Growth opportunities

Job performance   The most important action an individual can undertake to further his or her career is good job performance. The assumption of good performance underlies all career development activities. When performance is substandard, regardless of other career development efforts, even modest career goals are usually unattainable. Individuals who perform poorly are disregarded quickly by the personnel department and by management decision makers. *Career progress rests largely upon performance.*

Exposure   Career progress also is furthered by exposure.[19] *Exposure* means becoming known (and, it is hoped, held in high regard) by those who decide on promotions, transfers, and other career opportunities. Without exposure, good performers may not get a chance at the opportunities needed to achieve their career goals. Managers gain exposure primarily through their performance, written reports, oral presentations, committee work, community service, and even the hours they work. Simply put, exposure makes an individual stand out from the crowd—a necessary ingredient to career success, especially in large organizations.[20] For example, consider how one management trainee gained some vital exposure early in her career:

> Paula Dorsey noticed that two executives worked on Saturday mornings. As one of twelve new management trainees, she decided that coming to work on Saturday mornings would give her additional exposure to these key decision makers. Soon these two executives began greeting her by name whenever they passed in the halls. While still in the training program, she was assigned to the product introduction committee, which planned strategy for new products. At the end of the training program, Paula was made an assistant product manager for a new line of video recorders. The other eleven trainees received less important jobs.

In small organizations, exposure to decision makers is more frequent and less dependent upon reports, presentations, and the like. In some situations, especially in other nations, social status, school ties, and seniority can be more important than exposure.

Resignations   When an individual sees greater career opportunities elsewhere, a resignation may be the only way to meet his or her career goals. Some employees—managers and professionals in particular—change employers as part of a conscious career strategy. If done effectively, these resignations usually result in a promotion, a pay increase, and a new learning experience. Resigning in order to further one's career with another employer has been called *leveraging.*[21] Astute managers and professionals use this technique sparingly because too many moves can lead to the label of "job hopper." Those who leave seldom benefit their previous organization because they almost never return with their new experiences.

In a study of 268 mobile executives conducted by one of the authors of this book, only three percent (7 of the executives) ever returned to an organization that they had left during their careers.[22] This finding means that organizations seldom benefit from the return of managers who quit and go elsewhere. Thus personnel departments must work to develop the loyalty of their employees to reduce turnover and retain valuable human resources.

Organizational loyalty   In many organizations, people put career loyalty above organizational loyalty. Low levels of organizational loyalty are common among recent college graduates (whose high expectations often lead to disappointment with their first few employers) and professionals (whose first loyalty is often to their profession).[23] Career-long dedication to the same organization complements the personnel department's objective of reducing employee turnover. However, if the following findings are applicable to other organizations, there may be few benefits for such dedication.

In a study conducted by one of the authors of this book, it was found that a bare majority (51 percent) of the chief executives in the 100 largest industrial companies spent their entire careers with the same organization. The minority (49 percent) of presidents who changed employers at least once became chief executive officers at a younger age than those who spent their entire careers with the same organization.[24]

Mentors and sponsors   Many employees quickly learn that a mentor can aid their career development. A mentor is someone who offers informal career advice. Neither the mentor nor the employee always recognizes that such a relationship exists. Instead, a junior worker simply knows someone who gives good advice.

Mentors may help.

If the mentor can nominate the employee for career development activities —such as training programs, transfers, or promotions—then the mentor becomes a sponsor. A *sponsor* is someone in the organization who can create career development opportunities for others. Often an employee's sponsor is the immediate supervisor, although others may serve as nominators.[25]

Sponsors

Many Japanese firms rely on senior managers to use their storehouse of insights and wisdom to help junior managers with career development. In a relationship based on school ties or on some other non-work-related factor, the senior manager serves as a career counselor, mentor, and sponsor for the junior employee, who often works in a different department. In return, the senior manager's actions are reinforced by the respect he receives from other managers.

Key subordinates Successful managers rely on subordinates who aid the managers' development and performance. The subordinates may possess highly specialized knowledge or skills that the manager may learn from them. Or the employee may perform a crucial role in helping a manager achieve good performance. In either case, employees of this type are *key subordinates*. They exhibit loyalty and dedication to their bosses. They gather and interpret information, offer skills that supplement those of their managers, and work unselfishly to further their managers' careers. They benefit by also moving up the career ladder when the manager is promoted and by receiving important delegations that serve to develop their careers. These people complement personnel department objectives through their teamwork, motivation, and dedication. But when a manager resigns and takes a string of key subordinates along, the results can be devastating.[26]

Key subordinates

> A small Gulf Coast research firm had a ten-month lead in developing a new type of memory component for computers. A major electronics company hired away the project manager, the chief engineer, and their key subordinates. With this loss, the small firm was forced to recruit replacements at a higher salary and at a cost of several months' delay.

As a career strategy, perceptive subordinates are careful not to become attached to an immobile manager. One researcher calls such immobiles "shelf-sitters."[27] Not only do shelf-sitters block promotion channels, but their key subordinates can become unfairly labeled as shelf-sitters, too. Although working for a shelf-sitter may develop an employee's skill, such a label can arrest one's career progress.

Shelf-sitters

Growth opportunities When employees expand their abilities, they complement the organization's objectives. For example, enrolling in a training program, taking noncredit courses, pursuing an additional degree, or seeking a new work assignment can contribute to employee growth. These growth opportunities aid both the personnel department's objective of developing internal replacements and the individual's personal career plan.

> Rachael Holmes was the chief recruiter in the employment department of Brem Paper Products. Her department manager was 60 years old and had indicated that he planned to retire at age 65. At 37, with three years experience as a recruiter, Rachael felt she was in a dead-end job. She obtained a transfer to the wage and salary department. Two years later the company planned a new facility and made Rachael the personnel manager for it. She was selected because of her broad experience in recruiting and compensation—two major concerns in starting the new operation.

Rachael initiated the transfer through self-nomination because she wanted to further her career development. But the real opportunity she obtained from the transfer was a chance to grow—a chance to develop new skills and knowledge.

Besides self-nomination to find growth opportunities, other groups outside the organization may help. For years, men have used private clubs and professional associations to form "old-boy networks," which afforded growth opportunities and often a fair amount of exposure among organizational decision makers. Many of these organizations now admit women, but some do so grudgingly. However, a short piece in *The Wall Street Journal* noted:

"Old-boy" networks

> Women's groups spring up in a variety of occupations to aid members. These groups tend to push career advancement rather than general women's issues. Women in Information Processing, Washington, D.C., helps its 4,000 members achieve industry visibility in part by lining up speaking engagements.
>
> The National Association of Professional Saleswomen, Sacramento, stresses education for members. Its chapters in 35 cities hold monthly meetings to discuss sales training. Formed in 1980 with 900 members, it now has 5,000 saleswomen. The National Association of Black Women Entrepreneurs, Detroit . . . helps its 3,000 members get information about business opportunities for minorities.[28]

Women's networks, too

Personnel-Supported Career Development

Career development should not rely solely on individual efforts because such efforts are not always in the organization's best interest. For example, employees may move on to another employer, as in the Gulf Coast research example. Or employees may simply be unaware of opportunities within the company to further their careers or of the organization's staffing needs.

> The John Deere career information seminar offers a good example. It helps employees with education and information. The brochure handed out to attendees describes the range of jobs that are available at the job site. Personnel representatives also are available. But since the meetings are voluntary and on the employee's own time, the personnel department is able to emphasize that career development is the employee's responsibility.
>
> There can be little doubt that employees want such company-based programs if the results from the Harvester Works are representative. In the first two weeks after the program was announced, 50 percent of the eligible salaried employees enrolled in the program. For employees who attended the seminar, there was a 50 percent improvement in their understanding of career planning, compared with a control group that did not participate. And comments from participants have been favorable.[29]

A last look at John Deere Harvester

Personnel departments do more to help employee careers than just conduct career information seminars during off-hours. For example, the training and development programs discussed in Chapter 9 are a big stepping-stone in most people's careers.[30]

Personnel departments seek many goals through their career planning activities in addition to helping employees. A key goal is to develop an internal pool of talent. Career planning can help trainers identify training needs among employees. It also can be used to help guide members of protected classes into jobs where the employer has an underutilization of women and minorities. Improvements in performance, loyalty to the company, and motivation also may be outcomes of career planning. Simply put, career planning can make good business sense; it can enhance profits, productivity, and employees' quality of work life, as the following example underscores:

$1.95 million saved

One bank's career counseling program saved $1.95 million in a year. This estimate, based on tabulations by an industrial engineer, reflected a 65 percent reduced turnover, 25 percent increase in productivity and 75 percent increased promotability.[31]

However, for the benefits of career planning and development to accrue to the organization and its people, the personnel department must enlist the support of management, particularly top management.

Management support   Efforts by the personnel department to encourage career development have little impact unless supported by managers. Commitment by top management is crucial. Without it, middle-level managers may show much less support of their subordinates' career planning concerns. This commitment must go beyond mere permission; top management must lead through example by taking an active interest in the career plans of middle-level managers. When executives show active concern for career planning, other managers will emulate that behavior very quickly. Without broad-based support among all levels of operating management, others in the organization are likely to ignore career development and devote their attention elsewhere. Many North American and European managers do not have a tradition of giving meaningful peer recognition to those who voluntarily support employee development, but such recognition is common among managers in Japan.

Support for the career development of employees varies widely from company to company. Some organizations take the view that career planning is the employee's responsibility and that company involvement would be an intrusion of the employee's privacy. Others fear that career development may raise employee expectations about rapid promotions and lead to disappointment if those promotions do not materialize. However, among the leading companies in the United States, the development of successful employees is considered a hallmark of the organization. These successes could not exist without long-term support from generation after generation of top management. Some examples:

McGraw-Hill's philosophy

At McGraw-Hill, the publisher of this book, "The corporate point of view . . . is that management's involvement in career planning helps to ensure that the individual career plans of the employees mesh with the . . . goals of the corporation. In essence, the organization tries to ensure that 'the grass is greener at home than across the street.' "[32]

"In a 10-year period, General Electric produced a highly admirable earnings growth record while 61 of its 360 vice presidents became presidents of other companies. This means GE is producing talent for other companies.

GE's high-level turnover: is it good or bad?

"Donald Burnham was not the first chief engineer at GM to become the head of another company. He left . . . to lead Westinghouse.

"And finally . . . IBM. They give their employees such good training and experience that after five years these individuals can go to almost any company and name their price."[33]

Feedback Without feedback about their career development efforts, it is difficult for employees to sustain the years of preparation sometimes needed to reach career goals. Personnel departments can provide this feedback in several ways. One way is to give employees feedback about job placement decisions. An employee who pursues career development activities and is passed over for promotion may conclude that career development is not worth the effort. Unsuccessful candidates for internal job openings should be told why they did not get the career opportunity they sought. This feedback has three objectives:

1. *To assure* bypassed employees that they are still valued and will be considered for future promotions if they are qualified. Otherwise, valuable employees may resign because they think the organization does not appreciate their efforts.

Help those turned down.

2. *To explain* why they were not selected.

3. *To indicate* what specific career development actions they should undertake. Care should be exercised not to imply that certain career development actions automatically will mean a promotion. Instead, the individual's *candidacy* for selection will be influenced by appropriate career development actions.

Another type of feedback concerns job performance. Job performance feedback is, perhaps, the most important feedback an employee gets. As stated earlier in the chapter and worth emphasizing, career success rests largely upon job performance. In the long run, there can be no substitute for doing the job well. None. Although objective measures of performance are sometimes absent and some promotions are based on "whom you know," most managers are rational. They want to promote people who can do the job. If their subordinates are successful, they look good, too. To give employees feedback about their job performance, many personnel departments develop formal performance evaluation procedures. The resulting feedback allows the employee to adjust his or her performance and career plans. Chapter 11, "Performance Appraisal," addresses the many ways personnel departments have devised to give employees feedback about their performance.

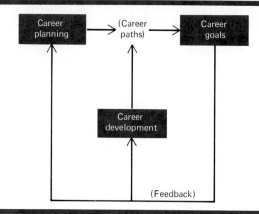

Figure 10-8
A Career Planning and Development Framework

SUMMARY

Career planning and development are relatively new concepts to personnel specialists. In recent years, personnel departments have begun to recognize the need for more proactive efforts in this area. As a result, some (mostly large) departments provide career education, information, and counseling. But the primary responsibility for career planning and development rests with the individual employee.

Figure 10-8 illustrates an overview of career planning and development. The planning process enables employees to identify career goals and the paths to those goals. Then through developmental activities the workers seek ways to improve themselves and to further their career goals. Even today, most developmental activities are individual and voluntary. Individual efforts include good job performance, favorable exposure, leveraging, and the building of alliances. Personnel departments become involved by providing information and obtaining management support. The personnel department helps make career planning and developing a success for both the employees and the organization.

Career planning does not guarantee success. But without it, employees are seldom ready for career opportunities that arise. As a result, their career progress may be slowed, and the personnel department may be unable to fill openings internally.

TERMS FOR REVIEW

Career	Career development
Career path	Job families
Career planning	Job progression ladder

Career counseling	Mentor
Life plan	Sponsor
Exposure	Key subordinates

REVIEW AND DISCUSSION QUESTIONS

1. Why should a personnel department be concerned about career planning, especially since employee plans may conflict with the organization's objectives? What advantages does a personnel department expect to receive from assisting career planning?

2. In what ways can a personnel department assist career planning?

3. If you were interested in making a career out of your ability to play a musical instrument, what types of career goals would you set for yourself? How would you find out about the career prospects for musicians before you took your first job?

4. Suppose you are in a management training position after completing college. Your career goal is not very clear, but you would like to become a top manager in your firm. What types of information would you seek from the personnel department to help you develop your career plan?

5. After you develop your first career plan while employed by a bank, what career development activities would you pursue? Why?

6. Suppose you are assigned to develop a career planning and development program for the employees of a large city. How would you go about developing employee interest in career planning? How would you enlist the support of managers throughout the organization?

7. Why is employee feedback an important element of any organization's attempt to encourage career development?

8. Suppose a hard-working and loyal employee is passed over for promotion. What would you tell this person?

INCIDENT 10-1

Career Planning and Development at Immobile, Inc.

Long-term employees at New York Electric nicknamed the company "Immobile, Inc." It seemed that the only time anyone received a promotion was when a manager retired or died. Even when job vacancies did occur, the personnel department frequently hired a replacement from some other electric utility, and so few employees received a promotion. Employee turnover was low partially because the jobs paid very well, provided high job security, and offered outstanding fringe benefits.

Top management became concerned about the negative attitude reflected by the nickname "Immobile, Inc." and hired a large New York City consulting firm to develop a career planning program. After several months, the consultants revealed a detailed plan, complete with a special office of career counseling in the personnel department. Initially, employees responded favorably and made extensive use of the counseling and career information services available to them. But by the fourth month, the chief career counselor asked the personnel manager for a transfer into any other part of the personnel department. When asked why, the counselor said that employees were not using the service and the job of counselor had become lonely and boring. The personnel manager gave the counselor an assignment to discover why the program had failed and what might be done to revitalize it.

1. What explanations can you offer to explain the initial enthusiasm for career planning assistance followed by an almost total avoidance by employees?

2. Assuming part of the problem was a lack of support by middle and first-level management, what recommendations would you make? Could this company learn a lesson from the approach used by the Japanese?

INCIDENT 10-2

The Shrinking Railroad

The North Railroad had undergone some unfavorable years. Year after year, losses piled up. Finally, management decided that it must close down many of its unprofitable operations in small towns. To ease the burden on long-term employees, a decision was made that no one with ten years of experience, or more, was to be laid off.

The personnel department developed a plan and notified each long-service employee in towns where rail service was to be discontinued. Since many of the jobs were those of station master and assistant station master, enough comparable openings in other cities did not exist. While the personnel department sought a permanent solution, these long-service employees were transferred into any other openings that were available.

Many of the transferees complained that they were being demoted. The union thought it unfair that these workers were paid their old salary when other workers on the same jobs received considerably less.

1. Under these circumstances, would career planning be a useful tool for the personnel department to reduce the ill feelings of these long-service workers?

2. How do you think these employees might react to career planning efforts by the personnel department? How do you think other unaffected employees might react to a new career planning effort?

REFERENCES

1. James W. Walker, "Let's Get Realistic about Career Paths," *Human Resource Management,* Fall 1976, p. 2.

2. Eugene E. Jennings, "How to Develop Your Management Talent Internally," *Personnel Administrator,* July 1981, p. 23.

3. John J. Leach, "The Career Planning Process," *Personnel Journal,* April 1981, pp. 283–287. See also Stephen L. Cohen, "Toward a More Comprehensive Career Planning Program," *Personnel Journal,* September 1979, pp. 611–615; see also Manuel London, "Toward a Theory of Career Motivation," *The Academy of Management Review,* October 1983, pp. 631–639; and Caela Farren and Beverly Kaye, "The Principles of Program Design: A Successful Career Development Model," *Personnel Administrator,* June 1984, pp. 109–118.

4. This individual-organizational dichotomy is useful for distinguishing between the role of the individual and the role of the personnel department. For a more detailed discussion of this distinction, see Elmer H. Burack, "Why All of the Confusion about Career Planning?" *Human Resource Management,* Summer 1977, pp. 21–23. See also Dorothy Heide and Elliot N. Kushell, "I Can Develop My Management Skills By:———," *Personnel Journal,* June 1984, pp. 52–54; and Warren R. Wilhelm, "Helping Workers to Self-Manage Their Careers," *Personnel Administrator,* August 1983, pp. 83–88.

5. Lawrence L. Ferguson, "Better Management of Managers' Careers," *Harvard Business Review,* March–April 1966, pp. 138–152. See also Ellyn Mirides and Andre Cote, "Women in Management: Strategies for Removing the Barriers," *Personnel Administrator,* April 1980, pp. 25–28, 48.

6. William F. Rothenbach, "Career Development: Ask Your Employees for Their Opinions," *Personnel Administrator,* November 1982, pp. 43–46, 51.

7. Ibid., p. 51.

8. James W. Walker and Thomas G. Gutteridge, *Career Planning Practices: An AMA Survey Report,* New York: AMACOM, 1979, p. 21.

9. Donald D. Bowen and Douglas T. Hall, "Career Planning for Employee Development: A Primer for Managers," *California Management Review,* Winter 1977, pp. 29–30. See also Douglas T. Hall, *Careers in Organizations,* Pacific Palisades, Calif.: Goodyear, 1976; and Frank W. Archer, "Charting A Career Course," *Personnel Journal,* April 1984, pp. 60–64.

10. Karl A. Hickerson and Richard C. Anderson, "Career Development: Whose Responsibility?" *Personnel Administrator,* June 1982, p. 46.

11. Jo Ellen E. Eng and Josephine S. Gottsdanker, "Positive Changes from a Career Development Program," *Training and Development Journal,* January 1979, p. 6.

12. Elmer H. Burack and Nicholas Mathys, "Career Ladders, Pathing and Planning: Some Neglected Basics," *Human Resource Management,* Summer 1979, pp. 2–8. See also Philomena D. Warihay, "The Climb to the Top: Is the Network the Route for Women?" *Personnel Administrator,* April 1980, pp. 55–60.

13. Hickerson and Anderson, op. cit.

14. Ted R. Gambill, "Career Counseling: Too Little, Too Late?" *Training and Development Journal,* February 1979, pp. 24–29.

15. Hall, op. cit., pp. 27–28.

16. Elmer H. Burack and Nicholas Mathys, "Work, Workers and Career Potential: Possibilities for a Common Language," *The Personnel Administrator*, May 1977, pp. 46–52.

17. Hickerson and Anderson, op. cit.

18. Ibid.

19. Eugene E. Jennings, *The Mobile Manager*, New York: McGraw-Hill, 1976.

20. Jennings, "How to Develop Your Management Talent Internally," op. cit., pp. 20–23.

21. *The Mobile Manager*, op. cit.

22. William B. Werther, Jr., "Management Turnover Implications of Career Mobility," *The Personnel Administrator*, February 1977, pp. 63–66. See also Ellen F. Jackofsky and Lawrence H. Peters, "The Hypothesized Effects of Ability in the Turnover Process," *Academy of Management Review*, January 1983, pp. 46–49.

23. Simeon J. Touretzky, "Changing Attitudes: A Question of Loyalty," *The Personnel Administrator*, April 1979, pp. 35–38.

24. Werther, op. cit.

25. Verne Walter, "Self-Motivated Personnel Career Planning: A Breakthrough in Human Resource Management (Part I)," *Personnel Journal*, March 1976, pp. 112–115, 136. See also Part II in the April 1976 issue of *Personnel Journal*, pp. 162–167, 185–186.

26. "How to Develop Your Management Talent Internally," op. cit.

27. *The Mobile Manager*, op. cit. See also John F. Veiga, "Plateaued Versus Nonplateaued Managers: Career Patterns, Attitudes, and Path Potential," *Academy of Management Journal*, September 1981, pp. 566–578.

28. Robert S. Greenberger, "Women's Groups Spring Up in a Variety of Occupations to Aid Members," *The Wall Street Journal*, Western ed., Jan. 11, 1983, p. 1.

29. Hickerson and Anderson, op. cit.

30. Beverly Kaye, "Career Development Puts Training in Its Place," *Personnel Journal*, February 1983, pp. 132–137.

31. Milan Moravec, "A Cost-Effective Career Planning Program Requires a Strategy," *Personnel Administrator*, 1982, p. 28.

32. "Is Career Development the Answer?" *Training and Development Journal*, March 1981, pp. 81–82.

33. Jennings, "How to Develop Your Management Talent Internally," op. cit., p. 20.

CHAPTER

11

The performance appraisal concept is central to effective management.

Harry Levison[1]

PERFORMANCE APPRAISAL

CHAPTER OBJECTIVES

After studying this chapter, you should be able to:

1 Identify the issues that influence selection of a performance appraisal system.

2 Explain the uses of performance appraisals.

3 Discuss rater biases in performance appraisals.

4 Describe commonly used appraisal methods.

5 Discuss the role of training and evaluation interviews in the appraisal process.

6 Explain how the results of performance appraisal affect personnel management.

Performance appraisal is the process by which organizations evaluate employee job performance. It is an essential function that supervisors and employees perform informally on an ongoing basis. Most people seek feedback on their performance, and those who manage others must evaluate individual performance in order to know what action to take. When performance is substandard, the manager or supervisor must take corrective action; likewise, when performance is good, that behavior should be reinforced.[2]

Informal versus formal

Informal and ongoing evaluations are necessary, but they are insufficient. Informal evaluations seldom leave any documentation of either good or poor performance. With formal, systematic feedback, the personnel department can identify good and poor performers. It also can identify specific training or career development needs. Feedback helps evaluate recruitment, selection, orientation, and placement procedures. Even decisions about future promotions, compensation, and other personnel actions depend on systematic and documented performance appraisal information.

When looked at from the perspective of a supervisor or manager, a formal performance appraisal often seems to be an unneeded interruption. And why not? The supervisor or manager knows how each employee is performing. Why go through some form developed by personnel when the rater already has his or her subjective opinion? The entire process is often poorly understood and poorly accepted by those outside the personnel department. The importance of a systematic performance appraisal from the organization perspective is, perhaps, best illustrated by an example from a major utility company.

Florida Power and Light's approach

Florida Power and Light Company is based in Miami, Florida, and serves nearly half the state. Since the utility faced pressures from Florida's rapid growth and was vulnerable to interruptions in the supply of fuel oil, management recognized the need for capable people to fill key positions in the company. To identify, select, and develop its key employees, the company sought an effective way to assess employee performance. Psychological testing and assessment center approaches were rejected in favor of a computerized, multiple-rater process where ratings made by different raters are combined to yield more objective results. The computerization of the process enables a large volume of assessments to be handled efficiently and reliably.

The talent assessment program (TAP) works on a two-year rating cycle that has three phases. During phase I, surveys are used to determine the criteria needed to rate professional and managerial employees. Although most of the criteria for managerial and professional positions are about the same, employees pointed out that leadership and delegation are particularly important for management positions. For professional jobs, the ability to learn and knowledge were rated as more important. The criteria used to rate managers and professionals are checked during each cycle to ensure that the process is relevant to the organization's current situation. From these surveys, specific behaviors are identified to be rated in the second phase.

Phase II requires each participant to select between five and nine people from among those who know the person's performance to serve as raters, for example, the participant's boss, subordinates, and peers. The only other requirement for selecting the raters is that they have worked with the employee during the last eighteen months. Then the computer generates a rating form that includes all the relevant job behaviors that are uncovered in phase I. Each rater evaluates all employees who selected him or her as a rater. If three employees, for example, named the same rater, that rater would evaluate each employee in comparison with the other two employees. Again, the rating would be based on each criterion uncovered in phase I. Each comparison on each criterion for each employee is tabulated by the computer to determine every employee's comparative standing.

Phase III includes the analysis, distribution, and discussion of the results. New employees are given a workshop in which their ratings are explained. Others receive a confidential mailing that summarizes their standings.[3]

The results of Florida Power and Light's talent assessment program are used to identify candidates for additional training and development. The information also helps managers develop replacement summaries and succession data to aid human resource planning (first discussed in Chapter 4). In short, TAP gives the individual, management, and the personnel department feedback on present managerial and professional employees. With this information, both the individual and the personnel department can better identify development (Chapter 9) and career planning information (Chapter 10).[4]

Feedback for both employee and the personnel department

Other uses of performance appraisal information are listed in Figure 11-1. Besides performance improvement, many companies use this information to determine compensation, especially when compensation is tied to performance. A good performance appraisal system also may identify problems in staffing or in the human resource information system. Poor performers may evidence incorrect selection, orientation, or training and development efforts. Or equally important, poor ratings may suggest that the job's design or external challenges have not been considered fully. Affirmative action is helped by an accurate appraisal, too, because it can ensure that internal placement decisions and other personnel actions are free from bias. As with virtually every other personnel activity, performance appraisal must be free from discrimination. Whatever form of evaluation the personnel department elects to use, that system should be both valid and reliable, as explained in Chapter 3.

General Motors, for example, was found guilty of discrimination in *Rowe v. General Motors* because a supervisor used an appraisal method that relied almost entirely on subjective evaluations of initiative and attitude. The "court ruled that a company could not rely solely on the recommendations of company foremen in selecting employees for promotion where the standards used by the foremen were vague and subjective."[5]

General Motors and EEO

● *Performance improvement.* Performance feedback allows the employee, manager, and personnel specialists to intervene with appropriate actions to improve performance.

● *Compensation adjustments.* Performance evaluations help decision makers determine who should receive pay raises. Many firms grant part or all of their pay increases and bonuses based upon merit, which is determined mostly through performance appraisals.

● *Placement decisions.* Promotions, transfers, and demotions are usually based on past or anticipated performance. Often promotions are a reward for past *performance.*

● *Training and development needs.* Poor performance may indicate the need for retraining. Likewise, good performance may indicate untapped potential that should be developed.

● *Career planning and development.* Performance feedback guides career decisions about specific career paths one should investigate.

● *Staffing process deficiencies.* Good or bad performance implies strengths or weaknesses in the personnel department's staffing procedures.

● *Informational inaccuracies.* Poor performance may indicate errors in job analysis information, human resource plans, or other parts of the personnel management information system. Reliance on inaccurate information may have led to inappropriate hiring, training, or counseling decisions.

● *Job design errors.* Poor performance may be a symptom of ill-conceived job designs. Appraisals help diagnose these errors.

● *Equal employment opportunity.* Accurate performance appraisals that actually measure job-related performance ensure that internal placement decisions are not discriminatory.

● *External challenges.* Sometimes performance is influenced by factors outside the work environment, such as family, financial, health, or other personal matters. If uncovered through appraisals, the personnel department may be able to provide assistance.

Figure 11-1
Uses of Performance Appraisals

As this example emphasizes, an organization cannot have just *any* performance appraisal system. It must be effective and accepted. Figure 11-2 shows the elements of an acceptable appraisal system. The approach must identify performance-related criteria, measure those criteria, and then give feedback to employees and to the personnel department. If performance measures are not job-related, the evaluation can lead to inaccurate or biased results.[6]

The personnel department usually develops performance appraisals for employees in all departments. One study found that in over 80 percent of the firms surveyed the development of appraisal systems is the responsibility of the personnel department.[7] This centralization is done to ensure uniformity. With uniformity in design and implementation, results are more likely to be comparable among similar groups of employees. Although personnel may develop different approaches for managers, professionals, workers, and other groups, uniformity within each group is needed to ensure useful results. Even though the personnel department usually designs the appraisal system, it seldom does the actual evaluation of performance. Instead, research shows that 95 percent of the time the employee's immediate supervisor performs the evaluation.[8] Although others may rate performance, the immediate supervisor is often in the best position to make the appraisal. So important is the evaluation of performance that over 70 percent of the firms in one study used appraisals for their office, professional, supervisory, and management employees.[9] To explain the importance of this widely used tool of personnel management, the rest of this chapter

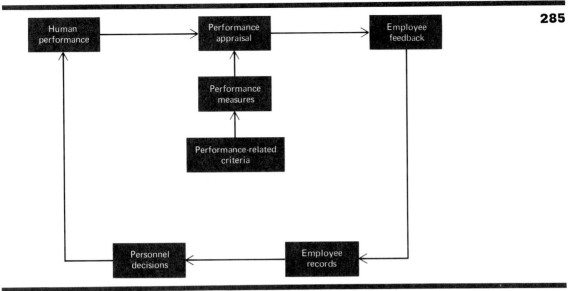

Figure 11-2
Key Elements of Performance Appraisal Systems

examines the preparation, methods, and implications of performance appraisals.

PREPARATION OF PERFORMANCE APPRAISALS

The appraisal should create an accurate picture of an individual's job performance. To achieve this goal, appraisal systems should be job-related and practical, they should have standards, and they should use dependable measures. *Job-related* means that the system evaluates critical behaviors that constitute job success. These behaviors normally are identified as part of the job analysis process, described in Chapter 5. If the evaluation is not job-related, it is invalid. Without validity and reliability, the system may discriminate in violation of equal opportunity laws. Even when discrimination does not occur, appraisals may be inaccurate and useless if they are not job-related. But a job-related approach also must be practical. A *practical* system is understood by evaluators and employees. A complicated, impractical approach may cause resentment, confusion, and nonuse.

A standardized system within an organization is helpful because it allows uniform practices to be established by the personnel department. Standardization among firms across different industries does not exist. However, two authorities believe that an emerging standard for performance appraisal systems may be found in the *Civil Service Reform Act* of 1978, which is enforced in the federal sector by the Office of Personnel Management. They believe that the act is noteworthy because its approach to performance appraisal is straightforward and eventually may be applied by the courts to private sector organizations with invalid systems.[10] Section 430 of the act encourages employee participation in

Civil Service Reform Act: A new standard?

286

developing performance standards based upon the critical elements of the jobs to be appraised. The method of identifying these elements would most likely be through job analysis procedures. But whatever method is used, there must be a written record of the standards. The employee also must be advised of these standards before the evaluation occurs, not afterward. The appraisal of each employee's performance must be based upon the employee's actual perform- ance on the critical elements.[11] The Florida Power and Light example earlier in this chapter does use employee participation to identify the critical elements. However, each employee is evaluated on those criteria in comparison with other employees. Even though the Florida Power and Light talent assessment program was an award-winning approach, the interpretation of the act might call into question the use of employee comparisons instead of the more straightforward evaluation of each employee on each criterion without matched comparisons.

Common elements

Before specific approaches to performance appraisal can be examined, however, common elements of most performance systems should be discussed. These include performance standards, performance measures, and rater biases.

Performance Standards

Standards are used as benchmarks.

Performance evaluation requires *performance standards*. They are the bench- marks against which performance is measured. To be effective, they should relate to the desired results of each job. They cannot be set arbitrarily. Knowledge of these standards is collected through job analysis. As discussed in Chapter 5, job analysis uncovers specific performance criteria by analyzing the performance of existing employees. As one pair of writers observed:

> It is important that management carefully examine the characteristics of effective performance. Job analysis coupled with a detailed performance analysis of existing employees should begin to identify what characteristics are required by a job and which of those are exhibited by "successful" employees. It is possible that such an investigation may reveal that what management has used in the past to define successful performance is inadequate or misleading. This should not deter management from the task of defining the criteria, but should reinforce management for the "house cleaning" which is being undertaken. This must be a careful scrutiny with an eye to what the performance criteria should be in the future, rather than what criteria have been used in the past.[12]

From the duties and standards listed in the job description, the analyst can decide which behaviors are critical and should be evaluated. When this information is lacking or unclear, standards are developed from observation of the job or discussions with the immediate supervisor.[13]

Performance Measures

Performance evaluation also requires dependable *performance measures*. They are the ratings used to evaluate performance. To be useful, they must be easy to use, be reliable, and report on the critical behaviors that determine performance. For example, a telephone company supervisor must observe each operator's:

- Use of company procedures—staying calm, applying tariff rates for phone-calls, and following company rules and regulations

- Pleasant phone manners—speaking clearly and courteously

- Call-placement accuracy—placing operator-assisted calls accurately

These observations can be made either directly or indirectly. *Direct* observation occurs when the rater actually sees the performance. *Indirect* observation occurs when the rater can evaluate only substitutes for actual performance. For example, a supervisor's monitoring of an operator's calls is direct observation; a written test on company procedures for handling emergency calls is indirect observation. Indirect observations are usually less accurate because they evaluate substitutes, or *constructs*. Since constructs are not exactly the same as actual performance, they may lead to errors.

Direct versus indirect observations

To test how well operators might respond to emergency calls, an independent telephone company developed a paper-and-pencil test. The test was intended to determine if each operator knew exactly how to proceed when emergency calls were received for such requests as police, ambulance, or fire equipment. After several hundred operators were tested, it was noticed that fast readers scored better. The personnel department decided to scrap the test and use false emergency calls to evaluate the operators.

Another dimension of performance measures is whether they are objective or subjective. *Objective performance measures* are those indications of job performance that are verifiable by others. For example, if two supervisors monitor an operator's calls, they can count the number of misdialings. The results are objective and verifiable since each supervisor gets the same call-placement accuracy percentage. Usually, objective measures are quantitative. They typically include items such as gross units produced, net units approved by quality control, scrap rates, number of computational errors, number of customer complaints, or some other mathematically precise measure of performance.

Objective versus subjective measures

Subjective performance measures are those ratings that are not verifiable by others. Usually, such measures are the rater's personal opinion. Figure 11-3 compares the accuracy of objective and subjective measures. It shows that subjective measures are low in accuracy. When subjective measures are also indirect, accuracy becomes even lower. For example, measurement of an operator's phone manners is done subjectively; supervisors must use their personal opinions of good or bad manners. Since the evaluation is subjective, accuracy is usually low even if the supervisor directly observes the operator. Accuracy is likely to be even lower when the rater uses an indirect measure, such as an essay test of phone manners. Whenever possible, personnel specialists prefer objective and direct measures of performance.

TYPES OF PERFORMANCE MEASURES	RELATIVE DEGREE OF ACCURACY	
	DIRECT	INDIRECT
OBJECTIVE	Very high	High
SUBJECTIVE	Low	Very low

Figure 11-3
Types and Accuracy of Performance Measures

Rater Biases

The problem with subjective measures is the opportunity for bias. *Bias* is the inaccurate distortion of a measurement. It is usually caused by raters who fail to remain emotionally unattached while they evaluate employee performance. The most common rater biases include:

Common biases

- The halo effect
- The error of central tendency
- The leniency and strictness biases

- Personal prejudice
- The recency effect

The halo effect   The *halo effect* occurs when the rater's personal opinion of the employee sways the rater's measurement of performance. For example, if a supervisor personally likes or dislikes an employee, that opinion may distort the supervisor's estimate of the employee's performance. This problem is most severe when raters must evaluate their friends or those they strongly dislike.

The error of central tendency   Some raters do not like to rate employees as effective or ineffective, and so the performance rating is distorted to make each employee appear to be average. On rating forms, this distortion causes evaluators to avoid checking extremes—very poor or excellent. Instead they place their marks near the center of the rating sheet.[14] Thus the term *error of central tendency* has been applied to this bias. Personnel departments sometimes unintentionally encourage this behavior by requiring raters to justify extremely high or low ratings.

The leniency and strictness biases   The *leniency bias* results when raters tend to be easy in evaluating the performance of employees. Such raters see all employee performance as good and rate it favorably. The *strictness bias* is just the opposite. It results from raters being too harsh in their evaluation of performance. Sometimes the strictness bias results because the rater wants others to think that he or she is a "tough judge" of people's performance. Both lenience and strictness errors more commonly occur when performance standards are vague.

Personal prejudice   A rater's dislike for a group or class of people may distort the ratings those people receive. For example, some personnel departments noticed that male supervisors give undeservedly low ratings to women who hold "traditionally male jobs." Sometimes raters are unaware of their prejudice, which makes such biases even more difficult to overcome. Nevertheless, personnel specialists should pay close attention to patterns in appraisals that suggest prejudice. Such prejudice prevents effective evaluations and may violate antidiscrimination laws. Where the halo bias affects one's judgment of an individual, prejudice affects entire groups. When prejudice affects the ratings of protected class members, this form of discrimination can lead to violations of equal employment laws.

Prejudice may mean illegal discrimination.

The recency effect   When using subjective performance measures, ratings are affected strongly by the employee's most recent actions. Recent actions—either good or bad—are more likely to be remembered by the rater.

When subjective performance measures must be used, personnel specialists can reduce the distortion from biases through training, feedback, and the proper selection of performance appraisal techniques. Training for raters should involve three steps. First, biases and their causes should be explained. Second, the role of performance appraisals in employee decisions should be explained to stress the need for impartiality and objectivity. Third, raters should be allowed to apply subjective performance measures as part of their training. For example, classroom exercises may require evaluation of the trainer or of videotapes showing workers and various working situations. Mistakes uncovered during simulated evaluations then can be corrected through additional training or counseling.

Once the use of subjective performance measures moves out of the classroom and into practice, raters should get feedback about their previous ratings.[15] When ratings prove relatively accurate or inaccurate, feedback helps raters adjust their behavior accordingly. Personnel departments also can reduce distortion through the careful selection of performance appraisal techniques.[16] For ease of discussion, these techniques are grouped into those that focus on past performance and those that are future oriented.

Raters need feedback, too.

PAST-ORIENTED
APPRAISAL METHODS

The importance of performance evaluations has led academicians and practitioners to create many methods to appraise past performance. Most of these techniques are a direct attempt to minimize some particular problem found in other approaches. No one technique is perfect; each has advantages and disadvantages.

Past-oriented approaches have the advantage of dealing with performance that has already occurred and, to some degree, can be measured. The obvious disadvantage is that past performance cannot be changed. But by evaluating past performance, employees can get feedback about their efforts. This feedback

Past performance is a common orientation.

then may lead to renewed efforts at improved performance. The most widely used appraisal techniques that have a past orientation include:

- Rating scales
- Checklists
- Forced choice method
- Critical incident method

- Comparative evaluation methods
- Behaviorally anchored rating scales
- Field review method
- Performance tests and observations

Rating Scales

Perhaps the oldest and most widely used form of performance appraisal is the *rating scale,* which requires the rater to provide a subjective evaluation of an individual's performance along a scale from low to high. An example appears in Figure 11-4. As the figure indicates, the evaluation is based solely on the opinions of the rater. And in many cases, the criteria are not directly related to job performance. Although subordinates or peers may use it, the form is usually completed by the immediate supervisor, who checks the most appropriate response for each performance dimension. Responses may be given numerical values to enable an average score to be computed and compared for each employee. The number of points attained may be linked to salary increases—so many points equal a raise of some percentage. Other advantages of this method are that it is inexpensive to develop and administer, raters need little training or

Figure 11-4
A Sample of a Rating Scale for Performance Evaluation

Instructions: For the following performance factors, please indicate on the rating scale your evaluation of the named employee.

Employee's Name _____   Department _____

Rater's Name _____   Date _____

	Excellent 5	Good 4	Acceptable 3	Fair 2	Poor 1
1. Dependability	—	—	—	—	—
2. Initiative	—	—	—	—	—
3. Overall Output	—	—	—	—	—
4. Attendance	—	—	—	—	—
5. Attitude	—	—	—	—	—
6. Cooperation	—	—	—	—	—
. .	.	.	.	.	.
. .	.	.	.	.	.
. .	.	.	.	.	.
20. Quality of Work Results	—	—	—	—	—
Totals	— +	— +	— +	— +	— = —
					Total Score

time to complete the form, and it can be applied to a large number of employees.[17]

Disadvantages are numerous. A rater's biases are likely to be reflected in a subjective instrument of this type. Specific performance criteria may be omitted to make the form applicable to a variety of jobs. For example, "maintenance of equipment" may be left off the form because it applies to only a few workers. But for some employees, that item may be the most important part of their jobs. This omission and others tend to limit specific feedback. These descriptive evaluations also are subject to individual interpretations that vary widely. And when specific performance criteria are hard to identify, the form may rely on irrelevant personality variables that dilute the meaning of the evaluation. The result is a standardized form and procedure that are not always job-related. And like the subjective evaluations in the General Motors case discussed earlier, these rating scales may prove to be discriminatory.

Biases may cause major problems.

Checklists

The *checklist* rating method requires the rater to select statements or words that describe the employee's performance and characteristics. Again, the rater is usually the immediate superior. But without the rater's knowledge, the personnel department may assign weights to different items on the checklist, according to each item's importance. The result is called a *weighted checklist.* The weights allow the rating to be quantified so that total scores can be determined. Figure 11-5 shows a portion of a checklist. The weights for each item are in parentheses but usually are omitted from the form the rater uses. If the list contains enough items, it may provide an accurate picture of employee performance. Although this method is practical and standardized, the use of general statements reduces its job-relatedness.

Checklist can be weighted.

The advantages of a checklist are economy, ease of administration, limited

Figure 11-5
An Example of a Weighted Performance Checklist

Instructions: Check each of the following items that apply to the named employee's performance.

Employee's Name _____   Department _____
Rater's Name _____   Date _____

Weights		Check Here
(6.5)	1. Employee works overtime when asked.	_____
(4.0)	2. Employee keeps work station or desk well organized.	_____
(3.9)	3. Employee cooperatively assists others who need help.	_____
(4.3)	4. Employee plans actions before beginning job.	_____
•	• •	•
•	• •	•
•	• •	•
(0.2)	30. Employee listens to others' advice but seldom follows it.	_____
100.0	Total of all weights.	

training of raters, and standardization. The disadvantages include susceptibility to rater biases (especially the halo effect), use of personality criteria instead of performance criteria, misinterpretations of checklist items, and the use of improper weights by the personnel department. Another disadvantage of this approach is that it does not allow the rater to give relative ratings. For example, on item 1 in the figure, employees who gladly work overtime get the same score as those who do so unwillingly.

Forced Choice Method

The *forced choice method* requires the rater to choose the most descriptive statement in each pair of statements about the employee being rated. Often both statements in the pair are positive or negative. For example:

1. Learns quickly. . . . . Works hard.

2. Work is reliable and accurate. . . . . Performance is a good example to others.

3. Absent too often.. . . . . Usually tardy.

Sometimes the rater must select the best statement (or even pair of statements) from four choices. However the form is constructed, personnel specialists usually group the items on the form into predetermined categories—such as learning ability, performance, interpersonal relations, and the like. Then effectiveness can be computed for each category by adding up the number of times each category is selected by the rater. The results can be reported to show which areas need further improvement. Again, the supervisor is usually the rater, although peers or subordinates may make the evaluation.

The forced choice method has the advantages of reducing rater bias, being easy to administer, and fitting a wide variety of jobs. Although practical and easily standardized, the general statements may not be specifically job-related. Thus it may have limited usefulness in helping employees improve their performance. Even worse, an employee may feel slighted when one statement is checked in preference to another. For example, if the rater checks "learns quickly" in number 1 above, the worker may feel that his or her hard work is overlooked.[18] This method is seldom liked by either the rater or ratee because it provides little useful feedback.

Critical Incident Method

The *critical incident method* requires the rater to record statements that describe extremely good or bad employee behavior related to performance. The statements are called critical incidents. These incidents are usually recorded by the supervisor during the evaluation period for each subordinate. Recorded incidents include a brief explanation of what happened. Several typical entries for a laboratory assistant appear in Figure 11-6. As shown in the figure, both positive and negative incidents are recorded and classified (either as they occur or later by the personnel department) into categories such as control of safety hazards, control of material scrap, and employee development.

Instructions: In each category below, record specific incidents of employee behavior that were either extremely good or extremely poor.

Employee's Name Kay Watts   (lab assistant)   Department Chemistry Lab

Rater's Name Nat Cordoba   Rating Period of 10/1   to 12/31

Control of Safety Hazards

Date	Positive Employee Behavior	Date	Negative Employee Behavior
10/12	Report broken rung on utility ladder and flagged ladder as unsafe	11/3	Left hose across storeroom aisle
10/15	Put out small trash fire promptly	11/27	Smoked in chemical storeroom

Control of Material Scrap

Date	Positive Employee Behavior	Date	Negative Employee Behavior
10/3	Sorted through damaged shipment of glassware to salvage usable beakers	11/7	Used glass containers for strong bases ruining glass
		11/19	Repeatedly used glass for storage of lye and other bases
			Poured acid into plastic container ruining counter top

Figure 11-6
A Critical Incidents Record for a Lab Assistant

The critical incident method is extremely useful for giving employees job-related feedback. It also reduces the recency bias. Of course, the main drawback is that supervisors often do not record incidents as they occur. Many start out recording incidents faithfully but lose interest. Then just before the evaluation period ends, they add new entries. When this happens, the recency bias is exaggerated, and employees may feel that the supervisors are building a case to support their subjective opinion. Even when the form is filled out over the entire rating period, employees may feel that the supervisor is unwilling to forget negative incidents that occurred months before.

Behaviorally Anchored Rating Scales

Behaviorally anchored rating scales (BARS) use specific named behaviors as benchmarks to help the rater. This method attempts to reduce some of the subjectivity and biases found in other approaches to performance measurement.[19] From descriptions of good and bad performance provided by incumbents, peers, and supervisors, job analysts or knowledgeable employees group behaviors into major categories of job performance. For example, a listing of job-related behaviors for a bartender in the category of customer relations appears in Figure 11-7. Other rating sheets would be assembled for other aspects

Ratings are "anchored" in relevant behaviors.

Behaviorally Anchored Rating Scale for <u>Hotel Bartender</u>

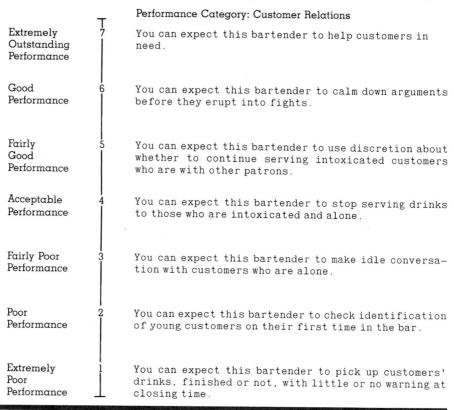

Performance Category: Customer Relations

Extremely Outstanding Performance	7	You can expect this bartender to help customers in need.
Good Performance	6	You can expect this bartender to calm down arguments before they erupt into fights.
Fairly Good Performance	5	You can expect this bartender to use discretion about whether to continue serving intoxicated customers who are with other patrons.
Acceptable Performance	4	You can expect this bartender to stop serving drinks to those who are intoxicated and alone.
Fairly Poor Performance	3	You can expect this bartender to make idle conversation with customers who are alone.
Poor Performance	2	You can expect this bartender to check identification of young customers on their first time in the bar.
Extremely Poor Performance	1	You can expect this bartender to pick up customers' drinks, finished or not, with little or no warning at closing time.

Figure 11-7

A Behaviorally Anchored Rating Scale for a Bartender's Customer Relations

of the bartender's job, such as ability to maintain equipment, to keep the bar area clean, and to mix drinks. Specific behaviors are ranked along a scale, from 1 to 7 in Figure 11-7, by the analyst or by a group of knowledgeable workers.

By allowing a group of incumbents to identify these behaviors, BARS—or

Behavioral expectation scales

behavioral expectation scales, as they also are known—can be expressed in terms with which the rater and the employee are familiar. The rater, usually the supervisor, can review the identified behavioral anchors and indicate those items the bartender needs to improve upon. Since these scales are "anchored" by specific behaviors within each category, the supervisor is better able to provide specific feedback to each bartender. If the rater also collects specific incidents during the rating period, the evaluation is apt to be more accurate, more legally defensible, and a more effective counseling tool.[20] One serious limitation of BARS is that they only look at a limited number of performance categories, such as, in the case of a bartender, customer relations or drink mixing. And each of these categories has only a limited number of specific behaviors. Like the critical incident method, most supervisors are reluctant to maintain records of critical incidents during the rating period, which reduces the effectiveness of this approach when it comes time to counsel the employee.[21]

Field Review Method

Whenever subjective performance measures are used, differences in rater perceptions cause bias. To provide greater standardization in reviews, some employers use the *field review method.* In this method, a skilled representative of the personnel department goes into the "field" and assists supervisors with their ratings. The personnel specialist solicits from the immediate supervisor specific information about the employee's performance. Then the expert prepares an evaluation based on this information. The evaluation is sent to the supervisor for review, changes, approval, and discussion with the employee who was rated. The personnel specialist records the rating on whatever specific type of rating form the employer uses. Since a skilled professional is completing the form, reliability and comparability are more likely. But the use of skilled professionals makes this approach costly and impractical for many firms.

Personnel specialists do ratings.

Performance Tests and Observations

With a limited number of jobs, performance appraisal may be based upon a test of knowledge or skills. The test may be of the paper-and-pencil variety or an actual demonstration of skills. The test must be reliable and validated to be useful. In order for the method to be job-related, observations should be made under circumstances likely to be encountered. Practicality may suffer when the cost of test development is high.

Pilots of all major airlines are subject to evaluation by airline raters and by the Federal Aviation Administration. Evaluations of flying ability are usually made in a flight simulator and in actual flight. The evaluation is based on how well the pilot follows prescribed flight procedures and safety rules. Although testing is expensive, public safety makes this approach practical in addition to being job-related and standardized.

Federal Aviation Administration checks pilots.

Comparative Evaluation Approaches

Comparative evaluation approaches are a collection of different methods that compare one person's performance with that of coworkers. Usually comparative appraisals are conducted by the supervisor. They are useful for deciding merit pay increases, promotions, and organizational rewards because they can result in a ranking of employees from best to worst. The most common forms of comparative evaluations are the ranking method, forced distributions, point allocation method, and paired comparisons. Although these methods are practical and easily standardized, they too are subject to bias and offer little job-related feedback.

Florida Power and Light's program, for example, uses an elaborate group evaluation method. Biases are reduced at this utility because multiple raters are used, and some feedback results when managers and professionals learn how they compared with others on each critical factor. However, many of the

Limited feedback

comparative examples described in this section offer employees little, if any, feedback. Often these comparative results are not shared with the employee because the supervisor and the personnel department want to create an atmosphere of cooperation among employees. To share comparative rankings may lead to internal competition instead of cooperation. However, two arguments in favor of comparative approaches merit mention before discussing specific methods.

Commonly done already

Arguments for a comparative approach are simple and powerful. The simple part of it is that organizations do it anyway, all the time. Whenever personnel decisions are made, the performance of the individuals being considered is ranked and compared. People are not promoted because they achieve their objectives, but rather because they achieve their objectives *better* than others.

The second reason (the powerful one) for using comparative as opposed to noncomparative methods is that they are far more reliable. This is because reliability is controlled by the rating process itself, not by rules, policies, and other external constraints.[22]

Ranking method   The *ranking method* has the rater place each employee in order from best to worst. All the personnel department knows is that certain employees are better than others. It does not know by how much. The employee ranked second may be almost as good as the one who was ranked first, or perhaps considerably worse. This method is subject to the halo and recency effects, although rankings by two or more raters can be averaged to help reduce biases. Its advantages include ease of administration and explanation.

Forced distribution   *Forced distributions* require raters to sort employees into different classifications. Usually a certain proportion must be put in each category. Figure 11-8 shows how a rater might classify ten subordinates. The criterion shown in the figure is for overall performance (but this method can be used for other performance criteria such as reliability and control of costs). As with the ranking method, relative differences among employees are unknown, but this method does overcome the biases of central tendency, leniency, and strictness errors. Some workers and supervisors at American Express's Western

Figure 11-8

The Forced Distribution Method of Appraisal of Ten Subordinates

Classification: Overall Performance				
Best 10% of Subordinates	Next 20% of Subordinates	Middle 40% of Subordinates	Next 20% of Subordinates	Lowest 10% of Subordinates
A. Wilson	G. Carrs M. Lopez	B. Johnson E. Wilson C. Grant T. Valley	K. McDougal L. Ray	W. Smythe

Instructions: Allocate all 100 points to all employees according to their relative worth. The employee with the maximum points is the best employee.

Points	Employee
17	A. Wilson
14	G. Carrs
13	M. Lopez
11	B. Johnson
10	E. Wilson
10	C. Grant
9	T. Valley
6	K. McDougal
5	L. Ray
5	W. Smythe
100	

Figure 11-9
The Point Allocation Method of Appraisal

Regional Operations Center strongly dislike this method because some employees received lower ratings than they or their supervisor-rater thought were correct. However, the personnel department's forced distribution required that some employees be rated low.

Point allocation method   The *point allocation method* requires the rater to allocate a fixed number of points among employees in the group, as shown in Figure 11-9. Good performers are given more points than poor performers. The advantage of the point allocation method is that the rater can recognize the relative differences between employees, although the halo effect and the recency bias are disadvantages that remain.

Paired comparisons   *Paired comparisons* force raters to compare each employee with all other employees who are being rated in the same group. An example of paired comparisons appears in Figure 11-10. The basis for comparison is usually overall performance. The number of times each employee is rated superior to another can be summed to develop an index. The employee who is preferred the most is the best employee on the criterion selected. In the figure, A. Wilson is selected nine times and is the top-ranking worker. Although subject to halo and recency effects, this method overcomes the leniency, strictness, and central errors because some employees must be rated better than others.

FUTURE-ORIENTED APPRAISALS

The use of past-oriented approaches is like driving a car by looking through the rearview mirror; you only know where you have been, not where you are going. Future-oriented appraisals focus on future performance by evaluating employee potential or setting future performance goals. Included here are four techniques used:

Instructions: Compare each employee on overall performance with every other employee. For each comparison, write the number of the employee who is best in the intersecting box. Each time an employee is found superior to another employee, the better employee receives one point. Employees then can be ranked according to the number of times each is selected as best by the rater.

Employee	2	3	4	5	6	7	8	9	10
1. G. Carrs	1	1	4	1	1	1	1	9	1
2. C. Grant		3	4	2	2	2	2	9	2
3. B. Johnson			4	3	3	3	3	9	3
4. M. Lopez				4	4	4	4	9	4
5. K. McDougal					6	5	8	9	10
6. L. Ray						6	8	9	10
7. W. Smythe							8	9	10
8. T. Valley								9	10
9. A. Wilson									9
10. E. Wilson									

Figure 11-10
The Paired Comparison Method
of Evaluating Employees

- Self-appraisals

- Management by objectives approach

- Psychological appraisals

- Assessment center technique

Self-Appraisals

Getting employees to conduct a self-appraisal can be a useful evaluation technique if the goal of evaluation is to further self-development. When employees evaluate themselves, defensive behavior is less likely to occur. Thus self-improvement is more likely. When self-appraisals are used to determine areas of needed improvement, they can help users set personal goals for the future. Obviously, self-appraisals can be used with any evaluation approach, past- or future-oriented. But the important dimension of self-appraisals is the employee's involvement and commitment to the improvement process.

Can be applied with other methods

At the Bechtel Company, the largest privately held construction and engineering firm in the world, the performance planning system involves the employees in a process of self-appraisal. The process starts with the supervisors telling the employees what is expected. Then the employees

Bechtel uses self-appraisal.

get a work sheet on which they write down their understanding of the job. About ten to fifteen days before a performance evaluation is to be done, the employees complete the work sheet by filling in the portions that relate to job accomplishments, performance difficulties, and suggestions for improvement. Not only does the work sheet get the employees involved in forming a self-appraisal of improvement areas, but it also indicates to the supervisors what they need to do to "eliminate roadblocks to meeting or exceeding job standards."[23]

Management by Objectives

The heart of the *management by objectives* (MBO) approach is that both employee and superior jointly establish performance goals for the future.[24] Ideally, these goals are mutually agreed upon and objectively measurable. If both of these conditions are met, the employees are apt to be more motivated to achieve their goals since they participated in setting them. Moreover, since they can measure their progress, employees can adjust their behavior periodically to ensure attainment of the objectives. However, in order to adjust their efforts, employees must receive performance feedback on a timely basis.

MBO can be motivating.

When future objectives are set, employees gain the motivational benefit of a specific target to organize and direct their efforts. Objectives also help the employee and supervisor discuss specific development needs of the employee. When done correctly, performance discussions focus on the job's objectives and not on personality variables. Biases are reduced to the extent that goal attainment can be measured objectively.

In practice, MBO programs have encountered difficulties. Objectives are sometimes too ambitious or too narrow. The result is frustrated employees or overlooked areas of performance. For example, employees may set objectives that are quantitatively measurable to the exclusion of subjectively measurable ones that may be equally important. The classic illustration is quantity versus quality of work. Objectives may focus on quantity to the exclusion of quality because quality is often more difficult to measure. When employees and managers do focus on subjectively measured objectives, special care is needed to ensure that biases do not distort the manager's evaluation.

Psychological Appraisals

Some (mostly very large) organizations employ full-time psychologists. When psychologists are used for evaluations, their role primarily is to assess an individual's future potential, not past performance. The appraisal normally consists of in-depth interviews, psychological tests, discussions with supervisors, and a review of other evaluations. The psychologist then writes an evaluation of the employee's intellectual, emotional, motivational, and other work-related characteristics that may predict future performance. The estimate by the psychologist may be for a specific job opening for which the person is being considered, or it may be a global assessment of his or her future potential. From these evaluations, placement and development decisions may be made to shape the person's career. Because this approach is slow and costly, it is usually

Company-hired counselors

reserved for bright young managers who others think may have considerable potential within the organization. Since the quality of these appraisals depends largely on the skills of the psychologists, some employees object to this type of evaluation.

Assessment Centers

Assessment centers are another method of evaluating future potential, but they do not rely on the conclusions of one psychologist. *Assessment centers* are a standardized form of employee appraisal that relies on multiple types of evaluation and multiple raters. The assessment center is usually applied to groups of middle-level managers who appear to have potential to perform at more responsible levels in the organization. Often the members in the group first meet at the center. During their stay they are individually evaluated. The process subjects selected employees to in-depth interviews, psychological tests, personal background histories, peer ratings by other attendees, leaderless group discussions, ratings by psychologists and managers, and simulated work exercises to evaluate future potential. The simulated work experiences usually include in-basket exercises, decision-making exercises, computer-based business games, and other joblike opportunities that test the employee in realistic ways. These activities usually are concentrated during a few days at a location physically removed from the jobsite. During this time, the psychologists and managers who do the rating attempt to estimate the strengths, weaknesses, and potential of each attendee at the center.[25] They then pool their estimates to arrive at some conclusion about each member of the group.

Assessment centers were first applied to business in 1956 by the director of human resources research at American Telephone and Telegraph. By the 1980s, more than 2000 corporate-operated assessment centers were in existence. This approach is both time-consuming and costly. Not only are the candidates away from their jobs with the company paying for travel and lodging, but the evaluators are often company managers who are assigned to the assessment center for short durations.[26] These managers are often supplemented by psychologists and personnel professionals who run the center and also make evaluations.[27] Some critics question whether the procedures used are objective and job-related, especially since rater biases are possible in forming the subjective opinions of attendees.[28] Nevertheless, assessment centers have gained widespread use, and personnel researchers are finding ways to validate the process.

The results can be extremely useful for aiding management development and placement decisions. From the composite ratings, a report is prepared on each attendee. This information goes into the personnel management information system to assist human resource planning (particularly the development of replacement charts) and other personnel management decisions. Interestingly, research indicates that the results of assessment centers are a good prediction of actual on-the-job performance in 75 percent of the cases.[29] Unfortunately, this accurate method is expensive since it usually requires both a separate facility and the time of multiple raters. Consider how the process works at Johnson Wax:

Multiple approaches and multiple raters reduce bias.

Useful for both placement and development

For years, the Consumer Products Division of S. C. Johnson & Son, Inc., ran a traditional assessment center. Twice a year, selected managers from each division in the company attended the assessment center for five days and were evaluated on a variety of skills. On the fourth day, the candidates attended a debriefing and career development session while the raters wrote their final evaluations. On the fifth day, attendees received a report of their performance and counseling. The assessment process was successful in helping management select sales representatives. However, the results of the center tended to be overemphasized; people were seen to have "passed" or "failed" the process. Those who "failed" became dissatisfied because they believed their career potential had been severely limited. Many people who attended the center "failed" because field management had few guidelines as to who should be sent and at what stage of their career development. Likewise, few programs existed to prepare people for the assessment center process, and no formal program existed to train people in management skills.

To overcome these shortcomings, a project group was formed that included people in personnel, field sales management, and a consultant. The group changed the thrust of Johnson Wax's assessment center by recommending that the center's results be given less importance and that it be used to identify strengths and weaknesses in individual skills. The group also recommended that field management become more involved in assisting management candidates with career planning and development activities. The project group also made sure that field management knew what the purpose of the center was and gave them guidelines for recommending people to attend the center. A voluntary program for skill development was also undertaken. Even the name of the center was changed to the Management Skill Identification Center.[30]

From assessment to skill identification

"Today, the MSI Center results are but one element in the 'management promotion equation.' This equation consists of four weighted elements which are used by management to make a promotion determination: (1) the individual's record of performance on the job; (2) the individual's sales experience level; (3) the individual's previous job-related experience (i.e., previous employment experience, education experience, etc.); and (4) the individual's MSI Center results."[31]

As this Johnson Wax example illustrates, the assessment center results must be kept in perspective. If they are the sole determinant of future career progress in the organization, people will see the assessment process as threatening. However, if it is used to appraise an individual's strength and weaknesses and the person has a way of improving areas of deficiency, the center can be a positive force for developing future talent within the organization.

To reduce the expense but still capture some of the benefits associated with assessment centers, some companies use "mail-in" assessments. A package of tests, exercises, and required reports is mailed to the individual who mails them to the raters for subsequent evaluation.[32] Not only does it cost less, but raters and employers do not spend the time needed to go to a centralized location.

"Mail-in" assessments

302

IMPLICATIONS OF
THE APPRAISAL PROCESS

Design of the appraisal system and its procedures is usually handled by the personnel department. The specific approach selected will be influenced by previous procedures and by the purpose of the new approach. If the goal is to evaluate past performance and allocate rewards, comparative approaches may be preferred. Other types of past-performance-oriented instruments may be used if the appraisal system exists primarily to give employees counseling about their behavior. Future-oriented approaches, such as MBO techniques, may focus on specific goals. Self-appraisals or assessment centers may seek to uncover specific weaknesses or to help with internal placement. Regardless of the technique selected by the personnel department, however, the approach must be converted into an ongoing practice among the line managers. Except in the field review or psychological appraisal methods, raters are often unfamiliar with the procedures or the forms. And they may not be very interested in self-study to learn more because the evaluation process may be seen as a project imposed by the personnel department and not as something of immediate concern to those who supervise others.

Appraisals must become an ongoing practice.

Evaluation systems that involve others in their design may gain greater acceptance. The Civil Service Reform Act and the Florida Power and Light Company's talent assessment program both support the need for having employees involved in the design of the appraisal system. Such involvement may increase interest and understanding. However, to operationalize the performance appraisal system, training may be required for those who will serve as raters.

Training Raters

Whether a simple comparative method or a sophisticated assessment center is used, the raters need knowledge of the system and its purpose. Just knowing whether the appraisal is to be used for compensation or for placement recommendations may change the rater's evaluation of those being rated.

Rater's handbook

Two major problems are rater understanding and consistency of evaluations. Some personnel departments provide raters with a handbook that describes the employer's approach. Guidelines for conducting the evaluation or for providing raters with feedback often are included, as well as definitions for key terms—such as "shows initiative" or "provides leadership."

Raters need training.

Companies like Bechtel and Glendale Federal Savings and Loan Association solve this knowledge gap through training. The training workshops are usually intended to explain to raters the purpose of the procedure, the mechanics of "how to do it," likely pitfalls or biases they may encounter, and answers to their questions. The training may include trial runs evaluating other classmates just to gain some supervised experience. Bechtel and Glendale even use videotapes and role-playing evaluation sessions to give raters both experience and insight into the evaluation process. During the training, the timing and scheduling of evaluations are discussed. Typically, most companies do formal evaluations annually near the individual's employment anniversary. For new employees or for those having performance problems, evaluations may be done more frequently as part of the personnel department's formal program or as the supervisor sees fit. Consider how the vice president and manager of human resources at Glendale Federal Savings and Loan viewed the implementation of his firm's program:

> With the new appraisal process and related forms in place, the next major step was educating managers and supervisors in the use of the program. Mandatory one-day training workshops were given, providing each manager an opportunity to review, discuss and understand the objectives of the program. The appraisal forms were reviewed in detail with an explanation of how to use the various sections in each form. A videotaped appraisal discussion was presented to demonstrate how performance appraisal worked. And finally, during the workshops, managers were given role-play situations using the new appraisal forms.[33]

> Then on the biweekly payroll sheets that included everyone in the department or branch, the manager received a notification of who was due to be evaluated during the next month. If the review date had passed, a reminder would appear on the payroll sheets showing that the review date for the indicated employee was past due. As a result, managers knew how to complete the forms, and few delinquencies occur. The human resource department at Glendale Federal also has valuable data that allow it to anticipate and respond to training needs and employee concerns.[34]

Once raters are trained, the appraisal process can begin. But the results of the appraisal do little to improve employee performance unless employees receive feedback. This feedback process is called the evaluation interview.

Evaluation Interviews

Evaluation interviews are performance review sessions that give employees feedback about their past performance or future potential. The evaluator may provide this feedback through several approaches: tell and sell, tell and listen, and problem solving.[35] The *tell-and-sell approach* reviews the employee's performance and tries to convince the employee to perform better. It is best used with new employees. The *tell-and-listen method* allows the employee to explain reasons, excuses, and defensive feelings about performance. It attempts to overcome these reactions by counseling the employee on how to perform better. The *problem-solving approach* identifies problems that are interfering with employee performance. Then through training, coaching, or counseling, goals for future performance are set to remove these deficiencies.

Regardless of which approach is used to give employees feedback, the guidelines listed in Figure 11-11 can help make the performance review session more effective.[36] The intent of these suggestions is to make the interview a positive, performance-improving dialogue. By stressing desirable aspects of employee performance, the evaluator can give the employee renewed confidence in her or his ability to perform satisfactorily. This positive approach also

304

1. *Emphasize* positive aspects of employee performance.

2. *Tell* each employee that the evaluation session is to improve performance, not to discipline.

3. *Conduct* the performance review session in private with minimum interruptions.

4. *Review* performance formally at least annually and more frequently for new employees or those who are performing poorly.

5. *Make* criticisms specific, not general and vague.

6. *Focus* criticisms on performance, not personality characteristics.

7. *Stay* calm and do not argue with the person being evaluated.

8. *Identify* specific actions the employee can take to improve performance.

9. *Emphasize* the evaluator's willingness to assist the employee's efforts and to improve performance.

10. *End* the evaluation sessions by stressing the positive aspects of the employee's performance.

Figure 11-11
Guidelines for
Effective Performance Evaluation Interviews

enables the employee to keep desirable and undesirable performance in perspective because it prevents the individual from feeling that performance review sessions are entirely negative. When negative comments are made, they focus on work performance and not on the individual's personality. Specific, not general and vague, examples of the employee's shortcomings are used so that the individual knows exactly which behaviors need to be changed.

The review session concludes by focusing on actions that the employee may take to improve areas of poor performance. In that concluding discussion, the evaluator usually offers to provide whatever assistance the employee needs to overcome the deficiencies discussed. Since the evaluation interview provides employees with performance-related feedback, it is not surprising that 95 percent of the firms in one study require managers to discuss the appraisal with employees.[37] The same study also reports that nearly 40 percent of these employers use appraisals at least annually.[38]

PERSONNEL MANAGEMENT FEEDBACK

The performance appraisal process also provides insight into the effectiveness of the personnel management function. Figure 11-12 summarizes the major concepts discussed so far in this book. As can be seen, performance appraisal serves as a "quality control check." If the appraisal process indicates that poor performance is widespread, many employees are excluded from internal placement decisions. They will not be promoted or transferred. In fact, they may be excluded from the organization through termination.

Appraisals give the personnel department feedback. Unacceptably high numbers of poor performers may indicate errors elsewhere in the personnel management function. For example, human resource development may be failing to fulfill career plans because the people who are hired during the selection process are poorly screened. Or the human resource

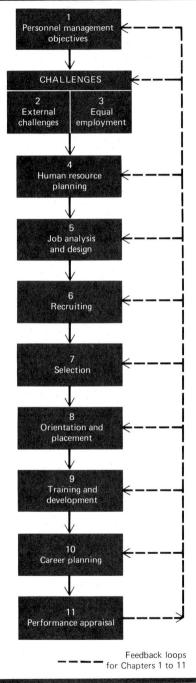

Feedback loops
for Chapters 1 to 11

Figure 11-12
The Personnel Management Process

plan may be in error because the job analysis information is wrong or the affirmative action plan seeks the wrong objectives. Likewise, personnel may be failing to respond to the challenges of the external environment or job design. Sometimes the personnel function is pursuing the wrong human resource objectives. Or the appraisal system itself may be faulty because of management resistance, incorrect performance standards or measures, or a lack of constructive feedback.[39]

Wherever the problem lies, personnel specialists need to monitor carefully the results of the organization's performance appraisal process. These results can serve as a barometer of the entire personnel function. As will be explained in Part IV, performance appraisal serves as a guide to compensation and to other personnel management activities as well.

SUMMARY

Performance appraisal is a critical activity of personnel management. Its goal is to provide an accurate picture of past and/or future employee performance. To do this, performance standards are established. Standards are based on job-related criteria that best determine successful job performance. Where possible, actual performance then is measured directly and objectively. From a wide variety of appraisal techniques, personnel specialists select those methods that most effectively measure employee performance against the previously set standards. Techniques can be selected both to review past performance and to anticipate performance in the future.

The appraisal process is usually designed by the personnel department, often with little input from other parts of the organization. When it is time to implement a new appraisal approach, those who do the rating usually have little idea about the appraisal process or its objectives. To overcome this shortcoming, the department may design and deliver appraisal workshops to train managers.

A necessary requirement of the appraisal process is employee feedback through an evaluation interview. The interview tries to balance positive areas of performance with those areas where performance is deficient, so that the employee receives a realistic view. Perhaps the most significant challenge raised by performance appraisals is the feedback they provide about personnel department performance. Personnel specialists need to be keenly aware that poor performance, especially when it is widespread, may reflect problems with previous personnel management activities.

TERMS FOR REVIEW

Performance standards   Error of central tendency

Performance measures   Recency effect

Halo effect   Rating scale

Forced choice method

Critical incident method

Behaviorally anchored ratings scales

Field review method

Comparative evaluation methods

Management by objectives

Assessment centers

Evaluation interviews

Constructs

REVIEW AND DISCUSSION QUESTIONS

1. What are the uses of performance appraisals?

2. Suppose the company you work for uses a rating scale. The items on the scale are general personality characteristics. What criticisms do you have of this method?

3. If you were asked to recommend a replacement for the rating scale, what actions would you take before selecting another appraisal technique?

4. If the dean of your college asked you to serve on a committee to develop a performance appraisal system for evaluating the faculty, what performance criteria would you identify? Of these criteria, which ones do you think are most likely to determine a faculty member's success at your school? What standards would you recommend to the dean, regardless of the specific evaluation instrument selected?

5. Why are direct and objective measures of performance usually considered superior to indirect and subjective measures?

6. If your organization were to use subjective measures to evaluate employee performance, what instructions would you give evaluators about the biases they might encounter?

7. Describe how you would conduct a typical performance evaluation interview.

8. How do the results of performance appraisals affect other personnel management activities?

INCIDENT 11-1

Multiple Appraisal Failures at Roget's Waterworks

For two years, the employees at Roget's Waterworks were evaluated with the same performance appraisal method as other employees of the Roget Municipal Services Corporation (a company-operated city utility). The personnel manager decided that the duties at the waterworks were sufficiently different that a specially designed appraisal should be developed. A weighted checklist was decided on and was used for about one year. The personnel manager left, and the replacement disliked weighted checklists. Specialists then implemented behaviorally anchored rating scales. But as soon as the method was installed, top management decided to shift all evaluations at the Roget corporation to the critical incident method.

The critical incident method worked well in all phases of the corporation's operations except at the waterworks. Supervisors in the waterworks would not keep a record of critical incidents until about a week before the incidents were due to be submitted to the personnel office. Training sessions were held for these supervisors, but little change in their behavior resulted. To evaluate the supervisors, the company conducted a survey of employees at the waterworks. Most employees thought the supervision was fair to good in all dimensions except supervisors showed too much favoritism. Thought was being given to other methods.

1. How would you suggest overcoming the resistance of the supervisors to using the critical incident method?

2. Should another evaluation method be tried?

3. What method would you recommend and why?

INCIDENT 11-2

The Malfunctioning Regional Personnel Department

For one month the corporate personnel department of Universal Insurance, Inc., had two specialists review the operations of their regional personnel department in Dallas, Texas. The review of the regional office centered on the department's human resource information base. A brief summary of their findings listed the following observations:

A. Each employee's performance appraisal showed little change from the previous year. Poor performers rated poor year in and year out.

B. Nearly 70 percent of the appraisals were not initialed by the employee even though company policy required employees to do so after they discussed their review with the rater.

C. Of those employees who initialed the evaluations, several commented that the work standards were irrelevant and unfair.

D. A survey of past employees conducted by corporate office specialists revealed that 35 percent of them believed that performance feedback was too infrequent.

E. Another 30 percent complained about the lack of advancement opportunities because most openings were filled from outside, and no one ever told these workers why they were unpromotable.

The corporate and regional personnel directors were dismayed by the findings. Each thought the problems facing the regional office were different.

1. What do you think is the major problem with the performance appraisal process in the regional office?

2. What problems do you think exist with the regional office's *(a)* job analysis information, *(b)* human resource planning, *(c)* training and development, *(d)* career planning?

REFERENCES

1. Harry Levinson, "Appraisal of *What* Performance?" *Harvard Business Review*, July–August 1976, pp. 30 ff.

2. Kenneth Blanchard and Spencer Johnson, *The One Minute Manager*, New York: William Morrow, 1982, p. 100.

3. "Tapping Managerial and Professional Talent at FPL," *The Career Development Bulletin*, vol. 3, no. 3, 1982, pp. 4–6.

4. Ibid.

5. Mary Green Miner and John B. Miner, *Employee Selection within the Law*, Washington, D.C.: Bureau of National Affairs, 1978, p. 27. See also Ronald G. Wells, "Guidelines for Effective and Defensible Performance Systems," *Personnel Journal*, October 1982, pp. 776–782.

6. John B. Miner, "Management Appraisal: A Review of Procedures and Practices," in W. Clay Hamner and Frank L. Schmidt (eds.), *Contemporary Problems in Personnel*, Chicago: St. Clair, 1977, p. 228. See also Michael H. Schuster and Christopher S. Miller, "Performance Appraisal and the Age Discrimination in Employment Act," *The Personnel Administrator*, March 1984, pp. 48–50, 52, 54–56.

7. Robert I. Lazer and Walter S. Wikstrom, *Appraising Managerial Performance: Current Practices and Future Directions*, New York: The Conference Board, 1977, p. 20.

8. Ibid., p. 26.

9. *Labor Policy and Practice—Personnel Management*, Washington: Bureau of National Affairs, 1974, p. 502.

10. Gary P. Latham and Kenneth N. Wexley, *Increasing Productivity through Performance Appraisal*, Menlo Park, Calif.: Addison-Wesley, 1981, pp. 28–29.

11. Ibid. See also Robert G. Pajer, "Performance Appraisal: A New Era for Federal Government Managers," *The Personnel Administrator*, March 1984, pp. 81–82, 84–86, 88–89.

12. James M. McFillen and Patrick G. Decker, "Building Meaning into Appraisal," *The Personnel Administrator*, June 1978, pp. 78–79.

13. Thomas C. Alewine, "Performance Appraisals and Performance Standards," *Personnel Journal*, March 1982, pp. 210–213. See also Robert Giles and Christine Landauer,

"Setting Specific Standards for Appraising Creative Staffs," *The Personnel Administrator,* March 1984, pp. 35–36, 38–41, 47.

14. Miner, op. cit.

15. McFillen and Decker, op. cit., p. 80.

16. Bruce McAfee and Blake Green, "Selecting a Performance Appraisal Method," *The Personnel Administrator,* June 1977, pp. 61–64.

17. H. John Bernardin, Robert L. Cardy, and Jarold G. Abbott, "The Effects of Individual Performance Schemata, Familiarization with Rating Scales and Rater Motivation on Rating Effectiveness," Unpublished paper, 1982.

18. John B. McMaster, "Designing on Appraisal System That Is Fair and Accurate," *Personnel Journal,* January 1979, pp. 38–40.

19. L. Fogli, C. L. Hulin, and M. R. Blood, "Development of First-Level Behavioral Job Criteria," *Journal of Applied Psychology,* January 1979, pp. 3–8.

20. Latham and Wexley, op. cit. 52–54.

21. Ibid. Also see Craig Eric Schneir and Richard W. Beaty, "Developing Behaviorally-Anchored Rating Scales (BARS)," *The Personnel Administrator,* August 1979, pp. 59–68; Aharon Tziner, "A Fairer Examination of Rating Scales When Used for Performance Appraisal in a Real Organizational Setting," Unpublished paper, 1982.

22. J. Peter Graves, "Let's Put Appraisal Back in Performance Appraisal: II," *Personnel Journal,* December 1982, p. 918.

23. Milan Moravec, "How Performance Appraisal Can Tie Communication to Productivity," *The Personnel Administrator,* January 1981, pp. 51–52.

24. William B. Werther, Jr., and Heinz Weihrich, "Refining MBO through Negotiations," *MSU Business Topics,* Summer 1975, pp. 53–58.

25. John P. Bucalo, Jr., "The Assessment Center—A More Specified Approach," *Human Resource Management,* Fall 1974, pp. 2–13. See also William C. Byham, "Starting an Assessment Center," *The Personnel Administrator,* February 1980, pp. 27–32.

26. Ibid.

27. "How to Spot Hotshots," *Business Week,* Oct. 8, 1979, pp. 62, 67.

28. Hubert S. Field and William H. Holley, "The Relationship of Performance Appraisal System Characteristics to Verdicts in Selected Employment Discrimination Cases," *Academy of Management Journal,* June 1982, pp. 392–406. See also George F. Dreher and Paul S. Sackett, "Some Problems with Applying Content Validity Evidence to Assessment Center Procedures," *Academy of Management Review,* October 1981, pp. 551–560; Steven D. Norton, "The Assessment Center Process and Content Validity: A Reply to Dreher and Sackett," *Academy of Management Review,* October 1981, pp. 561–566; Paul R. Sackett and George F. Dreher, "Some Misconceptions about Content-Oriented Validation: A Rejoinder to Norton," *Academy of Management Review,* October 1981, pp. 567–568.

29. Bucalo, op. cit., p. 11.

30. Leland C. Nichols and Joseph Hudson, "Dual-Role Assessment Center: Selection and Development," *Personnel Journal,* May 1981, pp. 380–386.

31. Ibid., p. 382.

32. "How to Spot the Hotshots," *Business Week,* Oct. 8, 1979, pp. 62, 67.

33. William J. Birch, "Performance Appraisal: One Company's Experience," *Personnel Journal,* June 1981, pp. 456–460. For another view see Virginia Bianco, "In Praise of Performance," *Personnel Journal,* June 1984, pp. 40–45, 47–48, 50.

34. Ibid.

35. Norman R. F. Maier, *The Appraisal Interview: Three Basic Approaches,* La Jolla, Calif.: University Associates, 1976.

36. Ibid. See also Robert L. Taylor and Robert A. Zawacki, "Trends in Performance Appraisal: Guidelines for Managers," *The Personnel Administrator,* March 1984, pp. 71–72, 74, 76, 78–80; and Brian L. Davis and Michael K. Mount, "Design and Use of a Performance Appraisal Feedback System," *The Personnel Administrator,* March 1984, pp. 91–97.

37. Miner, op. cit., p. 249.

38. Lazer and Wikstrom, op. cit., p. 31.

39. Kenneth S. Teel, "Performance Appraisal: Current Trends, Persistent Progress," *Personnel Journal,* April 1980, pp. 296–301. See also "Appraising the Performance Appraisal," *Business Week,* May 19, 1980, pp. 153–154.

PART

IV

COMPENSATION AND PROTECTION

Employees must be compensated for their efforts. But compensation goes beyond just wages and salaries. It may include incentives that help relate labor costs to productivity. Almost always, compensation includes a wide range of employee benefits and services that are part of the total compensation package each worker receives. Financial and physical security also are provided to employees because of a variety of federal and state laws.

Each of these topics is discussed in Part IV. They play an important role in any personnel department's attempts to obtain, maintain, and retain an effective work force. Understanding a personnel department's role in compensation and protection is important for your own well-being as an employee and also for the well-being of your present or future employees.

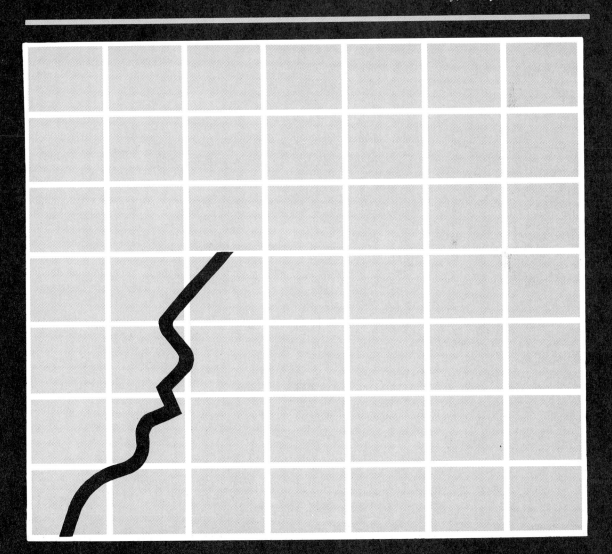

CHAPTER
12

Management's challenge is to create an environment which stimulates people in their jobs and fosters company growth, and a key aspect of the environment is compensation.

Milton L. Rock[1]

Something happened on the road to the 20th century. Employees became "wage earners"—pure and simple—not concerned about the overall success of the business because they did not have a *direct* stake in profits or ownership.

Bert L. Metzger[2]

COMPENSATION MANAGEMENT

CHAPTER OBJECTIVES

After studying this chapter, you should be able to:

1 Discuss the consequences of mismanaged compensation programs.

2 Explain the objectives of effective compensation management.

3 Describe how wages and salaries are determined.

4 Identify the major issues that influence compensation management.

5 Evaluate the advantages and disadvantages of incentive systems.

6 Explain the major approaches to group incentive plans.

Compensation is what employees receive in exchange for their work. The personnel department's management of this key activity helps ensure employee satisfaction, which in turn helps the organization obtain, maintain, and retain a productive work force. Without adequate compensation, current employees are likely to leave, and replacements will be difficult to recruit. Other implications of pay dissatisfaction are diagrammed in Figure 12-1.

The outcomes of pay dissatisfaction shown in Figure 12-1 may detract from the organization's productivity and evidence a decline in the quality of work life. In severe cases, the desire for more pay may lower performance, increase grievances, or cause workers to search for new jobs. And the lower attractiveness of poorly compensated jobs can lead to absenteeism and other forms of employee withdrawal. Even overpayment of wages and salaries can harm the organization and its people. Overpaid employees may feel anxiety, guilt, and discomfort.[3] High compensation costs can reduce the firm's competitiveness and lessen its future ability to provide attractive jobs. This balance between pay satisfaction and organization competitiveness underlies most of the personnel department's compensation efforts.

Within this balance of satisfaction and competitiveness, compensation

Figure 12-1
A Model of the Consequences of Pay Dissatisfaction

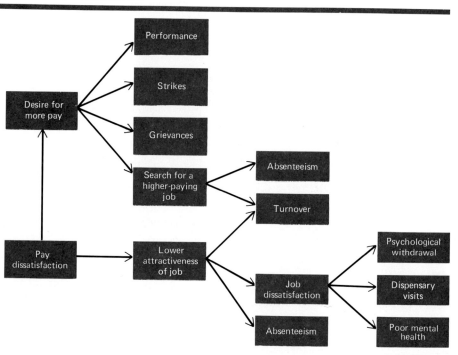

Source: Edward E. Lawler III, *Pay and Organizational Effectiveness: A Psychological View,* New York: McGraw-Hill Book Company, 1971, p. 233. Used with permission of the McGraw-Hill Book Company.

specialists can make a significant contribution to the organization's overall strategic objectives by the way they manage the firm's compensation program. An example comes from one of the twenty largest banks in the United States, the Marine Midland Bank.

As *Fortune* described it: "The Marine Midland Bank has always been an oddity. Founded in 1929, Marine grew over the decades through a series of acquisitions in which 75 local and regional banks in upstate New York were loosely joined with a money-center bank in New York City. With headquarters in Buffalo, Marine has had trouble attracting the kinds of talented young employees who flock to such slick, big-city banks as Morgan Guaranty and Citibank. Marine also has enjoyed little success in attracting the more lucrative kinds of customers—large corporations and wealthy individuals. . . . Now all this is changing."[4]

The bank is trying to reform itself by changing its policies, strategies, and organizational design in hopes of developing a more assertive organizational culture that will allow the bank to become a dominant force in its markets. Part of that strategy is to reshape employee attitudes. To change employee attitudes and become more assertive in its old and new markets, Marine Midland is revamping its approach to compensation management. Salaries and benefits are increasing rapidly. But these improvements are being tied to employee performance. Top performers, as measured against the new strategies, will be eligible for dramatic increases in their compensation. By rewarding employees and top management for actions that match the bank's new direction, Marine Midland plans to grow faster and make a bigger impact on the financial community.[5]

Strategy and compensation at Marine Midland Bank

It is too early to tell how successful Marine Midland will be in the difficult task of changing its organization's culture. However, by rewarding the types of results it wants from its management and employees, the bank's compensation policies are providing reinforcement so that new behaviors are more likely to occur.

Since compensation affects employees and the organization, this chapter examines the requirements of an effective compensation system and discusses the objectives and procedures used to administer it.[6] The chapter then concludes with a review of two financial incentives. Chapters 13 and 14 focus on employee benefits and services.

OBJECTIVES OF COMPENSATION MANAGEMENT

The management of compensation must meet several objectives. Sometimes these objectives, listed in Figure 12-2, conflict with one another, and trade-offs must be made.[7] For example, to retain employees and to ensure equity, wage and salary analysts pay similar amounts for similar jobs. But a recruiter may want to offer an unusually high salary to attract a qualified recruit. At this point, the personnel manager must

Trade-offs

- *Acquire qualified personnel.* Compensation needs to be high enough to attract applicants. Since companies compete in the labor market, pay levels must respond to the supply and demand of workers. But sometimes a premium wage rate is needed to attract applicants who are already employed in other firms.

- *Retain present employees.* When compensation levels are not competitive, some employees quit. To prevent employee turnover, pay must be kept competitive with that of other employers.

- *Ensure equity.* The administration of wages and salaries strives for internal and external equity. *Internal equity* requires that pay be related to the relative worth of jobs. That is, similar jobs get similar pay. *External equity* involves paying workers at a rate equal to the pay that similar workers receive in other companies.

- *Reward desired behavior.* Pay should reinforce desired behaviors and act as an incentive for those behaviors to occur in the future. Good performance, experience, loyalty, new responsibilities, and other behaviors can be rewarded through an effective compensation plan.

- *Control costs.* A rational compensation program helps an organization to obtain and retain its work force at a reasonable cost. Without a systematic wage and salary structure the organization could overpay or underpay its employees.

- *Comply with legal regulations.* As with other aspects of personnel management, wage and salary administration faces legal constraints. A sound pay program considers these constraints and ensures compliance with all government regulations that affect employee compensation.

- *Further administrative efficiency.* In pursuing the other objectives of effective compensation management, wage and salary specialists try to design the program so that it can be efficiently administered. Administrative efficiency, however, should be a secondary consideration compared with other objectives.

Figure 12-2
Objectives Sought Through
Effective Compensation Management

make a trade-off between the recruiting and the consistency objectives. Other objectives of compensation seek to reward desired behavior and to control costs. These objectives can conflict, too. For example, Marine Midland's top management wants to reward outstanding performance with raises, but every raise adds to costs.

Regardless of the trade-offs, an overriding objective is to maintain legal compliance. For example, the Fair Labor Standards Act of 1938 requires employers to pay minimum wages and time and a half for overtime. Periodically, Congress raises the minimum wage, and employers must comply regardless of their other objectives. Likewise, the Equal Pay Act requires employers to provide equal pay for equal work without regard to a person's sex. Discrimination in pay among workers 40 to 70 years of age is outlawed by the Age Discrimination in Employment Act. And Title VII of the 1964 Civil Rights Act prohibits discrimination in pay because of race, sex, religion, or national origin. (Each of these laws is discussed in Chapter 3). Regardless of its compensation strategy, each company must comply with the laws that affect wages and equal employment opportunity.

Compensation objectives are not rules. They are guidelines. But the better the objectives in Figure 12-2 are followed, the more effective the wage and salary administration will be. To meet these objectives, compensation specialists

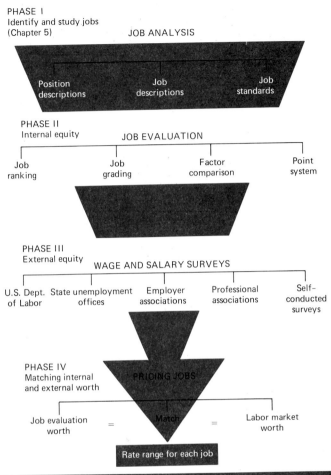

PHASE I
Identify and study jobs
(Chapter 5)   JOB ANALYSIS

Position descriptions   Job descriptions   Job standards

PHASE II
Internal equity   JOB EVALUATION

Job ranking   Job grading   Factor comparison   Point system

PHASE III
External equity   WAGE AND SALARY SURVEYS

U.S. Dept. of Labor   State unemployment offices   Employer associations   Professional associations   Self-conducted surveys

PHASE IV
Matching internal
and external worth   PRICING JOBS

Job evaluation worth   =   Match   =   Labor market worth

Rate range for each job

Figure 12-3
Major Phases of Compensation Management

evaluate every job, conduct wage and salary surveys, and price each job. Through these steps, the appropriate pay level for each job is determined. Figure 12-3 depicts these three major phases of compensation management. Each phase is discussed in the following sections.

JOB EVALUATION

Job evaluations are systematic procedures to determine the relative worth of jobs. Although there are several different approaches, each one considers the responsibilities, skills, efforts, and the work conditions of the job. The purpose of job evaluation is to decide which jobs should be paid more than others.

Since evaluation is subjective, it is conducted by specially trained personnel, called job analysts or compensation specialists. When a group of managers or specialists is used, it is called a *job evaluation committee.*[8] As explained in Chapter 5, the committee begins with a review of job analysis information to learn about the duties, responsibilities, and working conditions. With this knowledge, it determines the relative worth of jobs by selecting a job evaluation method. The most common ones are job ranking, job grading, factor comparison, and the point system.[9]

Job Ranking

The simplest and least precise method of job evaluation is *job ranking.* Specialists review the job analysis information. Then each job is ranked subjectively according to its relative importance in comparison with other jobs. These are overall rankings, although raters may consider the responsibility, skill, effort, and working conditions of each job. It is quite possible that important elements of some jobs may be overlooked while unimportant items are weighted too heavily. Even more damaging, these rankings do not differentiate the relative importance between jobs. For example, the job of janitor may be ranked as 1, the secretary's job may get a 2, and the office manager is ranked 3. But the secretarial position may be three times as important as the janitorial job and half as important as the job of office manager. The job ranking approach does not allow for these relative differences between jobs. Pay scales based on these broad rankings ensure that more important jobs are paid more. But since the rankings lack precision, the resulting pay levels may be inaccurate.

Job Grading

Job grading, or job classification, is a slightly more sophisticated method than job ranking, though still not very precise. It works by having each job assigned to a grade, as explained in Figure 12-4. The standard description in the figure that most nearly matches the job description determines the grade of the job. Once again, more important jobs are paid more. But the lack of precision can lead to inaccurate pay levels. The largest user of this approach has been the U.S. Civil Service Commission, which gradually is replacing this method with more sophisticated approaches.

Factor Comparison

The *factor comparison method* requires the job evaluation committee to compare critical job components. The critical components are those factors common to all the jobs being evaluated—such as responsibility, skill, mental effort, physical effort, and working conditions.[10] Each of these factors is compared, one at a time, with the same factor for the other jobs. This evaluation allows the committee to determine the relative importance of each job. The factor comparison method involves the following five steps:

Step 1: Determine the critical factors Analysts must first decide which factors are common and important in a broad range of jobs. The critical factors shown in Figure 12-5 are the ones most commonly used. Some or-

Directions: To determine appropriate job grade, match standard description with job description.

Job Grade	Standard Description
I	Work is simple and highly repetitive, done under close supervision, requiring minimal training and little responsibility or initiative. *Examples:* Janitor, file clerk
II	Work is simple and repetitive, done under close supervision, requiring some training or skill. Employee is expected to assume responsibility or exhibit initiative only rarely. *Examples:* Clerk-typist I, machine cleaner
III	Work is simple, with little variation, done under general supervision. Training or skill required. Employee has minimum responsibilities and must take some initiative to perform satisfactorily. *Examples:* Parts expediter, machine oiler, clerk-typist II.
IV	Work is moderately complex, with some variation, done under general supervision. High level of skill required. Employee is responsible for equipment or safety; regularly exhibits initiative. *Examples:* Machine operator I, tool and die apprentice
V	Work is complex, varied, done under general supervision. Advanced skill level required. Employee is responsible for equipment and safety; shows high degree of initiative. *Examples:* Machine operator II, tool and die specialist

Figure 12-4
A Job Classification Schedule
for Use with the Job Grading Method

ganizations use different factors for managerial, professional, sales, and other types of jobs if the factors in the figure are considered inappropriate.

Step 2: Determine key jobs   *Key jobs* are those that are commonly found throughout the organization and are common in the employer's labor market. Common jobs are selected because it is easier to discover the market rate for them. Ideally, these benchmark jobs should be accepted by employees as key jobs and should encompass a wide variety of critical factors to be evaluated.

Step 3: Apportion present wages for key jobs   The job evaluation committee then allocates a part of each key job's current wage rate to each critical factor as shown in Figure 12-5. The proportion of each wage assigned to the different critical factors depends on the importance of the factor.

For example, a janitor receives $4.50 an hour. This amount is apportioned in Figure 12-5 as follows: 40 cents for responsibility, 60 cents for skill, 30 cents for mental effort, $1.70 for physical effort, and $1.50 for working conditions. In apportioning these wage rates, the evaluation committee must make two comparisons. First, the amount assigned to each factor

CRITICAL FACTORS	MACHINIST	FORKLIFT DRIVER	SECRETARY	JANITOR	FILE CLERK
			KEY JOBS		
Responsibility	$ 2.20	$1.80	$1.20	$ .40	$ .95
Skill	4.00	1.50	1.60	.60	1.20
Mental effort	2.00	.80	1.30	.30	.90
Physical effort	2.00	1.10	.70	1.70	.70
Working conditions	.70	.60	.60	1.50	.60
Total	$10.90	$5.80	$5.40	$4.50	4.35
Wage rate	$10.90	$5.80	$5.40	$4.50	$4.35

Figure 12-5

The Apportionment of Wages for Key Jobs

should reflect its importance when compared with other factors of the job. For example, if $4 is assigned to skill and $2 is assigned to physical effort for a machinist, this implies that the skill factor is two times as important as the physical effort. Second, the amount allocated to a single factor should reflect the relative importance of that factor among the different jobs. For example, if the responsibility of a secretary is three times that of a janitor, then the money allocated to a secretary for responsibility ($1.20) should be three times that allocated to a janitor (40 cents).

Step 4: Place key jobs on a factor comparison Once the wage rates are assigned to the critical factors of each key job, this information is transferred to a factor comparison chart, such as the one in Figure 12-6. The titles of key jobs are placed in the columns according to the amount of wages assigned to each critical factor. In the responsibility column, for example, the secretary title is placed next to the $1.20 rate to reflect how much the secretary's responsibility is worth to the organization. This job also appears under the other critical factors according to the relative worth of these factors in the job of secretary. The same assignment process takes place for every other key job.

Step 5: Evaluate other jobs The titles of key jobs in each column of Figure 12-6 serve as benchmarks. Other nonkey jobs are then evaluated by fitting them on the scale in each column.

For the job of senior maintenance mechanic, the evaluation committee compares the responsibility of the mechanic with the responsibility of other key jobs already on the chart. It is decided subjectively that the mechanic's responsibility is between that of the forklift driver and the secretary. And since the mechanic's job requires about three-fourths of the mechanic's skills, the skill component of this job is placed just below that of the machinist in the skill column. This procedure is repeated for each critical factor. When the task is completed, the committee can determine the worth of the mechanic's job, which is:

Responsibility	$1.45
Skill	3.00
Mental effort	2.70
Physical effort	1.40
Working conditions	1.30
	$9.85

By using this same procedure, the committee can evaluate every other job in the organization. When the evaluations are completed, the job evaluation committee can rank every job according to its relative worth as indicated by its wage rate. These rankings should be reviewed by department managers to verify their appropriateness.[11]

Results should
be reviewed.

Point System

Research shows that the *point system* is used more than any other method.[12] This system evaluates the critical factors of each job. But instead of using wages, as the factor comparison method does, it uses points. Although more difficult to develop initially, the point system is more precise than the factor comparison method because it can handle critical factors in more detail. This system requires six steps and is usually implemented by a job evaluation committee or by an individual analyst.

Most popular method

Step 1: Determine critical factors   The point system can use the same factors as the factor comparison method, but it usually adds more detail by breaking down these factors into subfactors. For example, Figure 12-7 shows how the factor of responsibility can be broken down into *(a)* safety of others, *(b)* equipment and materials, *(c)* assisting trainees, and *(d)* product and service quality.

Step 2: Determine levels of factors   Since the extent of responsibility, or other factors, may vary from job to job, the point system creates several levels associated with each factor. Figure 12-7 shows four levels, although more or fewer may be used. These levels help analysts to reward different degrees of responsibility, skills, and other critical factors.

Step 3: Allocate points to subfactors   With the factors listed down one side of Figure 12-7 and the levels placed across the top, the result is a point system matrix. Starting with level IV, the job evaluation committee subjectively assigns points to each subfactor. This allocation allows the committee to give very precise weights to each element of the job. For example, if safety (100) is twice as important as assisting trainees (50), then it is assigned twice as many points.

Step 4: Allocate points to levels   Once the points for each job element are assigned under level IV, analysts allocate points across each row to reflect the importance of the different levels. For simplicity, equal point differences

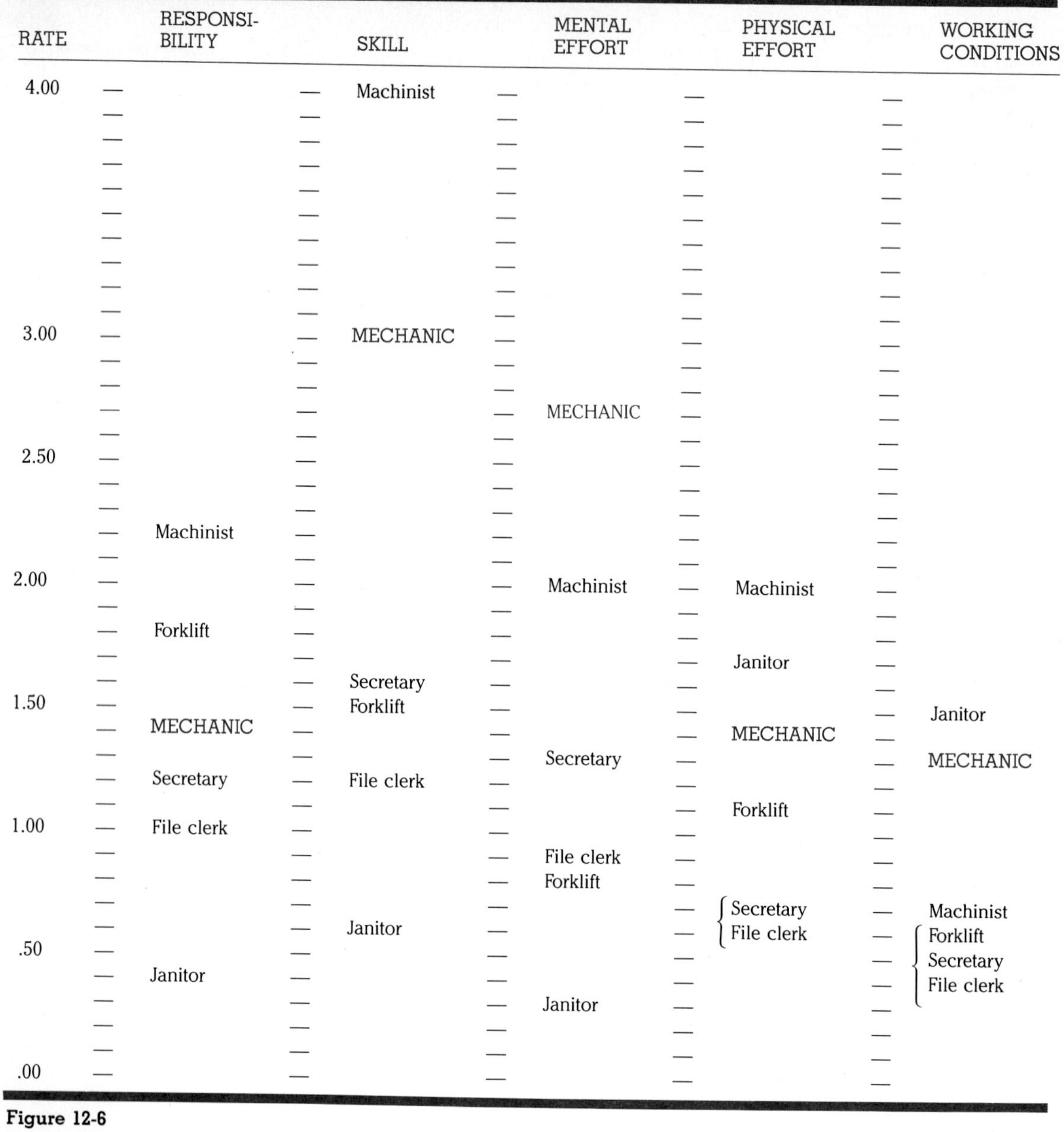

RATE	RESPONSI-BILITY	SKILL	MENTAL EFFORT	PHYSICAL EFFORT	WORKING CONDITIONS
4.00		Machinist			
3.00		MECHANIC			
			MECHANIC		
2.50					
	Machinist				
2.00			Machinist	Machinist	
	Forklift				
				Janitor	
		Secretary			
1.50		Forklift			Janitor
	MECHANIC			MECHANIC	MECHANIC
			Secretary		
	Secretary	File clerk		Forklift	
1.00	File clerk				
			File clerk / Forklift		
		Janitor		{ Secretary / File clerk	Machinist
.50					{ Forklift / Secretary / File clerk
	Janitor				
			Janitor		
.00					

Figure 12-6
A Factor Comparison Chart

usually are assigned between levels, as was done for "safety of others" in Figure 12-7. Or point differences between levels can be variable, as shown for "assisting trainees." Both approaches are used depending on the importance of each level of each subfactor.

CRITICAL FACTORS	LEVELS			
	MINIMUM I	LOW II	MODERATE III	HIGH IV
1. *Responsibility*				
a. Safety of others	25	50	75	100
b. Equipment and materials	20	40	60	80
c. Assisting trainees	5	20	35	50
d. Product/service quality	20	40	60	80
2. *Skill*				
a. Experience	45	90	135	180
b. Education/training	25	50	75	100
3. *Effort*				
a. Physical	25	50	75	100
b. Mental	35	70	105	150
4. *Working conditions*				
a. Unpleasant conditions	20	40	60	80
b. Hazards	20	40	60	80
Total points				1000

Figure 12-7
A Point System Matrix

Step 5: Develop the point manual Analysts then develop a point manual. It contains a written explanation of each job element, as shown in Figure 12-8 for responsibility of equipment and materials. It also defines what is expected for the four levels of each subfactor. This information is needed to assign jobs to their appropriate level.

Step 6: Apply the point system When the point matrix and manual are ready, the relative value of each job can be determined. This process is subjective. It requires specialists to compare job descriptions with the point manual for each subfactor. The match between the job description and the point manual statement reveals the level and points for each subfactor of every job. The points for each subfactor are added to find the total number of points for the job. Here, for example, is the matching process for a machine operator I:

> The job description of a machine operator I states that the "operator is responsible for performing preventive maintenance (such as, cleaning, oiling, and adjusting belts) and minor repairs." The sample point manual excerpt in Figure 12-8 states, "Level III: . . . performs preventive maintenance and minor repairs. . . ." Since the job description and the point manual match at level III, the points for the equipment subfactor are 60. Repeating this matching process for every subfactor yields the total points for the job of machine operator I.

After the total points for each job are known, the jobs are ranked. As with the job ranking, job grading, and factor comparison systems, this relative ranking should be reviewed by department managers to ensure that it is appropriate.

1. RESPONSIBILITY

   b. *Equipment and materials.* Each employee is responsible for conserving the company's equipment and materials. This includes reporting malfunctioning equipment or defective materials, keeping equipment and materials cleaned or in proper order, and maintaining, repairing, or modifying equipment and materials according to individual job duties. The company recognizes that the degree of responsibility for equipment and material varies widely throughout the organization.

   Level I.   Employee reports malfunctioning equipment or defective materials to immediate superior.

   Level II.   Employee maintains the appearance of equipment or order of materials and has responsibility for the security of such equipment or materials.

   Level III. Employee performs preventive maintenance and minor repairs on equipment or corrects minor defects in materials.

   Level IV.   Employee performs major maintenance or overhauls of equipment or is responsible for deciding type, quantity, and quality of materials to be used.

Figure 12-8

A Point Manual Description of "Responsibility: Equipment and Materials"

Variations

Beyond the four job evaluation methods discussed in this section, many other variations exist. Large organizations often modify standard approaches to create unique in-house variations. The Salt River Project, a large quasi-government utility, for example, has been working to make its job evaluation methods even more objective than a traditional point system.[13] The "Hay Plan" is another variation widely used by U.S. and Canadian firms. This proprietary method is marketed by a large consulting firm, Hay and Associates, and relies on a committee evaluation of critical job factors to determine each job's relative worth. Although other job evaluation approaches exist, all effective job evaluation schemes attempt to determine a job's relative worth to ensure internal equity.

WAGE AND SALARY SURVEYS

All job evaluation techniques result in a ranking of jobs based upon their relative worth. This ensures *internal* equity. That is, jobs that are worth more will be paid more. But how much should be paid? What constitutes *external equity?*

To determine a fair rate of compensation, most firms rely on *wage and salary surveys.* These surveys discover what other employers in the *same* labor market are paying for specific key jobs. The *labor market* is the area from which the employer recruits. Generally, it is the surrounding area within commuting distance from the employer. However, the firms may have to compete for some workers in a labor market that extends beyond their community. Consider how the president of one large university viewed the labor market:

External equity and labor markets

Our labor market depends on the type of position we are trying to fill. For the hourly paid jobs such as janitor, clerk, typist, and secretary, the labor market is the surrounding metropolitan community. When we hire professors, our labor market is the entire country. We have to compete with universities in other parts of the country to get the type of faculty member we seek. When we have the funds to hire a distinguished professor, our labor market is the free world.

Sources of Compensation Data

Wage and salary survey data are benchmarks against which analysts compare compensation levels. This survey information can be obtained in several ways. One source is the U.S. Department of Labor. It periodically conducts surveys in major metropolitan labor markets. Sometimes these surveys are out of date in a fast-changing labor market, and so other sources may be needed. Many state unemployment offices also compile wage and salary information for distribution to employers. If done frequently, this information may be current enough for use by compensation analysts. A third source of compensation data may be an employer association, which surveys member firms. Employer associations, or a fourth source—professional associations—may be the only source of compensation data for highly specialized jobs.

Sources of survey data

    The major problem with all of these published surveys is comparability. Analysts cannot always be sure that their jobs match the jobs reported in the survey. Matching job titles may be misleading. Federal, state, or association job descriptions may be considerably different, even though the jobs have the same title. Since most published surveys rely on the *Dictionary of Occupational Titles* (DOT), the company's descriptions should be compared with those in the DOT.

Survey Procedures

To overcome the limitations of published surveys, some personnel departments conduct their own wage and salary survey.[14] Since surveying all jobs is cumbersome and expensive, usually only key jobs are used. A sample of firms from the labor market is selected. Finally, these organizations are contacted by phone or mail to learn what they are paying for the key jobs. Most companies are willing to cooperate since they too need this information. Contacts through professional associations, such as the American Society for Personnel Administration or the American Compensation Association and their local affiliates, can further aid this process. Again, it is important to make sure that the comparisons are using similar jobs and not just similar titles.

    As a result of the job evaluation process, all jobs are ranked according to their relative worth. Through wage and salary surveys, the rate for key jobs in the labor market also is known. This leaves the last phase of wage and salary administration: pricing the jobs.

PRICING JOBS

Pricing jobs includes two activities: establishing the appropriate pay level for each job and grouping the different pay levels into a structure that can be managed effectively.

328

Pay Levels

The appropriate pay level for any job reflects its relative and absolute worth. A job's relative internal worth is determined by its ranking through the job evaluation process. The absolute worth of a job is controlled by what the labor market pays for similar jobs.

Scattergram

In order to set the right pay level, the job evaluation rankings and the survey wage rates are combined through the use of a graph called a *scattergram*. As Figure 12-9 shows, the vertical axis is for pay rates. If the point system is used to determine the ranking of jobs, the horizontal axis is for points. The scattergram is created by plotting the total points and wage level for each *key job*. Thus each dot represents the intersection of the point value and the wage rate for a particular key job. For example, key job A in Figure 12-9 is worth 500 points and is paid $6 an hour.

Wage-trend line

Through the dots that represent key jobs, a *wage-trend line* is drawn as close to as many points as possible. (This line can be done freehand or, more accurately, by a statistical technique called the *least squares method*.)[15]

The wage-trend line helps to determine the wage rates for nonkey jobs. There are two steps involved. First, the point value for the nonkey job is located on the horizontal axis. Second, a line is traced vertically to the wage-trend line, then horizontally to the dollar scale. The amount on the vertical scale is the appropriate wage rate for the nonkey job.

For example, nonkey job B is worth 700 points. By tracing a vertical line up to the wage-trend line and then across to the vertical (dollar) scale, it can be seen in Figure 12-9 that the appropriate wage rate for job B is $7 per hour.

Figure 12-9
The Development of a Wage-Trend Line

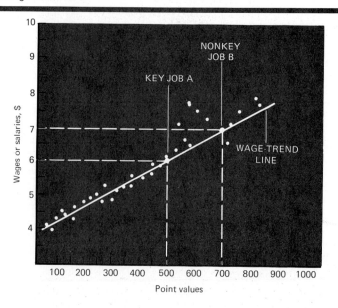

The Compensation Structure

A medium-sized organization with 2000 workers and 325 separately identifiable jobs would present the wage and salary analyst with complex problems. The existence of 325 separate wage rates would be meaningless because the differences in wages between each job might be no more than a few cents.

Compensation analysts find it more convenient to lump jobs together into *job classes*. In the job grade approach, jobs are already grouped into predetermined categories. With other methods, the grouping is done by creating job grades based on the previous ranking, pay, or points. In the point system, for example, classifications are based on point ranges: 0 to 100, 101 to 150, 151 to 200, and so forth. This grouping causes the wage-trend line to be replaced by a series of ascending dashes, as shown in Figure 12-10. Thus all jobs in the same class receive the same wage rate. A job valued at 105 points, for example, receives the same pay as a job with 145 points. Too many grades defeat the purpose of grouping; and too few groupings result in workers with jobs of widely varying importance receiving the same pay.

The problem with flat rates for each job class is that exceptional performance cannot be rewarded. To give a worker a merit increase requires moving the employee into a higher job class.[16] This upsets the entire balance of internal equity developed through job evaluations. To solve these problems, most firms use rate ranges for each class.[17]

Rate ranges are simply pay ranges for each job class. For example, suppose the wage-trend line indicates that $8 is the average hourly rate for a particular job class. Every employee in that class gets $8 if a flat rate is paid. With a rate range of $1 for each class, a marginal performer can be paid $7.50 at the bottom range, as indicated in Figure 12-11. Then an average performer is placed at the midpoint in the rate range, or $8. When performance appraisals (discussed in

Margin notes: Job classes · Rate ranges

Figure 12-10
The Impact of Job Classes on the Wage-Trend Line

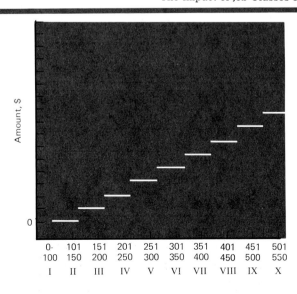

	0-100	101 150	151 200	201 250	251 300	301 350	351 400	401 450	451 500	501 550
	I	II	III	IV	V	VI	VII	VIII	IX	X

Amount, $

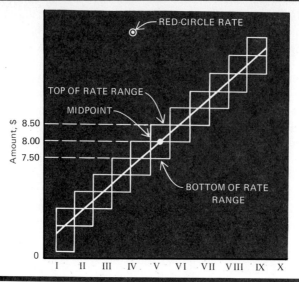

Figure 12-11
Varying Wage Rates for Job Classes

Chapter 11) indicate above-average performance, the employee may be given a *merit raise* of, say, 25 cents per hour.[18] If this performance continues, another merit raise of 25 cents can be granted. Once the employee reaches the top of the rate range, no more wage increases will be forthcoming. Either a promotion or a general across-the-board pay raise needs to occur for this worker's wages to exceed $8.50. An across-the-board increase moves the entire wage-trend line upward.[19]

As new jobs are created, the wage and salary section of the personnel department performs a job evaluation. From this evaluation, the new job is assigned to an appropriate job class. If rate ranges are used, the new incumbent will start at the bottom of the range and receive raises, where appropriate, to the top of the rate range.

CHALLENGES AFFECTING COMPENSATION

Even the most rational methods of determining pay must be tempered by several challenges. The implication of these contingencies may cause wage and salary analysts to make further adjustments to employee compensation.

Prevailing Wage Rates

Some jobs must be paid more than is indicated by their relative worth because of market forces.

In the late 1960s, there was a scarcity of computer specialists. Fitting these jobs onto a wage-trend line often resulted in a wage rate below prevailing rate. Since demand outstripped supply, market forces caused wage rates for these specialists to rise above their relative worth when compared with other jobs. Firms that needed these talents were forced to pay a premium. Diagrammatically, these rates appear on a wage chart as a *red-circle rate* (Figure 12-11). The term "red-circle rate" arises from the practice of marking out-of-line rates with a red circle on the chart.

Red-circle rates

Union Power

When unions represent a portion of the work force, they may be able to use their power to obtain wage rates that are out of proportion to the relative worth of the jobs. For example, wage and salary studies may determine that $6.50 an hour is appropriate for a truck driver. But if the union insists on $7, the personnel department may believe that paying the higher rate is less expensive than a strike. Sometimes the union controls most or all of a particular skill, such as carpentry or plumbing. This enables the union to raise the prevailing rate for those jobs.

Productivity

Companies must make a profit to survive. Without profits, the company cannot attract the investors necessary to remain competitive. Therefore, a company cannot pay its workers more than the workers give back to the firm through their productivity. However, if this should happen, (because of scarcity or union power), the company must either redesign those jobs, train new workers to increase their supply, automate, or go out of business.[20]

Productivity and survival

Wage and Salary Policies

Most organizations have policies that cause wages and salaries to be adjusted. One common policy is to give nonunion workers the same raises that are given to the unionized employees. Some companies have a policy of paying a premium above the prevailing wages to minimize turnover or to recruit the best workers. Also, some companies have automatic cost-of-living clauses that give employees automatic raises when the U.S. Department of Labor's cost-of-living index increases.[21] Raises or policies that increase employee compensation move the wage-trend line upward.

Government Constraints

The United States is a nation of wage earners. What people earn affects the economy and the general welfare of the population. Since the 1930s, the federal government has regulated some aspects of compensation.

The *Fair Labor Standards Act* (FLSA) of 1938 is the most comprehensive law affecting compensation management. It sets minimum-wage, overtime pay, equal pay, child labor, and record-keeping requirements. The minimum-wage and overtime provisions require employers to pay at least a minimum hourly rate of pay regardless of the worth of the job. (When the minimum is increased by law, it may mean that the wages of those who already earn above the minimum are adjusted accordingly. If those just above minimum wage do not also get raises, wage differentials are squeezed together.[22] This is called *wage compression*.) Overtime pay also is regulated. For every covered job, the

Wage compression

organization must pay 1½ times the employee's regular pay rate for all hours over forty per week. Executive, administrative, professional, and other groups of employees are exempt from the overtime provisions. Failure to comply can lead to serious back-pay claims. For example, the U.S. Postal Service agreed to pay $400 million to 800,000 present and past employees after it underpaid them from 1974 to 1978.

In 1963, the FLSA was amended by the Equal Pay Act. This amendment was passed to eliminate sex-based discrimination in pay. It requires employers to pay men and women equal wages when their jobs are equal in skill, effort, and responsibility.[23] As explained more fully in Chapter 3, the government enforces these provisions by requiring wrongdoers to equalize pay and make up past

AT&T   discrepancies. In one incident, for example, American Telephone and Telegraph was required to pay $6,300,000 to 6100 female employees whose pay suffered because of their sex.[24]

Comparable Worth versus Equal Pay

As first mentioned in Chapter 3, an important issue in compensation management and in equal opportunity is *comparable worth.* According to this idea, jobs of comparable value to the organization should be paid equally. Comparable worth goes beyond equal pay for equal work. The equal pay concept has been enacted into law and requires an employer to pay men and women the same

Equal pay exceptions   wage or salary when they do the same work. Exceptions to equal pay are allowed when a valid seniority or merit system exists. Employers can pay more to senior workers or to workers who perform better and merit higher pay. Exceptions also are allowed when pay is determined by the employee's production, such as in the case of sales commissions.[25]

The comparable worth theory, however, takes a slightly different perspective. It would require employers to pay equal wages for jobs of comparable value. For example, if a nurse and an electrician both received approximately the same number of job evaluation points under the point system, they would have to be paid the same wage or salary, regardless of market conditions. This approach to compensation is sought by some people as a means of eliminating the historical gap between the incomes of men and those of women. (In the United States women earn about 60 percent as much as men do.) This gap exists, in part, because women have traditionally found work in lower-paying occupations—such as teaching, retailing, and nursing. Part of the difference in earnings also results from women leaving the work force to have and care for children. And part of the difference may result from discrimination. Although comparable worth approaches may reduce the gap, this compensation theory

Theory versus   ignores marketplace realities. If, in the previous example, nurses were paid
market reality $20,000 a year and electricians were paid $30,000, comparable worth would require paying the nurses $30,000 a year even though wage and salary surveys showed the market rate to be $20,000. (To pay the electricians $20,000 would be appropriate under the comparable worth doctrine but impractical if their market rate was $30,000 a year.) Should legislative bodies or the courts mandate comparable worth, compensation analysts would face a major challenge in restructuring their wage and salary plans to comply while trying to obtain,

maintain, and retain an optimal and cost-effective work force.[26] They also might find it difficult to recruit for certain jobs because demand might exceed supply and rates could not easily be adjusted because of legal restraints.

FINANCIAL INCENTIVE SYSTEMS

Incentive systems link compensation and performance by paying employees for their actual results, not for seniority or for hours worked. Employees who work under a financial incentive system find that their performance determines, in whole or in part, their income. One of the most significant benefits of financial incentives is that better performance is reinforced on a regular basis. Unlike raises and promotions, the reinforcement is generally quick and frequent—usually with each paycheck. Since the worker sees the results of the desired behavior quickly, that behavior is more likely to continue. The employer benefits because wages are given in proportion to productivity, not for the indirect measure of time worked. And if the system motivates employees to expand their output, recruiting expenses for additional employees and capital outlays for new work stations are minimized. As one economist observed:

> With fixed wages individual workers also have little incentive to cooperate with management or to take the initiative in suggesting new ideas for raising productivity. At the level of the individual worker, higher productivity has no immediate payoff—wages are fixed for the length of the contract. The immediate effect of higher productivity is, in fact, negative. Less labor is needed, and the probability of layoffs rises.
>
> The higher productivity growth rates of the Japanese may also be due to their bonus system that encourages labor to take a direct interest in raising productivity.[27]

Offsetting these advantages are significant problems. The administration of an incentive system can be complex. As with any control system, standards have to be established and results must be measured. For many jobs, the standards and measures are too imprecise or too costly to develop. This means that the incentive system may result in inequities. For example, sometimes workers make more money than their supervisors, who are on salary. Another problem is that the employee may not achieve the standard because of uncontrollable forces, such as work delays or machine breakdowns.

Unions often resist incentive systems because they fear management will change the standard, and employees will have to work harder for the same pay. This fear of a speedup often leads to peer pressure against anyone who exceeds the group's output norms. The advantages of the incentive system are essentially lost when group pressures restrict output. Furthermore, incentives tend to focus efforts on only one aspect of the work (output, sales, or stock prices), sometimes to the exclusion of other dimensions (quality, service, and long-term objectives).

Limited focus

A discussion of some of the more common incentive systems follows.

Piecework

Piecework is an incentive system that compensates the worker for each unit of output. Daily or weekly pay is determined by multiplying the output in units times the rate per unit. For example, in agricultural labor, workers are often paid a specific amount per bushel of produce picked. Piecework does not always mean higher productivity, however. As the Hawthorne studies showed, group norms may have a more significant impact if peer pressure works against higher productivity. And in many jobs it may be difficult to measure the person's productive contribution (for example, a receptionist) or the employee may not be able to control the rate of output (as with an assembly-line worker, for example).

Production Bonuses

Production bonuses are incentives paid to workers for exceeding a specified level of output. They are used in conjunction with a base wage rate or salary. Under one approach, the employee receives a predetermined salary or wage. Then through extra effort that results in output above the standard, the worker gets a supplemental bonus, usually figured at a given rate for each unit of production over the standard. Another variation rewards the employee for saving time. For example, if the standard time for replacing an automobile transmission is four hours and the mechanic does it in three, the mechanic may be paid for four hours. A third method combines production bonuses with piecework by compensating workers on an hourly basis, plus an incentive payment for each unit produced. In some cases, the employee may get a higher piece rate once a minimum number of units are produced. For example, the employee may be paid $6 an hour plus 25 cents per unit for the first thirty units each day. Beginning with the thirty-first unit, the bonus may become 35 cents.

Commissions

In sales jobs, the salesperson may be paid a percentage of the selling price or a flat amount for each unit sold. When no base compensation is paid, the salesperson's total earnings come from commissions. Real estate agents and automobile salespeople are often on this form of straight commission.

Maturity Curves

Maturity curves

What happens when technical or scientific employees reach the top of their rate range? Generally, still higher increases can be achieved only by promotion into a management position. To provide an incentive for technical people, some companies have developed *maturity curves*, which are adjustments to the top of the rate range for selected jobs. Employees are rated on productivity and on experience. Outstanding contributors are assigned to the top curve, as shown in Figure 12-12. Good, but less outstanding, performers are placed on the next-to-top curve. Through this technique, high-performing professionals continue to be rewarded for their efforts without being required to seek a management position to increase their earnings.

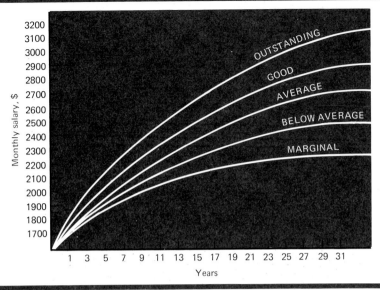

Figure 12-12
Maturity Curves for Professionals
with Varying Degrees of Performance

Executive Incentives

Executive incentives vary widely. Young and middle-aged executives are likely to desire *cash bonuses* to meet the needs of a growing or maturing family. As employees get older, they often feel that their need for present income is offset by retirement considerations. In some cases, bonuses may be deferred until the executive reaches the lower tax rates of retirement.

Executives are sometimes granted *stock options*—the right to purchase the company's stock at a predetermined price. This price may be set at, below, or above the market value of the stock. Thus the executive has an incentive to improve the company's performance. Stock options can be arranged so that the tax impact is minimized. If the stock option program meets Internal Revenue Service guidelines, the resulting income is taxed at the capital gains rate rather than at the higher personal income tax rates most executives face. This further increases the value of the incentive to the executive.

Stock options

Other forms of executive incentives exist, including incentive systems that allow executives to design their own compensation package. The common element in most executive incentive plans, however, is their relation to the performance of the organization. When these systems do not relate the incentive to performance, no matter what they are called, they are not incentive plans. And executive incentives are increasingly geared to promote long-term perform-ance.[28]

What focus should executive incentives have?

Group Incentive Plans

Performance is often a group effort. In recognition of this fact, several plans have been developed to provide incentive for teamwork. Most of them fall into one of the following categories: production incentives, profit sharing, or cost reduction plans.

Production incentive plans These plans allow groups of workers to receive bonuses for exceeding predetermined levels of output. They tend to be short-ranged and related to very specific production goals. For example, a work team may be offered a bonus for exceeding predetermined production levels. Or it may receive a per-unit incentive, which results in a group piece rate.

One well-publicized example comes from Nucor Corporation.

Corporate strategy and compensation tactics

Nucor's management transformed the company into a steel producer in the late 1960s, when the North American steel industry was beginning to face strong competition from European and Japanese producers. Nucor's strategy was to "build plants economically and run them very efficiently with high productivity."[29] One of Nucor's tactics was an incentive plan.

Nucor's nonunion production workers earn a base wage below that of employees in the United Steelworkers union. But if they reach progressively higher production targets, the Nucor workers can supplement their weekly pay with bonuses ranging from 100 to 200 percent of their base wage. If production does not reach the target, no bonuses are paid regardless of the reasons for the production shortfall.

The results? Workers are motivated to work as a team and find ways to improve productivity. Employees who do not do their share receive considerable peer pressure. Workers earn about 20 percent more than their unionized counterparts and about 250 percent more than the average hourly paid production worker in South Carolina, the home of Nucor's flagship steel mill. The company has been able to add mills in Texas, Nebraska, and Utah while producing steel at prices equal to or below foreign producers.[30]

Profit-sharing plans Profit-sharing plans share company profits with the workers. The effectiveness of these plans may suffer because profitability is not always related to the employee's performance. A recession or new competitors may have a significant impact. Even when outside sources do not seriously affect results, it is difficult for employees to perceive their efforts as making much difference. Some companies further reduce the effectiveness of the incentive by diverting the employee's share of profits into retirement plans. Thus the immediate reinforcement value of the incentive is reduced because the incentive is delayed. However, when these plans work well, they can have a dramatic impact on the organization and create a sense of trust and a feeling of common fate among workers and management. One example comes from the American Velvet Company, a leading producer of velvet.

A corporate turnaround through compensation

"Located in the rural seacoast town of Stonington, Connecticut, American Velvet is one of the largest manufacturers of velvet cloth in the United States. Within a remarkably stable industry whose product and process has not changed substantially since the Eighteenth Century, American Velvet has become a model of economic efficiency and effectiveness through the development of a 'people-oriented' organization.

"The company has experienced great success through the mechanisms of a profit-sharing plan (on top of high wages relative to the industry average) and open, sincere, personal communications based upon a healthy and cooperative management-union relationship.

"Deteriorating labor-management relations resulted in a bitter strike, a lockout, and the near demise of the company in 1939. In an effort to break the stalemate, the president (and major stockholders) shifted from the belligerent adversary relationship that had developed between management and labor. He agreed to reopen the plant and institute a major profit-sharing plan for all employees. The local union, suspicious of what was then an innovative, if not radical departure from common practice, declined the profit-sharing plan. They agreed to return to work for a wage increase and other work rule changes.

"At the end of the year, the president calculated the company profit; and with no legal contractual obligation, paid a profit-sharing bonus to the employees. Thus began a relationship built on mutual trust, understanding, and communications—a relationship that continues today.

"American Velvet regularly pays 27 percent of before-tax profits to employees through a plan that is now part of the union contract. The profit-sharing plan is considered a major factor in overcoming the adverse effects of undesirable working conditions."[31]

Cost-reduction plans   Some critics of group incentive plans argue that profit-sharing schemes, such as those found at American Velvet, do not always reward the employee's efforts if profits fall for reasons beyond the employee's control. For example, the average bonus received by workers at Lincoln Electric fell from $22,690 one year to $15,460 the next year because of a slowdown in the economy during the early 1980s. Although $15,460 is a considerable bonus, the amount is influenced by forces outside the employees' control.

Lincoln Electric

Another approach is to reward workers for something they can control: labor costs. Most cost-reduction plans seek ideas for ways to reduce costs. Many times, a committee of employees will be formed to open new lines of communication that allow these ideas to be heard. At the same time, the plans enable workers to participate more fully in the firm's day-to-day operations. Perhaps the best known of these approaches is the *Scanlon Plan*, which bases bonuses on improvements in labor costs as compared with historical norms.[32] Under a Scanlon type of group incentive, employees aim to reduce costs and then share in the savings that result. If, for example, employee productivity increases at the American Valve and Hydrant Manufacturing Company, the ratio of payroll costs to net sales revenue improves. These savings are then shared with employees in the form of a bonus. *Rucker* and *Improshare* plans are similar to the Scanlon approach, but they differ in how bonuses are calculated and in other administrative matters. All three of these approaches differ from profit-sharing in that they focus on something the employee can influence (costs) and not on something that the employees may control only indirectly (profitability).

Scanlon Plan

Compensation consists of more than wages, salaries, and bonuses. Remuneration includes an ever-growing list of fringe benefits and services. Although these benefits are referred to as noncash compensation, they are a significant part of most employer's total labor costs. The next chapter describes the range of fringe benefits and services offered by employers.

Next chapter

SUMMARY

Employee compensation, if properly administered, can be an effective tool to improve employee performance, motivation, and satisfaction. Pay programs that are mismanaged may lead to high turnover, high absenteeism, more grievances, poor performance, and job dissatisfaction.

For compensation to be appropriate, it must be internally and externally equitable. Through job evaluation techniques, the relative worth of jobs is determined. This ensures internal equity. Wage and salary surveys are then used to determine external equity.

The process of wage and salary administration is influenced by several challenges including union power, the productivity of workers, the company's compensation policies, and government constraints on pay. The Fair Labor Standards Act is the major federal law affecting compensation management. It regulates minimum wages, overtime, and child labor. The Equal Pay Act seeks to eliminate sex-based pay differentials.

Another dimension of compensation management is financial incentives. Individual incentives attempt to relate pay to productivity. Group plans have the same objectives, but the relationship is often not as direct or obvious to workers. Some approaches pay a bonus for reaching a production target, others share the company's profits with workers, and still other approaches share savings in labor costs.

TERMS FOR REVIEW

Job evaluations	Scanlon plan
Job ranking	Prevailing wage rates
Job grading	Comparable worth
Factor comparison method	Wage and salary surveys
Key jobs	Merit raise
Point system	Red-circle rate
Production bonuses	Fair Labor Standards Act
Profit sharing	Maturity curves
Stock options	Piecework
Rate range	Wage compression

REVIEW AND DISCUSSION QUESTIONS

1. Suppose you manage a small business with thirty employees. You discover that some employees are motivated by money, while others are motivated by security. For those who want more money you provide an incentive plan in which their income is determined by their productivity. The other employees have a fair salary. What problems might arise?

2. Why is job analysis information, discussed in Chapter 5, necessary before job evaluations can be performed?

3. Suppose that when you interview new employees, you ask them what they think is a fair wage or salary. If you hire them, you pay them that amount as long as it is reasonable and not below minimum-wage laws. What problems would you expect?

4. Assume your company has a properly conducted compensation program. If several employees ask you why they receive different hourly pay rates even though they perform the same job, how would you respond?

5. Why are the factor comparison method and the point system more widely used than the job ranking or the job grading approaches to job evaluation?

6. If you are told to find out what competitors in your area are paying their employees, how would you get this information without conducting a wage and salary survey?

7. Even after jobs are priced using a wage-trend line, what other challenges might cause you to adjust some rates upward? Downward?

8. Since financial incentives give employees feedback about their performance and relate pay to productivity, why do most companies pay wages and salaries rather than financial incentives?

INCIDENT 12-1

Compensation Administration at Reynolds Plastic Products

The Reynolds Plastic Products Corporation was recently purchased by a much larger organization: International Plastics, Inc. The personnel director of International Plastics is concerned that the wage and salary policies are irrational and, in some cases, actually violate federal laws. To evaluate the compensation system of the Reynolds Plastic subsidiary, a recent personnel management graduate, Thea Silverstein, was assigned to make an investigation. The key points of her report are summarized below:

A. The wage range for hourly employees is from $2.85 per hour to $6.98.

B. The amount of overtime paid by Reynolds is very modest; overtime is paid for all hours over 180 per month.

C. The wage rates for different workers vary widely even on the same job; those employees who are heads of households receive approximately 18 percent more than those workers who are not heads of households. Most of the heads of households are men.

D. On highly technical jobs, the firm pays a rate that is 20 percent above the prevailing wage rate for these jobs. All other jobs are paid an average of 15 percent below the prevailing rate.

E. Turnover averages a modest 12 percent. However, in technical jobs turnover is less than 2 percent; in nontechnical jobs turnover is nearly 20 percent. Absenteeism follows the same pattern.

1. What laws probably are being violated?

2. Develop a step-by-step plan of actions you would take and the order in which you would undertake them if you were made personnel director of the Reynolds subsidiary.

INCIDENT 12-2

Incentives at Karma Records

Joe Karma had owned and operated Karma records since its founding in 1979. Joe was often heard to say, "I believe in paying people for what they do, not for how many hours they work." This management philosophy was expressed through a variety of incentive plans that Joe designed himself. Although he was firmly committed to the use of incentives, he hired a management consulting team to make recommendations about his compensation program.

To help the consultants, Joe wrote down the major features of each incentive program. His notes were as follows:

A. Executives do not own any stock. But they each get $1000 for every dollar the stock price increases from the previous year.

B. Every time sales go up 10 percent, all the hourly employees get a day off with pay, or they can work one day at double-time rates.

C. Production workers get paid 18 cents for each record they press and 3 cents for each record they package.

D. Sales personnel get a $50 savings bond each time a new record store or department store starts stocking Karma records.

1. What problems do you see with the incentives for (a) executives, (b) hourly workers, (c) production workers, (d) salespeople?

2. If you were a member of the consulting team, what incentives would you recommend for each group?

REFERENCES

1. Milton L. Rock, *Handbook of Wage and Salary Administration,* New York: McGraw-Hill, 1972, p. xiii.

2. Bert L. Metzger, *Profit Sharing: A Natural for Today's Changing Work Force/Economy,* Evanston, Ill.: Profit Sharing Research Foundation, 1982, p. 7.

3. Edward E. Lawler III, *Pay and Organizational Effectiveness: A Psychological View,* New York: McGraw-Hill, 1971, p. 71.

4. Arthur M. Louis, "In Search of Style at the 'New Marine,'" *Fortune,* July 25, 1982, p. 40.

5. Ibid, p. 44.

6. George W. Bohlander, "A Statistical Approach to Assessing Minority/White Pay Equity," *Compensation Review,* Fourth Quarter, 1980, pp. 15–24. See also David W. Belcher, "Pay Equity or Pay Fairness," *Compensation Review,* Second Quarter, 1979, pp. 31–37. See also Elaine Wegener, "Does Competitive Pay Discriminate?" *The Personnel Administrator,* May 1980, pp. 38–43, 66.

7. *Elements of Sound Pay Administration,* Berea, Ohio: The American Society for Personnel Administration and the American Compensation Association, 1981, pp. 1–2. See also Thomas M. Hestwood, "Ensuring the Effectiveness of Compensation Programs," *Compensation Review,* First Quarter, 1979, p. 14, and Robert J. Greene, "Thoughts on Compensation Management in the '80s and '90s," *The Personnel Administrator,* May 1980, pp. 27–28.

8. Allan N. Nash and Stephen J. Carroll, Jr., *The Management of Compensation,* Monterey, Calif.: Brooks/Cole, 1975, pp. 109–111; and Richard I. Henderson, *Compensation Management,* Reston, Va.: Reston Publishing, 1976, pp. 158–159.

9. Marvin G. Dertien, "The Accuracy of Job Evaluation Plans," *Personnel Journal,* July 1981, pp. 566–570.

10. Nash and Carrol, op. cit., p. 132.

11. Eugene J. Benge, "Using Factor Methods to Measure Jobs," in Milton L. Rock (ed.), op. cit., pp. 242–256.

12. Nash and Carrol, op. cit., p. 128.

13. Dertien, op. cit.

14. Michael A. Conway, "Salary Surveys: Avoid the Pitfalls," *Personnel Journal,* June 1984, pp. 62–65. See also Edward Perlin, Irwin Bobby Kaplan, and John M. Curcia, "Clearing Up Fuzziness in Salary Survey Analysis," *Compensation Review,* Second Quarter, 1979, pp. 12–25.

15. The least squares method is explained in most introductory statistics books.

16. Lawrence B. Chonko and Ricky W. Griffin, "Trade-off Analysis Finds the Best Reward Combination," *The Personnel Administrator,* May 1983, pp. 45, 47, 99.

17. William A. Evans, "Pay for Performance: Fact or Fable," *Personnel Journal,* September 1970, p. 731.

18. Douglas L. Fleuter, "A Different Approach to Merit Increases," *Personnel Journal,* April 1979, pp. 225–226, 262. See also James T. Brinks, "Is There Merit in Merit Increases?" *The Personnel Administrator,* May 1980, pp. 59–64; and Richard E. Kopelman and Leon Reinharth, "Research Results: The Effect of Merit-Pay Practices on White Collar Performance," *Compensation Review,* Fourth Quarter, 1982, pp. 30–40.

19. Stephen H. Applebaum and John B. Millard, "Engineering a Compensation Program to Fit the Individual, Not the Job," *Personnel Journal,* March 1976, pp. 121–124.

20. Lester Thurow, "Productivity Pay," *Newsweek,* May 3, 1982, p. 69.

21. During the rapid deflation in early 1983, COLA caused some wages to drop. "The Wage Spiral Has Lost Its Bounce," *Business Week,* Apr. 11, 1983, p. 28.

22. Michael N. Wolfe and Charles W. Candland, "The Impact of the Minimum Wage on Compression," *The Personnel Administrator,* May 1979, pp. 24–28, 40. See also Allen Flamion, "The Dollars and Sense of Motivation," *Personnel Journal,* January 1980, pp. 51–52, 61.

23. *Elements of Sound Pay Administration,* op. cit., p. 23.

24. Ibid., p. 10.

25. Ibid.

26. Judy B. Flughum, "The Employer's Liabilities under Comparable Worth," *Personnel Journal,* May 1983, pp. 400–404, 406, 408, 410, 412. See also Thomas A. Mahoney, "Approaches to the Definition of Comparable Worth," *The Academy of Management Review,* January 1983, pp. 14–22; John R. Schnebly, "Comparable Worth: A Legal Overview," *The Personnel Administrator,* April 1982, pp. 43–48, 90; George L. Whaley, "Controversy Swirls over Comparable Worth Issue," *The Personnel Administrator,* April 1982, pp. 51–61, 92; and Gary R. Siniscalo and Cynthia L. Remmers, "A Special Update: Comparable Worth," *Employee Relations Law Journal,* Winter 1983–1984, pp. 496–499.

27. Thurow, op. cit.

28. Pearl Merey, "Executive Compensation Must Promote Long-Term Commitment," *The Personnel Administrator,* May 1983, pp. 37–38, 40, 42. See also Carl J. Loomis, "The Madness of Executive Compensation," *Fortune,* July 12, 1982, pp. 42–46; and Daniel Seligman, "Believe It or Not, Top-Executive Pay May Make Sense," *Fortune,* June 11, 1984, pp. 57–62.

29. Richard I. Kirkland, Jr., "Pilgrims' Profits at Nucor," *Fortune,* Apr. 6, 1981, p. 44.

30. Ibid., 43–44, 46. See also John Savage, "Incentive Programs at Nucor Corporation Boost Productivity," *The Personnel Administrator,* April 1981, pp. 33–36, 49.

31. William A. Ruch and James C. Hershauer, "Productivity in People-Oriented Organizations," *Arizona Business,* May 1975, pp. 12–13.

32. Robert J. Schulhop, "Five Years with the Scanlon Plan," *The Personnel Administrator,* June 1979, pp. 55–60, 62, 92. See also John Hoerr, "Why Labor and Management Are Both Buying Profit Sharing," *Business Week,* Jan. 10, 1983, p. 84; and Richard I. Henderson, "Designing a Reward System for Today's Employee," *Business,* July–August 1982, pp. 2–12.

CHAPTER

13

The very expensive but often forgotten stepchild
of the total compensation package is that
segment frequently called "fringe benefits."

Richard I. Henderson[1]

EMPLOYEE BENEFITS
AND SERVICES

CHAPTER OBJECTIVES

After studying this chapter, you should be able
to:

1 Describe the objectives of indirect
  compensation.

2 Identify policies that minimize fringe benefit
  costs.

3 Explain the key issues in designing pension
  plans.

4 Identify the administrative problems of
  employee benefits and services.

5 Explain how benefits and services can be
  better administered.

6 Cite benefits and services that are likely to
  become more common in the future.

Are fringe benefits fringes?

To many people, compensation means pay. Anything else an employer might provide is often considered so minor that it is a "fringe benefit." However, in recent years, fringe benefits have grown to become a major part of employee compensation and employer labor costs. According to a survey by the U.S. Chamber of Commerce, fringe benefits cost employers an average of $6627 per employee per year.[2] That figure represents more than 37 percent of the average firm's payroll costs. So for every dollar of payroll costs, 63 cents goes for wages and 37 cents goes toward employee fringe benefits.

Admittedly, wages and salaries are still the major part of most companies' labor costs. But the proportion of payroll costs devoted to employee benefits continues to climb year after year. Figure 13-1 shows a comparison of employee benefits over a twenty-year period for a select group of 175 companies. Although these firms spend a higher proportion of their payroll dollars on benefits (41.2 percent) compared with the average firm (37.3 percent), the growth of benefits as a percent of payroll approximates the experience of many U.S. and Canadian firms.[3]

By moving away from survey averages and looking at one employer's list of benefits, we can see why employee benefits are a major cost item to most companies. Consider just *some* of the fringe benefits one electronics firm provides its employees.

The Intel Corporation is a billion-dollar company that produces sophisticated microelectronics and electronic components for the computer, communications, automotive, and other industries. Although founded only in 1968, it is a fast-growing, profitable company that is responsible for some

Figure 13-1
A Historical Comparison of Major Benefit Categories for 175 Companies

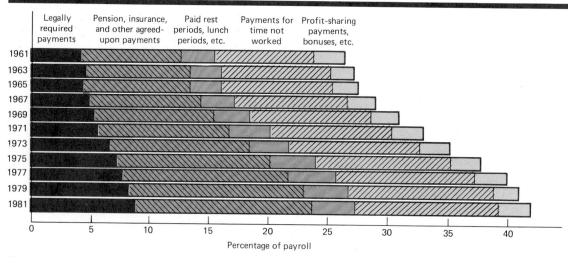

Source: Employee Benefits 1981, Washington, D.C.: Chamber of Commerce of the United States, 1982, p. 28
Redrawn by permission.

of the significant breakthroughs in the development of the computer-on-a-chip technology. Along the way, however, Intel has created a corporate climate that encourages innovation by giving employees rewards and security through its fringe benefit program.

Some of its fringe benefits are listed here: group life insurance, supplemental life insurance, business travel accident insurance, dependent life insurance, accidental death and dismemberment insurance, voluntary short-term disability plan, long-term disability plan, medical insurance, dental insurance, stock purchase plan, tuition reimbursement, vacation and personal absence time, holidays, profit-sharing retirement plan, sabbaticals, company subsidized cafeterias, free parking, rest breaks, and legally required services (social security, workers' compensation).

Intel's benefits and services

This is only a partial list. Other benefits exist at Intel. Moreover, most of these benefits and services are fully paid for by the company. And with the exception of sabbaticals, most large employers could produce a similar list.

The point of this Intel illustration is that fringe benefits encompass a broad range of benefits and services that employees receive as part of their compensation package. As with most employers, pay—or *direct compensation*—at Intel is based on critical job factors and performance. Benefits and services, however, are indirect compensation because they are usually extended as a condition of employment and are not directly related to performance. Included are insurance, security, time-off, and scheduling benefits in addition to educational, financial, and social services.

This chapter describes the objectives behind indirect compensation to explain its role in an organization's overall compensation program. Then common benefits and services are discussed. The chapter ends with an explanation of benefit administration. Legally required benefits and services are covered in Chapter 14.

This chapter

THE ROLE OF
INDIRECT COMPENSATION

Employee benefits and services seek to satisfy societal, organizational, and employee objectives.

Societal Objectives

Industrial societies have changed from rural nations of independent farmers and ranchers to urban nations of interdependent wage earners. This interdependence was illustrated forcefully by mass unemployment during the Great Depression in the 1930s and during the recession in the early 1980s. As a result, industrial societies seek group solutions to societal problems.

To solve social problems and to provide security for interdependent wage earners, governments rely on the support of employers. Through favorable tax treatment, employees can receive most benefits tax-free, while employers can deduct the cost of benefits as a regular business expense. The result has been a

Private versus public
sector burden

rapid growth in indirect compensation.[4] Although government tax collections are reduced by this tax break, these health care, disability, life insurance, and retirement benefits reduce the burden on government and charitable agencies when ill health, death, or retirement occur.

Organizational Objectives

Why employers
offer benefits

From these large outlays for fringe benefits, what do employers gain? Companies such as Intel must offer some fringe benefits if they are to recruit successfully in the labor market. If Intel did not offer health insurance and paid vacations, recruits and present employees would work for Motorola, Texas Instruments, National Semiconductor, or other competitors who did offer these "fringes." Similarly, many employees will stay with a company because they do not want to give up a benefit, and so employee turnover is lowered. For example, an employee who has been at Intel for 6½ years might stay through the seventh year to earn his or her eight-week sabbatical. Likewise, employees at other companies may stay to save pension credits or their rights to the extended vacations that typically come with greater seniority.

Vacations, along with holidays and rest breaks, help employees reduce fatigue and may enhance productivity during the hours the employees do work. Similarly, retirement, health care, and disability benefits may allow workers to be more productive by freeing them of concern about medical and retirement costs. Likewise, if these benefits were not available, employees might elect to form a union and collectively bargain with the employer. (Although collective action is legal, many nonunion employers such as Intel prefer to remain nonunion.) Therefore, it is accurate to state that indirect compensation may:

- Reduce fatigue
- Discourage labor unrest
- Satisfy employee objectives
- Aid recruitment
- Reduce turnover
- Minimize overtime costs

Employee Objectives

Employees usually seek employer-provided benefits and services because of lower costs and availability. For example, company insurance benefits usually are less expensive because the employer may pay some or all of the costs, as Intel does. Even when the workers must pay the entire premium, it is still less expensive because group plans save the insurer the cost of administering and selling many individual policies. With group plans, the insurer also can reduce

Adverse selection

the risk of *adverse selection,* which occurs when individuals sign up for insurance because they are heavy users. Actuaries—the specialists who compute insurance rates—can pass these savings on to policyholders in the form of smaller premiums.

Lower income taxes are another employee objective. For example, an employee in a 20 percent tax bracket has to earn $1000 to buy an $800 policy. But for $1000, the company can buy the same insurance policy and give the worker a $200 raise. After taxes, the employee has a policy and $160 of the raise, while the employer is no worse off. And in many cases the "buying power" of the company can allow it to negotiate a lower cost for the insurance policy. So the policy might cost only $600 instead of $800. Added to the $200 raise, the employer's outlay is only $800. If the employee were paid to buy his or her own policy, the cost would have been $1000. Whether employees will continue to avoid paying taxes on company-provided benefits is uncertain. Fiscal pressures and government deficits may lead to the taxation of these fringes in the future.[5]

When the employer pays for a benefit, the employee achieves "inflation protection." For example, a two-week paid vacation is not reduced in value by inflation. The employee still gets two weeks off with pay. Or if a completely employer-paid insurance premium rises from $800 to $900, the worker is protected (although pay raises may be smaller since the employer has less money available). For some employees, their primary objective may be to obtain benefits and services—especially health care and life insurance. Without employer-provided insurance, these policies may be unobtainable or unaffordable if the employee has a preexisting medical condition.

The objectives of society, organizations, and employees have encouraged rapid growth of benefits and services. This growth has affected all areas of fringe benefits and services including insurance, security, time-off, and work scheduling benefits.

INSURANCE BENEFITS

Insurance benefits spread the financial risks encountered by employees and their families. These risks are shared by pooling funds in the form of insurance premiums. Then when insured risks occur, the covered employees or their families are compensated.

Health-Related Insurance

Health-related coverage is the most common form of insurance provided by employers. In one survey of 994 companies, 99 percent reported making payments for health insurance.[6]

Medical insurance Medical insurance pays for sickness, accident, and hospitalization expenses, up to the dollar limits of the policy. In addition, most policies contain a schedule of benefits. This schedule sets forth which sickness, accident, or hospitalization costs are covered and how much of these expenses will be paid under the policy. Otherwise, the insurer agrees to pay "reasonable and customary" expenses.

If the company pays part or all of the premiums, personnel managers should require a deductible or coinsurance clause in addition to a ceiling on the policy's benefits. A *deductible clause* requires the covered employee to pay a specified amount (usually $100 or $200) before the insurer is obligated to pay. This clause has two significant cost advantages. First, most medical treatment is minor. If each minor illness resulted in a claim, premium costs would soar because of the added administrative burden. Second, a deductible discourages employees from abusing the benefit through overuse. A *coinsurance clause* requires the employee to pay a percentage of the medical expenses—typically,

20 percent. These clauses often specify a maximum liability for the employee. This sharing of costs discourages malingering and gives employees a reason to hold down the medical costs.

Even when deductibles, coinsurance, and policy ceilings have been used, premiums continue to increase rapidly. In one 10-year period, for example, the Ford Motor Company watched its health care costs balloon from 15 cents to 90 cents per hour per employee, and those costs are continuing to climb.[7] For General Motors, its biggest supplier is Blue Cross/Blue Shield of Michigan; the U.S. Steel Company is GM's second largest supplier. U.S. Steel has found it necessary to drop vision-care coverage for its 27,000 management and salaried employees.[8] As a health care adviser to the White House observed, "The cost of health care has risen so high for employers, it's undermining industrial efficiency and international competitiveness. . . ."[9]

Impact of health care costs

Benefit administrators in personnel departments are constantly searching for ways to meet the basic health care needs of employees in ways that minimize the costs to the employer. Some of the more innovative efforts include requirements for second opinions in nonemergency surgery, more extensive preadmission testing to reduce the time spent as a costly hospital inpatient, and a greater analysis of medical claim costs. Through analysis of claims costs, employers try to identify the most cost-effective doctors and hospitals in their area. More and more personnel departments also are publicizing the costs and value of health insurance to employees who too often view health care as "free" since the insurance company pays their medical bills above some nominal deductible.[10]

Other cost reduction methods

Some employers actually pay employees not to get sick, which may be especially effective if the firm uses self-funding to pay its health care benefits. (*Self-funding* occurs when an employer pays the insurance benefits rather than paying an insurance company to do it.) Companies such as Mobil, Chemical Bank, and Quaker Oats are using a method whereby the company sets aside a cash amount that employees can keep if they do not use those moneys for health care.[11]

Quaker Oats cost reduction plan

The Quaker Oats plan is a combination of a flexible spending account and a group plan. Each of the Quaker Oats 6000 employees is given $300 that can be applied to medical-related expenses or taken as cash. If taken as cash, the $300 is not tax-free; the employee then has to pay income taxes on the amount. If the employee does not need the $300 for medical-related expenses, he or she gets to keep what is left. If all 6000 employees reduce their medical expenses and Quaker Oats does not spend the full $1535 per employee that it has allocated for medical benefits, the unspent balance will be shared among employees. The director of employee benefits at Quaker estimates that each employee could receive as much as $200 while reducing the company's total outlays for medical care, and thus for insurance premiums.[12]

Many employers are turning to a different type of health care coverage: *Health Maintenance Organizations* (HMOs). HMOs are organizations that provide their own staff of doctors and facilities. Usually employees and their dependents can use the HMO's services for any health-related problem. Although the premiums are generally higher, employees usually have no deductible or coinsurance if this health-care option is elected. Most large employers in metropolitan areas (where the HMOs are located) offer this alternative to encourage preventive rather than remedial health care. The hope for HMOs is that through better management, preventative care, and fewer unneeded tests, exams, and other medical procedures, costs will rise slower than for those who receive only remedial care. Most large employers offer both HMOs and indemnity plans, which reimburse the employee for medical expenses according to the company's medical insurance plan.

Dental insurance   Dental insurance benefit plans pay for most preventative care and for a portion of needed dental work—sometimes including false teeth and braces. Since most insurance companies and employers have little experience with these plans, the policies tend to be limited in scope. Besides deductibles and coinsurance clauses, most plans have benefit ceilings of $1000 per year or less. On the average, dental insurance costs employers less than one-half of 1 percent of payroll.[13]

> Intel's dental plan, for example, pays for 90 percent of all routine care for employees who have been with the company for three years or more. It pays 70 percent in the first year and 80 percent in the second year. The plan has a one-time deductible of $25 and an annual maximum benefit of $1000 per year per person. Orthodontia is not covered, and other major costs are covered 50 percent by the company and 50 percent by the employee.

Mental health insurance   Mental health coverage is another relatively new area of health insurance. It pays for psychiatric care and counseling. In one study of 1800 firms, hospitalization costs for mental illnesses typically were covered through the company's health insurance program. Most policies, however, have special limits for this coverage. Nevertheless, there does appear to be a trend toward comprehensive, employer-provided mental health insurance. At Intel, for example, the coverage for outpatient psychiatric care is 50 percent of usual, customary, and reasonable charges up to a $25 benefit for each of fifty visits per year.

Life Insurance

Life insurance was the first form of insurance offered to workers by employers. As a result, "group life insurance has become a practically universal element in corporate employee benefit programs."[14] In the majority of firms, the amount of life insurance is a multiple of the employee's salary. For example, the multiple at Intel is 2, so a $20,000-a-year worker has $40,000 of coverage. A few firms provide a flat amount for all workers. Unlike health insurance, employer-provided life insurance is not typically extended to the worker's family members. Most personnel managers and benefits experts reason that life insurance is to

An early benefit

protect the family from the loss of the worker's income. Since group life insurance is considerably cheaper than most private policies, supplemental life insurance also may be available. These supplemental policies allow employees to increase their coverage or to include dependents. However, the employees must pay the premiums.

Disability Insurance

What happens when a worker is disabled and unable to work? Short-term disabilities usually are handled through the company's time-off benefits and *accident and sickness* policies. These policies usually provide $50 to $100 a week for up to six months a year. But if the worker is unable to work for a prolonged time, these solutions soon prove to be unsatisfactory. To protect workers from lost pay that results from extended illnesses or from injuries, most

Long-term disability

companies provide some form of *long-term disability* (LTD) insurance. LTD policies generally have a long waiting period (usually six months). They pay the employee only a fraction (usually 50 to 60 percent) of the income that working would have earned, and benefits usually end within a few years unless the insured is unable to perform any type of work. All of these features keep the employer's costs down while protecting the worker without encouraging malingerers. At Intel, there is a 180-day wait, after which the employee receives 65 percent of his or her base monthly earnings up to a maximum of $4000 a month. The payment is reduced by any social security or workers' compensation payments received by the employee.

EEO implications

Cost-saving measures may not discriminate against protected classes under equal employment laws. For example, disability payments must be extended to pregnant women if such payments are made to other workers for non-job-related disabilities. Personnel departments that discriminate against pregnant women in their disability policies (or in medical benefits) may be in violation of equal employment laws.[15]

Other Related Benefits

The economies of group plans have led a few companies to provide a variety of other insurance programs. Some employers offer group home owners' and group automobile insurance. Since individual rates vary widely, and not all employees have houses or cars, employers seldom contribute to the cost of these premiums. However, Procter & Gamble, Honeywell, Control Data, and others do provide financial assistance to employees who adopt children.[16]

Legal insurance

A new benefit that is likely to become widespread is group legal services. Under these plans employees gain access to low-cost legal aid. "The basic premise is akin to group medical programs. By pooling prepaid amounts, organized group members can obtain legal assistance that might not be readily available to individuals."[17] Personnel departments usually control these costs through maximum dollar limits on total services received per year or through a dollar limit on each type of legal service, such as selling a house, handling a divorce, or drawing up a will. At present, the unions are encouraging these plans through their negotiations with employers.

EMPLOYEE SECURITY BENEFITS

In addition to insurance, there are noninsurance benefits that enhance employee security. These benefits seek to ensure an income before and after retirement.

Employment Income Security

Discharges or layoffs hold potentially severe economic consequences for an employee. They can be cushioned by employer-provided benefits. *Severance pay* benefits entitle the worker to a lump-sum payment at the time of separation from the company. It is either a flat amount equal to a few weeks' pay or a graduated amount based on salary and length of service with the employer. For top executives, the figure can reach six months' or a year's pay. Personnel policies may limit severance pay to situations where the employee leaves involuntarily and has done nothing wrong, such as in the case of a layoff or a plant closing.

Severence pay

Layoffs also may be eased by accrued vacation pay. A few companies go so far as to provide a *guaranteed annual wage* (GAW). These plans ensure that the worker receives a minimum amount of work or pay. For example, employees may be promised a minimum of 1500 hours of work or pay a year (compared with the "normal" 52 forty-hour weeks for a total of 2080 hours). Some employers guarantee 30 hours per week. Even on layoff, the employees draw some income. Lincoln Electric in Euclid, Ohio, has such a plan, for example.

Guaranteed annual wage

The auto industry is a leader in another benefit: *supplemental unemployment benefits* (SUB). When employees are out of work, state unemployment benefits are supplemented by the employer from moneys previously paid to the SUB fund. This ensures covered employees of an income almost equal to their previous earnings for as long as the SUB fund remains solvent. Take the case of Alfredo Sedona:

Supplemental unemployment benefits

> Alfredo Sedona was put on indefinite layoff. Under the SUB plan, he is entitled to 95 percent of his previous take-home pay, less $12.50 that would otherwise go for commuting, lunches, and other work-related expenses.
>
> Alfredo typically took home $380 a week, therefore he will get $348.50 [($380 × .95) − $12.50]. Since the state unemployment benefits will pay Alfredo $98.50 a week, the SUB plan will pay him $250 a week ($348.50 − 98.50 = $250). Alfredo will get $348.50 until the SUB fund is depleted, he finds another job, or he is called back to work.

Although SUB plans are expensive, personnel specialists find that a very high percentage of workers is available for work when recalled. This high return rate occurs because few employees find jobs that pay as much as they receive while on layoff. One societal drawback is that these unemployed workers have little incentive to find other work, and so they may continue to draw public unemployment funds for a longer period of time than do unemployed workers who have no access to a SUB plan.

352   Retirement Security

Retirement plans originally were designed to reward long-service employees. Through employer generosity and union pressures, retirement plans have grown in scope and in coverage, so that the average firm spends 5.2 percent of its total payroll costs on private pensions in addition to social security costs.[18] And according to the Bureau of Labor Statistics, about 35 percent of the labor force is covered by retirement plans.[19] Of course, nearly all workers are covered by social security.

Developing a retirement plan   When a personnel department decides to develop a retirement plan, several critical questions must be answered. One concern is: Who shall pay for it? In a *noncontributory plan,* the employer pays the entire amount. *Contributory plans* require both the employee and the employer to contribute. Another question is: When will the pension rights vest?

Vesting gives the workers the right to pension benefits even if they leave the

Vesting company. Pension rights usually vest after several years of service. If an employee leaves before pension benefits are vested, the worker has no rights except to regain his or her contributions to the plan. Some pensions have

Portability *portability clauses,* which allow accumulated pension rights to be transferred to another employer.

A third question is: How will the firm meet its financial obligations? Some companies pay pensions out of current income when employees retire. This is

Funded versus
unfunded called an *unfunded plan. Funded plans* require the employer to accumulate moneys in advance so that the employer's contribution plus interest will cover the pension obligation.

Another important question is: Will the plan be *trusted* or *insured?* The trusted plan calls for all moneys to be deposited into a trust fund, usually in a bank. The bank manages and protects the funds; it does not guarantee that the employer's pension liabilities will be met. With an insured plan, the pension moneys are used to buy employee annuities from an insurer. Each annuity represents an insurance company's pledge to pay the worker a given amount per month upon retirement.

Two significant problems have developed in the administration of pension plans. First, some employers go out of business, leaving the pension plan unfunded or only partially funded. Second, some companies minimize their pension costs by having very long vesting periods. Thus an employee who quits or is fired often has no pension rights. Since both of these problems may impose hardships on employees and on the nation's welfare burden, Congress passed the *Employee Retirement Income Security Act* of 1974 (ERISA).

ERISA   ERISA imposed comprehensive restrictions on the operation of

Pension reform pension plans. As can be seen by Figure 13-2, this pension reform law sets forth participation, vesting, and funding requirements. To protect workers in the event of employer insolvency, employers are required to participate in a federal insurance program.

The insurance aspect of ERISA provides employees with a guarantee of a pension even if the employer should go out of business before the pension plan

MAJOR PROVISIONS	
PARTICIPATION	Prohibits plans from requiring an age of eligibility greater than 25 or a period of service longer than 1 year, whichever is later.
VESTING	Plan vesting provision must not be less liberal than one of three following minimum standards: 1. 100 percent vesting after 10 years of service 2. 25 percent vesting after 5 years of service, increasing yearly until 100 percent after 15 years 3. 50 percent vesting as soon as the sum of age and years of service (after 5 years) total 45, reach 100 percent 5 years later.
FUNDING	The plan must fund current year's benefit accruals and must amortize any unfunded costs over 30 years (40 years for existing plans and multi-employer plans).
FIDUCIARY STANDARDS	Establishes the "prudent man" rule as the basic standards of conduct, outlaws various transactions between parties-in-interest, and prohibits investment of more than 10 percent of fund assets in employer securities or real estate.
REPORTING AND DISCLOSURE	Requires the plan to provide participants with a comprehensive booklet describing pension plan provisions and to report annually to the Secretary of Labor on numerous operating and financial details of the plan.
PLAN TERMINATION INSURANCE	Creates a federal insurance organization to protect beneficiaries against loss of vested pension on plan termination where assets are inadequate. Protects benefits up to $750 per month. Initial annual premium for this coverage is $1 per participant (50¢ for multi-employer plan participants) and began on date of enactment for both single- and multi-employer plans
PORTABILITY	Encourages some voluntary portability by allowing a worker, if the employer agrees to it, to transfer his or her pension rights tax free from one employer pension fund to another by establishing a tax free individual retirement account.
JOINT AND SURVIVORSHIP OPTION	Unless a married worker specifically requests the plan's normal retirement benefit, the worker is required to receive a pension payable for his or her lifetime and continuing in 50 percent of that amount to the spouse if the spouse survives the employee. The worker's normal retirement benefit may be actuarially reduced to pay for the cost of this provision.

Source: The American Federationist, October 1975, p. 19. Used by permission.

Figure 13-2
Highlights of the Pension Reform Act

is fully funded. But ERISA is more than just an insurance plan. It requires employers to have their plans funded and vested. Moreover, it requires trustees to apply the "prudent man" rule when investing pension funds and to report annually on the plan's operations. For example, the fiduciary standards set by ERISA prohibit the pension plan from investing in stock or real estate. When the Grumman Corporation put more than 10 percent of its pension fund assets into its own stock to avoid a takeover by the LTV Corporation, the U.S. Department of Labor successfully sued Grumman for violating ERISA.

Portability was also encouraged by the act. *Portability* allows the pension credits earned in one employer's retirement plan to be transferred into another retirement plan when the worker changes companies. About 10 million, mostly unionized, employees have portability in their pension plans.

In the defense contracting industry, for example, engineers change employers when the government contracts they are working on come to an end. As a result, many of them never stay with an employer long enough to earn a vested pension. Lockheed Engineering & Management Services Company recognized this problem and modified its pension plan to make it a more attractive recruiting tool. At this Lockheed subsidiary the retirement program now offers immediate vesting once an employee joins the plan, and it allows portability when the employee leaves.[20]

A recruiting tool

Early retirement   As retirement plans mature, companies tend to liberalize them. Increasingly, this has meant early retirement provisions, which allow workers to retire before age 65. Benefits are normally reduced for early retirement because statistically the employee draws benefits longer, and the employer has less time to fund its share of the pension. Some pensions—those used by the military, for example—pay the retiree an amount based on years of service, regardless of age. When economic conditions require a layoff, the company may encourage senior employees to retire early by reducing or eliminating the penalty for early retirement. This lowers the employer's staffing levels in a voluntary manner.

Retirement counseling   As part of the retirement program, some employers conduct preretirement and postretirement counseling. The primary purpose of *preretirement counseling* is to encourage an employee to plan for retirement. The sooner counseling occurs, the more able the worker is to prepare emotionally and financially. These sessions also are used to explain the nature of the employee's retirement program to indicate the likely adjustments a retiree may face.

Postretirement counseling is designed to ease the transition from worker to retiree. The retiree is made aware of community and company programs for retired people. Retired employees of Mountain Bell Telephone Company, for example, can join an organization of other retired telephone workers. This type of association provides social contacts, community projects, and recreational opportunities.

TIME-OFF BENEFITS

Time periods when the employee is not working but is getting paid are the result of time-off benefits. Most time-off benefits are with pay. Although time-off benefits may seem minor, these outlays are a major contributor to fringe benefit costs, as can be seen in Figure 13-1.

On-the-Job Breaks

Some of the most common forms of time-off benefits are those found on the job. Examples include rest breaks, meal breaks, and wash-up time. A rest from the physical and mental effort of a job may renew employee energy and increase productivity. The major problem for personnel and line managers is the tendency of employees to stretch these time-off periods.

> When one personnel manager was confronted by a supervisor with the problem of stretched breaks, she suggested a simple solution. Each employee was assigned a specific break time—from 9:15 to 9:30 A.M., or 9:30 to 9:45 A.M., for example—but could not leave for break until the preceding employee returned. Since each clerk was anxious to go on break, the peer group policed the length of breaks, and the stretched breaks ended.

Sick Days and Well Pay

Some absences from work are unavoidable. Today, most companies pay workers when they are absent for medical reasons by granting a limited number of sick days per year. Unfortunately, this is often an abused fringe benefit; many workers take the attitude that these are simply extra days off. If the personnel policies prohibit employees from crediting unused sick leave to next year's account, absences increase near the end of the year.[21] To minimize abuses, some companies require medical verifications of illness or pay employees for unused sick leave. Payment for unused sick leave is sometimes called "well pay."

A few firms avoid the abuse question by granting "personal leave days," as Intel does, for example. This approach allows an employee to skip work for any reason and get paid, up to a specified number of days per year. *Sick leave banks* allow employees to "borrow" extra days above the specified number when they use up their individual allocation. Then when they earn additional days, the borrowed days are repaid to the sick leave bank.[22]

Personal leave days

Holidays and Vacations

The average company grants nine holidays. Like sick days, however, this benefit is subject to abuse. Employees sometimes try to stretch the holiday by missing the workday before or after it. Personnel policies that require attendance the day before and after the holiday as a condition of holiday pay lessen this problem. Other firms ignore this issue of "stretched holidays" by using the personal leave days concept instead of sick days. Then when an employee wants to extend a holiday, he or she takes a "personal" day.

"Stretched" holidays

Vacations usually are based on the employee's length of service: for example, one week for one year of service, two weeks for two years' of service, three weeks for five or ten years of employment, and so on. Policies for vacations vary widely. Some companies allow employees to use vacation days a few at a time. Other companies insist that the workers take the vacation all at once. A few employers actually close down during designated periods and require vacations to be taken during that time. (This "plant shutdown" approach is sometimes required to perform major maintenance on equipment.) Still other companies negate the reason for vacations completely by allowing employees to work and receive vacation pay as a bonus.

Intel, for example, created a sabbatical leave policy that is one of the more unusual industrial time-off benefits. It gives permanent U.S. and Canadian employees eight weeks off with full pay after seven years of service. And with executive staff management approval, employees can get up to six months leave with pay for public service, teaching, or exceptional educational opportunities.

Leaves of Absence

Leaves of absence are often granted for pregnancy, extended illness, accidents, summer military camps, jury duty, funeral services, and other reasons specified in a company's personnel policies. Extended leaves are normally without pay. Shorter absences—especially for jury duty or for funerals of close relatives—are often with pay.

WORK SCHEDULING BENEFITS

The length of the typical workweek has declined significantly since the early days of the industrial revolution, as illustrated by Figure 13-3. The norm of a five-day forty-hour workweek remained relatively unchanged from the 1930s to the early 1970s. During the 1970s, however, several new approaches to scheduling work gained popularity: the shorter workweek, flextime, and job sharing.[23]

Shorter Workweeks

A shorter workweek compresses forty hours of work into less than five full days. Some plans even shorten the workweek to less than forty hours. The most popular version has been forty hours of work compressed into four days. Figure 13-4 summarizes the major advantages and disadvantages commonly associated with shorter workweeks. The rankings of these factors are based on a survey of 223 firms. Although the U.S. Department of Labor reported that only 1.9 percent of employers use schedules of less than five days, the same report stated: "The 5-day week, which now seems so firmly entrenched, went through a developmental period in the 1920s that in some ways resembles the present situation in 4-day weeks."[24] It also noted that "the introduction from Europe of a different type of new workweek, flextime, apparently resulted in slower growth of 4-day weeks."[25]

Flextime

Flextime abolishes rigid starting and ending times for the workday. Instead, employees are allowed to report to work at any time during a range of hours. For example, starting time may be from 7 A.M. to 9 A.M., with all employees expected to work the *core hours* of 9 A.M. to 3 P.M. The workday usually remains unchanged at eight hours. Therefore, the end of the workday is also variable.

The outcome of a flextime program, however, is contingent upon the nature of the firm's operations. For example, the major disadvantage of flextime is the difficulty in meeting minimum staffing needs early and late in the day. Assembly-line and customer service operations find this problem to be especial-

Time Table of the Holyoke Mills,

To take effect on and after Jan. 3d, 1853.

The standard being that of the Western Rail Road, which is the Meridian time at Cambridge.

MORNING BELLS.

First Bell ring at 4.40, A. M.   Second Bell ring in at 5, A. M.

YARD GATES

Will be opened at ringing of Morning Bells, of Meal Bells, and of Evening Bells, and kept open ten minutes.

WORK COMMENCES

At ten minutes after last Morning Bell, and ten minutes after Bell which "rings in" from Meals.

BREAKFAST BELLS.

October 1st, to March 31st, inclusive, ring out at 7, A. M.; ring in at 7.30, A. M.
April 1st, to Sept. 30th, inclusive, ring out at 6.30, A. M.; ring in at 7, A. M.

DINNER BELLS.

Ring out at 12.30, P. M.; ring in at 1, P. M.

EVENING BELLS.

Ring out at 6.30.* P. M.

Source: Labor's Long, Hard Road, Air Line Employees Association, International, p. 4. Used by permission.

Figure 13-3
A Typical Work Schedule Prior to the Civil War

ly significant. But in most clerical operations, some users have reported noteworthy successes.[26] For example, Public Law 97-221 allows 325,000 federal employees to work longer hours on certain days in order to have other days, or partial days, off.[27]

Job Sharing

A third approach to employee scheduling that gained popularity during the 1970s is job sharing. *Job sharing* involves one or more employees doing the same job but working different hours, days, or even weeks. Most commonly, two people handle the duties of one full-time job.

Two people doing one job

Karen and Bob Rosen both taught English at Lincoln High School. After Karen had her first child one summer, Karen, Bob, and their principal agreed to a job-sharing arrangement. Bob taught three classes of English literature and composition in the morning. He then drove home, gave Karen the car, and she returned to school and taught three English classes in the afternoon. The school benefited because teachers normally had five classes and a planning period. With job sharing, the school received six

PERCEIVED ADVANTAGES OF THE SHORTER WORKWEEK

RANK ORDER	PERCENTAGE OF RESPONSES	POTENTIALLY ADVANTAGEOUS FACTORS
1	18.8	Less total time would be lost due to startup, washup, breaks, and cleanup.
2	15.8	Absenteeism and turnover rates will be lower.
3	13.2	Efficiency would increase through better utilization of our equipment.
4	12.9	Employee morale and loyalty will be higher.
5	8.1	It would be good public relations and create a progressive image.
6	7.9	It will stimulate employee motivation and higher productivity.
7	7.2	More employees could be scheduled at peak workload days or times.
8	6.2	It would be easier to recruit a large supply of good workers.
9	5.7	It would provide an opportunity to implement other important changes.
10	4.1	It would fulfill the firm's social responsibility to our employees.

PERCEIVED DISADVANTAGES OF THE SHORTER WORKWEEK

RANK ORDER	PERCENTAGE OF RESPONSES	POTENTIALLY DISADVANTAGEOUS FACTORS
1	22.1	Customers or suppliers would be inconvenienced.
2	20.3	It would create too many scheduling and communications problems.
3	12.9	Productivity would be lower once the novelty wore off.
4	12.1	All hours over 8 per day would probably have to be paid as overtime.
5	9.7	The long hours would be boring, monotonous, and tiresome for employees.
6	7.7	Too many employees would be fatigued from moonlighting on second jobs.
7	7.2	If it fails, returning to the five-day workweek would be difficult.
8	4.0	Absenteeism and/or turnover would be greater under a shorter workweek.
9	3.1	Employees would dislike and resist the idea.
10	0.9	Might get bad publicity because the program is not widely accepted.

Source: John W. Newstrom and William B. Werther, Jr., "Managerial Perceptions of the Shorter Workweek," *Arizona Business,* February 1973, pp. 10, 11. Used by permission.

Figure 13-4
Perceived Advantages and Disadvantages
of the Shorter Workweek

classes of English instruction. Bob and Karen also were able to share in raising their child with neither of them completely giving up his or her career.

The major advantage claimed for job sharing is increased productivity from workers who are not fatigued. Problems arise from the increased paperwork and administrative burden associated with two employees doing the job of one. Another problem is that of fringe benefits. Personnel specialists are forced to decide whether job sharers should be given benefits equal to those of other employees or whether the benefits should be scaled down in proportion to the employee's hours.[28] Most state unemployment offices will not scale down unemployment benefits when job sharers are put on layoff status. Instead, job sharers simply are considered ineligible for unemployment compensation.

EMPLOYEE SERVICES

Some companies go beyond pay and traditional benefits and provide services for their employees. The most common ones are educational, financial, and social programs.

Educational Assistance

Tuition refund programs are among the more common employer services. These programs partially or completely reimburse employees for furthering their education. This reimbursement may be limited to courses that are related to the employee's job, or the employer may pay for any educational expenditure. Some companies make the amount of reimbursement contingent upon grades. Beckman Instruments, Inc., for example, refunds 100 percent of the college tuition for an A or a B, 50 percent for a C, and nothing for grades of D or F. In the future, more companies may follow the lead of Kimberly-Clark Corporation:

> Kimberly-Clark created an educational savings account for employees and their dependents. The company gives employees credits for each year of service. Then when an employee or dependent wants to go to college, he or she can be reimbursed partially from the educational savings account established by the company.

Financial Services

Probably the oldest service is the employee discount plan. These programs—common among retail stores and consumer goods manufacturers—allow workers to buy products from the company at a discount. For example, employees of Broadway Department Stores may buy clothes from the store at 10 percent off the retail price.

Credit unions are another well-established employee service. The interest collected by the credit union on loans and investments is distributed to members in the form of dividends. The dividends (interest payments) are allocated in proportion to the amount employees have in their share (savings) account. The lower interest rate on loans, the higher interest on deposits, and the payroll deductions for savings or loan repayment are the major employee advantages.

Stock purchase programs are another financial service. These plans enable employees to buy company stock—usually through payroll deductions. In some stock purchase programs, employee outlays may be matched by company contributions, or the stock may be purchased by employees at a discount from its market value. At Intel, for example, employees in the stock purchase plan can buy company stock at 85 percent of its market price.

An *employee stock option plan* (ESOP) enables the employer to raise money and also encourages employee ownership of stock. The employer sells a block of stock to an employee group, which uses it as collateral for a loan. The proceeds from the loan then repay the company for the stock. The dividends and purchases of stock from the ESOP retire the loan. Employees end up with stock

ESOPs

in the company and share in its prosperity. Of course, if the company faces hard times, the employees may find that their jobs *and* their investments are at risk.

Social Services

A wide range of social services is provided by employers. At one extreme are simple interest groups such as bowling leagues and baseball teams. At the other extreme are comprehensive *employee assistance programs* (EAPs) designed to help employees with personal problems.

EAPs

> Valley National Bank had a high turnover rate among its entry-level workers. After conducting a study, the bank discovered that many new workers had transportation, housing, child-care, and other problems. These difficulties were sometimes insurmountable, and so the employees would quit. To combat this situation, the bank created its "Contact" program. Each employee was informed of the program and given a telephone number to call whenever a work or non-work-related problem occurred. The Contact staff provided individual counseling and/or referred the employee to groups in the community that could help. The program was not limited to recently hired workers, however. To help build better employee relations, the Contact staff tried to assist with all types of problems. This involved the staff in resolving employee quarrels, advising managers of employee complaints, and even helping workers solve family disputes.

Although employee assistance programs like the one at this bank are not a universal benefit, personnel managers realize that workers' problems affect company performance. Employer services that can lessen these problems offer potential dividends in employee performance, loyalty, and turnover.

One employer service with a growing record of success is alcoholic and drug rehabilitation. For example, personnel experts formerly recommended the discharge of alcoholic workers. During recent years, however, an increasing number of personnel departments have implemented *alcohol and drug rehabilitation programs*. This service has saved many otherwise good employees in companies such as Kennecott Copper, Motorola, and General Motors. After the worker is rehabilitated, the company usually gains a hard-working, loyal employee.

Alcohol and drug rehabilitation program efforts

> General Motors Corporation evaluated the job performance of seventy-one alcoholic employees who had been treated in an alcoholic rehabilitation program. The results of a several-month-long experiment showed over an 85 percent decline in employee lost time and a 72 percent reduction in accident and sickness benefits claims.[29] Whether these savings repaid the company's outlays was not reported. However, this limited study indicates that positive benefits accrue to employers who sponsor such programs either separately or as part of a comprehensive employee assistance plan.

Another fast-growing company service is child care. With 49 percent of all mothers with children under age 6 in the work force, reliable child care is a much-sought benefit.[30] A poll of human resource executives revealed that two-thirds of them thought that child care at the workplace would be a common benefit before the end of the 1980s. And since child-care expenses average 10 percent of a working family's gross income, employer-provided child care appears to offer strong recruiting and retention value. Intermedics, Inc., a Texas manufacturer of heart pacemakers, reports a 23 percent drop in turnover and an approximately 2 percent decline in absenteeism since offering its heavily subsidized child-care benefit.[31]

Child-care benefits

Relocation programs are the support in dollars or services that a company provides to its transferred or new employees. At a minimum, this benefit includes payment for moving expenses. Some employees receive fully paid house-hunting trips with their spouses to the new location before the move, subsidized home mortgages, placement assistance for working spouses, and even family counseling to reduce the stress of the move. A transferred employee also may be able to sell his or her home to the employer for the appraised value.[32]

ADMINISTRATION OF BENEFITS AND SERVICES

A serious shortcoming of personnel management has been poor administration of indirect compensation. Even in otherwise well-managed personnel departments, benefits and services have grown in a haphazard manner.[33] Those costly supplements were added in response to social trends, union demands, employee pressures, and management wishes, and so personnel departments seldom established objectives, systematic plans, and standards to determine the appropriateness of the programs. This patchwork of benefits and services has caused several problems.

Problems in Administration

The central problem in supplementary compensation is a lack of employee participation. Once a fringe benefit program is designed by the personnel department and by the labor union, if there is one, employees have little discretion. For example, the same pension and maternity benefits usually are granted to all workers. Younger employees see pensions as distant and largely irrelevant; older workers feel that maternity benefits are unneeded. This uniformity fails to recognize individual differences and wishes. Admittedly, uniformity leads to administrative and actuarial economies; but when employees receive benefits they neither want nor need, these economies are questionable.

Unwanted benefits

Since employees have little choice in their individual benefit packages, most workers are unaware of all the benefits to which they are entitled.

Two researchers designed a study to learn how knowledgeable selected workers were about their benefits. In two different plants—one with a union and one without a union—they asked employees to list all the benefits that they could think of. The average employee could not recall 15 percent of the employer-provided benefits.[34]

This lack of knowledge and the inability to choose appropriate benefits often cause employees to request more benefits to meet their needs. For example, older workers may want improved retirement plans, while younger workers seek improved insurance coverage for dependents. Often the result is a proliferation of benefits and increased employer costs. And perhaps even worse, employee confusion can lead to complaints and dissatisfaction about their fringe benefit package.

Traditional Remedies

The traditional remedy to benefit problems has been to increase employee awareness, usually through publicizing employee benefits.[35] This publicity starts with orientation sessions that explain the benefit programs and provide employee handbooks. Company newspapers, special mailings, employee meetings, bulletin-board announcements, and responses to employee questions are also used to further publicize the organization's benefit package.

In-house "advertising"

The Massachusetts Mutual Life Insurance Company has developed an interesting variation of these traditional approaches. With the consent of the employer, this insurer evaluates the benefits each employee receives and provides a booklet that summarizes this information. A representative of the insurer explains the booklet and indicates gaps in the employee's coverage (with the object of selling the worker any needed insurance).

Publicizing the benefits and services only attacks a symptom of the problem: employee disinterest. Moreover, this reactive approach further adds to the costs of administration through increased "advertising" expenses.

A Proactive Solution: Cafeteria Benefits

Custom designed benefit packages

Cafeteria benefit programs, or variable fringe benefit programs, allow employees to select benefits and services that match their individual needs. Workers are provided a benefit and services account with a specified number of dollars in it. With the money from this account, employees choose and "purchase" specific benefits from among those offered by the employer. The types and prices of benefits are provided to each worker in the form of a computer printout. This cost sheet also describes each benefit. Then, as illustrated in Figure 13-5, employees elect their package of benefits and services for the coming year.

Figure 13-5 indicates how two different workers might spend the $5500 the company grants each employee. Workers A and B elect two different sets of benefits because their personal situations differ dramatically. Worker A is a young parent who is supporting a family and her husband. If they were to

WORKER A	WORKER B
Age 27, female, married with one child. Husband in graduate school.	Age 56, male, married with two grown and married children. Wife does not work.

WORKER A		WORKER B
	Health insurance:	
$ 245	Maternity	0
1935	$100 deductible	0
0	$1000 deductible	$1625
	Life insurance:	
100	$20,000 for worker	100
150	$10,000 for spouse	0
600	Vacations	900
300	Holidays	300
200	Pension plan	1270
0	Jury duty pay	0
100	Disability insurance	100
1870	Sick pay	1205
$5500	Total	$5500

Figure 13-5

Hypothetical Benefit Selection
by Two Different Workers

have another child or if they had some other health-related expense, it might seriously affect their plans, and so they have elected to be well insured for pregnancy and health costs. Worker B can more easily afford unexpected medical expenses, and so he bought health insurance with a larger deductible and allocated fewer dollars for sick pay. Instead, he put a large portion of his benefit moneys into the company pension plan.

Although this approach creates additional administrative costs and an obligation for the personnel department to advise employees, there are several advantages. The main advantage is employee participation. Through participation, workers understand exactly what benefits the employer is offering and can better match their benefits with their needs.[36]

Beyond the wide range of benefits and services described in this chapter, employers are required to provide social security, workers' compensation, and a workplace free from recognizable safety and health hazards. These legally imposed benefits and services are described in Chapter 14, which will conclude this section of the book.

Next chapter

SUMMARY

Employee benefits and services are the fastest-growing component of compensation. Employers have sought to expand them to discourage labor unrest, respond to employee pressures, and remain competitive in the labor market. Employees have desired to obtain benefits and services through their employer because of the low costs, tax advantages, and inflation protection they provide.

Benefits are classified into four major types: insurance, security, time-off, and scheduling benefits. Services include educational, financial, and social programs. This diversity contributes to several serious administrative problems. The most significant problem is the orientation of managers and personnel specialists toward cost savings. In pursuit of administrative and actuarial economies, most companies and unions do not allow individualized benefit packages in indirect compensation programs.

TERMS FOR REVIEW

Adverse selection

Coinsurance clause

Long-term disability insurance

Severance pay

Legal insurance

Portability clauses

Contributory plans

Well pay

Employee Retirement Income
    Security Act (ERISA)

Guaranteed annual wage

Supplemental annual wage

Vesting

Self-funding

Health Maintenance Organizations

Personal leave days

Shorter workweeks

Flextime

Cafeteria benefit program

REVIEW AND DISCUSSION QUESTIONS

1. What factors have contributed to the rapid growth of fringe benefits as a percentage of most employers' total payroll costs?

2. Suppose you were a benefits administrator at the Ford Motor Company and you discovered that health-care costs have increased from 15 to 90 cents per hour in recent years. What actions would you recommend to control these rising costs?

3. Suppose you were requested to explain why employees are better off receiving pay and benefits rather than just getting larger paychecks that include the monetary value of benefits. What arguments would you use?

4. Briefly describe the benefits that an organization might give employees to provide them with greater financial security.

5. Why was the Employee Retirement Income Security Act needed? What are its major provisions?

6. For each of the following groups of employees, what types of problems are likely if a company goes from a five-day forty-hour week to a four-day forty-hour week: (*a*) working mothers, (*b*) laborers, (*c*) assembly-line workers?

7. What are the common problems you would expect to find with the benefits and services program of a large company?

8. If you were asked to increase employee awareness of fringe benefits, what actions would you take without changing the way the company provides benefits? If you could change the entire benefits program, what other methods might you use to increase employee awareness?

INCIDENT 13-1

Soap Producers and Distributors, Inc.

Soap Producers and Distributors, Inc., faced a severe employee turnover problem. The company's annual turnover rate was nearly 40 percent among technical and white-collar workers. Among hourly paid employees, the rate was almost 75 percent.

Wage and salary surveys repeatedly showed that the company's pay levels were 10 to 12 percent above those for comparable jobs in the labor market. The fringe benefit program was not as impressive, but management thought it was competitive. Employees received health and life insurance, paid vacations and holidays, and a Christmas bonus of $100 each. Although some employees complained about the company's benefits, complaints varied widely and no one benefit seemed to be the key issue.

To make Soap Producers and Distributors' problems worse, they operated in a tight labor market. Thus jobs sometimes took weeks to fill. To hire specialized workers almost always meant recruiting them from other cities and paying their moving expenses.

1. What changes do you think should be made in the company's fringe benefit program?

2. What problem in the incident might be solved by a cafeteria approach?

3. To overcome the company's recruitment problems, what other changes do you suggest?

INCIDENT 13-2

Electron Products Pension Plan

Since 1963, Electron Products, Inc., has had a pension plan for all workers with twenty years or more of service with the company. Workers are eligible for a pension beginning at age 65. The amount of the pension is based on the employee's average salary over the last five years of employment. For each year of service, an employee receives 2½ percent of his or her average salary upon retirement. The company, until 1972, always paid pensions out of current earnings. In that year the board of directors decided to fund the pension plan by putting 2 percent of each year's total payroll into either company stock or real estate. Although employees were told that there was an employer-paid pension fund, little explanation was given. Whenever the general manager of the company was questioned about the retirement plan, the only explanation given was that "the company takes care of loyal employees."

1.   What changes must be made in this company's pension plan to comply with the Employee Retirement Income Security Act?

2.   What other changes do you recommend to increase the effectiveness of the pension plan in improving employee morale?

REFERENCES

1.   Richard I. Henderson, *Compensation Management,* Reston, Va.: Reston Publishing, 1976, p. 283.

2.   *Employee Benefits 1981,* Washington, D.C.: Chamber of Commerce of the United States, 1982, p. 5.

3.   Ibid.

4.   J. H. Foegen, "The Creative Flowering of Employee Benefits," *Business Horizons,* May–June, 1982, pp. 9–13.

5.   "Proposal to Tax Employer-Paid Health Plans," *San Francisco Chronicle,* Nov. 26, 1982, p. 4.

6.   *Employee Benefits 1981,* op. cit.

7.   "A Joint Look at Cutting Health Care Costs," *Business Week,* Nov. 17, 1975, p. 49. See also "How to Earn 'Well Pay,'" *Business Week,* June 12, 1978, pp. 143, 146.

8.   "Painful Pinch: More Companies Reduce Health Benefits to Save Cash," *The Wall Street Journal,* Western ed., Jan. 4, 1983, p. 1.

9.   Susan J. Duncan, "What's Next on Health Cost Control," *Nation's Business,* November 1982, p. 24. See also "Shifting Health Costs to Employees 'More Expensive'," *Resource,* June 1984, p. 12.

10. Ibid.

11. Ronald Bujan, "A Primer on Self-Funding Health Care Benefits," *The Personnel Administrator,* April 1983, pp. 61–64.

12. "Paying Employees Not to Go to the Doctor," *Business Week,* Mar. 21, 1983, p. 150. See also Thomas N. Fannin and Teresa Ann Fannin, "Coordination of Benefits: Uncovering a Buried Treasure," *Personnel Journal,* May 1983, pp. 386–391.

13. *Employee Benefits 1981,* op. cit.

14. Mitchell Meyer and Harland Fox, *Profile of Employee Benefits,* New York: The Conference Board, 1974, p. 22.

15. Patricia M. Lines, "Up-date: New Rights for Pregnant Employees," *Personnel Journal,* January 1979, pp. 33–37. See also Nancy Norman and James T. Tedeschi, "Paternity Leave: The Unpopular Benefit Option," *The Personnel Administrator,* February 1984, pp. 39–40, 42–43.

16. "More Companies Aid Employees on Adoptions," *The New York Times,* Aug. 18, 1982, pp. C1, C13.

17. Dave Stack, "Legal Services: An Evolving Union Benefit," *The American Federationist,* January 1975, p. 18.

18. *Employee Benefits 1981,* op. cit., p. 19.

19. Donald R. Bell, "Prevalence of Private Retirement Plans," *Monthly Labor Review,* October 1975, p. 17. See also Douglas C. Kimmel, Karl F. Price, and James W. Walker, "Retirement Choice and Retirement Satisfaction," *Journal of Gerontology,* April 1978, pp. 575–585; and "Inflation Is Wrecking the Private Pension System," *Business Week,* May 12, 1980, pp. 92–96, 99.

20. "Pension Plans Get More Flexible," *Business Week,* Nov. 8, 1982, pp. 82, 87; see also Larry Lang, "The Impact of Job-Hopping on Retirement Benefits," *The Personnel Administrator,* February 1984, pp. 55–56, 58–60.

21. Barron H. Harvey, "Two Alternatives to Traditional Sick Leave Programs," *Personnel Journal,* May 1983, pp. 374, 376–378. See also Richard E. Kopelman, George O. Schneller, IV, and John J. Silver, Jr., "Parkinson's Law and Absenteeism: A Program to Rein In Sick Leave Costs," *The Personnel Administrator,* May 1981, pp. 57–58, 60, 62, 64; Patrick M. Towle, "Calculating Sick Leave and Vacation Time with an Hourly Accrual System," *Personnel Journal,* May 1979, pp. 303–306; and Malcolm H. Morrison, "Retirement and Human Resource Planning for the Aging Workforce," *The Personnel Administrator,* June 1984, pp. 151–152, 154–159.

22. Barron H. Harvey, Judy A. Schultze, and Jerome F. Rogers, "Rewarding Employees for Not Using Sick Leave," *The Personnel Administrator,* May 1983, pp. 55–56, 58–60.

23. John W. Newstrom and Jon L. Pierce, "Alternative Work Schedules: The State of the Art," *The Personnel Administrator,* October 1979, pp. 19–23.

24. Janice Niepert Hedges, "How Many Days Make a Workweek?" *Monthly Labor Review,* April 1975, pp. 33–34.

25. Ibid., p. 33. See also Robert D. Brinton, "Effectiveness of the Twelve-Hour Shift," *Personnel Journal,* May 1983, pp. 393–398.

26. "Flexible Work Hours Get an Enthusiastic Review from Three Companies," *The Wall Street Journal,* Apr. 13, 1976, p. 1. See also Keith E. Barnard, "Flextime's Potential for Management," *The Personnel Administrator,* October 1979, pp. 51–58; Cary B. Barad, "Flextime under Scrutiny: Research on Work Adjustment and Organizational Performance," *Personnel Administrator,* May 1980, pp. 69–74; and David E. Nelson, "Employee Control Is an Important Option in Variable Work Schedules," *The Personnel Administrator,* June 1983, pp. 118–119, 121, 123.

27. "New Laws You May Have Missed," *U.S. News & World Report,* Oct. 4, 1982, p. 74.

28. Michael Frease and Robert A. Zawacki, "Job Sharing: An Answer to Productivity Problems," *The Personnel Administrator,* October 1979, pp. 35–39.

29. "More Help for Emotionally Troubled Employees," *Business Week,* Mar. 12, 1979, p. 102. See also Robert Witte and Marsha Cannon, "Employee Assistance Programs: Getting Top Management's Support," *The Personnel Administrator,* June 1979, pp. 23–28.

30. Foegen, op. cit.

31. "Child Care Grows as a Benefit," *Business Week,* Dec. 21, 1981, pp. 60, 63. See also Sandra E. LaMarre and Kate Thompson, "Industry-Sponsored Day Care," *The Personnel Administrator,* February 1984, pp. 53–55, 58, 60, 62, 64–65.

32. John M. Moore, "The Role Relocation Plays in Management Planning," *The Personnel Administrator,* December 1982, pp. 31–34. See also Earl C. Gottschalk, Jr., "Firms Increasingly Help Spouses of Transferred Employees Find Jobs," *The Wall Street Journal,* Western ed., Jan. 21, 1981, p. 25.

33. Randall B. Dunham and Roger A. Formisano, "Designing and Evaluating Employee Benefit Systems," *The Personnel Administrator,* April 1982, pp. 29–35. See also Philip Kienast, Douglas McAlister, and David Sampson, "The Modern Way to Redesign Compensation Packages," *The Personnel Administrator,* June 1983, pp. 127, 129–130, 133.

34. William H. Holley, Jr., and Earl Ingram II, "Communicating Fringe Benefits," *The Personnel Administrator,* March–April 1973, pp. 21–22. See also Robert Krogman, "What Employees Need to Know about Benefit Plans," *The Personnel Administrator,* May 1980, pp. 45–47.

35. Stephen N. Gerberding, "Communicate Your Benefits Program through an Employee Fair," *The Personnel Administrator,* May 1983, pp. 51–53.

36. Albert Cole, Jr., "Flexible Benefits Are a Key to Better Employee Relations," *Personnel Journal,* January 1983, pp. 49–53. See also William B. Werther, Jr., "A New Direction in Rethinking Employee Benefits," *MSU Business Topics,* Winter 1974, pp. 36–37. See also "Labor Letter," *The Wall Street Journal,* Western ed., Jan. 30, 1979, p. 1; and "IRS Proposes Long-Awaited Flexible Benefit Rules," *Resource,* June 1984, pp. 1, 8.

CHAPTER
14

In recent years, a rapid expansion of government controls has been associated with a growing dissatisfaction with the effects of regulation.

John T. Dunlop[1]

SECURITY, SAFETY AND HEALTH

CHAPTER OBJECTIVES

After studying this chapter, you should be able to:

1 Explain how government furthers employee security.

2 Describe the required employee security programs.

3 Identify the implications of employee security programs.

4 List the objectives of safety and health programs.

5 Describe some of the efforts of OSHA to help employers reduce the burden of its regulations.

6 Summarize the safety and health responsibilities of employers and employees.

C hapter 13 described the benefits and services that employers voluntarily give to their employees. This chapter examines those that are legally required.

Legally required benefits and services are imposed upon an organization by government. They include social security, unemployment compensation, workers' compensation, and occupational safety and health. Since government actions carry the force of law, employers must comply or face legal sanctions.

Why have these benefits and services?

These forms of financial and physical security are required to further societal objectives. In wealthy societies, composed largely of working men and women, it is common to find laws that help employees alter work-related hardships and protect them from future workplace hazards. Long ago industrial nations decided that the consequences of unregulated employment relationships imposed burdens on society. For example, before workers' compensation laws required payment for job-related injuries, much of the burden for those injuries fell on society through government or charitable organizations. Today employers must compensate workers for their on-the-job injuries. Even better than reactive reimbursement are proactive prevention efforts. Here again, laws exist that require employers to provide safe and healthy worksites.

Since all but the smaller employers must comply, the challenge for personnel specialists becomes how to comply proactively with the least costs to the employer and the greatest benefit for the employees. In the area of employee safety and health, few companies have managed better than Du Pont.

Du Pont's nylon fiber plant in Seaford, Delaware, provides an example of the company's safety efforts. The last accident at the plant that was serious enough to cause an employee to miss a day happened when an employee tripped in the parking lot and fractured her wrist. "Like any other accident serious enough to keep one of Du Pont's 140,000 employees off the job for a day or more, this one was reported to Du Pont's chairman within 24 hours."[2] Since that accident, the plant has operated for more than two years without a lost-time case.

Top management involvement at Du Pont

This commitment to safety by top management is reflected by other managers within Du Pont. The plant manager at the Seaford plant, for example, has his staff conduct regular one-hour safety tours that look for deviations from sound safety practices. On one tour, the three safety defects that were found included a worker without his hearing protectors, a ladder leaning against a wall without anyone attending to it, and an open desk drawer that could trip someone. Although these items are seemingly minor in a large nylon plant, attention to such minor "safety defects" prevents them from growing into accidents.

This level of attention to safety does not just happen because top management is notified of accidents. Employee safety and health must be part of an ongoing concern by top management that is built into the firm's culture. Du Pont has been fortunate to have had that concern from its beginning: Pierre Samuel Du Pont founded the American branch of the family and set an early example of top management involvement.

In 1817 he left his sickbed at age 77 to help put out a fire at a gunpowder mill. Today, that aspect of Du Pont's organizational character is reflected in the regular Friday meetings of Du Pont's top management in Wilmington, Delaware; safety is the first agenda item at each meeting. This pattern occurs at lower-level management meetings, too. People inside the company realize that to do a job right, it must be done safely. Supervisors and managers also realize that promotions are hindered by poor safety records.

Has all this attention to safety paid off? "Du Pont, which probably has the lowest accident rate of any major manufacturer, counts savings in the tens of millions a year from its safety programs."[3] For example, in one year, it had 129 lost-time accidents at all of its operations, for an annual rate of 0.12 accidents per 100 workers. This accident rate was 1/23 of the National Safety Council's average for all manufacturers. If Du Pont's rate had been average, its workers' compensation and related costs would have been $26 million higher. That $26 million is equivalent to 3.6 percent of Du Pont's profits. Said another way, Du Pont would have had to sell another $500 million worth of products to make as much money as its safety program saved the company.[4]

An estimated $26 million saved

The apparent key to Du Pont's successful safety record is top management's active commitment. That commitment cascades down the organization to all levels of management. But not all organizations exhibit the commitment that Du Pont does. The result has been government-imposed measures to assure working men and women a base level of financial security along with safe and healthy working conditions. The primary sources of financial and physical protection for workers are outlined in Figure 14-1.

None of the sources of protection shown in the figure fully meet the needs of workers. Instead, employees are provided a floor of protection that is supplemented with company-provided benefits and services. The objective of providing financial security is to ease the monetary burdens of retirement, death,

Figure 14-1
Sources of Financial and Physical Protection for Workers

PROTECTION FOR WORKERS	SOURCES OF PROTECTION
FINANCIAL SECURITY	
Retirement	Social Security Act, 1935
Survivors and dependents	1939 amendments to Social Security
Total disability	1956 amendments to Social Security
Involuntary unemployment	Title IX of the 1935 Social Security Act
Industrial accidents	State workers' compensation acts
PHYSICAL SECURITY	
Unsafe situations and unhealthful work environments	Occupational Safety and Health Act, 1970, and its enforcement agency, the Occupational Safety and Health Administration

long-term disability, and injury. The loss of income from these causes is cushioned by social security. The financial problems of involuntary unemployment are lessened by unemployment compensation. And job-related injuries and death are compensated under workers' compensation laws. The objective in providing physical security is to protect employees from unhealthy environments and from injury-causing situations. These goals are partially achieved through health and safety legislation.

Legally required benefits and services are important to the personnel department for three reasons. First, top management holds the personnel department responsible for meeting these legal obligations. If the department is to meet this responsibility, it must keep the firm in compliance. Second, if the obligations are improperly handled, the result can be severe fines, more taxes, or higher insurance premiums for the company. And third, effective management of these legal requirements can help the personnel department contribute to the organization's objectives, as the safety program at Du Pont illustrates.

FINANCIAL SECURITY

The United States is a nation of workers financially dependent on a paycheck. Anything that keeps people from earning a paycheck threatens their financial security. If enough people are affected, the well-being of society is harmed, and government action becomes likely. Because retirement, disability, layoffs, and injuries limit the earning power of many citizens, government has intervened with social security, unemployment compensation, and a variety of state workers' compensation acts. Each of these interventions into the employment relationship will be discussed.

Social Security

Social security is one of the most comprehensive and least understood social programs ever enacted in the United States. To some, it is a high-priced pension. Others see it as a wide-ranging program of social insurance. Since social security results in payroll deductions, questions and complaints often end up in the personnel department.[5] Personnel specialists then must contend with widely differing views, such as the following:

Chuck DeLeon: With five children and a wife to support, I can't afford social security, even if it is a good deal. More money is taken out of my paycheck every week for social security than for income taxes. My grandfather gets a check every month that amounts to around $240. If he didn't live with my parents, how would he survive? I pay in nearly $70 a month. If I put $70 in a bank every month until I'm 65, I would get a lot more than $240 a month when I retire. I'm against social security.

Martha Kearny: Social security is a great bargain. My parents, who retired last year, receive $490 every month and that goes up with inflation! Even their medical bills are paid by the medicare provisions of social security. I even know one 29-year-old man who gets social security checks because he is disabled.

● *Disability benefits.* After a six-month waiting period, disabled workers can collect social security checks. To qualify, the disability must prevent the individual from working and be expected to last twelve months or result in death.

● *Death benefits.* The surviving spouse or other family member may receive a lump-sum payment upon the death of a worker. This nominal amount is designed to assist with the burial expenses.

● *Survivors benefits.* Dependents of a retired, disabled, or deceased worker may also receive monthly social security checks. Such payments generally are limited to dependent children, parents, or spouse.

● *Health insurance benefits.* Medicare is the portion of social security that helps those over 65 (or under 65 if disabled) meet the costs of health care. Medicare coverage includes hospital insurance (to pay hospital costs), medical insurance (to pay physicians and other nonhospital costs), and payment for kidney transplants or dialysis.

Figure 14-2
Nonretirement Provisions of the Social Security Act,
as Amended

Social security is more than a compulsory retirement plan, although it does provide an income for life at retirement. There are several nonretirement provisions, as the listing in Figure 14-2 explains. These provisions give covered workers and their families disability, death, survivor, and health insurance benefits.

Coverage and administration   The Social Security Act covers virtually all workers in the United States. Benefits are determined by the amount and duration of the worker's earnings. The more an employee earns (up to a limit that changes annually), the more the payroll department is required to deduct from each paycheck. This figure is matched by the employer and paid to the federal government.

Employees with contributions for forty quarters (ten years) are *fully insured* workers. They are eligible for a pension at retirement and for all the benefits   Fully insured workers
explained in Figure 14-2. Those who are fully insured and have paid in at the highest rate receive the largest benefits. The total benefits received may be more or less than the amount credited to the individual's social security account. There also are certain eligibility requirements. For example, if a retired employee takes a part-time job, that employee may lose social security income or have it reduced. This federal program is administered by the Social Security Board in the Department of Health and Human Services.

Implications for personnel management   The implications of social security for personnel departments are several. First, personnel specialists should explain social security to workers. Some employees do not realize that the employer must make these deductions by law. Other employees—especially those with large families and low incomes, like Chuck DeLeon in the previous example—do not understand why social security is a bigger deduction than income tax. Like many people, he also appears to be unaware of the nonretirement benefits explained in Figure 14-2. Personnel specialists can reduce

374

employee confusion and morale-lowering resentment by explaining how social security works. This explanation is an especially important part of any preretirement counseling program, discussed in Chapter 13. The local social security administration office often is able to provide informative booklets that can be used in orientation and in preretirement counseling sessions.

A second implication for personnel experts is to consider social security when designing other benefits and services. For example, one hospital discovered an unintended outcome of its pension plan:

> Exit interviewer: Why are you taking early retirement at age 62?
>
> Housekeeper: I cannot afford to stay here. I can make more money if I retire.
>
> Exit interviewer: How can that be? According to our retirement plan, you are eligible for only 80 percent of your average salary based on the last three years. That's still 20 percent less than you earn now.
>
> Housekeeper: Not if you consider social security. Even with the lower social security rates of early retirement at age 62, I figure I will make $7 more a week by not working. If I stay and work, the government will reduce my social security benefits.

That hospital's retirement plan probably did not intend to encourage retirement in this way. A less expensive program might have freed resources for other employee benefits and services. Likewise, thought should be given to social security when designing health insurance. Kidney dialysis and transplants should be excluded from the company's major medical policy since both types of treatment are covered under social security.

Although social security affects morale and the design of fringe benefits, another obvious implication is cost.[6] The U.S. Chamber of Commerce has reported that the average firm pays 6.3 percent of its payroll for social security.[7] And if declines in the social security reserve fund continue, employer costs are nearly certain to climb as Congress attempts to match revenues and costs of the program through higher payroll taxes.[8]

Unemployment Compensation

Unemployment compensation represents payments to those who lose their jobs. It began as a voluntary fringe benefit in such companies as General Electric and Eastman Kodak.[9] But with the massive unemployment of the 1930s, Congress decided that unemployment compensation should be widely available.

Legally required unemployment compensation began in 1935 under Title IX of the Social Security Act. Under Title IX, the federal government imposed a tax of 3 percent on payrolls. The tax applied to the first $3000 of each covered employee's annual earnings. To encourage state participation, employers could reduce this federal tax from 3.0 percent to 0.3 percent if they paid the difference (2.7 percent) into a qualified state unemployment plan. This tax-offset feature prompted *every* state to create an unemployment compensation program. The moneys collected by each state created the funds from which unemployment compensation claims are paid. The federal share finances the U.S. Employment Service and supports emergency funds against which states can borrow during severe economic downturns. This state-federal partnership still works the same way. However, the tax rate and the tax base have changed. The U.S. Employment Service determines the federal tax rate and tax base and allows each state to set its own tax rates and tax base.[10]

Coverage and administration   Employers with four or more employees must participate in their state unemployment program.[11] Their employees are eligible for compensation if they meet two tests. First, the employee must be *involuntarily separated.* That is, the employee's actions did not cause the unemployment. For example, if a drop in sales causes an employee to be laid off, the employee is considered involuntarily separated. Applicants for unemployment compensation who quit or who are fired for just cause may be denied payments.

Eligibility for unemployment compensation

    The second test requires that the applicant must make a *good-faith attempt* to secure *suitable employment.* A "good-faith attempt" means that the individual is *willing and able* to accept employment. Willingness is usually evidenced by actively looking for another job. This means at least pursuing job interviews arranged by a counselor at the state unemployment office. Being "able" means being available, which explains why full-time college students are often denied unemployment compensation.

> Tim Tara is a junior majoring in management at Midwest University. Three days before he was going to quit his job and return to college, he was laid off. The following week he applied for unemployment compensation, but his application was denied. The clerk at the state unemployment office told Tim that he was considered unable to work since he was a full-time student.

    The phrase "willing and able" does not require acceptance of just any job. Only suitable employment must be accepted. An unemployed engineer cannot be told to accept the job of a janitor, for example, because the job of janitor is not suited to the engineer's training and experience. If an unemployed individual rejects a suitable job, that person is considered unavailable for employment and, therefore, ineligible for unemployment compensation.

    When a claim is received by a state unemployment office, the past employer is allowed to comment. If the claim appears proper, the worker receives weekly compensation until another job is found or for the maximum duration of benefits. Weekly payments typically amount to half or two-thirds of a worker's previous pay, except for highly paid workers who receive up to their state's maximum benefit. If the employer can show that the unemployment was caused by the employee's actions, the claim may be denied or, if paid, not charged to the employer. The benefits do not continue indefinitely. An unemployed worker only receives benefits for a specified period or until a new job is found. During periods of severe unemployment, Congress often extends the duration of benefits for states with high levels of unemployment. As a result, benefits vary from state to state.

Implications for personnel management The unemployment tax is controllable. Employers pay the maximum tax rate in their state *minus* credits for favorable experience. The use of *experience rating* encourages employers to stablize their employment levels in order to pay a lower payroll tax. By stabilizing employment, personnel specialists can make a measurable contribution to the company: a lower unemployment tax.

There are six major ways a personnel department can lower the unemployment tax rate.[12] First, as explained in Chapter 4, human resource planning minimizes overhiring and subsequent layoffs; shortages and surpluses of personnel are anticipated. Then retraining or attrition can lead to proper staffing levels without layoffs. Second, personnel departments can educate other decision makers—particularly production planners and schedulers. Production specialists may not realize that "hire-then-layoff" policies increase payroll costs, which in turn raise production costs and selling prices. Third, personnel can review all discharges to make sure that they are justified. Unjustified dismissal decisions by supervisors can be reversed or changed into intracompany transfers in order to prevent higher payroll taxes.[13]

A fourth approach is to challenge all unjustified claims for unemployment compensation made against the employer. Those claims that are successfully challenged may reduce the employer's costs in the future.

> Kevin Hirtsman was fired for stealing from the company. (The employee manual stated that stealing was grounds for immediate dismissal.) When his claim for unemployment insurance was sent to the company for its comments, the personnel manager replied that Kevin was terminated for cause. Kevin's claim for unemployment compensation was denied. Had the personnel manager not objected to Kevin's claim, the company's unemployment tax rate might have increased.

A fifth way to reduce the tax is to use workweek reductions instead of layoffs. When a company must lower its labor costs, a reduction in everyone's hours rather than a partial layoff does not create claims for unemployment compensation under the plans in most states. And even the smaller paycheck for a short workweek usually exceeds unemployment compensation.

A final means of reducing the unemployment tax is to adopt the "rings of defense" strategy used by Control Data and other companies. As described at the end of Chapter 8, the company contracts some tasks to outside firms. When the work for the permanent full-time Control Data employees is insufficient, these workers begin doing jobs previously handled by outside contractors in order to avoid layoffs.

Experience rating

Ways to reduce this tax

Workers' Compensation

Work-related accidents and illnesses are another threat to the financial security of employees. In the nineteenth century a worker could get compensation for an industrial accident or illness only by suing the employer. With the cost of medical treatment, the loss of income, or the loss of a wage earner, many workers or their families found it financially impossible to bring these suits. The result was a severe burden on society in general and on the affected workers and their families in particular.

Once again the problem became widespread and government acted. Starting in 1908, states began passing *workers' compensation laws.* Today, every state has these laws, which are designed to compensate workers, at least partially, under a wide range of situations. Covered under these laws are the following:

- Medical expenses.

- Lost income due to total disabilities that prevent working. Such disabilities may be temporary (sprains, burns, broken limbs) or permanent (loss of limbs, blindness).

- Death benefits including funeral allowances and survivor benefits.

Services paid for by workers' compensation

For example, every state requires at least partial payment of the medical bill that results from a work-related accident or illness; all but seven states pay the entire bill. Every state pays disabled employees between 55 and 75 percent of their average weekly earnings up to a limit. And all states pay benefits to survivors in the event of death. The actual operation of the law is straightforward. A covered employee with a compensable injury or illness files the proper documentation with the state agency, insurer, or employer. After a waiting period of three to seven days, the employee is compensated at the rate determined by the state.

Coverage and administration   Most employees in the United States are covered under workers' compensation laws. The major exceptions are farm workers, domestics, casual labor, athletes, and small businesses with less than five full-time workers. Since these laws vary from state to state, there are some significant difference in how the law is administered. Most states have compulsory laws, although a few have elective laws.

Compulsory laws require employers to comply fully with the decision of the state agency that administers the law. Some states administer their own insurance fund and compel the employer to contribute to it. Other states permit employers to buy policies from insurance companies or allow the employer to be self-insuring by paying compensation claims out of reserves or company income. But however the fund is financed, the employer must compensate affected employees according to the decision of the state agency.

Elective laws allow the employer to refuse coverage under the state's workers' compensation laws. In these states, the decision of the state agency that administers these laws is *not* binding on the employer. If the employer rejects the state agency's decision on the amount of compensation for an affected worker, the worker can sue.[14]

Implications for personnel management Workers' compensation claims are expensive. If the employer is self-insuring or uses some other insurance pool, the funds devoted to workers' compensation increase with each injured or disabled employee. Efforts to restrain these costs are an ongoing concern to those in personnel management in small and large organizations alike. Besides providing a safe and healthy work environment, personnel professionals can help restrain workers' compensation costs by getting injured employees back on the job as quickly as possible. Not only does returning to work stop the costly benefit payments, but the sooner the employee returns to the workplace, the less likely that the person will treat the injury as a permanent disability. In other words, the sooner the injured employee returns—even if it is not to his or her "old job"—the less likely that the employee will become used to receiving compensation without working.

The IAM and Boeing program

The International Association of Machinists Union and Boeing used some federal funds to retrain 200 disabled ex-Boeing workers. The union provides job counseling information about rehabilitation programs and then works with Boeing to find jobs for these people. The injury may mean that the employee cannot do the job that he or she had done previously. But if other jobs that require different physical attributes are available and if those who are disabled are reached soon enough with retraining, the company may be able to reduce the number of short-term disabilities that become long-term ones. As one union counselor said, "We try to get them within six months of their accident, before they learn to live on compensation payments and lose their work habits."[15]

Another problem is that employees often are only vaguely aware of these compensation laws and even less aware of their rights. Consider the comments one employee made to a personnel specialist:

> It really came as a shock to learn that the state would only pay me 60 percent of my wages while I was unable to work. On top of that the state paid nothing for the first seven days I was out. I guess I am lucky that the disability wasn't permanent or else my weekly benefit would have been even lower.

As this incident illustrates, employees are sometimes shocked by workers' compensation rules that pay only a fraction of the regular paycheck. For example, every state pays disabled claimants only part of their regular pay to discourage self-inflicted accidents or malingering. Also to encourage a speedy return to work, payments are less than wages. Another universal state rule includes a waiting period to lessen claims for trivial accidents. Payments eventually are reduced or even discontinued to encourage the permanently disabled to seek rehabilitation.

The inadequacy of workers' compensation coverage holds two related implications for personnel departments. First, workers need to be informed by the personnel department of the limited financial security provided by these laws. Second, gaps in the employee's financial security need to be closed with supplemental disability and death insurance. These voluntary actions by personnel departments help to illustrate a genuine concern for employee welfare. Personnel specialists also need to be concerned about reducing accidents to lower the cost of workers' compensation. These costs are directly related to the claims made against the company by employees. The more that must be paid to these employees, the greater the cost. Beyond cost considerations, many managers feel an obligation to provide a safe working environment, as is the case at Du Pont. Unfortunately, too few personnel departments have achieved such dramatic success as Du Pont. As a result, government interest in the physical security of workers has increased and resulted in safety laws.

Financial security threatened

PHYSICAL SECURITY

Workers' compensation programs have a serious defect: They are after-the-fact efforts. These laws attempt to compensate employees for accidents and illnesses that have already occurred. Once again, government intervened. This time Congress passed a comprehensive safety and health law: *The Occupational Safety and Health Act of 1970* (OSHA). The statistical support justifying this safety legislation was overwhelming. As *Business Week* noted, several years after the act was passed:

> Few argue that OSHA—or something like it—was not needed. For example, during World War II, 292,000 U.S. servicemen were killed in battle—and 300,000 workers were killed in factory accidents. Some 53,000 workers lost major limbs, compared with 17,000 combatants who returned minus an arm or leg.[16]

Since there were many more workers than soldiers, these figures are deceptive. Although the physical security of employees improved during the twenty-five years between the end of World War II in 1945 and the passage of OSHA in 1970, accidents and injuries remained a serious problem. The agency that now administers the act viewed the situation as follows.

Toward reducing the human costs of work

In 1970 Congress considered annual figures such as these:

- Job-related accidents accounted for more than 14,000 worker deaths.

- Nearly 2½ million workers were disabled, either temporarily or permanently.

- Ten times more workdays were lost from job-related disabilities than from strikes.

- Estimated new cases of occupational diseases totaled 300,000.[17]

		INCIDENCE RATES PER 100 FULL-TIME WORKERS		
YEAR	TOTAL INJURIES	NONFATAL INJURIES WITHOUT LOST WORKDAYS		LOST WORKDAY INJURIES
1972	10.5	=	7.3	+	3.2
1981	8.1	=	4.4	+	3.7

Source: "Occupational Injury Incidence Rates and Average Lost Workdays per Lost Workday Injury, 1972–1981," *News*, U.S. Department of Labor, Nov. 17, 1982, p. 4.

Figure 14-3
Total Lost Workday and Non-Lost Workday Injuries
for 1972 and 1981

Trends

Figure 14-3 tells the story of workplace injuries since OSHA began collecting injury statistics in 1972. The trend from 1972 to 1981 shows that total injuries per 100 full-time workers have declined from 10.5 to 8.1. The incidence of injuries without lost workdays has declined also, from 7.3 to 4.4. However, the injuries that have led to lost workdays have actually increased from 3.2 to 3.7 incidents per 100 full-time workers. Part of the increase in lost workday figures may be due to more accurate recording and reporting of lost-time accidents.[18]

Purpose and objectives

In passing OSHA, Congress declared its purpose was "to assure so far as possible every working man and woman in the nation safe and healthful working conditions and to preserve our human resources." Figure 14-4 summarizes the major objectives of this legislation. As the figure indicates, Congress sought improved attention to safety and health by employees and employers. It also sought to enforce tough safety standards and to uncover causes of accidents. OSHA has been one of the most far-reaching efforts by government to control the work environment.[19] Since OSHA directly affects human resources, the personnel department typically is responsible for compliance.

Coverage and administration   OSHA covers all workers, except those who are self-employed, those who are protected under other federal agencies or statutes, and those who work on family-owned and operated farms. It is administered and enforced by the secretary of labor through the *Occupational Safety and Health Administration* (also called OSHA). This organization conducts safety and health inspections according to its targeting system. Besides cases of serious accident, fatality, or complaint, the agency's 1200 inspectors focus their efforts on high-hazard industries. Within these industries, OSHA inspectors try to pinpoint those manufacturing firms with injury rates above the national average. The result is to concentrate inspections where accidents are most common. These inspections help the agency directly meet some of the objectives in Figure 14-4.

These objectives contain goals that the agency pursues and that the safety sections of most personnel departments could support. Employers want to reduce safety and health hazards through effective programs. However, many line managers and personnel professionals have found some aspects of OSHA

1. To encourage employers and employees to reduce safety and health hazards

2. To encourage employers and employees to perfect safety and health programs

3. To authorize the Secretary of Labor to establish mandatory occupational health and safety standards

4. To create an Occupational Safety and Health Review Commission to hear appeals under the act

5. To provide health and safety research through the National Institute for Occupational Safety and Health

6. To discover the causal connections between diseases and work, and to establish appropriate standards to eliminate industrial disease

7. To establish medical criteria to assure no employee will suffer diminished health, ability, or life expectancy

8. To implement training programs to improve the quantity and quality of people engaged in the safety and health field

9. To provide an effective program of enforcement of safety and health standards

10. To encourage the states to assume responsibility for administration and enforcement of safety and health regulations

11. To provide appropriate reporting procedures with regard to safety and health

12. To encourage joint labor-management efforts to reduce injuries and disease.

Source: The Occupational Safety and Health Act of 1970.

Figure 14-4
Objectives of OSHA

burdensome, such as the required government reporting requirements, the on-site OSHA inspections, and the fines for violations. To meet these objections, OSHA has eliminated some of the more trivial safety requirements, exempted some low-hazard industries from routine inspections, allowed some industries to drastically reduce their reporting requirements, and even exempted some employers from routine safety inspections and allowed them to begin their own self-policing of worksite safety and health. Combustion Engineering, Inc., provides an example of two voluntary worker protection programs called "Star" and "Try."

OSHA's burden on employers

OSHA's "Star" and "Try" programs

Combustion Engineering has 121 worksites that employ about 45,000 workers worldwide who make a variety of energy-related products. Its in-house safety and health programs at six different worksites qualified for various self-policing programs initiated by OSHA. The Air Preheater plant in Wellsville, New York, was the first facility in the nation to qualify for the Star program. To qualify in both safety and health, the plant met all requirements including an internal audit procedure, safety and health accountability for first-line supervisors, an industrial hygiene program, and both an injury and incidence and lost workday case rate below the national average for their industry for the past three years."[20]

Although OSHA remains responsible for investigating fatal or serious accidents and worker complaints, the Wellsville plant management is responsible for policing the other aspects of the plant's safety and health.

As long as this plant qualifies under the Star program, it will be free from OSHA safety inspections.

Combustion Engineering

The innovative aspect of Combustion Engineering's internal effort is that its insurance carrier independently audits the company's safety efforts. The company also has established both a corporatewide and an individual plant review committee as an appeal mechanism for internal complaints. When the secretary of labor gave the congratulatory letter to the president of Combustion Engineering, the secretary said that the firm "is precisely the kind of employer for which the voluntary programs were designed, one which goes beyond the minimum requirements of OSHA standards to provide protection."[21]

Besides the Star program that Combustion Engineering earned for its Wellsville plant, five other plants qualified under OSHA's Try program. The Try program allows employers to implement experimental safety efforts that may differ from traditional safety and health programs. If OSHA thinks a company's Try program meets the minimum qualifications of reasonable safety, the program is approved as long as OSHA has the budgetary and other resources to monitor the plan's implementation and operation.

OSHA's "Praise" program

The third voluntary program that OSHA has implemented is the "Praise" program. This OSHA effort is an attempt to recognize the lowest hazard firms in low-hazard industries. It is a performance recognition program by OSHA for firms that have an exceptional safety and health program but do not normally receive inspections because they are in a low-hazard industry.[22]

Inspections   A variety of situations can lead to an OSHA inspection. When an inspection occurs, an employer *and* an employee representative normally accompany the OSHA compliance officer.[23] Situations of interest to OSHA that lead to inspections are summarized below.

1. *Imminent danger.*   A condition likely to cause death or a serious injury if allowed to continue. Included are situations that could cause severe bodily damage, disability, or life-shortening illness. Improperly shored ditches, machines with open gears, and toxic fumes and dust are examples. Compliance officers must seek an immediate voluntary solution or obtain a court order to correct any imminent dangers. Cases of imminent danger receive OSHA's highest priority for inspection.

2. *Catastrophes and fatal accidents.*   Catastrophes, deaths, or accidents resulting in hospitalization of five or more employees merit a high priority from compliance officers. The compliance officer determines if any OSHA standards have been violated and how similar events can be avoided in the future.

3. *Employee complaints.*   Employees can complain to OSHA about safety violations or about unsafe or unhealthy conditions; these allegations receive OSHA's attention and an inspection. Employees have the right under OSHA to request an inspection when they believe improper safety and health conditions

exist. When complaints of imminent danger are made, the employee's name is withheld from the employer if the employee wishes.

4. *Special emphasis programs.* Occupations, industries, or substances that lead to high levels of accidents or illnesses receive special attention and extra inspections under OSHA. Meat cutting, sheet metal working, logging, and their associated industries are examples of target occupations and industries. Asbestos and lead are examples of hazardous health substances.

5. *Random inspections.* To encourage all employers to comply with the act, inspections are conducted randomly among firms in hazardous industries, with emphasis on those employers whose safety records are worse than industry norms.

6. *Reinspections.* Employers who have been cited for violations of OSHA are reinspected to ensure that hazards have been corrected and that compliance is maintained.[24]

Standards and appeals The standards to which employers must adhere are extremely detailed. Although the cowboy in Figure 14-5 is an obvious exaggeration, OSHA does have jurisdiction over every chemical substance, piece of equipment, and work environment that possesses even a potential

Figure 14-5
The Cowboy after OSHA

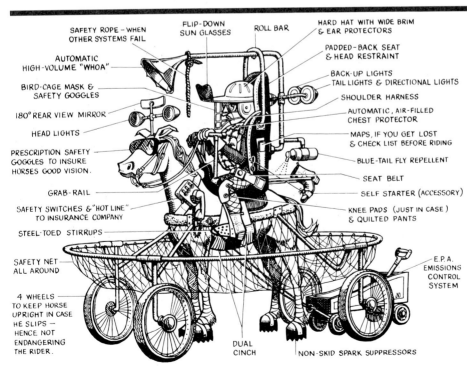

Source: Copyright © 1972 by James N. Devin. Used by permission.

NIOSH

threat to worker health or safety. To conduct research and develop additional safety and health standards, the act also created the *National Institute of Occupational Safety and Health* (NIOSH).[25] Although NIOSH's standards are sometimes viewed by industry as arbitrary, those standards can be the basis for serious fines.

> NL Industries, Inc., was hit with a proposed fine of $155,000 by OSHA for allowing excessive levels of lead in the air at its Indiana lead recycling plant and for other related violations. Even after the company installed $800,000 worth of control equipment in its plant, OSHA inspectors found that lead concentrations were from 2 to 109 times the permissible levels.[26]

Appeals and reviews

Violations are cited and can lead to fines, as happened with NL Industries. Figure 14-6 summarizes the type and extent of fines that are imposed on a noncomplying employer. Note that fines are imposed for *each* violation, no matter how many violations are discovered per inspection. If an employer wants to challenge a citation, a "notice of contest" can be filed with the nearest area director of OSHA. This appeal is reviewed by a judge from the *Occupational Safety and Health Review Commission*. The judge's decision can be appealed to the review commission and even to the federal courts.

State participation   As with unemployment compensation, state involvement was encouraged under the law. Any state that wanted to assume the duties of enforcing safety and health standards could submit a qualified plan to the U.S. Department of Labor. If the state plan was considered "at least as effective as" the federal program, the department allowed the state to have jurisdiction. Fifty percent of the operating costs of a qualified state plan is paid for by the federal government.

Implications of OSHA for Personnel

The act requires that an employer:

> 1.   shall furnish to each of his employees . . . a place of employment . . . free from recognized hazards that are . . . likely to cause death or serious physical harm to his employees;
>
> 2.   shall comply with occupational safety and health standards promulgated under this Act.[27]

Likewise, the act imposes certain duties on employees:

> Each employee shall comply with occupational safety and health standards and all rules, regulations, and orders issued pursuant to this Act.[28]

These two quotes from the act hold several implications for personnel managers: They must obtain organizationwide compliance, maintain records,

TYPE	DESCRIPTION	PENALTY
DE MINIMIS	Violation with no direct or immediate relationship to job safety or health.	None
NONSERIOUS VIOLATION	Violation of safety or health standards that would not likely cause serious physical harm or death.	Up to $1000 per day beyond the abatement period allowed by OSHA. Penalty is discretionary and may be reduced because of the employer's size, past actions, and good-faith cooperation.
SERIOUS VIOLATION	Violation likely to cause death or serious injury due to hazard of which the employer was, or should have been aware.	A $1000 mandatory penalty that can be reduced by 50 percent because of the employer's size, past actions, and good-faith cooperation.
IMMINENT DANGER	Violation that is expected to cause death or serious physical harm immediately or before usual enforcement procedures can eliminate the danger.	Immediate voluntary abatement or court order closing the operations. Financial penalties same as serious violation, unless a willful or repeated violation.
WILLFUL OR REPEATED	Intentional or continuous violations of safety and health standards.	Up to $10,000 per violation. A willful violation that leads to death of an employee can be fined up to $10,000 and/or six months imprisonment. These maximums are doubled for second convictions.
FALSIFYING RECORDS	Any improper and willful falsification of records.	Fine of up to $10,000 and six months in jail.
POSTING VIOLATIONS	Failure to post OSHA notices after violations are cited by OSHA.	Civil penalty of up to $1000.
INTERFERING WITH COMPLIANCE	Assaulting a compliance officer or otherwise resisting or obstructing a safety inspection.	Fine of up to $5000 and up to three years imprisonment.

Figure 14-6
Violations and Penalties under OSHA

seek consistent enforcement, and permit workers to exercise their rights without punishment.

Compliance   Organizationwide compliance requires a detailed safety program. To be effective, the program should have several characteristics.[29] Top management support is crucial to the personnel department's plans. Without such backing, other managers often fail to make the necessary commitment of time and resources. The Du Pont example earlier in this chapter illustrates how strong top management commitment can lead to organizationwide compliance.

Personnel
department actions

With this support, the personnel department needs to conduct a self-inspection so that health and accident hazards can be eliminated and unsafe practices corrected. Then training should include safety awareness programs for both employees and supervisors, whose support is essential. Firm enforcement of safety rules by the supervisor quickly establishes a safety-conscious work environment. Supervisory commitment also requires that rewards (such as pay increases and promotions) depend on a good safety record, as they do at Du Pont. Finally, personnel must communicate directly with employees about safety. Not only do communications elevate safety awareness, but they reinforce supervisory actions as well. Some companies even develop safety slogan contests or offer rewards to employees to increase safety awareness.

> In Gainesville, Florida, a city-owned utility conducted a successful safety program managed by a city employee who had been seriously injured on his job as a utility lineman. Once a week, he changed a large sign in the office showing how many total hours had been worked since the last departmental accident. When the figure reached 10,000 hours (about three months), every employee and spouse was entitled to a free dinner at any restaurant in the city. This program succeeded because safety was reinforced: weekly by the sign and quarterly by the free dinners.

Records   The personnel department must maintain proper records, as shown in Figure 14-7. Not only are they required by OSHA, but they can be used to identify the causes of accidents. From these records, safety experts can detect patterns of accidents or illnesses and then undertake corrective action. Accurate record keeping is also important because falsification can lead to severe fines and jail sentences.

Enforcement   Another personnel management implication of OSHA is

Stern enforcement is often needed.

consistent enforcement of safety and health rules. Is management too harsh when it fires a worker who refused to wear safety shoes? Probably not. If personnel policies allow one worker to violate the safety rules, others may do the same. If an accident results, it is the employer that is fined by OSHA. By being firm—even if this means discharge—management quickly convinces employees that safety is important. Sometimes just the threat of discipline is sufficient to get employees to comply with safety regulations. And a strong record of enforcing safety rules also may convince OSHA to reduce penalties when citations are received.

Employee rights   Figure 14-8 explains the last major implication of OSHA for personnel management: employee rights to safe working conditions. To ensure the effectiveness of OSHA, the law permits employees to refuse to work when working conditions are unsafe. This is not an unqualified right. Employees first are expected to ask the employer to correct the situation if it is reasonable to do so. They may also request an OSHA inspection and have an employee representative accompany the inspector. When employees exercise their rights under the act, they are protected from discrimination by the employer. Management may not retaliate against workers who have sought changes in unsafe or unhealthful working conditions.[30]

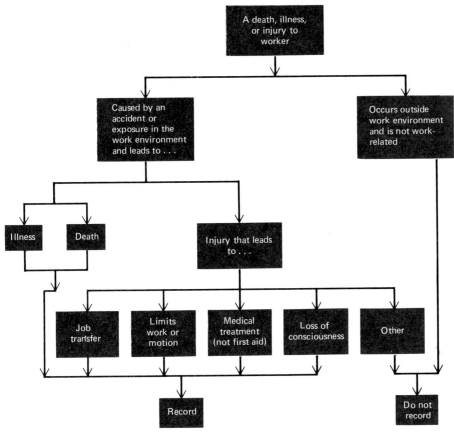

Source: *What Every Employer Needs to Know about OSHA Recordkeeping*, U.S. Department of Labor, 1975, p. 2.

Figure 14-7
Recordability of Cases under OSHA

SUMMARY

Legally required benefits and services are imposed by government to further societal objectives. The government—primarily the federal government—seeks to provide workers with financial and physical security.

Financial security is achieved partially through such benefits as social security, unemployment compensation, and workers' compensation. Social security provides income at retirement or upon disability. It also provides the family members of a deceased worker with a death benefit and a survivor's annuity, under certain conditions.

Unemployment compensation pays the worker a modest income to reduce the hardships of losing a job. These payments go to employees who are involuntarily separated from their work. Payments last until the worker finds suitable employment or until the worker receives the maximum number of payments permitted by the state.

Workers' compensation pays employees who are injured in the course of their employment. The payments are made to prevent the employee from having

IT'S AGAINST THE LAW FOR YOUR EMPLOYER TO PUNISH YOU
FOR EXERCISING YOUR OSHA RIGHTS

Section ELEVEN-C of the OSHA law was written to protect you from discrimination or punishment by your employer if you do such things as:

- Complain to your employer about job safety or health conditions.
- Discuss health or safety matters with other workers.
- Participate in union activities concerning health and safety matters.
- Participate in workplace health and safety committee activities.
- File health or safety grievances.
- File a complaint about workplace health or safety hazards with OSHA, state agencies, your local health department or fire department, or any other government agency.
- Participate in OSHA inspections.
- Testify before any panel, agency, or court about job hazards.
- File ELEVEN-C complaints.
- Give evidence in connection with ELEVEN-C complaints.
- Refuse a dangerous task, but only under certain conditions.

Section ELEVEN-C of the OSHA law makes it illegal for your employer to do any of the following as punishment for exercising your OSHA rights:

- Fire you.
- Demote you.
- Assign you to an undesirable job or shift.
- Take away your seniority.
- Deny you a promotion.
- Deny you benefits you've earned, such as sick leave or vacation time.
- Spy on you.
- Harass you.
- Blacklist you with other employers.
- Take away your company housing.
- Try to cut off your credit at banks or credit unions.

OSHA can protect you from these and other punishments only if they result from your exercising OSHA rights. If you want to protest discrimination or punishment which is not related to your OSHA rights, you should contact your union or the appropriate government agency. OSHA cannot protect you if you are disciplined solely for refusing to comply with OSHA regulations or valid health or safety rules established by your employer.

Source: "OSHA: Your Workplace Rights in Action," U.S. Department of Labor, 1980, pp. 2–3.

Figure 14-8
Worker Rights under OSHA

to sue to be compensated for injuries. If an employee dies, benefits are paid to the survivors.

The government has tried to provide physical security through the Occupational Safety and Health Act of 1970. This act imposes a duty on employers to provide a safe and healthy place of employment. Violations of this law, which can lead to serious injuries or to industrial diseases, are subject to severe penalities. The success of a personnel department's program depends heavily on top management's support and commitment to employee safety and health.

TERMS FOR REVIEW

Social security

Fully insured workers

Unemployment compensation

Suitable employment

Experience rating

National Institute of Occupational Safety and Health (NIOSH)

Occupational Safety and Health Review Commission (OSHRC)

Lost-time accidents

Workers' compensation

Occupational Safety and Health Act (OSHA)

Occupational Safety and Health Administration

Imminent danger

REVIEW AND DISCUSSION QUESTIONS

1. Why has government been interested in providing financial security to workers through laws? What areas in the future do you think are likely to receive federal attention to ensure employee financial security?

2. Some people feel that social security is greatly overpriced for the benefits it delivers. But many people who are retired or permanently disabled think it is an excellent social program. What is your opinion of social security? Why?

3. Explain why someone from the personnel department should follow up on employees who are injured on the job and who are beginning to receive workers' compensation checks at home.

4. Suppose a friend of yours contracted lead poisoning on the job. What sources of income could this person rely on while recovering during the next two months? What if it took two years for your friend to recover? Are other sources of income available?

5. If you worked at the same lead processing plant as your ill friend, what actions would you take?

6. Besides retirement income, what benefits are provided by social security?

7. Indicate whether each of the following people would be eligible for unemployment compensation and why: (*a*) a worker who took voluntary retirement at age 62, (*b*) a disabled employee who was confined to a hospital bed, (*c*) a soldier who is on active duty.

8. When must an accident or illness be recorded by an employer?

INCIDENT 14-1

Cutting the K & D Company's Tax Bill

Karen Carrea, a personnel specialist, recently was hired by the K & D consulting firm. The president of the firm was concerned about the taxes the company paid for such employee benefits as social security, workers' compensation, and unemployment compensation. The president assigned Karen to uncover ways that the firm legally could reduce its labor costs by reducing tax liability.

Karen's report contained several novel solutions. To reduce workers' compensation costs, she suggested that the personnel department request OSHA to inspect the company's printing shop, which produced the firm's reports and most of its accidents. To reduce unemployment compensation costs, Karen suggested that personnel change its policy of hiring additional consultants on a project basis. She had found that every time a project ended, the temporary consultants were laid off and filed for unemployment compensation. She suggested that the company subcontract its overload to free-lance consultants at the nearby university. Since the consultants would be independent contractors, their loss of consulting business would not reflect on the firm's unemployment insurance taxes, and as independent consultants they would pay their own social security taxes. Karen was unable to suggest any other way that social security taxes could be lowered, since they were a percentage of payroll.

1. What is your evaluation of Karen's suggestions?

2. What other methods might Karen suggest to hold down the cost of these required benefits?

REFERENCES

1.   John T. Dunlop, "The Limits of Legal Compulsion," *Labor Law Journal*, February 1976, p. 67.

2.   Jeremy Main, "When Accidents Don't Happen," *Fortune*, Sept. 6, 1982, p. 62.

3.   Ibid.

4.   Ibid., pp. 62, 64, 68.

5.   Richard Schultz, Peter J. Ferrara, and Richard C. Keating, "Social Security: Three Points of View," *The Personnel Administrator*, May 1981, pp. 45–49.

6.   Michael J. Boskin (ed.), *The Crisis in Social Security: Problems and Prospects*, 2d ed., San Francisco: Institute for Contemporary Studies, 1979.

7.   *Employee Benefits 1981*, Washington, D.C.: Chamber of Commerce of the United States, 1982, p. 11.

8.   Dwight K. Bartlett III, "Current Developments in Social Security Financing," *Social Security Bulletin*, September 1980, pp. 10–20.

9.   Russell L. Greenman and Eric J. Schmertz, *Personnel Administration and the Law*, Washington, D.C.: Bureau of National Affairs, 1972, p. 129.

10. "The Hidden Crisis in Jobless Pay," *Business Week*, Jan. 24, 1977, p. 21.

11. Allan N. Nash and Stephen J. Carroll, Jr., *The Management of Compensation* Monterey, Calif.: Brooks/Cole, 1975, p. 230.

12. Philip Kaplan, "Unemployment Taxes Are Variable, Controllable Expenses Which Employers Must Recognize as Growing Profit Drain," *Personnel Journal*, April 1976, pp. 170–172, 184–185.

13. Kathleen Classen-Utsoff, "Unemployment Insurance: What Does It Really Do?" *Business Horizons*, February 1979, pp. 53–56.

14. Greenman and Schmertz, op. cit., pp. 152–153.

15. "Disabled Workers Get Training to Begin New Careers in a Union Program," *The Wall Street Journal*, Western ed., July 7, 1981, p. 1.

16. "Why Nobody Wants to Listen to OSHA," *Business Week*, June 14, 1976, p. 65; "Sticking Uncle Sam for On-the-Job Injuries," *Business Week*, Nov. 6, 1978, p. 182.

17. "All about OSHA," U.S. Department of Labor, April 1980, p. 1.

18. "Occupational Injuries and Illnesses in 1981," *News*, U.S. Department of Labor, Nov. 17, 1982, p. 4.

19. Joseph Barry Mason, "OSHA: Problems and Prospects," *California Management Review*, Fall 1976, p. 21. See also "A Lead Recycler Contests a Huge Fine," *Business Week*, Nov. 13, 1978, pp. 38, 40; and Neil Maxwell, "How Johns-Manville Mounts Counterattack in Asbestos Dispute," *The Wall Street Journal*, Western ed., June 30, 1980, pp. 1, 10.

20. "Donovan Announces OSHA Approval of Six Combustion Engineering Facilities for Voluntary Protection Programs," *News*, U.S. Department of Labor, Nov. 10, 1982, p. 1-2.

21. Ibid.

22. Barbara Gray Gricar and H. Donald Hopkins, "How Does Your Company Respond to OSHA?" *The Personnel Administrator*, April 1983, pp. 53–57.

23. Mary Hayes, "What Can You Do When OSHA Calls?" *The Personnel Administrator*, November 1982, pp. 65–66.

24. "All about OSHA," op. cit., pp. 22–23.

25. Richard E. Gallagher, "Setting Priorities for NIOSH Research," *Monthly Labor Review*, March 1975, pp. 41–43. See also James P. Carty, "The Politics of Regulation: Understanding the Regulatory Complex," *The Personnel Administrator*, June 1980, pp. 25–30.

26. "A Lead Recycler Contests a Huge Fine," op. cit., pp. 38, 40.

27. Occupational Safety and Health Act of 1970.

28. Ibid.

29. Randall S. Schuler, "Occupational Health in Organizations: Strategies for Personnel Effectiveness," *The Personnel Administrator*, January 1982, pp. 47–55.

30. John J. Hoover, "Workers Have New Rights to Health and Safety," *The Personnel Administrator*, April 1983, pp. 47–51.

PART

V

EMPLOYEE
RELATIONS

Previous parts of the book have focused on obtaining, training, and compensating employees. This part addresses employee relations—maintaining and motivating a productive work force. The major theories of motivation and satisfaction are explored in Chapter 15 with particular attention to the personnel department's role. Other issues include stress, counseling, and discipline, which are covered in Chapter 16. Personnel communications systems are described in Chapter 17. Change and organizational development challenges are presented in Chapter 18 to provide a useful background to the productivity and quality of work life efforts described in Chapter 19.

Regardless of the job you hold, you will use many of the concepts discussed here. If you are planning a career in personnel management, Part V will introduce you to many of the skills and procedures used by personnel professionals.

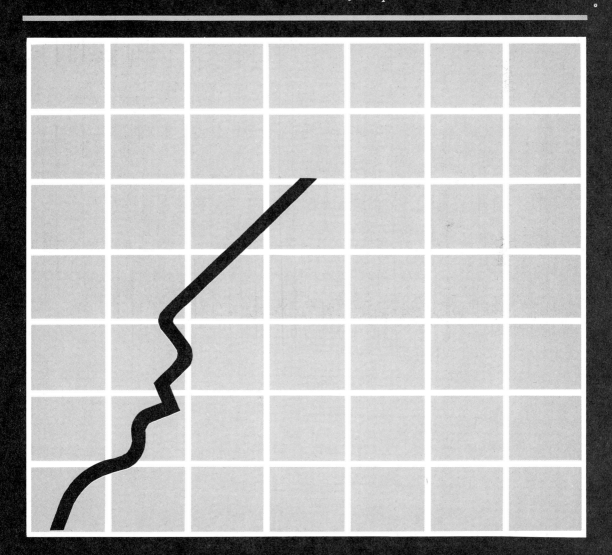

CHAPTER 15

In golf and work, goals are a major component of motivation!

William H. Mobley[1]

Organization behavior is a function of its consequence.

Fred Luthans and Robert Kreitner[2]

EMPLOYEE MOTIVATION AND SATISFACTION

CHAPTER OBJECTIVES

After studying this chapter, you should be able to:

1 Explain how the personnel function helps with motivation and job satisfaction.

2 Discuss how employee needs may affect motivation.

3 Interpret differences among models of motivation.

4 Analyze employee performance in terms of models of motivation.

5 Explain the relationship between job satisfaction and performance.

6 Describe the implications of low levels of job satisfaction.

An organization's productivity is determined by many factors; employee motivation and satisfaction are just two of them. Nevertheless, they are important factors in any organization.[3] Personnel departments affect employee motivation and satisfaction through almost every activity that they perform. Consider the topics of the last few chapters: training and development; performance appraisals; compensation; benefits and services; security, safety, and health.[4] Employee motivation and satisfaction certainly are affected by how personnel departments handle these challenges. Personnel professionals also serve as human resource consultants for managers in other departments. More and more well-managed personnel departments want other managers to use the department as a source of employee relations expertise. When these other managers seek assistance with human resource problems, they often want personnel professionals to suggest ways to motivate employees to perform in a more productive manner. So for the manager and for the personnel professional, understanding employee motivation and satisfaction is an important topic.

But understanding employee motivation and satisfaction is more than knowing a handful of theories or performing some set of activities. Motivation and satisfaction are affected by virtually every aspect of the organization, and many of these aspects the personnel department cannot directly control, such as supervisory treatment of employees, promotions, merit raises, and other personnel actions normally reserved for line managers. Personnel specialists can contribute to employee motivation and satisfaction, however, by assisting these decision makers. Given the commitment and leadership of top management, personnel specialists can help the organization achieve high levels of productivity and quality through a motivated and satisfied work force.[5] An interesting example comes from a Sharp Corporation plant in Memphis, Tennessee:

RCA's problems
versus Sharp's
success

When plans were announced to build the facility in Memphis, many people thought Sharp had made a bad decision. As the *Wall Street Journal* observed: "After all, RCA Corp. had built a TV plant in Memphis in 1966—and shut it down five years later. That facility had suffered just about every labor management affliction imaginable: wildcat strikes, union-authorized strikes, apparent sabotage of the product and a series of layoffs that took the payroll from 4,200 workers down to 1,600. At times, so many hundreds of defective TV sets clogged the assembly-line aisles that technicians had difficulty repairing them. Finally, RCA pulled the plug, shipped most of the machinery and work off to Taiwan. . . ."[6]

Paul Hogusa, the president of Sharp Manufacturing Company of America, did not think it was labor problems that closed the RCA plant. He thought it was RCA's poor product quality at that factory. At the rate of a quarter of a million high-quality TV sets and microwave ovens per year, Sharp has proved the skeptics wrong. Sharp's success was not caused by special machinery or by automation; its competitors use the same equipment. Instead, Sharp's management focused on producing quality products while making employees feel that they are an important member of the "Sharp family." Management demands high standards from employees and is constantly pushing for improvements in quality or in productivity. But at the same time, the organization has managed to create a work environment that is motivating and satisfying to the employees. Although all of their Memphis employees do not sing the company song, dress in uniforms, or exercise before work (as they do in Japan), the American workers at this Japanese-owned plant produce high-quality products at high levels of productivity.

What makes the difference between RCA's plant in the 1960s and Sharp's plant in the 1980s? Many factors are different. But Mr. Hogusa attributes it all to "the quality of the people."[7] But since Sharp recruits from the same labor pool that RCA used for its assemblers, the real difference must be the day-to-day management of human resources.

A key difference between Sharp and RCA

People make the difference. If a personnel department can contribute toward the motivation and satisfaction of an organization's employees, then the department can make a meaningful contribution toward the organization's productivity. In fact, a growing recognition among managers, consultants, and professors that people are the key to organizational success has led to a parade of popular books that share this theme.[8]

This chapter discusses the basic framework within which the personnel function operates to influence motivation and job satisfaction. Then it discusses different models for motivating employees and explains how motivation and job satisfaction are related.

This chapter

HOW PERSONNEL INFLUENCES MOTIVATION AND SATISFACTION

The personnel function has both a direct and an indirect influence on employee motivation and satisfaction. As Figure 15-1 illustrates, the personnel function makes direct contact with employees and supervisors in ways that influence them. For example, orientation, training and development, career planning, and counseling activities may directly motivate employees through one-to-one or group meetings. At the same time, these activities may help a supervisor do a better job of motivating employees.[9]

Direct and indirect influences

Personnel policies and practices also influence motivation and satisfaction indirectly. Rigorously enforced safety and health programs, for example, can give employees and supervisors a greater sense of safety from accidents and industrial health hazards. Likewise, compensation policies may motivate and satisfy employees through incentive plans, or they may harm motivation and satisfaction through insufficient raises or outright salary freezes. The motivation and satisfaction of employees act as feedback on the organizational climate and on the personnel function's day-to-day activities.

Organizational Climate

Personnel policies and activities have a major impact on an organization's climate. *Organizational climate* is the favorableness or unfavorableness of the environment for people in an organization. Some organizations live by the rules

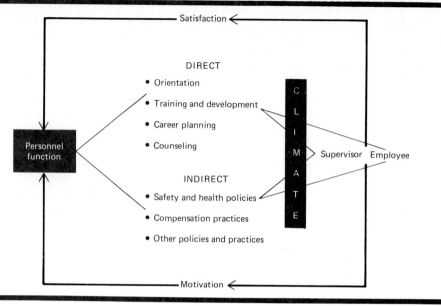

Figure 15-1

Influence of the Personnel Function
on Motivation and Satisfaction

**Work versus
teamwork**

and are bureaucratic. Other firms are friendly and easygoing. Some companies emphasize work; others emphasize teamwork. The difference between work and teamwork may appear small, but it is a significant one in the climate of an organization.

For example, one study compared the relationship between organizational climate and job satisfaction.[10] The study covered 695 employees in a large utility. Climate was studied along with such dimensions of satisfaction as attitudes toward pay and supervision. The results showed a significant relationship between organizational climate and job satisfaction. When the climate was favorable, satisfaction was high; but when climate was unfavorable, satisfaction was low.

Day-to-Day Activities

The policies and activities of the personnel department affect all employees in a number of ways, and personnel has daily opportunities to strengthen or weaken the organization in the eyes of employees. As the saying goes, almost by itself personnel can "make or break" the humanness of an organization. Since personnel's influence on the climate is widespread and important, personnel specialists need to ask themselves day by day as they do their work:

- Do we show people that we care?

- Are we seen as a help to people or as a problem?

- Do we encourage the growth of cooperation and teamwork?

- Do we encourage the growth of people?

To illustrate the importance of these questions, we will examine some basic ideas about motivation and job satisfaction so that we can see how personnel activities relate to these issues.

MOTIVATION

Motivation is a complex subject. It involves the unique feelings, thoughts, and past experiences of each of us as we share a variety of relationships within and outside organizations. To expect a single motivational approach to work in every situation is probably unrealistic. In fact, even the theorists and researchers take different points of view about motivation. Nevertheless, some basic guidelines do exist that can be useful in improving motivation under some circumstances.

Motivation is a person's drive to take an action because that person wants to do so. If people are pushed, they are merely reacting to pressure. They act because they feel that they have to. However, if they are motivated, they make the positive choice to do something because they see this act as meaningful to them. Their actions, for example, may satisfy some of their needs.

No universal motivation method exists.

Definition

Content Theories of Motivation

Content theories of motivation describe the needs or desires within us that initiate behavior. Figure 15-2 compares three of the most common theories. Each of these theories is discussed in the following pages.

Figure 15-2

A Comparison of Content Motivation Theories

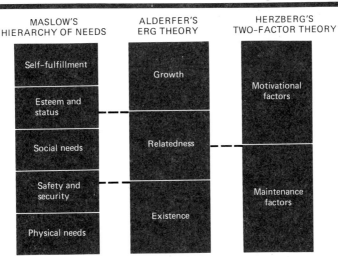

400

Maslow's hierarchy of needs   One model of motivation is Maslow's hierarchy of needs.[11] Since all needs cannot be expressed at once, they tend to have some priority in which they find expression. The result is that people have different levels of needs, as shown in Figure 15-3. If one's lowest needs are not satisfied, they claim priority, and one turns to their satisfaction in preference to higher-order needs.

When first-level needs begin to be satisfied, then second-level needs become more important and gradually tend to dominate a person's behavior. As each succeeding level of needs becomes reasonably satisfied, the next level of needs becomes more important. This model does not apply to all people all of the time. It is possible to suppress some needs in favor of others; and some people have greater or lesser needs at each level in the hierarchy. Even with these cautions, the model is considered a general relationship that applies to large numbers of people in normal situations.

Lower-order needs include the physical level of needs and the safety and security level of needs shown in Figure 15-3. The *physical (or physiological) needs* concern those actions required to maintain life and physical aspects of well-being. *Safety and security* needs are closely related to the first level of needs because they concern longer-run maintenance of life and well-being. People want to be free of workplace hazards (safety needs), which are partially addressed by the Occupational Safety and Health Act discussed Chapter 14. At the same time, people also want the reassurance that they will continue to meet these basic needs if they are injured or retired, which partially explains the use of disability and retirement benefits offered by many compensation programs. The first two levels of Maslow's hierarchy are called lower-order needs because they usually take minimum amounts of satisfaction before higher-order needs are activated. Lower-order needs are met by food, clothing, housing, pay to

Figure 15-3

Hierarchy of Needs According to Maslow

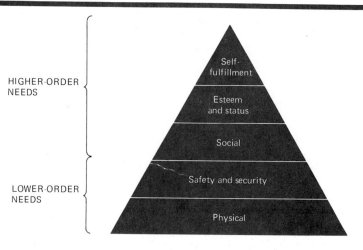

purchase these items, fringe benefits, and safe working conditions. Fair rules and supervision provide psychological security from unfair treatment.

Higher-order needs are different from lower-order ones. Lower-level needs generally are useful only in limited quantities. One can have too much food, for example. Higher-order needs, however, are not so easily oversupplied. Satisfaction of *social needs,* such as belonging and love, is difficult to overdo. Likewise, the need for *esteem*, which is met by the recognition of others or by a personal sense of growth and achievement, is seldom oversatisfied. Lower needs are substantially physical and economic; money will buy food, clothing, and hospital care. But money becomes less useful as a means to secure most higher needs, such as self-esteem. Essentially the higher needs relate more to feelings and values than to physical needs. The highest need is *self-fulfillment,* also called self-actualization. It is met when people become all that they are capable of becoming. In this manner they find inner fulfillment. This state of mind is achieved only rarely, and it usually does not assume priority until after other needs are reasonably satisfied.

Higher-order needs

Alderfer's ERG theory   Alderfer's theory is similar to Maslow's except that it condenses Maslow's hierarchy into three categories: existence (E), relatedness (R), and growth (G).[12] Figure 15-2 shows these categories in comparison with Maslow's approach.

Existence needs include those desires that meet Maslow's lower-order needs—physiological, safety, and security. *Relatedness* needs encompass interpersonal relationships and include the acceptance, belonging, and security that come from the approval of those in the organization. This division of Alderfer's model parallels Maslow's social needs but slightly overlaps with his security and self-esteem levels. *Growth* needs include those that challenge the individual's capabilities and may cause personal growth on the job. Included here are esteem and self-fulfillment needs found in levels 4 and 5 of Maslow's model.

ERG explained

The ERG theory rests on three suppositions:

1.   The less the need is satisfied, the stronger the desire for that need.

2.   The strength of desire for higher-level needs goes up the more lower-level needs are satisfied.

3.   The more frustration one finds in meeting higher-level needs, the more lower-level needs will be desired.

Unlike Maslow's theory, which is based on a progression of satisfaction up the hierarchy, Alderfer's ERG theory includes a frustration-regression viewpoint. In circumstances where higher-order needs remain unsatisfied, frustration occurs and the individual "regresses" to fulfilling more basic needs. Also unlike Maslow, Alderfer's model acknowledges that more than one need may be operative at any one time. A common element in both approaches is that people have needs. And each need varies in its intensity depending on how well it and other needs are being satisfied.

Maslow versus Alderfer

Herzberg's two-factor model of motivation   Another popular content theory is Herzberg's two-factor model of motivation. Herzberg and his associates have developed a model of motivation based on motivational and maintenance needs. They interviewed employees to determine what conditions led to strong positive or negative feelings about their jobs. The result was that most employees named different types of causes for their good and bad feelings. That is, if recognition led to a good feeling, lack of recognition seldom led to a bad feeling.[13]

Motivational factors

The conclusion was that some factors primarily build higher motivation and satisfaction, but their absence is not strongly negative. These factors are known as *motivational factors,* motivators, or satisfiers because they tend to motivate and satisfy. They give the employee a built-in generator that provides an internal drive toward better performance. Ideally, the job itself—the actual work the person does—should provide these sources of internal motivation.

Maintenance or hygiene factors

Other factors primarily dissatisfy employees when they are absent, but their presence does not provide strong motivation. They are called *maintenance factors,* hygiene factors, or dissatisfiers. An example is fringe benefits. Employees can be quite unhappy when they lack them, but their presence is not strongly motivating. For many years personnel people had been wondering why generous fringe benefits did not increase employee motivation. The concept of maintenance factors explained why. Fringe benefits are needed to maintain an employee (prevent dissatisfaction), but they are not by themselves strong motivators.

As shown in Figure 15-4, each of the two factors operates primarily, but not always, in one direction. Since each of the two is different, the Herzberg model is often called a *two-factor model of motivation.*

Figure 15-5 shows the factors reported in the original Herzberg study. The motivational factors occur mostly in direct connection with the job so that performance of the work becomes self-rewarding. Employees obtain this

Figure 15-4

Motivational Factors Compared with
Maintenance Factors

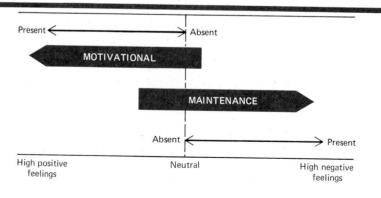

MOTIVATIONAL FACTORS	MAINTENANCE FACTORS
Work itself	Status
Achievement	Relationships with supervision
Possibility of growth	Relationships with peers
Advancement	Relationships with subordinates
Recognition	Supervision: technical
	Company policy and administration
	Job security
	Working conditions
	Salary
	Personal life

Figure 15-5
Motivational and Maintenance Factors

reward for themselves. On the other hand, the maintenance factors occur mostly in the environment that surrounds the job. Employees typically have minimum control over these conditions.

The Herzberg model has been strongly criticized because a number of studies do not support the idea of two separate factors in motivation.[14] In spite of criticism, it remains a popular model because it helps managers and personnel specialists label conditions that are more likely either to motivate employees or to dissatisfy them.

Equity Theory

Although needs-oriented theories may explain what factors motivate employees, they offer little insight as to why people behave as they do. *Equity theory* suggests that people are motivated to close the gap between their efforts and the amount of reward they receive.[15] When rewards are perceived as insufficient, either more rewards are sought or less effort is put forth. These issues are most likely to arise through comparisons with other people in the organization or with people who do similar work outside of the organization. When an employee compares his or her job inputs (performance, effort, skills, or education) with those of another person, the worker usually feels that comparable inputs should have comparable results. If the other person receives more pay, recognition, status, promotions, or other favorable outcomes with no more inputs, the situation is seen to be inequitable. When inequity exists between inputs and outcomes, the person is motivated to reduce the inequity by obtaining an increase in the rewards (a raise or a promotion, for example) or by decreasing the inputs (be less productive, for example) or some combination of both.

Comparative fairness of rewards

The research on equity theory supports the contention that people will be motivated to reduce the inequities that result from insufficient rewards. The research on rewards that represent overpayments, however, is less clear.[16] Nevertheless the theory does emphasize to personnel professionals the need to scrutinize diligently an organization's reward structure to ensure equity. Otherwise, inequities may lead to turnover, absenteeism, or even strikes.

Reconsider the comparison between Sharp and RCA in their efforts to make television sets in the Memphis area. Even if RCA had an equitable pay structure, employees may have sensed inequities because unionized workers typically receive different benefits than do nonunionized employees, particularly managers. The result can sometimes be an "us-versus-them" syndrome. Since workers can do little to increase their rewards until the next union contract is negotiated, some may have elected to reduce their quantity or quality of work as a way to reduce the perceived inequities of the reward system.

Expectancy Theory

Desire and likelihood shape motivation.

A more sophisticated view of motivation is found in Vroom's expectancy theory. *Expectancy theory* states that motivation is a result of the outcomes one seeks and one's estimate that action will lead to these desired outcomes.[17] In more straightforward terms, if a person wants something strongly enough, and if the path looks sufficiently open to get it, that person will go for it.

For example, Peter Rizzo, a clerk in an X-ray laboratory, strongly wanted the outcome of promotion to X-ray technician. As he assessed the situation, he saw that the present technicians have medical or technical backgrounds. Since he lacks either type of background, he sees little chance of promotion, and so he is not motivated. Regretfully, the hospital seeks technicians and would consider him for training, but its objectives and his needs have not been mutually communicated, and so he remains unmotivated.

Valence and expectancy   The strength of a person's preference for one outcome in relation to others is called *valence.* Since a person also may desire not to have an outcome, valence may range from -1 to $+1$.

The strength of a person's belief that an act will lead to a particular outcome is called *expectancy.* If an employee is certain that an act has no chance to lead to an outcome, then expectancy is zero. At the opposite end of the scale, if an employee is sure that an act will lead to an outcome, expectancy is $+1$. The result is that expectancy may range anywhere from zero to $+1$. In short, valence is one's *desire* for an outcome, and expectancy is the *probability* that the action will achieve the outcome. When valence and expectancy are multiplied, the product is a person's approximate state of motivation. The equation is as follows:

$$\text{Valence} \times \text{expectancy} = \text{motivation}$$
$$\text{(or) Desire} \times \text{probability} = \text{motivation}$$

Application of the expectancy model   The expectancy model suggests that people use their experience and judgment to determine which kinds of desired outcomes are available, and then they judge which ones they have the best probability of reaching. What they perform is a type of cost-benefit analysis to determine whether a reward is worth its costs. If the reward is enough to justify the cost of more effort, then they tend to go for it.

A criticism of the model is its applicability for use by personnel profession- **Complexity** als. The model can be extremely complex. Although that complexity may reflect the complexity of motivation, few personnel practitioners can apply this complex model to everyday motivational situations. Furthermore, the probabilities used are subjective, whether those probabilities are estimated by the employee or others. An employee's estimate of a particular outcome may be inaccurate because the probabilities that someone assigns vary from person to person. And little evidence suggests that employees become motivated through careful assignment and multiplication of probabilities.

Even with these criticisms, a personnel department can reduce costs and increase benefits for employees whose motivation is shaped by a careful reflection of desired outcomes (valence) and their likelihood of attainment (expectancy). Personnel may be able to increase employee motivation through counseling, training, compensation, and other activities that stimulate employee desires for rewards such as promotions. Likewise, personnel's efforts may strengthen an employee's belief that training, hard work, and other efforts lead to wanted rewards (outcomes). This approach is a *path-goal personnel strategy* in **Path-goal strategy** which the personnel department improves the path toward the goal (such as reducing red tape) and then tries to improve the outcomes at the end of the path (such as developing an award program for suggestions). In this way the personnel function is building a better organizational climate for motivation.

Reinforcement Theory and Behavior Modification

All of the models of motivation that have been discussed are based on needs determined internally by each person. They are called *cognitive models of motivation* because they depend on the thinking and feeling (that is, cognition) within each person. They relate to the internal psychological person and how that person views the world.

The problem with cognitive models is that they are not subject to precise scientific measurement and observation. We can never be sure whether needs really exist as we see them because we can only infer them from what people say and do. It is argued that we could understand motivation better if we gave more attention to models that are more subject to scientific analysis. The principal model of this type is behavior modification, which has evolved from the work of Skinner and others.[18]

Behavior modification states that behavior depends on its consequences. **Behavior modification** While cognitive models argue that *internal* needs lead to behavior, behavior **defined** modification states that *external* consequences tend to determine behavior. We no longer have to figure out what is in a person's mind because we can affect a person's behavior by modifying the consequences.

Since behavior depends on its consequences, the *law of effect* states that **Law of effect** people learn to repeat behavior that has favorable consequences, and they learn to avoid behavior that has unfavorable consequences. Thus favorable consequences are used to reinforce desired behavior so that one tends to repeat it.

> Brent Parks discovered that 'nearly every time he tried to use his own judgment or take initiative on the job, he received support and recognition from his supervisor. For example, his supervisor commended him for making an operating decision "on the spot" without delay until advice could be sought. Brent liked these favorable consequences, and so he worked hard to improve his competence and increase his on-the-job judgment and initiative.

Figure 15-6 illustrates the law of effect. An antecedent or cue in the environment triggers a behavior. The behavior has a favorable consequence that reinforces it and makes it more likely to occur when the appropriate cue or antecedent happens again. For example, if someone notices that it is lunchtime (the antecedent), they then eat lunch (behavior), which has the favorable outcome of reducing hunger (consequence).

Reinforcement schedules   Reinforcement may be given in different ways, called *reinforcement schedules.* There is *continuous reinforcement,* which follows each desired behavior. For example, each time an agent sells an automobile, the agent earns a commission.

Intermittent reinforcement does not follow every desired behavior. Instead, the timing of reinforcers follows one of four schedules:

- *Fixed interval.* After a certain period of time, such as a weekly paycheck

- *Variable interval.* After a random or varied number of time periods

- *Fixed ratio.* After a certain number of correct responses

- *Variable ratio.* After a random or varied number of correct responses

Variable-ratio reinforcement   Variable-ratio reinforcement tends to be the most powerful motivator among the four schedules. For example, slot machines in casinos pay on a variable-ratio

Figure 15-6
The Law of Effect

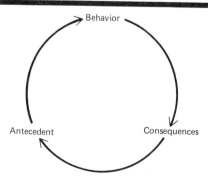

schedule. It is difficult for gamblers to leave them because the gamblers keep hoping to beat the odds, and payoffs are unpredictable. However, since work situations are more complex than slot machines, variable-ratio schedules are not always the most successful ones to use on the job.

Interpreting behavior modification Behavior modification is criticized as being manipulative because it controls one's environment and largely ignores one's internal needs. It is seen as a threat to the classical concepts of human dignity and autonomy. Others claim that it is an oversimplified explanation of a complex situation.

Application of behavior modification is somewhat limited. In addition to objections concerning its use, there are numerous difficulties installing behavior modification so that it applies a specific reinforcement for specific correct behaviors. On the other hand, when the behavior-and-reinforcement connection is rather direct, behavior modification is successful.[19] An example is control of absences.

A small electronics plant had trouble with employee absenteeism, and so it developed a lottery for those who had no absences or tardiness during each month.[20] Winners of each lottery received $10 cash. In addition, all eligible employees had their names posted on the bulletin board.

The result was that absences were reduced. For sick leave alone there was a savings of $3125 the first year. In comparison, the reinforcement cost was $120 cash ($10 monthly for twelve months).

Some managers have problems using positive reinforcement to motivate employees because it is a long-run approach. Using it once or twice is not likely to change an employee's behavior patterns. Figure 15-7 illustrates the problem. Dashed line *A* represents an employee's average performance. The actual performance varies, both good and bad. Whenever an employee's performance is unacceptable, it falls below line *P*, and the employee is disciplined. The discipline may be no more than a corrective comment, or it may be as severe as several days off without pay or worse. After discipline (shown as a minus), performance improves in most cases. The manager learns that discipline apparently improves performance. Therefore, the manager is reinforced to use discipline when poor employee performance is observed.[21] However, improvement may have occurred without discipline because the poor performance is well below the employee's average or normal efforts.

Where many managers go wrong is that they do not put in an upper threshold (line *S*), which signifies superior performance. Even when managers do reward superior performance, outstanding results may not occur the next time because the high-level performance is also an exception to the employee's normal level of effort. The manager observes that the superior performance received some positive reinforcement (shown as a plus), and then it subsequently dropped. The consequences of using rewards seem to be a return to lower levels of performance. After several tries at reinforcing performance and having it drop back toward the average, many managers stop using positive reinforce-

Short-run perspective

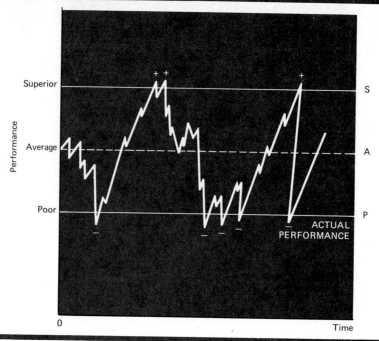

Figure 15-7

A Hypothetical Range of Employee Performance

ment. However, if they continued using it, episodes of superior performance would become more likely, and then the average level of performance would increase.

A Reward-Performance Model

All models of motivation have their strengths and weaknesses. No model is perfect, but each one adds something to our understanding of motivation. The *reward-performance model*, for example, combines strengths from others. It is shown as a wheel in Figure 15-8 because it is a circular relationship that regularly reinforces performance so that it will continue.

Environmental impact   As the figure shows, employee motivation occurs in an environmental system that consists of the following factors:

- The job itself
- The organization
- Small groups
- The external environment

These four factors make up the *environmental system for motivation.* As shown on the figure, all of these factors are interacting in a complex system relationship. Each factor must be considered when planning a motivational action. The personnel function's task is to help build a repetitive system of rewards so that the desired performance continues for a long period of time. If

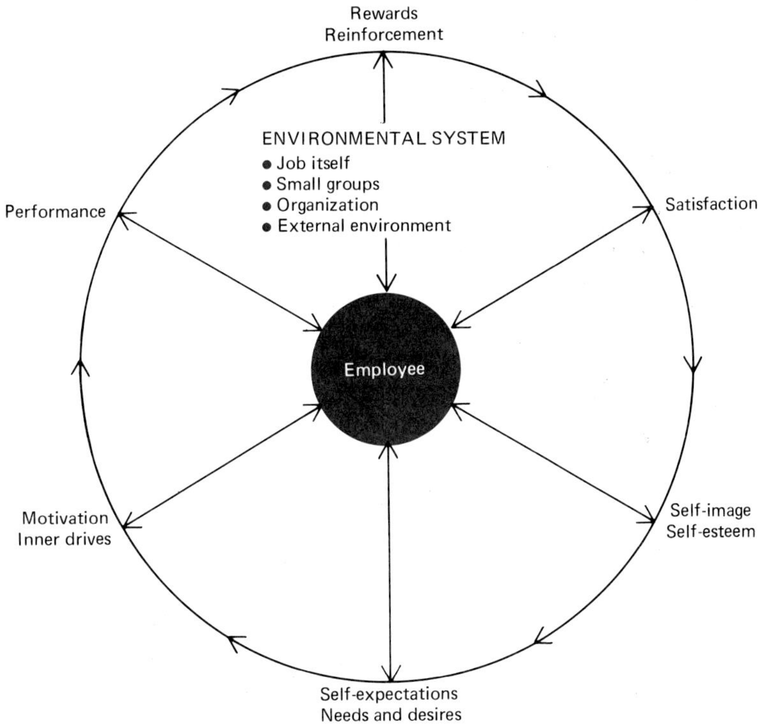

Figure 15-8
A Reward-Performance Model of Motivation

the proper rewards can be developed, they reinforce performance, provide satisfaction of needs, and build one's self-image.[22]

Enhanced self-image is a key in the motivational sequence. People must have an acceptable self-image in order to function effectively. A favorable self-image releases the creativity and potential that are in all people, so that growth is encouraged. It helps them cope with the world around them, and it encourages them to make decisions and accept responsibility for their own actions. A favorable self-image leads to higher self-expectations about one's performance. Expectancy is increased, thus further encouraging employee drives. Motivation is built up and released in the form of performance to accomplish desired results. At this point, rewards and reinforcement occur, and the reward-performance sequence repeats itself.

The self-image key

The model shows that suitable rewards must continue if motivated performance is to be maintained. But what are suitable rewards? They are rewards that meet the employee's self-expectations and fulfill his or her needs. However, built into the model are other sources of rewards that are not readily apparent. For example, most people will be motivated to perform at a level that is consistent with their self-image. When that level of performance is achieved, it reaffirms the individual's self-image and sense of self-esteem, which further reinforces the

Suitable rewards

person's self-expectations about future performance. If the environmental system continues to provide reinforcement, the person's self-image is likely to grow. The individual will be motivated by higher self-expectations to perform at a higher level that is more congruent with the stronger self-image and self-esteem. If suitable rewards are received at the higher level of performance, self-image, self-expectations, motivation, and performance are all likely to increase again.

JOB SATISFACTION

Definition   ■■■■■■■■■■■■■■■■ *Job satisfaction* is the favorableness or unfavorableness with which employees view their work. As with motivation, it too is affected by the environmental system shown in Figure 15-8. The job itself impacts satisfaction through its job design, as discussed in Chapter 5. Jobs that are rich in behavioral elements—such as autonomy, variety, task identity, task significance, and feedback—contribute to an employee's satisfaction. Likewise, orientation was emphasized in Chapter 8 because the employee's acceptance into the small work group and into the organization is important for high levels of satisfaction. And Chapter 2 outlined some of the major environmental challenges that can directly impact a personnel department and indirectly affect an organization's human resources. In short, each element of the environmental system can add to, or detract from, job satisfaction.

As was shown in Figure 15-1, the personnel function is substantially concerned with job satisfaction. It monitors job satisfaction closely because satisfaction affects turnover, absences, grievances, and other vital personnel issues. In many organizations personnel specialists periodically conduct job satisfaction surveys and study other indexes of satisfaction is order to be aware of employee feelings. In addition, satisfaction is affected by the way personnel specialists administer personnel activities. Bureaucratic, rules-oriented personnel departments have been the source of much employee dissatisfaction in the past. In contrast, more helpful, human-oriented personnel departments build employee motivation, growth, and satisfaction.

Job Satisfaction and Performance

Are high job satisfaction and high performance related? If so, what is the relationship? Historically, it was assumed that more satisfied workers performed better. There often are positive relationships between high satisfaction and improved performance, but most of these are not significant.[23] There are many satisfied workers who are not high producers. They remain content to perform only an average job. Satisfaction by itself is not a strong motivator, but it may maintain employees so that they are more receptive to a motivational environment when it is provided. This relationship probably accounts for the connection often found between satisfaction and performance.

Satisfied workers are not always the best producers.

For example, George Moore liked his employer and was satisfied with his job, but his performance was average. However, when the personnel department developed a program that increased his participation in job issues and encouraged small work teams, George was receptive and developed strong motivation. During the next few months his performance improved substantially.

A basic issue is whether satisfaction leads to better performance, or whether better performance leads to satisfaction. Which comes first? The relationship between satisfaction and motivation or performance is not as straightforward as might be expected. Various studies have shown that high *and* low performance can be associated with *either* high *or* low job satisfaction. This lack of causation may not be as strange as it first seems. The fact that workers are satisfied does not mean that they are motivated. It only means that they are satisfied. They may be satisfied because they do not have to work hard, and yet they have an environmental system that is very favorable to them personally. Conversely, employees who work very hard are not always highly satisfied. They may be working diligently because they fear discipline or because they personally hold high work standards. The reason for the apparent uncertain relationship between performance and satisfaction is because rewards intervene, as shown at the top of Figure 15-8. Whether satisfaction is going to be improved depends on whether the rewards at the top of the diagram match the expectations, needs, and desires held by the employee at the bottom of the figure. If better performance leads to higher rewards and if these rewards are seen as fair and equitable, then improved satisfaction results. It results because employees feel that they are receiving rewards in proportion to their performance.[24] On the other hand, if rewards are seen as inadequate for one's level of performance, dissatisfaction tends to occur. In either case, one's level of satisfaction becomes feedback that affects one's self-image and motivation to perform. The total performance-satisfaction relationship is a continuous system, making it difficult to assess the impact of satisfaction on motivation or on performance and vice versa.

The role of rewards

For example, a military doctor in a remote field hospital may be very dissatisfied with the long working hours or with the remote location. However, that same doctor may be motivated by a self-image of doing a good job and by expectations of working hard, regardless of the rewards or level of satisfaction. If the doctor gets appropriate rewards (extra or long vacations, for example), satisfaction may climb. For the personnel specialists at the military hospital, however, job satisfaction is an important determinant of whether the military doctors will reenlist.[25]

Job Satisfaction, Turnover, and Absences
Although research has been unable to specify the exact relationship between satisfaction and performance, personnel professionals should be very concerned about job satisfaction. Research has shown that there is a strong relationship between job satisfaction and employee turnover and absenteeism.[26] And as RCA discovered at its television plant in Memphis, extreme employee dissatisfaction can lead to union activity, strikes, and other causes of disruption.

Turnover and absences are an important concern for the personnel function,

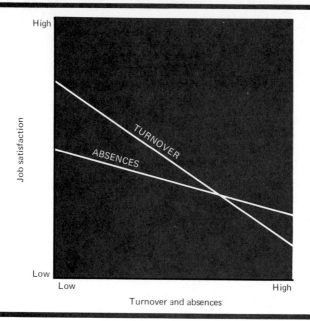

Figure 15-9
A General Model Relating Job Satisfaction to
Turnover and Absences

Increased satisfaction lowers turnover and absenteeism.

and job satisfaction does affect them, although it is only one of many influences.[27] As might be expected, when job satisfaction goes up, turnover declines. The reverse is also true. As shown in Figure 15-9, those employees who have lower satisfaction usually have higher turnover. They are more likely to leave their employer and seek greener pastures elsewhere, while their more satisfied associates remain.

A similar relationship applies to absences. Those employees who have less satisfaction tend to be absent more often. They do not necessarily plan to be absent, but when some reason for absence arises, a dissatisfied employee finds it easier to respond to that reason. As shown by the steepness of the lines in Figure 15-9, job satisfaction may not have quite as strong an effect on absences as it does on turnover.

Personnel costs for turnover and absences can be rather easily computed. For example, a bank calculated that each turnover costs $4500 for records, recruitment, and training of a replacement. When a job satisfaction problem developed in one of its branches, three clerks resigned. The personnel department calculated a direct cost of $13,500 ($4500 × 3) and used this cost as leverage to persuade the manager to improve branch practices.

Parkinson's law of sick leave

As one group of writers observed about absenteeism: "Imaginary illnesses are especially likely to occur in those organizations which have a paid sick leave program. A common behavioral outcome of such a program might be labeled Parkinson's Law of Sick Leave Abuse: the days lost due to sickness expand to equal the number of paid sick days allowed."[28]

Perhaps the only sure ways for personnel to repeal this version of Parkinson's law is to provide high levels of job satisfaction.

Age and Job Satisfaction

As workers grow older, they tend to be more satisfied with their jobs. There are a number of reasons for this satisfaction, such as lowered expectations and better adjustment to their work situation because of experience. Younger workers, on the other hand, tend to be less satisfied because of higher expectations, less adjustment, and other causes. There may be expectations, but the trend of higher job satisfaction with age is shown by most studies. This general relationship is illustrated in Figure 15-10. The trend applies to both men and women, and to managers as well as workers.[29]

For example, one study of nearly 4000 managers showed a steadily rising job satisfaction index with advancing age.[30] The age groups and satisfaction indexes are as follows:

Satisfaction grows with age.

Under 30 years	3.41
30 to 40 years	3.42
41 to 55 years	3.57
Over 55 years	3.63

Figure 15-10

A General Model Relating Job Satisfaction to Age and Occupational Level

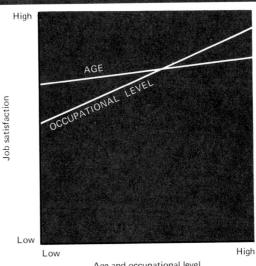

Occupational Level and Job Satisfaction

Figure 15-10 also shows that people with higher-level occupations tend to be more satisfied with their jobs. They usually have better pay and better working conditions. Their jobs make fuller use of their abilities, and so they have good reasons to be more satisfied. The result is that managers and professionals usually are more satisfied than skilled workers, who tend to be more satisfied than semiskilled and unskilled workers. The steepness of the lines in Figure 15-10 shows that occupation is more strongly related to job satisfaction than age is. Those who work in high occupational levels are considerably more satisfied than unskilled workers.

Organization Size and Job Satisfaction

Organization size tends to be inversely related to job satisfaction. As organizations grow larger, job satisfaction tends to decline moderately unless corrective action is taken to offset the trend.[31] Without corrective action large organizations tend to overwhelm people and disrupt supportive processes, such as communication, coordination, and participation. Employees begin to feel that they are losing control over the events that affect them because decision-making power is so far removed. The work environment also loses elements of personal closeness, friendship, and small-group teamwork that are important to the satisfaction of many people.

The term "organization size" refers to the size of an operating unit, such as a branch plant, rather than the size of an entire corporation or governmental group. For example, a large manufacturer could operate with thirty decentralized units, all of small size. Other things being equal, each of the decentralized units should be able to maintain high job satisfaction, even though the entire corporation is large. Because of the size-satisfaction relationship, the personnel function in larger organizations may have a more difficult job in maintaining employee satisfaction. Large size puts a personnel department on notice that it needs to give more attention to job satisfaction issues.

Satisfaction is more difficult to provide in large organizations because people do not feel as though they are as important an element in a large organization as they are in a small one. As a result, the personnel department must deal with stress, counseling, and discipline, which are the subjects of the next chapter. Personnel specialists also can help people feel more satisfied through effective communication, as discussed in Chapter 17.

SUMMARY

The personnel function is directly and indirectly involved with organizational climate, motivation, and job satisfaction. Organizational climate is the favorableness or unfavorableness of the environment as seen by the people who work there. Personnel policies and programs have a major effect on the climate in an organization.

Motivation is a person's drive to take an action because that person wants to do so. It is a complex system of relationships that are affected by forces inside and outside of the organization. Major frameworks for understanding motivation include a hierarchy of needs, ERG needs, motivation and maintenance factors, equity theory, expectancy theory, and behavior modification. These may be combined into a reward-performance model that responds to needs within the environment of the job, small groups, the organization, and the social system. The model is portrayed in a circular manner to show that it rewards and reinforces desired behavior on a regular basis. It builds satisfaction, self-image, and self-expectations so that motivation is encouraged to continue.

Job satisfaction is the favorableness or unfavorableness with which employees view their work. The personnel function tries to develop and monitor job satisfaction because of its close association with certain measures of performance. Satisfaction is inversely related to turnover, absences, and organizational size. On the other hand, it is positively related to age and occupational level.

TERMS FOR REVIEW

Organizational climate

Motivation

Hierarchy of needs

Higher-order needs

Existence-relatedness-growth theory

Reinforcement schedules

Reward-performance model

The expectancy model

Valence

Expectancy

Path-goal personnel strategy

Cognitive models of motivation

Behavior modification

Law of effect

Motivational factors

Maintenance factors

Equity theory

Environmental system for
   motivation

Job satisfaction

REVIEW AND DISCUSSION QUESTIONS

1. In what ways is the personnel function involved with organizational climate, motivation, and job satisfaction?

2. Discuss similarities and differences among cognitive models of motivation. Do you see any major differences among them?

3. Are you personally motivated by higher-order or by lower-order needs? Think about this issue and discuss it.

4. In relation to the expectancy model, think of a situation in which a person had strong desires for an outcome, but low expectancy frustrated that person. Discuss corrective action that could have been taken.

5. Explain why the application of positive reinforcement by managers sometimes fails. If you had to use behavior modification, which reinforcement schedule do you think is best?

6. Contrast and explain how Alderfer's ERG theory differs from Maslow's needs hierarchy.

7. Why should a plant personnel manager be concerned about the level of job satisfaction? Explain the consequences of low levels of job satisfaction.

8. Interview two employees in large organizations and two others in small organizations. Do you find differences in their job satisfaction that may be related to organization size? Discuss your findings.

INCIDENT 15-1

Empire Machinery Company

Marge Jones, age 45, is a machinist in a small factory. She has been there for six months. She had not been in the job market prior to her training to become a machinist at a trade school a year ago.

Marge Jones's quality of work has been borderline during the last several weeks, and so Carl Bunyan, her supervisor, decided to have a conference with her. After a routine discussion of other matters, Carl asked her how she felt about her quality of output during the last few weeks. Marge replied, "I know that I haven't been doing as good a job as I should. I have thought about this a great deal; and, though I regret to tell you this, my conclusion is that you are the cause of my poor work! The problem is the way you talk to me and the others in this department. You talk to all of us so gruffly and in such a loud voice that I am upset all day long. I just can't get motivated."

Carl was visibly upset by Marge's comments because he realized he was gruff and talked in a loud voice, but this was his normal personality.

1. Can Maslow's hierarchy of needs help Carl understand this situation? Can the idea of motivational and maintenance factors help? What about the expectancy model? Discuss.

2. What action do you recommend for Carl? Discuss.

INCIDENT 15-2

Health-More Foods Corporation

Health-More Foods Corporation of Lincoln, Nebraska, has been growing at a compounded rate of 30 percent for the last seven years. It entered the vitamin and health food business at a time when many people were concerned about natural foods and vitamins, and it sells high-quality products. The firm has captured a dominant position in its regional market, and it now has about 150 employees.

Because of its growth Health-More Foods has had difficulty maintaining trained clerical employees. At one point billing errors reached 9 percent, and accounts payable errors were at 8 percent. The new personnel director proposed and installed a simple two-step program to correct this situation. First, supervisors and employees in each work unit met to discuss and set goals for improvement. Then supervisors regularly praised employees who had fewer errors than standard, and results for each work unit were charted daily. Within one month the error rates for both billing and accounts payable declined to less than 1 percent and remained there.

1.   Discuss the two-step program and its results in terms of each of the models of motivation presented in this chapter.

2.   How many of the models apply? Does one apply better than others? Discuss.

REFERENCES

1.   William H. Mobley, "Where Have All the Golfers Gone?" *Personnel Journal,* July 1977, p. 340.

2.   Fred Luthans and Robert Kreitner, *Organizational Behavior Modification,* Glenview, Ill.: Scott, Foresman, 1975.

3.   David Macarov, *Worker Productivity,* Beverly Hills, Calif.: Sage, 1982.

4.   Erwin S. Stanton, "A Critical Reevaluation of Motivation, Management and Productivity," *Personnel Journal,* March 1983, pp. 208–214.

5.   Edward E. Lawler III and Gerald E. Ledford, Jr., "Productivity and the Quality of Work Life," *National Productivity Review,* Winter 1981–82, pp. 23–36.

6.   L. Erik Calonius, "Factory Magic: In a Plant in Memphis Japanese Firm Shows How to Attain Quality," *The Wall Street Journal,* Western ed., Apr. 29, 1983, p. 1.

7.   Ibid., p. 12.

8.   See for example, Kenneth Blanchard and Spencer Johnson, *The One Minute Manager,* New York: William Morrow, 1982; William G. Ouchi, *Theory Z, How American Business Can Meet the Japanese Challenge,* New York: Avon, 1981; and Thomas J. Peters and Robert H. Waterman, Jr., *In Search of Excellence, Lessons from America's Best-Run Companies,* New York: Harper & Row, 1982.

9.   Stanton, op. cit.

10.   Paul M. Muchinsky, "Organizational Communication: Relationships to Organizational Climate and Job Satisfaction," *Academy of Management Journal,* December 1977, pp. 592–607.

11.   A. H. Maslow, "A Theory of Human Motivation," *Psychological Review,* vol. 50, 1943,

pp. 370–396; and A. H. Maslow, *Motivation and Personality*, New York: Harper & Row, 1954.

12. Clayton P. Alderfer, *Existence, Relatedness, and Growth*, New York: Free Press, 1972.

13. Frederick Herzberg, Bernard Mausner, and Barbara Snyderman, *The Motivation to Work*, New York: Wiley, 1959. See also Clifford E. Jurgensen, "Job Preferences (What Makes a Job Good or Bad?)," *Journal of Applied Psychology*, June 1978, pp. 267–276.

14. Gerald R. Salancik and Jeffrey Pfeiffer, "An Examination of Need-Satisfaction Models of Job Attitudes," *Administrative Science Quarterly*, September 1977, pp. 427–456. This article also criticizes other need-satisfaction models, such as those of Maslow and Alderfer.

15. J. Stacy Adams, "Toward an Understanding of Inequity," *Journal of Abnormal and Social Psychology*, November 1963, pp. 422–436.

16. M. R. Carrell and J. E. Dettrich, "Equity Theory: The Recent Literature, Methodological Considerations, and New Directions," *Academy of Management Review*, April 1978, pp. 202–210; also see Richard A. Cosier and Dan R. Dalton, "Equity Theory and Time: A Reformulation," *Academy of Management Review*, April 1983, pp. 311–319.

17. Victor H. Vroom, *Work and Motivation*, New York: Wiley, 1964.

18. B. F. Skinner, *Science and Human Behavior*, New York: Macmillan (Free Press), 1953; and B. F. Skinner, *Contingencies of Reinforcement*, New York: Appleton-Century-Crofts, 1969. See also Luthans and Kreitner, op. cit.

19. Charles A. Snyder and Fred Luthans, "Using OB Mod to Increase Hospital Productivity," *The Personnel Administrator*, August 1982, pp. 67–68, 70–73.

20. Jerry A. Wallin and Ronald D. Johnson, "The Use of Positive Reinforcement to Reduce the Costs Associated with Employee Absenteeism," *Proceedings of the Twenty-Eighth Annual Winter Meeting*, Madison, Wis.: Industrial Relations Research Association, 1976, pp. 41–46.

21. Arthur C. Beck and Ellis D. Hillman, "The Power of Positive Management," *Personnel Journal*, February 1983, pp. 126–131; see also Philip C. Grant, "Why Employee Motivation Has Declined in America," *Personnel Journal*, December 1982, pp. 905–909.

22. J. H. Kerr Inkson, "Self-Esteem as a Moderator of the Relationship between Job Performance and Job Satisfaction," *Journal of Applied Psychology*, April 1978, pp. 243–247. See also Leonard Ackerman and Joseph P. Grunenwald, "Help Employees Motivate Themselves," *Personnel Journal*, July 1984, pp. 55–57.

23. Lawler and Ledford, op. cit., p. 26.

24. See Edward E. Lawler III, and Lyman W. Porter, "The Effect of Performance on Job Satisfaction," *Industrial Relations*, October 1967, pp. 20–28.

25. Lyman W. Porter and Edward E. Lawler, *Managerial Attitudes and Performance*, Homewood, Ill.: Irwin, 1968.

26. Lyman W. Porter and Richard M. Steers, "Organizational, Work, and Personal Factors in Employee Turnover and Absenteeism," *Psychological Bulletin*, August 1973, pp. 151–176; see also Richard T. Mowday, Lyman W. Porter, and Richard M. Steers, *Employee-Organization Linkages*, New York: Academic Press, 1981.

27. Richard M. Steers and Susan R. Rhodes, "Major Influences on Employee Attendance: A Process Model," *Journal of Applied Psychology*, August 1978, pp. 391–407; William H. Mobley, Stanley O. Horner, and A. T. Hollingsworth, "An Evaluation of Precursors of Hospital Employee Turnover," *Journal of Applied Psychology*, August 1978, pp. 408–141; and Richard T. Mowday and Daniel G. Spencer, "The Influence of Task and Personality Characteristics on Employee Turnover and Absenteeism Incidents," *Academy of Management Journal*, September 1981, pp. 634–642.

28. Richard E. Kopelman, George O. Schneller IV, and John J. Silver, Jr., "Parkinson's Law and Absenteeism: A Program to Rein In Sick Leave Costs," *The Personnel Administrator*, May 1981, p. 28.

29. Timothy J. Keaveny, John H. Jackson, and John A. Fossum, "Are There Sex Differences in Job Satisfaction?" *The Personnel Administrator*, March 1978, pp. 55–58.

30. Frank J. Smith, Kenneth D. Scott, and Charles L. Hulin, "Trends in Job-Related Attitudes of Managerial and Professional Employees," *Academy of Management Journal*, September 1977, pp. 454–460.

31. Keith Davis, *Human Behavior at Work*, 6th ed., New York: McGraw-Hill, 1981, pp. 87–88; and Lyman W. Porter, Edward E. Lawler III, and J. Richard Hackman, *Behavior in Organizations*, New York: McGraw-Hill, 1975, pp. 248–252.

CHAPTER

16

My problems are just as important to me as the company president's problems are to him.

An Employee

STRESS, COUNSELING AND DISCIPLINE

CHAPTER OBJECTIVES

After studying this chapter, you should be able to:

1 Explain causes of stress and describe how stress affects performance.

2 Discuss employee burnout.

3 Define employee counseling and the major types of counseling.

4 Describe differences between directive and nondirective counseling.

5 Explain how progressive discipline works.

6 Discuss differences between preventive and corrective discipline.

The City of Phoenix has developed a counseling program called Project Concern for employees with troublesome personal problems.[1] The program is operated mostly by trained professionals on the city staff. City employees are used rather than outside professionals for several reasons: The in-house location is more convenient, many problems brought to the counselors are partly job-related, and the staff-operated program is more economical.

The counseling program is available to all employees, and 5 to 10 percent of them use it annually. Many workers are referred by a supervisor because their problems are affecting job performance. The supervisors receive a six-hour training course that helps them to be more sensitive to employee problems and encourages them to make early referrals before the situation becomes serious. Most counseling problems are related to the job, alcohol and drug abuse, marital relations, one's family, and personal finances.

Program results   The program has produced successful results. About 50 percent of the counselees have returned to full productivity, resulting in large cost savings for the city. Other organizations have reported similar successes. For example, Kimberly-Clark, a paper and forest products firm, compared the records of participants for one year before and one year after their involvement in its program. These workers had a 43 percent reduction in absences and a 70 percent reduction in accidents.[2] Substantial cost savings will result. In the case of accident reductions, chances for long-term employee disability and long-run disability costs are reduced.

Programs such as those in the City of Phoenix and at Kimberly-Clark are needed, and they are part of the services of many personnel departments. All of us from time to time face problems and emotional upsets, and frequently another person can help us cope with them. Some difficulties occur off the job, and others are job-related. In either case, the problems may affect performance on the job and be of concern to management.

The first section of this chapter discusses stress, which is one of the major conditions that creates a need for counseling. The next section explains counseling programs and discusses how they are applied. If counseling is not successful and an employee continues with inadequate performance, some form of disciplinary action may be necessary, as discussed in the final section.

EMPLOYEE STRESS

Stress and distress   Stress both on and off the job may create a need for counseling and other personnel services such as training and job transfers. *Stress* is a condition of strain that affects a person's emotions, thought processes, and physical condition.[3] Excessive amounts of stress can lead to *distress,* which is an overload on an employee's ability to cope with the total job and nonjob environment. The result usually is a variety of negative symptoms that can harm job performance. As shown in Figure 16-1, these symptoms involve both mental and physical health. Persons who have an overload of stress may become easily provoked to anger and are unable to relax. They may even develop stress-related medical problems such as stomach ulcers or alcoholism.[4]

- Nervousness and tension
- Chronic worry
- Digestive problems
- High blood pressure
- Inability to relax

- Excessive use of alcohol and/or tobacco
- Difficulties with sleep
- Uncooperative attitudes
- Feelings of inability to cope
- Anger and aggression

Figure 16-1
Typical Symptoms of Stress

These conditions are common symptoms of stress, although other causes for them exist.

The basic theory of stress, often called a *person-environment fit*, states that "when the resources and demands of the work environment do not fit the needs and abilities of the worker, the worker will develop symptoms of strain."[5] These symptoms eventually can lead to problems with job performance, physical health, and mental health. Conditions that tend to cause stress are called *stressors*. Although major distress can occur from only one stressor, usually stressors combine to affect an employee in a variety of ways until distress develops.

Person-environment fit

Stressors

> The experience of Bill Jenkins, an office supervisor, illustrates how stressful conditions multiply and become nearly overwhelming. Bill felt that he was doing well, but then he failed to get a promotion that he had sought. At about the same time, two of his key employees quit, and he had difficulty replacing them. Then his son got into trouble in high school, and the transmission failed on an automobile that he had planned to sell the following week. So many different problems were hitting Bill that he began to show signs of distress. He became easily upset, less considerate of employees, and less productive in meeting his deadlines.

Job Causes of Stress

Almost any job condition may cause stress depending upon an employee's response to it. For example, one employee will accept a new work procedure, while another employee rejects it. There are, however, a number of job conditions that frequently cause stress for employees, as shown in Figure 16-2.[6] Major causes are work overload and time urgency, which put employees under pressure.[7] Often some of this pressure arises from ineffective supervision. For example, the following stressful conditions are mostly created by supervisors: an insecure political climate, lack of performance feedback, and inadequate authority to match one's responsibilities. Another cause of stress is *role ambiguity,* which is a situation in which people in the organization have different expectations of an employee in a job. Sometimes an employee cannot meet all of these expectations and is confused about what to do. As a result, stressful feelings gradually build up.[8]

Role ambiguity

Frustration is a result of repeated interferences or blockages that prevent an employee from reaching a desired goal. It is a major cause of stress.[9] For

Frustration

- Work overload
- Time urgency
- Poor quality of supervision
- Insecure political climate
- Insufficient performance feedback
- Inadequate authority to match responsibilities
- Role ambiguity
- Frustration
- Interpersonal and intergroup conflict
- Differences between company and employee values
- Change of any type

Figure 16-2
Typical Causes of Stress on the Job

example, if you are trying to finish a report before quitting time, you are likely to become frustrated by repeated interferences. You may become irritable, develop an uneasy feeling in your stomach, or have some other reaction. These reactions to frustration are known as *defense mechanisms* because you are trying to defend yourself from the psychological effects of the blocked goal.

Both interpersonal and intergroup conflicts may cause stress. As people with different backgrounds, points of view, needs, and personalities interact, disagreements and other conflicts may cause stressful feelings.[10] Another cause **Value differences** of stress is the existence of important differences between company values and employee values. In a sense, these differences "tear the employee apart" with mental stress as the worker makes an effort to meet the requirements of both sets of values.[11] For example, a salaried employee may value home life and an early quitting time, but that worker's manager may expect salaried employees to work overtime to meet department objectives. Or perhaps the company values employee loyalty, but the employee's loyalty is family-centered.

A widely recognized cause of stress is change of any type, which will be discussed in Chapter 18. It requires adaptation by employees and tends to be especially stressful when it is major, unusual, or frequent.

For example, a sales representative named Dorothy Wang developed job stress as a result of repeated management changes. During the last twelve months she has had three different sales managers. Each manager used a different leadership style; and as soon as Dorothy adjusted to the style of one manager, she was forced to learn how to deal with the style of another. She felt insecure and under constant pressure. She longed for the day when she would have only one sales manager for two or three years and hoped that a measure of stability would return to her world.

Off-the-job Causes of Stress

Stress outside of one's employment also may affect job performance. Causes of stress off the job are the full range of problems that can occur to people. Certain causes, though, are fairly common, including financial worries, problems with children, marital problems, change in residence, death of a spouse or other close family member, and major injury or illness. At these times the personnel department needs to be especially helpful with counseling and other services, such as those at Kimberly-Clark and in the City of Phoenix.

Burnout

Burnout is a condition of mental, emotional, and sometimes physical exhaustion that results from substantial and prolonged stress. It can happen to any employee whether one is a manager, professional, clerk, or factory worker. Even human resource managers may experience it.[12] Burned out employees tend to feel used up, worn out, and "at the end of their rope."

Burnout can happen to anyone.

People with burnout tend to have a variety of symptoms, such as depression and a low self-image.[13] They may become withdrawn and detached from interpersonal contacts and day-to-day activities. They tend to be irritable and blame others for their difficulties and may even develop health problems, such as sleep disorders and excessive use of alcohol. They eventually can become so emotionally exhausted that they go through the motions of work but accomplish very little. As one employee described a burned-out associate, "His body is here today, but his mind stayed home."

Symptoms of burnout

With regard to burnout, the personnel department's role is a proactive one to help employees prevent burnout before it occurs. For example, the personnel department can train supervisors to recognize stress and rearrange work assignments to reduce it. Jobs may be redesigned, personal conflicts resolved, counseling provided, and temporary leaves arranged. Many other approaches to stress reduction are discussed throughout this book. The popular statement that "prevention is better than curing" definitely applies to burnout because it has high human and economic costs. Weeks or months of rest, reassignment, and/or treatment may be required before recovery occurs. Some emotional or health damage can be permanent.

Personnel department role

Stress and Job Performance

Stress can be either helpful or harmful to job performance depending upon the amount of it. Figure 16-3 presents a *stress-performance model* that shows the relationship between stress and job performance.[14] When there is no stress, job challenges are absent, and performance tends to be low. As stress increases, performance tends to increase because stress helps a person call up resources to meet job requirements. It is a healthy stimulus that encourages employees to respond to challenges. Eventually the stress reaches a plateau that represents approximately a person's top day-to-day performance capability. At this point additional stress tends to produce no further improvement.

Stress-performance model

Finally, if stress becomes too great or continues for too long, performance begins to decline. An employee loses the ability to cope, becomes unable to make decisions, and is erratic in behavior. At this point the worker is approaching burnout. If stress increases to a breaking point, performance becomes zero. The employee has a breakdown, becomes too ill to work, is fired, quits, or refuses to come to work to face the stress.

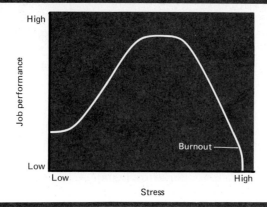

Figure 16-3
A Stress-Performance Model

Stress Thresholds

Stress threshold

People have different tolerances for stressful situations. The level of stress that a person can tolerate before feelings of distress begin to occur is known as one's *stress threshold.* Some persons are easily upset by the slightest change or emergency. Others are cool, calm, and collected, partly because they have a high self-image and confidence in their ability to cope. They feel very little stress unless a stressor is major or prolonged.

> Mabel Kelly worked at the driver's license desk in a state office. She faced a variety of problems, complaints, angry citizens, and red tape during the day, but it did not seem to trouble her. On the other hand, Malcolm Morgan, her associate at an adjoining desk, had difficulty with the complaints, anger, and abuse that he received. He began taking longer breaks and then extra breaks. He seemed nervous. Finally, he asked for a transfer to another state office. The two employees had different stress thresholds.

Type A and Type B Persons

Type A people

Reactions to stressful situations often are related to type A and type B people.[15] *Type A people* are those who are aggressive and competitive, set high standards, and put themselves under constant time pressures. They even make excessive demands on themselves in recreational sports and leisure activities. They often fail to realize that many of the pressures they feel are of their own making, rather than in their environment. Because of the constant stress, they are more prone to physical ailments related to stress, such as heart attacks.

Type B people

Type B people are more relaxed and easygoing. They accept situations and work within them, rather than fight them competitively. They are especially relaxed regarding time pressures, and so they are less prone to problems associated with stress.

Recovery from Stress

Different recovery patterns

Some persons recover from stressful situations easily. For example, they recuperate at home each evening and return to work the next day refreshed.

Others can recover during the weekend. Although stress builds up during the week, they return to work the following Monday ready to absorb more stress. Other persons, however, allow stress to build up week after week without relief, and it is these employees who are of special concern to the personnel department.

Figure 16-4 shows the stress responses of three employees with the same job. Each employee responded differently. For example, employee A showed moderate stress in the beginning but adapted rapidly. Employee B showed higher stress. There was some recovery during weekends, but stress built up again during the week. In the case of employee C the stress reaction was cumulative, becoming higher and higher.

Personnel Actions to Reduce Stress

The human resources department should play a leading role in reducing employee stress and burnout. Since it is responsible for the care of personnel, the department needs to take the following actions:

• Develop a basic stress management policy for company approval.[16]

• Communicate the policy to all employees in a sensitive, caring way. Then continue communication so that employees are always aware of the programs that are available to help them.

• Train managers to be sensitive to the early symptoms of stress so that they can take corrective action before it becomes severe. For example, an employee with signs of distress may be given less demanding work, encouraged to take a vacation, or referred to a counselor.

• Train employees to recognize and cope with stress.

• Improve communication and participation throughout the organization so

Figure 16-4

Stress Responses of Three Employees to the Same Job

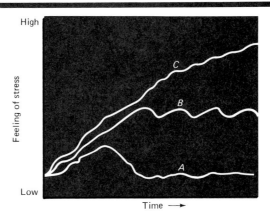

that employees understand what is affecting them and feel that they have a useful role in dealing with it.

• Monitor company activities to discover any conditions that unnecessarily lead to stress. The theory of person-environment fit (discussed earlier in this chapter) helps management understand and correct stressful situations.

• Improve job and organization design to avoid stressful working conditions.[17] For example, the records clerk should not be located in an area with a high noise level where there will be frequent interruptions.

• Provide counseling and other employee assistance programs to help employees in stressful situations.[18] For example, New York Telephone Company provides a meditation room and meditation training to give employees a quiet break from job pressures. Any employee who is found to be experiencing stress can use the facility.[19]

In summary, the human resources department must be alert to stressful symptoms and situations and take the necessary action to prevent them. Potential benefits to the organization include less absenteeism, reduced turnover, increased productivity, reduced medical costs, better decision making, improved employee satisfaction, and a better climate for work.[20]

EMPLOYEE COUNSELING

Theory of counseling

Counseling is the discussion of a problem with an employee, with the general objective of helping the worker cope with it. The purpose is to help employees either resolve or cope with the situation so that they can become more effective persons.[21] The basic theory supporting counseling is that stress and personal problems are likely to affect both performance and an employee's general life adjustment; therefore, it is in the best interests of all those concerned (employer, employee, and community) to help the employee return to full effectiveness. Most counselees are healthy people who are experiencing stress and need help to return to emotional wellness. Emotions are a normal part of life, but they can get out of control and cause workers to do things that are harmful to their own best interests and to those of the firm. Sometimes employees may leave the organization because of a trifling conflict that seems large to them, or they may undermine morale in their departments. Managers want their workers to maintain a reasonable emotional balance and channel their emotions along constructive lines so that everyone will work together effectively. Counseling is a useful tool to help accomplish this goal. The success rate from counseling programs often is substantial, as described in the Phoenix and Kimberly-Clark examples at the beginning of this chapter.

Counseling Programs

Counseling programs usually are administered by the human resources department, which uses various combinations of in-house and external counseling services.[22] Large firms often employ their own counseling staff. Some are full-time counselors while others may be part-time counselors in the community who are available on the company premises for certain hours during the week. Other firms refer most problems to community agencies, even though there may be an in-house counselor who coordinates the program. If the employer is located in a large city, expert community counseling services usually are available, so both large and small firms tend to use them. Community services are especially useful to smaller firms that would be unable to employ a full-time counselor.

An example of a comprehensive employee counseling service is Control Data Corporation's Employee Advisory Resource (EAR) program.[23]

One of the program's slogans is: "Employees are bright and well-trained enough to handle just about any problem—except their own." The program is available to employees and their families, and it covers both personal and work-related problems. It maintains a twenty-four-hour hot line and uses both company counselors and community agencies. The service is strictly confidential.

An average of 750 employees use the service each month. Many successes have been reported, although the program is unable to solve every employee problem. Control Data's more specific study of alcoholic employees reported a remarkable 85 percent reduction in lost work hours, a 47 percent reduction in sick leave, and a 72 percent reduction in sickness and accident benefit payments. In a survey 93 percent of the employees reported that they believe EAR is a worthwhile service.

Company and community counseling services

Control Data's approach

Characteristics of Counseling

Counseling has a number of characteristics that make it a useful activity in the personnel department. As shown in Figure 16-5, counseling requires two people: a counselor and a counselee. It is their exchange of ideas that creates a counseling relationship, and so counseling is an act of communication. Counseling can improve organizational performance because the employee

Figure 16-5
Characteristics of Counseling

- Requires two people, a counselor and a counselee.
- Is an act of communication.
- Helps employees cope.
- Reduces employee problems and emotional upsets.
- Improves organizational performance.
- Helps organization be more human and considerate.
- Performed by both professionals and nonprofessionals.
- Involves both job and personal problems.
- Is confidential and private.

becomes more cooperative, worries less about personal problems, or makes progress in other ways. Because it deals with people problems, counseling also helps organizations to be more human and considerate.

Counseling usually is performed by both professionally trained counselors and nonprofessionals. For example, both personnel specialists and supervisors engage in counseling activities.

Supervisors as counselors

> A study of supervisors in seven companies reported that they spent an average of 2.5 hours a week discussing moderately serious personal problems with their employees. The most frequently discussed problems were work-related, such as difficulties with associates; but more personal subjects, such as marital problems, also were discussed. The researchers' conclusion was that most supervisors "felt positively about being cast in the interpersonal helper role and considered that to be an important part of their job."[24]

Some firms, however, advise managers to avoid giving personal, nonjob advice to employees because the managers are not professionally qualified to do so. There is a chance that they will give inappropriate or wrong advice that will increase an employee's problem. In some instances an employee may sue the company under the principle of agency, which makes the employer liable for the acts of its supervisors and managers.

Counseling is confidential.

Counseling is strictly a confidential relationship, and records of it should be restricted to persons directly involved in solving the counseling problem. These practices are necessary to protect employee privacy and to protect the employer from possible lawsuits for such liabilities as invasion of privacy or alleged slander. The policy of some firms is to refer all marital and family counseling to community agencies. These companies believe that, for reasons of employee privacy, they should not be involved in these problems. Employers also must be certain that their counseling programs comply with EEO regulations by providing equal counseling services to all protected employee groups.

Counseling Functions

Counseling functions are the activities performed by counseling, such as:

•   *Advice.* Counselors often give advice to counselees in order to guide them toward desired courses of action.

•   *Reassurance.* The counseling experience often provides employees with reassurance, which is confidence that they are following a suitable course of action and have the courage to carry it out.

•   *Communication.* Counseling is a communication experience. It initiates upward communication to management and also gives the counselor an opportunity to interpret management problems and give work insights to employees.

- *Release of emotional tension.* People tend to get emotional release from their tensions when they have an opportunity to discuss their problems with someone else.

- *Clarified thinking.* Serious discussion of problems with someone else helps a person think more clearly.

- *Reorientation.* Reorientation involves a change in an employee's basic self through a change in goals and values. Professional counseling by psychologists and psychiatrists often helps employees reorient their values. For example, a better self-image helps a person to be more effective. It is said, "The person you see in yourself is the person you will be."

Self-image

Types of Counseling

When we look upon counseling in terms of the amount of direction that a counselor gives a counselee, we see that it is a continuum from full direction (directive counseling) to no direction (nondirective counseling), as shown in Figure 16-6. Between the two extremes is participative counseling. These three counseling types will be discussed in order to show how counselors may vary their direction of a counselee in a counseling situation.

Directive counseling   Directive counseling is the process of listening to an employee's problems, deciding with the employee what should be done, and then telling and motivating the employee to do it. Directive counseling mostly accomplishes the counseling function of *advice,* but it also may reassure, communicate, give emotional release, and (to a minor extent) clarify thinking. Reorientation is seldom achieved in directive counseling. Almost everyone likes to give advice, counselors included, and it is easy to do. But is it effective? Does the counselor really understand the employee's problem? Does the counselor have the knowledge and judgment to make a "right" decision? Even if the decision is right, will the employee follow it? The answer to these questions is usually "no," and this is why advice often is not helpful in counseling. On other occasions an employee welcomes guidance because of a counselor's broader knowledge and contacts in a situation.

Directive counseling has limitations.

Ronald Clark came to a personnel counselor, Vince Mardian, to discuss a conflict he was having with Margie DeLaval, an employee in another department. Ronald alleged that Margie reduced his incentive earnings by delivering products late from her department. He said that several loud arguments had developed. Vince offered some insights into interdepart-

Figure 16-6
Counseling Types According to Amount of Direction
that Counselors Give Counselees

TYPE OF COUNSELING	Nondirective	Participative	Directive
AMOUNT OF DIRECTION	Low	Intermediate	High

mental difficulties, so that Ronald could see that his problem was not unique. Vince advised, "Sit tight and don't rock the boat while I check this with the people involved."

Vince discovered that the problem resulted from some misunderstood instructions that caused Margie to deliver the products after her lunch rather than before. She also was upset by the conflict and was glad to try to settle it. Instructions were changed to provide delivery before lunch, and the problem was easily solved.

Nondirective counseling   Nondirective, or client-centered, counseling is at the opposite end of the continuum. It is the process of skillfully listening and encouraging a counselee to explain bothersome problems, understand them, and determine appropriate solutions. It focuses on the counselee rather than on the counselor as judge and adviser; hence it is "client-centered." Some variation of such counseling usually is practiced by professional counselors.

Professional counselors often accomplish four of the six counseling functions. Communication occurs both upward and downward through the counselor. Emotional release takes place, even more effectively than with directive counseling, and clarified thinking tends to follow. The unique advantage of nondirective counseling is its ability to encourage the employee's reorientation.

Emphasis on personal change It emphasizes changing the person, instead of dealing only with the immediate problem in the usual manner of directive counseling. Here is the way nondirective counseling typically works.

Assume that Harold Pace comes to a counselor, Janis Peterson, for assistance. Janis attempts to build a permissive relationship that encourages Harold to talk freely. At this point Janis defines the counseling relationship by explaining that she cannot tell Harold how to solve his problem, but that she may be able to help him understand his problem and deal satisfactorily with it.

Harold then explains his feelings, and Janis encourages their expression, shows interest in them, and accepts them without blame or praise. Eventually the negative feelings are drained away, giving Harold a chance to express tentatively a positive feeling or two, a fact that marks the beginning of Harold's emotional growth. Janis encourages these positive feelings and accepts them without blame or praise, just as she did the negative feelings.

If all goes well, Harold should at this point begin to get some insight into his problem and to start to develop alternative solutions. As he continues to grow, he should be able to choose a course of positive action and see his way clear to try it. He will then feel a decreasing need for help and recognize that the counseling relationship should end.

Participative counseling   Nondirective counseling by employers is limited because it requires professional counselors and is costly. Directive counseling often is not accepted by modern, independent employees. This means that the type of counseling used by many supervisors and personnel department employees is between the two extremes of directive and nondirective counseling. This middle ground is called participative (or cooperative) counseling because the counselor and the counselee participate in discussing a problem and developing a possible solution. *Participative counseling* is a mutual counselor-employee relationship that establishes a cooperative exchange of ideas to help solve an employee's problems. It is neither wholly counselor-centered nor wholly counselee-centered. Rather, the counselor and counselee use mutual discussion to apply their different knowledge, perspectives, and values to problems. Participative counseling integrates the ideas of both participants in the counseling relationship. It is, therefore, a balanced compromise that combines many advantages of both directive and nondirective counseling while throwing off most of their disadvantages. It also is best fitted to the skills of most company people who counsel employees.[25]

Mutual discussion

Participative counseling starts by using the listening techniques of nondirective counseling; but as the interview progresses, participative counselors may play a more active role than a nondirective counselor does. They may offer bits of information and insight. They may discuss the situation from their broader knowledge of the organization, thus giving an employee a different view of the problem. In general, participative counselors apply the four counseling functions of reassurance, communication, emotional release, and clarified thinking.

> For example, Mario Ponti came to see his supervisor concerning the insecurity he was feeling about his job. Because of technological changes in the type of work he did, he was losing confidence in his ability to retain his position. His supervisor did not tell Mario what to do (directive approach), and he did not merely listen to Mario (nondirective approach). Instead, the supervisor listened, recommended some training programs that were available, and helped Mario gain confidence that he could overcome his problem. The result was that Mario developed clarified thinking and chose to follow a training program to prepare himself for the new technology.

Although the success rate of counseling is substantial, as mentioned in the City of Phoenix example at the beginning of this chapter, failures sometimes occur. In these instances, disciplinary action and even termination may be appropriate, as discussed in the next section.

DISCIPINE

Discipline is management action to encourage compliance with organization standards. It is a type of training that seeks to correct and mold employee knowledge, attitudes, and behavior so that the worker strives willingly for better cooperation and performance. There are two types of discipline: preventive and corrective.

Preventive Discipline

Preventive discipine is action taken to encourage employees to follow standards and rules so that infractions are prevented. The basic objective is to encourage self-discipline among employees. In this way the workers maintain their own discipline, rather than having it imposed by management.

Personnel department role

The personnel department has a major responsibility for preventive discipline. For example, it develops programs to control absences and grievances. It communicates standards to employees and encourages workers to follow them. It also gives training programs to explain the reasons behind standards and to build a positive spirit of self-discipline. On other occasions, it encourages employee participation in setting standards, since workers will give better support to rules that they have helped create. Employees also will give more support to standards stated positively instead of negatively, such as "safety first!" rather than "don't be careless!" Workers usually want to know the reasons behind a rule so that it will make more sense to them. Effective discipline is a system relationship, so the personnel department needs to be concerned with all parts of the system.[26]

Corrective Discipline

Corrective discipline is an action that follows a rule infraction. It seeks to discourage further infractions and to ensure that future acts are in compliance with standards.[27] Typically the corrective or *disciplinary action* is a penalty of some type for the offending employee, such as a warning or suspension without pay.

Corrective discipline usually is governed by the hierarchy of an organization. It is initiated by an employee's immediate supervisor, but actions may require approval by a higher-level manager and/or procedural approval by the personnel department. The purpose is to prevent subsequent labor union or legal actions and to assure uniform application of rules throughout the organization. Any appeals then go to higher levels in the company and in the union hierarchy.

The objectives of corrective discipline are as follows:

- To reform the offender

- To deter others from similar actions

- To maintain consistent, effective group standards

The objectives of corrective discipline are positive. They are educational and corrective, rather than a negative slapping back at employees who have done wrong. The goal is to improve the future rather than punish for the past. A negative, punishing approach introduces too many undesirable side effects —such as apathy, absences, and fear of the supervisor.[28]

"Sandwich model"

The corrective disciplinary interview often follows a "sandwich model," which means that a corrective comment is sandwiched between two positive comments in order to make the corrective comment more acceptable. For example: "Your attendance is excellent, Roy (a positive comment), but your late return from coffee breaks disrupts our repair operations (negative). Otherwise your work is among the best in our department (positive)." The supervisor then focuses on ways in which the two of them can work together to correct the problem.

Dismissal

The ultimate disciplinary action is *dismissal,* which is separation from the employer for cause. (Other terms used in this situation are fired, terminated, discharged, or separated.) Usually there is a carefully planned termination interview to ensure that the separation is as positive and constructive as possible.[29] It has been said that every employee dismissal is evidence of management and personnel department failure, but this view is not realistic. Neither managers nor employees are perfect; so some problems cannot be solved regardless of how hard people try. Sometimes dismissal is better for both the worker and the company. This action gives the employee a chance to seek a new job where his or her abilities and temperament may be more appropriate. Many discharged employees move to another company and are successful, sometimes receiving promotions to top positions.

Termination interview

Restrictions on Corrective Discipline

In general, discipline is substantially restricted by the rules, laws, and regulations of unions and government. Corrective discipline is an especially sensitive subject with unions. They see it as an opportunity to protect employees from unreasonable management authority and to show employees that the union leadership cares for their interests. Employees also are sensitive about disciplinary issues because they can be a threat to employee pay and jobs. If there is a hint of unfairness in a disciplinary action, it can lead to a prolonged, costly dispute and eventually to arbitration. Walkouts and strikes can occur, and new bargaining issues about discipline may develop for the next bargaining session. The personnel department's job is to reduce chances for conflict by working with supervisors and union representatives to ensure that corrective discipline is fairly and uniformly applied.

Union restrictions

Government is increasing its regulation of discipline, making it more difficult to justify. The historical employer right to terminate an employee at any time without cause (the *termination-at-will doctrine*) is being restricted by the courts in many ways.[30] Normally an employee cannot be disciplined or dismissed for any of the following reasons:

Government restrictions

• Conditions controlled by equal opportunity laws—such as race, religion, national origin, sex, and age (40 to 70)[31]

• Union activities, as determined by law[32]

• Reporting Occupational Safety and Health Act violations

• Refusing to perform an unusual work assignment that the employee believes is hazardous or even life-threatening

• Refusing to perform an act that is clearly in violation of law, such as cooperating in a price-fixing scheme[33]

Other employment restrictions also may apply depending on the circumstances and local laws. In general, a dismissal may be challenged if it is arbitrary and unjust. It also cannot be contrary to clear public policy. For example, an employee was fired for serving on a jury after the employer asked the worker to try to avoid service. The court decided in favor of the employee because jury duty is a high public obligation.[34]

Due process for discipline is required by courts of law, arbitrators, and labor unions, especially where employee handbooks, labor agreements, or even verbal promises apply. *Due process* means that established rules and procedures for disciplinary action are followed and that employees have an opportunity to respond to charges made against them.[35] It is the personnel department's responsibility to ensure that all parties in a disciplinary action follow the correct rules and procedures so that due process will be used.

Due process

Documentation

If a disciplinary action is challenged, the personnel department also must have sufficient documentation to support the action; therefore, personnel policy usually requires proper documentation for all employer disciplinary actions.[36] Proper documentation should be specific—beginning with the date, time, and location of an incident. It should also describe the nature of the undesirable performance or behavior and show how it relates to job and organizational performance. Specific rules and regulations that relate to the incident should be identified. Documentation should also state what the manager said to the employee and how the employee responded, including specific words and acts. If there were witnesses, they should be identified. All documentation must be recorded promptly while the supervisor's memory is still fresh. It should be objective, based on observations and not on impressions. Documentation need not be lengthy, but it should be complete, precise, and accurate. If a supervisor follows these practical documentation guidelines, then the employer is reasonably protected in case of challenges—by employees, unions, regulatory bodies such as the Equal Employment Opportunity Commission—and lawsuits.

The Hot-Stove Rule

A useful guide for corrective discipline is the hot-stove rule, as shown in Figure 16-7. The *hot-stove rule* states that disciplinary action should have the same characteristics as the penalty a person receives from touching a hot stove. These characteristics are that discipline should be with warning, immediate, consistent, and impersonal. Warning is essential, and it requires communication of the rules to all employees. If an employee can show that management failed to give adequate notice of rules, management has difficulty justifying the discipline before a union or arbitrator.

With warning

> Dorothy Settler was given a one-day suspension for smoking in a restricted area. She was able to show that there were no "No Smoking" signs and she had no other notice that smoking in the area was a fire hazard. The arbitrator revoked the penalty and ordered one day of back pay for Dorothy.

Figure 16-7
The Hot-Stove Rule for Discipline

Discipline also should be immediate. When the discipline quickly follows an infraction, there is a connection between the two events in the employee's mind, and there is less probability of a future infraction.

Consistent discipline is required because consistency is an important part of fairness. Lack of consistency causes employees to feel discriminated against. If the person receiving the more severe penalty is a minority employee, then a charge of illegal discrimination may be filed, and the employer may be required to prepare a costly defense of the action. On the other hand, occasional exceptions can be accepted if they are justified.[37]

> Walter Miller, who had worked eighteen years without a disciplinary infraction, came to work slightly intoxicated three weeks after the death of his wife. Different treatment for him was justified, compared with the penalty for Betina Rouse, who had only two years of seniority, had been warned twice in the last six months about coming to work intoxicated, and again committed the same infraction.

The hot-stove rule also requires impersonal discipline—just as a stove equally burns men and women, young and old. The supervisor's personal feelings about an employee are not relevant to disciplinary action. The idea is to condemn the employee's wrongful act, not the employee as a person. There is a difference between applying a penalty for a job not performed and calling an employee a lazy loafer. However, unlike a hot stove, managers should be considerate of employee feelings by administering discipline in private.

Progressive Discipline
Most employers apply a policy of *progressive discipline,* which means that there are stronger penalties for repeated offenses. The purpose is to give an employee an opportunity to take corrective action before more serious penalties are applied. Progressive discipline also gives management time to work with an employee to help correct infractions, such as unauthorized absences.

When Margaret Stoner had two unauthorized absences, the personnel department provided counseling. It also arranged for her to join a ride pool that allowed her to leave home thirty minutes later, compared with public transportation. Afterward her unauthorized absences stopped.

A typical progressive discipline system is shown in Figure 16-8, and more detailed examples may be found in most labor union contracts. The first infraction leads to a verbal reprimand by the supervisor. The next infraction leads to a written reprimand, with a record placed in the files. Further infractions build up to stronger discipline, leading finally to discharge. Usually the personnel department is involved in step 3 or sooner in order to ensure that company policy is followed consistently in all departments.

Some progressive systems remove minor offenses from the record after one to three years, allowing each employee to return to step 1. Specified serious offenses, such as fighting or major theft, usually are exempted from progressive discipline. An employee who commits these offenses may be discharged for the first occurrence.

A Counseling Approach to Discipline

Most organizations use counseling in connection with discipline, but a few firms have moved a step further and taken a counseling approach to the entire procedure. For example, an employee is counseled rather than progressively penalized for the first few breaches of organizational standards. Here is how the program works in one firm.[38]

Counseling versus progressive discipline

The philosophy is that violations are employee malfunctions that can be constructively corrected without penalty. The first violation results in a private discussion with the supervisor. The second violation brings further discussion with the supervisor with a focus on correcting causes of the behavior. A third violation leads to counseling with the immediate supervisor and the shift supervisor to determine roots of the employee's malfunction. For example, does the employee dislike the job and want a transfer? Is the employee prepared to abide by the standard? The result of the discussion is given to the employee in a letter.

A fourth infraction within a reasonable amount of time, such as a year, results in final counseling with the superintendent. The offender is released from duty with pay for the remainder of the day to consider willingness to abide by standards. The offender is told that a further violation regretfully

Figure 16-8
A Progressive Discipline System

1. Verbal reprimand by supervisor
2. Written reprimand, with a record in personnel file
3. One- to three-day suspension from work
4. Suspension for one week or longer
5. Discharge for cause

will result in termination because it will show that the employee is unable or unwilling to work within the standards of the organization.

The focus of the counseling approach is fact-finding and positive. It attempts to guide the employee toward improved behavior rather than penalize to discourage infractions. In this manner the employee's self-image and dignity are retained, and the supervisor-employee relationship remains cooperative and constructive. A Frito-Lay manufacturing plant tried the counseling approach to discipline and in the first nine months reduced disciplinary terminations from fifty-two to sixteen.[39]

A positive approach

SUMMARY

Counseling sometimes is necessary for employees because of job and personal problems, many of which are associated with stress. The stress-performance model indicates that excessive stress reduces job performance, but a moderate amount may help employees respond to job challenges. Type A people tend to show more stress compared with type B people. Personnel department programs to help reduce stress include job design, communication, training, and counseling.

Counseling is the discussion of a problem with an employee to help the worker cope with the situation. It is performed by personnel department professionals as well as supervisors. In the typical firm most counseling for day-to-day problems is in the broad middle ground between directive and nondirective methods. Counseling programs include both job and personal problems, and there is extensive cooperation with community counseling agencies.

Discipline is management action to enforce organizational standards, and it is both preventive and corrective. The hot-stove rule is a useful general guide for corrective discipline. Most disciplinary action is progressive, with stronger penalties for repeated offenses. Some disciplinary programs primarily emphasize a counseling approach.

TERMS FOR REVIEW

Stressors	Counseling functions
Role ambiguity	Directive counseling
Burnout	Nondirective counseling
Stress-performance model	Participative counseling
Stress threshold	Preventive discipline
Type A persons	Corrective discipline
Type B persons	Hot-stove rule
Counseling	Progressive discipline

REVIEW AND DISCUSSION QUESTIONS

1.   Think of a part-time or full-time job that you have had. Discuss the stressors you experienced on the job.

2.   Discuss how stress and job performance are related.

3.   Do you feel that you are a type A or type B person? Do you have a high or low stress threshold? How would you rate your best friend on these items, and what are your reasons for choosing these ratings?

4.   Discuss what the personnel department can do to help people cope with stress.

5.   Explain the three types of counseling and the ways in which they differ.

6.   Discuss differences between preventive and corrective discipline. What examples of either one were applied to you on the last job you had?

7.   Discuss different government restrictions on an employer's right to discipline or dismiss an employee "at will," and explain why each of these restrictions probably exists.   935,   1108

8.   Discuss what progressive discipline is and how it works. Is its basic approach realistic in work situations?

INCIDENT 16-1

The Machinist's Abusive Comments to the Supervisor

William Lee, a machine operator, worked as a machinist for Horace Gray, a supervisor. Horace told William to pick up some trash that had fallen from William's work area, and William replied, "I won't do the janitor's work."

Horace replied, "When you drop it, you pick it up." William became angry and abusive, calling Horace a number of uncomplimentary names in a loud voice and refusing to pick up the trash. All employees in the department heard William's comments.

The situation was as follows. Horace had been trying for two weeks to get his employees to pick up trash in order to have a cleaner workplace and prevent accidents. He talked with all employees in a weekly department meeting and to each employee individually at least once. He stated that he was following the instructions of the superintendent. Only William objected with the comment, "I'm not here to do the janitor's work. I'm a machinist."

William had been in the department for six months and with the company for three years. Horace had spoken to him twice about excessive horseplay, but otherwise his record was good. He was known to have a quick temper.

After William finished his abusive outburst, Horace told him to come to the office and suspended him for one day for insubordination and abusive language to a supervisor. The discipline was within company policy, and similar acts had been disciplined in other departments.

When William walked out of Horace's office, Horace called the personnel director, reported what he had done, and said that he was sending a copy of his action for William's file.

1. As a personnel director, what comments would you make?

2. What follow-up actions should the personnel director take or recommend that Horace take? For example, do you recommend counseling for William? Would you reconsider disciplinary procedures and policies?

EXERCISE 16-1

A Counseling Program for Drug Abuse

Copeland Electronics, a growing electronics manufacturing firm, has increasingly faced problems with employees who abuse the use of alcohol and other drugs. Supervisors have been dealing with these employees in whatever ways seemed appropriate. However, both the supervisors and the personnel director agree that drug abuse problems are now serious enough to require a company policy and a procedure to implement it. They also believe that the company needs a consistent, dependable policy to protect itself from possible EEOC complaints of discrimination in counseling or treatment.

The personnel director has asked the assistant personnel director, Carolyn Stevens, to prepare a policy and procedure for working with employees when drug abuse is suspected. Carolyn has been in the personnel department for three years following her graduation with a major in personnel management from a nearby university.

Form teams of three to five members and develop an appropriate drug abuse policy and procedure for Carolyn. Be sure to include specific steps covering who will work with drug abusers and what they should do. Then present your report to your entire classroom group and compare it with statements by other teams.

REFERENCES

1. William G. Wagner, "Assisting Employees with Personal Problems," *The Personnel Administrator*, November 1982, pp. 59–64.

2. David Hill, "Employee Assistance Programs: The Helping Hand That's Good for All," *Corporate Fitness and Recreation*, October–November 1982, pp. 43–49.

3. For a thorough stress model and discussion of stress see James C. Quick and

Jonathan D. Quick, *Organizational Stress and Preventive Management,* New York: McGraw-Hill, 1984. See also John M. Ivancevich and Michael T. Matteson, *Stress and Work: A Managerial Perspective,* Glenview, Ill.: Scott, Foresman, 1981; and Walter H. Gmelch, *Beyond Stress to Effective Management,* New York: Wiley, 1982. Two significant earlier books on stress are Hans Selye, *The Stress of Life,* rev. ed., New York: McGraw-Hill, 1976; and Hans Selye, *Stress without Distress,* Philadelphia: Lippincott, 1974.

4.   Current material on this subject may be found in the journal *Alcoholism.*

5.   "Coping with Job Stress," *ISR Newsletter,* (Institute for Social Research, University of Michigan), Winter 1982, p. 4, referring to work by John R. P. French, Jr., and others at the institute.

6.   For research examples see Saroj Parasuraman and Joseph A. Alutto, "An Examination of Organizational Antecedents of Stressors at Work," *Academy of Management Journal,* March 1981, pp. 48–67; and James B. Shaw and John H. Riskind, "Predicting Job Stress Using Data from the Position Analysis Questionnaire," *Journal of Applied Psychology,* May 1983, pp. 253–261.

7.   Kenneth E. Friend, "Stress and Performance: Effects of Subjective Work Load and Time Urgency," *Personnel Psychology,* Autumn 1982, pp. 623–633; and Thomas F. Bateman, "Work Overload," *Business Horizons,* September–October 1981, pp. 23–27.

8.   Ahmed A. Abdel-Halim, "Effects of Role Stress–Job Design–Technology Interactions on Employee Work Satisfaction," *Academy of Management Journal,* June 1981, pp. 260–273; and R. Stephen Wunder, Thomas W. Dougherty, and M. Ann Welsh, "A Causal Model of Role Stress and Employee Turnover," *Proceedings of the Academy of Management,* 1982, pp. 297–301.

9.   A model of frustration is reported in Paul E. Spector, "Organizational Frustration: A Model and Review of the Literature," *Personnel Psychology,* Winter 1978, pp. 815–829.

10.   Janina C. Latack, "Person/Role Conflict: Holland's Model Extended to Role-Stress Research, Stress Management, and Career Development," *Academy of Management Review,* January 1981, pp. 89–103. See also L. David Brown, *Managing Conflict at Organizational Interfaces,* Reading, Mass.: Addison-Wesley, 1983.

11.   Kurt R. Student, "Personnel's Newest Challenge: Helping to Cope with Stress," *The Personnel Administrator,* November 1978, pp. 20–24.

12.   Oliver L. Niehouse, "Burnout: A Real Threat to Human Resources Managers," *Personnel,* September–October 1981, pp. 25–32. For books on burnout see Robert L. Veninga and James P. Spradley, *The Work Stress Connection: How to Cope with Job Burnout,* Boston: Little, Brown, 1981; and Herbert J. Freudenberger, with Geraldine Richelson, *Burn-Out: The High Cost of High Achievement,* New York: Anchor/Doubleday, 1980.

13.   For discussion see Harry Levinson, "When Executives Burn Out," *Harvard Business Review,* May–June 1981, pp. 73–81; Susan E. Jackson and Randall S. Schuler, "Preventing Employee Burnout," *Personnel,* March–April 1983, pp. 58–68; and Morley D. Glicken and Katherine Janka, "Executives under Fire: The Burnout Syndrome," *California Management Review,* Spring 1982, pp. 67–72.

14.   For discussion and research see Herbert Benson and Robert L. Allen, "How Much Stress Is Too Much?" *Harvard Business Review,* September 1980, pp. 86–92; and R. Douglas Allen, Michael A. Hitt, and Charles R. Greer, "Occupational Stress and Perceived

Organizational Effectiveness in Formal Groups: An Examination of Stress Level and Stress Type," *Personnel Psychology,* Summer 1982, pp. 359–370.

15. John M. Ivancevich, Michael T. Matteson, and Cynthia Preston, "Occupational Stress, Type A Behavior, and Physical Well Being," *Academy of Management Journal,* June 1982, pp. 373–391. A basic book on types A and B behavior is Meyer Friedman and Ray H. Rosenman, *Type A Behavior and Your Heart,* New York: Knopf, 1974.

16. Charles R. Stoner and Fred L. Fry, "Developing a Corporate Policy for Managing Stress," *Personnel,* May–June 1983, pp. 66–76. The article also has two excellent lists of corrective policies and action programs for reducing stress.

17. Robert A. Karasek, Jr., "Job Demands, Job Decision Latitude, and Mental Strain: Implications for Job Redesign," *Administrative Science Quarterly,* June 1979, pp. 285–308.

18. Morley D. Glicken, "A Counseling Approach to Burnout," *Personnel Journal,* March 1983, pp. 222–228.

19. William A. McGeveran, Jr., "Meditation at the Telephone Company," *Wharton Magazine,* Fall 1981, pp. 29–32.

20. Heather R. Sailer, John Schlacter, and Mark R. Edwards, "Stress: Causes, Consequences, and Coping Strategies," *Personnel,* July–August 1982, pp. 35–48.

21. The beginning and early history of modern counseling are reported in F. J. Roethlisberger and William J. Dickson, *Management and the Worker,* Cambridge, Mass.: Harvard University Press, 1939, especially pp. 189–205, 593–604.

22. Surveys of counseling practices are reported in Helen LaVan, Nicholas Mathys, and David Drehmer, "A Look at the Counseling Practices of Major U.S. Corporations," *The Personnel Administrator,* June 1983, pp. 76ff.; Hermine Zagat Levine, "Employee Counseling Services," *Personnel,* March–April 1981, pp. 4–11; and Robert C. Ford and Frank S. McLaughlin, "Employee Assistance Programs: A Descriptive Survey of ASPA Members," *The Personnel Administrator,* September 1981, pp. 29–35.

23. David J. Reed, "One Approach to Employee Assistance," *Personnel Journal,* August 1983, pp. 648–652; and information supplied to the authors by Control Data Corporation. The Reed article has a list of the major personal and work problems reported by employees. For other counseling programs see Sheila H. Akabas and Seth A. Akabas, "Social Services at the Workplace: New Resource for Management," *Management Review,* May 1982, pp. 15–20; and Hana Rostain, Peter Allan, and Stephen Rosenberg, "New York City's Approach to Problem-Employee Counseling," *Personnel Journal,* April 1980, pp. 305–309, 321.

24. Elizabeth M. Kaplan and Emory L. Cowen, "Interpersonal Helping Behavior of Industrial Foremen," *Journal of Applied Psychology,* October 1981, pp. 633–638.

25. A participative counseling program is discussed in Steven H. Appelbaum, "A Human Resources Counseling Model: The Alcoholic Employee," *The Personnel Administrator,* August 1982, pp. 35–44.

26. James A. Belohlav and Paul O. Popp, "Making Employee Discipline Work," *The Personnel Administrator,* March 1978, pp. 22–24.

27. For discussion of a corrective discipline program using employee-supervisor shared responsibility see Ira G. Asherman, "The Corrective Discipline Process," *Personnel*

444

Journal, July 1982, pp. 528–531. For a corrective discipline program for absences see Frank E. Kuzmits, "No Fault: A New Strategy for Absenteeism Control," *Personnel Journal,* May 1981, pp. 387–390.

28. Henry P. Sims, Jr., "Tips and Troubles with Employee Reprimand," *The Personnel Administrator,* January 1979, pp. 57–61; and Henry P. Sims, Jr., "Further Thoughts on Punishment in Organizations," *Academy of Management Review,* January 1980, pp. 133–138.

29. Laurence J. Stybel, Robin Cooper, and Maryanne Peabody, "Planning Executive Dismissals: How to Fire a Friend," *California Management Review,* Spring 1982, pp. 73–80; and Stanley J. Schwartz, "How to Dehire: A Guide for the Manager," *Human Resource Management,* Winter 1980, pp. 22–25; and Robert Coulson, "The Fine Art of Informing an Employee: You're Fired!" *Management Review,* February 1982, p. 37.

30. Maria Leonard, "Challenges to the Termination-at-Will Doctrine, *The Personnel Administrator,* February 1983, pp. 49–56; Lawrence Z. Lorber and others, *Fear of Firing: A Legal and Personnel Analysis of Employment at Will,* Alexandria, Va.: The ASPA Foundation, 1984; and Edward Mandt, "Employee Termination: Proceed with Care," *Management Review,* December 1980, pp. 25–28. For a general discussion of restrictions on the right to dismiss see David W. Ewing, *Do It My Way or You're Fired!* New York: Wiley, 1983.

31. Janis Klotchman and Linda L. Neider, "EEO Alert: Watch Out for Discrimination in Discharge," *Personnel,* January–February 1983, pp. 60–66.

32. Edward L. Harrison, "Legal Restrictions on the Employer's Authority to Discipline," *Personnel Journal,* February 1982, pp. 136–141.

33. David W. Ewing, "Your Right to Fire," *Harvard Business Review,* March–April 1983, pp. 33–42.

34. Jeffrey C. Pingpank and Thomas B. Mooney, "Wrongful Discharge: A New Danger for Employers," *The Personnel Administrator,* March 1982, pp. 31–35.

35. David W. Ewing, "Due Process: Will Business Default?" *Harvard Business Review,* November–December 1982, pp. 114–122; and Bryan P. Heshizer and Harry Graham, "Discipline in the Nonunion Company: Protecting Employer and Employee Rights," *Personnel,* March–April 1982, pp. 71–78.

36. Ira G. Asherman and Sandra Lee Vance, "Documentation: A Tool for Effective Management," *Personnel Journal,* August 1981, pp. 641–643.

37. For differences between disciplinary policies for professional and nonprofessional employees see Irene Unterberger and S. Herbert Unterberger, "Disciplining Professional Employees," *Industrial Relations,* October 1978, pp. 353–359.

38. John Huberman, " 'Discipline without Punishment' Lives," *Harvard Business Review,* July–August 1975, pp. 6–8.

39. Richard C. Grote, "Positive Discipline: Keeping Employees in Line without Punishment," *Training,* October 1977, pp. 42–44. A related type of positive discipline at a General Electric Company plant is reported in Alan W. Bryant, "Replacing Punitive Discipline with a Positive Approach," *The Personnel Administrator,* February 1984, pp. 79–87.

CHAPTER 17

Much of the civilized world is already . . . into an information revolution, and this phenomenon is touching the souls of men and women everywhere in countless and multiplying ways.

Gordon L. Lippitt[1]

Communication is the lifeblood of an organization; it pervades all activities in an organization.

Everett M. Rogers and Rekha Agarwala-Rogers[2]

PERSONNEL COMMUNICATIONS SYSTEMS

CHAPTER OBJECTIVES

After studying this chapter, you should be able to:

1 Explain the personnel function's role in organizational communication.

2 Describe the communication process.

3 Identify barriers to communication.

4 Discuss the common forms of downward communication used by personnel departments.

5 Interpret how the grapevine works.

6 Explain different approaches to improving upward communication.

Information is the engine that drives organizations.[3] Information about the organization, its environment, its products and services, and its people is essential to management and workers. Without information, managers cannot make effective decisions about markets or resources, particularly human resources. Likewise, insufficient information may cause stress and dissatisfaction among workers. This universal need for information is met through an organization's communication system. *Communication systems* provide formal and informal methods to move information through an organization so that appropriate decisions can be made. This chapter discusses the personnel department's role in managing the human resource communication system. Our focus is on organizationwide communication efforts, rather than on the primarily one-to-one communications of employee counseling and discipline discussed in Chapter 16.

The need for communication

The *human resource communication system* includes formal and informal procedures used to acquire and distribute information about an organization's human resources. All organizations have human resource communication systems. In small or unsophisticated firms, communications may be informal and subject to infrequent management intervention. In large multi-billion-dollar enterprises, specialists may serve as employee communications directors. Most organizations use a blend of the formal, systematically designed communications efforts and the informal, ad hoc arrangements. Consider, for example, just a few parts of IBM's human resource communication system.

IBM example

The IBM Corporation is one of the world's premier organizations. It is the leading producer of computers and microelectronic devices. In fact, IBM has been so dominant in its field that it is known in the industry as "Snow White and the Seven Dwarfs," which is a reference to IBM's former dress rule of white shirts and its relationship to its competitors. Technology and market dominance aside, IBM also excels in the management of its human resources.

Long ago top management at IBM realized that the company's future success rested with the people who developed its technology and sold its products. One example of IBM's commitment to its workers is a 1940s policy against putting full-time permanent employees on layoff. That policy has remained in effect since then. Another example comes from its view of human resources as found in an IBM training program: "The success of the IBM Company is related directly to the ability and skill of its employees. Improvement of this ability and skill is a major objective of the Company and the responsibility for bringing it about is shared by each member of management. This steady self-development of employees is as important to the IBM organization as would be a technological breakthrough or the creation of a new product."[4]

The management at IBM recognizes that the treatment of human resources must be approached from a systems viewpoint. Personnel activities, such as appraisal or training, lose their effectiveness if they occur in isolation and are not related to other aspects of employee development. To tie the various employee development activities together and to facilitate motivation and satisfaction, IBM relies heavily on communication. Some of its approaches to employee communication include extensive career planning information and assistance, attitude surveys, suggestion systems, open-door policies, daily newspapers at some sites, and near-daily bulletins on educational opportunities and promotions.

Beyond these formal methods, personnel specialists and line managers informally communicate with employees. This "management by walking around" is known at IBM as "trolling for open doors." IBM has an open-door policy whereby employees are free to walk into any manager's office with their problems. However, IBM management realizes that most workers are reluctant to take a problem to their boss's boss.[5] Therefore, personnel specialists and line managers leave their offices and go out among the employees to learn what problems exist. As one IBM executive explained, "The only open-door policy that works is one where the manager gets up from the desk and goes through the door to talk to employees." *"Trolling for open doors"*

These informal management-by-wandering-around approaches combined with formal, systematic communications efforts enhance other aspects of the personnel department's efforts. By creating an atmosphere of informed employees, IBM develops a sense of trust and commitment. In turn, trust and commitment help further motivation and satisfaction (as discussed in Chapter 15) while reducing job-related stresses for managers and employees (as discussed in Chapter 16). Effective communication does not guarantee a successful personnel department or organization. However, neither the department nor the organization is likely to achieve high levels of productivity and quality of work life without effective human resources communication.

Following an overview of communication concepts, the remainder of this chapter focuses on ways the personnel department can improve human resource communication in organizations. *This chapter*

COMMUNICATIONS OVERVIEW

Communication is the transfer of information and understanding from one person to another. It is a bridge of meaning among people so that they can share what they feel and know. When handled correctly, the result is open communication. *Open communication* occurs when people feel free to communicate all relevant messages. Without open communication, cooperation becomes virtually impossible because people cannot communicate their needs and feelings to others. We can say with some confidence that *every act of communication influences the organization in some way.* *Communication defined*

Open communication

The Communication Process
The *communication process* is the method by which a sender reaches a receiver. It consists of six steps, as shown in Figure 17-1. Step 1 is to *develop the idea* or thought that the sender wishes to transmit. This is a key step because unless

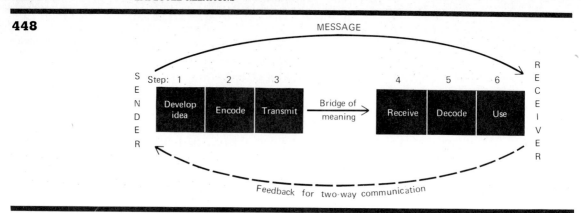

Figure 17-1
The Communication Process

there is a worthwhile message, all the other steps are somewhat useless.[6] Step 2 is to *encode* the idea into suitable words, charts, or other symbols for transmission. When the message is finally developed, step 3 is to *transmit* it. Transmission allows another person to *receive* the message, which is step 4. At this point the message becomes the receiver's responsibility. If the message is not received, no communication has occurred. Step 5 is to *decode* the message so that it can be understood. When the message is received and understood, then step 6—the receiver's use of the message—can occur. This step completes the communication process.

Feedback and Two-Way Communication

The sender usually wants some type of feedback to ensure that the message has been understood. Feedback initiates a new communication that must pass through the same six steps. The result is a completed communication circuit known as two-way communication.[7] *Two-way communication* means that a sender and a receiver are exchanging messages so that a regular flow of communication is maintained. An important job of the personnel function is to help management and employees build two-way communication systems so that they can work together more effectively. One key to improve this two-way flow of information is to give workers feedback about their job performance. Most companies give feedback through the performance appraisal process (discussed in Chapter 11). However, this type of feedback occurs only once or twice a year. Some companies, such as American Express, provide more frequent performance feedback and try to keep the feedback loop (shown on the bottom of Figure 17-1) working continuously.

Two-way communication

American Express

In the customer service department of American Express's Western Regional Operation Center, the number of customer calls and the average time to resolve each call are recorded for each team. This information is communicated through charts posted on the walls. The posters show the trend line in call volume and average duration. Management uses this tool to decide on staffing levels and to evaluate supervisory performance. The employees benefit from being able to see and compare their performances.

To aid in the establishment of two-way communication, personnel specialists need to understand the roles of listening, nonverbal communication, and barriers in the two-way communication process.

Listening

Listening is a receiver's positive effort to receive and understand a message transmitted by sound. It has many benefits. Good listening helps receivers understand the feelings, emotions, and needs of communicators so that the receiver can better relate to the sender. Good listening is good manners, too, because it shows others that we care and are interested in them and in their ideas. In turn, their attitudes toward us improve, and so they are likely to be more receptive to what we have to say. For example, supervisors who listen effectively are judged to be better bosses, better communicators, and more interested in their people. From a manager's point of view, good listening provides inputs for better decision making. Managers who do not know what is happening in their organization are unlikely to make sound decisions, so good listening often can be the difference between a successful manager and an unsuccessful one.

Since good listening is of major importance, personnel activities try to encourage it. The personnel department may even offer guidelines for improving listening skills, as shown in Figure 17-2. The goal is to convince managers that

Listening guidelines

Figure 17-2
Listening Guides for Display at the Workplace

1. Stop talking. You cannot listen if you are talking.
2. Put the talker at ease.
3. Show the talker that you want to listen.
4. Remove distractions.
5. Empathize. See the situation from the other person's point of view.
6. Be patient.
7. Hold your temper.
8. Go easy with argument and criticism. When you argue, even if you win, you lose.
9. Ask questions to show interest and encourage response.
10. Stop talking. This is first and last because all other guides depend on it.

- Nature gave people two ears but only one tongue, which is a gentle hint that they should listen more than they talk.
- Listening requires two ears, one for meaning and one for feeling.
- Decision makers who do not listen have less information for making sound decisions.

listening is important and that it requires active, interested effort. This goal is difficult to sell because most of us would rather speak our own ideas than listen to the ideas of others. As Figure 17-2 suggests, listening carefully is much more than merely hearing the other person talk. *Active listening* requires the listener to stop talking, remove distractions, be patient, and empathize with the talker.

Studies of the amount of time managers spend listening show that listening takes more managerial time than any other form of communication. One study followed forty-six managers for a number of working days.[8] Most were middle-level managers, and they reported that their communication time was spent as follows:

Listening	33 percent	Reading	19 percent
Speaking	26 percent	Writing	22 percent

Nonverbal Communication

People often do not realize that their actions communicate as well as their words. In fact, the message received from actions is often stronger than the one from words. As the saying goes, "Actions speak louder than words." Actions that communicate are called *nonverbal communication.*[9] This kind of communication is involved in almost everything that a manager does—*or fails to do, because lack of action also communicates.*

Martin Carnes, an office supervisor, often said that he wanted suggestions from employees. He mentioned this fact in departmental meetings, and he even issued a bulletin calling for suggestions. However, his actions indicated otherwise. He became angry when employees offered suggestions, rejected useful ones, and "lost" some suggestions in his files. His employees believed his actions, not his words.

Body language   Another part of nonverbal communication is *body language,* which communicates by body movements during face-to-face discussion. There are many subtle movements, and some not so subtle, that people make when they are talking to each other. For example, smiles, frowns, eye contact, and countless other body movements communicate to others. A weak handshake may mean lack of interest, and a bowed head may mean worry. All employees need to be aware of how body movements are used to communicate so that they can interpret these movements effectively.

Barriers to Communication

Even when the receiver receives the message and makes a genuine effort to decode it, a number of interferences may limit the receiver's understanding.[10] These interferences are known as *barriers to communication.* They may prevent a communication entirely, filter part of it out, or give it incorrect meaning. The three types of barriers are personal, physical, and semantic (see Figure 17-3).

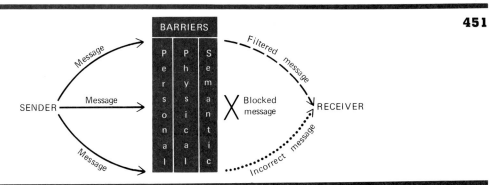

Figure 17-3
Operation of Communication Barriers

Personal barriers *Personal barriers* are communication interferences that arise from human emotions, values, and limitations. They are the most common type of barrier in work situations and include poor listening habits. We all have experienced how our personal feelings can limit our communications with other people.

For example, a personnel specialist tried to explain the company policy to an employee who had been bypassed for a promotion. The employee was unhappy, and so she did not want to hear what the actual policy was. She let her emotions block her understanding.

Physical barriers *Physical barriers* are communication interferences that occur in the environment. A typical physical barrier is a distracting noise of some type. Other physical barriers include distances between people, walls, or static that interferes with radio messages.

Semantic barriers *Semantic barriers* arise from limitations in the symbols with which we communicate. Words are our main form of communication, but they have so many different meanings that they are often misunderstood. The different meanings place an obligation on the sender to create a total environment (context) that pinpoints only one meaning for key words that are used.

For example, an electric utility crew was constructing a substation about seventy-five miles from the company warehouse. The workers needed certain supplies quickly, and so they called the warehouse on their radio. The supply superintendent wrote out the list of supplies and handed it to a new warehouse loader-truck driver with the comment, "Here, take this to our crew at the substation. They are waiting for it." The driver hurriedly drove to the substation with *the list,* not the supplies.

DOWNWARD COMMUNICATION SYSTEMS

Goals of in-house communications

The personnel department operates a large communication system in order to keep people informed. To do this effectively, personnel specialists must be aware that barriers to communication may exist in any type of message. What personnel departments try to do is create in-house approaches that overcome as many of these barriers as possible.[11] Although the goal is to facilitate an open two-way flow of information, most messages in organizations are of the top-down variety. *Downward communication* is information that begins at some point in the organization and proceeds down the organization hierarchy to inform or influence others. Top-down methods are necessary for decision makers to have their decisions carried out. These communications also help give employees knowledge about the organization and feedback on how their efforts are perceived. In fact, a nationwide survey revealed that 42 percent of the people thought that "more and better information from management about decisions that affect employees" would improve productivity.[12]

Multiple channels of communication

Organizations use a variety of downward communications. The reason for this diversity is that multiple channels are more likely to overcome barriers and reach the intended receivers. Some common examples of downward communication approaches include house organs, information booklets, employee bulletins, television films, jobholder reports, and meetings. Each of these techniques will be discussed in the following sections before concluding this chapter with a discussion of upward communication systems.

House Organs

Many organizations publish company magazines, newspapers, or bulletins for employees. These publications are also called *house organs.* Their purpose is to inform workers about current developments and to build long-run understanding about company activities and goals.[13] Large organizations are able to publish well-designed magazines and/or newspapers, while small organizations may have only a weekly personnel information bulletin. Workers are encouraged to take these magazines and newspapers home so that family members also may develop a better understanding of the organization. Frequently there are items about company bowling teams, discount theater tickets, and hobbies. These articles are designed to appeal to family members as well as employees.

> IBM's Boulder, Colorado, facility publishes a daily paper called *Boulder Today,* plus almost daily flyers about promotions and educational opportunities. In addition, the Information Systems Division at the Boulder site prints its own newspaper every two months. These local house organs are supplemented by other divisional and corporate publications that try to keep IBM employees in Boulder informed. Similar house organs are published at other IBM facilities around the world.

Editors of in-house magazines and newspapers occasionally make readership surveys to determine which parts of their publication are being read and what additional information readers desire. In this way they can improve content, readability, and other features for better communication.[14] Samples of questions asked on readership surveys are as follows:

- What sections do you read regularly? (A list follows for checking.)

- What articles did you read in the July issue? (A list of the articles follows for checking.)

- What article in the July issue did you like most?

- What additional subjects would you like information about?

Information Booklets

Personnel departments often distribute information booklets on various subjects to their employees. A well-known booklet is the employee handbook that is given to new employees to inform them about regulations and benefits. Other booklets are distributed on specialized subjects relating to personnel work— such as suggestion programs, wage incentives, retirement, and fringe benefits. When benefits such as life and medical insurance are purchased through an insurance company, that firm usually supplies the booklets. Following are examples of information booklets distributed by personnel departments:

- *How to Read Your Future* (the retirement program)

- *You've Got Something There* (the suggestion program)

- *Steps to Security* (programs for employee security)

- *The Employee Health Insurance Plan*

Employee Bulletins

Personnel departments publish a number of bulletins that concern their day-to-day operations.[15] Usually these are placed on employee bulletin boards, and copies are sent to each manager. For example, job openings are announced so that all employees have an equal opportunity to apply for them. Holidays are announced along with the regulations that govern payment and absences the day before and the day after them. Announcements are made about awards, retirements, and similar events. As a service activity it is the personnel function's responsibility to keep employees informed about all events that are relevant to their employment.

Television and Films

Since the public is conditioned to watching television, some organizations tape their own television programs for later replay to employees. These programs are viewed on television screens in company lunchrooms and in other locations. Large firms with branch operations especially use this approach to keep their branch employees informed about corporate developments or to assist with training. Other firms prepare information films for the same kind of use. As viewed by one program producer, "It doesn't always beat the office grapevine, but it quickly gets out the facts that are garbled in the grapevine."[16] Some organizations use recorded telephone messages to present the latest information. Employees can dial a certain number from any telephone, and a recorded message is played to them. In a typical program the message takes one minute, and a new one is prepared daily.

Jobholder Reports and Meetings

Jobholder reports

A few organizations distribute *jobholder reports* to employees.[17] These are reports to workers about a firm's economic performance. The reasoning is that company economic information is just as important to employees as it is to stockholders. The report is presented in the same style as the annual stockholder report, except that the jobholder report shows how the annual economic results affect employees.

> Some organizations follow the jobholder reports with jobholder meetings that are organized and conducted in the same way as stockholder meetings. Top management attends the meetings, and all employees are invited. Management presents its reports, and employees are invited to question management and make proposals in the same way that owners do in stockholder meetings. These meetings improve communication and give jobholders a stronger feeling of belonging.

UPWARD COMMUNICATION SYSTEMS

Personnel professionals need to understand the communication process, the role of feedback, the barriers to communication, and the downward communication process. With that knowledge, personnel experts can help improve their organization through more effective upward communications systems.[18] Perhaps no other area of communications is more in need of improvement in most organizations than upward communications.

Upward communication

Upward communication consists of information initiated by people who seek to inform or influence those higher up in the organization's hierarchy. The cornerstone of all such messages is the employee and the supervisor.[19] When a free flow of information travels between an employee and the supervisor, informal day-to-day communications are often sufficient for most situations (which helps explain why the counseling skills discussed in Chapter 16 are so important to supervisors and personnel specialists). When open communications do not exist, or exist for only a limited range of issues, other tactics are needed. For example, an employee may have a good, open relationship with the supervisor about job-related matters such as supplies, work performance, quality of outputs, and the like. However, that same employee and supervisor may not be able to discuss effectively interpersonal issues such as peer relations or career expectations. If the personnel department is to help build effective communications, then it must provide additional channels through which messages can flow, such as IBM's active open-door policy.

How do organizations create open, upward communications? No universal formula exists. Each organization's personnel department must take an approach that is contingent upon the situation. However, one common element in most organizations is a genuine concern for employee well-being combined with meaningful opportunities for ideas to flow up the organization's hierarchy. Some of the more common upward communications channels include the grapevine, in-house complaint procedures, rap sessions, suggestion systems, and attitude survey feedback.

Living with the Grapevine

There are two types of communication systems in an organization: the formal system and the informal one, usually called the "grapevine." A formal communication system is the one established by the organization for the official conduct of its activities. Examples of formal communications are job instructions, surveys, reports, and bulletins. *Grapevine communication* is an informal system that arises spontaneously from the social interaction of people in the organization.[20] It is the people-to-people system that arises naturally from the human desire to make friends and share ideas. When two employees chat at the water fountain about their trouble with a supervisor, that is a grapevine communication.

Definition

The personnel department has a major interest in the grapevine for several reasons:

- It is a source of upward communications.

- It affects motivation and job satisfaction.

- It provides valuable feedback of personnel information.

- It is poorly understood by supervisors.

Grapevine patterns   Management did not establish the grapevine and it cannot control it. This means that the grapevine can fly across chains of command or between departments as quickly as a telephone call or a chance meeting in the hallway. It is impossible to control these freewheeling communications. Even if control were possible, it is not desirable because grapevines help satisfy social needs. Whenever normal people are together, they are going to share their ideas. All that management can do is learn to live with the grapevine. Management perhaps can influence it, but control is impossible.

Figure 17-4 shows how a grapevine easily moves across chains of command in an organization. It also can bypass levels of authority and even move to and from the community as it runs its course. Employee J originated the communication, which was interesting gossip about the love affair of employee H. The grapevine network then developed as follows:

J told I at the same organizational level.
I told L, a subordinate.

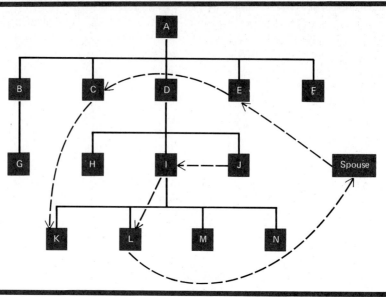

Figure 17-4
A Grapevine Network Compared with
a Chain of Command

L told his wife, who did not work for the organization.
The wife told a friend, E, who was two levels higher in the organization than L.
E told C, an associate.
C told K, who was two levels lower.

It is evident that the people involved in this grapevine could ignore chains of command because they were communicating on the basis of their interests and friendships.

Grapevine feedback from employees   The grapevine provides a large amount of useful off-the-record feedback from employees. Workers often
> Feedback to personnel

feel somewhat free to talk to personnel specialists because the field of personnel management is oriented toward human needs and resources. In addition, employees feel safe to express their feelings because personnel specialists do not directly supervise employees in other departments. The result is a large amount of useful input, provided that the personnel department is prepared to listen, understand, and interpret the information. Some of the types of grapevine feedback that come to the personnel department are shown in Figure 17.5.

If the personnel department shows that it is responsive and can handle
> Confidence is crucial.

off-the-record information in confidence without putting the communicator in jeopardy, then open communication is further encouraged. There are risks in this kind of communication because supervisors may feel threatened by disclosures about their departments, but usually the benefits of more complete information are greater than the disadvantages. A further point is that even when

- Information about the problems and anxieties that employees have

- Incorrect feedback that is evidence of breakdowns in communication

- Insights into goals and motivation of employees

- Identification of job problems that have high emotional content, because intense feelings encourage grapevine communication

- Information about the quality of labor relations, including grievance settlements

- Information about the quality of supervision. Complaints about supervision often are brought informally to the attention of personnel specialists with the hope that they will do something

- Information about areas of job dissatisfaction

- Feedback about acceptance of new policies and procedures

Figure 17-5
Types of Grapevine Feedback
to the Personnel Department

personnel specialists know that a grapevine input is incorrect, they should still listen because the input may be helpful. Incorrect inputs tell management that there are communication breakdowns that need to be remedied. A useful guide to follow is: Listen to the grapevine, it may be trying to tell you something.

In-House Complaint Procedures

How does an employee solve a complaint if the supervisor is not receptive? In some organizations, the employee has no other option except to talk to the supervisor's superior. Although this may seem reasonable, most people in organizations are reluctant to do so because they do not want to create negative feelings between themselves and their supervisor. To lessen the burden of "going over the boss's head" some organizations have installed in-house complaint procedures.

In-house complaint procedures are formal methods through which an   Definition
employee can register a complaint. Normally these procedures are operated by the personnel department and require the employee to submit the complaint in writing. Then an employee relations specialist investigates the complaint and advises its author of the results. In some companies, the investigator is the only one who knows the employee's name. However, in many cases if a supervisor is questioned about the issue, it is obvious who filed the complaint, so the person's anonymity is lost.

> IBM's program is called "Speak Up!" It uses a confidential form designed as a prepaid envelope. On the inside the employee completes a home address section and then writes the complaint, opinion, or question. When the Speak Up! administrator receives the envelope, the name and address sections are removed, and the issue is investigated. Once an answer is found, the envelope is mailed to the employee's home address. No one but the Speak Up! administrator knows who submitted the form. If the employee does not provide a name and address, the issue and the response may be printed in the company newspaper. If the employee is not satisfied

with the answer, an interview with an executive from corporate headquarters will be arranged, regardless of where the employee's jobsite is located.

Managers at IBM "troll for open doors" to avoid Speak Ups! that cause an executive to visit a disgruntled employee. If that employee is dissatisfied with some improper management action and talks to an executive about it, the manager's career with IBM may be adversely affected. What makes IBM's complaint procedure and open communications so effective is that IBM executives support the program with their actions; they are willing to get on an airplane and fly to a meeting with a dissatisfied employee. That level of commitment from top managers causes lower-level managers to pay close attention to employee communications.

Rap Sessions

Closely related to in-house complaint procedures are rap sessions. *Rap sessions* are meetings between managers and groups of employees to discuss complaints, suggestions, opinions, or questions. These meetings may begin with some information sharing by management to tell the group about developments in the company. However, the primary purpose of these gatherings is to encourage upward communications, often with several levels of employees and lower-level management in attendance at the same time. When these meetings are face-to-face informal discussions between a higher-level manager and

Deep-sensing
meetings

rank-and-file workers, the process is called *deep-sensing* because it attempts to probe in some depth the issues that are on the minds of employees.[21] These sessions also are called *vertical staffing meetings* because they put higher-level managers directly in touch with employees.[22]

"Birthday club"

Attendance at rap sessions varies according to how the meetings are planned. One plant manager runs a "birthday club." All employees who have a birthday during the month meet with the plant manager and the personnel manager to have coffee and birthday cake. The occasion is used to discuss what changes these people think are needed.

Two common problems often arise from these meetings. First, the top manager must be careful not to undermine other managers by countermanding orders without getting all of the facts. Sometimes employees present a compelling case. If the top manager reacts too quickly, a bad decision may result. Second, initial meetings tend to focus on employee complaints. Many of these complaints concern hygiene factors—as defined by Herzberg—such as housekeeping, pay, working conditions, fringe benefits, and the like. Many managers and personnel specialists become discouraged by the lack of constructive ideas and sometimes abandon these approaches too quickly. Personnel departments that respond to employee complaints promptly and continue the rap sessions into a second year often receive constructive suggestions for improvement of operations policies and practices. Sometimes constructive suggestions emerge in the earlier meetings, as the president of Hyatt Hotels discovered.

In one eight-month period, Patrick Foley, president of Hyatt Hotels Corporation, held a dozen meetings with hotel employees. "Sometimes he hears of serious problems that require immediate attention. More often, he hears seemingly trivial complaints—but they concern matters that can make day-to-day life miserable. 'Every time I do one of these meetings, I realize it's the little things that most often affect morale,' Mr. Foley says. 'This is a way to make the employee feel like we care.' "[23]

Suggestion Systems

Suggestion systems are a formal method for generating, evaluating, and implementing employee ideas. If even one of these three elements—generating, evaluating, or implementing—is missing, the suggestion plan fails. All three are crucial.

Definition

Figure 17-6 shows the key steps in a successful suggestion system. It begins with the employee's idea and a discussion with the supervisor. Once the suggestion form is completed, the supervisor reviews and signs the form, indicating awareness of the suggestion but not necessarily approval. The suggestion system office or committee receives the idea and sends an acknowledgment to the employee through company mail. The idea is then evaluated, and the decision is communicated to the employee. If it is a good idea, implementation follows with the employee receiving recognition and usually some award.[24] (Typically, awards are equal to 10 percent of the first year's savings.) The savings from the idea accrue to the organization.

Success is likely if management provides prompt and fair evaluations, if supervisors are trained to encourage employee suggestions, and if top management actively supports the program. Unfortunately, this source of upward communications is not very effective in many companies because evaluations often take months to process or supervisors see suggestions as too much work for them with few personal benefits. As a result, many company suggestion plans exist on paper but are not very effective.[25]

Although most suggestion systems pay employees a percentage of the first

Figure 17-6
Suggestion System Steps

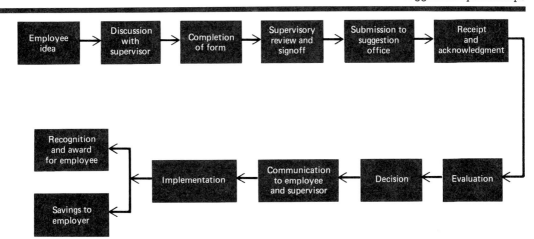

year's savings, some companies pay a flat dollar amount in order to minimize the need for precision in evaluating the suggestion's exact dollar value. This approach means that employees receive feedback about their suggestions much faster. At Honeywell, supervisors' performance appraisals are based, in part, on how effective the suggestion system has been among their employees. Obviously, this approach causes supervisors to encourage employee suggestions. Another way of encouraging supervisory support is to give them a reward for accepted suggestions from their employees. At a Penn Central subsidiary, supervisors are given $25 for each accepted employee idea.

Honeywell's approach

Beech Aircraft goes even a step further. At Beech, supervisors are given the authority to make "quick look" awards. These $10 checks can be authorized by supervisors and issued the following week whenever they receive an idea that looks useful. If the formal evaluation procedure rejects the suggestion, the employee may still keep the ten dollars. This method communicates feedback to the employee quickly and involves the supervisor in distributing awards as a means of encouraging ideas from employees.

Beech Aircraft's "quick look"

Not all organizations have suggestion programs because problems can develop if they are not administered carefully. Some employees feel that the award is not enough, and others resent the fact that their suggestions are not accepted. Workers may object to an idea because it changes their jobs. They show their feelings by retaliating against the suggester, who is discouraged from offering further ideas. In spite of the problems, suggestion programs offer an opportunity for management to explain job improvement needs to employees and for workers to offer ideas to management. This exchange of ideas builds two-way communication, improves the organization's productivity, and can further the quality of work life for employees.[26]

Attitude Survey Feedback

What do employees think about the organization? Do they have problems or concerns? Do they understand the personnel department's fringe benefit plan? Compensation plan? Career planning efforts? Answers to these and to many other questions can make a useful addition to the personnel department's human resource information system.[27]

Attitude surveys are systematic methods of determining what employees think about their organization. These surveys may be conducted through face-to-face interviews, but they are usually done through anonymous questionnaires. An attitude survey typically seeks to learn what employees think about working conditions, supervision, and personnel policies. Questions about new programs or special concerns to management may also be included. The resulting information can be used to evaluate specific concerns, such as how individual managers are perceived by their employees.

Attitude surveys can be a frustrating experience for employees if they do not see any results. It is only natural that people would like to know what the survey questionnaire uncovered. Otherwise the survey has little meaning to them, especially if it is readministered in the future. Therefore, a summary of upward communication should be provided to employees for their reactions. When this feedback loop is closed, the overall process is called *attitude survey feedback.* However, feedback is not enough. Action is needed. Employees need to see that the survey resulted in the resolution of problems.[28] Feedback of the results and action on the problem areas make "attitude survey feedback a powerful communication tool." However, providing feedback in a constructive manner may require considerable assistance from the personnel department, especially for first-level supervisors who may have little experience in running meetings and listening to employee criticisms.

> In the Automotive Division of Bendix, supervisors are given a workbook to help them analyze the survey. Trained internal facilitators assist the supervisors in the interpretation of these results. Then the facilitators conduct a role-playing exercise with the supervisors to prepare them for the questions that employees are likely to ask.
>
> After the role playing, the supervisor meets with the employees and presents the results. Together, problems are identified and solutions are sought. From this meeting a prioritized list is drawn up with completion dates indicated for each action item. Bendix's approach to attitude survey feedback not only gives employees an explanation of what the results showed but develops an action plan to resolve problems that emerged from the process.

Bendix and survey feedback

Whether attitude survey feedback is appropriate for an organization depends on several factors. Is top management truly willing to take action based on the results of the survey feedback process? Are resources available to conduct the survey, to train the facilitators that might be needed, and to follow up on the prioritized action items? But, perhaps, the key question is whether the organization and its leadership are ready for change. Dealing with change as a means of developing a more productive and satisfying organization is an ongoing concern of most proactive personnel departments. Chapter 18 discusses the personnel department's role in change and in organizational development.

Next chapter

SUMMARY

Communication is the transfer of information and understanding from one person to another. It is a bridge of meaning among people. The sender of a message develops an idea, encodes it, and transmits it. The receiver takes the message, decodes it, and uses it. When the receiver replies to the sender, two-way communication is established. Sometimes personal, physical, and semantic barriers interfere with communication and must be overcome.

The personnel department's role in organizational communication is to create an open two-way flow of information. Part of the foundation of any organizational communication effort is the view held by management of employees. If that view is one that sincerely strives to provide an effective downward and upward flow of information, then the personnel department can help develop and maintain appropriate communication systems.

Perhaps the greatest difficulty in organizational communication is to provide an effective upward flow of information. In-house complaint procedures, rap sessions, suggestion systems, and attitude survey feedback are commonly used tools.

Downward communication approaches include house organs, information booklets, employee bulletins, television and films, and jobholder reports and meetings. Multiple channels are used to help ensure that each message reaches the intended receivers.

TERMS FOR REVIEW

Communication	Open communication
Communication process	Downward communication
Two-way communication	Upward communication
Nonverbal communication	Grapevine communication
Body language	Attitude survey feedback
Barriers to communication	House organs
Semantic barriers	Suggestion programs
Vertical staffing meetings	Rap sessions
Deep-sensing meetings	Open-door policy
In-house complaint procedures	

REVIEW AND DISCUSSION QUESTIONS

1. Prepare a list of the ways others have communicated to you nonverbally during the last twenty-four hours. Discuss. What could you do to improve your awareness of nonverbal communication signals?

2. Discuss the various barriers to communication.

3. Discuss how grapevines work in an organization and the kinds of feedback management can get from them.

4. Think of a situation in which you learned some new information from the grapevine and took action on the basis of that information. Discuss.

5. List and discuss different programs that the personnel department manages in order to improve communications.

6. Describe why the best open-door policy is one where "the manager gets up from behind the desk and goes through the door to talk to employees."

7. Most organizations have a significant accounting department to collect data about the organization and its performance. However, very few organizations have even one person whose full-time responsibility is collecting information about employee attitudes. Why do you think this lack of a full-time person is common?

8. What reasons can you list that might explain why many suggestion systems do not work or do not work very well?

REFERENCES

1. Gordon L. Lippitt, *Organization Renewal*, 2d ed., Englewood Cliffs, N.J.: Prentice-Hall, 1982, p. 104.

2. Everett M. Rogers and Rekha Agarwala-Rogers, *Communication in Organizations*, New York: Free Press, 1976, p. 26.

3. Ibid.

4. "Techniques of Appraising Performance," *IBM Fundamentals of Management Course*, N.D., p. 4-1.

5. Walter D. St. John, "Successful Communications between Supervisors and Employees," *Personnel Journal*, January 1983, p. 73.

6. Edward H. Rockey, *Communications in Organizations*, Cambridge, Mass.: Winthrop, 1977, pp. 21–23.

7. Frederick E. Schuster, "A Tool for Evaluating and Controlling the Management of Human Resources," *The Personnel Administrator*, October 1982, pp. 63–69.

8. J. Donald Weinrauch and John R. Swanda, Jr., "Examining the Significance of Listening: An Exploratory Study of Contemporary Management," *The Journal of Business Communication*, Fall 1975, pp. 25–32.

9. See a special issue on nonverbal communication in *The Journal of Communication*, December 1972, pp. 339–477; and Mark L. Knapp, *Nonverbal Communication in Human Interaction*, 2d. ed., New York: Holt, Rinehart and Winston, 1978.

10. Lynn R. Cohen, "Minimizing Communication Breakdowns between Male and Female Managers," *The Personnel Administrator*, October 1982, pp. 57ff.

11. Walter D. St. John, "In-House Communications Guidelines," *Personnel Journal*, November 1981, pp. 872–878.

12. Amitai Etzioni, *Perspectives on Productivity: A Global View*, Philadelphia: Louis Harris, 1981, p. 45.

13. For example, see Roger M. D'Aprix, "The Believable House Organ," *Management Review*, February 1979, pp. 23–28. American Express Company publications for employees are summarized in "How Amex Employees Learn What's Happening," *Management Review*, February 1980, pp. 48–49.

14. "In-House Communications Guidelines," op. cit., p. 873.

15. Ibid., p. 876.

16. "TV That Competes with the Office Grapevine," *Business Week,* Mar. 14, 1977, pp. 49–54.

17. "Spreading the Word about the Facts of Life in the Corporation," *Personnel,* May–June 1976, pp. 4–5.

18. For discussion of upward and downward communication programs see the special section on communication in *The Personnel Administrator,* July 1979, pp. 23–55.

19. St. John, "Successful Communications between Supervisors and Employees," op. cit., p. 73. See also Robert W. Hollmann and Mary Ellen Campbell, "Communications Strategies for Improving HRM Effectiveness," *The Personnel Administrator,* July 1984, pp. 93, 95–98.

20. See Keith Davis, *Human Behavior at Work: Organizational Behavior,* 6th ed., New York: McGraw-Hill, 1981, pp. 335–346.

21. "Deep Sensing: A Pipeline to Employee Morale," *Business Week,* Jan. 29, 1979, pp. 124–128.

22. "Vertical Staffing Meetings Open Lines of Communication at Rocketdyne Plant," *World of Work Report,* April 1979, pp. 27–28.

23. Lawrence Rout, "Hyatt Hotels' Gripe Sessions Help Chief Maintain Communications with Workers," *The Wall Street Journal,* Western ed., July 16, 1981, p. 25.

24. "Employee Recognition: A Key to Motivation," *Personnel Journal,* February 1981, pp. 103–106.

25. *The "Key Program",* Chicago: National Association of Suggestions Systems, 1983.

26. Lee A. Graf, "Suggestion Program Failure: Causes and Remedies," *Personnel Journal,* June 1982, pp. 450–454.

27. William J. Rothwell, "Conducting an Employee Attitude Survey," *Personnel Journal,* September 1982, pp. 689–691.

28. Ibid.

CHAPTER

18

It must be considered that there is nothing more difficult to carry out, nor more doubtful of success, nor more dangerous to handle, than to initiate a new order of things.

Niccoló Machiavelli[1]

CHANGE AND ORGANIZATION DEVELOPMENT

CHAPTER OBJECTIVES

After studying this chapter, you should be able to:

1 Explain the personnel department's role in implementing change.

2 Discuss barriers and resistance to change.

3 Describe the organizational learning curve for change.

4 Discuss practices that support change.

5 Describe the characteristics of organization development.

6 Explain steps necessary to implement organization development.

The Mead Corporation faced some difficult decisions that required changes throughout several of its paper mills.[2] Its productivity was low, and its competitive ability was declining. One of the company's major decisions to help overcome its decline was a broad program of organization development in which the personnel department was heavily involved. According to the senior vice president for human relations, a key idea was to develop better work teams in each paper mill and to encourage them to improve both product quality and quantity.

The move toward better quality and quantity required many small changes day by day until the company's whole organizational culture was changed. For example, all workers at one mill were put on salary rather than being paid hourly wages. They were called members, not workers or employees, and were carefully trained in both human relations and technical skills so that they could work better as a team. Union involvement was required in order to change work rules so that teamwork could develop. These changes, and many others, combined to build a strong spirit of teamwork and productivity.

Results of the program were significant. Costs of making paper cartons decreased by 20 to 30 percent in a Georgia plant. In an Ohio plant the labor hours required to make a ton of paper were reduced from 21 to 13, which was a reduction of 38 percent in two years. The company became more competitive, and jobs were more secure because the firm had successfully responded to necessary changes.

Change is everywhere. Change, such as that faced by the Mead Corporation, is normal and natural in every organization. It exists because the world both inside and outside of the organization is dynamic, not static. Within a company people retire or problems develop that must be solved. Outside of the company there are thousands of changes ranging from new products to new government regulations. For example, when an employer installs industrial robots, hundreds of hours of time may be required for the personnel department to develop new work rules and negotiate them with the union. And employees may spend thousands of hours retraining for new jobs.

This chapter discusses how change affects the entire organization and how the personnel department works to implement it. Then the chapter focuses on organization development, a major way to help a company deal with change.

THE PERSONNEL DEPARTMENT AND CHANGE

The personnel department in a firm such as the Mead Corporation both initiates change and responds to it. The department creates change by developing new policies and programs for employees. It also responds to change introduced by others inside and outside the organization. Examples are as follows:

- *Production change.* Affects training, job descriptions, motivation, working conditions, and grievances

- *New office computer.* Affects training, employee transfers, job descriptions, employment, pay, and quality of work life

- *Company growth.* Affects career planning, employment, employee development, promotions, pay, and working conditions

Before change is undertaken, managers and personnel specialists must recognize the trade-offs involved. Of particular concern are the costs and other effects of change on the organizational system. The personnel department also must work to reduce barriers to change. In the next few pages the costs and benefits, effects, and barriers to change are explored. Then the discussion centers on implementing change in an organization.

Costs and Benefits

The *objective of the personnel department* is to manage *change* in ways that increase the benefits and reduce the costs. All types of benefits and costs are considered, including human and economic ones. The approach is proactive rather than reactive, in order to make a positive contribution to the situation. The personnel department strives to provide a *net benefit,* as shown in Figure 18-1, which means that there will be a surplus of benefits after all costs are included. If a change produces more unfavorable results than favorable ones, then the change probably is undesirable and should not be implemented.

> The change objective: net benefits

All changes are likely to produce some costs. For example, a new procedure may require the inconvenience of learning new practices, may disrupt work, or may temporarily reduce motivation. These conditions are costs, and they must

Figure 18-1
Net Benefits Are the Surplus of Benefits above Costs

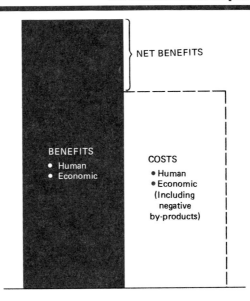

NET BENEFITS

BENEFITS
- Human
- Economic

COSTS
- Human
- Economic (Including negative by-products)

be considered along with the potential benefits of the new procedure. One difficulty with introducing change is that different people are affected by it in different ways. Some may benefit while others suffer a loss. In these instances, the personnel department works especially to assist those who will be affected negatively. In most cases it cannot prevent the costs, but perhaps it can encourage offsetting benefits in a related area such as working conditions. In other instances, the personnel department provides training to help employees adjust to change with minimal disruption. It also builds communication to help employees understand the net benefit that the organization will receive.

Personnel's varying role

For example, a state office introduced a new procedure as required by legislation. People throughout the office were affected in different ways as follows:

- *Employees directly affected.* A long-run cost because they performed more work without added benefits, and there was a temporary decline in job satisfaction

- *Accounting employees.* A minor benefit, because they performed slightly less work

- *Other employees.* No effect

- *Supervisor where change was made.* A temporary cost of more problems during the change period

- *Other supervisors.* No effect

- *Management.* Minor temporary cost to plan and implement change

- *Personnel department.* Intermediate-term costs to make job analysis and evaluation of jobs having new duties and to advise supervisor on problems of job satisfaction caused by change

In situations such as the one just described, there is no clear-cut 100 percent gain for the office. Rather, a series of separate costs and benefits must be managed on an individual basis. Other departments as well as the personnel department will become involved in working with these problems.

Psychic Costs of Change

Persons who experience change usually also experience some *psychic costs,* which are the stress, strain, and anxiety that affect a person's inner self during a period of change. Obviously an undesirable, troublesome change may produce stress, but a desirable change such as a promotion may also be stressful. A promotion may require a person to learn new skills, develop new work contacts, and form new friendships; and all of these requirements can be stressful.

For example, Glenda Cortez was promoted from a clerical job in the back office of a bank to the consumer loan department. She wanted the job, and she looked forward to the opportunities it offered. In her new job she was required to learn new skills and make new friendships. She also had to discuss problems with customers, but her clerical background had given her little experience in customer contacts.

Glenda found these new experiences stressful, even though she wanted them for promotion and growth. Soon she sought the help of her supervisor and the personnel department in order to cope with the psychic costs of her new job.

After a number of employees experienced costs similar to Cortez's, the personnel department developed a course on coping with change in order to help employees adjust.[3] Workers who received a promotion were required to take the course, and other employees were encouraged to do so. The personnel department also improved its monitoring of promotions and transfers in order to assist individual employees when problems developed.

Costs of Relocation

Promotions and transfers tend to have especially high psychic costs when they require employees to move to another location. These changes involve the employee's family, and so coping may be more difficult.[4] The children may not want to move from their friends and familiar surroundings. The spouse may have a job and not want to leave it. Companies that require employees to relocate have found that they need thoughtful personnel policies that reduce the psychic costs involved. These policies are applied situationally so that each employee's individual needs can be considered.[5] Effective relocation policies often include an advance company-paid orientation trip to the new location for the employee and spouse, allowances for moving household goods, travel expenses to the new location, and assignment of one or more employees to help the family get acquainted after arrival. These policies greatly ease the stress of the move.

Environmental Effects on Change

Change is influenced partly by the environment in which an organization operates. Government, customers, labor unions, communities, and others initiate changes in organizations. For example, if union policy strongly favors seniority for promotion, then there will be pressures to change personnel policies in that direction. If customers want better product quality, then the personnel department will need to initiate training programs that upgrade labor skills. Each company's personnel policies and problems depend on the external environment in which the firm operates. Stable environments mean less change. Firms in dynamic industries encounter more change.

Dynamic versus stable environments

One study covered dynamic companies having an employee growth rate of 20 percent or more for at least four years.[6] Most of these companies were chosen to have similar human resource problems as follows:

- The need to make quick decisions

- Rapidly changing jobs

- Large recruiting and employment demands

- Increased training needs

- Stress from frequent change, often unanticipated

- Strain on personnel resources

Barriers to Change

Resistance to change

Barriers are environmental factors that interfere with the acceptance and implementation of change. Among them are economic costs, difficulties in securing financing, problems with new technology, and lack of resources. However, usually the most difficult barrier—and the one of concern to the personnel department—is frequent employee opposition or *resistance to change.*[7] People sometimes stand like a wall against needed change. At other times they are responsive to it and cooperative with management. Their reactions depend largely on their own values and self-interests, and so their responses often are different from those of management. As shown in Figure 18-2, employee resistance to change is of three different types, and each type contains the word "logical."

- *Logical.* Based on rational reasoning

Figure 18-2

Types of Employee Resistance to Change

LOGICAL; RATIONAL

- Time required to adjust
- Extra effort to relearn
- Possible less desirable conditions, such as skill downgrading
- Costs of change
- Different assessment of the change

PSYCHOLOGICAL; EMOTIONAL

- Fear of the unknown
- Low tolerance of change
- Dislike of management or other change initiator
- Lack of trust in others
- Need for security; desire for status quo

SOCIOLOGICAL; GROUP INTERESTS

- Political coalitions
- Opposing group values
- Parochial, narrow outlook
- Vested interests
- Desire to retain existing friendships

- Psycho*logical.* Based on emotions, sentiments, and attitudes

- Socio*logical.* Based on group interest and values

Logical-rational resistance arises from the time and effort required to adjust to the change and learn the new job duties. These are true costs borne by the employees. Even though a change may be favorable for workers in the long run, these short-run costs must first be paid. *Logical resistance*

Psychological resistance is concerned with attitudes and feelings of individual employees about change. They may fear the unknown, mistrust management's leadership, or feel that their security is threatened. Even though management may believe there is no justification for these feelings, they are real and must be recognized. *Psychological resistance*

Mike Thornton was one of five skilled machine operators at St. Regis Company. His supervisor introduced a job change to provide a minor improvement in efficiency. For many years Mike had feared that any efficiency improvement would cause him to lose his job. Even though his job was not threatened in any way, his fear caused him to fight the change.

Sociological resistance is more concerned with group interests and values. There are political coalitions, opposing labor union values, and even different community values. On a small-group level there are work friendships that may be disrupted by changes. Social values are powerful forces in the environment, and so they must be carefully considered by personnel specialists. *Sociological resistance*

The office manager at Winthrop Company reorganized departments in a way that moved Susan Maxwell to another department on a different floor of the building. The move was reasonable, and it should give Susan more professional contacts for better training; however, she strongly resisted it. She belonged to a closely knit group in her department and did not want to leave it.

It can be seen that psychological resistance and sociological resistance are not illogical or irrational; rather, they are logical according to different sets of values. They are based on the tune of a different drummer.

Possible Benefits of Employee Resistance

Resistance interferes with management efforts to implement changes; therefore, it is usually viewed by management as undesirable. On the other hand, it has some possible benefits. For example, resistance may encourage management to reexamine its change proposals so that it can be more sure of their appropriateness. In this way employees operate as a check and balance to ensure that management properly plans and implements a change. Not all changes are beneficial. Some have undesirable results in the long run, and if reasonable employee resistance causes management to screen more carefully its proposed changes, then employees have discouraged careless management decisions. *Resistance may be beneficial.*

Resistance also may identify specific problem areas where a change is likely to have difficulty, so that management can take corrective action before a problem becomes serious. At the same time management may be encouraged to do a better job of communicating the change, an approach that in the long run should lead to better acceptance. Resistance also gives management information about the intensity of employee emotions on an issue, provides emotional release for pent-up employee feelings, and may encourage employees to think and talk more about a change so that they are better acquainted with it.

Personnel specialists become involved with change because they are seen as the "people" experts. Even when technical changes occur, managers may seek the advice of specialists in the personnel department. When managers draw on the personnel department's human resource expertise, barriers to change may be lowered and the change may be implemented more smoothly.

IMPLEMENTING CHANGE

Supporting and resisting forces

The personnel department actively works with both employees and managers to implement change. In general, it encourages change by increasing the supporting forces for change and reducing the forces that resist change.[8] As shown in Figure 18-3, an organization at any time is a dynamic balance of forces supporting and resisting any practice. These practices will continue in a steady way until a change is introduced. However, the change is not likely to be accepted unless supporting forces are added to

Figure 18-3
A General Model of Organizational Change

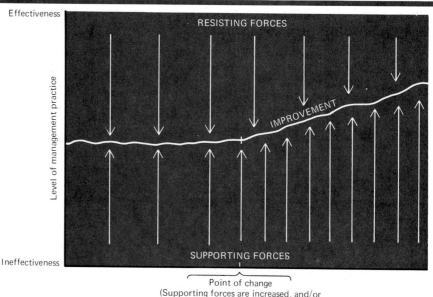

Time ⟶

give it acceptance. Resisting forces also need to be removed to the extent possible. In this manner the old practice will be replaced by the desired change because organizational forces support the change.

Both the number and the strength of supporting and resisting forces may be influenced by the personnel department. For example, a larger amount of feedback about quality of work should be a supporting force for it, and also more pride in work should support high quality. In the same situation, resisting forces may be reduced by decreasing high noise levels that interfere with work.

For example, the Peerless Company was growing rapidly and needed more parking spaces for employees. The only space available was on the other side of the manufacturing-office building where all employees worked. One problem was that this new lot was far from the building, and so employees might find it inconvenient to use. Following the advice of the personnel department, the company added a long covered walkway from the parking lot to the building. Since weather in this area frequently was wet and the other lot had no covered walkway, employees were motivated to use the new parking lot.

The Organizational Learning Curve for Change

It takes time for people to adapt. This period of adjustment can be charted as the organization's *learning curve for change.* Figure 18-4 shows the learning curve for a change that was designed to reduce costs. As the figure shows, in the beginning costs increased rather than decreased because of the difficulties people had adjusting to the change. This pattern is fairly typical. Procedures are upset, and communication patterns are disrupted. Conflicts develop about the change, and cooperation declines. Problems arise, and time must be taken to

Learning curve for change

Figure 18-4
Typical Organizational Learning Curve for Change

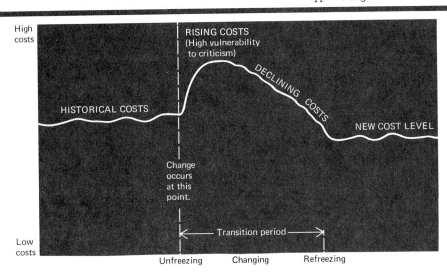

High costs

RISING COSTS
(High vulnerability to criticism)

HISTORICAL COSTS

DECLINING COSTS

NEW COST LEVEL

Change occurs at this point.

Low costs

|← Transition period →|

Unfreezing   Changing   Refreezing

resolve them. The result is that, as the statement goes, "things are likely to get worse before they get better."

Reactions during transition period

During the transition period when people are adjusting to a change, they may become discouraged because of the problems that develop. At this time the change is especially subject to criticism, attack, and even failure because it appears not to be working. Only after the passage of time, when teamwork and efficiency are restored, is the change likely to produce the favorable results intended.

The learning curve shown in Figure 18-4 reflects three basic steps in the theory of change:

Unfreezing, changing, and refreezing

- *Unfreezing* (also *unlearning*).[9] Casting aside old ideas and practices so that new ones can be learned.

- *Changing.* Learning new ideas and practices so that an employee can think and perform in new ways.

- *Refreezing.* Integrating what has been learned into actual practice.

Three steps are necessary.

All three steps are necessary to make a successful change. For example, merely knowing a new practice is not enough. Unless the old practice is unfrozen, an employee tends to use an ineffective combination of both the old and the new. Also the new ideas will be useless until an employee can refreeze them into actual practice.

Practices That Support Change

When a company such as the Mead Corporation faces change, it needs to develop practices that will support the change, such as the following:

Planning is essential.

Planning   Careful planning is fundamental for the success of a change, and it is important for the personnel department to be involved in planning from the beginning.[10] Often when other departments initiate change, they tend to plan independently and bring in the personnel department only after plans are well advanced. The result is that many human factors are overlooked, and the change needs to be delayed while its human effects are reconsidered. In other instances, the change is introduced hastily without giving enough thought to people, and so it fails.

> Management in a state auditor's office, for example, introduced certain changes in work assignments. It was the management's intention to notify the personnel department after the changes became effective so that new job evaluations could be made to reflect the revised duties. Employees, however, saw the change as a move that would give some of them secondary positions with reduced status.
>
> When the employees refused to go along with the change, there was a tardy call to the personnel department. At this point the situation was more difficult to handle than it would have been with the personnel department

involved in the beginning. Personnel specialists also found that several personnel practices in addition to job evaluation were involved in the change—such as recruitment patterns, employment needs, career plans, training needs, and personnel policies.

Participation   For many of the same reasons that the personnel department needs to be involved in change, employees also need to be considered. Participation is a key personnel practice that encourages employees to discuss, to communicate, to make suggestions, and to become interested in change.[11] Participation often operates through committees and task forces, such as those used in Japan to improve employee productivity and thus enable their products to compete aggressively with those manufactured in the United States. Participation encourages commitment, rather than mere compliance with change. Commitment implies a motivation to support a change and to ensure that it operates effectively.

As shown in Figure 18-5, a general model of participation and change indicates that as participation increases, resistance to change tends to decrease. Resistance declines because employees have less cause to resist. Their needs are being considered, and so they feel secure in a changing situation. Participation reaches deep into the wellsprings of human nature to produce security, cooperation, and feelings of personal worth.

Participation reduces resistance.

It is essential for employees to participate in a change *before* it occurs, not after. When workers can be involved from the beginning, they are protected from surprises and feel that their ideas are wanted. They begin to see personally the need for change and want to help management implement it.[12] On the other hand, employees are likely to feel that involvement after a change is nothing more than a selling device and manipulation by management.

Many managers and supervisors think that they are supposed to make

Figure 18-5
A General Model of Participation
in Relation to Resistance to Change

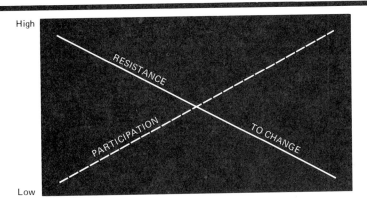

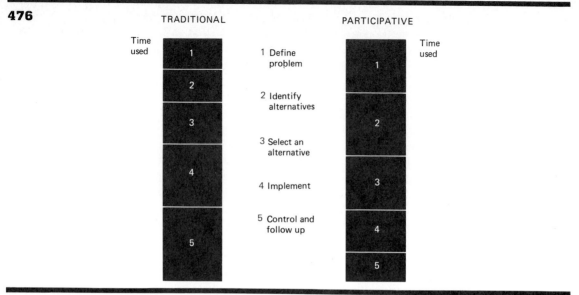

Figure 18-6
Traditional versus Participative Approaches to
Decision Making

decisions. So they unilaterally make these decisions and deprive employees of an opportunity to participate. Figure 18-6 illustrates a time bar for two approaches to decision making. The bar on the left is labeled "traditional." Here managers believe that their role is to make decisions. To do so efficiently, they define their problems (step 1), identify alternatives (step 2), and select one of them (step 3). Then the managers implement their decision only to encounter resistance from the employees, who feel no "ownership" because they did not participate in the decision-making process.

Participative decision making frequently takes longer because employees are allowed to participate. As the longer time bar shows for steps 1, 2, and 3, these stages are time-consuming. However, the next step, implementation, goes quicker because employees do not resist their own decisions. In addition, since employees are likely to be more committed to those decisions in which they participated, the need for controls and follow-up by management is probably much less. The lower levels of resistance and control may mean that when all five steps are considered, the participative approach is not slow at all. And as will be explained in Chapter 19, employee involvement in decision making also may lead to a higher quality of work life and more productivity.

Which employees should be involved? Essentially, any employee who is likely to be affected by a change should know about it and be involved in it. When large numbers of workers are affected, representatives may be used to keep change committees to a manageable size. Management seeks to involve both those who support a change and those who oppose it, because involvement tends to reduce opposition. Occasionally management chooses an opposition leader to chair a committee or task force. In this way opponents are assured a fair hearing, and the leader may develop a more balanced viewpoint as a result of intense involvement. Participation does not always require official committees or task forces. When employees feel that there is open communication and that their ideas are wanted, change may be implemented through informal discussions.

Communication   Communication encourages understanding. It is a major activity of the personnel department. Employees are unlikely to give their support to any change that they do not understand. The personnel department needs to ensure that supervisors, managers, staff people, and personnel specialists are fully communicating about any impending change.[13]

> In one instance a textile plant faced a temporary increase in product demand.[14] New manufacturing equipment could not be secured, and the plant was operating twenty-four hours a day for five days a week. The only alternative was to use the plant on Saturdays and Sundays. The personnel department was assigned to implement the entire change in a manner that would gain cooperation of employees.
> The department used communication to inform employees about the problem and to seek their ideas. Communication revealed that employees did not want to work overtime or in a rotation with a fourth shift; so a solution appeared to be difficult. Over a period of time employee surveys and bulletins were used to inform employees and to ask their reactions to different proposed solutions. Based on feedback, a task force finally selected a separate part-time group to work only on Saturdays and Sundays. The plan was established, proved to be effective, and was well received by employees. It was evident that thorough two-way communication helped management make a correct decision and gain the support of employees.

Additional communication practices that are useful with change are discussed in Chapter 17, "Personnel Communications Systems."

Supplementary rewards   Another way to build employee support for change is to be sure that there are enough rewards for employees in the change situation. It is only natural for employees to ask, "What's in this for me?" If they see that a change brings them only losses and no gains, they can hardly be enthusiastic about it.

Rewards say to employees, "We care. We want you to benefit from this change as well as us." Rewards also give employees a sense of progress with a change. Both financial and nonfinancial rewards are useful. Employees appreciate a pay increase or a promotion, but they also appreciate emotional support, training in new skills, and recognition from management.[15]

> In an electronics firm the personnel department held a "half-way banquet" when the group had implemented about half of a major change. When the

478

change was fully implemented, a "success banquet" was held, and special recognition was given to key employees who helped install the change. This additional recognition was a reward to employees for their extra effort, and it helped build their support for the change.

It can be seen that personnel practices such as those just discussed are a strong encouragement for employees to accept change. When these practices are added to those discussed in other chapters, such as training, the personnel department has a powerful kit of tools for implementing change. In a dynamic environment the personnel department also may provide specialists in organizational development, as discussed in the next section.

ORGANIZATION DEVELOPMENT

Definition of OD   *Organization development* (OD) is a change process that has the potential to bring major improvements in cooperation, teamwork, and productivity. The results can be impressive. OD is an intervention strategy that uses group processes to focus on the whole organization in order to bring about planned change.[16] It seeks to change beliefs, attitudes, values, structures, and practices—in fact, the entire operational system—so that the organization can better adapt to change. It especially focuses on team building and on group problem solving. An excellent by-product is human resource development since employees gain skills in coping with their mutual problems.[17]

Supports change   A major reason for the growth of OD is that it builds support for changed behavior and thus overcomes a limitation of traditional training. The problem with traditional training is that the reward structure on the job often fails to reinforce the training, and so there is excessive loss of training momentum in the transition from the classroom to the work situation.[18] The personnel department administers most training programs using skilled company and noncompany trainers, but the trainers rarely supervise those same trainees back on the job. Consequently, the trainers are unable to guide the day-to-day trainee decisions or to change job rewards to encourage trainees to apply what they have learned.

For example, Margie Myers, shipping supervisor, returned from her course on supervisory effectiveness eager to try some of the new human relations practices she had learned. The first thing she did was to plan some participative problem-solving meetings with her employees, but her manager rejected the idea. Then she attempted to make some schedule changes to fit the needs of her employees, but she could not get them approved. She planned some other changes to make her supervision more employee-centered, but she abandoned them when she found that her performance rating continued to emphasize mostly production and costs.

About the only long-run result of her training was that she became less happy with her job because the company system discouraged efforts to try what was learned.

Characteristics of OD

OD has a number of characteristics that are implied in its definition. Most of these characteristics are substantially different from a typical training program.

Focus on the whole organization   OD's objective is to improve the whole organization or one of its major units so that it can respond to change more uniformly and capably. OD builds teamwork and cooperation. It also encourages more frequent and open communication. It seeks to build problem-solving capability by improving group relationships and problem confrontation. In short, it reaches into all parts of the organization in order to make it more humanly responsive.

Systems orientation   OD is concerned with interactions of various parts of the organization as they affect each other. It is concerned with intergroup relationships as well as interpersonal ones. It is concerned with structure and process as well as attitudes. And it may even become involved in the politics of the organization.[19] The basic issue to which it is directed is: How do all these parts work together?

Use of a change agent   OD uses one or more *change agents*, who are persons with the role of stimulating and coordinating change within a group.[20] Often the primary change agent is a consultant from outside of the company. In this way the agent can operate independently without ties to the hierarchy and politics of the firm. As shown in Figure 18-7, which presents an *OD change model*, the personnel director is the in-house change agent who coordinates the program internally with both management and the external agent. The external agent also works with management, and so the result is a three-way relationship of the personnel director, management, and an outside consultant as they develop the OD program. In rare cases the organization has its own in-house professional who replaces the outside consultant and works with the personnel director and management. This in-house consultant is usually a specialist on the personnel staff.

Change agents

Problem solving   OD emphasizes problem solving. It seeks to solve problems, rather than to discuss them theoretically as in a classroom. These problems are real problems that the participants face in their organization; therefore, they are stimulating and interesting. This focus on real, ongoing problems, not artificial ones, is called *action research*.[21] It is such a key characteristic that OD sometimes is defined as organizational improvement through action research.

Action research

Experiential learning   *Experiential learning* means that participants learn by experiencing in the training environment the kinds of behavioral situations they face on the job. Then they can discuss and analyze their own immediate experience and learn from it. This approach tends to produce more changed behavior than traditional lecture and discussion methods in which

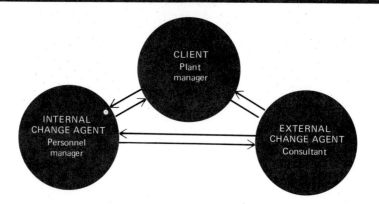

THE IN-HOUSE MANAGER'S SIDE

- Knowledge of specific sociotechnical systems

- Perspective limited to organization (local outlook)

- Dependency on organization for financial rewards

- Company-person career bond

WHAT THE CONSULTANT BRINGS

- Knowledge of OD techniques

- Experience in many organizations, variety of perspectives (cosmopolitan outlook)

- Independence

- No bond; easily dispensable relationship

Source: Redrawn, by permission of the publisher, from Thomas H. Patten, Jr., "Team Building, Part 1, Designing the Intervention," *Personnel,* January–February 1979, copyright © 1979 by AMACOM, a division of American Management Associations, p. 19. All rights reserved.

Figure 18-7
The OD Change Model

people talk about abstract ideas. Theory is necessary and desirable, but the ultimate test is how one applies the theory in a real situation. OD helps to provide some of the answers. Participants work on real problems in real situations, and the experience helps to solidify their new learning.

Group processes Another characteristic is group processes. There are group discussions, intergroup conflicts, confrontations, and team building. There is an effort to improve interpersonal relations, open communication channels, build trust, and encourage responsiveness to others.

Feedback OD relies heavily on feedback so that participants will have concrete data on which to make decisions. Feedback encourages them to understand a situation and take self-correcting action, rather than wait for someone else to tell them what to do.

A feedback exercise An example is a feedback exercise in one OD program. Participants are separated into two groups representing two different departments in the organization. Both groups are asked to develop answers to the following questions:

- What characteristics best describe our group?

- What characteristics best describe the other group?

- How will the other group describe us?

After the separate groups have prepared their answers, they assemble and present their answers to the other group. They give concrete feedback about impressions each group has of the other, and there are usually major misunderstandings. In this presentation no arguments are allowed. Questions are accepted only to clarify what the other group is saying.

The groups again are separated to discuss two other questions:

- How did these misunderstandings occur?

- What can we do to correct them?

Based on this new feedback the groups meet together to develop specific plans of action for solving their misunderstandings. In each instance feedback about themselves is the basis for their activities.

In summary, by focusing on the whole rather than on the parts, OD tends to integrate the various activities of the firm that often go their separate ways. The result should be improved organizational performance.

Implementing an OD Program

The steps necessary to apply an OD program are often called *the OD process.*   **The OD process**
This process is complex and difficult. It tends to take a year or more and may continue indefinitely. For a program of this magnitude, top-management support is essential. This support must be seen as active commitment, not just passive permission. There are many different approaches to OD, but a typical complete program includes the following steps.[22]

1. *Initial diagnosis.* Top management meets with the consultant to determine the type of OD program that is needed. During this phase the consultant may seek inputs from various persons in the organization.

2. *Data collection.* Surveys may be made to determine organizational climate and behavioral problems. The consultant usually meets with groups away from work to develop information from questions such as:

- What kinds of conditions contribute most to your job effectiveness?
- What kinds of conditions interfere with your job effectiveness?
- What would you most like to change in the way this organization operates?

3. *Data feedback and confrontation.* Work groups are assigned to review the data collected, to mediate among themselves areas of disagreement, and to establish priorities for change.

4. *Action planning and problem solving.* Groups use the data to develop specific recommendations for change. Discussion focuses on real problems in the organization. Plans are specific, including who is responsible and when the action should be completed.

5. *Team building.* During the entire period of group meetings the consultant has been encouraging the groups to examine how they work together.[23] The consultant helps them see the value of open communication and trust as prerequisites for improved group functioning. Team building is further encouraged by having individual managers and their subordinates work together in small-group OD teams.

6. *Intergroup development.* Following the development of small-group teams, larger teams may be developed to improve interdepartmental cooperation.

7. *Evaluation and follow-up.* The consultant helps the organization evaluate the results of its OD program and develop additional programs in areas where further efforts are needed. As an example of follow-up in one organization, the consultant asked managers to provide tapes of committee meetings that they chaired subsequent to the program. The consultant analyzed these tapes and used them to discuss with the managers how well each was applying what was learned in the OD program.

Team building is encouraged.

The steps in OD are part of a whole process, and so all of them need to be applied if an organization expects to gain the full benefits. A firm that applies only two or three steps, such as diagnosis and team building, is likely to be disappointed with the results. However, the whole process can produce quite favorable results. In a manufacturing plant, for example, an OD program led to a productivity increase of 22 percent in two years and 69 percent in four years.[24]

Benefits of OD

When OD is successful, a number of variables may be improved. Three major areas of benefit are performance, job satisfaction, and self-change, as shown in Figure 18-8.[25] However, the success rate is limited. Only 42 to 63 percent of the OD programs reported improved results for these areas.

Performance Performance benefits occur on three levels: individual, group, and organization. On the individual level, if the performance ratings of employees in the program improve, evidence suggests that the OD program is associated with the improved performance. The improvement may not have been *caused* by the OD program, but at least there is an *association.* The evidence is even stronger if there is a control group of nonparticipants and if this group fails to show any rating improvement during the same period.

Performance improves.

A strong likelihood for improvement in group performance exists, since OD emphasizes group processes. Examples are improved cooperation, better meetings, and reduced conflict.[26] In the long run these group improvements should be associated with broad organizational improvements, such as lower unit costs of products and higher return on investment. These improvements

VARIABLE	NUMBER OF STUDIES	PERCENTAGE REPORTING IMPROVEMENT
PERFORMANCE		
Individual		
(*Example:* performance ratings)	14	42
Group		
(*Example:* quality of meetings)	8	63
Organization		
(*Example:* return on investment)	12	47
GENERAL JOB SATISFACTION	7	43
(*Example:* job satisfaction surveys)		
SHELF-CHANGE FOR INDIVIDUAL	10	62
(*Example:* openness to ideas and others)		

Source: Adapted from Jerry L. Porras and P. O. Berg, "The Impact of Organization Development," *Academy of Management Review,* April 1978, tables 1 to 3, pp. 249–266.

Figure 18-8
Proportion of OD Programs Reporting Improved Results

often are called "bottom-line results" because they affect the bottom-line figure of profit on the profit and loss statement. These cost savings are usually the principal reason that management establishes an OD program.

Job satisfaction   As shown in Figure 18-8, job satisfaction often increases following an OD program. Since teamwork, cooperation, and communication may improve, employees are likely to feel that they have a better place to work.

Satisfaction increases.

> A supervisor, Gus Anka, participated in an OD program with supervisors from other departments. During the meetings the participants were encouraged to express conflicts and use a problem-solving approach to them. For three years Gus had an intense conflict with a supervisor in another department. This conflict was revealed during the OD meetings and discussed. Gus felt that his problem was adequately resolved, and afterward he felt more accepted by the other supervisors and more involved in his work. His job satisfaction substantially increased.

Self-change   An important result of many OD programs is self-change. Participants learn to be more aware of their own feelings and the feelings that others have toward them. They are encouraged to share their feelings with others, be more open in their communication, and become more cooperative. At least some of these new behaviors are likely to be carried back to the workplace and affect both self-perceptions and individual behavior on the job.

Self-change occurs.

Problems with OD

OD is often criticized because of several problems and weaknesses. As shown in Figure 18-9, an OD program is difficult and costly to apply. Some programs even

There are problems.

- Difficult to initiate; fails before completion
- Costly, including consultant and participant costs
- Slow and time-consuming, often requiring one to three years
- Possible psychological damage when misused
- Conceptual ambiguities
- Possible elitist, top-down imposition of values
- Narrow focus mostly on people
- Antibureaucratic, at cross-purposes with authority systems

Figure 18-9
Typical Problems Associated with OD

fail before completion because employees dislike the methods used. OD also consumes much time as it continues through months or even years. Some of the techniques may invade privacy, and they can be misused. For these reasons, management needs to assure itself that benefits will be clearly higher than costs, and the personnel director must be sure that the program is administered professionally.

A number of conceptual and philosophical questions about OD merit review.[27] Some critics maintain that its ambiguities prevent it from being applied consistently. They also feel that it is an elitist top-down program that tries to force humanistic values on people, even when they may not want them. The values usually emphasize group processes and decisions, and so they may be contrary to the organization's authority structure. Some critics say that OD would be more effective if it were fine-tuned to have a better fit with authoritative organizations, rather than try to change them.[28] Also better research is needed to verify the benefits claimed by practitioners.[29]

In spite of the numerous weaknesses and problems, OD is an accepted practice in personnel management. It is widely used, and practitioners feel that its benefits are substantial in creating more humanly effective organizations.

Next chapter   Other approaches to employee involvement are discussed in Chapter 19. Through these approaches, personnel departments can contribute to the organization's quality of work life and productivity, the subjects of the next chapter.

SUMMARY

The personnel department is actively involved with change because it affects people. The objective is to manage change in ways that increase the benefits and reduce the costs. The personnel department is especially concerned with barriers to change and the psychic costs. Major personnel practices that tend to support change include careful planning, participation, communication, and supplementary rewards.

Organization development is widely used to improve a firm's skills for working with change. OD is defined as an intervention strategy that uses group processes to focus on the whole organization in order to bring about planned change. It attempts to build the organization into a cooperative team. Although there are problems associated with OD, it is an accepted practice in personnel management because of its benefits.

TERMS FOR REVIEW

Net benefit	Refreezing
Psychic costs	Organization development (OD)
Barriers to change	Change agents
Resistance to change	OD change model
Learning curve for change	Experiential learning
Unfreezing	OD process

REVIEW AND DISCUSSION QUESTIONS

1. Analyze your own responses to change during the last six months. What types of changes do you tend to accept more readily than others and why? Can you apply any of the change models in this chapter to help you understand your responses to change?

2. Discuss the relationship of costs and benefits of change. Can an organization implement a major change without costs? What are psychic costs?

3. Select a change that occurred within the classroom environment and discuss logical, psychological, and sociological resistance to it, if any.

4. If you were a supervisor in a government office and were required to make a major change in work methods, what practices would you use to support the change and why?

5. How are participation and resistance to change related?

6. Define and explain the characteristics of OD.

7. In which of the following situations would OD tend to be more effective and why?
    a. Scientists in a product development laboratory
    b. Workers on a television assembly line

8. What are the potential benefits of OD and what are its problems?

9. If you were a participant in an OD program in an information processing office, what personal benefits would you attempt to gain from it?

486

INCIDENT 18-1

First National Bank

First National Bank is a large bank in an eastern state. It has about eighty branches throughout the state. For some months management has been considering a change in training evaluation procedures—a change that will affect both the personnel department and branch managers. The plan has been discussed with those who will be affected, and a number of them oppose the change. The training supervisor, Ramona Spelman, is one of them.

After discussion with other bank officers, the vice president for personnel, Gary Reynolds, decided to adopt the change. He selected a task force to implement it and chose Ramona as chairperson. When he asked her to accept, she did so, and then commented, "You know I am opposed to this change. Why did you select me as chairperson?"

Gary replied, "Yes, we know of your opposition. We chose you because we knew that if any flaws exist, you will find them. And we believe you can correct them."

Nothing more was said.

1. Why would a manager such as Gary choose a leader of the opposition to implement a change? What models or basic ideas about change may have guided his thinking?

2. What degree of success do you predict for Ramona in implementing the change?

REFERENCES

1. Niccoló Machiavelli, *The Prince*, 1532.

2. Ralph E. Winter, "Firms' Recent Productivity Drives May Yield Unusually Strong Gains," *The Wall Street Journal*, Western ed., June 14, 1983, pp. 33 and 49.

3. For an example see "Coping with Anxiety at AT&T," *Business Week*, May 28, 1979, pp. 95–106.

4. Thomas P. Gullotta and Kevin C. Donohue, "Preventing Family Distress during Relocation: Initiatives for Human Resource Managers," *The Personnel Administrator*, December 1982, pp. 37–43.

5. For a discussion of the personnel department's role in relocation see John M. Moore, "Employee Relocation: Expanded Responsibilities for the Personnel Department," *Personnel*, September–October 1981, pp. 62–69. See also Lawrence W. Foster and Marilyn L. Liebrenz, "Corporate Moves—Who Pays the Psychic Costs?" *Personnel*, November–December 1977, pp. 67–75.

6. John P. Kotter and Vijay Sathe, "Problems of Human Resource Management in Rapidly Growing Companies," *California Management Review*, Winter 1978, pp. 29–36.

For several articles discussing how the environment will change personnel practices in the twenty-first century, see the special issue on "Change in the 21st Century," *The Personnel Administrator,* December 1983.

7. Joseph Stanislao and Bettie C. Stanislao, "Dealing with Resistance to Change," *Business Horizons,* July–August 1983, pp. 74–78; Irving G. Calish and R. Donald Gamache, "How to Overcome Organizational Resistance to Change," *Management Review,* October 1981, pp. 21–28 and 50; and George S. Odiorne, "The Change Resisters," *The Personnel Administrator,* January 1981, pp. 57–63.

8. For a discussion of implementing change see John P. Kotter and Leonard A. Schlesinger, "Choosing Strategies for Change," *Harvard Business Review,* March–April 1979, pp. 106–114; and Stephen R. Michael, "Organizational Change Techniques: Their Present, Their Future," *Organizational Dynamics,* Summer 1982, pp. 67–80. The change process in a personnel department is reported in Tana Pesso, "A Pathway to Change: The Honeywell Study Model," *Personnel,* January–February 1984, pp. 75–80.

9. John W. Newstrom, "The Management of Unlearning: Exploding the 'Clean Slate' Fallacy," *Training and Development Journal,* August 1983, pp. 36–39.

10. For extensive discussion see Charles Margerison, *Influencing Organizational Change: The Role of the Personnel Specialist,* London: Institute of Personnel Management, 1978.

11. Peter Brownell, "Participative Management," *Wharton Magazine,* Fall 1982, pp. 38–43; William E. Zierden, "Managing Workplace Innovations: A Framework and a New Approach," *Management Review,* June 1981, pp. 57–61; and Marshall Sashkin, *A Manager's Guide to Participative Management,* New York: American Management Association, 1982.

12. Alexander Mikalachki, "Does Anyone Listen to the Boss?" *Business Horizons,* January–February 1983, pp. 18–24.

13. Marsha Sinetar, "Mergers, Morale, and Productivity," *Personnel Journal,* November 1981, pp. 863–867.

14. Richard C. Huseman and others, "Managing Change through Communication," *Personnel Journal,* January 1976, pp. 20–25.

15. Kotter and Schlesinger, op. cit.

16. For a comparison of OD and human resource development see C. Edward Kur, "OD: Perspectives, Processes, and Prospects," *Training and Development Journal,* April 1981, pp. 28–34. For an OD planning model see Anthony R. Marchione and Jon English, "Managing the Unpredictable—A Rational Plan for Coping with Change," *Management Review,* February 1982, pp. 52–57.

17. Milan Moravec, "Is HRD Enough?" *Personnel,* January–February 1979, pp. 53–57.

18. Ronald H. Gorman and H. Kent Baker, "That's Okay in Theory, But . . .," *Personnel,* July–August 1978, pp. 48–54. For a study of the perceived effectiveness of training methods as seen by training directors, see John W. Newstrom, "Evaluating the Effectiveness of Training Methods," *The Personnel Administrator,* January 1980, pp. 55–60.

19. Anthony T. Cobb and Newton Margulies, "Organization Development: A Political Perspective," *Academy of Management Review,* January 1981, pp. 49–59.

20. For discussions of change agents and how they work see Phillip L. Hunsaker,

"Strategies for Organizational Change: The Role of the Inside Change Agent," *Personnel,* September–October 1982, pp. 18–28; and Richard N. Ottaway, editor, *Change Agents at Work,* Westport, Conn.: Greenwood Press, 1979.

21. For a discussion of action research and other OD activities see Gordon L. Lippitt, *Organization Renewal: A Holistic Approach to Organization Development,* 2d. ed., Englewood Cliffs, N.J.: Prentice-Hall, 1982, especially pp. 307–310.

22. For a more extensive discussion of the OD process see John P. Kotter, *Organizational Dynamics: Diagnosis and Intervention,* Reading, Mass.: Addison-Wesley, 1978; and Glen H. Varney, *Organizational Development for Managers,* Reading, Mass.: Addison-Wesley, 1977.

23. For an extensive discussion of team development see Francis X. Mahoney, "Team Development, Part 1: What Is TD? Why Use It?" *Personnel,* September–October 1981, pp. 13–24; and Parts 2–7 in issues of *Personnel* extending through September–October 1982.

24. Rensis Likert and M. Scott Fisher, "MBGO: Putting Some Team Spirit into MBO," *Personnel,* January–February 1977, pp. 40–47. Other applications of OD are reported in a special section of OD in *Personnel,* March–April 1979, pp. 31–52, 62–68.

25. For further support see John M. Nicholas, "The Comparative Impact of Organization Development Interventions on Hard Criteria Measures," *Academy of Management Review,* October 1982, pp. 531–542; and Gene Milbourn and Richard Cuba, "OD Techniques and the Bottom Line," *Personnel,* May–June 1981, pp. 34–42.

26. For approaches to resolving conflict see Michele Stimac, "Strategies for Resolving Conflict: Their Functional and Dysfunctional Sides," *Personnel,* November–December 1982, pp. 54–64.

27. A readable summary of criticisms is Patrick E. Connor, "A Critical Inquiry into Some Assumptions and Values Characterizing OD," *Academy of Management Review,* October 1977, pp. 635–644. A book reporting failures and problems is Philip H. Mirvis and David N. Berg (eds.), *Failures in Organization Development and Change: Cases and Essays for Learning,* New York: Wiley, 1977. Insights into the philosophy and processes of OD are provided in a special issue entitled "Collaboration in Work Sessions," *Journal of Applied Behavioral Science,* vol. 13, no. 3, 1977.

28. Virginia E. Schein and Larry E. Greiner, "Can Organization Development Be Fine Tuned to Bureaucracies?" *Organizational Dynamics,* Winter 1977, pp. 48–61.

29. Achilles A. Armenakis, Arthur G. Bedeian, and Samuel B. Pond III, "Research Issues in OD Evaluation: Past, Present, and Future," *Academy of Management Journal,* April 1983, pp. 320–328; and W. Alan Randolph, "Planned Organizational Change and Its Measurements," *Personnel Psychology,* Spring 1982, pp. 117–139.

CHAPTER

Although improvements in QWL do not always lead to improvement in productivity, there is reason to believe that some new approaches to management can do a good job of increasing both of these factors.

Edward E. Lawler III[1]

QUALITY OF WORK LIFE

CHAPTER OBJECTIVES

After studying this chapter, you should be able to:

1 Explain how newer approaches to QWL differ from typical management approaches used in the past.

2 Describe the personnel department's role in QWL.

3 Discuss the connection between QWL and employee involvement.

4 Explain the quality circle process.

5 Identify international influences on North American QWL efforts.

6 Prepare a summary of the barriers to organizational QWL efforts.

Q *uality of work life (QWL)* efforts are systematic attempts by organizations to give workers a greater opportunity to affect their jobs and their contributions to the organization's overall effectiveness.[2] Too often

Tapping
employee ideas

employers have sought a worker's labor but have not tapped his or her ideas. Since employees' ideas often were not used, workers felt little responsibility for the success or failure of management's unilateral decisions. In extreme cases, the result became an "us-versus-them" contest with the rules being formulated by the union and management as part of a collective bargaining agreement.

Need for QWL
A union view of
the steel industry

Cooperation was replaced by formal rules. Teamwork seldom existed. When it did, it rarely bridged the gap between workers and management. Productivity suffered. And eventually foreign competition gained a significant market share in the steel, automobile, tires, consumer electronics, and other industries. At the same time an entire generation of workers began entering the factories and offices with different work attitudes and expectations. This combination of economic necessity and a changing work force has led a growing number of organizations to embrace QWL efforts. The assistant to the president of the United Steelworkers of America summarized these issues as follows:

> For decades the steel industry has operated basically as an autocratic industrial institution. Simply put—workers were hired to do exactly as ordered by their foreman. No questions, no backtalk. A good worker was one who showed up on time, everyday, did as he was told and did not complain. Thus, a steelworker learned quickly that he was just a check number, hired to labor, with no right to use his experience or mind or to fulfill his desire to participate.
>
> A worker was stripped of dignity and pride. A worker wanted to believe in our system of democracy, but was puzzled by the absence of industrial democracy in the workplace for the major part of his life span.
>
> Today this workplace dissatisfaction is compounded by the growing fear of more layoffs and plant shutdowns—a combination that has resulted in workers being alienated from their company with no real concern or interest in production and product quality.
>
> The problem has become more acute due to the fact that steelworkers hired in the last two decades are part of the new generation with changing cultural attitudes, who want more out of life than a job that robs them of their self-dignity. They are demanding a job that offers satisfaction for personal input, and a feeling of having contributed something more than just their guts and sweat in the work process.
>
> The steel crisis—combined with workers' desire for job satisfaction and dignity—has given us an opportunity to take an important step forward. It was against this backdrop that steel management finally concluded that autocratic management does not promote productivity, that management cannot successfully legislate or order people to become conscious of quality or production.[3]

And the steel industry is not the only one coming to these realizations. More and more employers are installing QWL efforts as a way to gain productivity through improved employee motivation and satisfaction, reduced employee stress, improved communications, and reduced resistance to change. A properly executed QWL effort also can result in many of the benefits associated with organizational development, as discussed in Chapter 18.

Contrast the bleak picture described by the United Steelworkers official with the comments of employees in Figure 19-1. These workers have jobs in organizations with QWL efforts already in place. As those few employee quotes illustrate, worker attitudes and motivation can be positively affected by QWL efforts.

Employee reactions to QWL

THE PERSONNEL DEPARTMENT'S ROLE

The role of the personnel department in QWL efforts varies widely, although personnel is involved in almost every undertaking. In some organizations such as TRW, Bank America, Control Data, and NASA, top management has appointed an executive to ensure that QWL and productivity efforts occur throughout the organization.[4] In most cases, these executives have a small staff and must rely on the personnel department for help with employee training, attitude survey feedback, and so forth.[5] In other organizations, the personnel department is responsible for initiating and directing the firm's QWL and productivity efforts, as is the case at a large subsidiary of Consolidated Foods, for example.

QWL executives

Perhaps the most crucial role that the personnel department plays is winning the support of key managers. Management support—particularly top

Figure 19-1
Employee Perceptions of QWL Efforts

"As you begin to feel better about yourself, you begin to be more concerned about your job."

> John Ecke
> Lock Spike Operator
> USWA 1374
> Bethlehem Steel Corp.

"A self-fulfilled person who is willing to assume his own responsibilities makes a better employee and, therefore, produces a better product."

> Bonnie Lou Oda
> Ball Joint Assembler
> General Motors Company

"'Participating in the QWL effort gives me a chance to be heard, maybe improve something, work together with my co-workers and get to know them."

> Danny Lopez
> General Plant
> Boise Cascade Company

Source: "The Pulse Report," February 1982, pp. 2, 3, 6. Published by the American Productivity Center, 123 North Post Oak Lane, Houston, Texas.

management support—appears to be an almost universal prerequisite for successful QWL programs.[6] When full support from all levels of management does not exist, proactive departments seek ways to document the success of individual QWL efforts.[7] By substantiating employee satisfaction and financial benefits, which range from lower absenteeism and turnover to higher productivity and fewer accidents, the personnel department can help convince doubting managers.[8] Ohio Bell, for example, achieved better sales from its phone installers, a reduction in lost inventory, fewer strikes, better employee attitudes, and improved productivity as a result of its QWL effort. Without the documentation of these favorable results, top management at Ohio Bell perhaps would not have given its ongoing and strong support.

Ohio Bell's results with QWL

The remainder of this chapter provides an overview of the QWL concept and discusses how employee involvement in decision making enhances an organization's QWL and productivity. Then we will review some specific approaches to QWL and employee involvement before concluding with a discussion of barriers that personnel departments are likely to encounter.

This chapter

QWL OVERVIEW

Quality of work life is determined by how people feel about their role in the organization. Although people seek slightly different outcomes from their affiliation with an organization, research over the last several decades reveals two important observations.[9] First, significant, long-term improvements in productivity must be accompanied by improvements in QWL. In the short run, autocratic management may lead to enhanced productivity even though QWL is made worse. However, autocratic managers can seldom sustain significant productivity gains in the long run because declining QWL usually leads employees to withdraw from the organization. This withdrawal may be seen as increases in absenteeism and turnover. Or if employees have poor mobility and elect not to leave physically, they may withdraw psychologically—which is sometimes evidenced by the statement, "I will do my job and no more." Anything out of the ordinary is simply labeled "not my job" and ignored. Thus in the long run, QWL and employee productivity go hand in hand.[10]

Key observations

"Not my job"

The second observation is that most people report high QWL when they feel that they are contributing to the success of the enterprise in some meaningful way. Merely doing their job is often insufficient if their work does not allow them to influence the decisions that affect them. People want to know that they make a difference.

"Make a difference"

The implication for managers and personnel specialists is to create an organizational climate that truly treats people as though they are experts at their jobs. When management does this, a *Pygmalion effect* may result, which occurs when people live up to the high expectations that others have of them.[11] If management further assumes that people want to contribute and seeks ways to tap that contribution, better decisions, improved productivity, and a higher QWL are likely.

Pygmalion effect

QWL THROUGH
EMPLOYEE INVOLVEMENT

One of the most common methods used to create QWL is employee involvement. *Employee involvement* (EI) consists of a variety of systematic methods that enable employees to participate in the decisions that affect them and their relationship with the organization. Through EI, employees feel a sense of responsibility, even "ownership" of decisions in which they participated. To be successful, however, EI must be more than just some systematic approach; it must become part of the organization's culture by being part of management's philosophy of management.[12] Some companies have had this philosophy ingrained in their corporate structure for decades. Hewlett-Packard, IBM, and Tektronix are just a few examples. Other companies like U.S. Steel, General Motors, and Ford are trying to create a high QWL corporate culture through employee involvement approaches. Through EI, these firms hope that better quality, productivity, and employee satisfaction will result. Consider, for example, Ford's Sharonville operation.

EI defined

The Sharonville plant was built in 1957. Over the years it had developed a "confrontational" form of labor-management relations. Plant management was autocratic, and employment had dropped from 5000 in 1979 to 2500 within a few years. A new plant manager who was not satisfied with the old autocratic style observed, "Times have changed and we have to take a new approach."[13]

Ford's Sharonville operation

Shortly after his arrival, he proposed a joint union-management coordinating committee to be cochaired by the head of the union's bargaining group and a top-ranked management employee. This committee helped create several groups of six or seven hourly employees. To each group was added a representative from quality control and one from process engineering. The groups were formed to identify and recommend solutions to workplace problems. One of the hourly members was elected leader, and meetings were held for one hour each week. During the next several months, other hourly employees asked to create similar groups so that they too could identify and solve work-related problems.

Soon members of the original committee could no longer keep up with the demand for creating and training more groups. Additional "minicoordinators" were used, and within two years the small problem-solving groups existed throughout the entire plant. "In effect, a parallel organization overlay the regular hierarchical structure. EI had become a permanent process interlocking at all points with the formal organization."[14]

Parallel organization

Efforts like these at Ford—or similar ones at General Motors, Westinghouse, IBM, Motorola, Texas Instruments, AT&T, Citibank, TRW, Phillips Petroleum, Pennzoil, General Electric, NASA, American Express, Reynolds Metals, and many others shown in Figure 19-2—indicate that interest in improving the quality of work life is no accident. It parallels, and some might say reflects, societal changes. Workers are more educated today and are less likely to accept authority

Allen Bradley Company	General Telephone and Electric Co.
American Express, Inc.	General Tire Company
American Telephone and Telegraph	Honeywell, Inc.
AmHoist, Inc.	Ideal Basic Industries
Arizona Public Service	Inland Steel Company
Atwood Vacuum Machine Company	International Business Machine Co.
Arcata Redwood Company	Lincoln Electric Company
Babcock & Wilcox	Motorola, Inc.
Bank of America	N.A.S.A.
Beech Aircraft Corporation	Owens-Illinois, Inc.
Bendix Company	Penn Central, Inc.
Boeing, Inc.	Pennzoil, Inc.
Boise Cascade Company	Philadelphia Electric Company
Citibank Corporation	Phillips Petroleum Company
City of Phoenix	Reynolds Metals Company
Champion International	Tektronix, Incorporated
Chrysler Corporation	Texas Instruments, Inc.
Consolidated Foods, Inc.	TRW, Inc.
Control Data Corporation	Union Carbide
Flemming Foods, Inc.	Valley National Bank
Ford Motors Company	Waters Associates Inc.
General Dynamics, Inc.	Western Electric
General Electric Company	Westinghouse, Inc.
General Motors Company	W.R. Grace and Company

Figure 19-2
A Partial List of North American Organizations
Concerned with Quality of Work Life
and Employee Involvement

without question. As a result, there is greater interest in the quality of working life.[15] These changes have led employees to seek a larger voice in the shape of the work environment around the world. In Europe, this trend is often labeled *industrial democracy*.[16]

APPROACHES TO QWL AND EI

This book already has introduced a variety of approaches to employee involvement. Attitude survey feedback and suggestion systems were described in Chapter 17, "Personnel Communications Systems." Chapter 12 on compensation discussed profit sharing and gain sharing. Even the performance evaluation interviews are a form of involvement, as explained in Chapter 11. Each of these approaches, however, is a traditional function of the personnel department. In the last decade, proactive departments, along with progressive business and union leaders, increasingly have sought new approaches to quality of work life through employee involvement.

Overseas origins

The economic dominance of the United States during the post-World War II period created little need for evolutionary changes in the way people were managed. However, in Europe and in Japan, national economic survival during the late 1940s and early 1950s meant that new, innovative ways in human resource management were needed. Some of these innovations began in the legislative halls, while other developments started on the shop floor. Most of these approaches were based upon sound behavioral and sociological research, much of which had been initially conducted in the United States and Canada but first applied in Japan and in Northern Europe. During subsequent decades these EI approaches to QWL were modified and in many cases "imported" back into North America. Some of the more commonly used approaches to attain QWL through EI are discussed in the following pages.

Quality Circles

Quality circles are small groups of employees who meet regularly with their common leader to identify and solve work-related problems.[17] When quality circles started in Japan, they were called "quality control circles" because their primary focus was to improve the poor quality of products manufactured in Japan.

    Definition

Origins of circles   Following World War II, the small island nation of Japan lacked virtually all types of resources except human ones. Japan—smaller than the state of Montana with about half the population of the United States—found that to buy sufficient foodstuffs and raw materials it had to export. But in the 1950s and even in the early 1960s, "Made in Japan" meant poor quality to many buyers. Government and business leaders realized that to import raw goods, to add value, and to export required production of quality products that the world would buy. With the assistance of such U.S. experts as Drs. Demming and Juran, the concept of quality control circles was born in Japanese factories in the early 1960s. This concept was based squarely upon behavioral research conducted in U.S. factories and universities during the previous thirty years. By the 1980s most medium- and large-sized Japanese firms had quality control circles for hourly employees. This effort began as a quality improvement program but has since become part of the routine procedures of many Japanese managers and a key part of the QWL effort in many Japanese firms.

    A drive for high quality

    In the 1970s, Lockheed Corporation and others imported this approach to QWL back from Japan and, with a few modifications, began using it in the United States. The imported version is simply called "quality circles" or "employee participation groups," although many firms customize the name. For example, Tektronix, Inc., calls them "Tek circles"; Control Data Corporation calls them "involvement teams"; and Union Carbide calls them "pride circles," which stands for *p*roductivity through *r*ecognition, *i*nvolvement, and *d*evelopment of *e*mployees.

Unique characteristics   Whatever they are called, quality circles (QC) are unique among the many QWL efforts being tried by North American firms. First, membership in the circle is voluntary for both the leader (usually the supervisor) and the members (usually hourly workers).[18] Typically, supervisors are given a brief explanation of the QC concept and asked if they want to start a circle. If the answer is "yes," the supervisor's employees are given a briefing, and volunteers are sought.

Second, the creation of quality circles is usually preceded by in-house training. For supervisors these sessions typically last for two or three days. Most of the time is devoted to discussions of small group dynamics, leadership skills, and indoctrination in the QWL and quality circle philosophies. About a day is spent on the different approaches to problem solving, such as those explained in Figure 19-3. Then the employees are usually given one day of intensive training

Training is necessary.

Figure 19-3

Quality Circle Decision-Making Tools

BRAINSTORMING

Brainstorming is a process by which members of the circle provide their ideas on a stated problem during a free-wheeling group session. Some circles do request that members present their ideas in turn to ensure that each one participates.

PARETO ANALYSIS

Pareto analysis is a means of collating data provided to employees by staff assistants or collected by the workers themselves. Often the data are collected in reference to types or causes of production problems, then arranged in descending order of frequency. This information is usually shown as a bar chart, like the one below, to help workers identify the most important causes of problems in priority order.

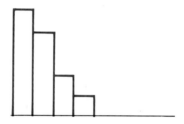

CAUSE AND EFFECT

A cause-and-effect, or fishbone, diagram begins with a known effect, such as a defective part. From that effect, members of the circle use brainstorming and their knowledge of the production or service process to identify possible causes in such standard areas as machines, people, methods, or materials. The term "fishbone" results from the appearance of the diagram.

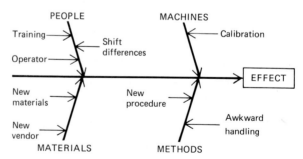

Each "bone" or branch in the diagram represents a possible cause of the effect under study. Once the group identifies these possible causes through brainstorming, members usually collect data on the most likely causes to determine if there is a relationship.

STATISTICAL TOOLS

Workers also are taught a variety of statistical concepts to help them objectively determine causes of production problems. Common methods include random sampling, probability sampling, and computation of arithmetical means and variances.

primarily in the same problem-solving techniques. The workers also receive an explanation of the supervisor's role as the group's discussion leader and information on the quality circle concept.

Third, as is pointed out in the training, the group is permitted to select the problems it wants to tackle. Management may suggest problems of concern, but the group decides which ones to select. Ideally, the selection process is not by democratic vote but is arrived at by consensus, whereby everyone agrees on the problem to be tackled. (If management has pressing problems that need to be solved, these problems can be handled in the same way that they were resolved before the introduction of quality circles.) The reason for relying on group consensus to select the problem rather than on management is to allow employees to take on problems of concern to them.

At Solar Turbines International (a Caterpillar Tractor Company subsidiary), employees were frustrated by the lack of power hand tools. They studied the lost production time caused by waiting for tools and showed management how to save more than $30,000 a year by making a $2200 investment in additional hand tools.

The employees did not select this problem to save management money; they did it because of the inconvenience that insufficient tools caused them. The fact that the solution saved more than a dozen times what it cost was the type of by-product that many companies report from successful quality circle efforts.

When employees are allowed to select the problems they want to work on, they are likely to be more motivated to find a solution. And they are also more likely to be motivated to stay on as members of the circle and solve additional problems in the future.

QC process   After the training is completed, employees and their supervisor begin meeting—usually once a week for an hour. First the supervisor reviews the ground rules. Circles are intended to tackle problems in that group's area of responsibility. Company pay policies, union contracts, problems in remote departments, and personality issues are usually excluded from consideration. Instead, employees are asked to focus on how they can make their job easier. As a quality circle leader at Control Data Corporation once stated, "If we find ways to make the job easier, we cannot help but improve the QWL and productivity."

Following the ground rules discussion, the group uses brainstorming to create a list of problems worth solving. Then through discussion, one of them is selected for further study and research. Data are collected about the problem and analyzed to see if there is a pattern from which causes and effects may be identified. If no pattern exists, the effect under study may be put into a "fishbone" diagram for further brainstorming sessions. Possible causes are then ranked by the group, and the most significant ones are researched.

Once a cause has been found for the problem, the group develops a solution. During training, the workers are taught how to justify the cost of their solutions. For example, at Solar Turbines, the employees believed that a $2200

Workers pick problems.

QCs at Solar Turbines

Excluded topics

outlay by the company was justified because of the potential to save more than $30,000 in the first year.

At this point the group assembles its research, its proposed solution, and its justification for presentation to management. This presentation explains the problem and the circle's recommended course of action. It also gives the circle members an opportunity to be recognized by more than the managers in the firm. Management, of course, reserves the right to accept or reject the recommendation, although more than 80 percent of a circle's ideas are typically accepted at Northrup Aircraft, Solar Turbine, Control Data Corporation, Tektronix, and at other organizations with which the authors are familiar.[19]

80 percent acceptance is common.

Once an idea is presented, the burden is on management to give the circle a timely authorization to implement the solution or an explanation as to why the suggestion is rejected. In the meantime, the circle begins the process again and starts on another problem. This cycle repeats itself until the group solves all of the problems it wishes to handle or until the members of the circle decide to disband. Circles usually disband when supervisors act autocratically rather than participatively or when upper levels of management repeatedly and arbitrarily reject circle recommendations.

Facilitators and circle coordination   Most organizations with multiple circles find that a coordinator or a facilitator is needed. This person may be a line manager or a personnel specialist. Facilitators need good interpersonal skills, particularly the ability to communicate and train. The first facilitator usually receives five days of specialized training through the International Association of Quality Circles or the American Productivity Center. These training programs focus on teaching the facilitator about quality circles and how to administer a QC effort. Sessions on teaching and consulting skills are typical, too. Likewise, the facilitator also receives considerable training in group dynamics and in the ability to coach supervisors. He or she reports to the *steering committee,* which includes the top manager and staff. Once the circles are operating, the facilitator may serve as a consultant to those supervisors who need additional help. The facilitator also serves as a link between the circles and others in the company who may have specialized knowledge needed by the circle to solve its problems.

Steering committee

Costs and benefits of quality circles   Quality circles have few costs. The primary expenditures are related to training—including the costs of developing the materials and teaching the facilitators, supervisors, and employees. Perhaps the major expenses are the wages and salaries paid to the trainees while they are being trained. Interestingly, the time spent in the weekly one-hour circle meetings is not considered a significant expense because most facilitators and supervisors find that circle members get as much work done in thirty-nine hours as they did in forty hours before the quality circles were formed.

Solar Turbines International kept detailed track of their start-up expenses over the first eighteen months—including the costs of training materials, facilitator salaries, and the wages for employees while they were in training and attending circle meetings. The total amount spent was $79,000. However, during the same time period, documented and fully audited first-year savings from circle suggestions amounted to $90,000. And most of the circle ideas continued to save the company money during the second and subsequent years. After the start-up period, the facilitator estimated in a conversation with one of the authors that the annual savings amounted to $3 for every dollar Solar Turbines spent on its quality circle effort.[20]

499

300 percent return

The measurable dollar savings from quality circle efforts are probably not the major benefits, however. Companies like Solar, Tektronix, and Westinghouse report that circles mean increased QWL for employees. Communications between supervisors and employees improve because of the less autocratic relationships. Supervisors and employees also learn to think more like business-men and businesswomen because they begin to solve problems systematically and cost-justify their recommendations. Often higher-level managers can spot particularly articulate employees who show promise as future supervisors based on their efforts in the circle group. In fact, some plant managers view the circles as their primary employee and supervisor development program. They see quality circles as an effective way to train supervisors and workers because circles allow the application of newly learned skills. The result may be a growing cadre of managers and personnel specialists with exceptional people skills.[21]

Cost and QWL benefits

Team Building Variations

Quality circles are a very specialized form of team building. Some companies have undertaken other approaches to create cohesiveness among their supervi-sors and employees. These approaches, such as Motorola's participative management program discussed in Chapter 2, are a slight variation of the quality circle method. The "involvement teams" at Champion International's Paper Division, for example, are not truly quality circles even though they have a similar structure and purpose. The major difference is that the teams at Champion consist of people from different departments, so they are more like a task force. In addition, teams may exist only to solve one problem and then disband. Boeing uses a similar single-focus task force approach called "tiger teams." Generally these teams are assembled to solve some production-delaying problem that the supervisor and employees cannot overcome.

Other approaches to EI

These various forms of team building share a common underlying philoso-phy: Groups of people usually are better at solving problems than an individual. And even though the "purpose" of these teams may be to find a solution, a by-product is improved quality of work life.[22]

Sociotechnical Systems

Another approach to QWL efforts is the use of sociotechnical systems. *Socio-technical systems* are interventions into the work situation that restructure the work, the work groups, and the relationship between workers and the technolog-ies they use to do their jobs. More than just enlarging or enriching a job, these approaches may result in more radical changes in the work environment.

Definition

At a Siemens plant in Karlsruhe, West Germany, workers assembling electronics products used to perform simple tasks over and over, spending less than one minute on each unit as it moved along a belt conveyor. Today many employees work in groups of three to seven at well designed "work islands," where they can avoid boredom by rotating jobs, socializing, and working in cycles of up to 20 minutes rather than a few seconds.[23]

This rearrangement of the social and technical relationships on the job offers workers an opportunity for greater QWL. The "humanization" of the workplace efforts seems to be most advanced in West Germany, where the government even funds 50 percent of selected work restructuring and retraining efforts of private industry.[24]

Ergonomics

West Germany also has done considerable work in the area of ergonomics. *Ergonomics* is the study of the biotechnical relationships between the physical attributes of workers and the physical demands of the job. The objective is to reduce the physical and mental strain in order to increase productivity and QWL. The Germans have made considerable strides in reducing the strain of lifting, bending, and reaching through their ergonomic approach to structuring jobs, arranging equipment, and lighting. Through ergonomics and sociotechnical approaches to work, the West Germans appear to lead the world in modifying assembly lines and increasing the worker's job cycle to minimize boredom and dissatisfaction.

Individual work stations

Individual work stations are used to allow workers to assemble significant subassemblies that may take ten minutes or more. Through buffer stocks of partially completed products, employees are increasingly freed from the tedium of the assembly line.

Codetermination

A formal voice for employees

One of the first attempts at industrial democracy on a broad scale occurred in West Germany under the name codetermination. Through formal sessions with company management, *codetermination* allows workers' representatives to discuss and vote on key decisions that affect the workers. This form of industrial democracy has since spread throughout most of free Europe. As a result, decisions to close plants or to lay off large numbers of employees meet with far more formal resistance in Europe than they do in North America. On the plus side, however, European firms are forced to plan their human resource needs more carefully and to seek export markets to offset national economic cycles. Since major North American corporations operate in Europe under codetermination, personnel management in multinational corporations is affected. For international personnel experts, codetermination is a consideration in the design of overseas jobs. In North America, the first steps toward codetermination may have begun in the early 1980s when Chrysler Corporation appointed the president of the United Automobile Workers to its board of directors.

Autonomous Work Groups

A more common, albeit still rare, approach to employee involvement is the use of autonomous work groups. *Autonomous work groups* are teams of workers, without a formal company-appointed leader, who decide among themselves most decisions traditionally handled by supervisors. These groups of workers typically decide daily work assignments, the use of job rotation, new employee orientation, training, and production schedules. Some groups even handle recruitment, selection, and discipline. In the United States, companies such as TRW and Gaines Pet Food have used these approaches. Perhaps the two best known experiments in this area are at the Gaines Pet Food plant and at Volvo's Kalmar plant in Sweden. Both are summarized in Figure 19-4.

Whether attempts at Gaines and Volvo herald a radically new approach to the quality of work life is still uncertain. These innovations do indicate a demand by some employers and employees for more novel solutions to the trade-offs between efficiency and behavioral elements of job design, as discussed more fully in Chapter 5. More, not less, attention will have to be paid by personnel experts to changing the sociotechnical relationship in order to meet changing expectations about jobs. Improving the quality of work life may mean completely redesigning factories and workplaces—as Volvo and Gaines have done to satisfy efficiency, environmental, and behavioral requirements of jobs.

QWL is more likely to improve as workers demand jobs with more behavioral elements. These demands will probably emerge from an increasingly educated work force that expects more challenges and more autonomy in its jobs—such as worker participation in decisions traditionally reserved for management. Through codetermination, this trend in Europe has lasted more

Popularity may grow.

Figure 19-4
A Summary of Gaines's and Volvo's Experiences with
Autonomous Work Groups

GAINES PET FOOD

At the Gaines Pet Food plant, jobs were radically changed. No longer are workers assigned specific tasks in traditional jobs. Instead, teams of workers are held responsible for a group of tasks that previously constituted several separate jobs. For example, the work group is held responsible for packing and storing the completed products, instead of each worker having a narrow job that includes only a few tasks in the packaging and storing operations. Employees are assigned to a work group, not a job. They are free to participate in the group decision-making processes. Members develop work schedules, interview new employees, perform quality control checks, maintain machinery, and perform other diverse activities. The work-group enrichment led to reduced overhead, higher productivity, better product quality, and lower turnover and absenteeism.

VOLVO'S KALMAR PLANT

Volvo, the Swedish automobile producer, sought to design a more humane car production environment. It built the Kalmar plant around the concept of work teams, rather than the traditional assembly line. Again, workers are assigned to teams, not jobs. Teams build subsystems of the car: doors, cooling systems, engines, and other key components. Buffer stocks of partially completed cars reduce the dependence of one group on another. The physical work environment is as quiet as the latest technology permits.

Results of this experiment with autonomous work groups are not clear. Volvo claims higher satisfaction levels among employees because of the design changes, but productivity has remained behind other plants for years.

than thirty years and is still growing in popularity. And experiments by Gaines, Volvo, TRW, and other employers indicate that such new arrangements are economically feasible.[25]

Changing social and demographic forces

If the population of industrial countries continues to grow at the slow rates of the last two decades, the scarcity of new workers entering the labor force will allow employees to be more selective. Then employers may be forced by economic necessity to redesign jobs to achieve a higher quality of work life.[26] Or as has happened in Europe, government may decree programs to improve the quality of work life.[27] In any event, increased on-the-job autonomy and participation in decision making seem likely to occur during coming decades.

Personnel departments will play an even more important role in organizations as social expectations increase the pressure for more autonomy. Job rotation, enlargement, enrichment, and other job-design changes will be coming. The training of present workers will likely receive additional attention from personnel departments, too. And to attract scarce human resources, personnel departments may even have to offer a wide variety of part-time and full-time work schedules that allow employees to pick the hours and days they wish to work. Whether these changes mean that any one approach to employee involvement will become more common is uncertain. What seems virtually certain, however, is the growing desire of employees to participate in decisions that affect them.

BARRIERS TO QWL AND EI

As with many personnel department programs, barriers to implementation can undermine the success of any quality of work life effort. These barriers are commonly erected by employees, management, or unions. Each of these groups usually fears the effect of unknown change. Even when the process and results of the change are explained, the incentives may be too few. This situation can lead to resistance, as explained in Chapter 18.

Initial suspicion

To overcome these barriers, the personnel department usually must explain the need for change, as well as the hoped-for results, and provide whatever assurances it can. Workers and unions are sometimes suspicious because they may feel that any program to management's advantage is not likely to benefit them. Western workers seldom have the job security that career employees in large Japanese firms have—unless, of course, the western employee works for one of the growing number of overseas Japanese plants. Feelings of suspicion are likely to be much less among employees with high QWL, especially if job security also is available. Consider one Tennessee worker's attitude.

> "Nissan says my employment is for life and all I have to worry about is doing the best quality job I can," says Vic Williams, a plant maintenance technician from Smyrna who recently returned from a company-sponsored trip to Japan. "Sometimes I pinch myself because things are going so smoothly. For me this is a dream come true."[28]

Management often resists change because it doubts that the benefits justify the potential disruption of production or service. Besides, when it comes to changing to new approaches, many key decision makers feel that their present style has worked well. Even when productivity, quality, or QWL is declining, many managers are reluctant to adopt new approaches that may be quite foreign to their more traditional methods of management. And in this regard, union leaders are much like managers; they too are reluctant to give up "proven" roles and approaches to problem solving. The lack of top management and union support for QWL and EI methods is probably the most significant barrier to change, not resistance from workers.

Although there is no one certain way to gain the support of each group, most successful attempts at implementing quality of work life require broad participation.[29] Through the involvement of key managers, union officials, and affected employees—as in the Ford example earlier—personnel specialists are more likely to overcome the barriers to new programs. For example, consider how General Motors Corporation was able to implement such a program in what was then one of its least productive plants.[30]

Faced with high absenteeism, labor turnover, and operating costs, the Tarrytown, New York, plant of General Motors represented one of its least productive facilities. The plant manager approached an admittedly suspicious union leadership and asked them to help change the atmosphere in the plant. Reluctantly, they agreed.

After some initial experiments in the trim departments, a large-scale program was planned. To ensure its support, the company formed a policy group. It consisted of the personnel manager, the production manager, the plant manager, top union officers, and two specialists in quality of work life. This group arranged for all members of management, union officials, and eventually production employees to go through a three-day training program. The object of the program was to teach everyone about the idea of improving the quality of work life, to explain the functions of the plant, and to instruct all employees—from managers to hourly workers—in how to become more effectively involved with problem solving.

Through this several-year-long program, employees were able to better participate in solving work-related production problems. The increased participation of workers in day-to-day problems gave them increased recognition and additional feedback on their performance. But had management not involved the union leaders and employees from the start, it is doubtful that the program would have succeeded. The proof of this program's success is evidenced by the General Motors' decision to use the Tarrytown plant for the difficult task of building the first "X" body front-wheel cars.

A turnaround at GM

Successful QWL and productivity efforts, such as those at GM's Tarrytown site, have some common elements. One of the most important is top management commitment. Top management at Tarrytown meant the plant manager. Commitment, however, is different from permission. Top management must show through its actions and commitment of resources that it stands squarely behind the effort. At TRW, for example, the chairman of the board, Rube Mettler,

Commitment versus permission

actually wrote the corporate productivity objectives and then initiated a productivity measurement system so that progress toward productivity and quality of work life could be evaluated.

Another key point for successful QWL efforts is a long-term perspective. The Tarrytown effort took several years; the groundwork was done back in 1973 when top GM and union officials agreed to a corporate wide commitment. The reason for the long time horizons is that in order to create an ongoing QWL effort in an organization the culture of the company must often change. Until QWL begins, managers in most organizations are evaluated on measures of production that seldom include employee feelings about their jobs or work relationships. To make QWL for employees an integral part of the corporate management philosophy takes years of reinforcement.

Often a personnel department lacks the resources or the organizational clout to direct the company toward a large-scale QWL effort. However, when top management decides to undertake such a journey, the personnel department is often called upon to provide its "people expertise" along with its staffing, training, and communications abilities.

Next chapters   When organizations fail to consider the QWL needs of employees, dissatisfaction is likely to grow. Left unattended long enough, this dissatisfaction may focus on collective action. Chapters 20 and 21 will discuss unionization, negotiations, and collective bargaining administration.

SUMMARY

Quality of work life efforts are systematic attempts by organizations to give workers a greater opportunity to affect the way they do their jobs and the contributions they make to their organization's overall effectiveness. These efforts are not a substitute for good, sound personnel practices and policies. However, effective QWL can supplement other personnel actions and provide improved employee motivation, satisfaction, and productivity. QWL is most commonly improved through employee involvement. Whether that involvement is in solving workplace problems or in merely participating in the design of one's job, it gives people a feeling that their contributions matter. People want to know that they make a difference.

Many approaches to QWL exist. One of the most popular is an import from Japan: quality circles. A quality circle is a small group of employees from the same work area who meet regularly with their supervisor to identify and solve workplace problems. It affords workers a chance to make a meaningful contribution by participating in decisions that affect them. Other forms of team building are similar to quality circles, although different groupings or objectives might be sought. Sociotechnical systems seek to change the human and technical relationship that exists in the workplace. Typically, employees are involved in making these changes.

Codetermination gives workers a formal voice in management decisions. Although common in Europe, it is almost nonexistent in North America. Autonomous work groups also are uncommon in North America, though they are more widely used in the United States than codetermination. These work groups consist of employees who collectively assume the supervisor's role of deciding work schedules, job assignments, and so forth.

Management support and a long-term perspective are essential to any successful QWL effort. Unless the barrier of management support is overcome, even short-term success is unlikely.

TERMS FOR REVIEW

Quality of work life	Facilitators
Pygmalion effect	Ergonomics
Employee involvement	Codetermination
Quality circles	Autonomous work groups
Steering committee	Brainstorming
Sociotechnical systems	Cause and effect diagrams

REVIEW AND DISCUSSION QUESTIONS

1. Describe the forces that are causing organizations and personnel departments to become more interested in QWL efforts. Why did these changes not occur sooner?

2. Since many QWL efforts are initiated by top management or by other line managers, what is the personnel department's role in a QWL effort?

3. What are the characteristics of a work relationship that is high in QWL?

4. Suppose you are a plant or division manager and you want to create a high QWL environment. Why could you not simply order it done and expect a high QWL environment almost immediately?

5. What is the relationship between QWL and employee involvement?

6. Explain where quality circles started and what makes them unique compared with other QWL efforts. What is management's responsibility after a quality circle group makes its presentation to management?

7. If TRW and Gaines Pet Food have had success with autonomous work groups, why, in your opinion, have so few other employers used this innovative way to manage?

8. From your experience in organizations, what are the major barriers that prevent workers from having better, more satisfying jobs?

INCIDENT 19-1

Automation and QWL Efforts

During the 1970s and the early 1980s, the role of the United States as a leading manufacturer became tarnished. Although the country continued to lead in most categories of manufacturing, Japanese, German, and other foreign-based producers began to excel. In 1980, for the first time this century, the United States fell to second place in the number of cars produced. Japan—with little iron ore, coal, and other ingredients necessary for automobile production—took first place.

However, advances in computer-controlled machine tools and other equipment indicate that the manufacturing processes of recent years are likely to give way to highly automated procedures. Factories already exist where the machines operate in total darkness untended by humans, except for an occasional maintenance mechanic. These "factories of the future" will employ very few workers. And the workers who are employed are likely to be skilled technicians rather than unskilled or semiskilled assemblers. The result will be very high levels of productivity along with high quality products.

For many years the dream of an automated factory was not practical because most production is done in short production runs. After a batch of product is made, the machines are reset to produce another product. But with the advances in computer controlled equipment, firms that rely on manual setup of equipment may become too ineffective to compete against a factory that can go through setup in the few minutes it takes to change a computer program.

1. What are the implications for QWL if the factory of the future becomes common?

2. Some experts think that the total employment in direct manufacturing occupations will drop to 5 percent of the work force by the year 2000. If the factory of the future causes these predictions to become true, what new pressures are personnel departments likely to face?

3. Given that the birth rate in the industrialized free world has been declining for more than two decades, what implications do these demographic changes hold for the personnel departments of highly automated factories of the future?

INCIDENT 19-2

Cooperation, QWL, and Space

Psychologists Joseph Brady and Henry Emurian at Johns Hopkins Hospital have been doing research to learn how to increase productivity and reduce friction on future space missions. Under research grants from NASA, they are "studying the psychological and physiological efforts of prolonged confinement on two- and three-person 'microsocieties.' Their goal is to develop behavioral guidelines for the most productive individual and group performance, with the least social friction, on future space and underwater missions."[31]

Their studies have revealed the not-too-surprising conclusion that rewards and incentives are better motivators than sanctions and controls. Cooperation leads to greater individual performance and greater satisfaction in the group.

Assume for the sake of this incident that these findings are applicable to larger societies called organizations.

1. What implications do you see in these studies for improving the QWL in organizations?

2. If you were a supervisor with six employees working for you, how could these findings make your quality circle group more effective? Suggest specific actions you would implement to improve the effectiveness of the quality circle based on this brief research summary.

INCIDENT 19-3

Corporate Strategy and the People Factor

The Sony Corporation has been responsible for numerous innovations in the field of consumer electronics in its post-World War II history. "What their long-range plan boils down to is balancing revenues among three roughly equivalent sources: consumer electronics equipment, nonconsumer electronics hardware, and a hodgepodge of other businesses, including products related to the electronic segments, such as video and audio recording tape." As the chairman of the board commented, "Kodak is making much more from film than cameras. [However] Consumer Electronics is still our main business."

One of the elements that makes Sony such an interesting company to study is that the firm has a strong commitment to its people. As *Business Week* observed, "Some of the markets in which the company is dabbling—sphaghetti shops and cosmetics, in particular—seem to have absolutely no connection with Sony's traditional expertise."[32] Chairman Morita explains this unusual hodgepodge by observing that he wants to give the widest possible latitude to the new workers that Sony hires. With these varying businesses, new and unique career paths open up to Sony's young and middle managers.

1. Although Sony is a leader in consumer electronics, what is your opinion of their approach toward their human resources?

2. Describe the advantages and disadvantages you would see for a western business organization to adopt a program of "guaranteed lifetime employment," as Japanese organizations such as Sony have done.

3. What aspects of personnel management as described in this book so far would change because of this total commitment to quality of work life that is exhibited by Sony's approach to corporate strategy and its people?

508   ## REFERENCES

1. Edward E. Lawler III, "Strategies for Improving the Quality of Work Life," *American Psychologist,* May 1982, p. 487.

2. Lisa Copenhaver and Robert H. Guest, "Quality of Work Life: The Anatomy of Two Successes," *National Productivity Review,* Winter 1982–1983, p. 5.

3. Sam Camens, "Steel—An Industry at the Crossroads," *Productivity Brief 17* (American Productivity Center), September 1982, p. 3.

4. William B. Werther, Jr., and William A. Ruch, "Chief Productivity Officer," Working Paper, Bureau of Business Research, College of Business Administration, Arizona State University, 1982.

5. William A. Ruch and William B. Werther, Jr., "Productivity Strategies at TRW," *National Productivity Review,* Spring 1983, p. 116.

6. William B. Werther, Jr., "Out of the Productivity Box," *Business Horizons,* September–October 1982, p. 56.

7. Martha Glenn Cox and Jane Covey Brown, "Quality of Work Life: Another Fad or Real Benefit?" *The Personnel Administrator,* May 1982, pp. 49–53.

8. Werther, "Out of the Productivity Box," op. cit., pp. 51–52.

9. Edward E. Lawler III, and Gerald E. Ledford, Jr., "Productivity and the Quality of Work Life," *National Productivity Review,* Winter 1982–1983, pp. 23–36.

10. Ibid., p. 26; see also D. L. Scantlebury, "Productivity Sharing Programs: Can They Contribute to Productivity Improvement?" United States General Accounting Office Study, Mar. 3, 1981, p. 1.

11. J. Sterling Livingston, "Pygmalion in Management," *Harvard Business Review,* July–August 1969, pp. 81–89.

12. William B. Werther, Jr., "Productivity Improvement through People," *Arizona Business,* February 1981, pp. 14–19.

13. Copenhaver and Guest, op. cit., p. 11.

14. Ibid.

15. Ted Mills, "Human Resources—Why the New Concern?" *Harvard Business Review,* March–April 1975, pp. 120–134. See also Cary L. Cooper, "Humanizing the Work Place in Europe: An Overview of Six Countries," *Personnel Journal,* June 1980, pp. 488–491.

16. Ibid.

17. William B. Werther, Jr., "Quality Circles: Key Executive Issues," *Journal of Contemporary Business,* vol. 11, no. 2, N.D., pp. 17–26.

18. Frank Shipper, "Quality Circles Using Small Group Formation," *Training and Development Journal,* May 1983, p. 82.

19. See for example, "Tektronix, Inc.," *Case Study 17* (American Productivity Center), 1981, pp. 1–3.

20. "Quality Circles: Key Executive Issues," op. cit., p. 26.

21. "A Serendipitous Training Ground for Managers," *Business Week,* Feb. 15, 1982, p. 52T.

22. Dutch Landen, "Beyond Quality Circles," *Productivity Brief 12* (American Productivity Center), April 1982, pp. 1–7.

23. "Moving beyond Assembly Lines," *Business Week,* July 27, 1981, pp. 87, 90.

24. Ibid.

25. Daniel Zwerdling, *Democracy at Work,* Washington: Association for Self-Management, 1978.

26. Timothy J. Keaveny, Robert E. Allen, and John H. Jackson, "An Alternative to Legislating the Quality of Work Life," *The Personnel Administrator,* April 1979, pp. 60–64, 79. See also Keith Davis and William C. Frederick, *Business and Society,* 5th ed., New York: McGraw-Hill, 1984, pp. 175.

27. Ted Mills, "Europe's Industrial Democracy: An American Response," *Harvard Business Review,* November–December 1978, pp. 143–152. See also Kenneth A. Kouach, Ben F. Sands, Jr., and William W. Brooks, "Is Codetermination a Workable Idea for U.S. Labor-Management Relations?" *MSU Business Topics,* Winter 1980, pp. 49–55.

28. David A. Vise, "Nissan Truck in Tennessee," *QC News,* August 1982, p. 1.

29. George W. Bohlander, "Implementing Quality-of-Work Programs: Recognizing the Barriers," *MSU Business Topics,* Spring 1979, pp. 37–39.

30. Robert H. Guest, "Quality of Work Life—Learning from Tarrytown," *Harvard Business Review,* July–August 1979, pp. 76–89. See also William T. Horner, "Tarrytown: A Union Perspective," *National Productivity Review,* Winter 1981–82, pp. 37–41.

31. Guest, op. cit., pp. 86–89.

32. For a more detailed explanation of this study, see Berkeley Rice, "Space-Lab Encounters," *Psychology Today,* June 1983, pp. 50–58.

33. Quotations in Incident 19-3 are from Sony: A Diversification Plan Tuned to the People Factor," *Business Week,* Feb. 9, 1981, pp. 88, 90.

PART

VI

UNION-MANAGEMENT RELATIONS

Employees sometimes form unions. This action changes the framework of employee relations. It causes the personnel department to deal with the challenges of union organizing and bargaining. Then the labor agreement needs to be administered to ensure that the employer, the union, and the employees have their rights and duties properly defined.

The next two chapters explain the challenges that you can expect when employees join unions. Your job is likely to be affected whether you are in the personnel department, in management, or in the union. By understanding labor-management relations, you can avoid serious errors that may harm your career success.

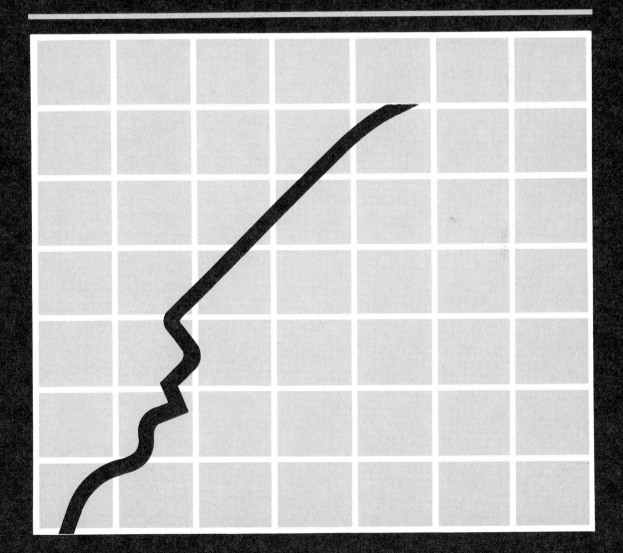

CHAPTER

20

America is fortunate to have a durable, refined and proven system of collective bargaining to meet the demands of change.

W. J. Usery, Jr.[1]

Wage earners join unions for a great many different reasons.

John T. Dunlop[2]

THE UNION-MANAGEMENT FRAMEWORK

CHAPTER OBJECTIVES

After studying this chapter, you should be able to:

1 <u>Explain</u> the relationship between unions, employers, and government.

2 <u>Describe</u> the nature and priorities of union objectives.

3 <u>Identify</u> illegal management and union activities.

4 <u>Distinguish</u> between various government agencies that enforce labor laws.

5 <u>Discuss</u> the major reasons why workers join unions.

6 <u>Describe</u> how personnel departments respond to unions.

Personnel department professionals are largely responsible for handling employee relations, as discussed in Part V of this book. When employee relations efforts are not effective, quality of work life suffers and employee dissatisfaction may result. When employees are dissatisfied, they may band together and form a union. It does not mean the end of an organization's success. Many successful companies have one or more unions. But the use of collective action confronts personnel management with new limits and challenges. Even more significant, unions affect the manner in which line managers manage. Because of the many constraints that a unionized work force can place upon an organization, some companies try to avoid them.

Unions do not mean disaster.

For many years, the Emerson Electric Company was a high-cost producer of fans, motors, tools, and defense equipment. However, during the twenty-year reign of W. R. "Buck" Persons, Emerson became a low-cost manufacturer and consistently outperformed other firms in the electrical and electronics industry.

Emerson's "southern strategy"

Part of this transformation was achieved by Persons's "southern strategy," which involved opening new small factories throughout the rural South. (Most of Emerson's 116 plants are located in the mid-South.) Also as part of its strategy, the company bases 10 percent of the division managers' bonuses on keeping their plants union-free.[3]

Unions and industry

Emerson resists unionization because it must operate in an industry that is only partially organized. By staying nonunion, it hopes to retain lower labor costs through lower wages and greater management flexibility in the day-to-day operations of its plants. However, in industries that are largely unionized, management often takes a more conciliatory view of the union-management relationship. Consider the comments of Roger B. Smith, former chairman and chief executive officer of General Motors Corporation, about a recently negotiated agreement with the United Automobile Workers Union.

General Motors and the United Auto Workers

The new agreement between General Motors and the United Auto Workers will be seen as historic because it recognizes the unprecedented changes taking place in world competition. And more than that, it brings GM management and GM employees together in a united effort to meet and overcome that competition.

Our new agreement commits us to continuing and expanding the quality-of-work-life process. But it seeks to take us even further. It seeks to directly involve the union and its members in the effort to make GM more competitive, and thereby to provide more job security.[4]

The differences between Emerson Electric and General Motors are common in industry. Some employers view unions as outsiders; others see them as an integral part of their human resource efforts. As domestic and worldwide competition grows ever more demanding, many union-management relationships are undergoing a change toward more cooperation.[5] However, before discussing these trends toward cooperation in Chapter 21, this chapter will describe the union-management framework and its principal "actors." It will review the impact unions have on personnel management by discussing union goals and structure. The role of government, with its laws and regulatory bodies, will be reviewed, too. The chapter will end with a discussion of why workers join unions and the union organizing process.

This chapter

ACTORS IN THE SYSTEM

The union-management framework consists of three principal actors: workers and their representatives (unions); managerial employees (management); and government representatives in the legislative, judicial, and executive branches (government).[6] Each of these parties depends upon the other, as shown in Figure 20-1. For example, the union relies on management for jobs and on the government for protection of workers' rights. Government protection means that employers cannot legally fire employees who want to start a union. Managers depend on the union to honor its contract obligations. The government relies on both unions and management to provide productive organizations that meet society's needs. Although each party depends on the other, the parties are not equals. Government is the dominant force because it defines the roles of management and unions through laws. Within these laws, unions and management may use their respective powers to shape their relationship. For example, a powerful union may force management to make concessions in order to avoid a crippling strike. Likewise, when the union is weak, management can get concessions because the threat of an effective

Three main actors

Figure 20-1
The Interdependence of Unions, Management, and Government

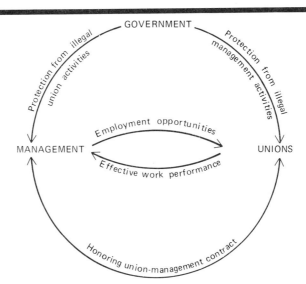

strike is remote. The power of each side depends on the capacity of each to influence or threaten the other.

Durability is another characteristic of the labor-management framework. The process of collective bargaining between employers and unions has survived in its present form since the 1930s. Admittedly, the framework has undergone continuous refinement as a result of laws and practices. And unions, management, and the government have grown more sophisticated. But the three-way relationship has shown considerable stability while remaining flexible enough to adjust to countless legal, social, and economic challenges.

Continuous refinement

LABOR UNIONS AND PERSONNEL MANAGEMENT

Labor unions do alter the work environment. Their presence changes the relationship between employees and the organization. It especially changes the roles of supervisors and the personnel department, which are altered by the addition of more formal rules and regulations that shape their day-to-day activities. In many other ways the environment remains unchanged. Supervisors and managers retain their primary responsibility for employee performance. Profit objectives and budgetary goals are not bargained with the union. Nor do unions reduce the need for effective personnel procedures. In short, management must still manage; and the union does not assume the responsibilities of the personnel department.

To understand how and why unions influence human resource management, it is necessary to examine their goals and structure.

Union Goals and Philosophy

Like other organizations, unions are social systems that pursue objectives. Their objectives are influenced internally by the wishes of their members, the aspirations of their leaders, and the financial and membership strength of the union. And like other organizations, unions are open social systems that are affected by their external environment. The financial condition of the employer, the gains of rival unions, the inflation and unemployment rates, and government policies influence the union's objectives.

Among these internal and external considerations, there does exist a common core of widely agreed upon objectives. These objectives were stated by Samuel Gompers, the first president of the American Federation of Labor. Although published in 1919, Gompers's philosophy remains valid today and is summarized in Figure 20-2.[7]

The mission Gompers set forth for the union movement was to protect workers, increase their pay, and improve their working conditions. This approach became known as *business unionism* primarily because it recognizes that a union can survive only if it delivers a needed service to its members in a businesslike manner. But Gompers also realized that unions must address broader social issues of politics and economics when these are in the best interest of union members.[8] This second area of concern, called *social unionism,* includes the economic and social policies of government at all

Business unionism

Social unionism

The ground-work principle of America's labor movement has been to recognize that first things must come first. The primary essential in our mission has been the protection of the wage-worker, now; to increase his wages; to cut hours off the long workday, which was killing him; to improve the safety and the sanitary condition of the work-shop; to free him from the tyrannies, petty and otherwise, which serve to make his existence a slavery. These, in the nature of things, I repeat, were and are the primary objects of . . . unionism.

Our great Federation has uniformly refused to surrender this conviction and to rush to the support of any one of the numerous society-saving or society-destroying schemes which decade by decade have been sprung upon this country. A score of such schemes . . . have gone down behind the horizon and are now but ancient history. But while our Federation has thus been conservative, it has . . . had its face turned toward whatever reforms in politics or economics could be of direct and obvious benefit to the working class. It has pursued its avowed policy with the conviction that if the lesser and immediate demands of labor could not be obtained now from society as it is, it would be mere dreaming to preach and pursue that will-o'-the-wisp, a new society constructed from rainbow materials—a system of society on which even the dreamers themselves have never agreed.

These demands of organized labor are comprehended in this larger and ultimate ideal—to enrich, enlarge, and magnify humanity. . . .

Source: Samuel Gompers, *Labor and the Common Welfare,* Freeport, N.Y.: Books for Libraries Press, 1919, p. 20.

Figure 20-2
Union Philosophy and Objectives

levels—city, state, and federal. In practice, union leaders pursue the objectives of social unionism by speaking out and taking actions for or against government programs. They also further their social unionism goals by working to elect favored politicians. For example, many union leaders actively supported the Civil Rights Act of 1964 because it would benefit their members and other workers.

Business and social unionism present unions with multiple, and sometimes conflicting, objectives. Figure 20-3 explains these trade-offs. For example, when the union bargains with management, it seeks high pay and good working conditions. But higher costs may cause the company to hire fewer workers or encourage management to use more automation. The social unionism trade-offs are less obvious. For example, successful lobbying by unions helped to ensure the passage of the Occupational Safety and Health Act. This act improved working conditions for all people. But the cost of compliance may have lessened

Trade-offs

Figure 20-3
Trade-offs Faced by Unions
under Business and Social Unionism

PHILOSOPHICAL APPROACHES	TRADE-OFFS BETWEEN UNION OBJECTIVES		
BUSINESS UNIONISM	Maximize number of employed members.	OR	Maximize pay and benefits of members.
SOCIAL UNIONISM	Maximize welfare of members.	OR	Maximize welfare of working people.

the ability of unionized employers to provide pay raises. Thus social unionism causes labor organizations to face the trade-off of maximizing the well-being of all workers without minimizing the welfare of its members.[9]

Personnel management is influenced by both business and social unionism goals. The growth of fringe benefits discussed in Chapter 13 has resulted partly from union pressure. Even nonunionized employers have added many benefits in order to remain competitive in the labor market or to forestall unionization among their employees. Social unionism goals also affect personnel management through such union-supported actions as the Employee Retirement Income Security Act.

Union Structure and Functions

Some writers believe that as organizations grew, employees lost direct contact with the owners, and so unions emerged to help workers influence workplace decisions.[10] Through unions, workers were able to exert control over "their jobs" and "their work environment."[11] Then when attempts were made by employers to cut wages, the employees relied on their unions to resist these actions.[12]

Early attempts to control the work environment were local efforts because most companies were small operations. As employers—particularly the railroads—began to span city and then state boundaries, labor organizations formed national unions composed of locals from all over the country. When social problems affected several national unions at once, these unions joined together and formed multiunion associations. The most successful of these has been the *American Federation of Labor and Congress of Industrial Organizations* (AFL-CIO). A brief review of the three levels—locals, nationals, and multiunion associations, as represented by the AFL-CIO—illustrates the functions and structure of unions as seen by the personnel department.[13]

The three levels of unions

Local unions   For personnel administrators, the *local unions* are the most important part of the union structure.[14] They provide the members, the revenue, and the power of the entire union movement. There are three types of local unions: craft, industrial, and mixed locals. *Craft unions* are composed of workers who possess the same skills or trades. These include, for example, all the carpenters who work in the same geographical area. *Industrial unions* include the unskilled and semiskilled workers employed at the same location. When an employer has several locations that are unionized, employees at each location are usually represented by a different local union. Such is the case with the United Automobile Workers, for example. A local may even combine both unskilled and skilled employees. This arrangement is common in the electric utility industry where the International Brotherhood of Electrical Workers includes skilled, semiskilled, and unskilled workers, which results in a mixed local.

Craft unions versus industrial unions

Figure 20-4 shows the structure of a typical local. The *steward* is the first level in the union hierarchy and usually is elected by the workers. Stewards help employees present their problems to management. If the steward of an industrial or mixed local cannot help a worker, then the problem is given to the *grievance committee,* which takes the issue to higher levels of management or to the

Grievance committee

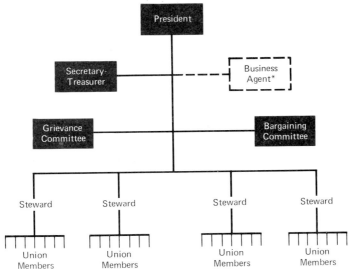

*The position of business agent is common in craft union locals.

Figure 20-4

Organization Structure of a Typical Local Union

personnel department.[15] In craft unions, the steward—who is also called the representative—usually takes the issue directly to the *business agent*, who is a full-time employee of the union.   **Business agent**

This process of resolving employee problems, called the *grievance procedure*, limits personnel specialists and line managers because it challenges their decisions. If the challenge is successful, the result may serve as a precedent that limits future decisions.

Personnel specialists also find that employee perceptions of the local union's administration can influence worker attitudes, satisfaction, and even complaints to the personnel department about the union. Yet little is known about how union members view their local. After surveying 3000 members of nine different locals, one researcher concluded:

> Union members were largely satisfied with contract terms, with the commu-   **Research summary**
> nications and informational materials received from officials, and with the
> opportunity to participate in local union affairs. Members were moderately
> satisfied with the effectiveness of union leadership, the overall worth of
> union meetings, and the administration of grievances. The main dissatisfac-
> tion uncovered in this survey was in the areas of adequacy of union training,
> the willingness of union leaders to act on the personal views of constituents,
> and the usefulness of union meetings to serve job-related needs.[16]

An even more important limitation on supervisors and personnel specialists is the labor contract. It normally specifies wages, hours, working conditions, and related issues such as grievance procedures, safety standards, probationary periods, and benefits. It usually is negotiated between the local union's *bargaining committee* and the personnel or industrial relations department.

National unions Most local unions are chartered by a larger association called the *national union,* which organizes and helps the locals. National unions also pursue social objectives of interest to their members and maintain a staff that helps the local unions with legal assistance, negotiations, training of local officers, grievance handling, and expert advice. In return, locals share their dues with the national union, and they must obey its constitution and bylaws. Among the craft unions, the national tends to leave many decisions to the locals. Industrial nationals, though, are more likely to be involved with their locals. For example, a national union may require that locally bargained contracts receive its approval to ensure consistent treatment among locals and a floor under wages. Sometimes the national union actually may bargain a companywide contract, as is the case with the United Automobile Workers.[17]

Multiunion associations The *AFl-CIO* is the principal multiunion associ-ation. It is composed of affiliated national unions, and most major unions are members. The AFl-CIO is not a union; it is an association of unions. Its primary purpose is to further the social unionism goals of organized labor. Through lobbying, education, and research efforts, it supports new laws and social changes that benefit workers and affect personnel management. The AFL-CIO's influence over national unions is limited. It charges them a small per capita tax to finance its programs. Any national union that fails to pay the tax or fails to support the AFL-CIO's policies may be removed as a member. At one time the United Automobile Workers union was expelled for nonpayment of dues. It has subsequently reaffiliated with the AFL-CIO.

GOVERNMENT AND PERSONNEL MANAGEMENT

Government shapes the union-management framework through laws and their interpretation. Its role comes from the obligation to protect the welfare of society and from the authority found in Section VIII of the U.S. Constitution, which states that Congress shall have the power "to regulate commerce . . . among the . . . states. . . ." Congress has used this authority several times to regulate union-management relations and to produce legislation that influences the role of personnel management. These laws are discussed in the following sections.

National Labor Relations Act

The *National Labor Relations Act* (NLRA), also known as the Wagner Act, became law in 1935. It was passed during the Great Depression in an attempt to minimize the disruption to interstate commerce caused by strikes.[18] The act gave employees the right to collective action free of employer interference, except in small businesses that have little impact on interstate commerce. It allowed employees to form labor organizations and to bargain with management about wages, hours, and working conditions.

To prevent employers from interfering with these new employee rights, the law prohibited five *unfair labor practices* by management. These legal prohibitions are summarized in Figure 20-5. The act required that management neither interfere nor discriminate against employees who undertake collective action. Unfair labor practices also outlaw the firing of employees, "blacklisting," and "yellow dog" contracts.

Unfair labor practices

A common personnel policy was to require new employees to sign a "yellow dog" contract. This employment contract meant that if a worker assisted a union in any way, that person could be fired. Those who agreed to these contracts were often called "yellow dogs." The NLRA made yellow dog contracts illegal, as well as the management practice of "blacklisting" an employee by giving a negative reference.

The NLRA also makes company-dominated unions illegal. Some employers believed that if they could not prevent their employees from organizing, then the next best thing was to encourage a union that they could dominate. Through threats, bribes, or infiltration, some companies tried to control union activities. For example:

During the 1930s, when the United Auto Workers were trying to organize General Motors, GM hired private detectives to infiltrate the union. In time, some detectives were elected to important posts. When this action was discovered by the government, GM was found guilty of interference and domination and was ordered to cease these actions.

The law also prohibits employers from discriminating against anyone who brings charges against a company for violating the law. To make the result of

Figure 20-5
Unfair Labor Practices by Management

The National Labor Relations Act makes it an unfair labor practice for members of management to:

1. *Interfere*, restrain, or coerce employees who desire to act collectively or refrain from such activities

2. *Dominate* or interfere with the formation or administration of any labor organization by contributing money or other support to it

3. *Discriminate* against anyone in hiring, stability of employment, or any other condition of employment because of their union activity or lack of involvement

4. *Discharge*, discipline, or otherwise discriminate against employees who have exercised their rights under the act

5. *Refuse* to bargain in good faith with employee representatives

unionization meaningful, employers must bargain with the union in good faith over wages, hours, and working conditions. Refusal to do so is a violation of the act, as the National Football League owners discovered.

NFL versus the players

The NFL owners were charged with a violation of their duty to bargain in good faith, according to a formal complaint issued against them. The complaint stemmed from a strike by the National Football League Players Association. It charged that the players' strike "was caused and has been prolonged by the unfair labor practices of respondents—the NFL management council."[19] The owners had failed to give the union required "information essential to bargaining, changing working conditions . . . coercing players and interfering with their rights, as well as attempting to bypass the union in dealing with individual players."[20]

National Labor Relations Board

To make the National Labor Relations Act work, Congress also created the *National Labor Relations Board* (NLRB) to enforce it. This federal agency prosecutes violators and conducts secret-ballot elections among employees. It was the NLRB that filed the complaint against the NFL owners and conducted the elections at Emerson Electric's plants.

The enforcement procedures of the NLRB are summarized in Figure 20-6. This agency does not search for violations until someone files a complaint with local offices, which are located in major cities.[21] Then the complaint is investigated. If a violation appears to have occurred, a judge from the NLRB hears the case and renders a decision. A guilty employer must refrain from these illegal actions in the future. If an employee was fired as a result of the violation, that person is entitled to back pay, plus interest, and reinstatement with no loss of seniority.

Figure 20-6
NLRB Procedures to Redress Unfair Labor Practices

1. The aggrieved individual or organization contacts the nearest NLRB regional office and explains the alleged violation.

2. If the case appears to have merit, the regional director assigns the case to an NLRB employee for investigation.

3. The investigator determines if the facts are accurate.

4. The NLRB employee reports the findings to the regional director. If a violation appears to have occurred, the wrongdoer is charged with a violation of the act.

5. The local NLRB office prosecutes the alleged violator (who is defended by counsel) before an administrative law judge who renders an opinion after receiving final written arguments from both sides.

6. If innocent, the procedure ends. If guilty, the party may appeal the case to a five-member board in Washington, D.C.

7. If the board's ruling upholds the original finding, the guilty party may appeal to the federal courts.

When charges are filed against the employer, the personnel department usually assists the company's attorney in preparing the case. The department compiles performance appraisals, attendance records, and other documents that help the company prove its case. Sometimes the department's investigation reveals that the company is guilty. At this point, time and legal costs are saved by admitting guilt and accepting the NLRB's proposed settlement.

Law violations and personnel's role

Personnel departments also become involved when the NLRB holds an employee election. This other function of the NLRB takes place when a substantial number of employees (at least 30 percent) request a government-supervised election. The election is to determine if the workers want a union. Through its local offices, the NLRB conducts a secret-ballot election at the employer's place of business. To win, the union must get a majority of the votes. If the union loses, then another election among the same employees cannot be held for one year. If the union wins, then the personnel department must prepare to bargain with the union and reach a labor agreement.

Labor Management Relations Act

After World War II, the public objected to the inflationary economic conditions, strikes, and the lack of legal constraints on unions. As a result, Congress passed the *Labor Management Relations Act* (LMRA) in 1947.

Why LMRA happened

> One illustration of this lack of constraint concerns a powerful union that arranged for a large number of its unemployed members to picket a small trucking firm. The pickets so severely interfered with deliveries that the owner was forced to recognize the union against the wishes of his employees.
>
> When negotiations on the first contract began, the union leader refused to meet with the company's attorney. The owner was told to pick someone else to represent the firm. Having no legal remedies and fearing more disruption, the owner hired a new attorney. Then the union presented the lawyer with a completed contract and said, "Sign or we strike." There were no negotiations, and the company signed.

Although most unions did not abuse their power, isolated cases such as this contributed to the legal restrictions.

The Taft-Hartley Act, as the LMRA also is called, amended the earlier National Labor Relations Act by adding unfair labor practices by unions. These prohibitions appear in Figure 20-7. The act made it illegal for unions to force employees to join them or to interfere with an employer's selection of its collective bargaining representatives. It also required unions to bargain with management in good faith, and it outlawed union picketing and strikes under certain circumstances. Violations are prosecuted by the NLRB.

This law allows employers and their personnel departments to deal with unions on a more equal basis. No longer can unions legally force one employer to stop doing business with another as a way of winning their demands. Unions can no longer threaten employees with high initiation fees if they do not actively

Reduces union power

524

The Labor Management Relations Act made it an unfair labor practice for unions to:

1. *Restrain* or coerce employees or employers in the exercise of their legal rights.

2. *Force* an employer to discriminate against an employee because of that employee's membership or nonmembership in the union.

3. *Refuse* to bargain with an employer in good faith.

4. *Engage* in strikes or threats to force members of management to join a union (usually to collect large initiation fees) or to force an employer to cease doing business with another employer.

5. *Require* an employer to bargain with a union other than the one employees have selected.

6. *Demand* excessive or discriminatory initiation fees.

7. *Picket* an employer in order to force it to recognize the union as the employees' representative without requesting a government election within a reasonable time period.

Figure 20-7
Unfair Labor Practices by Unions

support the union's organizing efforts. Although some union leaders called Taft-Hartley the "slave labor act," the law meant that unions had to organize employees on the merits of unionization, not through unfair economic pressure on workers or their employer.

To further minimize the disruptions caused by strikes, the Labor Management Relations Act made two other changes in union-management relations. It created the Federal Mediation and Conciliation Service, and it authorized Taft-Hartley injunctions.

Federal Mediation and Conciliation Service (FMCS) As its name implies, the FMCS helps union and management bargainers to remain friendly (conciliate) during the process of bargaining a contract.[22] When bargaining leads to deadlocks, the agency suggests compromises (mediates). Although it has no power to force a settlement of disputes, the agency helps both sides reach an agreement without the need for a strike. Consider how one commissioner from the FMCS avoided a strike at a paint factory.

Third-party
assistance

All of the bargaining issues were settled when the FMCS commissioner arrived, except the size of the pay raise. Management had offered 35 cents an hour, and the union was demanding 64 cents more. The two sides had broken off negotiations, and so the commissioner asked them to reconvene.

After he learned of their differences, he separated union and management bargainers. Then he asked management how high it would go to avoid a strike. Management said 55 cents an hour. When the union's bargaining committee was asked how little it would accept, the members said 50 cents an hour.

The commissioner reconvened both sides after the union agreed to propose a new demand of 60 cents, down from 64 cents. Then the commissioner asked if management would be willing to offer 40 cents. This give-and-take process continued until both sides agreed to a 53-cent-an-hour raise.

Taft-Hartley injunctions   When serious strikes threaten national securi-ty or create a national emergency, the Taft-Hartley Act allows the President of the United States to seek a court-ordered injunction to delay the strike for eighty days. During this "cooling-off" period, the government investigates the facts surrounding the dispute. The results of the fact-finding activities are turned over to the parties, and the office of the President urges a negotiated settlement. If no agreement is reached at the end of eighty days, the strike can resume. Public pressure and the potential for congressional action usually cause both sides to find a solution eventually even if the strike does start up again at the end of the eighty-day cooling-off period.

Eighty-day cooling-off period

Labor-Management Reporting and Disclosure Act
During the twelve years following the passage of the Taft-Hartley Act, it became evident that a few union leaders were not properly representing their members' interests. To correct this problem, the *Labor-Management Reporting and Disclosure Act* was passed in 1959.[23]

Figure 20-8 summarizes the major provisions of this act. In general, the law sought two broad objectives. First, it made union officials responsible for properly using union funds by establishing detailed reporting requirements. It backed up these requirements with the possibility of prison sentences for those found guilty of serious violations. Second, the act sought to make unions more democratic by providing members with certain rights. In fact, Title I of the law is often referred to as the union members' "bill of rights."

Union members' bill of rights

If an employee has a complaint about the union's treatment, the personnel department need not get involved. Instead, it can direct workers to the nearest

Figure 20-8
Major Provisions of
the Labor-Management Reporting and Disclosure Act

- *Title I* created a bill of rights for union members in dealing with their union. It assured members equal rights, freedom of speech and assembly, the right to sue the union, and other safeguards.

- *Title II* imposed detailed reporting requirements upon those who handle union funds.

- *Title III* established safeguards to ensure that the rights of members to elect leaders will not be lost when a national union takes over a local union and creates a trusteeship.

- *Title IV* requires that fair elections for union officers be held periodically.

- *Title V* sets forth the fiduciary responsibility of union officers and prohibitions against certain people from holding union office (primarily convicted felons).

- *Title VI* grants the Secretary of Labor the right to conduct investigations into possible abuses under this act.

- *Title VII* includes a series of miscellaneous provisions that limit strikes, picketing, and boycotts.

office of the Department of Labor. Specialists within the department then investigate and ensure that employee rights are not being ignored by the union leaders.

CAUSES OF UNIONS

Unions do not just happen. They are caused—not by laws and government agency procedures but by some management action or inaction that seems unfair to workers. The causes of unions vary from person to person and from worksite to worksite. Even workers in the same organization may have different reasons for joining a union because of their different perceptions.[24] However, common reasons are often shared by employees. And as Figure 20-9 shows, these reasons vary for different types of unions.

Craft Unions

Common skills People join craft unions for practical reasons. They hope to learn a useful skill through the union's apprenticeship program, which offers them both a job and training. Workers who already have a trade often use craft unions to find jobs. In the construction industry (where many skilled tradespeople are employed), craft workers are hired on a per-project basis. When the project is over, the contractor

Figure 20-9

Workers' Major Reasons for Joining or Not Joining Unions

TYPE OF ORGANIZATION (AND WORKERS)	MAJOR REASONS FOR JOINING	MAJOR REASONS FOR NOT JOINING
CRAFT UNIONS (Blue-collar workers)	• Learn an enjoyable trade • Find employment through union • Receive union benefits • Acquire collective power	• Dislike unions • Possess steady employment • Have fair treatment
INDUSTRIAL UNIONS (Blue- and white-collar workers)	• Seek change in management practices • Dislike supervision • Receive peer pressure • Required by union shop • Want benefits promised during organizing drive	• Want a management position • Are afraid of strikes • Dislike dues • Dislike unions • Have fair treatment
PROFESSIONAL ASSOCIATIONS (White-collar workers)	• Seek professional contacts • Dislike supervisory practices • Resolve professional issues • Want better pay	• Reject as unprofessional • Are unneeded for self-employed • Want a management position Have fair treatment

lays them off. Then the workers typically ask the union for a referral to another contractor who has requested their skills. Thus membership in a craft union makes it easier to find a job. Craft unions also offer other services—such as health insurance, life insurance, and pension plans—that are financed through employer payments. In addition, the union's collective bargaining power can mean favorable wages and working conditions.

Not all skilled workers join craft unions, however. Some employees dislike them, while others already have acceptable management, personnel policies, employment security, and fringe benefits.

Industrial Unions

Workers usually form industrial unions when personnel policies or supervisors cause mistreatment. Personnel policies that affect discipline, layoffs, compensation, job design, and communications are especially important. When these policies are ignored or when employees are indifferent to employee needs, a union may be formed by workers to bring about changes. Possibly even more important that policies are the first-level supervisors. These people serve as the link between employees and management. If supervisors do not provide fair treatment, workers may look to unions for protection.

Once a union exists, members may pressure their peers to join. This *peer pressure* is most effective on new workers, who often are uncertain of their roles and want to "feel like they belong." The pressure also can affect other employees, who might otherwise be indifferent. Sometimes labor leaders and management agree to a *union shop.* Under this arrangement, all workers are obligated to join the union. If they fail to do so, management must fire them. Union shops are allowed in thirty states.[25]

Union shop

The reasons for nonmembership are equally diverse. Workers who want to become managers may believe that union membership damages their chances for promotion. Other employees view unions as "just another boss" that costs them money, in the form of union dues or lost wages from strikes. Likewise, past experiences or isolated stories of union wrongdoing may cause some people to form negative opinions of collective action.[26] Or more simply, personnel policies and supervisory treatment may be fair, and so employees lack the motivation to join a union.

Professional Associations

Most professionals do not join unions. Instead, they belong to *professional associations* that are designed to further their knowledge and improve the image of their profession. But when professionals are also employees, their associations may become more like unions and are sometimes referred to as quasi unions.[27]

Quasi unions

Some professional groups—state education associations and state nurses' associations, for example—have evolved into unions, usually as a result of poor management treatment. These "unions" emerge when supervisory practices, personnel policies, or professional issues are unacceptable. For example, a few years ago many members of the Florida Education Association conducted a statewide strike centered on the issues of better student-teacher ratios and higher pay.

There are several reasons why professionals do not join unions. Those who are self-employed would receive few benefits from membership. Even those who work for an employer have little to gain if their treatment is favorable. Besides, many professionals view unions as inappropriate.

UNION ORGANIZING

It is worth remembering that a union begins only when the workers create it.[28] Although this is a simple observation, it is a key to understanding the process of unionization. Sure, unions use professional organizers; however, the outcome of the organizing drive depends primarily on the employees. As George Meany, the first president of the AFL-CIO, once commented:

What organizers organize

> Despite the well-worn trade union phrase, an organizer does not organize a plant. Now, as in the beginning, the workers must organize themselves. The organizer can serve only as an educator; what he organizes is the thinking of the workers.[29]

Union organizers educate the workers by explaining how the union can reduce mistreatment. These professionals only assist workers; they do not cause workers to join a union. Organizers are less successful when confronted with a proactive personnel department, because then there is little that a union can offer. Even the most experienced organizers find it difficult to organize a truly well-managed and growing company. IBM provides an appropriate example:

IBM's proactive approach

> During the past thirty-five years, IBM claims that it has never laid off a worker for economic reasons. Instead, it retrains those who are not needed in one job and assigns them to another. In one five-year period, the company retrained and physically relocated 5000 employees as part of the most extensive corporate education program in the United States.
>
> Not surprisingly, IBM has never been the target of a major union organizing drive. "I don't know what a union at IBM would do," says one salesperson incredulously, when asked if employees would join a union.[30]

Signs of Organizing Activity

Personnel departments can estimate the chances of union organizing by looking for the proper signs. One set of signs is found in the work environment. Figure 20-10 lists specific questions that can alert a personnel department to union

Key questions

activity. The higher the number of "yes" answers to the questions in the figure, the more likely that union activity will occur. The external factors shown in the figure are largely outside the personnel department's control. But external developments can alert personnel to pay greater attention to the internal factors over which it has influence.

EXTERNAL FACTORS

- Have there been recent changes in the labor laws that affect your industry which might cause interest in your firm by union organizers?
- Has there been a sudden increase in unionization activity in your community or industry?
- Is your company planning a major increase in its work force that might stimulate union interest in organizing the firm before it becomes larger and more expensive to organize?

INTERNAL FACTORS

- Has your organization failed to resolve systematically the union complaints made during previous, unsuccessful organizing attempts?
- Are employee turnover and absenteeism rates worse than the norms for your industry or community?
- Has the company failed to conduct job satisfaction surveys? Or if conducted, do they reveal a trend toward dissatisfaction?
- Are pay and fringe benefits below the average for the industry, community, or unionized firms?
- Is the company's procedure for resolving employee complaints largely unused by workers?

Figure 20-10

Environmental Factors that May Lead to Unionization

When Congress changed the labor laws to include nonprofit health-care facilities, many personnel managers in hospitals realized that union organizing was more likely. Rather than wait for a union drive to begin, proactive personnel managers began an assessment of the internal factor over which they had control. Their prompt action gave them a wide range of options to improve the work environment. Their counterparts who did not respond to this external sign had less flexibility once union activity started.

Another set of signs comes from changes in employee behavior that suggest a union drive may be underway. Figure 20-11 indicates the type of behavior supervisors and personnel specialists should watch for. Again a high number of "yes" answers may mean that unionization is occurring. It is important to remember that these are only indications, not proof.

One manager who observed some suspicious activities notified the personnel department. A few days later she was "pleasantly" embarrassed when the employees presented her with a Christmas present. What this manager had seen was a group of workers passing around a card and collecting contributions for a gift. She thought they were signing up to join a union.

Limits on Management's Response

Once a union drive begins, management's response is limited in several important ways. First, the National Labor Relations Board (NLRB) protects

• Do some employees seem to be suddenly popular?

• Are workers making unusual inquiries about fringe benefits, wage levels, raises, promotions, grievance procedures, or other employee-related matters?

• Do criticisms of management decisions and policies seem more vocal?

• Have employee directories been disappearing at a high rate?

• Are employees asking about management's reaction to unions?

• Are questions being asked about company rules on solicitation?

• Have employees discussed past or future group meetings?

• Are there strangers in the cafeteria or parking lots?

• Do employees exclude supervisors from their conversations?

• Are cards or handbills being distributed?

Figure 20-11

Employee Behavior that Suggests Unionization Activity

Union organizing committee
workers from management reprisals. For example, the discipline of union supporters can result in legal violations unless the employer can prove that the wrongdoer received the same punishment as other employees normally receive.[31] Even a previously unscheduled *increase* in wages or fringe benefits during an organizing drive is considered a violation because the employer is trying to "buy" employee support.

Another limitation results when a *union organizing committee* is present.[32] This committee, which consists of those workers who are leading the union drive, tries to convince other employees to join them. To do this, they use handbills, speeches, conversations, and even home visits. The committee's goal is to get workers to sign *authorization cards,* which show the employees' interest in the union. Once 30 percent of the employees sign cards, the committee can then ask the NLRB to conduct a representation election. The outcome of the election determines if there will be a union. During this process, the committee may raise questions about management activities that affect employees, even if these activities are fair.

A third limitation during unionization concerns the actions of management. Personnel administrators should caution every manager, from supervisor to chief executive officer, with the following two questions:

• Will management actions be ruled as unfair labor practices?

• Will management actions provide fuel for the organization drive?

Milliken and Company had to pay $5 million to workers who were fired when the company closed its Darlington, South Carolina, mill in 1956. The $5 million back-pay award, however, was probably less than Milliken's legal expenses from 1956 (when the plant was closed) until 1980 (when the legal aftermath ended).[33]

When an unfair labor practice is committed by any member of management, it can lead to expensive, time-consuming lawsuits. Equally damaging, the organizing committee can point to violations as further justification for a union. Even when management actions are legal, union leaders may claim credit for new policies favorable to employees.

> The personnel manager and president of a small insurance company were surprised by what happened after they gave a 10 percent raise during a union organizing campaign. The day after the pay raise was announced, the union circulated handbills that read as follows: "Beware! Management is trying to trick you. They gave you a 10 percent raise to con you into voting against the union next week. What will happen if the union loses? Will it take another drive to get a raise? Isn't it odd that with the union here, management suddenly cares about your pay? Don't be tricked! Vote for the Teamster's Union! Show management that you are smarter than they think. . . ."
>
> Even worse than the union's counterattack, the NLRB charged the employer with an unfair labor practice. The union then promptly circulated another handbill that was entitled, "NLRB Catches Company Breaking Labor Laws." The union won the election: 37 to 14.

Management's Campaign

Most employers mount a careful campaign to counteract the union drive. Normally, the personnel department is responsible for fending off the union, although outside consultants and labor lawyers often help.[34] The campaign usually begins by getting needed information. The most important information is top management's attitude toward unionization. Although management officials often oppose unions, the personnel department must determine what response, if any, top management wants to make. Assuming management wants to keep the company nonunion, the personnel department collects data about the union's dues, strike record, salaries of officers, and any other relevant facts that might cause workers to vote against it.

Armed with detailed information about the union, the personnel department arranges for speeches to workers about the need to stay nonunion. Speeches are usually supplemented with group meetings, handbills, letters to employees, and articles in the company paper. To coordinate these activities, an *information clearing office* may be established in the personnel department. This office provides information to supervisors about the need to stay nonunion and answers their questions. Sometimes telephone "hot lines" are installed so that supervisors and employees can get quick answers to questions raised during the organizing drive. The personnel department uses the clearing office to remind employees of the company's good points while refuting the union's claims. Ideally, the employer's case is presented in a factual, honest, and straightforward manner. However, the personnel department's success is determined only partially by its campaign. More important is the treatment employees receive before the organizing drive begins.

Clearing house and "hot lines"

SUMMARY

The labor-management framework consists of unions, governments, and management. Each union is unique, but all share the goals of protecting and improving members' wages, hours, and working conditions. To further these objectives, the union movement has created local and national structures. Moreover, most unions are loosely united by the AFL-CIO.

The federal government plays a dominant role in the labor-management framework because it regulates the behavior of unions and employers. The government's most comprehensive vehicle for controlling the other two parties has been the NLRA and its amendments, which establish specific requirements by which unions and employers must abide.

Management's role is to integrate resources to meet society's needs within an environment substantially shaped by union and government constraints. Although unions may represent the employees, management remains ultimately responsible for obtaining organizational performance and effectively utilizing the human resources. Only through proper utilization of human resources can management fulfill its labor-management role.

A union-management relationship occurs when workers perceive the need for a union. Their perceptions depend upon many factors. However, treatment by management is the single most important factor in most cases. Union organizing usually begins with a small group of dissatisfied workers. Cases of an outside organizer suddenly appearing and gaining widespread employee support seldom occur. Even when this does happen, it is because of basic dissatisfactions among the work force. The organizing process finds workers (with or without a professional organizer) trying to convince others to join the union. Management's response is limited by several laws and by employee activities. The employer's primary defense is sound personnel policies implemented by competent supervisors *before unionization begins*.

TERMS FOR REVIEW

Business unionism

Social unionism

Local unions

Craft unions

Industrial unions

National unions

Union shop

Authorization cards

Union organizers

Unfair labor practices

American Federation of Labor
   and Congress of Industrial
   Organizations (AFL-CIO)

National Labor Relations Act (NLRA)

National Labor Relations Board (NLRB)

Federal Mediation and Conciliation
   Service (FMCS)

Labor-Management Reporting and
   Disclosure Act

1.   In your own words, summarize the primary objectives of unions.

2.   What distinguishes craft, industrial, and mixed unions from one another?

3.   Suppose an employee in your department is an active member of the union and is performing improperly. After several sessions with the worker, you find that the performance is still unacceptable. What type of support would you want to gather before you terminated that employee? What legal complications might result from your action?

4.   What roles does the National Labor Relations Board serve in labor-management relations?

5.   Suppose you are a personnel specialist, and you are having the following problems. For each problem, which government agency would you turn to for assistance?
   a. The union is trying to get the personnel department to fire a union critic.
   b. An employee complains to you that the union will not allow members to speak up at the local meetings.
   c. The company and the union are deadlocked over the terms of a new labor agreement.

6.   In your own words, summarize the reasons why workers join (*a*) craft unions, (*b*) industrial unions, and (*c*) professional associations.

7.   "Unions do not happen, they are caused by management." What arguments can you use to agree or disagree with that statement?

8.   The major role of personnel departments occurs before union organizing begins. In what ways does the personnel department influence employee decisions to unionize?

INCIDENT 20-1

A Routine Discharge at ITC

On October 2, 1984, Pete Ross was discharged from ITC. The supervisor requested that the personnel department discharge him because he was caught drinking in the employees' locker room. Drinking on company property was prohibited, as it has been since the 1971 publication of the ITC Employee Handbook.

All employees of ITC were given a copy of the handbook. It states in part: "The consumption of alcoholic beverages on company premises is grounds for immediate termination. . . ."

The discharge appeared rather routine to personnel and to the plant manager. Although drinking violations were uncommon, the plant manager believed that clear-cut infractions of company policy should be punished.

Besides, he was frequently heard to say, "We must support our first-line managers."

Pete's fellow machinists did not see it as a "routine discharge." John Briggs, a fellow worker, summed up the group's feelings:

> Pete was a darn good machinist. He was seldom tardy, never absent, and always did a first-class job. If Pete did it, it was done right! That bugged George (the supervisor). He would pressure Pete to get out the work and say, "Don't worry about the quality; they only measure quantity." But Pete wasn't slow. He'd turn out a quality product as fast as some people turned out junk. I don't think George liked Pete. I don't know if Pete took a "belt" before leaving the plant Wednesday evening, but I think George just wanted to "can" him.

The following Monday, October 6, 1984, John Briggs spent his rest breaks and lunch hour talking to the other machinists, telling them that "if we don't want to end up like Pete, we'd better get a union here." He even had cards from the International Association of Machinists Union. By Monday evening, Briggs had thirty-two signatures. (There were thirty-nine machinists in the shop.)

On a Tuesday morning John Briggs was called into the supervisor's office. The plant manager and George grilled him. They asked him if he had been distributing authorization cards, who had signed them, and how many he had obtained. Briggs simply replied by saying, "That is none of your business." The plant manager adjourned the meeting without saying a word.

On Thursday (payday at ITC), Briggs received a termination notice with his paycheck. The notice was effective immediately. It said that termination was for low productivity and excessive absences during the previous twelve months.

1. What unfair labor practices may have occurred?

2. Should management offer reinstatement to Pete Ross or to John Briggs? Why?

3. Was Briggs correct when he said, "That is none of your business," to the questions about the authorization cards?

REFERENCES

1. W. J. Usery, Jr., "Collective Bargaining: A Stable Process for Unstable Times," in *Proceedings of the Eleventh Annual Labor-Management Conference on Collective Bargaining and Labor Law*, Tucson: Division of Economic and Business Research, University of Arizona, 1975, p. 69.

2. John T. Dunlop, "The Development of Labor Organization: A Theoretical Framework," in Richard L. Rowan (ed.), *Readings in Labor Economics and Labor Relations*, rev. ed., Homewood, Ill.: Irwin, 1972, p. 74.

3. "Emerson Electric: High Profits from Low Tech," *Business Week,* Apr. 4, 1983, p. 60.

4. Roger B. Smith, "Toward a New Alliance with Labor," a Robert S. Hatfield Fellow's Speech at the Cornell Forum, Ithaca, New York, Apr. 7, 1982.

5. "The New Industrial Relations," *Business Week,* May 11, 1981, pp. 84–93.

6. John T. Dunlop, *Industrial Relations Systems,* New York: Henry Holt, 1958, pp. 7–8; and J. W. Miller, Jr., "Power, Politics, and the Prospects for Collective Bargaining: An Employer Viewpoint," in Stanley M. Jacks (ed.), *Issues in Labor Policy,* Cambridge, Mass.: The MIT Press, 1971, pp. 144–157.

7. Samuel Gompers, *Labor and the Common Welfare,* Freeport, N.Y.: Books for Libraries Press, 1919.

8. Ibid., p. 20.

9. Miller, op. cit., pp. 3–10.

10. Frank Tannenbaum, *The Labor Movement, Its Conservative Functions and Consequences,* New York: Knopf, 1921.

11. Selig Perlman, *A Theory of the Labor Movement,* New York: Macmillan, 1928.

12. John R. Commons et al., *History of Labor in the United States,* New York: Macmillan, 1918. See also A. H. Raskin, "From Sitdowns to Solidarity," *Across the Board,* December 1981, pp. 22–25.

13. Reed C. Richardson, *American Labor Unions, An Outline of Growth and Structure,* 2d ed., Ithaca, N.Y.: New York State School of Industrial and Labor Relations, Cornell University, 1970, p. 19.

14. Leonard Sayles and George Strauss, *The Local Union,* New York: Harcourt, Brace & World, 1967.

15. Harry Graham and Brian Heshizer, "The Effect of Contract Language on Low-Level Settlement of Grievances," *Labor Law Journal,* July 1979, pp. 427–432; see also James E. Martin, John M. Magenau, and Mark Peterson, "Variables Related to Patterns of Commitment among Union Stewards," an unpublished paper presented to the Academy of Management, 1982.

16. George W. Bohlander, "How the Rank and File Views Local Union Administration— A Survey," *Employee Relations Law Journal,* Autumn 1982, p. 232.

17. "Labor's Marriages of Convenience," *Business Week,* Nov. 1, 1982, pp. 28–29.

18. Irving Berstein, *A History of the American Worker, 1933–1941: Turbulent Years,* Boston: Houghton Mifflin, 1971, p. 332; and Foster Rhea Dulles, *Labor in America,* New York: Crowell, 1966, pp. 264–279.

19. "NLRB Complaint Blames Football Owners," *AFL-CIO News,* Oct. 30, 1982, p. 8.

20. Ibid.

21. John S. Irvin, Jr., "Why Do We Need a Labor Board?" *Labor Law Journal,* July 1979, pp. 387–395.

22. Perry A. Zirkel and J. Gary Lutz, "Characteristics and Functions of Mediators: A Pilot Study," *The Arbitration Journal,* June 1981, pp. 15–20; see also Joseph Krislov and Amira

Galin, "Comparative Attitudes towards Mediation," *Labor Law Journal,* March 1979, pp. 165–173.

23. George W. Bohlander and William B. Werther, Jr., "The Labor-Management Reporting and Disclosure Act Revisited," *Labor Law Journal,* September 1979, pp. 582–589.

24. Tom Herriman, "A Union at J. P. Stevens," *The AFL-CIO American Federationist,* December 1980, pp. 1–7.

25. The twenty states that have declared union shop clauses illegal are Alabama, Arizona, Arkansas, Florida, Georgia, Iowa, Kansas, Louisiana, Mississippi, Nebraska, Nevada, North Carolina, North Dakota, South Carolina, South Dakota, Tennessee, Texas, Utah, Virginia, and Wyoming. These states are usually referred to as "right-to-work" states.

26. Joseph W. R. Lawson, II. *How to Meet the Challenge of the Union Organizer,* Chicago: Dartnell Corporation, 1973, pp. 7–24.

27. Charles A. Hill, Jr., "The Void in Collective Bargaining: Professional Employees," *The Personnel Administrator,* August 1979, pp. 51–57.

28. George Meany, "Organizing: A Continuing Effort," *The American Federationist,* July 1976, p. 1.

29. Ibid.

30. "How IBM Avoids Layoffs through Retraining," *Business Week,* Nov. 10, 1975, pp. 110, 112.

31. Edward F. Murphy, *Management vs. the Union,* New York: Stein and Day, 1971, pp. 47–64.

32. Edward S. Haines and Alan Kistler, "The Techniques of Organizing," *The American Federationist,* July 1967, pp. 30–32. See also James F. Rand, "Preventative-Maintenance Techniques for Staying Union-Free," *Personnel Journal,* June 1980, pp. 497–499.

33. "Darlington Closing Case Finally Resolved," *Vantage Point,* January 1981, p. 2.

34. "How Union-Busters Beat Labor Law," *AFL-CIO News,* Dec. 25, 1982; see also "Unions Move into the Office," *Business Week,* Jan. 25, 1982; and "Organizing Today," *Industrial Union Department Digest,* November–December 1982, pp. 1–2.

CHAPTER

21

Contract administration is the joint activity with which labor and management are most involved in terms of time.

John A. Fossum[1]

A new industrial revolution is under way. With it will come a new age of harmony in industrial relations.

Roger B. Smith[2]

BARGAINING AND CONTRACT ADMINISTRATION

CHAPTER OBJECTIVES

After studying this chapter, you should be able to:

1 Explain the key steps in negotiating a union contract.

2 Define the major topics of collective bargaining.

3 Explain how a labor agreement limits personnel management.

4 Discuss common techniques to resolve disputes.

5 Identify the personnel department's role in grievance handling and arbitration.

6 Suggest ways to build union-management cooperation.

Labor-management relations do not occur in isolation. The day-to-day treatment that employees receive from their supervisors, the employer's compensation program, and the personnel department's employee relations efforts all shape the workers' feelings about the organization, whether a union exists or not. With a union, however, employees can take collective action.

The actions that employees take depend upon the treatment they have received. When that treatment is perceived to be unacceptable by nonunionized employees, a union is one likely outcome. If a union already exists, members seek to negotiate an agreement with management that changes the worse features of their relationship. When negotiations fail to resolve the major causes of friction, a strike is likely. Consider the situation surrounding a strike by 11,000 federal employees.

After members of the Professional Air Traffic Controllers' Organization (PATCO) went on strike, they were fired and barred from further federal employment because strikes by U.S. government workers are illegal. The traditional economic motives of most strikes were not the primary cause for the action taken by these Federal Aviation Administration (FAA) employees. According to research done by the University of Michigan's Institute for Social Research, the strike "was bred in and precipitated by the deteriorating conditions created by the Federal Aviation Administration's own organizational and management practices."[3]

A survey of more than 33,000 FAA employees revealed that morale among air traffic controllers was low from the bottom to the top of the organization. Strikers and nonstrikers alike produced similarly negative assessments of their jobs. "FAA employees holding managerial positions gave relatively high approval to an autocratic, no-questions-asked style of management, while the generally younger technicians and controllers— strikers and nonstrikers alike—strongly rejected such a style."[4]

Discontent was caused by the controllers' belief that little concern was shown for their well-being, rewards, work loads, or satisfaction. Many felt that ability had little to do with promotions. The principal researcher concluded: "A less directive bureaucratic style would have buffered the problem of the strike . . . and a participative style would have solved it. The implementation of participatory management . . . can go far toward preventing future labor relations disasters like the massive federal strike and employee dismissals suffered by the FAA."[5]

The economic warfare of strikes extends to innocent victims, too. The PATCO strike meant restrictions on air traffic during the peak summer flying season. Passengers were inconvenienced, airlines lost money, and many employees were laid off for lack of work. And since the strike was illegal, the Federal Labor Relations Authority (which administers federal sector labor regulations) decertified PATCO. This meant that the union could no longer represent air traffic controllers. For most PATCO leaders and employees, the strike-caused decertification meant a loss of their jobs, too.

539

Although personnel professionals are not always the primary negotiators on management's negotiating team (attorneys may be used instead), they are included as members of the team in order to provide useful data and guidance. After the contract is negotiated personnel professionals become involved in administering its terms and conditions. Understanding the negotiations process can facilitate the contract administration duties that follow. This chapter reviews the bargaining and administrative aspects of labor-management relations. It ends with a discussion of union-management cooperation.

COLLECTIVE BARGAINING

Figure 21-1 shows that the process of collective bargaining has three overlapping phases. Preparation for negotiations is the first and the most critical stage. It may involve ongoing data collection with

Three-phase process

Figure 21-1
The Stages of Collective Bargaining

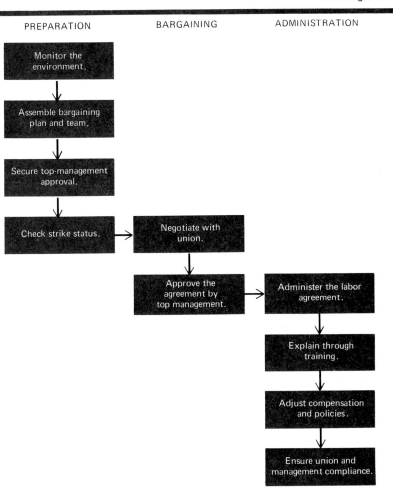

PREPARATION   BARGAINING   ADMINISTRATION

Monitor the environment.

Assemble bargaining plan and team.

Secure top-management approval.

Check strike status.

Negotiate with union.

Approve the agreement by top management.

Administer the labor agreement.

Explain through training.

Adjust compensation and policies.

Ensure union and management compliance.

formal preparations beginning six months to a year before the contract expires. The success of the second stage, face-to-face negotiations, largely depends on how well each side has prepared in the first stage. The third phase involves the follow-up activities of contract administration. To conduct these new duties, a labor relations department may be added to personnel.

Preparations for Negotiations

The purpose of negotiations is to develop a contract. The contract—or *labor agreement,* as it is also called—specifies the rights and responsibilities of management and the union. Detailed preparations are required if the agreement is to achieve a balance of rights and responsibilities.[6] Figure 21-1 shows that several steps are needed before actual negotiations begin.

Labor agreement defined

Monitor the environment Collective bargaining does not occur in a vacuum. Labor relations specialists need to monitor the environment to find clues about likely union concerns. These clues can be found in several ways. First, the personnel department must be sensitive to the inflation rate and to the gains made by other unions. Since union leaders are elected, they seldom accept wage increases that are less than those of rival unions. If they do, they may be voted out of office. Acceptable increases have tended to exceed the inflation rate by a small percentage, unless the employer cannot afford this amount. For example, the United Auto Workers allowed Chrysler Corporation to give a smaller wage increase because of its weaker financial position in comparison with General Motors and Ford. Necessity required that *pattern bargaining*—the same contract for all firms—be broken.

Pattern bargaining

A second set of clues can be found among union promises made during the organizing drive or among unmet demands from previous negotiations.

> While organizing a Los Angeles television station, union leaders complained about poor life insurance benefits. These benefits were a minor issue until the station's helicopter pilot died in a fiery crash. Then the union made life insurance a key issue. After an emotional speech by the pilot's widow, the union won by a vote of 54 to 9. In the negotiations that followed, the union demanded an increase in death benefits from $5000 per employee to $50,000 and asked the station to pay the entire insurance premium. Management granted a larger policy but insisted that employees pay one-half of the premium.

Management rights

A third source of bargaining issues is *management rights.* These rights are the freedoms that supervisors and managers need to do their jobs effectively, such as the right to reassign employees to different jobs, to make hiring decisions, and to decide other matters important to management. If these rights are not protected in the contract, the union may hinder management's effectiveness. For example, supervisors may want all job descriptions to include the phrase "and other duties assigned by management" to prevent employees from refusing to do work because it is not in their job descriptions. This phrase also gives supervisors greater freedom in assigning workers. Labor relations specialists in the personnel department discover which rights are important to supervisors and managers based on discussions and surveys.[8]

Assemble a bargaining plan   After monitoring union demands and management rights, the organization puts together a *bargaining book.* The "book," or more commonly a computer tape, contains estimates of likely union demands and management's counterproposals. It represents the employer's plan for the upcoming negotiations. To implement the plan, a bargaining team is assembled. The team usually is led by the director of labor relations or by an attorney. It also may include specialists in wages and benefits and line managers familiar with company operations.

Bargaining "book"

Secure top-management approval   Top management should approve of the overall bargaining goals. These goals serve as controls that enable top management to gauge the bargaining team's effectiveness. Goals also help the bargaining team know the limits of its authority.

Check strike status   Most contracts are negotiated without a strike. But labor specialists usually plan for one in order to strengthen their bargaining position. The extent of these preparations depends upon the likelihood of a strike. If employees strongly support union demands, a strike is more likely and plans are more thorough.

A good defense is an offense.

    The goal of labor specialists is to reduce the damage from a strike if it does occur. Special arrangements are made with important buyers and suppliers. If operations are to be stopped during a strike, close-down and start-up plans are included. When top management seeks to continue production or service, work schedules for managers and nonstriking employees are developed. These preparations signal union leaders that the employer is ready for a strike and may cause the leaders to rethink their demands and agree to a negotiated settlement.

Bargaining

After preparations, the second phase of collective bargaining is face-to-face negotiations with the union. Discussions usually start sixty to ninety days before the end of the present contract. If negotiations are occurring for the first time, they begin after the union is recognized by the employer or after it wins an NLRB election.

Negotiate with the union   Negotiations cover wages, hours, and working conditions. These three areas are interpreted broadly. *Wages* mean all forms of compensation such as pay, insurance plans, retirement programs, and other benefits and services. *Hours* include the length of the workday, breaks, holidays, vacations, and other actions that shape the work schedule. *Working conditions* involve safety, supervisory treatment, and other elements of the work environment.[9]

Wages, hours, and working conditions

    Once face-to-face bargaining begins, it is important to follow the techniques listed in Figure 21-2. Otherwise confusion may develop that can cause needless delays or even a strike.[10]

THE "DOS" OF NEGOTIATIONS

1. Do seek more (or offer less) than you plan to receive (or give).

2. Do negotiate in private, not through the media.

3. Do let both sides win; otherwise the other side may retaliate.

4. Do start with easy issues.

5. Do remember that negotiations are seldom over when the agreement is concluded; eventually the contract will be renegotiated.

6. Do resolve deadlocks by stressing past progress, another point, or counterproposals.

7. Do enlist the support of the Federal Mediation and Conciliation Service if a strike seems likely.

THE "DON'TS" OF NEGOTIATIONS

1. Do not make your best offer first; that is so uncommon that the other side will expect more.

2. Do not seek unwanted changes; you may get them.

3. Do not say "no" absolutely, unless your organization will back you up absolutely.

4. Do not violate a confidence.

5. Do not settle too quickly; union members may think a quick settlement is not a good one.

6. Do not let the other side bypass your team and go directly to top management.

7. Do not let top management actually participate in face-to-face negotiations; they are often inexperienced and poorly informed.

Figure 21-2
Guidelines for Negotiations

Boulwarism

General Electric used to use an approach called *Boulwarism*.[11] Instead of following the suggestions in the figure, GE simply presented the union with its final offer at the beginning of negotiations. This approach created confusion because the unions did not believe that GE's first offer was its best one. Politically, the union leaders did not dare accept it. As a result, bitter strikes occurred. Eventually, the NLRB ruled this approach to be illegal because GE was not really bargaining. It simply made an offer on a take-it-or-leave-it basis.

Successful bargaining usually begins with easy issues to build a pattern of give-and-take. This give-and-take occurs in private since off-the-record comments may be embarrassing to either side when repeated out of context. This way management does not have to worry about what stockholders may think of its bargaining comments, and union leaders can focus on bargaining without guarding against member reactions.

Bargaining deadlocks

When deadlocks do occur, several tactics can keep negotiations moving toward a peaceful settlement. By solving the easy issues first, bargainers often can point to this progress and say, "We've come too far to give up on this impasse. Surely, we can find a solution." This sense of past progress may increase the resolve of both sides to find a compromise, which may be achieved by offering counterproposals that meet the objectives of the other party. Sometimes progress is made by simply dropping the issue temporarily and moving on to other items. Further progress on other issues may lead to compromises regarding earlier impasses. If no progress results, bargainers may turn to the Federal Mediation and Conciliation Service. This government agency provides mediators who can help both parties reach a settlement without a strike, as discussed in Chapter 20.[12]

The suggestions in Figure 21-2 also imply common bargaining strategies. For example, most management teams exclude top executives. They are kept out of negotiations because top managers often are inexperienced at collective bargaining. But their exclusion also gives management bargainers a good reason to ask for a temporary adjournment when the union produces demands that require a careful review. Rather than refusing the union's suggestions, management bargainers may ask for a recess to confer with top management. Experienced management bargainers also realize that the union must "win" some concession. If the employer is powerful enough to force an unacceptable contract on the union, union leaders may seek revenge by refusing to cooperate with management once the contract goes into effect. They may encourage slowdowns, large numbers of grievances, and other uncooperative actions. Or when the contract is renegotiated, the union may be strong enough to cause a long strike. Besides, an unfavorable agreement may not be ratified by union members. If it is rejected, union leaders must then reopen negotiations.[13] During severe recessions, management bargainers may seek outright concessions from the union. However, unions can be expected to demand reinstatement of most concessions when the economy improves, as the United Automobile Workers Union did when Chrysler regained its economic health in the early 1980s.[14]

Approve the agreement   The negotiation stage of collective bargaining is completed when the agreement is approved. Often final approval for the employer rests with top management, although the bargaining team may have   **Approvals needed** the authority to commit the company. But negotiations are not complete until the union also approves the agreement. Union bargainers usually submit the contract to the membership for ratification. If a majority of the members vote for the new contract, then it replaces the prior arrangements. When members reject the contract offer, union and management bargainers reopen negotiations and seek a new compromise. Administration of the contract begins when both sides sign the agreement.

THE SCOPE OF CONTRACT ADMINISTRATION

A labor agreement affects many areas of personnel management. As a result, its administration often limits personnel practices in a number of ways. These limitations come from the contract provisions, past practices, and resolution of disputes.

Contract Provisions

Every labor agreement contains specific terms and provisions. The most common ones are listed in Figure 21-3. These clauses are important because they define the rights and obligations of the employer and the union. Since

● *Union recognition.* Normally near the beginning of a contract, this clause states management's acceptance of the union as the sole representative of designated employees.

● *Union security.* To ensure that the union maintains members as new employees are hired and present employees quit, a union security clause commonly is demanded by the union. Forms of union security include:

  a. *Union shop.* All new workers must join the union shortly after being hired.

  b. *Agency shop.* All new workers must pay to the union an amount equal to dues.

  c. *Checkoff.* Upon authorization, management agrees to deduct the union dues from each union member's paycheck and transfer the moneys to the union.

● *Wage rates.* The amount of wages to be paid to workers (or classes of workers) is specified in the wage clause.

● *Cost of living.* Increasingly, unions are demanding and receiving automatic wage increases for workers when price levels go up. For example, a common approach is for wages to go up by one cent an hour for each 0.3 or 0.4 percent increase in the consumer price index.

● *Insurance benefits.* This section specifies which insurance benefits the employer provides and how much the employer contributes toward these benefits. Frequently included benefits are life, hospitalization, and surgical insurance.

● *Pension benefits.* The amount of retirement income, years of service required, penalties for early retirement, employer and employee contributions, and vesting provisions are described in this section if a pension plan exists.

● *Income maintenance.* To provide workers with economic security, some contracts give guarantees of minimum income or minimum work. Other income maintenance provisions include severance pay and supplements to state unemployment insurance.

● *Time-off benefits.* Vacations, holidays, rest breaks, wash-up periods, and leave-of-absence provisions typically are specified in this clause.

● *Strikes/Lockouts.* It is common to find clauses in which the union promises not to strike for the duration of the contract in return for management's promise not to lock employees out of work during a labor dispute.

● *Seniority clause.* Unions seek contract terms that cause personnel decisions to be made on the basis of seniority. Often senior workers are given preferential treatment in job assignments, promotions, layoffs, vacation scheduling, overtime, and shift preferences.

● *Management rights.* Management must retain certain rights to do an effective job. These may include the ability to require overtime work, decide on promotions into management, design jobs, and select employees. This clause reserves to management the right to make decisions that management thinks are necessary for the organization's success.

● *Discipline.* Prohibited employee actions, penalties, and disciplinary procedures are either stated in the contract or included in the agreement by reference to those documents that contain the information.

● *Dispute resolution.* Disagreements between the union and management are resolved through procedures specified in the contract.

Figure 21-3

Common Provisions in Union-Management Agreements

nearly every provision affects the management of human resources, these clauses merit the attention of personnel specialists.

Whether the contract contains all of the provisions found in Figure 21-3 depends on the parties. For example, the employer is never required by law to grant a union security clause. Management bargainers may agree to a *union* **Union shop** *shop* (which requires all employees in the bargaining unit to join the union) or *checkoff* provision (which requires the employer to deduct union dues from employees' paychecks and remit the proceeds to the union) when such agreement leads to a lessening of other union demands. Often these security clauses are given in return for a provision that protects important management rights.

With the exception of clauses on management rights, most provisions in the agreement limit personnel actions. Some of these limitations are minor and similar to the self-imposed policies of well-managed organizations. For example, even without a union, most employers provide competitive wages, benefits, and working conditions. The labor agreement merely formalizes these obligations. But other contract terms may change the policies used before the contract was negotiated. Seniority and discipline clauses are two common constraints that are added.

Seniority   Unions typically prefer to have employee-related decisions determined by the length of the worker's employment, called *seniority*. Seniority ensures that promotions, overtime, and other employee concerns are handled without favoritism. But as the following example illustrates, seniority may limit management's flexibility in making personnel decisions.[15]

Uses of seniority

Three weeks before the retirement of the senior clerk in the parts department, the manager of the Anderson Buick dealership sought a replacement. The labor agreement required that "all job openings must be posted on the employee bulletin board for one week. Interested employees must submit their bids during the one-week open period. After the open period, the most senior, qualified employee will be selected from among those who submitted job bids."

Two workers applied. One, Jacob Marls, had been with the car agency for almost three years. His performance as a junior clerk was efficient and courteous. In fact, many parts customers asked for Jacob by name. John Abbott also submitted a bid. He had been with the dealership for three years and two months. John was dependable, but sometimes he was moody in dealing with customers. The general manager wanted to reward Jacob's good performance. But the contract required that the promotion go to John since he was qualified and had the most seniority.

Seniority also is used to decide vacations, training, shift assignments, overtime, and layoff rights. As with promotions, merit cannot always be rewarded. For example, a supervisor may need three subordinates to finish a job. Since seniority must be honored, the supervisor cannot select the best employees. Likewise, when a company plans a layoff, the most recently hired workers are the first to go. Those who are left probably get higher wages if there is a premium for longevity. Thus the higher-paid employees are retained even though the layoff was probably needed to reduce costs. And these layoffs may undermine the company's affirmative action plan since covered employees hired through the program may have low seniority.

Discipline Unions often challenge the discipline of a union member. Therefore, disciplinary action must be in accordance with the contract and must be backed with evidence. The need for proof requires management to document employee discipline, which results in more essential (but not necessarily productive) paperwork. Even when discipline is done correctly, the union may argue that special circumstances should be considered.

Past Practices

The actions of managers and union officials sometimes change the meaning of the agreement. Suppose a supervisor fails to discipline an employee who performs poorly. The result might be a precedent. A *precedent* is a new standard that arises from the past practices of either party. Once a precedent results from unequal enforcement of disciplinary rules, the new standard may affect similar cases in the future. In time, for example, it may become difficult for management to control tardiness because precedents created exceptions to the rules. When a personnel manager believes that an exception is appropriate, the union and the company can sign a letter stating that this exception is not a binding precedent. Then other employees cannot rely on the precedent to win exceptions from the rules.

The fear of setting precedent usually causes two changes in personnel procedures. First, more employee-related decisions are made by the personnel department. Supervisors are stripped of their authority to decide layoffs, discipline, and other employee matters. Instead, they are required to make recommendations to the personnel department to ensure uniformity. The other change concerns the training of supervisors in contract administration. This training is needed to ensure that supervisors administer the remaining portions of the contract uniformly.

(margin note: Precedent)

RESOLUTION OF CONTRACT DISPUTES

Constraints on management during contract administration also come from the resolution of disputes with the union. Generally, there are three ways that differences between union and management can be settled during the life of the contract. One method is to sue the other party in court for violation of the agreement. Although possible, this method seldom is used. It is too expensive and too time-consuming, not to mention the hard feelings and adversary relationship that such suits foster. The second way is for the union to strike the employer. Through economic pressure the union hopes to change management's position. Again, this approach is seldom used because it is expensive and time-consuming. Besides, 91 percent of all contracts limit the use of strikes during the term of the contract.[16] The third method is to file a formal complaint called a grievance. Grievance procedures are found in 98 percent of all labor-management agreements.[17]

(margin note: Strikes are limited)

Grievance Procedures

Either management or the union may file a grievance when the contract is violated. But since most decisions are made by management, there are few

- *Preliminary discussion.* The aggrieved employees discuss the complaint with the immediate supervisor with or without a union representative.

- *Step 1.* The complaint is put in writing and formally presented to the first-level supervisor. Normally, the supervisor must respond in writing within a contractually specified period, usually two to five days.

- *Step 2.* The union representative or the union grievance committee takes the written complaint to the supervisor's boss or the personnel department. A written response is required, usually within a week.

- *Step 3.* The local union president or other high-ranking union official takes the complaint to a member of top management or the personnel director. Again, a written response typically is required.

- *Step 4.* The company and the union present its viewpoints to an outside neutral arbitrator who hears the case and renders a decision much as a judge would do.

Figure 21-4
Typical Steps in
a Union-Management Grievance Procedure

opportunities for the union to break the agreement. More commonly, unions file grievances because of alleged violations by management. The *grievance procedure* consists of an ordered series of steps to resolve disputes. Figure 21-4 describes the steps through which an employee's grievance typically passes.

    The number of steps in the grievance procedure depends upon the size of the organization. A three-step grievance procedure is most common. In very large firms (often in manufacturing), four and even five steps are possible. The additional steps are used to reduce the number of cases reaching top union and company officials.

> Solving employee complaints

Types and causes of grievances Even though personnel may not handle grievances in their early stages, the department plays an important role. Each supervisor sees only a small number of complaints. But personnel has an organizationwide view from which it can identify the types and causes of grievances. With this information, personnel can create programs to improve grievance handling.[18] Grievances can be classified into three types: legitimate, imagined, and political. *Legitimate grievances* occur when there is a reasonable cause to think that there has been a contract violation. Even in a cooperative environment, contract clauses have different meanings to different people.

> Legitimate grievances

    Imagined grievances occur when employees believe that the agreement has been violated even though management is exercising its contract rights in a reasonable manner. Again, misunderstanding is the primary cause of these grievances. A cooperative union can help settle such complaints quickly by explaining management's rights. Otherwise, when a manager says that the complaint is without merit, the worker may feel that management is trying to save face for a bad decision.

> Imagined grievances

    Political grievances are the most difficult to solve. They are most common just before contract negotiations and union elections. They also occur when a complaint is pursued to further someone's political aspirations. For example, a union representative may be reluctant to tell union members that their grievanc-

> Political grievances

es are without merit. To do so may mean a loss of political support in the next union election. Instead, the union leader may process a worthless grievance. Likewise, management also files political grievances.[19]

Handling grievances Once a grievance is submitted, management should seek to resolve it fairly and quickly. Failure to do so can be seen as a disregard for employee needs. In time, morale, motivation, performance, and company loyalty may be damaged.

In adjusting grievances, several precautions should be followed.[20] Most important, grievances should be settled on their merits. Political considerations by either party weaken the grievance system. Complaints need to be carefully investigated and decided on the facts, not on emotional whim. Otherwise, damaging precedents may result. Second, the cause of each grievance should be recorded. Many grievances coming from one or two departments may indicate personality conflicts or a poor understanding of the contract. Third, employees should be encouraged to use the grievance procedure. Problems cannot be solved unless management and union officials know what they are. But before employees can use the grievance process, it must be explained through meetings, employee handbooks, or bulletin-board notices. And finally, whatever the solution may be, it needs to be explained to those affected. Even though union leaders do this, management should not fail to explain *its* reasoning to the worker.[21]

Arbitration

The grievance procedure does not always produce a satisfactory solution. When a deadlock results, 96 percent of all labor agreements call for arbitration.[22] *Arbitration* is the submission of a dispute to a neutral third party. The arbitrator acts in the role of a judge and hears both sides of the dispute. After weighing the facts, the arbitrator renders a binding decision.

Benefits of arbitration

Arbitration clauses are common because they allow a complaint to be resolved once and for all. Although a court action would have the same result, arbitration has several advantages. Unlike court decisions, an arbitrator's ruling usually is not subject to several levels of appeal. The lack of extensive appeals means a quicker decision. Since arbitration also is private, it is not an open proceeding as court cases are. Best of all, arbitration is less expensive than a court case.[23]

Arbitration holds two potential problems for personnel administrators: costs and unacceptable solutions. Although the employer and the union usually share the expenses, each case may cost several hundred to several thousand dollars. Admittedly, court costs and legal fees usually are more. Nevertheless, personnel needs to consider the costs involved. Another potential problem occurs when an arbitrator renders a decision against management's best interests. Since the ruling is binding, it may drastically alter management's rights. Suppose, for example, that management lays off several hundred workers, and the union convinces an arbitrator that management did not follow the contract's layoff procedure. The arbitrator may rule that all workers get their jobs back with back pay. Or if an arbitrator accepts the union's argument of extenuating circumstances in a disciplinary case, those extenuating circumstances may be cited in future cases. For instance, consider what happened in a chain of convenience markets.

The Quick Foods Market had a policy that stealing from the company was grounds for immediate discharge. Sam Anglin, a new employee, took a sandwich and a beer from the cooler and consumed them without paying for them. He was fired when caught by the store manager. The union argued that Sam should get a second chance since he was a new employee. The arbitrator upheld management but added that discharge for such a minor theft might be too harsh a penalty had Sam not been a probationary employee. If a senior employee is ever caught stealing, the union may use this opinion to claim that discharge is the wrong penalty. And another arbitrator might agree.

In cases like Sam's, a prompt arbitration decision is essential. The employee may be reluctant to look for a new job, and personnel may be reluctant to train a replacement until a final decision is made. To speed up the arbitration process, the company and the union may agree to use *expedited arbitration*. Under this approach the arbitrator usually gives an oral opinion at the end of the hearing or a written decision within a few days. Otherwise, arbitrators usually are allowed thirty days in which to render their decisions, and some arbitrators take considerably longer.[24]

It is important for personnel specialists to seek a solution with the union before arbitration. In this manner they avoid additional costs, delays, and the possibility of an unsatisfactory decision. When arbitration is unavoidable, personnel specialists should follow the guidelines in Figure 21-5. These suggestions offer the best chance of winning a favorable decision. If these guidelines reveal serious flaws with the employer's case, a compromise solution with the union before arbitration is usually advised.

UNION-MANAGEMENT COOPERATION

Although dispute resolution techniques stop most complaints from erupting into a strike, they are after-the-fact measures. Even the "winner" of a favorable arbitration decision loses the time and money it took to argue the case. Through cooperation, both parties can replace reactive measures with proactive approaches. Proactive efforts benefit the union and the company by saving time and expenses. These savings can mean higher profits for the employer and better contracts for the union.

Winners can be losers.

As personnel manager for the Oregon Logging Company, Joe VonKampen spent about 40 percent of his time on some phase of dispute resolution. Although the Teamsters represented only 125 of the employees, there were usually 275 to 300 grievances a year. About 10 percent of these cases went to arbitration. These costs seriously affected the company's profitability, which forced the union to accept the lowest wage rates in the area. To change the situation, the town's mayor offered to help.

1. Study the original grievance and review its history through every step of the grievance machinery.

2. Determine the arbitrator's role. It might be found, for instance, that while the original grievance contains many elements, the arbitrator is restricted by the contract to resolving only certain aspects.

3. Review the collective bargaining agreement from beginning to end. Often, other clauses may be related to the grievance.

4. Assemble all documents and papers you will need at the hearing. Where feasible, make copies for the arbitrator and the other party. If some of the documents you need are in the possession of the other party, ask in advance that they be brought to the arbitration.

5. Make plans in advance if you think it will be necessary for the arbitrator to visit the plant or job site for on-the-spot investigation. The arbitrator should be accompanied by representatives of *both* parties.

6. Interview all witnesses. Make certain that they understand the whole case and the importance of their own testimony within it.

7. Make a written summary of what each witness will say. This serves as a useful check-list at the hearing to make certain nothing is overlooked.

8. Study the case from the other side's point of view. Be prepared to answer the opposing evidence and arguments.

9. Discuss your outline of the case with others in your organization. A fresh viewpoint often will disclose weak spots or previously overlooked details.

10. Read as many articles and published awards as you can on the general subject matter in dispute. While awards by other arbitrators for other parties have no binding precedent value, they may help clarify the thinking of parties and arbitrators alike.

Source: Labor Arbitration Procedures and Techniques, New York: American Arbitration Association, 1972, pp. 15–16. Used with permission.

Figure 21-5
Preparation Guidelines for Arbitration Hearings

The mayor devised a training program that consisted of the union leader and the personnel manager taking turns reading the contract to an audience of supervisors and union representatives. After each paragraph, the personnel manager and the union president both summarized what the paragraph meant. The mayor did not let them go on to the next paragraph until both agreed on the meaning of the previous one. After several sessions, the entire contract was reviewed. Lower-ranking union and management officials learned what the contract meant and that they were expected to cooperate with each other. The following year, fourteen grievances were filed and only one went to arbitration. The company's profitability improved dramatically, and the local union obtained its largest wage increase in the next negotiations.

Union-Management Attitudes

Severe conflicts between a company and the union often can be traced to the attitudes each holds about the other.[25] In the Oregon Logging example, supervisors felt that the union was intruding on their rights. When the supervisors, in turn, denied workers their rights, the union fought back with grievances. Sometimes members of a union get so upset that they conduct a *wildcat strike.* These strikes are spontaneous acts that take place in violation of the contract, regardless of the objections raised by union leaders. Even after the strike is over, the underlying problems still have to be settled.[26]

If the attitudes beween the parties remain hostile, the organization suffers from poor performance. Serious disruptions can affect even the survival of the organization and the union.[27] Sometimes extreme disruptions may require both parties to cooperate in order to prevent bankruptcy and massive layoffs.

Building Cooperation

Proactive personnel departments cannot wait for disaster to occur before attempting to build cooperation with the union. Such departments realize that cooperation is not automatic and must be initiated by human resource specialists. However, there are several obstacles to cooperation.

Obstacles to cooperation Personnel specialists often seek union cooperation to improve the organization's effectiveness. But effectiveness usually is far less important to union leaders. Quite naturally, these officials are more concerned about the welfare of their members and winning reelection to union office. So when cooperation fails to be attractive politically, union leaders have little incentive to cooperate. In fact, if leaders do cooperate, they may be accused by workers of forgetting the union's interests. These accusations can mean defeat by political opponents within the union. Thus cooperation may not be in the leader's best interest.

For many years, negotiations in the steel industry were marked by strikes and threats of strikes. The result was lower profitability and even a loss of markets to foreign producers. In turn, many members of the United Steelworkers union were laid off. Both the union and the steel companies were suffering.

Both parties reached a cooperative arrangement called the *Experimental Negotiations Agreement.* This agreement called for concessions from the steel producers and no nationwide strikes by the union. The cooperative move was intended to benefit both the union and employees. But some members saw it as a loss of rights, particularly the right to strike. In the union's national elections, a splinter group was able to make a serious challenge to the established leadership by attacking this cooperative agreement.

Besides political obstacles, union leaders may mistrust the personnel department. For example, bitter remarks during the organizing drive may convince union officials that personnel specialists are antiunion. Within this climate, cooperative gestures by personnel may be seen as tricks. If mistrust increases, cooperation usually fails.

Cooperative methods Once personnel specialists realize the political concerns and suspicions of union leaders, several cooperative methods can be

Managers and personnel specialists can build cooperation between the employer and the union through:

- *Prior consultation* with union leaders to defuse problems before they become formal grievances

- *Sincere concern* for employee problems and welfare even when management is not obligated to do so by the labor agreement

- *Training programs* that objectively communicate the intent of union and management bargainers and reduce biases and misunderstandings

- *Joint study committees* that allow management and union officials to find solutions to common problems

- *Third parties* who can provide guidance and programs that bring union leaders and managers closer together to pursue common objectives.

Figure 21-6
Methods of Building Union-Management Cooperation

tried. These techniques are summarized in Figure 21-6 and are explained in the following paragraphs.

Prior consultation

One of the most basic actions is *prior consultation* with the union. Not every management decision must be approved by the union. But actions that affect the union or its leaders may cause a grievance unless explained before the action is taken. Suppose a senior employee was passed over for promotion because the use of profanity by this employee could mean a loss of customers. Suppose further that the personnel department explains to the union leaders that the use of profanity by the most senior worker could mean a loss of valuable business and jobs for union members. Perhaps the union leaders might accept the promotion of the junior worker. At least politically, the union president would be less likely to challenge the promotion decision. Some managers even ask union leaders to talk to problem employees before management has to take action that might lead to a grievance.

Sincere concern

Management and personnel also can build cooperation through a *sincere concern* for employees. This concern may be shown through the prompt settlement of grievances, regardless of who wins. Or management can bargain sincerely with the union to reduce the need for a strike. Even when a strike occurs, management can express its concern for workers. For example, during one strike at General Motors, GM continued to pay the strikers' insurance premiums to prevent a lapse in coverage. Sometimes this concern is initially expressed by management's acceptance of the union. The disciplining of a member of management for a flagrant violation of the union's rights is one example. Ford Motor Company provides another:

Ford Motor Company

The president of Ford Motor Company issued a policy letter to all Ford divisions, subsidiaries, and affiliated companies. In that policy letter, entitled "Employee Involvement," he stated: "It is the policy of the Company to encourage and enable all employees to become involved in and contribute to the success of the Company. A work climate should be created and maintained in which employees, at all levels, can achieve individual goals and work satisfaction by directing their talents and energies toward clearly defined Company goals.

• Methods of managing should encourage employee participation in identifying and solving work-related problems.

• Communications programs and procedures should be implemented that encourage frequent, timely and constructive two-way communications with employees concerning work-related problems."[28]

Training programs are another way to build cooperation. After a new contract is signed, the personnel department usually trains managers so that they understand the contract terms. The union does the same for its leaders. As a result, both sides continue their biases and misunderstandings. If personnel sponsors training for both the union and management, then a common understanding of the contract is more likely. The training can be as simple as taking turns paraphrasing the contract. Or outside neutrals can be hired to do the training. Either way, supervisors and union officials end the training with a common understanding of the contract and a new basis for cooperation.

When a complex problem confronts the union and the employer, *joint study committees* are sometimes formed.[29] For example, the three largest automobile companies agreed to create separate committees with the United Auto Workers union to study health-care costs. If successful, costs will grow slower, and there will be more money available for other benefits.[30] Productivity committees are another common form of union-management cooperation. According to the Department of Labor, 97 of 1550 contracts surveyed had provisions for union-management committees to study production.[31]

A final method of building cooperation is through third parties, such as consultants or government agencies, who may act as catalysts. For example, the Federal Mediation and Conciliation Service (FMCS) has a program entitled *relations by objectives* (RBO).

> In a series of meetings, which at first are held separately with labor and management, FMCS staff members determine company and union viewpoints on what the "other party" should do to improve relations, and then on what each party should do itself. Following these sessions, meetings are held, attended by all management officials—including top executives and line supervisors—and by all union officials including shop stewards. Respective viewpoints are discussed, clarified, and incorporated into mutually acceptable lists of objectives for improvement of labor-management relations.
>
>   The list then is discussed by the two parties separately and jointly. The joint sessions develop an agreement on action steps for attaining each objective, assigning responsibility for starting and completing steps, and implementing a timetable for achievement of each objective.[32]

There is no single best approach to building cooperation. Since each relationship is unique, the methods used will depend upon the situation. But if

Joint training

Joint study committees

Third parties

RBO

personnel administrators can build more cooperative relations with their unions, the employer gains higher productivity. In turn, there are more resources against which the union and its members can make demands. Improving union-management relations, therefore, is a potentially significant role for personnel departments in unionized organizations.

> At Ford Motor Company the fruits of their employee involvement effort have been widespread throughout their multiple plant locations. Some of the benefits from a more cooperative labor-management environment are listed below. Although each saving is small, those savings multiplied by thousands of other ideas already received may eventually affect Ford's survival.
>
> • *The Chicago Stamping Plant and UAW Local 588* began recycling damaged sheet metal. By fixing sheets or using them for smaller jobs, savings averaged $6812 per week. This plant had an 800 percent increase in the productivity of saw blades because of employee suggestions. Savings equalled more than $14,000 per year.
>
> • *The Sandusky Plant and UAW Local 1216* discovered that loading starter pinions into the furnace differently reduced defects by 95 percent.
>
> • *The Michigan Truck Plant and UAW Local 900* began using poly-knit gloves in the trim department at a savings of $38,000 per shift per year.[33]

THE CHALLENGE TO PERSONNEL MANAGEMENT

Today many personnel managers and union leaders perceive government intervention as a potential threat to the traditional freedoms that they have all enjoyed. Their common concern rises out of the fear that more government laws will control their affairs. And since existing laws are enforced by agencies with the power to "make laws" by their interpretation of existing ones, regulations are bound to grow.

Closer union and management cooperation to improve labor relations is a major way to slow the growth of government regulations. This does not mean that either party must abandon its constituency: rank-and-file members and stockholders. On the contrary, both sides must continue to perform. What is needed is a realization that cooperation, not legalistic advocacy, represents the shortest route away from additional government intervention. Otherwise, political expediency and public welfare will demand, for better or for worse, further legislative action, new agency decisions, and more government constraints.[34]

Personnel's Proactive Response

Unions cause changes in the behavior of managers and in the operation of the personnel department. In nonunionized facilities, an implicit objective of personnel management often is to remain nonunion. Since the National Labor Relations Act prohibits the use of coercion or discrimination, management must rely on a proactive approach. That is, it must use *effective* personnel practices that discourage unionization, if that is the company's policy. For example, this approach requires that personnel specialists (within the constraints of organizational effectiveness and efficiency, law, technology, and other challenges) carefully do the following:

- *Design* jobs that are personally satisfying to workers.

- *Develop* plans that maximize individual opportunities and minimize the possibility of layoffs.

- *Select* workers who are qualified.

- *Establish* fair, meaningful, objective standards of individual performance.

- *Train* workers and managers to enable them to achieve expected levels of performance.

- *Evaluate* and reward behavior based upon actual performance.

In other words, personnel managers need to apply actively the ideas discussed in earlier chapters of this book! Failure to implement sound personnel policies and practices provides the justification *and* motivation for workers to form unions.

Personnel Management Implications

When unions are present, the personnel department is expanded by the addition of a labor relations section. This section allows labor specialists to deal with such critical areas as negotiations and contract administration, while personnel professionals attend to their more traditional roles. In fact, personnel and labor relations may form two equal divisions within a broader department, typically called *industrial relations.*

Operationally, the personnel section seeks sound employee relations through effective practices. Open-door policies and in-house complaint procedures are two examples. The labor relations section has a complementary role. It wants to minimize restrictions on management by diligent negotiations and fair administration of the union contract. Or to use a sports analogy, personnel serves as the offensive team and labor relations is the defensive team.[35]

SUMMARY

If workers form a union, the National Labor Relations Board requires management and the union to bargain in good faith. The success of the personnel department at the bargaining table is affected by its actions before negotiations begin. Labor relations specialists must monitor changes in the collective bargaining environment and assemble a detailed bargaining plan. Then after top management approval and strike preparations, bargainers begin to negotiate. Negotiations with the union result in a contract that must be approved by union members and by top management. Once negotiated, the agreement is administered by both the union and management.

In administering the agreement, personnel specialists face several challenges. First, contract clauses place limits on management. Second, day-to-day administration of the contract can lead to precedents. And finally, limitations can arise from the dispute resolution procedures. Grievance handling and arbitration help interpret the contract, sometimes in ways that limit management.

Within these constraints, managers still must manage. Only through increased cooperation between the company and the union can these limitations be lessened. Responsibility for improving the relationship must be assumed by the personnel department if political barriers and mistrust are to be overcome. Through prior consultation, concern for employees, training programs, or joint committees, personnel specialists can lay the foundations for a cooperative union-management relationship.

TERMS FOR REVIEW

Labor agreement	Political grievances
Management rights	Arbitration
Seniority	Wildcat strikes
Bargaining book	Relations by objectives
Precedent	Boulwarism
Techniques to resolve disputes	Pattern bargaining
Grievance procedure	

REVIEW AND DISCUSSION QUESTIONS

1. In preparing to negotiate a contract with a union, what types of information would you gather before arriving at the bargaining table?

2. If you were asked to explain why various types of people are on the employer's bargaining team, what reasons would you give for (a) the company lawyer, (b) the director of industrial relations, (c) a wage and salary specialist, (d) a benefit specialist, (e) the assistant plant manager, and (f) an experienced supervisor?

3. If you have to advise the manager of a small chain of bakeries on how to prepare for a possible strike, what would you suggest?

4. Suppose you decide to make the union the best offer you could at the beginning of negotiations. What problems might you expect?

5. In your own words, explain why unions usually file most grievances.

6. During one union organization drive, a plant manager told employees: "A union means less flexibility in dealing with your individual problems. With a

union present, the company must follow the labor agreement." Explain how this loss of freedom might be to the employee's disadvantage.

7.   Suppose one of your unionized employees wanted to leave work early to see her child play in Little League. Further, suppose she agreed to work through her lunch hour so that no loss of work or production would occur. If you agreed to her suggestions, what problems might result?

8.   What are the disadvantages of using arbitration as a last step in the grievance procedure?

INCIDENT 21-1

In-Flight Food Services Company

The In-Flight Food Services Company provides prepared meals for several airlines at a major airport in the Southeast. Food handlers cook and package meals to be reheated in airplane galleys for service to passengers while in flight. Most of the 535 food handlers belong to the Independent Food Handlers Union, which has represented these employees for over five years.

Each year, the industrial relations department noticed that the number of grievances filed by members of the union had increased about 15 percent. The time spent by union representatives, employees, and supervisors as a result of these grievances was affecting productivity in the company's cafeteria. The general manager was concerned that the company's costs and the low productivity could lead to a loss of several key contracts with major airlines.

The industrial relations department studied all of the grievances during the past year and provided the following analysis.

Total grievances filed	803
Number settled at:	
First-level supervision	104
Second-level supervision	483
General manager level	205
Arbitration	11

Although some grievances involved more than one issue, most of them were single-issue matters. When the industrial relations department classified the grievances, the following results were reported:

Tardiness or absence control	349
Overtime disputes	265
Other discipline or discharge	77
Incorrect job schedules	75
Multiple-issue disputes	37

1.   Assuming the industrial relations director asked you to design a training program to reduce the high number of grievances, who do you think should attend the training sessions?

2.   What topics would you cover in the training?

3.   If you felt that many of the grievances resulted from poor wording in the contract, what could you do to make changes before the contract expired?

REFERENCES

1.   John A. Fossum, *Labor Relations: Development, Structure, Process,* Dallas: Business Publications, 1979, p. 348.

2.   Roger B. Smith, "Toward a New Alliance with Labor," a Robert S. Hatfield Fellow's Speech at the Cornell Forum, Ithaca, N.Y., Apr. 7, 1982. For a contrary view see "Why the UAW May Go Back to Old-Style Bargaining," *Business Week,* March 12, 1984, pp. 98, 100.

3.   "Management vs. Labor," *IRS Newsletter,* Autumn 1982, p. 3.

4.   Ibid.

5.   Ibid.

6.   Gerald I. Nierenberg, *The Art of Negotiating,* New York: Cornerstone Library, 1968, pp. 47–61. See also Jeremy Main, "How to Be a Better Negotiator," *Fortune,* Sept. 19, 1983, pp. 141–146.

7.   Edward F. Murphy, *Management vs. the Union,* New York: Stein and Day, 1971, pp. 47–64.

8.   George E. Constantino, Jr., "Defining Line and Staff Roles in Collective Bargaining," *Personnel Journal,* October 1979, pp. 689–691, 717.

9.   Fred W. Elarbee, Jr., "How Management Will Bargain in the 1980s," *Business,* March–April 1979, pp. 9–11. See also Tony Zivalich, "How Labor Will Bargain in the 1980s," *Business,* March–April 1979, pp. 12–14.

10.   David Ignatius and George Getschow, "Chances to End Strike Are Hurt by Weakness of UMW's Leadership," *The Wall Street Journal,* Western ed., Feb. 25, 1978, pp. 1, 29. See also "U.S. Workers and Their Unions, 1959–1979," *The Federationist,* March 1980, pp. 5–8.

11.   Herbert R. Northrup, *Boulwarism,* Ann Arbor: Bureau of Industrial Relations, Graduate School of Business, The University of Michigan, 1964. For an excellent discussion of negotiations see Richard E. Walton and Robert B. McKersie, *A Behavioral Theory of Labor Negotiations,* New York: McGraw-Hill, 1965, pp. 13–46; also see Nierenberg, op. cit., pp. 7–12.

12.   Perry A. Zirkel and J. Gary Lutz, "Characteristics and Functions of Mediators: A Pilot Study," *The Arbitration Journal,* June 1981, pp. 15–20.

13.   Ignatius and Getschow, op. cit. See also John G. Kilgour, "How to Respond to an Impending Strike," *Personnel Journal,* February 1979, pp. 98–101.

14.   John W. Falahee, "Concession Bargaining: The Time Is Now!" *The Personnel Administrator,* January 1983, pp. 27–28; see also "Why Eastern Is on a Short String," *Business Week,* Apr. 11, 1983, pp. 116, 118.

15.   Harry Graham and Brian Heshizer, "The Effect of Contract Language on Low-Level Settlement of Grievances," *Labor Law Journal,* July 1979, pp. 427–432.

16. *Basic Patterns in Union Contracts,* Washington: Bureau of National Affairs, 1975, p. 90. See also Ben Burdetsky and Marvin S. Katzman, "Is the Strike Iron Still Hot?" *Personnel Journal,* July 1984, pp. 48–52.

17. *Basic Patterns in Union Contracts,* op. cit., p. 32.

18. William B. Werther, Jr., "Reducing Grievances through Effective Contract Administration," *Labor Law Journal,* April 1974, pp. 211–216.

19. Ross Stagner and Hjalmar Rosen, *Psychology of Union-Management Relations,* Belmont, Calif.: Wadsworth, 1965, pp. 110–11.

20. Thomas F. Gideon and Richard B. Peterson, "A Comparison of Alternate Grievance Procedures," *Employee Relations Law Journal,* Autumn 1979, pp. 222–233. See also "The Antiunion Grievance Play," *Business Week,* Feb. 12, 1979, pp. 117, 120.

21. James C. McBrearty, *Handling Grievances: A Positive Approach for Management and Labor Representatives,* Tucson: Division of Economics and Business Research, University of Arizona, 1972, pp. 3–6. See also George W. Bohlander, "Fair Representation: Not Just a Union Problem," *The Personnel Administrator,* March 1980, pp. 36–40, 82.

22. *Basic Patterns in Union Contracts,* op. cit., p. 37.

23. William B. Werther, Jr., and Harold C. White, "Cost Effective Arbitration," *MSU Business Topics,* Summer 1978, pp. 59–64. See also Mollie H. Bowers, "Grievance-Mediation: Another Route to Resolution," *Personnel Journal,* February 1980, pp. 132–136, 139.

24. Werther and White, op. cit.

25. Joseph Tomkiewicz and Otto Brenner, "Union Attitudes and the 'Manager of the Future,'" *The Personnel Administrator,* October 1979, pp. 67–70, 72.

26. "In Wildcat Strikes, Court Rules: Union Leaders Safe from Discipline," *Resource,* May 1983, pp. 1, 10.

27. Richard E. Walton and Robert B. McKersie, *A Behavioral Theory of Labor Negotiations,* New York: McGraw-Hill, 1965, pp. 184–221.

28. Philip Caldwell, "Policy Letter 13–14, Subject: Employee Involvement," Ford Motor Company, Nov. 5, 1979, p. 1.

29. Edger Weinberg, "Labor-Management Cooperation: A Report on Recent Initiatives," *Monthly Labor Review,* April 1976, p. 13.

30. "A Joint Look at Cutting Health Care Costs," *Business Week,* Nov. 17, 1975, p. 49.

31. Weinberg, op. cit.

32. National Center on Productivity and Quality of Working Life, *Recent Initiatives in Labor-Management Cooperation,* U.S. Government Printing Office, 1976.

33. "EI . . . It Makes the Difference," *UAW-Ford National Joint Committee on Employee Involvement,* N.D., pp. 2, 3, 16.

34. William B. Werther, Jr., "Government Control vs. Corporate Ingenuity," *Labor Law Journal,* June 1975, pp. 360–367.

35. John R. Bangs, *Collective Bargaining,* New York: Alexander Hamilton, 1964, pp. 29–34.

PART

VII

PERSONNEL MANAGEMENT IN PERSPECTIVE

A personnel department cannot become content with its performance. It must search for new ways to help its firm and its people. One way is through an audit of its activities. Audits point to changes that can improve the department's performance. Another way personnel can help is by planning for the future. Proactive departments anticipate new challenges.

As a manager or personnel professional, you need to understand audits and the future challenges that affect you. They can change the procedures you use and the way in which you manage employees.

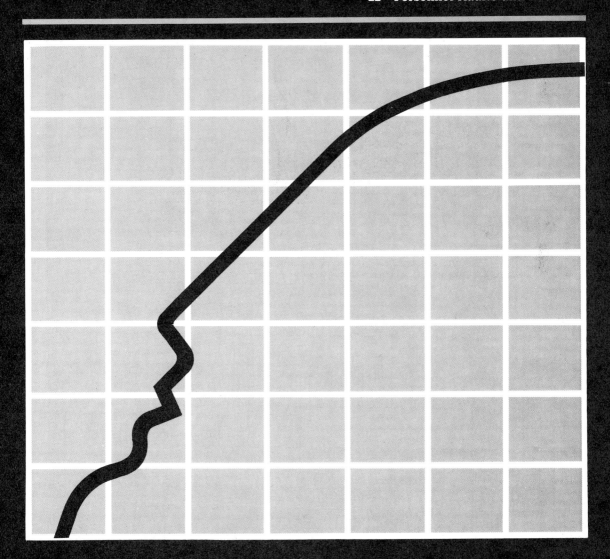

CHAPTER

Acceptance of personnel research seems to have grown over time . . . because of its demonstrated usefulness.

Dean F. Berry[1]

Personnel has the opportunity to help . . . in ways that will both increase productivity and enhance the quality of working life.

Fred K. Foulkes[2]

PERSONNEL AUDITS AND RESEARCH

CHAPTER OBJECTIVES

After studying this chapter, you should be able to:

1 <u>Identify</u> the benefits of a personnel audit.

2 <u>Describe</u> the most common approaches to personnel audits.

3 <u>List</u> the research tools used in a personnel audit.

4 <u>Explain</u> the major challenges facing personnel practices in the future.

5 <u>Describe</u> how third parties cause changes in personnel management.

6 <u>List</u> major workplace innovations that are likely to occur by the year 2000.

Personnel departments cannot assume that everything they do is correct. Errors do happen, and policies become outdated. By checking its activities, the personnel department can find problems before they become serious. If the evaluation is done correctly, it can build support between the department and the operating managers. An audit of past practices and policies also may reveal outdated assumptions that can be changed to help the department better meet future challenges. Research into those practices and procedures may uncover better ways for the department to contribute to the objectives discussed in Chapter 1.

Evaluating past practices and researching better procedures grow more important with each passing year for three reasons. First, personnel work carries with it many legal implications for the employer. Failure to comply with equal employment or safety laws, for example, can subject the organization to lawsuits. Second, personnel costs are significant. Compensation and benefits often are a major operating expense for most employers. Improper pay or benefit plans can be costly, even fatal, to the company's survival. Third, the personnel department's activities help shape an organization's productivity and its employees' quality of work life. But most of all, the growing complexity of personnel work makes audits and research necessary.[3] Consider, for example, the range of benefits described in an in-house publication of State Farm Insurance. Figure 22-1 provides a pictorial summary of the State Farm "building blocks" approach, which is explained in the following paragraphs:

State Farm wants to help its employees succeed. That's why the company provides a variety of benefits, programs, and policies . . . all designed to help you *build personnel success.*

"An easy way to picture this is to view what State Farm provides employees as a set of building blocks," says Bruce Callis, then Vice President–Personnel. "It's an integrated, never-finished set of blocks, with each one representing an employee relations program. Together, they are the ingredients for personal success.

"We've decided to divide the building blocks into five categories:

- Career
- Personal interests
- Health
- Retirement
- Finance

"From the categories, you can see we look at an employee as a *whole* person, not just a worker. The building blocks help employees achieve not only career success, but also success in other aspects of their lives—their finances, health, personal interests, and retirement.

"This is a *holistic* approach to employee relations. It encourages employees to seek a more balanced and healthier lifestyle."

Why does the company provide these building blocks for success? "We want our employees to be successful," explains Callis. "When our people are successful, our company is, too. There's no doubt about it—that

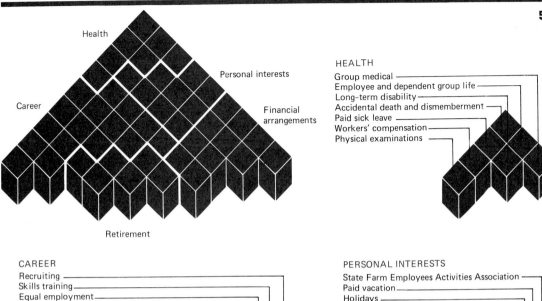

Health

Personal interests

Career

Financial arrangements

Retirement

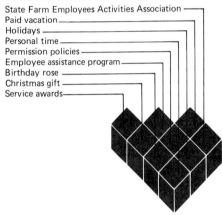

HEALTH
Group medical
Employee and dependent group life
Long-term disability
Accidental death and dismemberment
Paid sick leave
Workers' compensation
Physical examinations

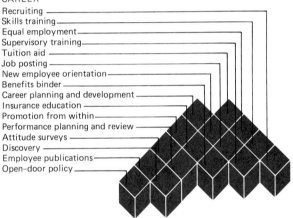

CAREER
Recruiting
Skills training
Equal employment
Supervisory training
Tuition aid
Job posting
New employee orientation
Benefits binder
Career planning and development
Insurance education
Promotion from within
Performance planning and review
Attitude surveys
Discovery
Employee publications
Open-door policy

PERSONAL INTERESTS
State Farm Employees Activities Association
Paid vacation
Holidays
Personal time
Permission policies
Employee assistance program
Birthday rose
Christmas gift
Service awards

FINANCIAL ARRANGEMENTS
Mutual funds
Foundation scholarships
Incentive and thrift
Savings bonds
Credit union
IRA
Salary surveys
Benefits statement
Moving assistance program
Merit raises
COLA

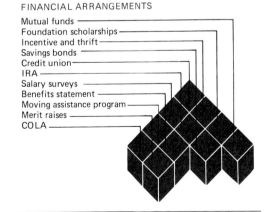

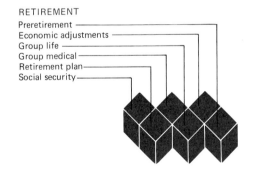

RETIREMENT
Preretirement
Economic adjustments
Group life
Group medical
Retirement plan
Social security

Source: Operation Understanding, April/May, 1983. Used by permission of the State Farm Insurance Companies.

Figure 22-1
State Farm's Building Block Approach

principle works at State Farm. Our leadership in the insurance industry is a tribute to the success of our people."

Management has a key role in continuing State Farm's success by continuing to help employees succeed. "Supervisors should think of their job as *helping employees succeed,*" Callis suggests. "To do that, you must think of each employee as an individual, not just a worker. You help employees see how the demands of one's job can be compatible with one's personal interests. And, by doing that, you'll get improvements in productivity while also meeting the personnel needs of employees."

Let's take a look at each category of building blocks for personal success.

Career

The building blocks for career success allow employees the opportunity to grow both personally and professionally. They help employees build skills, set goals, and take on new career challenges.

A State Farm career begins with *recruiting.* We seek the best qualified people to carry on our insurance business.

Then comes *new employee orientation.* Here we say "Welcome to State Farm," and introduce the new employees to their job and the company benefits.

An ongoing part of your career is the *Performance Planning and Review* process. This program gives each employee the opportunity to set realistic performance goals to work toward. Progress is reviewed so employees can be recognized for their achievements at salary time.

At State Farm, school is never out. You can continue your education through *skills training, insurance education, and tuition aid.*

Skills training programs are available for all levels of employees—support, technical/professional, and management.

There are several *insurance education* programs offered . . . at State Farm right now, with many . . . people enrolled in courses.

Health

We know that people are most happy and most productive when they're in good health. So each regional office has a medical department to provide *physical exams* and other preventative health services.

For those times when you're not in good health, there's *PSL* [Personal Sick Leave]. And, four *group insurance plans* are available to protect you from financial hardship due to illness, disability, or death.

Finance

State Farm, one of the most financially secure companies in our industry, provides a variety of building blocks for your financial strength.

The company is known for competitive salaries, to which we add *merit raises* and promotional increases. So you have a place to save and invest money, there are the company-sponsored *credit unions* available to all employees, as well as the *Mutual Funds.*

The *Incentive and Thrift Plan* allows eligible employees to share in the companies' profit while they save for retirement. *IRA's* are also available for tax-deductible, tax-deferred savings.

Personal Interests

The Personal Interests building blocks include the programs that pay employees for time away from work—*holidays, vacation, personal time, and permission absences.* We all need time away from work to develop the other interests in our lives. These programs give us that opportunity.

The newest building block in the personal interests group is *employee assistance.* This is a process where State Farm associates who have personal problems which are interfering with their personal success and job performance can get confidential assistance. This is generally done through personnel's medical department.

The assistance program has helped State Farm employees with health, chemical dependency, or emotional problems return to a more productive life.

Retirement

Your retirement years can be golden years, if you plan for them. Your income during these years will come from three sources: State Farm's Retirement Plan, Social Security, and your personal savings.

State Farm's *Retirement Plan* is fully funded by the Company. You don't have to make any contributions—State Farm pays for it all. Your retirement income is determined by your salary over the years and your length of State Farm service. Four times since 1976, *economic adjustments* have been made which increased retirees' incomes.

Under the Retirement Plan, many employees may continue their *Group Medical* coverage. State Farm continues to pay over half of the total premium cost for this. Also, retiring employees may be eligible to continue a portion of their insurance coverage from *Group Life.* This Group Life coverage is paid for entirely by State Farm.

Social Security, a hotly debated item these days, is a second source of retirement income. The amount you will receive from Social Security will depend on your average earnings over the years.

Both your Retirement Plan income and Social Security should be supplemented by personal savings and investments, such as Incentive & Thrift Plan savings. Some retirees are even adding a fourth source of income by working part-time or embarking on a 'new' career.

To help employees make the transition to retirement, *pre-retirement planning,* beginning at age 55, is provided by the personnel department. At that time, employees receive information they'll need to prepare for the time they choose to retire."[4]

The scope of State Farm's personnel function reads like a summary of this book. Other large, well-managed, and proactive personnel departments do many of these same activities. Only through an audit can the former vice

568

president for personnel, Bruce Callis, be certain that his personnel managers in the United States and Canada are providing these benefits and services in the ways intended. Through auditing the home office and regional personnel departments, compliance with national and local laws can be verified, too. Then periodically, the regional personnel managers are brought to company head-quarters in Bloomington, Illinois, for discussions about the department's upcoming plans to ensure that the personnel department is preparing for future challenges.

Expanded personnel model

Only through a comprehensive audit can a personnel department hope to assess the various subsystems of the overall personnel management model in Figure 22-2, which is an expanded version of the model first introduced in Chapter 1. An effective audit does more than just assess the subsystems; it ensures that the subsystems mesh to form a rational approach to the creation and delivery of personnel management services.

This chapter

This chapter examines the scope, approaches, and tools used in personnel audits and research. It concludes with a review of future challenges that arise from the personnel department's day-to-day practices.

THE SCOPE OF PERSONNEL AUDITS

Definitions

A *personnel audit* evaluates the personnel activities used in an organization. The audit may include one division or an entire company. It gives feedback about the personnel function to operating managers and personnel specialists. It also provides feedback about how well managers are meeting their human resource duties. In short, the audit is an overall quality control check on personnel activities in a division or company.[5]

Benefits of audits

Several benefits result from a personnel audit. Figure 22-3 lists the major ones. An audit reminds members of the department and others of its contribution. It also creates a more professional image of the department among managers and personnel specialists. The audit helps clarify the department's role and leads to greater uniformity, especially in a geographically scattered and decentralized personnel function like the one at State Farm. Perhaps most important, it finds problems and ensures compliance with a variety of laws. These benefits explain why over two-thirds of the personnel departments in one survey conduct audits.[6]

The scope of an audit extends beyond the personnel department's actions. The department does not operate in isolation. Its success depends on how well it performs *and* on how well its programs are carried out by others in the organization. For example, consider how supervisors at the American Guard Agency reduced the effectiveness of the performance appraisal process.

To become a sergeant at the American Guard Agency, employees need two years of good or superior performance evaluations. The agency uses a critical incident appraisal form, which means that supervisors should record both positive and negative incidents as they occur. In practice, supervisors stressed employee mistakes when they recorded incidents. As

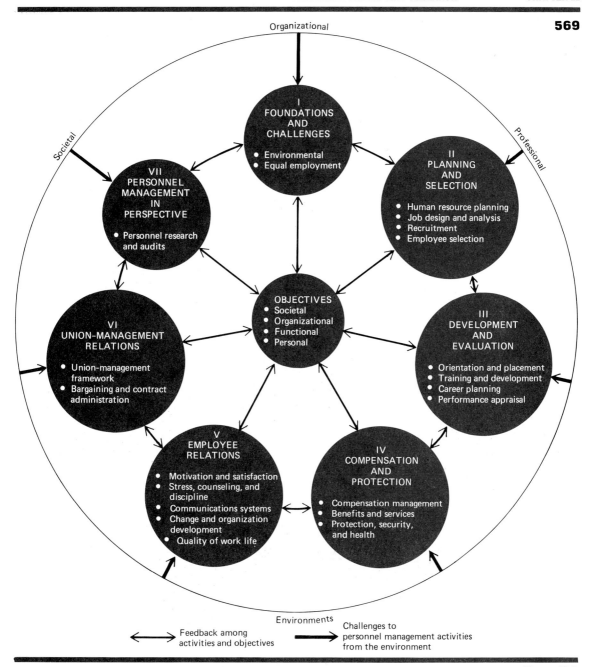

Figure 22-2

A Personnel Management Model

- *Identifies* the contributions of the personnel department to the organization.

- *Improves* the professional image of the personnel department.

- *Encourages* greater responsibility and professionalism among members of the personnel department.

- *Clarifies* the personnel department's duties and responsibilities.

- *Stimulates* uniformity of personnel policies and practices.

- *Finds* critical personnel problems.

- *Ensures* timely compliance with legal requirements.

- *Reduces* human resource costs through more effective personnel procedures.

- *Creates* increased acceptance of needed changes in the personnel department.

- *Requires* a thorough review of the department's information system.

Figure 22-3
Benefits of a Personnel Management Audit

a result, few guards received good enough ratings to qualify for sergeant. Many of them blamed the personnel department's appraisal process for their lack of promotions.

An audit uncovered the misuse of the program and recommended additional training for supervisors in the use of the critical incident method. If the audit had not uncovered this problem, employee dissatisfaction may have grown worse.

As this example illustrates, personnel problems seldom are confined to the personnel department. Thus audits should be broad in scope to be effective. They should evaluate the personnel function, the use of personnel procedures by managers, and the impact of these activities on employee goals and satisfaction.

Audit of the Personnel Function

Audits logically begin with a review of the personnel department's work.[7] Figure 22-4 lists the major areas covered. An audit touches on virtually every subject discussed in this book. To review only a few aspects of the personnel management system may ignore topics that affect the department's performance. For each item in the figure, the audit team of personnel specialists should:

Audit activities
- *Identify* who is responsible for each activity.

- *Determine* the objectives sought by each activity.

- *Review* the policies and procedures used to achieve these objectives.

- *Sample* the records in the personnel information system to learn if policies and procedures are being followed correctly.

- *Prepare* a report commending proper objectives, policies, and procedures.

PERSONNEL MANAGEMENT INFORMATION SYSTEM

AFFIRMATIVE ACTION PLANS

- Underutilization and concentration
- Affirmative action goals
- Progress toward goals

HUMAN RESOURCE PLANS

- Supply and demand estimates
- Skills inventories
- Replacement charts and summaries

JOB ANALYSIS INFORMATION

- Job standards
- Job descriptions
- Job specifications

COMPENSATION ADMINISTRATION

- Wage and salary levels
- Fringe benefit package
- Employer-provided services

STAFFING AND DEVELOPMENT

RECRUITING

- Sources of recruits
- Availability of recruits
- Employment applications

SELECTION

- Selection ratios
- Selection procedures
- Equal opportunity compliance

TRAINING AND ORIENTATION

- Orientation program
- Training objectives and procedures
- Learning rates

CAREER DEVELOPMENT

- Internal placement success
- Career planning program
- Human resource development effort

ORGANIZATION CONTROL AND EVALUATION

PERFORMANCE APPRAISALS

- Standards and measures of performance
- Performance appraisal techniques
- Evaluation interviews

LABOR-MANAGEMENT RELATIONS

- Legal compliance
- Management rights
- Dispute resolution problems

HUMAN RESOURCE CONTROLS

- Employee communications
- Discipline procedures
- Change and development procedures

PERSONNEL AUDITS

- Personnel function
- Operating managers
- Employee feedback on personnel

Figure 22-4
Major Areas Covered by a Personnel Function Audit

- *Develop* an action plan to correct errors in objectives, policies, and procedures.

- *Follow up* on the action plan to see if it solved the problems found through the audit.[8]

Admittedly, an audit of every personnel activity is time-consuming. As a result, small firms use ad hoc arrangements that often evaluate only selected areas.[9] Very large organizations have full-time audit teams similar to those used to conduct financial audits. These teams are especially useful when the personnel department is decentralized into regional or field offices, as is the case with State Farm. Through the use of audits, the organization can maintain consistency in its practices even though there are several personnel offices in different locations. And the mere existence of a corporate audit team encourages compliance and self-audits by the regional offices between visits.

> Cliff Swain, a regional personnel manager, realized that his chances for promotion to the corporate headquarters depended on how well his region's personnel offices performed. The corporate personnel audit team reviewed his region's performance every June. In preparation for the audit, he had each personnel office in the southwest region conduct a self-audit in April. Then in early May, the personnel administrators from the four branches met in Phoenix to review the results. Errors uncovered through the audit were corrected if possible. When the corporate audit team completed its review in June, they always gave Cliff's region high marks for compliance with company policies and employment laws.

Audit of Managerial Compliance

An audit also reviews how well managers comply with personnel policies and procedures. If managers ignore personnel policies or violate employee relations laws, the audit should uncover these errors so that corrective action can be started. Compliance with laws is especially important. When equal opportunity, safety, compensation, or labor laws are violated, the government holds the company responsible.

Managers may be breaking the law.

Besides ensuring compliance, the audit can improve the personnel department's image and contribution to the company. Operating managers may gain a higher respect for the department when an audit team seeks their views. If the comments of managers are acted upon, the department will be seen as more responsive to their needs. And since personnel is a service department, these actions may improve its contribution to organizational objectives. For example, consider what one audit team learned when it talked to managers of local claims offices.

> After several interviews with claims office managers, the audit team discovered a pattern to their comments. Most managers believed that the personnel department filled job vacancies quickly. The major criticism was that the department did not train recruits before assigning them to a claims office. The day-to-day pressures in the claims offices caused training to be superficial and led to many errors by new adjusters. Most managers felt that the training should be done by the personnel department at the regional office.
>
> After reading the team's report, the regional personnel manager felt confident that the selection process was satisfactory. To solve the complaints about field training, she created a two-week program for claims adjusters with her next budget increase.

Audit of Employee Satisfaction

Effective personnel departments meet both company objectives and employee needs. When employee needs are unmet, turnover, absenteeism, and union activity are more likely. To learn how well employee needs are met, the audit team gathers data from workers. The team collects information about wages, benefits, supervisory practices, career planning assistance, and the feedback employees receive about their performance.[10]

Responding to employee needs

The audit team of an automobile parts distributor received one common complaint from employees: they felt isolated because they worked in retail stores or in warehouses located all over the Midwest. They had little sense of belonging to the large company of which they were a part. To bolster sagging morale and to help employees feel that they were members of a fast-growing and dynamic organization, the personnel department started a biweekly "Payroll Action Newsletter." The two-page letter was stuffed into every pay envelope each payday. It gave tips on new developments at headquarters and at different field locations. In this way, the department used the audit to make the firm more responsive to its employees' needs.

RESEARCH APPROACHES TO AUDITS

Personnel activities are evaluated through research.[11] At times, the research may be advanced, relying on sophisticated designs and statistics.[12] Whether informal or rigorous, this research seeks to improve the personnel department's performance. Applications-oriented efforts are called *applied research*. The most common forms of applied personnel research are described in Figure 22-5 and explained in the following paragraphs.[13]

Applied research

Figure 22-5
Research Approaches of Personnel Audits

- *Comparative approach.* The personnel audit team compares its firm (or division) with another firm (or division) to uncover areas of poor performance. This approach commonly is used to compare the results of specific personnel activities or programs. It helps to detect areas of needed improvement.

- *Outside authority approach.* The audit team relies on the expertise of a consultant or published research findings as a standard against which personnel activities or programs are evaluated. The consultant or research findings may help diagnose the cause of problems.

- *Statistical approach.* From existing records, the audit team generates statistical standards against which activities and programs are evaluated. With these mathematical standards, the team may uncover errors while they are still minor.

- *Compliance approach.* By sampling elements of the personnel information system, the audit team looks for deviations from laws and company policies or procedures. Through their fact-finding efforts, the team can determine whether there is compliance with company policies and legal regulations.

- *MBO approach.* When an MBO approach is applied to the human resource area, the audit team can compare actual results with stated objectives. Areas of poor performance can be detected and reported.

Perhaps the simplest form of research is the *comparative approach.* It uses another division or company as a model. The audit team then compares their results or procedures with those of the other organization. This approach often is used with absence, turnover, and salary data. It also makes sense when a new procedure is being tried for the first time. For example, if a company installs an alcoholic rehabilitation program, it may copy a similar program at another firm or division. Then the results of both programs are compared. IBM conducts a common staffing study to compare employment levels among its various plants and facilities.

Or the personnel department may rely on an *outside authority approach.* Standards set by a consultant or from published research findings serve as a benchmark for the audit team. For example, the consultant or industrywide research may indicate that the personnel budget is usually about three-fourths of 1 percent of gross sales. This figure then serves as a rough guidepost when evaluating the personnel department's overall budget. Over half of the personnel departments in one study relied on comparisons with outside figures to evaluate their activities and services.[14]

A third approach is to develop statistical measures of performance based on the company's existing information system. For example, research into the company's records reveals its absenteeism and turnover rates. These data indicate how well personnel activities and operating managers control these problem areas. A *statistical approach* usually is supplemented with comparisons against external information, which may be gathered from other firms or industry sources. This information often is expressed as ratios that are easy to compute and use. For example, a company that averages 200 employees during the month and has 12 quit finds that its turnover rate is 6 percent.[15]

Absenteeism and turnover rates

$$\frac{\text{Number of separations}}{\text{Average number of employees}} = \frac{12}{200} \times 100 = 6 \text{ percent}$$

Likewise, if 8 employees miss work on a particular day, the absenteeism rate is 4 percent.

$$\frac{\text{Number of employees absent}}{\text{Total number scheduled to work}} = \frac{8}{200} \times 100 = 4 \text{ percent}$$

The *compliance approach* is another personnel audit strategy. This method reviews past practices to determine if those actions followed legal requirements and company policies and procedures. Often the audit team examines a sample of employment, compensation, discipline, and employee appraisal forms. The purpose of the review is to ensure that field offices and operating managers comply with internal rules and legal regulations.

A final approach is for personnel specialists and operating managers to set objectives in their area of responsibility. This *MBO* (management by objectives) *approach* creates specific goals against which performance can be measured.[16] Then the audit team researches actual performance and compares it with the previously set objectives. For example, operating managers may set a goal of resolving a higher percentage of grievances before they reach arbitration. Then the audit evaluates the trends in this area. Over two-thirds of the personnel departments in one study use this approach.[17]

No one of these audit approaches can be applied to all parts of personnel management. More commonly, audit teams use several of these strategies depending on the specific personnel activities under evaluation. Then as Figure 22-6 suggests, the audit team gives feedback on personnel activities to those in the personnel function and to operating managers and employees. Unfavorable feedback leads to corrective action that improves the contribution of personnel activities.

TOOLS OF PERSONNEL RESEARCH

Several techniques serve as information-gathering tools to collect data about the firm's personnel activities. Each tool provides partial insight into the firm's personnel activities. If these tools are used skillfully, the team can weave these insights into a clear picture of the organization's personnel activities. The tools include:

- Interviews
- Questionnaire surveys
- Record analysis
- External information
- Personnel experiments

Figure 22-6
An Overview of
the Personnel Management Audit Process

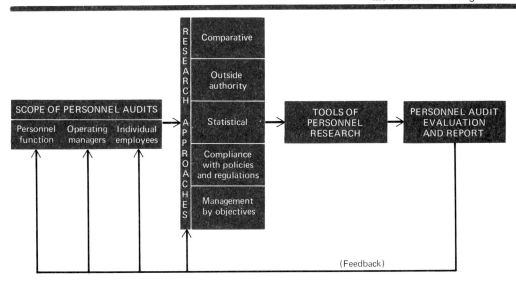

(Feedback)

576

Interviews

Interviews with employees and managers are one source of information about personnel activities. Their comments help the audit team find areas that need improvement. Criticisms by workers may pinpoint those actions that the department should take to meet employees' needs. Likewise, suggestions by managers may reveal ways to provide them with better service. When the criticisms are valid, changes should be made. But when the personnel department is correct, it may have to educate others in the firm by explaining the procedures that are being questioned.[18]

Exit interviews

Another useful source of information is the exit interview.[19] *Exit interviews* are conducted with departing employees to learn their views of the organization. Figure 22-7 shows the typical questions that are asked. The workers' comments are recorded and later reviewed during the audit to find the causes of employee dissatisfaction and other personnel management problems. Since many employees are reluctant to criticize, the exit interviewer must take time to probe and listen carefully. Then the results must be studied to uncover trends by departments, divisions, or managers.

Questionnaire Surveys

Many personnel departments supplement interviews with questionnaires. This technique is used because interviews are time-consuming, costly, and usually limited to only a few people. Through questionnaire surveys, a more accurate picture of employee treatment can be developed. Also questionnaires may lead

Figure 22-7
An Exit Interview Form

Employee's Name _____   Date Hired _____

Interviewed by   _____   Interviewed on _____

Supervisor's Name _____   Department _____

1. Were your job duties and responsibilities what you expected? _____
   If not, why: _____
2. What is your frank and honest opinion of:
   a. Your job? _____
   b. Your working conditions? _____
   c. Your orientation to your job? _____
   d. Your training provided by the company? _____
   e. Your pay? _____
   f. Your company-provided benefits and services? _____
   g. Your treatment by your manager? _____
3. What is your major reason for leaving the company? _____
   _____
4. What could we have done to keep you from leaving? _____
   _____
5. What could be done to make this a better place to work? _____
   _____

EMPLOYEE ATTITUDES ABOUT SUPERVISORS

● Are some supervisors' empolyees exceptionally satisfied or dissatisfied?

● Do specific supervisors need training in supervisory and human relations skills?

● Have attitudes improved since the last survey?

EMPLOYEE ATTITUDES ABOUT THEIR JOBS

● What are common elements of jobs that cause negative attitudes? Positive attitudes?

● Can jobs that cause poor attitudes be redesigned to improve satisfaction?

● Can jobs that cause poor attitudes be given alternative work schedules (such as shorter workweeks or flextime)?

PERCEIVED EFFECTIVENESS OF THE PERSONNEL DEPARTMENT

● Do employees think they work for a good or bad employer?

● Do employees think they merely have a job or a career?

● Do employees feel they have some place to turn in order to solve their problems besides their immediate superior?

● Do employees feel informed about company developments?

● Do employees know what is expected of them in their jobs?

● Are employees satisfied by the amount and type of feedback they get about their performance?

● Are employees satisfied by their pay? Benefits?

Figure 22-8
Critical Concerns to Be Answered by Attitude Surveys

to more candid answers than face-to-face interviews. As discussed in Chapter 17, attitude survey feedback can find answers to the concerns found in Figure 22-8. One study indicated that 45 percent of the firms use some form of attitude survey to gain feedback about employee perceptions.[20]

Record Analysis

Not all problems are revealed through employee attitudes. Sometimes insight can be obtained by studying personnel records. These reviews are done to ensure compliance with company procedures and laws. The records normally reviewed by an audit team are listed in Figure 22-9 and discussed in the following paragraphs.

Safety and health audits   An analysis of safety and health records may reveal violations of the Occupational Safety and Health Act. Under the record-keeping requirements of OSHA, the personnel audit team should find detailed records of all safety and health violations. Patterns of accidents by job classifications, location, supervisor, employee seniority, age, sex, and type of violation may uncover targets for additional safety training or equipment. Insurance companies or private consultants may assist the audit team in analyzing safety and health statistics.

Looking for patterns

Grievance audits   The audit team also may be able to uncover a pattern to employee grievances. Patterns may emerge by job classification, supervisor, union representative, age group, or contract provision. If patterns are detected, personnel specialists seek out the underlying causes of grievances. And if union officials participate in finding such patterns, they may support management's suggested changes.

Compensation audits   Audit teams carefully review the personnel department's compensation practices.[21] Primarily, they study the level of wages, benefits, and services that are provided. If jobs have been priced properly

Figure 22-9

Records Commonly Reviewed
as Part of a Personnel Audit

SAFETY AND HEALTH RECORDS

- Determine differences before and after personnel programs aimed at lowering turnover or absenteeism.

GRIEVANCE RECORDS

- Are there patterns to grievances arising from specific contract clauses or supervisors?
- Are there sections of the agreement that are unclear to union or management officials?

COMPENSATION STUDIES

- Are wages externally and internally equitable?
- Are fringe benefits understood by employees?
- Does the fringe benefit package compare favorably with local firms and national competitors?

AFFIRMATIVE ACTION PLANS

- Is the firm in compliance with all equal employment laws?
- Does the affirmative action plan address those areas where the firm is not in compliance?
- Has the firm made acceptable progress toward meeting its affirmative action goals?

PROGRAM AND POLICY STUDIES

- Does each personnel program meet its stated goals?
- Are personnel policies and procedures being followed by the personnel department and line managers?

SCRAP RATES

- Determine if training, bonuses, or other personnel programs have reduced scrap rates.

TURNOVER/ABSENTEEISM

- Are there patterns or discernable causes? By age? Sex?
- How do these records compare with those of other employers?
- Determine differences before and after personnel programs aimed at lowering turnover or absenteeism.

PRETEST/POSTTEST SCORES

- Determine if orientation or training programs improve test scores or job performance.
- How well do test scores relate to job performance?

INTERNAL PLACEMENT RECORDS

- What percentage of jobs are filled internally?
- How well do internally promoted candidates perform?
- Do replacement charts/summaries indicate sufficient promotable talent?

SELECTION RECORDS

- Is the performance of recruits better according to the source from which they were recruited?
- Are recruitment and selection costs comparable with other firms?

EMPLOYEE FILES

- Are employee files in order, properly completed?
- Do records contain accurate, up-to-date information that is useful for making employee decisions?
- Is this employee making reasonable career progress?
- Is this employee a source of discipline or interpersonal problems?

SPECIAL PROGRAMMING REPORTS

- Are special programs achieving the desired results?

Figure 22-9
(Continued)

through job evaluations and salary surveys, pay levels are fair. Benefits and services also are studied to learn if they are competitive with those of other employers and in compliance with government regulations.

Affirmative action audits The audit team also reviews the firm's compliance with equal opportunity laws.[22] Although most large employers have a compliance officer to monitor the affirmative action program, the audit team serves as a further check. The team usually concentrates its attention on hiring, placement, and compensation practices as applied to protected groups. If discrimination exists, the audit team informs management of the need for corrective action.

Program and policy audits Besides safety, grievance, compensation, and affirmative action programs, audits evaluate many other personnel programs and policies to determine if they are doing what was intended.

Two years after Seafood Canners, Inc., adopted a "promotion-from-within" policy, most supervisors still were recruited from outside the firm. Few workers applied for supervisory openings, even though these jobs were posted throughout the plant and employees were encouraged to apply. The audit team learned that during peak seasons, production workers earned more money than supervisors because of overtime pay and the incentive system. Many employees viewed supervisory jobs as more responsibility with less pay. To remedy the problem, supervisors were given a percentage of their department's production bonus. A year later, 90 percent of the supervisory openings were filled internally.

Conflict among
policies

As the Seafood Canners example illustrates, policies (promote from within) may conflict with other programs (the incentive system). And legal requirements (overtime pay) may conflict with the department's goals. Virtually every personnel policy or program affects another. Thus a thorough audit needs to include all of the major personnel policies and programs and a study of how they relate to one another.

External Information

Another tool of the audit team is external information.[23] Research that is limited to the organization's internal attitudes and records may uncover unfavorable trends. But outside comparisons also give the audit team a perspective against which their firm's activities can be judged. Some needed information is readily available, while other data may be difficult to find.

Department of Labor

Perhaps the most significant source of external information is the federal government.[24] Through the Department of Labor, numerous statistics and reports are compiled. The department regularly publishes information about future employment opportunities, employee turnover rates, work-force projections, area wage and salary surveys, severity and frequency rates of accidents, and other data that can serve as benchmarks for comparing internal information.

State agencies

State unemployment offices and industrial development commissions often provide information that also can be used for comparative purposes. Work-force demographics—age, sex, education, and racial composition—are commonly available from state agencies and are useful for evaluating affirmative action programs.

Associations

Industry associations usually make specialized data available to members. Of most use to audit teams are statistics on industry norms—such as turnover rates, absenteeism rates, standard wage rates, growth rates, standardized job descriptions, accident rates, fringe benefit costs, and sample union-management agreements.

Professional associations often provide similar information to members of the profession. Studies conducted by the association may include salary and benefit surveys, demographic profiles, and other data that can serve as standards against which the personnel department's efforts are measured. Consultants and university research bureaus may be able to provide information as well.

Personnel Experiments

Field experiment

The final tool available to personnel departments and audit teams is the research experiment, particularly the *field experiment* that compares an experimental and a control group under realistic conditions. For example, the personnel department may implement a safety training program for half of the supervisors. This half is the experimental group. The control group contains the supervisors who are not given training. Subsequent safety records of both groups are compared several months after the program is completed. If the experimental group has a significantly lower accident rate, then there is evidence that the safety training program was effective.

Experimentation does have some drawbacks. Many managers are reluctant to experiment with workers because of morale problems and potential dissatisfaction among those who were not selected. Employees involved in the experimental group may feel manipulated. And the experiment may be confounded by changes in the work environment or simply by the two groups talking to each other about the experiment.

THE AUDIT REPORT

Research approaches and tools are used to develop a picture of the organization's personnel activities. For this information to be useful, it is compiled into an audit report. The *audit report* is a comprehensive   Definition description of personnel activities that includes both commendations for effective practices and recommendations for improving practices that are ineffective. A recognition of both good and bad practices is more balanced and encourages acceptance of the report.

Often an audit report contains several parts. One part is for line managers, another is for managers of specific personnel functions, and the final part is for the personnel manager. For line managers, the report summarizes their personnel objectives, responsibilities, and duties. Examples of personnel duties include interviewing applicants, training employees, evaluating performance, motivating workers, and satisfying employee needs.

The report also identifies personnel problems. Violations of personnel policies and employee relations laws are highlighted. Poor management practices are revealed in the report along with recommendations where appropriate.

The specialists who handle employment, training, compensation, and other personnel activities also need feedback. The audit report that they receive isolates specific areas of good and poor performance. For example, one audit team observed that many jobs did not have qualified replacements. This information was given to the manager of training and development along with the recommendation for more programs to develop promising supervisors and managers. The report also may provide other feedback, such as attitudes of operating managers about the specialists' efforts. Sometimes external data show what other companies are doing and provide standards for comparison.

The personnel manager's report contains all of the information given to line managers and specialists within the personnel department. In addition, the personnel manager gets feedback about:

Attitudes of operating managers and employees about the personnel department's benefits and services

A review of the department's objectives and its plans to achieve them

- Human resource problems and their implications

- Recommendations for needed changes and the priority for their implementation

With the information contained in the audit report, the personnel manager can take a broad view of the personnel function. Instead of solving problems in a random manner, the manager now can focus on those that have the greatest potential for improving the department's contribution to the firm.[25] Perhaps most important, the audit serves as a map to future efforts and as a reference point for future audits. With knowledge of the department's present performance, the manager can make long-range plans to upgrade crucial activities. These plans identify new goals for the department, which serve as standards for future audit teams.

A PROACTIVE
PERSONNEL DEPARTMENT

Personnel management must seek a balance between company objectives, societal demands, and employee needs. To be responsible, personnel must do more than audit itself. Audits are necessary but backward-looking. They only uncover the results of past decisions. Although past performance should be evaluated, personnel departments also should look to the future in order to be more proactive.

*Backward- versus
forward-looking*

Without a future orientation, the personnel department becomes reactive, not proactive. And reactive approaches allow minor problems to become major ones. A proactive approach, however, is insufficient by itself. A systems orientation also is needed. Personnel specialists must view company objectives and employee needs as part of the total system. When managers fail to keep this perspective in mind, they may misuse human resources to achieve company objectives. They also may pursue employee needs to the exclusion of organizational goals.[26] The appropriate focus is a proactive human resource approach to personnel management within a systems framework. As explained in Chapter 1:

- *Proactive approach* means having a future orientation in order to anticipate challenges before they arise. Therefore, personnel management needs to be sensitive to emerging trends.

- *Human resource approach* means that employees should be treated with dignity. Since the standards of fair treatment change through time, personnel management should be sensitive to future developments.

- *Systems approach* means that personnel management takes place within a larger context; the organization and its environment. The department can be evaluated only with respect to its contribution to the organization. And since organizations are open systems, personnel management needs to relate to the external environment.

By applying these three approaches, personnel departments are better able to meet the future challenges that arise from the department's day-to-day practices and from the external challenges discussed throughout this book. With an effective contribution from human resource professionals, our organizations will become more productive, leading to higher standards of living through improved productivity.[27]

SUMMARY

A personnel audit evaluates the personnel activities used in an organization. Its purpose is to ensure that operating managers and personnel specialists are following personnel policies and maintaining an effective work force.

The scope of the audit involves personnel specialists, operating managers, employees, and the external environment. Inputs are sought from all four sources because each has a unique perspective. And to be truly effective, personnel activities must do more than meet the wishes of personnel experts. They also must meet the needs of employees and operating managers and the challenges from the environment.

The audit team uses a variety of research approaches and tools to evaluate personnel activities. Along with internal comparisons, the team compares the firm's efforts against those of other companies or against standards developed by external authorities and internal statistics. It may also evaluate compliance with laws or objectives set by management.

Data are gathered through interviews, questionnaires, surveys, internal records, external sources, or experimentation. Through these tools, the audit team is able to compile an audit report. The audit report gives feedback to top management, operating managers, personnel specialists, and the personnel manager. Armed with this information, the personnel manager can then develop plans to ensure that personnel activities make an effective contribution to the organization. If personnel management is to be responsible, it needs to review its past performance through audits and research. At the same time, it needs a future orientation to anticipate upcoming challenges. Finally, a proactive view encourages personnel to contribute to both employee and company goals.

With all of the challenges facing personnel management, its role is sure to grow in scope and importance. The key to this growth is unlocking the contribution that people make to organizations. It is through their contribution that an organization prospers. And it is through these life-giving and life-sustaining organizations that we prosper as individuals and as a society.

TERMS FOR REVIEW

Personnel audit

Audit team

Applied research

MBO approach

Employee assistance programs

Exit interviews

Attitude survey

Field experiment

Audit report

REVIEW AND DISCUSSION QUESTIONS

1.   In your own words, what are the benefits of a personnel audit to an organization?

2.   Why does a personnel audit go beyond the actions of personnel special-ists?

3.   What research approach do you think should be followed for each of these areas of concern to the personnel audit team: (a) the evaluation of a new company-sponsored drug rehabilitation program, (b) an analysis of employee tardiness patterns, (c) the appropriateness of present recruiting costs?

4.   Why are exit interviews an effective source of insight into employee problems in the organization?

5.   Describe how you would design a field experiment to evaluate the advantag-es of two different employee compensation programs.

6.   What types of information should be put in an audit report for (a) em-ployment manager, (b) assistant plant manager, and (c) personnel director?

7.   In the last two decades, many cultural values have changed, some rather drastically. Briefly describe how personnel management might be affected by these changes: (a) a trend toward smaller families, (b) increased participation of women in the work force, (c) increased acceptability by society of divorce.

8.   Explain why a personnel department should be proactive in its approach.

INCIDENT 22-1

United Coal Industries, Inc.

United Coal Industries ran two underground coal mines and a coke oven for converting coal into industrial coke. The locations were about sixty miles apart, and so each operation had a branch personnel office. The branch offices did their own hiring, administration of employee benefits, safety programs, and labor relations with the local union. After reading an article about the merits of the personnel management audit, the personnel director at United, Gabe Kowlowski, discussed the need for an audit with the three branch personnel officers. Their individual reactions are summarized below:

Tony Masone: We don't need an audit. It will take weeks to conduct, and it won't change a thing. Each of us branch personnel managers does the best job we know how. Besides, most of our actions are audited daily by the union. If we make a mistake in employee treatment, pay, benefits, safety, or most of the traditional audit areas, the union lets us know promptly. When you have a union, an audit is unneeded.

Joyce Laskowski: I disagree with Tony. The union would complain if we made an error against their members. But if our error is against the best interests of

United, I doubt if the union would say anything. Besides, in the affirmative action area—recruiting, selection, orientation, and training—the union has little to say of interest. An audit might even reveal areas where each branch might improve. I for one welcome an audit and a chance to see how my office compares with the other two.

Duke Cush: Joyce makes a good case for an audit, but if we were having problems in training, selection, or the other areas she mentions, we'd know it. We have gotten along for years without an audit; I see no need to put in a lot of overtime and disrupt everything else just to compile a report that will tell us what we already know.

1.   Assuming you agree with Joyce, what other arguments would you add to justify the overtime and disruption that worry Duke?

2.   Even though the union contract specifies many areas in detail, briefly describe the possible benefits from an audit of United's (a) compensation program, (b) safety program, (c) grievance process, and (d) labor relations training for supervisors.

3.   Do you think Tony and Duke would have a different attitude if they and Joyce were assigned to the audit team? Why

INCIDENT 22-2

Employee Attitudes at Anko, Inc.

Anko, Inc., rents sports equipment. Its main business involves the rental of skis and snowmobiles. During the winter, the number of employees ranges from fifty to sixty at five locations in various western resort areas.

Al Anko, the owner, hired a management consultant to evaluate employee satisfaction and attitudes. After interviewing nearly twenty workers and supervisors, the consultant developed an attitude survey that was mailed to all employees. From the interviews and attitude surveys, the consultant made the following observations:

- Nearly two-thirds of the employees felt little loyalty to the firm because they considered their jobs temporary.

- Many employees applied for work at Anko because they were interested in skiing.

- Although the firm gave few benefits, many workers commented that reduced rental rates on equipment were an important "extra."

- Every supervisor mentioned that the most important selection criterion was whether an applicant knew how to fit and adjust ski bindings.

- Over half of the employees worked split shifts from 7 to 10 A.M. and from 4 to 7 P.M., which were the hours most skis were rented and returned. Some employees liked those hours so they could ski during the day. However, employees who lived in the resort area all year long generally disliked them.

- Employee turnover was very low. But many employees indicated that they would quit if they could find a better paying job.

- Several employees who had worked for Anko in previous years thought it was unfair that they received the same hourly wage as new employees.

1. If you were the consultant, what recommendations would you make to the owner about (*a*) the use of split shifts, (*b*) the types of people recruited, and (*c*) the treatment of employees who have worked for Anko more than one season?

2. Should Anko treat employees who permanently live in the resort areas differently than they treat those who move there just for the ski season? If so, what differences in treatment do you recommend?

REFERENCES

1. Dean F. Berry, *The Politics of Personnel Research,* Ann Arbor: Bureau of Industrial Relations, Graduate School of Business Administration, University of Michigan, 1967, p. 28.

2. Fred K. Foulkes, "The Expanding Role of the Personnel Function," *Harvard Business Review,* March–April 1975, p. 84.

3. For example, one researcher found that the more "respondents reported they were aware of their employer's investment in personnel activities, the more they expressed satisfaction with the activities and the more they reported that they believed the activities had a positive effect on their performance." See Harold C. White, "Personnel Administration and Organizational Productivity: An Employee View," *The Personnel Administrator,* August 1981, p. 46.

4. State Farm Insurance Company, *Operation Understanding,* April–May 1983, pp. 1–4. (Quoted by permission of the State Farm Insurance Company.)

5. Walter R. Mahler, "Auditing PAIR," in Dale Yoder and Herbert G. Heneman, Jr. (eds.), *Planning and Auditing PAIR,* Washington: Bureau of National Affairs, Inc., 1976, p. 2-92.

6. "Personnel Policies: Research and Evaluation," ASPA-BNA Survey No. 37, *Bulletin to Management,* Mar. 22, 1979, p. 6.

7. Vytenis P. Kuraitis, "The Personnel Audit," *The Personnel Administrator,* November 1981, pp. 29–34. See also Mahler, op. cit., pp. 2–95, to 2–98; and Dow Scott, Diana Deadrick, and Stephen Taylor, "The Evolution of Personnel Research," *Personnel Journal,* August 1983, pp. 624–629.

8. Berry, op. cit., pp. 89–103.

9. Robert L. Mathis and Gary Cameron, "Auditing Personnel Practices in Smaller-Sized Organizations: A Realistic Approach," *The Personnel Administrator,* April 1981, pp. 45–50.

10. Victoria Kaminski, "There's a Better Way to Conduct Attitude Surveys," *The Personnel Administrator*, July 1983, pp. 62–63.

11. Fred Crandall, "Personnel Research for Problem-Solving," *The Personnel Administrator*, September 1978, pp. 13–16.

12. Fred Luthans and Terry L. Maris, "Evaluating Personnel Programs through the Reversal Technique," *Personnel Journal*, October 1979, pp. 692–697.

13. George Odiorne, "Evaluating the Personnel Program," in Joseph Famularo (ed.), *Handbook of Modern Personnel Administration*, New York: McGraw-Hill, 1972, chap. 8.

14. "Personnel Policies: Research and Evaluation," loc. cit.

15. Thomas F. Cawsey and William C. Wedley, "Labor Turnover Costs: Measurement and Control," *Personnel Journal*, February 1979, pp. 90–95, 121; and Joseph Lowman and Tom Snediker, "Pinpointing Avoidable Turnover with 'Cohort Analysis,'" *Personnel Journal*, April 1980, pp. 310–315.

16. Odiorne, loc. cit.

17. "Personnel Policies: Research and Evaluation," op. cit., p. 7.

18. Kaminski, op. cit.

19. Wanda R. Embrey, R. Wayne Mondy, and Robert M. Noe, "Exit Interview: A Tool for Personnel Management," *The Personnel Administrator*, May 1979, pp. 43–48.

20. "Personnel Policies: Research and Evaluation," op. cit., p. 4; and Bonnie Goldberg and George G. Gordon, "Redesigning Attitude Surveys for Management Action," *Personnel Journal*, October 1978, pp. 546–549.

21. Carl H. Driessnack, "Financial Impact on Effective Human Resources Management," *The Personnel Administrator*, January 1976, pp. 22–26.

22. Richard W. Beatty, "Research Needs of PAIR Professions in the Near Future," *The Personnel Administrator*, September 1978, pp. 17–20. See also Jac Fitz-Enz, "Measuring Human Resource Effectiveness," *The Personnel Administrator*, July 1980, pp. 33–36.

23. Beatty, op. cit.

24. Harvey S. Cohen, "Public Rewards as a Source of Employment Information," *Personnel Journal*, June 1978, pp. 313, 314, 336. Price Waterhouse and Co., "Government Information Sources," *The Personnel Administrator*, June 1980, pp. 81–82.

25. Dennis C. King and Walter G. Beevor, "Long-Range Thinking," *Personnel Journal*, October 1978, pp. 542–545; and William C. Byham, *The Uses of Personnel Research*, (American Management Association Research Study 91), New York: American Management Association, 1968.

26. Walter R. Nord and Douglas E. Durand, "What's Wrong with the Human Resources Approach to Management?" *Organizational Dynamics*, Winter 1978, pp. 13–25.

27. Jean A. Briggs and James Cook, "Help Wanted," *Forbes*, Apr. 25, 1983, p. 58; Joan Lindroth, "How to Beat the Coming Labor Shortage," *Personnel Journal*, April 1982, pp. 268–272; William B. Werther, Jr., "Out of the Productivity Box," *Business Horizons*, September–October 1982, pp. 51–59; "The Revival of Productivity," *Business Week*, February 1984, p. 92; and Edward J. O'Connor, Lawrence H. Peters, Cathy Rudolf Kline, and Donald H. Brush, "Work Constraints: Barriers to Productivity," *The Personnel Administrator*, May 1984, pp. 90–92, 94–95, 97–98.

APPENDIX

JOURNALS IN PERSONNEL MANAGEMENT AND HUMAN RESOURCES

Academy of Management Journal
Academy of Management Proceedings
Academy of Management Review
Across the Board
Administrative Management
Administrative Science Quarterly
American Journal of Sociology
Business Horizons
Business Management
Business Week
California Management Review
Canadian Business
*Compensation Review
Dun's Review
*Employee Relations
Fortune
Futurist
Harvard Business Review
Human Organizations
Human Relations
*Human Resource Management

*Publications marked with an asterisk are those devoted primarily to the field of personnel management and human resources.

*Industrial and Legal Relations Review
*Industrial Relations
Industry Week
Journal of Applied Behavioral Science
Journal of Applied Psychology
*Journal of the American Society of Training Directors
Journal of Business Communication
*Journal of Management Development
Journal of Management Studies
*Labor Law Journal
*Labor Studies Journal
*Management of Personnel Quarterly
Management Review
Monthly Labor Review
Occupational Hazards
*Organizational Behavior and Human Performance
*Organizational Dynamics
*Personnel
*Personnel Administrator
*Personnel and Guidance Journal
*Personnel Journal
*Personnel Management
*Personnel Management Abstracts
*Personnel·Psychology
*Public Personnel Management
*Public Personnel Quarterly
Supervisory Management
Wall Street Journal

GLOSSARY

Absentees. Absentees are employees who are scheduled to be at work but are not present.

Accident and sickness policies. Accident and sickness policies usually provide a minimum-care stipend for several weeks up to six months to help employees defray the loss of income while they are sick or recovering from an accident.

Accreditation. Accreditation is a process of certifying the competence of a person in an area of capability. The American Society for Personnel Administration operates an accreditation program for personnel professionals.

Active listening. Active listening requires the listener to stop talking, to remove distractions, to be patient, and to empathize with the talker.

Adverse selection. Adverse selection occurs when an insurance company has a disproportionately high percentage of insureds who will make claims in the future. Adverse selection often results when people are given a chance to buy insurance without prescreening, which often means that a higher than normal proportion have a condition that is likely to cause them to be frequent claimants.

Advisory authority. See *Staff authority*.

Affirmative action programs. Affirmative action programs are detailed plans developed by employers to undo the results of past employment discrimination, or to ensure equal opportunity in the future.

Age Discrimination in Employment Act of 1967. This act prohibits discrimination in employment because of age against those who are between 40 and 70.

American Federation of Labor and Congress of Industrial Organization (AFL-CIO). The AFL-CIO is a federation of most national unions. It exists to provide a unified focal point for the labor movement, to assist national unions, and to influence government policies that affect members and working people.

American Society for Personnel Administration (ASPA). ASPA is the major association for professional personnel specialists and administrators.

Applied research. Applied research is a study of practical problems, the solutions of which will lead to improved performance.

Arbitration. Arbitration is the submission of a dispute to a neutral third party.

Assessment centers. Assessment centers are a standardized form of employee appraisal that relies on multiple types of evaluation and multiple raters.

Attitude surveys. Attitude surveys are systematic methods of determining what employees think about their organization. The surveys are usually done through questionnaires. Attitude survey feedback results when the information collected is reported back to the participants. This process then is usually followed by action planning to identify and resolve specific areas of employee concern.

Attrition. Attrition is the loss of employees who leave the organization's employment.

Audit report. The audit report is a comprehensive description of personnel activities. It includes both commendation for effective practices and recommendations for improving practices that are ineffective.

Audit team. An audit team consists of those people who are responsible for evaluating the performance of the personnel department.

Authorization cards. Authorization cards are forms that prospective union members sign. The cards indicate their wish to have an election to determine whether a labor organization will represent the workers in their dealings with management.

Autonomous work groups. Autonomous work groups are teams of workers, without a formal company-appointed leader, who decide among themselves most decisions traditionally handled by supervisors.

Autonomy. Autonomy is having control over one's work.

Bargaining book. A bargaining book is a compilation of the negotiation team's plans for collective bargaining with labor or management. Increasingly, the bargaining book is being replaced by information stored in a company or union computer.

Bargaining committee. The union bargaining committee consists of union officials and stewards who negotiate with management's representatives to determine the wages, hours, and working conditions to be embodied in the labor agreement.

Barriers to change. Barriers to change are factors that interfere with employee acceptance and implementation of change.

Barriers to communication. Barriers to communication are interferences that may limit the receiver's understanding.

Behavioral modeling. Behavioral modeling relies on the initiation or emulation of a desired behavior. A repetition of behavior modeling helps to develop appropriate responses in specified situations.

Behaviorally anchored rating scales (BARS). BARS rate employees on a scale that has specific behavioral examples on it to guide the rater.

Behavior modification. Behavior modification states that behavior depends on its consequences.

Blind ads. Blind ads are want ads that do not identify the employer.

Bona fide occupational qualifications (BFOQ). A BFOQ occurs when an employer has a justified business reason for discriminating against a member of a protected class. The burden of proving a BFOQ generally falls on the employer.

Bottom-line test. The bottom-line test is applied by the Equal Employment Opportunity Commission to determine if a firm's overall selection process is having an adverse impact on protected groups. Even though individual steps in the selection process might exhibit an adverse impact on a protected group, the firm will be considered in compliance if the overall process does not have an adverse effect.

Boulwarism. Boulwarism is a negotiation strategy developed by General Electric. Using this approach the company made its "best" offer to the union at the beginning of negotiations. Then it remained firm unless the union could find where management had erred in the calculations used to arrive at the offer. This strategy has been ruled as an unfair labor practice by the National Labor Relations Board and by the federal courts.

Brainstorming. Brainstorming is a process by which participants provide their ideas on a stated problem during a freewheeling group session.

Buddy system The "buddy system" of orientation exists when an experienced employee is asked to show a new worker around the jobsite, conduct introductions, and answer the newcomer's questions.

Burnout. Burnout is a condition of mental, emotional, and sometimes physical exhaustion that results from substantial and prolonged stress.

Business agent. A business agent is a full-time employee of a local (usually craft) union. The business agent helps employees resolve their problems with management.

Business unionism. Business unionism describes unions that seek to improve the wages, hours, and working conditions of their members in a businesslike manner. (See *Social unionism.*)

Buy-back. Buybacks occur when an employee who attempts to resign is convinced to stay in the employment of the organization. Normally the person is "bought back" with an offer of increased wages or salary.

Cafeteria benefit programs. Cafeteria benefit programs allow employees to select the fringe benefits and services that answer their individual needs.

Career. A career is all the jobs that are held during one's working life.

Career counseling. Career counseling assists employees in finding appropriate career goals and paths.

Career development. Career development consists of those experiences and personal improvements that one undertakes to achieve a career plan.

Career goals. Career goals are the future positions that one strives to reach. These goals serve as benchmarks along one's career path.

Career path. A career path is the sequential pattern of jobs that form one's career.

Career planning. Career planning is the process by which one selects career goals and paths to those goals.

Career plateau. A career plateau occurs when an employee is in a position that he or she does well enough not to be demoted or fired but not well enough to be promoted.

Cause and effect diagrams. Cause and effect or fishbone diagrams begin with a known effect such as a defective part. From that effect, an individual or group attempts to brainstorm the various possible contributing factors—usually people, machines, materials, and methods. Then each element that could be contributing toward this effect undergoes further scrutiny.

Change agents. Change agents are people who have the role of stimulating and coordinating change within a group.

Change objective of the personnel department. The change objective of the personnel department is to manage change in ways that increase the benefits and reduce the costs.

Checkoff. A checkoff provision in a union-management labor agreement requires the employer to deduct union dues from employee paychecks and to remit those moneys to the union.

Civil Rights Act of 1964. This act was passed to make various forms of discrimination illegal.

Closed shop. A closed shop is a workplace where all employees are required to be members of the union *before* they are hired. These arrangements are illegal under the National Labor Relations Act.

Codetermination. Codetermination is a form of industrial democracy first popularized in West Germany. It gives workers the right to have representatives vote on management decisions.

Cognitive dissonance. Cognitive dissonance results from a gap between what one expects and what one experiences.

Cognitive models of motivation. Cognitive models of motivation depend on the thinking or feeling (that is, cognition) within each individual.

Coinsurance clause. A coinsurance clause is a provision in an insurance policy that requires the employee to pay a percentage of the insured's expenses.

Communication. Communication is the transfer of information and understanding from one person to another.

Communication overload. A communication overload occurs when employees receive more communication inputs than they can process or more than they need.

Communication process. A communication process is the method by which a sender reaches a receiver. It requires that an idea be developed, encoded, transmitted, received, decoded, and used.

Communication system. A communication system provides formal and informal methods for moving information throughout an organization so that appropriate decisions are made.

Comparable worth. Comparable worth is the idea that a job should be evaluated as to its value to the organization and then paid accordingly. Thus jobs of comparable worth would be paid equally. For example, two people with widely different jobs would both receive the same pay if the two jobs were of equal value to the employer.

Comparative evaluation approaches. Comparative evaluation approaches are a collection of different methods that compare one person's performance with that of coworkers.

Compensation. Compensation is what employees receive in exchange for their work.

Comprehensive Employment and Training Act of 1973 (CETA). CETA was a broad-ranging act designed to provide job training, employment, and job-hunting assistance to less advantaged persons. It has since been replaced by the *Job Partnership Training Act.*

Concentration in employment. Concentration exists when an employer (or some subdivision such as a department) has a higher proportion of employees from a protected class than is found in the employer's labor market. (See *Underutilization*.)

Conciliation agreement. A conciliation agreement is a negotiated settlement agreeable to the EEOC and to all parties involved. Its acceptance closes the case.

Constructs. Constructs are substitutes for actual performance. For example, a score on a test is a construct for actual learning.

Content theories of motivation. Content theories of motivation describe the needs or desires within us that initiate behavior.

Contract labor. Contract labor consists of people who are hired (and often trained) by an independent agency that supplies companies with needed human resources for a fee.

Contributory plans. Contributory plans are fringe benefits that require both the employer and the employee to contribute to the cost of the insurance, retirement, or other employer benefit.

Corrective discipline. Corrective discipline is an action that follows a rule infraction and seeks to discourage further infractions so that future acts are in compliance with standards.

Counseling. Counseling is the discussion of an employee problem with the general objective of helping the worker cope with it.

Counseling functions. Counseling functions are the activities performed by counselors. They include advice, reassurance, communication, release of emotional tension, clarified thinking, and reorientation.

Craft unions. Craft unions are labor organizations that seek to include all workers who have a common skill, such as carpenters or plumbers.

Critical incident method. The critical incident method requires the rater to report statements that describe extremely good or extremely bad employee behavior. These statements are called critical incidents, and they are used as examples of good or bad performance in rating the employee.

Decision-making authority. See *Line authority.*

Deductible clause. A deductible clause is a provision in an insurance policy that requires the insured to pay a specified amount of a claim before the insurer is obligated to pay.

Deferral jurisdictions. Deferral jurisdictions are areas in the United States where the EEOC will refer a case to another (usually a state or local) agency.

Delegation. Delegation is the process of getting others to share a manager's work. It requires the manager to assign duties, grant authority, and create a sense of responsibility.

Delphi technique. The Delphi technique solicits predictions from a panel of experts about some specified future development(s). The collective estimates are then reported back to the panel so that the members may adjust their opinions. This process is repeated until a general agreement on future trends emerges.

Demographics. Demographics is the study of population characteristics.

Demotions. Demotions occur when an employee is moved from one job to another that is lower in pay, responsibility, and organizational level.

Development. Development represents those activities that prepare an employee for future responsibilities.

Dictionary of Occupational Titles (DOT). The *Dictionary of Occupational Titles* is a federal government publication that provides detailed job descriptions and job codes for most occupations in government and industry.

Differential validity. Differential validity is used to demonstrate that tests or other selection criteria are valid for different subgroups or protected classes.

Directive counseling. Directive counseling is the process of listening to an employee's emotional problems, deciding with the employee what should be done, and then telling and motivating the employee to do it. (See *Nondirective counseling.*)

Discipline. Discipline is management action to encourage compliance with the organization's standards.

Dismissal. Dismissal is the ultimate disciplinary action because it separates the employee from the employer for a cause.

Disparate impact. Disparate impact occurs when the results of an employer's actions have a different effect on one or more protected classes.

Disparate treatment. Disparate treatment occurs when members of a protected class receive unequal treatment.

Downward communication. Downward communication is information that begins at some point in the organization and then feeds down the hierarchy to inform or influence others in the firm.

Dual responsibility for personnel management. Since both line and staff managers are responsible for employees, production, and quality of work life, a dual responsibility for personnel management exists.

Due process. Due process means that established rules and procedures for disciplinary action are followed and that employees have an opportunity to respond to the charges made against them.

Early retirement. Early retirement occurs when a worker retires from an employer before the "normal" retirement age.

Employee assistance programs (EAPs). EAPs are company-sponsored programs to help employees overcome their personal problems through direct company assistance, counseling, or outside referral.

Employee handbook. The employee handbook explains key benefits, policies, and general information about the employer.

Employee involvement (EI). Employee involvement consists of a variety of systematic methods that enable employees to participate in the decisions that affect them.

Employee Retirement Income Security Act (ERISA). ERISA was passed by Congress to ensure that employer pension plans meet minimum participation, vesting, and funding requirements.

Employment freeze. An employment freeze occurs when the organization curtails future hiring.

Employment function. The employment function is that aspect of personnel responsible for recruiting, selecting, and hiring new workers. This function is usually handled by the employment section or employment manager of a large personnel department.

Employment references. Employment references are evaluations of an employee's work performance. They are provided by past employers.

Employment tests. Employment tests are devices that assess the probable match between the applicants and the job requirements.

Equal Employment Act of 1972. This act strengthened the role of the Equal Employment Opportunity Commission by amending the Civil Rights Act of 1964. The 1972 law empowered the EEOC to initiate court action against noncomplying organizations.

Equal employment opportunity. Equal employment opportunity means giving people a fair chance to succeed without discrimination based on factors unrelated to job performance—such as age, race, or national origin.

Equal Employment Opportunity Commission (EEOC). The EEOC is the federal agency responsible for enforcing Title VII of the Civil Rights Act, as amended.

Equal employment opportunity laws. Equal employment opportunity laws are a family of federal and state acts that seek to ensure equal employment opportunities for members of protected groups.

Equal Pay Act of 1963. This act prohibits discrimination in pay because of a person's sex.

Equifinality. Equifinality means that there are usually multiple paths to an objective.

Equity theory. Equity theory suggests that people are motivated to close the gap between their efforts and the perceived amount and appropriateness of the rewards they receive.

Ergonomics. Ergonomics is the study of biotechnical relationships between the physical attributes of workers and the physical demands of the job. The object is to reduce physical and mental strain in order to increase productivity and quality of work life.

Error of central tendency. The error of central tendency occurs when a rater evaluates employee performance as neither good nor poor, even when some employees perform exceptionally well or poorly. Instead, the rater rates everyone as average.

Evaluation interviews. Evaluation interviews are performance review sessions that give employees feedback about their past performance or about their future potential.

Executive order. Executive orders are presidential decrees that normally apply to government contractors or managers in the executive branches of the federal government.

Existence-relatedness-growth theory. Alderfer's existence-relatedness-growth theory suggests that lower-order needs can be grouped under the heading of existence. Relatedness needs encompass interpersonal relationships and include the acceptance, belonging, and security that come from approval of those in the organization. Growth needs challenge an individual's capabilities and cause personal growth on the job.

Exit interviews. Exit interviews are conversations with departing employees to learn their views of the organization.

Expectancy. Expectancy is the strength of a person's belief that an act will lead to a particular outcome.

Expectancy theory. Expectancy theory states that motivation is the result of the outcome one seeks and one's estimate that action will lead to the desired outcome.

Expedited arbitration. Expedited arbitration is an attempt to speed up the arbitration process. It may include an arrangement with the arbitrator for him or her to be available on short notice (one or two days) and to render a quick decision at the conclusion of the hearings (sometimes an oral decision is used in these cases).

Experience rating. Experience rating is a practice whereby state unemployment offices determine an employer's unemployment compensation tax rate based on the employer's previous experience in providing stable employment.

Experiential learning. Experiential learning means that participants learn by experiencing in the training environment the kinds of problems they face on the job.

Experimental Negotiations Agreement (ENA). The ENA was an arrangement between major steel producers and the United Steelworkers Union. It included an agreement by the union not to strike at the conclusion of the contract in return for management's agreement to submit unresolved issues to arbitration.

Exposure. Exposure means becoming known by those who decide on promotions, transfers, and other career opportunities.

Extrapolation. Extrapolation involves extending past rates of change into the future.

Facilitator. A facilitator is someone who assists quality circles and the quality circle leader in identifying and solving workplace problems.

Factor comparison method. The factor comparison method is a form of job evaluation that allocates a part of each job's wage to key factors of the job. The result is a relative evaluation of the organization's jobs.

Fair employment practices. Fair employment practices are state and local laws that prohibit employer discrimination in employment against members of protected classes.

Fair Labor Standards Act of 1938 (FLSA). FLSA is a comprehensive federal law affecting compensation management. It sets minimum-wage, overtime pay, equal pay, child labor, and record-keeping requirements.

Federal Mediation and Conciliation Service (FMCS). The FMCS was created by the Labor Management Relations Act of 1947 to help labor and management resolve negotiation impasses peacefully through mediation and conciliation without resort to a strike. The FMCS also is a source of qualified labor arbitrators.

Feedback. Feedback is information that helps evaluate the success or failure of an action or system.

Field experiment. A field experiment is research that allows the researchers to study employees under realistic conditions to learn how experimental and control subjects react to new programs and to other changes.

Field review method. The field review method requires skilled representatives of the personnel department to go into the "field" and assist supervisors with their ratings. Often it is the personnel department's representative that actually fills out the evaluation form after interviewing the supervisor about employee performance.

Flextime. Flextime is a scheduling innovation that abolishes rigid starting and ending times for each day's work. Instead, employees are allowed to begin and end the workday at their discretion, usually within a range of hours.

Flexyear. Flexyear is an employee scheduling concept that allows workers to be off the job for part of the year. Employees usually work the normal workyear in less than twelve months.

Forced choice method. The forced choice method of employee performance evaluation requires the rater to choose the most descriptive statement in each pair of statements about the employee being rated.

Forecasts. Forecasts predict the organization's future needs.

Four-fifths rule. The four-fifths rule is a test used by the EEOC. When the selection ratio of protected-class applicants is less than 80 percent (or four-fifths) of the selection ratio for majority applicants, adverse impact is assumed.

Fully insured workers. Fully insured workers are employees who have contributed forty quarters (ten years) to social security.

Functional authority. Functional authority allows staff experts to make decisions in specified circumstances that are normally reserved for line managers.

Funded plan. Funded plans require an employer to accumulate moneys in advance so that the organization's contribution plus interest will cover its obligation.

Funded retirement plans. A funded retirement plan is one in which the employer sets aside sufficient money to meet the future payout requirements.

Grapevine communication. Grapevine communication is an informal system that arises spontaneously from the social interaction of people in the organization.

Grievance procedure. A grievance procedure is a multistep process that the employer and union jointly use to resolve disputes that arise under the terms of the labor agreement.

Griggs v. Duke Power Company. The U.S. Supreme Court case held that when an employment criterion disproportionately discriminates against a protected class, the employer is required to show how the criterion is job-related.

Guaranteed annual wage. A guaranteed annual wage assures workers of receiving a minimum amount of work or pay during the course of a year.

Halo effect. The halo effect is a bias that occurs when a rater allows some information to disproportionately prejudice the final evaluation.

Harassment. Harassment occurs when a member of an organization treats an employee in a disparate manner because of the worker's sex, race, religion, age, or other protected classification.

Health maintenance organizations (HMOs). HMOs are a form of health insurance whereby the insurer provides the professional staff and facilities needed to treat their insured policyholders for a predetermined monthly fee.

Hierarchy of needs. Since all needs cannot be expressed at once, there is a priority in the way these needs find expression. This ordering or priority forms a hierarchy, beginning with physical and security needs and continuing with social, esteem, and self-fulfillment needs.

Higher-order needs. Higher-order needs include the need for social acceptance, esteem, and self-fulfillment.

Hot-stove rule. The hot-stove rule states that disciplinary action should have the same characteristics as the penalty a person receives from touching a hot stove. That is, the discipline should be with warning, immediate, consistent, and impersonal.

House organs. A house organ is any regularly published organizational magazine, newspaper, or bulletin directed to employees.

Human resource forecasts. Human resource forecasts predict the organization's future demand for employees.

Human resource planning. Human resource planning systematically forecasts an organization's future supply of, and demand for, employees.

Human resources. Human resources are the people who are ready, willing, and able to contribute to organizational goals.

Imminent danger. An imminent danger is a situation that is likely to lead to death or serious injury if allowed to continue.

Incentive systems. Incentive systems link compensation and performance by paying employees for actual results, not for seniority or hours worked.

Indexation. Indexation is a method of estimating future employment needs by matching employment growth with some index, such as sales growth.

Industrial democracy. Industrial democracy refers to giving employees a larger voice in making the work-related decisions that affect them.

Industrial unions. Industrial unions are labor organizations that seek to include all of an employer's eligible workers regardless of whether they are skilled, semiskilled, or unskilled.

In-house complaint procedures. In-house complaint procedures are organizationally developed methods for employees to register their complaints about various aspects of the organization.

Job analysis. Job analysis systematically collects, evaluates, and organizes information about jobs.

Job analysis schedules. Job analysis schedules are checklists or questionnaires that seek to collect information about jobs in a uniform manner. (They are also called job analysis questionnaires.)

Job banks. Job banks exist in state employment security offices. They are used to match applicants with job openings.

Job code. A job code uses numbers, letters, or both to provide a quick summary of the job and its content.

Job description. A job description is a written statement that explains the duties, working conditions, and other aspects of a specified job.

Job enlargement. Job enlargement means adding more tasks to a job in order to increase the job cycle.

Job enrichment. Job enrichment means adding more responsibilities, autonomy, and control to a job.

Job evaluations. Job evaluations are systematic procedures to determine the relative worth of jobs.

Job families. Job families are groups of different jobs that require similar skills.

Job-Flo. Job-Flo is a monthly report of frequently listed openings from job banks throughout the country.

Job grading. Job grading is a form of job evaluation that assigns jobs to predetermined classifications according to the job's relative worth to the organization. This technique is also called the job classification method.

Jobholder reports. Jobholder reports are reports to employees about the firm's economic performance.

Job Information Service. The Job Information Service is a feature of state employment security agencies that enables job seekers to review job bank listings in their efforts to find employment.

Job instruction training. Job instruction training is training received directly on the job. It is also called "on-the-job training."

Job performance standards. Job performance standards are the work requirements that are expected from an employee on a particular job.

Job posting. Job posting informs employees of unfilled job openings and the qualifications for these jobs.

Job progression ladder. A job progression ladder is a particular career path where some jobs have prerequisites.

Job ranking. Job ranking is one form of job evaluation that subjectively ranks jobs according to their overall worth to the organization.

Job rotation. Job rotation is the process of moving employees from one job to another in order to allow them more variety in their jobs and the opportunity to learn new skills.

Job satisfaction. Job satisfaction is the favorableness or unfavorableness with which employees view their work.

Job sharing. Job sharing is a scheduling innovation that allows two or more workers to share the same job, usually by each working part-time.

Job specifications. A job specification describes what a job demands of employees who do it and the human skills that are required.

Job Training Partnership Act of 1983. This act provides federal funds to authorized training contractors, often city or state government agencies. These moneys are used to train people in new, employable skills. (It replaces the Comprehensive Education and Training Act of 1973.)

Joint study committees. Joint study committees include representatives from management and the union who meet away from the bargaining table to study some topic of mutual interest in the hope of finding a solution that is mutually satisfactory.

Juniority. Juniority provisions require that layoffs be offered first to senior workers who may accept or refuse them. If sufficient senior workers do not accept the layoffs, then management is free to lay off the least senior workers.

Key jobs. Key jobs are those that are common in the organization and in its labor market.

Key subordinates. Key subordinates are those employees who are crucial to a manager's success in a particular job.

Labor agreement. A labor agreement, which is also called a labor contract, is a legal document that is negotiated between the union and the employer. It states the terms and conditions of employment.

Laboratory training. Laboratory training is a form of group training primarily used to enhance interpersonal skills.

Labor Management Relations Act of 1947 (LMRA). The LMRA, also known as the Taft-Hartley Act, amended the National Labor Relations Act of 1935 by designating specific union actions that were considered to be unfair labor practices. The act also created the Federal Mediation and Conciliation Service and enabled the President of the United States to call for injunctions in national emergency strikes.

Labor-Management Reporting and Disclosure Act of 1959 (LMRDA). The LMRDA, also called the Landrum Griffin Act, amended the National Labor Relations Act. It created the union members' "bill of rights" by giving union members certain rights in dealing with their union. The law also established detailed reporting requirements for those who handle union funds.

Labor market. The labor market is the area in which the employer recruits.

Labor market analysis. Labor market analysis is the study of the employee's labor market to evaluate the present or future availability of workers.

Landrum-Griffin Act. See *Labor-Management Reporting and Disclosure Act of 1959.*

Law of effect. The law of effect states that people learn to repeat behaviors that have favorable consequences, and they learn to avoid behaviors that have unfavorable consequences.

Layoffs. Layoffs are the separation of employees from the organization for economic or business reasons.

Learning curve. A learning curve is a visual representation of the rate at which one learns given material through time.

Learning curve for change. The learning curve for change is a charted representation of the period of adjustment and adaptation to change required by an organization.

Learning principles. Learning principles are guidelines to the ways in which people learn most effectively.

Legal insurance. Legal insurance is usually a group insurance plan provided by the employer that reimburses the insureds when they have specified legal expenses or provides the insureds with access to legal assistance at predetermined (and usually low) rates.

Leniency bias. A leniency bias occurs when employees are rated higher than their performance justifies.

Leveraging. Leveraging refers to resigning in order to further one's career with another employer.

Life plan. A life plan is that often ill-defined series of hopes, dreams, and personal goals that each person carries through life.

Line authority. Line authority allows managers to direct others and to make decisions about the organization's operations.

Listening. Listening is a receiver's positive effort to understand a message transmitted by sound.

Local unions. Local unions are the smallest organizational unit of a union. They are responsible for representing the members at the worksite.

Long-term disability. Long-term disability insurance provides a proportion of a disabled employee's wage or salary. These policies typically have long waiting periods and seldom allow the employee to attain the same income level that existed before the disability.

Lost-time accidents. These are severe job-related accidents that cause the employee to lose time from his or her job.

Maintenance factors. Maintenance factors are those elements in the work setting that lead to employee dissatisfaction when they are not adequately provided. These factors are also called hygiene factors or dissatisfiers. They include working conditions and fringe benefits.

"Make-whole" remedies. When an individual is mistreated in violation of employment laws, the wrongdoer usually is required to make up the losses that were suffered by the employee because of the wrongdoing.

Management by objectives (MBO). MBO requires an employee and superior to jointly establish performance goals for the future. Employees are subsequently evaluated on how well they have obtained these agreed upon objectives.

Management inventories. Management inventories summarize the skills and abilities of management personnel. (See *Skills inventories*, which are used for nonmanagement employees.)

Management rights. Management rights are the rights and freedoms that an employer needs to manage the enterprise effectively. These areas of discretion usually are reserved by management in the labor agreement.

Maturity curves. Maturity curves are used to compensate workers based on their seniority and performance. Normally, these compensation plans are limited to professional and technical workers.

Mentor. A mentor is someone who offers informal career advice.

Merit-based promotions. Merit-based promotions occur when an employee is promoted because of superior performance in the present job.

Merit raises. Merit raises are pay increases given to individual workers according to an evaluation of their performance.

Motivation. Motivation is a person's drive to take action because that person wants to do so.

Motivational factors. Motivational factors are those elements in the work environment that motivate the individual. They are sometimes called motivators and satisfiers.

National Institute of Occupational Safety and Health (NIOSH). NIOSH was created by the Occupational Safety and Health Act to conduct research and to develop additional safety and health standards.

National Labor Relations Act of 1935 (NLRA). The NLRA, also known as the Wagner Act, was passed by Congress to ensure that covered employees could join (or refrain from joining) unions for the purpose of their own mutual aid and protection and for negotiating with employers. The act also created the National Labor Relations Board.

National Labor Relations Board (NLRB). The NLRB was created by the National Labor Relations Act to prevent unfair labor practices and to conduct union representation elections.

National unions. National unions are the parent body that helps organize, charter, guide, and assist their affiliated local unions.

Needs assessment. Needs assessment diagnoses present problems and future challenges that can be met through training and development.

Net benefit. Net benefit means that there will be a surplus of benefits after all costs are included.

Nominal group techniques (NGT). NGT is a group method of drawing out ideas from people on a specified topic. It requires participants to list their ideas and then share them in round-robin fashion with the group and a facilitator. Once all the ideas of the group are vented, duplicate ideas are eliminated and clarification follows. Then the members of the group vote on what they believe to be the best or the most important items they uncovered through the NGT process.

Noncontributory benefit plans. Noncontributory benefit plans are fringe benefits that are paid entirely by the employer. (See *Contributory benefit plans.*)

Nondeferral jurisdictions. Nondeferral jurisdictions are areas where the EEOC finds no qualified agency to which it may defer cases.

Nondirective counseling. Nondirective, or client-centered, counseling is the process of skillfully listening to an employee and encouraging him or her to explain bothersome problems, to understand them, and to determine appropriate solutions.

Nonverbal communication. Nonverbal communication is action that communicates without spoken words.

Obsolescence. Obsolescence results when an employee no longer possesses the knowledge or ability to perform successfully.

Occupational Outlook Handbook. The *Occupational Outlook Handbook* is published by the U.S. Department of Labor. It indicates the future need for certain jobs.

Occupational Safety and Health Act of 1970 (OSHA). OSHA is a broad-ranging law that requires employers to provide a work environment that is free of recognized safety and health hazards.

Occupational Safety and Health Administration. The Occupational Safety and Health Administration is located in the U.S. Department of Labor and is responsible for enforcing the *Occupational Safety and Health Act.*

Occupational Safety and Health Review Commission. The Occupational Safety and Health Review Commission is the federal agency that reviews on appeal the fines given to employers by the Occupational Safety and Health Administration for safety and health violations.

Open communication. Open communication exists when people feel free to communicate all relevant messages.

Open-door policy. An open-door policy encourages employees to go to their manager or even to higher management with any problem that concerns them.

Open system. See *System.*

Organizational climate. Organizational climate is the favorableness or unfavorableness of the environment for people in the organization.

Organizational development (OD). OD is an intervention strategy that uses group processes to focus on the whole organization in order to bring about planned changes.

Organizational development process. The OD process is complex and difficult to implement. It consists of seven steps: initial diagnosis, data collection, data feedback and confrontation, action planning and problem solving, team building, intergroup development and evaluation, and follow-up.

Organization character. An organization's character is the product of all the organization's features—such as its people, objectives, technology, size, age, unions, policies, successes, and failures. It is the organization's "personality."

Organizing committee. An organizing committee consists of employees who guide the efforts needed to organize their fellow workers into a labor organization.

Orientation programs. Orientation programs familiarize primarily new employees with their roles, the organization, its policies, and other employees.

Outplacement. Outplacement occurs when an organization assists its present employees in finding jobs with other employers.

Pareto analysis. Pareto analysis is a means of collecting data about the types or causes of production problems in descending order of frequency.

Participation rates. Participation rates are the percentages of working-age men and women in the work force.

Participative counseling. Participative counseling seeks to find a balance between directive and nondirective counseling techniques, with the counselor and the counselee participating in the discussion and solution of the problem.

Part-time layoffs. Part-time layoffs occur when an employer lays off workers without pay for a part of each week, such as each Friday.

Paternalism. Paternalism exists when management assumes that it alone is the best judge of employee needs and therefore does not seek or act upon employee suggestions.

Path-goal personnel strategy. The path-goal personnel strategy is used by the personnel department when it attempts to improve the path toward a goal (such as reducing red tape) and then tries to improve the outcomes at the end of the path (such as improving the amount of merit pay or other rewards).

Pattern bargaining. Pattern bargaining occurs when the same or essentially the same contract is used for several firms, often in the same industry.

Patterns and practices. When discrimination is found to exist against a large number of individuals who are in a protected class, a *pattern and practice* case exists.

Performance appraisal. Performance appraisal is the process by which organizations evaluate employee performance.

Performance measures. Performance measures are the ratings used to evaluate employee performance.

Performance standards. Performance standards are the benchmarks against which performance is measured.

Personnel barriers. Personnel barriers are communication interferences that arise from human emotions, values, and limitations.

Personal leave days. Personal leave days are normal workdays that an employee is entitled to take off. (In some firms personal leave days are used instead of sick days.)

Personnel audit. A personnel audit evaluates the personnel activities used in an organization.

Personnel management. Personnel management is the study of how employers obtain, develop, utilize, evaluate, maintain, and retain the right numbers and types of workers. Its purpose is to provide organizations with an effective work force.

Peter Principle. The Peter Principle states that in a hierarchy, people tend to rise to their level of incompetence.

Piecework. Piecework is a type of incentive system that compensates workers for each unit of output.

Placement. Placement is the assignment of an employee to a new or different job.

Point system. The point system is a form of job evaluation that assesses the relative importance of the job's key factors in order to arrive at the relative worth of jobs.

Political grievances. Political grievances are filed or supported because of their political implications, not their merits.

Portability clauses. Portability clauses allow workers to transfer accumulated pension rights to their subsequent employer when they change jobs.

Position analysis questionnaire (PAQ). The PAQ is a standardized, preprinted form that collects specific information about jobs.

Precedent. A precedent is a new standard that arises from past practices of either the company or the union.

Preferential quota systems. Preferential quota systems exist when a proportion of the job openings, promotions, or other employment opportunities is reserved for members of a protected class who have been previously discriminated against.

Pregnancy Discrimination Act of 1978. This act prevents discrimination in employment against women who are pregnant and able to perform their jobs. The law amends the Civil Rights Act of 1964.

Prevailing wage rates. Prevailing wage rates are the rates most commonly paid for a given job in a specific geographical area. They are determined by a wage and salary survey.

Preventive discipline. Preventive discipline is action taken to encourage employees to follow standards and rules so that infractions are prevented.

Private placement agencies. Private placement agencies are for-profit organizations that help job seekers find employment.

Proactive management. Proactive management exists when decision makers anticipate problems and take affirmative steps to minimize those problems rather than wait until after a problem occurs before taking action.

Problem-solving interviews. These types of interviews rely on questions that are limited to hypothetical situations or problems. The applicant is evaluated on how well the problems are solved.

Production bonuses. Production bonuses are a type of incentive system that provides employees with additional compensation when they surpass stated production goals.

Productivity. Productivity is the ratio of a firm's output (goods and services) divided by its input (people, capital, materials, energy).

Professional associations. Professional associations are groups of workers who voluntarily join together to further their profession and their professional development. When these associations undertake to negotiate for their members, they are also labor organizations.

Profit sharing. Profit sharing exists when an organization shares a proportion of its profits with the workers, usually on an annual basis.

Profit-sharing plans. Profit-sharing plans enable eligible employees to receive a proportion of the organization's profits.

Progressive discipline. Progressive discipline requires strong penalties for repeated offenses.

Promotion. A promotion occurs when an employee is moved from one job to another that is higher in pay, responsibility, and/or organizational level.

Protected groups. Protected groups are classes of people who are protected from discrimination under one or more laws.

Psychic costs. Psychic costs are the stresses, strains, and anxieties that affect a person's inner self during a period of change.

Pygmalion effect. The Pygmalion effect occurs when people live up to the highest expectations others hold of them.

Qualifiable worker. A qualifiable worker is one who does not currently possess all of the requirements, knowledge, skills, or abilities to do the job, but who will become qualified through additional training and experience.

Qualified handicapped. The qualified handicapped are those mentally or physically handicapped individuals who, with reasonable accommodations, can perform successfully.

Quality circles. Quality circles are small groups of employees who meet regularly with a common leader to identity and solve work-related problems.

Quality of work life. Quality of work life means having good supervision, good working conditions, good pay and benefits, and an interesting, challenging, and rewarding job.

Quality of work life efforts. Quality of work life efforts are systematic attempts by an organization to give workers a greater opportunity to affect their jobs and their contributions to the organization's overall effectiveness.

Rap sessions. Rap sessions are meetings between managers and groups of employees to discuss complaints, suggestions, opinions, or questions.

Rate ranges. Rate ranges are pay ranges for each job class.

Rating scale. A rating scale requires the rater to provide a subjective evaluation of an individual's performance along a scale from low to high.

Rational validity. Rational validity exists when tests include reasonable samples of the skills needed to perform successfully or where there is an obvious relationship between performance and other characteristics that are assumed to be necessary for successful job performance.

Reactive management. Reactive management exists when decision makers respond to problems instead of anticipating problems before they occur. (See *Proactive management.*)

Realistic job preview (RJP). An RJP allows the job applicant to see the type of work, equipment, and working conditions involved in the job before the hiring decision is finalized.

Recency effect. The recency effect is a rater bias that occurs when a rater allows recent employee performance to sway the overall evaluation.

Recruitment. Recruitment is the process of finding and attracting capable applicants for employment.

Red-circle rates. Red-circle rates are wages or salaries that are inappropriate for a given job according to the job evaluation plan.

Refreezing. Refreezing requires the integration of what has been learned into actual practice.

Regulations. Regulations are legally enforceable rules developed by government agencies to ensure compliance with laws that the agency interprets and administers.

Rehabilitation Act of 1973. This act prohibits discrimination against those who are handicapped but qualified to perform work. It applies to employees who receive federal moneys and to federal agencies.

Reinforcement schedules. Reinforcement schedules are the different ways that behavior reinforcement can be given.

Relations by objectives. Relations by objectives is a program created by the Federal Mediation and Conciliation Service to improve labor-management cooperation between participating parties.

Reliablity. Reliability means that a selection device (usually a test) yields consistent results each time an individual takes it.

Relocation programs. Relocation programs are company-sponsored fringe benefits that assist employees who must move in connection with their jobs.

Repetition. Repetition facilitates learning through repeated review of the material to be learned.

Replacement charts. Replacement charts are visual presentations of who will replace whom in the organization when a job opening occurs.

Resistance to change. Resistance to change arises from employee opposition to change.

Résumé. A résumé is a brief listing of an applicant's work experience, education, personal data, and other information relevant to the applicant's employment qualifications.

Reverse discrimination. Reverse discrimination occurs when an employer seeks to hire or to promote a member of a protected class over an equally (or better) qualified candidate who is not a member of a protected class.

Reward-performance model. The reward-performance model combines the strengths of other motivational approaches. It argues that properly reinforced behavior enhances an individual's self-image and, therefore, the individual's self-expectations. These self-expectations lead to greater effort, and the rewards for this effort continue to reinforce the behavior.

Role ambiguity. Role ambiguity results when people are uncertain of what is expected of them in a given job.

Role playing. Role playing is a training technique that requires the trainee to assume different identities in order to learn how others feel under different circumstances.

Sandwich model of discipline. The sandwich model suggests that a corrective comment should be sandwiched between two positive comments in order to make the corrective comment more acceptable.

Scanlon Plan. The Scanlon Plan is an incentive program that compensates eligible employees for improvements in labor costs that are better than the previously established company norms.

Search firms. Search firms are private for-profit organizations that exist to help employers locate hard-to-find applicants.

Selection interviews. Selection interviews are a step in the selection process whereby the applicant and the employer's representative have a face-fo-face meeting.

Selection process. The selection process is a series of specific steps used to decide which recruits should be hired.

Selection ratio. The selection ratio is the ratio of the number of applicants hired to the total number of applicants.

Self-actualization. See *Self-fulfillment needs.*

Self-fulfillment needs. Self-fulfillment needs are the needs people have that make them feel they are becoming all that they are capable of becoming. This need also is called self-actualization.

Self-funding. Self-funding occurs when an organization agrees to meet its insurance obligations out of its own resources.

Semantic barriers. Semantic barriers are limitations that arise from the words with which we communicate.

Seniority. Seniority means the length of a worker's employment in relation to other employees.

Seniority-based promotions. Seniority-based promotions result when the most senior employee is promoted into a new position.

Severance pay. Severance pay is a payment made to workers when they are dismissed from the company. Employees who are terminated because of their poor performance or behavior are usually not eligible.

Shelf-sitters. "Shelf-sitters" is a slang term for upwardly immobile managers who block promotion channels.

Shorter workweeks. Shorter workweeks are employee scheduling variations that allow full-time workers to complete their week's work in less than the traditional five days. One variation is forty hours work in four days.

Skills inventories. Skills inventories are summaries of each employee's skills and abilities. (Skills inventories usually refer to nonmanagement workers. See *Management inventories.*)

Socialization. Socialization is the ongoing process by which an employee adapts to an organization by understanding and accepting the values, norms, and beliefs held by others in the firm. Orientation programs—which familiarize primarily new employees with their role, the organization, its policies, and other employees—speed up the socialization process.

Social Security Act of 1935. This act established the social security program of the federal government, which taxes workers and employers in order to create a fund from which medicare, retirement, disability, and death payments are made to covered workers and their survivors.

Social unionism. Social unionism describes unions that seek to further their members' interests by influencing the social, economic, and legal policies of government at all levels—city, county, state, and federal. (See *Business unionism.*)

Sociotechnical systems. Sociotechnical systems are interventions in the work situation that restructure the work, the work groups, and the relationship between the workers and the technology they use to do their jobs.

Specialization. Specialization occurs when a very limited number of tasks are grouped into one job.

Sponsor. A sponsor is a person in an organization who can create career development opportunities for others.

Staff authority. Staff authority is the authority to advise, not direct, others.

Staffing table. A staffing table lists anticipated employment openings for each type of job.

State employment security agency. A state employment security agency (or unemployment office) matches job seekers with employers who have job openings.

Steering committee. The steering committee is part of a quality circle or other employee involvement effort and usually includes the top manager of the worksite (such as a plant manager) and his or her direct staff.

Steward. A union steward is elected by workers (or appointed by local union leaders) to help covered employees present their problems to management.

Stock options. Stock options are fringe benefits that give the holder the right to purchase the company's stock at a predetermined price.

Strategic plan. A strategic plan identifies a firm's long-range objectives and proposals for achieving those objectives.

Stress. Stress is a condition of strain that affects one's emotions, thought processes, and physical condition.

Stress interviews. Stress interviews rely on a series of harsh, rapid-fire questions that are intended to upset the applicant and show how the applicant handles stress.

Stressors. Stressors are conditions that tend to cause stress.

Stress-performance model. The stress-performance model shows the relationship between stress and job performance.

Stress threshold. A stress threshold is the level of stressors that a person can tolerate before feelings of distress begin.

Strictness bias. A strictness bias occurs when employees are rated lower than their performance justifies.

Structural unemployment. Structural unemployment occurs when people are ready, willing, and able to work, but their skills do not match the jobs available.

Structured interviews. Structured interviews use a predetermined checklist of questions that usually are asked of all applicants.

Suggestion systems. Suggestion systems are a formal method for generating, evaluating, and implementing useful employee ideas.

Suitable employment. Suitable employment means employment for which the person is suited as a result of education, training, or experience.

Supplemental unemployment benefits (SUB). SUB is an employer-provided fringe benefit that supplements state unemployment insurance when an employee is laid off.

System. A system is two or more parts (or subsystems) working together as an organized whole with identifiable boundaries. An open system is one that is affected by the environment.

Taft-Hartley Act. See *Labor-Management Relations Act* of 1947.

Taft-Hartley injunctions. Taft-Hartley injunctions allow the President of the United States to seek a court order to delay a labor-management strike for eighty days. During this cooling off period, the government investigates the facts surrounding the dispute.

Task identity. Task identity means doing an identifiable piece of work, thus enabling the worker to have a sense of responsibility and pride.

Task significance. Task significance means knowing that the work one does is important to others in the organization and outside of it.

Time studies. Time studies are measurements of how long a job takes to perform.

Title VII. Title VII refers to the part of the *Civil Rights Act* of 1964 that requires equal employment opportunities without regard to race, color, religion, sex, pregnancy, or national origin.

Training. Training represents activities that teach employees how to perform their present jobs.

Transference. Transference refers to how applicable the training is to actual job situations, as evaluated by how readily the trainee transfers the learning to his or her job.

Transfers. Transfers occur when an employee is moved from one job to another that is relatively equal in pay, responsibility, and organizational level.

Turnover. Turnover is the loss of employees by the organization. It represents those employees who depart for a variety of reasons.

Two-tiered orientation program. A two-tiered orientation program exists when both the personnel department and the immediate supervisor provide an orientation for new employees.

Two-way communication. Two-way communication means that a sender and a receiver are exchanging messages so that a regular flow of communication is maintained.

Type A people. Type A people are those who are aggressive and competitive, set high standards, and put themselves under constant time pressures.

Type B people. Type B people are more relaxed and easygoing. They tend to accept situations and work within them rather than fight them or put themselves under constant time pressures.

Underutilization. Underutilization occurs when a department or an entire organization has a smaller proportion of members of a protected class than is found in the firm's labor market. (See *Concentration in employment.*)

Unemployment compensation. Unemployment compensation is payment to those who lose their jobs, are unemployed, are seeking new employment, and are willing and able to work.

Unfair labor practices (ULPs). ULPs are violations of the National Labor Relations Act, as amended. These unfair practices are specific activities that employers and labor organizations are prohibited from doing.

Unfreezing. Unfreezing means casting aside old ideas or practices so that new ones can be learned.

Union-management agreement. See *Labor agreement.*

Union members' bill of rights. The union members' bill of rights refers to Title I of the Labor-Management Reporting and Disclosure Act of 1959, which established the specific rights of union members in dealing with their unions.

Union organizers. Union organizers are people who assist employees in forming a local union.

Union shop. A union shop is a workplace where all employees are required to join the local union as a condition of employment. New employees are usually given thirty, sixty, or ninety days in which to join.

Unstructured interview. An unstructured interview uses few, if any, planned questions to enable the interviewer to pursue, in depth, the applicant's responses.

Upward communication. Upward communication is communication that begins at some point in the organization and then proceeds up the hierarchy to inform or influence others.

Valence. Valence is the strength of a person's preference for a particular outcome.

Validity. Validity means that the selection device (usually a test) is related significantly to job performances or to some other relevant criterion.

Variety. Variety in jobs means being able to use different skills and abilities.

Vertical staff meetings. Vertical staff meetings occur when managers meet with two or more levels of subordinates to learn of their concerns.

Vestibule training. Vestibule training occurs off the job on equipment or methods that are highly similar to those used on the job. This technique minimizes the disruption of operations caused by training activities.

Vesting. Vesting is a provision in retirement plans that gives workers rights to retirement benefits after a specified number of years of service, even if the employee quits before retirement.

Vietnam Era Veteran's Readjustment Act of 1974. This act prohibits certain government contractors from discriminating in employment against Vietnam era veterans.

Wage and salary surveys. Wage and salary surveys are studies made by an organization to discover what other employers in the same labor market are paying for specific key jobs.

Wage compression. Wage compression occurs when the difference between higher- and lower-paying jobs is reduced. This compression usually results from giving larger pay increases to lower-paying jobs.

Wagner Act. See *National Labor Relations Act.*

Walk-ins. Walk-ins are job seekers who arrive at the personnel department in search of a job without any prior referrals and not in response to a specific ad or request.

Want ads. Want ads describe the job and its benefits, identify the employer, and tell those who are interested how to apply.

Weighted checklist. A weighted checklist requires the rater to select statements or words to describe an employee's performance or characteristics. After those selections are made, different responses are given different values or weights in order to determine a quantified total score.

Welfare secretary. The welfare secretary was a forerunner of the modern personnel specialist. Welfare secretaries existed to help workers meet their personal needs and to minimize any tendency of workers to join unions.

Well pay. Well pay is a fringe benefit, provided by some employers, that pays employees for unused sick leave.

Wildcat strikes. Wildcat strikes are spontaneous work stoppages that take place in violation of the labor contract and are officially against the wishes of the union leaders.

Workers' compensation. Workers' compensation is payment made to employees for work-related injuries or to their families in the event of the workers' job-caused death.

Work flow. Work flow is the sequence of jobs in an organization needed to produce the firm's goods or service.

Work measurement techniques. Work measurement techniques are methods for evaluating what a job's performance standards should be.

Work practices. Work practices are the set ways of performing work in an organization.

Work sampling. Work sampling means using a variety of observations on a particular job to measure the length of time devoted to certain aspects of the job.

Work simplification. Work simplification means simplifying jobs by eliminating unnecessary tasks or reducing the number of tasks by combining them.

Write-ins. Write-ins are those people who send in a written inquiry, often seeking a job application.

INDEXES

NAME INDEX

SUBJECT INDEX